PERSPECTIVES
on Contemporary Issues

Readings Across the Disciplines

FIFTH EDITION

Katherine Anne Ackley
Emerita, University of Wisconsin at Stevens Point

D0001989

WADSWORTH
CENGAGE Learning

Australia • Brazil • Japan • Korea • Mexico • Singapore • Spain • United Kingdom • United States

WADSWORTH
CENGAGE Learning™

Perspectives on Contemporary Issues:
Readings Across the Disciplines, Fifth Edition
Katherine Anne Ackley

Publisher: Lyn Uhl
Development Editor: Laurie K. Runion
Editorial Assistant: Megan Power
Associate Development Project Manager:
   Emily Ryan
Marketing Manager: Mandee Eckersley
Marketing Coordinator: Kathleen Remsberg
Marketing Communications Manager:
   Stacey Purviance
Project Manager, Editorial Production:
   Tiffany Kayes
Creative Director: Rob Hugel
Art Director: Cate Barr
Print Buyer: Susan Carroll
Permissions Editor:
   Margaret Chamberlain-Gaston
Production Service/Compositor: Newgen/G&S
Text Designer: Hearthside Publishing Services
Photo Researcher: Jill Engebretson
Photo Manager: Sheri Blaney
Copy Editor: Beth Burke
Cover Designer: Joyce C. Weston
Cover Image: © Georg Gorster

For product information and technology assistance, contact us at
Cengage Learning Customer & Sales Support
1-800-354-9706
For permission to use material from this text or product, submit all requests online at
www.cengage.com/permissions
Further permissions questions can be emailed to
permissionrequest@cengage.com

Library of Congress Control Number: 2008923116

ISBN-13: 978-1-413-03397-7

ISBN-10: 1-413-03397-0

Wadsworth
25 Thomson Place
Boston, MA 02210-1202
USA

Cengage Learning products are represented in Canada by Nelson Education, Ltd.

For your course and learning solutions, visit
academic.cengage.com.

Purchase any of our products at your local college store or at our preferred online store
www.ichapters.com.

For My Mother, Phyllis
In Memory of My Father and
My Brother Mike

Printed in Canada
3 4 5 6 7 14 13 12 11 10 09

CONTENTS

PREFACE

Perspectives on Contemporary Issues: Readings Across the Disciplines, Fifth Edition, presents an approach to thinking, reading, and writing that views learning as the interconnectedness of ideas and disciplinary perspectives. Contemporary issues engage the students, while the readings provide rich material for both class discussion and writing topics. The essays focus on individual, national, and global issues by authors from a variety of disciplines and professions. Likewise, the writing assignments enhance the skills that students will use, regardless of their majors.

The goals of *Perspectives on Contemporary Issues: Readings Across the Disciplines* are

- to sharpen students' thinking skills by presenting them with a variety of perspectives on current issues;
- to give students practice in both oral and verbal expression, by providing questions for discussion and writing after each selection;
- to provide students with a variety of writing assignments representing the kinds of writing they will be asked to do in courses across the curriculum; and
- to encourage students to view issues and ideas in terms of connections with other people, other disciplines, or other contexts.

The questions for discussion and writing encourage critical thinking by asking students to go well beyond simple recall of the readings and to use higher-order skills such as integration, synthesis, or analysis of what they have read. Most of the questions are suitable for work in small groups, as well as for class discussion.

NEW TO THIS EDITION

New Chapter

A new Chapter 2, The Writing Process, takes students through the writing process, from prewriting, discovery, and planning to composing multiple drafts and then editing and proofreading.

New Readings   There are 42 new readings in this edition, almost all of them published in the 2000s. Every chapter has at least one new reading, some as many as three.

Among the new readings are essays that focus on topics of recent interest, such as the national discussion of radio shock jock Don Imus's racist and sexist language, the importance of word choice in describing America's involvement in foreign wars, the controversy over mandatory HPV virus for teenage girls, America's responsibility to under-developed nations, and Internet networking sites like MySpace and Facebook. In addition, the classic essay "Fifth Avenue, Uptown" by James Baldwin is included in the chapter on poverty and homelessness. The chapter on natural sciences has been deleted at the suggestion of reviewers.

Expanded Discussions of Writing in Part I   All of the chapters in Part I have been revised and in many cases expanded. For instance, Chapter 3 provides additional guidelines for writing summaries and explains the difference between formal and informal summaries, and Chapter 5 on writing an argument has a greatly expanded section on structuring an argument.

READING SELECTIONS

The reading selections are divided into four sections within the book, representing four broad disciplinary areas: the arts and media studies, the social sciences, the natural sciences, and business and economics. Within each broad division are chapters on specific topics related to the larger subject. Part Two, The Arts, Media Studies, and Popular Culture, contains chapters with readings on music and video games, media violence, advertising, Hollywood films, television, and the visual arts. In Part Three, Social and Behavioral Sciences, the chapters address such matters as education, poverty and homelessness, criminal behavior, gender and sex roles, race and ethnicity, terrorism, and war. In Part Four, Science and Technology, writers from a variety of disciplines explore such subjects as the relationships among science, technology, and society; public-health issues; computers and digital technology; and the ethical implications of technology and human genetic experimentation. Finally, in Part Five, Business and Economics, the essays address marketing and the American consumer, the work place, the economic impact of outsourcing, and the United States in the global marketplace.

The selections in each chapter encourage students to consider issues from different perspectives because their authors come from a wide range of disciplinary backgrounds and training. Sometimes the writers cross disciplinary lines in their essays. For example, a historian extols the virtues of reading. The individual perspectives of the writers may differ markedly from students' own perspectives, thus generating discussion and writing topics.

ACTIVITIES AND ASSIGNMENTS

Following each selection, students have an opportunity to make a *Personal Response* to some aspect of the reading. Each reading is also followed by several *Questions for Class or Small-Group Discussion.* These questions invite students to consider rhetorical strategies of the piece, to think of larger implications, to discuss related issues, or to make connections between the readings and their own experiences. Many of these questions are appropriate for writing topics as well, and many others will prompt students to discover related topics on which to write.

The selections in each chapter are followed by a section called *Perspectives on . . . ,* which provides writing topics based on ideas generated by the collected readings in that chapter. These writing assignments are arranged in two categories:

- **Suggested Writing Topics** suitable for synthesis, argumentation, and other modes of writing such as the report, the letter, the personal essay, and the comparison and contrast essay; and
- **Research Topics** suitable for development into research papers.

Finally, each chapter in Parts Two through Five concludes with a section called *Responding to Visuals,* which features two photographs or other visual images. These images relate to the thematic focus of the chapter and are accompanied by questions on rhetorical strategies and other relevant matters.

A DEFINITION OF ISSUES

Given the title of this textbook, a definition of "issues" is in order. An issue is usually taken to mean a topic that is controversial, that prompts differences of opinion, or that can be seen from different perspectives. It often raises questions or requires taking a close look at a problem. While this is not primarily an argument textbook, the inclusion of topics and essays guaranteed to spark controversy is deliberate. Many of the readings will surely prompt students to take opposing positions. Some of the readings are provocative; others may anger students. Such differences of opinion will not only generate lively class discussions, but they will also result in writing opportunities that engage students.

ACKNOWLEDGMENTS

I would like to thank the following reviewers for their helpful suggestions on this new edition and on previous editions:

Lynn Alexander, *University of Tennessee*
Valerie K. Anderson, *York College, The City University of New York*

Bim Angst, *Penn State Schuykill*

M. Susan Bonifer, *Mountain State University*

Robert Brown, *Champlain College*

Charlene Bunnell, *University of Delaware*

Joan Canty, *Columbia College*

Edward Carmien, *Westminster Choir College of Rider University*

Jo Cavins, *North Dakota State University*

N. Bradley Christie, *Erskine College*

Judith Cortelloni, *Lincoln College*

Robert Con Davis-Undiano, *University of Oklahoma*

Stacey Donohue, *Central Oregon Community College*

Clark L. Draney, *Idaho State University*

Sarah Duerden, *Arizona State University*

David Elias, *Eastern Kentucky University*

Virginia Fambrough, *Baker University*

James Gifford, *Mohawk Valley Community College*

Fatin Morris Guirguis, *Polk Community College*

Keith Hale, *South Texas Community College*

Letitia Harding, *University of the Incarnate Word*

M. Hunter Hayes, *University of Southern Mississippi*

Kathy Henkins, *Mt. San Antonio College*

Hyo-Chang Hong, *Marshall University*

Elizabeth Huston, *Eastfield College*

William T. Hyndman, III, *Rosemont College*

Karen R. Jacobs, *Louisiana Tech University*

Margaret Johnson, *Idaho State University*

Howard Kerner, *Polk Community College*

Joyce Kessel, *Villa Maria College*

James Kirpatrick, *Central Piedmont Community College*

Mary Kramer, *University of Massachusetts, Lowell*

Linda Lawliss, *College of the Desert*

Lindsay Lewan, *Arapahoe Community College*

Jun Liu, *California State University, Los Angeles*

Jeanette Lugo, *Valdosta State University*

Christopher Mattson, *Keene State College*

James McNamara, *Alverno College*

Brett J. Millan, *South Texas Community College*

Deborah Montuori, *Shippensburg University*

Rosemary Moore, *Iowa Western Community College*
Sean Nighbert, *St. Philip's College*
Debbie Ockey, *Fresno City College*
Debbie Olson, *Central Washington University*
Marc Prinz, *Hofstra University*
Louise Rosenberg, *University of Hartford*
Kiki Leigh Rydell, *Montana State University*
Daniel Schenker, *University of Alabama in Huntsville*
Judith Schmitt, *Macon State College*
Marilyn Schultz, *Delta State University*
Allison D. Smith, *Middle Tennessee State University*
Harvey Solganick, *LeTourneau University*
Shannon C. Stewart, *Coastal Carolina University*
Rosalee Stilwell, *Indiana University of Pennsylvania*
Steve Street, *The State University of New York*
William Tashman, *Baruch College, The City University of New York*
Tiffany Trent, *Virginia Polytechnic Institute and State University*
Sandi Ward, *West Virginia University*
Gwen Wilkinson, *University of Texas at San Antonio*

As always, I thank my husband, Rich, and my family: Heather, Brian, Elizabeth, and Lucas Schilling; Laurel, Gianni, Zack, and Celia Yahi; and Jeremy, Jenni, and Che White. Special thanks are due Matthew Diomede, who made several sound recommendations for the section on MLA style.

I am grateful to my colleagues in the English Department at the University of Wisconsin at Stevens Point. In particular, Tom Bloom and Ann Bloom shared their suggestions on writing an opinion paper, which I have incorporated into the discussion of the research paper, and Don Pattow, former Director of Freshman English, gave me materials on writing across the curriculum. I also want to thank the following students in my English classes who gave permission to use material from their course papers: Erin Anderson, Josanne Begley, Margo Borden, Morris Boyd, Sam Cox, Rita Fleming, Nathan Hayes, Missy Heiman, Linda Kay Jeske, Kelley Kassien, Kari Kolb, Steph Niedermair, Barbara Novak, Shawn Ryan, Lauren Shimulunas, Jodi Simon, Jennifer Sturm, and Cory L. Vandertie, Melinda Vang.

Finally, I owe special thanks and gratitude to my editor, Laurie Runion, who has given me good advice and much appreciated support throughout the revision of this edition.

PART • ONE

Writing Critically
and Conducting Research

CHAPTER 1

Reading Critically

READING CRITICALLY IN PREPARATION FOR WRITING CRITICALLY

Reading critically does not necessarily mean that you object to what someone has written or that you view it negatively. Rather, it means that you read something carefully, thoughtfully, and thoroughly for two reasons: first, to understand it, and second, to assess it. You read for meaning first because, obviously, you must understand what you read before it can be examined. Once you develop a clear understanding of a piece of writing, you have a solid basis for moving beyond comprehension to evaluation.

Reading critically involves examining an author's ideas and the evidence the author has supplied in support of those ideas. It means that you try to recognize the difference between reasonable, logical assertions and those that are unreasonable or lack credibility. It requires you to distinguish between fact and opinion, to sort out the evidence an author cites, and to evaluate that evidence in terms of its relevance, accuracy, and importance. Thus, reading critically means that you actively engage in what you read, that you analyze it, and that you evaluate it. Learning to be a critical reader also helps to make you a better writer. If you pay attention to the ways in which professional writers and scholars use language, structure their essays, and develop their ideas, you will learn some valuable lessons for your own writing.

The following guidelines are not ironclad rules for reading critically, but they are useful suggestions to help you get the most from your reading. These guidelines for reading will also be very helpful for any kind of writing required in your college courses, especially the one for which you are using this textbook. If you read the assigned selections carefully, you will very likely be fully prepared to write on one of the topics that end each chapter. Certainly, reading critically is a necessity for any of the varieties of writing and strategies discussed in Part 1: summary, critique, argument, synthesis, and the research paper.

Read the Title.   Before you read, consider the title. A title often not only reveals the subject of the piece, but it can also tell you something about the way in which the subject will be treated. It may indicate the position the author takes on the subject or reflect the tone of the piece. ("Tone" refers to the writer's attitude toward the subject and audience, which is conveyed largely through word choice and level of language usage, such as informal or formal, colloquial, or slang.) A number of essays in this textbook have revealing titles. For instance, the title "Smallpox Shots: Make them Mandatory" in Chapter 21 clearly indicates the position of its author, Charles Krauthammer, on the subject of mandatory smallpox shots. You cannot tell from the title alone what his arguments are, but you can expect him to favor requiring smallpox shots for everyone. Similarly, the title "Stop Blaming Kids and TV" in Chapter 10 indicates that the subject will be young people and television viewing and that the author believes they are being unfairly blamed for something—though what that is will not be clear until you read the essay. Sometimes authors ask questions in their titles, as in "Sacred Rite or Civil Right?" As readers, we assume that the author of that essay in Chapter 15, Howard Moody, answers the question he poses in his title. There is no indication in that title, however, of how he answers it.

Find Out About the Author.   If information about the author is provided, read it. Knowing who the author is, what his or her publications are, and what his or her profession is, for example, gives you an idea of the authority from which the author writes. In magazines, journals, and collections of essays, such as those you will use in many of your college courses, the headnote often tells you about the author. The headnote is the information located between the title and the beginning of the essay, usually highlighted or set off from the body of the essay itself. Here is the headnote for Lisa Curtis's "Efforts to Deal with America's Image Abroad: Are They Working?" (Chapter 18):

> *Lisa Curtis is a Senior Research Fellow in the Asian Studies Center at The Heritage Foundation whose research focuses on analyzing America's economic, security, and political relationships with India, Pakistan, Sri Lanka, Bangladesh and Nepal. She has served as a professional staff member of the Senate Foreign Relations Committee, as a Senior Adviser in the State Department's South Asia bureau, and as a political analyst on South Asia for the Central Intelligence Agency. The testimony here was delivered to the United States House of Representative Committee on Foreign Affairs' Subcommittee on International Organizations, Human Rights, and Oversight on April 26, 2007.*

The information about Curtis's professional activities including her positions as a senior research Fellow focusing on America's relationship with several Asian countries, a member of the Senate Foreign Relations Committee, an advisor in the State Department's South Asia bureau, and a political analyst in South Asia for the Central Intelligence Agency, all indicate her qualifications to write and speak as a professional on a subject related to her research interests and professional experience. The fact that she has served as a consultant to various government agencies that work with other countries provides further evidence of her qualifications to write and speak on America's image abroad.

Determine the Purpose.   Good writers have clear purposes in mind as they plan and draft their writing. Most nonfiction writing falls into the categories of persuasive, expository, and expressive writing. These forms of writing are used to achieve different goals, and they adopt different strategies for achieving those goals. In persuasive writing, the emphasis is on the reader: The writer's purpose is to convince the reader of the validity of his or her position on an issue and sometimes even to move the reader to action. In expository writing, the goal is to inform or present an objective explanation. The emphasis is on ideas, events, or objects themselves, not on how the writer feels about them. Much of the writing in college textbooks is expository, as are newspaper, magazine, and professional journal articles, and nonfiction books. Expository writing can take many forms, including cause–effect analysis, comparison–contrast, definition, and classification. Expressive writing emphasizes the writer's feelings and subjective view of the world. The writer's focus is on personal feelings about, or attitude toward, the subject. A journal or diary includes expressive writing. Persuasive, expository, and expressive writing often overlap, but usually a writer has one main purpose. From the opening paragraphs of a written work, you should be able to determine its general purpose or aim. A clearly implied or stated purpose helps the writer to shape the writing, and it helps the reader to understand and evaluate the work.

Try to Determine the Intended Audience.   Writers make assumptions about the people they are writing for, including whether their audience will be sympathetic or opposed to their positions, how informed their readers are about the subjects they are writing on, how intelligent they are, and similar considerations. These assumptions that writers make about their readers directly influence the tone they use, the evidence they select, the way in which they organize and develop their writing, and even their sentence structure, word choice, and diction level. Knowing whom the writer is addressing helps you to understand the writer's point of view and to explain the choices the writer has made in writing the piece. In writing for college courses, students usually assume a general audience of people like themselves who are reasonably intelligent and interested in what they have to say. However, professional writers or scholars often write for specific audiences, depending on the publications in which their writing appears. Knowing whether an audience is familiar with a subject or whether the audience is specialized or general also governs what kind of evidence to offer and how much to include. Where the writing is published gives you a good idea of who the audience is. Take, for instance, the essays by Mike Males in Chapter 10 and Arnold S. Relman in Chapter 21. You know from the headnote that accompanies "Stop Blaming Kids and TV" that it was first published in the *Progressive*. It is fair to assume that readers of the magazine share the magazine's mission, which is, according to its website (http://www.progressive .org), to be "a journalistic voice for peace and social justice at home and abroad." From the word "progressive" and the stated mission, it is reasonable to assume that Males anticipated an audience that is likely to be liberal in its political, social, and philosophical views. On the other hand, it is not immediately clear whether the audience is liberal or conservative for "Restructuring the U.S. Health Care System," first published in *Issues in Science and Technology,* an online journal for discussion of public policy related to the interactions of science, engineering and medicine. According to its website (http://www.issues.org), this journal provides a forum for those with a strong interest in public policy to share ideas and suggestions. This forum differs from a popular magazine or professional journal by offering "authorities an opportunity to share their insights directly with a broad audience." Thus, the target audience has a special interest but includes those with both general interest and specialized expertise in science and technology.

Locate the Thesis Statement or Main Idea.
The thesis states the main idea of the entire essay. Sometimes it is embodied in a single sentence—the thesis statement—and sometimes it is stated in several sentences. If the main idea is not explicitly stated, it should be clearly implied. The thesis statement answers the question, What is the main point of this essay? Whether the thesis is explicit or implicit, it is a necessary component of a clearly written work. A thesis helps the writer to focus the writing and guides the organization and development of key ideas. It also helps to provide direction to the reader and assists in the reader's understanding of the piece.

Locate Key Ideas and Supporting Evidence or Details.
For this step in your critical reading, you should underline or highlight the major points of the essay. One important tool for an active, critical reader is a pen or pencil. As you read, underline, star, or in some way highlight major points of development. Look for topic sentences of paragraphs. The thesis statement answers the question, What is this essay about? In the same way, the topic sentence answers the question, What is this paragraph about? If a topic sentence is not clearly stated, it should be clearly implied.

Make Marginal Notes as You Read.
In the margins, write your response to a passage or make note of words, phrases, or entire passages you think are important to the piece. Make notes about the evidence or details that support major points. If you have a question about something the author says, write it in the margin for later consideration. If you are not sure of the meaning of a word, circle it and look it up in a dictionary after you have finished reading. Finally, if you are struck by the beauty, logic, or peculiarity of a passage, note marginal comments on that as well.

Summarize What You Have Read.
This is the point at which you test your understanding of what you have read. Go back now and look at your underlining and notations. Then try to state in your own words what the writing is about and the main points the writer makes. If you can accurately summarize a piece of writing, then you probably have a good idea of its meaning. Summarizing also helps you to recall the piece later, perhaps in class or in small-group discussions. Incidentally, summarizing is also a good strategy for your own study habits. After reading an assignment for any of your courses, try to write or tell someone a summary of your reading. If you cannot express in your own words the major ideas of what you have

just read, it should be reread. For a more detailed discussion of writing a summary, see Chapter 3.

Evaluate What You Have Read.   When you are sure that you understand what you have read and can summarize it objectively, you are ready to respond. You can evaluate something in a number of ways, depending on its purpose. First, consider whether the author achieves the stated or implied purpose and whether the thesis or main idea is thoroughly explained, developed, or argued. Has the writer supplied enough details, examples, or other evidence? If you are evaluating an argument or persuasion essay, is the evidence convincing to you? Does the piece make a logical and reasonable argument? Are you persuaded to the writer's position? What questions do you have about any of the writer's assertions? Do you wish to challenge her or him on any points? If the purpose of the essay is to describe, has the writer conveyed to you the essence of the subject with appropriately vivid language? For any piece of writing, you can assess how well written it is. Is it organized? Is the writing clear to you? Does the introduction give you enough information to get you easily into the essay, and does the conclusion leave you satisfied that the writer has accomplished the purpose for the essay? In Chapter 4, Writing a Critique, you will find a more detailed discussion of how to evaluate a passage or entire essay.

GUIDELINES FOR READING CRITICALLY

- Consider what the title tells you about the essay.
- Try to learn something about the author.
- Determine the purpose of the writing.
- Determine the audience for whom the piece was written.
- Locate the thesis statement or main idea.
- Locate key ideas and supporting evidence or details.
- Make marginal notes as you read, including not only a summary of key ideas but also your questions about the content.
- Summarize what you have read.
- Evaluate what you have read.

ILLUSTRATION: READING CRITICALLY

A demonstration of how a reader might apply the guidelines for critical reading accompanies the following essay "What's in a Name? More than You Think" by Joe Saltzman. Read the essay first, noticing words and passages that are underlined and addressed in the marginal comments. After you have read the essay, prepare for class by writing a response to the personal response question and preparing your answers to the questions for class or small-group discussion. Then read the discussion following "What's in a Name?" and consider the ways in which your own critical reading might differ from the comments there. Would you add anything? What other words or passages would you underline or highlight? What other marginal comments would you make?

WHAT'S IN A NAME?
MORE THAN YOU THINK

JOE SALTZMAN

Academic and professional credentials.

Joe Saltzman is associate mass media editor of USA Today; *associate dean and professor of journalism, University of Southern California Annenberg School for Communication, Los Angeles; and director of the Image of the Journalist in Popular Culture, a project of the Norman Lear Center. He is author of* Frank Capra and the Image of the Journalist in American Film. *Recipient of more than fifty awards, Saltzman produces medical documentaries, functions as a senior investigative producer for* Entertainment Tonight, *and writes articles, reviews, columns, and opinion pieces for hundreds of magazines and newspapers. In this piece, which first appeared in the July 2003 issue of* USA Today Magazine, *Saltzman's use of the phrase "the war in Iraq" refers to the period between the invasion of Iraq by a coalition of American, British, and Australian forces on March 20, 2003, and President George W. Bush's declaration on May 1, 2003, that combat operations in Iraq were over. "The aftermath" is that period immediately following President Bush's declaration.*

His subject.
His thesis—note word choice.

<u>Television coverage of the Iraqi war and postwar</u> illustrates once again how <u>American television news is obsessed with show business terminology that at the very least is poor journalism and at its worst corrupts and ignores a basic rule of journalism: fairness and accuracy in all reporting.</u>

Re-states thesis.

With the government's public relations arm pushing hard, phrases to describe the war and postwar stories moved from a fair account of what was going on to an oppressive vocabulary that gave a spin to the coverage. <u>Colorful phrases, sometimes</u>

patriotic, sometimes just plain wrong, gave much of the TV news coverage a convenient anti-Iraqi/pro-American stance. Some examples:

"Operation Iraqi Freedom" was used constantly by Fox and MSNBC as a banner for summing up the coverage of the war in the Middle East. Few would dispute that "Operation Iraqi Freedom" sounded noble and gave a heroic and honorable reason for going to war as opposed to the accurate and more evenhanded "The War in Iraq" or "The Iraqi Conflict." Fighting for a country's freedom brings images of the American and French revolutions, of World War II soldiers fighting against Hitler and the Japanese, and of friendly, grateful citizens waving American flags to greet soldiers who had liberated their country. These images neatly fit with a title like "Operation Iraqi Freedom." "The War in Iraq" conjures up destruction and death. It is one thing for the Administration to use favorable phrases to win support for its policies, quite another for the American media to use such phrases in trying to describe what is going on in a Middle East war.

4   "Coalition forces" sounds as if a worldwide coalition of military force is being used to fight the war. It's certainly the Bush-approved term for the American and British forces fighting in Iraq. News organizations, however, shouldn't use phrases that do not adequately describe the situation. It was American soldiers in Baghdad, not coalition forces, but most of the news media used the phrase "coalition forces" throughout the coverage of the war.

Going into a foreign country to get rid of "weapons of mass destruction" makes sense. As *Time* magazine put it, "they sound so much more fearsome than chemical or biological weapons. A few papers, like the *New York Times*, have been careful to use 'unconventional weapons' or other terms instead."

If you were trying to figure out whether the war in Iraq was justified, see which sentence would convince you: "Operation Iraqi Freedom was underway as coalition forces went into Iraq to discover and destroy weapons of mass destruction"; or "The war in Iraq was underway as American and British forces went into Iraq to discover and destroy unconventional weapons."

"Collateral damage" doesn't sound as horrific as civilian casualties or, even more accurately, civilians who were wounded, maimed, or killed by American bombs and ground fire.

8   Certain phrases make a difference in our perception of what goes on in our world. Catchphrases that make unpopular events less difficult to accept should not be a part of daily news media coverage. It demeans both the journalist and the viewer.

Shifts focus to visual images.

Says "embedded journalists" give distorted view of war.

Many watching the television war coverage were impressed with the pictures sent back by "embedded" journalists traveling with various military units in the field. And many of the images and reports were spectacular, but at what cost? No one would deny that reporters embedded with individual units would be partial to the people around them saving their lives. No one would deny that this kind of coverage simply gives the viewer a glimpse at specific moments in war. No embedded reporter has the chance or the ability to interview the other side during a battle. In many ways, this coverage, while unique in the history of war reporting, gave an even more-distorted view of what was going on in the field than battle reports issued by reporters safely away from the sounds and sights of immediate warfare.

Not opposed to embedded reporters, but there should be a broader perspective of what's going on. Check definition of "myopic."

None of this is to say that we shouldn't have reports from embedded reporters. It is one more attempt to figure out what is going on during wartime. It must be put into proper perspective, however. The British broadcasters and the Middle East press did an effective job in showing other sides of the war, other sides that were either not reported by the American news media or given short shrift next to the action-packed, myopic reports from embedded correspondents in the field.

Journalists guilty of censorship— kept pictures of POWs and wounded civilians out of media.

Perhaps even more damaging was the news media's attempt to "censor" unpleasant sights and sounds from the battlefield because they were worried about offending American sensibilities. The most-grievous example was the failure of U.S. news media to show the footage of the American prisoners of war when the entire world was watching what was happening to them. Moreover, other pictures of wounded Iraqi civilians were also missing in much of the American news media coverage. Many viewers turned to other sources for news of the war—newspapers, magazines, the Internet, the BBC, and cable stations showing some of the foreign coverage.

Showing "offensive" pictures might balance the picture of war. TV news media need to change approach to reporting war.

12   The TV news media never should assume the role of a parent deciding what images and sounds the American people should be allowed to see. While it is true that pictures of wounded Iraqi civilians and abused POWs do not give viewers an accurate and complete picture of the war by themselves, they would have been an important addition to the embedded war coverage of bullets and sand-clouded battles. One wonders what the news media would have shown, however, if an embedded reporter was suddenly blown to bits on camera.

War is always brutal and the images always horrible and hard to watch. If the American TV news media want to cover modern warfare, they will have to do far more than give us fancy showbiz titles and only the sounds and images that they deem suitable for G-rated TV news.

PERSONAL RESPONSE

Thinking about television news coverage of Americans engaged in war, do you believe that you are swayed by the language that news reporters use in that coverage? Do you agree with Saltzman that television news media in effect "assume the role of a parent" (paragraph 11)?

QUESTIONS FOR CLASS OR SMALL-GROUP DISCUSSION

1. What is Saltzman's central idea or thesis?
2. How convincing do you find Saltzman's strategy for developing or supporting his thesis?
3. What do you see as the strengths and weaknesses of this essay?

DISCUSSION OF "WHAT'S IN A NAME? MORE THAN YOU THINK"

Title.   The title tells readers the subject of the article—names and their connotations—but not what kinds of names. The title does suggest that the author is going to be critical of whatever sort of naming he discusses in the paper (names mean "more than you think").

Author.   The information in the headnote suggests that the author seems well qualified to write critically of news reporting. He is a mass media editor of a major news magazine and a professor of journalism. He is active in his discipline, has published a book on the image of journalists in film, and has received numerous awards for his professional work.

Audience.   The headnote also says that "What's in a Name? More than You Think" was first published in *USA Today Magazine,* a publication for a general audience of urban readers who like to get the essentials of news stories quickly. Saltzman likely assumed an audience of educated readers who want analyses of important national and international developments but who do not necessarily have the time to read lengthy articles on those topics. Saltzman therefore writes in a style appropriate to newspapers and news magazines—that is, he avoids informal language such as slang or colloquialisms as well as specialized terms or difficult vocabulary. He uses words and terms that would be familiar to an audience of readers who keep up on America's involvement in Iraq. His word choice and sentence structure are appropriate for educated adults who take an interest in the news.

Purpose and Main Idea.   Saltzman states his subject and main idea in his first sentence: he believes that television coverage of the Iraqi war and postwar is unfair and inaccurate. He elaborates in the second paragraph by suggesting that TV reporters gave in to pressure from the government and adopted "an oppressive vocabulary" to give "spin" to their coverage of the war. We know from the headnote that Saltzman was writing not long after President Bush declared that the coalition invasion of Iraq was over, so his use of present tense is appropriate for reporting what was going on at the time he wrote his piece. He uses language that makes his view of such reporting quite clear when he accuses television news of being "obsessed with show business terminology," which "corrupts and ignores" the basic rule of journalism to be fair and accurate in its reporting. It is clear from those opening paragraphs that his purpose is to argue that American television news reporters have been unfair, inaccurate, and demeaning in their reporting of the war in Iraq and its aftermath.

Key Ideas and Supporting Evidence.   Saltzman primarily uses **exemplification** to develop his **argument**. In paragraphs 3–6, he gives examples of the phrases that he finds offensive in American television news reporting, along with his explanation of why their use is very bad journalism. He believes that the phrase "Operation Iraqi Freedom," with its associations of patriotism and nobility, is appropriate for the administration but not for reporters, who are supposed to remain neutral and unbiased. His preferred phrase would be "The War in Iraq." Next he cites the phrase "coalition forces," which suggests a worldwide joining of military forces, when, he asserts, it was only British and American soldiers who were fighting in Baghdad. He goes on to "weapons of mass destruction," which suggests something quite fearsome, as opposed to a more neutral phrase like "unconventional weapons." His last example is "collateral damage," which downplays or helps soften the reality that the phrase refers to "civilian casualties" or "civilians who were wounded, maimed, or killed by American bombs and ground fire" (paragraph 6).

After arguing that the language of American television news reporters is unfair and biased, he goes on to discuss the images that were broadcast on television. He believes that using " 'embedded' journalists" gave a very narrow, distorted view of the battlefield and that viewers did not get a proper perspective of what was going on in the war. His last example is the "even more damaging" attempts by the media to " 'censor' unpleasant sights and sounds from the battlefield" because they did not want to offend "American sensibilities." His point about both embedded journalists and attempts to withhold disturbing images is that reporters give a narrow and distorted perspective of what was happening during the war and what has been going on after it. He argues for a broader picture of the realities of war. Saltzman concludes by asserting that if American television news media want to cover modern warfare, they must drop the "fancy showbiz titles" and stop "censoring" images they believe Americans would find disturbing.

Summary.   In "What's in a Name? More than You Think," Joe Saltzman argues that American television news reporters violate the basic rules of reporting by using language and making choices that give an unfair, inaccurate, and distorted view of the war in Iraq and its aftermath. He gives a number of examples of language to make his point. He cites the phrase "Operation Iraqi Freedom," which stirs up patriotic feelings, more appropriately the business of the government's public relations people than reporters. Saltzman then asserts that "coalition forces" is a misleading and inaccurate phrase because there were only American soldiers in Baghdad, not an alliance of many forces from around the world. His remaining two examples are "weapons of mass destruction," with its connotations of terror, and "collateral damage," which softens the reality of what the term actually denotes. From language, Saltzman moves to the images that were broadcast on television. The use of embedded reporters to cover the war was not a bad idea, he says, but it narrowed the view of the war rather than helped present a broad perspective of what was going on. Worse, he argues, was the decision not to show images of the abuses of prisoners of war and wounded Iraqi citizens. Such a failure amounts to censorship. He concludes by reasserting his major point that American television journalists failed in their coverage of the war in Iraq and the period after the war, and he suggests that they change their ways if they want to report modern warfare accurately and fairly.

Evaluation.   Saltzman's essay is organized sensibly and logically written in clear, straightforward prose. His use of specific examples and his reasons why they are inappropriate make a convincing case for his argument that American television journalists were inaccurate and unfair in their reporting of the Iraq war. The repetition of "no one would deny" in paragraph 8 lends emphasis to the point he is making about the limited perspective of embedded reporters. Furthermore, the disclaimer in the first sentence of paragraph 9 is his concession, in a way, to readers who may think that he is being overly critical of embedded reporters, and it leads to his repeating—and emphasizing—his opinion. Despite Saltzman's excellent use of examples to support and develop his central idea, he does not go into real depth in his analysis of any of them. It is quite possible that space limitations imposed by the magazine kept him from a fuller discussion. The fact that many of his paragraphs are short—one or two sentences in several cases—may reflect his training in journalism: the physical space of newspaper and in some cases magazine columns requires shorter paragraphs.

Saltzman is an accomplished writer who is not afraid to express opinions that may not be popular with the general public, and these opinions raise questions that bear further exploration and thought. His assertion that American television news reporting of war should give a broader picture, showing if possible the perspective of the enemy and the effects of war on the people we are fighting, is fair. On the other hand, is it the place of the press to be critical of the administration or to challenge the decisions of its country's leaders in time of war? Is it not important to keep up morale on the home front as well as on the battlefield? What is gained by a press hostile to or even subversive of its government in a time when patriotism and public support of its military are crucial to the war effort? These are tough questions that both the press and its critics have been struggling with, and Saltzman's essay is a good starting place for an open discussion of the issues he raises.

THE WAR AND THE WORDS

CHARLES KRAUTHAMMER

Charles Krauthammer earned a medical degree from Harvard and began his career as a psychiatrist at Massachusetts General Hospital but quit medical practice to serve as director of psychiatric planning in the Carter administration. He began contributing articles to magazines such as the New Republic *and* Time *and became a regular contributor to the* Washington Post *in 1985. In addition to a Pulitzer Prize for distinguished commentary in 1987, Krauthammer has won numerous other awards, including the first $250,000 Bradley Prize. This piece appeared in the February 9, 2007, issue of the* Washington Post.

National Intelligence Estimates are not supposed to be amusing. And the latest NIE on the situation in Iraq was uniformly grim. But the document's determined effort to split the difference on the use of the phrase "civil war" did verge on the comical. One can only imagine the interagency wrangling that produced the classic bureaucratic compromise: "The Intelligence Community judges that the term 'civil war' does not adequately capture the complexity of the conflict," but "nonetheless, the term 'civil war' accurately describes key elements of the Iraqi conflict."

In other words: yes, no, maybe. Multiple civil strife, but way too messy to rank with the classics such as America in the 1860s or Spain in the 1930s. I don't deny that this is a fair application of "civil war" to the current situation. What I note with dismay, however, is how important—and absurdly irrelevant—the application of certain loaded words to the situation has become.

What is striking is how much of the debate in Washington about Iraq has to do not with the war but with the words. Who owns them, who deploys them, who uses them as a bludgeon. NBC's announcement in November that it would henceforth use the term civil war—a statement far more political than analytical, invoking the same fake authority with which the networks regally "declare" election winners (e.g., Florida to Al Gore, Nov. 7, 2000)—set the tone of definitional self-importance.

4   Words. We had weeks of debates in the Senate about Iraq. They eventually went nowhere, being shut down (temporarily) by partisan procedural disputes. But they were going nowhere anyway. The debates were not about real fighting in a real

place. They were about how the various senators would position themselves in relation to that real fighting in that real place. At issue? With what tone and nuance and addenda to express disapproval of a troop surge that the president was going to order anyway.

When it came to doing something serious about the surge, the Senate ducked. It *unanimously* (81–0) approved sending Gen. David H. Petraeus to Baghdad to do the surge—precisely what a majority of the senators said they did not want done.

If you really oppose the surge, how can you not oppose the appointment of the man whose very mission is to carry it out? Yet not one senator did so. Instead, they spent days fine-tuning the wording of a nonbinding—i.e., entirely toothless—expression of disapproval. A serious legislative body would not be arguing over degrees of disapproval anyway, but about the elements of three or four alternative plans that might actually change our course in Iraq, something they all say they desire. But instead of making a contribution to thinking through how the war should be either prosecuted or liquidated, they negotiate language that provides precisely the amount of distancing a senator might need as political insulation should the surge either succeed or fail.

Words. The Democrats are all in favor of "redeployment" and pretend that this is an alternative plan. But the word redeployment is meaningless. It simply means changing the position of our soldiers and, implicitly, changing their mission. Unless you're saying where you're redeploying to, and with what mission, you've said nothing. It's a statement of opposition, yet another expression of disapproval of the current strategy—much like an empty, nonbinding congressional resolution—until you say whether you want to redeploy to Kansas or Kurdistan.

8   Words. Consider "surge." It carries an air of energy, aggression and even hope. That, in fact, is a fairly good reflection of Petraeus's view of it—not just more troops but a change in the rules of engagement, with more latitude to fight, less political interference by the Iraqi government and a much tougher attitude toward foreign, especially Iranian, agents in Iraq.

The opposition prefers "escalation," as featured, for example, in the anti-surge commercial that aired in certain markets during the Super Bowl. The main reason for using escalation, of course, is that it is a Vietnam word. And the more Vietnam words you can use in discussing Iraq, the more you've won the debate without having to make an argument.

The problem with this battle over words is that it is entirely irrelevant to what is happening in Iraq. There will be real troops on real missions regardless of what label they are given. The country is engaged in a serious debate about exactly what strategy to pursue to either prosecute the war or withdraw in an orderly fashion. The Senate might consider putting such a debate on its agenda.

PERSONAL RESPONSE

How crucial do you consider word choice to be in the context of describing the war in Iraq and determining policy there?

QUESTIONS FOR CLASS AND SMALL GROUP DISCUSSION

1. Summarize in your own words the criticism Krauthammer has of debates over appropriate wording to describe the war in Iraq. What exactly is his objection to the focus on words?

2. To what extent do you sympathize with Krauthammer when he writes that he is dismayed at "how important—and absurdly irrelevant—the application of certain loaded words to the situation has become" (paragraph 2). Do you agree that a discussion of wording is "irrelevant?" Do you find his examples of "loaded words" convincing? Does he use any loaded words himself?

3. Comment on Krauthammer's strategy of repeating the single word "words" at the beginnings of paragraphs 4, 7, and 8. What effect does that repetition have?

4. What do you understand Krauthammer to mean when he writes: "And the more Vietnam words you can use in discussing Iraq, the more you've won the debate without having to make an argument" (paragraph 9)?

RHETORICAL ANALYSIS OF VISUALS

Rhetorical considerations apply to visual images as well as to written forms of communication. "Analysis" as a process involves taking something that is whole and complex and breaking it into its individual components to better understand it. Thus, a rhetorical analysis is a close examination of not just what a work says but, just as importantly, how it says it. Whether you are critiquing an essay in a book or periodical, a visual art form, or an Internet website, questions of audience, tone, purpose, organization, content, and meaning apply. With visuals, as with written works, you must consider perspective or point of view, context, and connotation. Connotation—the emotional associations of a thing—is perhaps even more important when viewing visuals than in reading words. Just as words have associations that go beyond or add layers of meaning to what they denote ("the dictionary definition"), images have powerful associations. Images often have the ability to express things—emotions, nuances, insights—in a way that words often cannot. They can reveal what is difficult to put into words by conveying impressions or depicting in sharp detail what it would take a great many words to describe or explain, including subtleties of meaning that emerge only after thoughtful consideration and careful perusal of the image. Visuals also have the potential to argue a viewpoint or persuade an audience; their authors use strategies to present a viewpoint or make a statement that is similar to those used by authors of written text.

We see images daily in a variety of forms—in photographs, drawings, paintings, pictures, brochures, advertisements, CD album covers, posters, and Internet web pages, and of course on television and in film. Most of these images go unexamined because we see so many images in our lives that we simply would not have time to analyze them all. But when we find it useful to consider an image closely, how do we analyze it? What can we say about it? How can we express in words what an image means or implies? The answer to these questions is that analyzing images critically requires skills that are quite similar to those for analyzing a piece of writing critically. Just as writers select details and organize essays to make specific points, so, too, do artists shooting a scene or painting a picture select details and arrange them in order to convey specific ideas or impressions. Writers and artists alike make judgments that in turn shape how readers or viewers perceive their work.

Analyzing visuals involves doing a close "reading" of the image and asking a series of questions about it. In looking critically at a visual image, you want to consider many aspects of it: What do you see when you first look at it? How do you respond initially? What details does the image highlight? What else is included and what might have been excluded? How does the positioning of various elements of the image emphasize its meaning? The following list of questions will help you analyze the visual images that are located throughout the textbook in each of the chapters of Parts 2–5. The answers you get when you ask these questions can give you a greater understanding of the images you are scrutinizing. Most of the visual images reproduced in this textbook are photographs or paintings, so the first set of questions is designed to help you in your analysis of them. However, the questions can easily be adapted to other kinds of images, such as advertisements, newspaper page layouts, and Internet web pages. Furthermore, television, film, music videos, and documentaries also convey messages through images that can be analyzed rhetorically in much the same way as the other forms of visual communication can be.

Questions to Ask about a Visual Image:

- What is your overall immediate impression of the image? First impressions often linger even after rethinking one's initial response, so what strikes you immediately about an image is particularly important.
- What detail first catches your attention? After noting your immediate overall response, consider what detail or details first attract you. Is it the prominence, size, or positioning of the subject? Is it the colors or absence of them? Is it the size, the physical space it occupies? More than likely, the artist wanted you to notice that detail first, and very likely, it is an integral part of the "message" or "statement" the image makes.
- What details emerge after you have studied the image for a while? Do you detect any pattern in the arrangement of details? If so, how does the arrangement of details function to convey the overall impression?
- How does the arrangement of objects or people in the picture help draw your attention to the central image, the one you are initially drawn to? Are some things placed prominently in the center or made larger than others? If so, what is the effect of that arrangement? How does the background function in relation to what is placed in the foreground?
- If the image is in color, how does the artist use color? Are the colors selected to represent certain emotions, moods, or other qualities? If it is in black and

white, what use does the artist make of the absence of color? Does the artist use degrees of shading and brightness? If so, to what effect?

- From what perspective is the artist viewing the subject? Is it close to or far away from the subject? Is the subject viewed straight-on or from the side? Why do you think the artist selected this particular perspective? How might a shift in perspective alter the view of the subject, not just physically but on the level of meaning as well?
- What emotions does the image evoke in you? Why? Which details of the image convey the strongest emotion?
- Has anything important been left out of the image? What might have been included, and why do you think it was left out?
- What is happening in the picture? Does it tell a story or give a single impression?
- What does the picture tell you about its subject? How does it convey that message?
- If there are people in the image, what can you tell about them? What details tell you those things? Is it the way they are dressed? Their physical appearance? What they are doing?
- Does the picture raise any questions? What would you like to ask about the image, the activity, or the people in it? How would you find the answers to your questions?

EXERCISE

Ask the questions for analyzing visuals listed above as you study the following photograph (Figure 1.1). Then, selecting the details you believe are important, write an analysis of the photograph. Begin your analysis with an introductory paragraph that includes a thesis statement or a statement of the main idea of the photograph. This thesis should reflect your understanding of what the photograph means to you—its message, its story, what it suggests symbolically, or whatever ultimately you decide about the photograph. The rest of the paper should draw on details from your answers to the questions as you explain or support your thesis statement.

Here are some questions specific to this photograph that you might want to think about as you work through the questions listed above: Besides showing the tattoo, what effect is achieved by taking the picture from behind the man? What does the tattoo suggest to you about the man? Does the earring in his left ear add anything to your image of him? Can you tell the race or ethnicity of the man and, if so, does that detail add a layer of meaning or implication to the picture? Does the man's stance—the way he is standing, the shape of his shoulders, the position of his arms—tell you anything about what he is thinking or what he is about to do? Is the man anticipating a challenge? Is he preparing to climb the dune? Does it make a difference that this is a sand dune and not a mountain or some other challenge? What do you anticipate happening if the man tries to climb the dune? Do the clouds represent anything? Why is the sunlight hidden by the clouds? Is the sun trying to break through the clouds, or are the clouds preventing the sun from shining?

© Herb Watson/CORBIS

Figure 1.1: *Tattooed man looking at sand dune.*

Questions to Ask about an Advertisement.   Advertising is a powerful and pervasive force in our world. Ads have the ability to affect how we think, act, and even feel about ourselves and others. Ads can shape, reflect, or distort both individual perceptions and social values, and they do so by employing some of the classic strategies of argument and persuasion: they have a proposition, they know their audience, they make appeals, they use comparisons and examples, and they particularly want to persuade us to action. In addition to the questions to ask about visual images, the following questions will help you analyze both print and nonprint advertisements:

- What is the message of the advertisement? What does it say to potential buyers of the product? That is, what is its argument?
- Who is the intended audience? How can you tell?

- What strategies does the ad use to convey its message? What appeals—to logic, to emotion, to ethics, or to shared values—does it use? Does it rely primarily on one appeal only or does it combine them? How do the specific details convey that message?
- How does the text—the actual words used—convey the message of the advertisement? How are words arranged or placed in the ad and why are they placed that way? If a non-print ad, how are the voice-overs or dialogue used to convey the message?
- How would you describe the style and tone of the advertisement? How do they help convey the message or sell the product?

EXERCISE

1. Select a print advertisement for analysis. Ask the questions noted above and write an analysis based on your notes in which you assess the effectiveness of the ad in achieving its purpose. Attach the advertisement with your analysis when you hand it in to your instructor.
2. Select two advertisements for the same kind of product (for instance, clothing, toothpaste, or laundry detergent). Apply the questions noted above and choose the one that you think is more effective at selling or promoting the product. Formulate a thesis sentence that states your preference and use details from your scrutiny of both of them to support that statement.

Questions to Ask about a Newspaper Page.   Newspapers can shape reader response in the choices they make about the layout of text and photographs. While we like to think that newspapers are unbiased in their reporting of news items, reading just two different newspapers on the same subject reveals that the choices a newspaper makes about a news item have a huge influence on the impressions it leaves on readers. Just the visual effect of a page layout alone tells us many things. What page an article or picture appears on and where on the page it is located represent a judgment on the part of the paper about the importance of the article or image and cannot help but shape how readers respond to it. Consider the following list about photographs and news articles when looking at a newspaper page:

- Where in the paper is the article or photograph placed? Front-page placement indicates that the newspaper considers it more important as a news item than placement on the inside pages.
- How are photographs and news articles positioned on the page? Items that are placed high on the page or in the center of the page are likely to draw the attention more readily than those placed low or off center.
- How large are the photographs or the headlines? Visually, larger photographs or headlines are likely to draw attention and interest quicker than small ones.

- Are photographs in color or black and white? Choosing to run a picture in color indicates a value judgment that the paper has made about the interest or newsworthiness of the image.

EXERCISE

1. Select a newspaper page for analysis. Front pages are particularly important in newspapers for attracting reader attention, so perhaps you will want to analyze the front page of the newspaper. Ask the questions listed above and write an analysis based on the answers to your questions. What article(s) does the newspaper think more important than others? How are photographs used on the page? Attach the page with your analysis when you hand it in to your instructor.
2. Select two different newspapers covering the same news story and compare their treatment of the story. How do the two newspapers compare and contrast in their handling of the story? Is one more effective than the other in reporting it? Formulate a thesis that reflects your ultimate judgment of the two papers' treatment of the news story and support that thesis with details gathered from your comparison of the two.

RHETORICAL ANALYSIS OF WEBSITES

The Internet provides a seemingly endless variety of sites to visit for every taste and interest. Web pages can function rhetorically to influence visitors to the site in much the same way as other forms of discourse. The very way in which the web page is constructed can work to produce a desired effect, especially if the constructor of the site wishes to persuade an audience, sway opinion, or impose a particular point of view. A rhetorical analysis looks at the ways a site achieves its stated or implied purpose. Because websites vary considerably in their reliability and currency, you will find additional information about evaluating them in Chapter 7. Many of the same questions one asks when evaluating a website apply when doing a rhetorical analysis of it. What follows are some of the components of a web page and questions to ask about it as you analyze its rhetorical effectiveness.

Questions to Ask about a Website:

- **Domain.** What is the URL (Uniform Record Locator) of the site? The domain—the logical or geographical location of the site on the Internet, indicated by the very last part of the URL—tells you something about the site. Domains differ according to the entity sponsoring them: *edu* for educational institutions, *gov* for government agencies, *com* or *net* for commercial or personal enterprises, *org* for organizations. These broad categories give you the first piece of information about the site. Within the categories, there are countless subcategories.

- **Author.** Who created the web page? Is it an individual, an organization, a government agency, an educational institution, or a corporation? Does the text at the site give you information about the author? If not, why do you think that information is not provided? Does the site tell you how to contact the author?
- **Audience.** What audience does the web page target? How can you tell? Is the intended audience stated or implied? Does it make assumptions about values, beliefs, age, sex, race, national origin, education, or socioeconomic background of its target audience?
- **Purpose.** Does the web page want to inform, entertain, sell, argue a position, or persuade people to change their minds or to take action? If it has more than one purpose, what combination of purposes does it have? Is the implied purpose the same as the stated purpose? Does the text state one purpose, while word choice, graphics, and page layout suggest or imply another? For instance, a political candidate's website might state that it has no intention of bringing up an opponent's past wrongdoings, while the very fact of stating that there are past wrongdoings to bring up casts doubt on the character of the opponent.
- **Text.** What rhetorical appeals does the written text of the website make? Does it appeal to logic or reason? Does it appeal to emotions? If emotions, which ones does it appeal to—pity, fear, joy, anger, sympathy?
- **Content.** Does the website cover the topic thoroughly? Does it use language that you understand? Does it offer links and if so, how many links? Are the links still active? What is the quality of the links?
- **Background color.** How does the background color choice affect the mood and tone of the page? Is it a vibrant color or a sober one? Does it intrude on the text or enhance it?
- **Page layout.** Is there space between items on the page or are things cramped together? How does the use of space on the page affect your overall impression of the page and your ability to read it?
- **Loading and positioning of items.** What gets loaded first when you go to the web page? Where is that material positioned? What is loaded later or positioned low on the page? Sometimes certain components of a web page are purposely programmed to load first in order to further emphasize the purpose of the site.
- **Graphics.** Are graphics on the web page static or active? Is the print used for the text large, small, or a mix of both? If a mix, what does larger print emphasize that smaller print doesn't? What font is used? Are bold print, italics, or underlining used, and if so, to what effect? Is there a banner? What purpose does the banner serve?
- **Photographs or drawings.** If photographs or other images are used, what is their function? Do they illustrate or help explain something, give information, or serve to decorate the page?
- **Lighting and contrast.** Does the web page make use of contrasts of light and dark? If so, what is the effect of those contrasts?

Forums on the Web: Listservs and Blogs

In addition to websites that people go to for information, entertainment, or news, the Internet also has available a number of forums for people to participate in, such as chat rooms, newsgroups, discussion lists (listservs), and blogs. While most websites are fairly dynamic in that they are (or should be) regularly updated, forums typically change at least daily and sometimes multiple times a day. Two very popular forums are **listservs** and **blogs.** Both are capable of influencing people's views or the way they think about the topics for discussion at the sites, but blogs in particular have gotten a great deal of attention for their potential to actually bring about changes. Blogs are able to effect change because of the high degree of involvement that they have generated among visitors to their sites. Another distinguishing characteristic of listservs and blogs is that people are invited to participate in an ongoing, ever-changing discussion. People who become members of listservs or who visit blog sites have an opportunity to be not just passive readers but also active writers.

Listservs.   Listservs are e-mail based discussion groups linked to specific topics. Listservs function as forums for the exchange of ideas, where members can debate, discuss, post news items, seek or give advice, and share in a community of people who have in common their interest in the topic of the listserv. Although listservs have official websites where people can subscribe, read the guidelines for posting, and locate archived postings, among other things, the real activity takes place through e-mail. Members can elect to receive messages either individually as they are posted or in digests that are sent daily or whenever a specific number of messages have posted. Members are usually required to follow certain rules or guidelines, primarily those related to conduct and appropriate content, and often the listserv has a moderator who monitors the content of messages to make sure that posts do not violate those rules. Listservs typically archive messages by date, subject of message, and/or author, and these archives can be viewed by nonmembers as well as members. They vary widely in membership numbers, from just a few people to thousands. For instance, a listserv devoted to British novelist Barbara Pym has a small membership of around 100, and posts to the site are occasional and few. In contrast, DorothyL, a discussion and idea list for lovers of the mystery genre, has almost 3,000 subscribers and fifty to 100 postings each day. Since listservs attract people with at least the subject of the listserv in common, they can create a strong sense of community among subscribers. While listservs are good for reading what many people have to say on various subjects related to the primary topic of the discussion group, postings are, in general, unedited and may not be completely reliable. On the other hand, a posting that seems wrongheaded or erroneous is likely to be corrected or at least commented on by other members of the group.

Blogs.   The term "blog" (we**b log**) is a relatively new word to describe an activity that people had been doing long before the term was coined: maintaining a website where they record personal thoughts and provide links to other sites. Many of them are essentially personal pages that bloggers (owners of the sites) update daily. They provide a forum for the bloggers themselves to argue, explain, comment on, vent frustrations, air opinions, or just gossip, while visitors to the site can express their own opinions or make observations. Membership is not required; anyone can read and respond to anyone's blog. In addition to online journals, blogs can be news summaries, collections of bits and pieces from other websites, and valuable resources for instant access to the latest news. Thus blogs have been described as a cross between an online diary and a cybermagazine, but one of the key characteristics of the most successful or popular blogs is that they are constantly updated. While just a few years ago there were only a small number of blogs, today there are millions of them. Many blogs are run by professionals like educators, reporters, researchers, scientists, and political candidates, with visits to the sites numbering in the thousands and in a few cases millions, but the vast majority are run by individuals who see them as chatty, stream-of-consciousness journals and whose readership is very limited.

A few blogs have attracted so many readers that they have achieved or exceeded the kind of readership that large newspapers enjoy. Because of the sheer number of readers and their ability to communicate instantly with other bloggers around the world, a few blogs have been responsible for bringing to light events or issues that mainstream media have ignored. For instance, bloggers played a key role in focusing public attention on talk-show host Don Imus's racist and sexist comments about the Rutgers women's basketball team in 2007. As a result, Imus lost his show. Blogs with the most impact on public affairs appear to be those with large numbers of daily visitors, and they tend to have the most influence in politics. One of the oldest blogs is Drudge Report (www.drudgereport.com), which records 8 to 10 million visits daily and provides many links to a wide variety of news sources. For instance, it has links to the front pages of most of the major newspapers in the world, links to all the wire services, links to the opinion columns of perhaps a hundred columnists who are read in newspapers around the United States, links to constant updates on America's involvement in foreign countries, and many more features that make it an excellent site for keeping up on what is being said, thought, and done around the world. Many other respected sites attract millions of visits daily or weekly.

Blogs have certain common features, including making it convenient for people to post or respond to the blog owner, posting messages in reverse chronological order for others to read, and providing links to other blogs and websites. However, blogs differ greatly in the quality and reliability of the information at the site. Blogs by definition are logs or journals and as such are often unedited, not-very-well-thought-out musings on a variety of topics. Be very careful when choosing blogs to follow and even more careful in accepting as truth what you read on a blog. You can apply the same questions to blogs that you would use for analyzing other websites rhetorically, but keep in mind the special nature of blogs and how their unrestricted, constantly changing content is very likely slanted or biased to fit the viewpoint of the blogger.

EXERCISE

1. Locate two websites on the same topic and compare and contrast their rhetorical effectiveness by applying the previous guidelines. After deciding which one you think is more effective, write an analysis in which your thesis states which site you prefer. Use details from your perusal of both of them as proof or evidence to support your thesis statement.

2. Locate two listservs on topics that interest you and read a few days' worth of posts. How do they compare and contrast? What is your impression of the sense of community among the members? What sorts of posts do people send? Do they stay on topic? Do the listservs have moderators? If you were going to join a list-serv, which one would you prefer?

3. Locate several blogs on a topic that interests you—baseball, water skiing, crime prevention, politics, a hobby, your major—and assess their rhetorical effective-ness, using the guidelines discussed.

CHAPTER 2

The Writing Process

Writing for any purpose involves a progression of stages, from prewriting, discovery, and planning to composing multiple drafts and then editing and proofreading. This process begins with determining your purpose, then inventing or discovering what you want to say, developing a strategy, planning how to organize your thoughts, writing a rough draft, revising as many times as necessary, proofreading, and then producing and editing the final copy. All writers, not just college students, benefit from treating a written endeavor as a process. Even professional writers plan, draft, revise, and edit before turning in their work. This chapter gives you a brief overview of the writing process. The guidelines presented here assume that you are writing for a college class and that your instructor has given you at least a general or broad subject area to write about and has specified what your purpose is. Often instructors give students a number of choices, but they still outline their expectations for the assignment.

PREWRITING

Prewriting is the first stage of any writing project and includes everything you do before you write your first draft. At this stage, you want to think about the best approach to your subject. Whether your instructor has given you a specific assignment or you are to select your own from a variety of possibilities, you need to spend time thinking about the assignment, generating ideas for it, identifying what you already know about it, discovering what you need to know, and narrowing your focus from a general subject to a specific topic. You also want to determine your purpose, identify your audience, and generate ideas before you even begin to write your paper. The practices used in prewriting usually spill over into other stages of the writing process as well. Through drafting, revising, editing, and producing the finished product, you are thinking about your topic, discovering new strategies or information, and determining how best to organizing, develop, and polish your piece.

Determine Your Purpose.   Your first step in the writing process is to determine your purpose, or your reason for writing. Are you going to argue a position, explain a phenomenon, analyze an event, narrate an experience, or come to some conclusion about something? Are you to write a summary or a critique? Perhaps you are to examine the ideas of several people on a specific topic, come to your own conclusions, and then incorporate the comments of those people into your own argument or explanation. It is crucial that you know what you hope to accomplish with the piece of writing at the beginning of each written assignment. Knowing your purpose puts you on the right track for the other stages of the process.

Identify Your Audience.   For college work, your audience may be your instructor alone but more often it includes your writing group or your classmates. For college writing classes where your work is not likely to be read outside of the classroom context, your instructor may ask you to imagine an audience or even suggest a specific audience to write for. Whether your instructor tells you what audience to write for or leaves the selection of an audience up to you, knowing whom you are writing to or for will help you determine what details you need to include in your paper.

Ask yourself who is going to read your work and what you know about the people in that audience. If you are writing an argument, anticipating readers who are not already convinced will help sharpen your argument. If your purpose is to explain, illustrate, or analyze, your audience is likely to be informed in general but not have a deep understanding of your subject. Unless instructed otherwise, assume an intelligent audience of nonspecialists who are interested in learning more about the topic of your paper. Imagining this audience will keep you from having to define or explain every term or concept and give you room for interesting, informative, and/or intriguing material about the topic.

Generate Ideas.   After establishing your purpose and audience, it is time to concentrate on how best to narrow your focus and develop your central idea. A number of useful exercises will help you discover what you know about your subject, generate ideas for your paper, and open up ways for you to narrow your subject to a workable topic. These include the following:

- **Brainstorming** or **freewriting.** This act involves simply writing without stopping for a set time, putting on paper everything that occurs to you as you think about your subject. To brainstorm or freewrite, spend five or ten minutes listing on a blank sheet of paper everything that occurs to you about your topic. Do not think too hard about what you are doing. Do not stop to check grammar or spelling. When your time is up, read through everything that you have written. Look for ideas that you think are promising for your assignment and, if you need to explore them further, brainstorm or freewrite on those, or try one of the other exercises for generating ideas.
- **Asking questions.** A good way to find out more about your subject is to simply ask questions about it. The most obvious questions are those that journalists routinely use: Who? What? When? Where? Why? How? Depending on your initial broad subject area, any of the following may help

you generate ideas for your paper: Who is affected? Who is responsible? What does it mean? When did it happen or take place? How is it done? Why does it matter? How does it work? What are its components? What happened? Where did it happen? Why did it happen? What does it mean? As you can tell, not every question is relevant for a subject, but asking some of them about your subject when appropriate alerts you to areas that you may need to explore and helps anticipate the kinds of questions readers may have when reading your paper.

- **Making lists.** List everything you know about or are curious about the subject you are working on. Listing is similar to brainstorming but involves just making a simple list of ideas, thoughts, or information related to your subject. Sometimes seeing ideas, concepts, or key words in a list leads to further development of those things.

- **Clustering around a central idea.** Clustering involves placing a key word or central idea in the center of your page and writing related words, phrases, or ideas around this central idea. As you move out from the central point by creating related ideas, you may see patterns emerge or recognize ways to develop your topic.

- **Researching.** Reading about or researching your subject will give you information, details, or arguments that you can use in the essay. If you use the Internet to locate information, be cautious about which sources you accept. Keeping in mind the guidelines in Chapter 1 on evaluating Internet sources, choose your search engine from among the best known or most used; they are likely to be the most reliable. The following search engines and databases, which will be particularly useful for researched writing, are well known, quite reliable, and likely to give you the results you seek in your search:

    - **Google (www.google.com),** which daily gives millions of people around the world access to billions of documents, is the search engine used most by people searching for information on the web. Using crawler-based technology, Google has many features that make it attractive to users. Besides providing links to web pages containing the key words of your search, the top of the search box on Google's home page offers links to images, discussion groups, news sites, shopping (Froogle), and its many other web features such as catalogs, web directories, and special searches. Google offers many web tools, including "Blogger," which lets you create your own blog and links you to other blogs, a translation tool, and Google's toolbar.

    - **Yahoo (www.yahoo.com)** is the web's oldest directory, having been established in 1994. It is easy to search and suitable for both experienced and novice Internet users. In addition to links to websites, you can use the tabs above the search box on its home page to find, among other things, groups, Yellow Pages listings, and shopping sites. Yahoo used to use human editors to organize websites into categories, but in 2002 shifted to crawler-based listings, getting most of its sites from Google. In 2004 it created its own search technology.

- **Ask.com (www.ask.com)** has over 2 billion fully indexed, searchable pages. Formerly known as Ask Jeeves and powered by ExpertRank algorithm, it is a good resource for locating articles on a variety of subjects.
- **Alta Vista (www.altavista.com)** at one time had the largest index in the industry, but attempts to change its nature caused it to fall behind the larger Google and Yahoo. Alta Vista is still a good, reliable source of information and, in addition to the usual links like news, images, and shopping, lets you find MP3/audio, video, and human category results.
- **InfoTrac® College Edition (www.infotrac.thomsonlearning.com** provides a searchable database of some 15 million periodical articles from over 5,000 journals, newspapers, and magazines covering the last twenty years. It is a rich resource of readings on just about any topic. InfoTrac College Edition is a subscription service that requires a pass code to access the database.
- **LookSmart (www.looksmart.com)** is a human-compiled directory of websites. Its best feature is likely its index of articles, which provides access to the contents of thousands of periodicals. You can search by subject, author, or title in your choice of all periodicals, certain categories of periodicals, or a specific periodical.
- **Lycos (www.lycos.com),** like Yahoo, was established in 1994 and is therefore one of the oldest search engines on the web. It provides both human-powered results from LookSmart for some queries, usually the most popular, and crawler-based results for others.
- **Excite (www.excite.com)** provides a full-text index of some 50 million web pages, lets you search from over 60,000 reviewed sites, and rates each site it lists.
- **Search.com (www.search.com)** is a collection of tools designed to find all kinds of information, from World Wide Web sites to phone numbers to movies to stock quotes. It searches Google, Ask.com, LookSmart, and dozens of other search engines to give you a broad range of responses to your queries.
- **Talking to others.** Discussing your subject with other people can be enormously helpful, whether it be friends, classmates, or your instructor. Oftentimes discussing a subject out loud with someone else helps to clarify thoughts or to discover new ideas or approaches.

Narrow your focus.   Along with settling on a subject, look for ways to narrow your focus to a specific topic. Keep in mind the distinction between **subject** and **topic:** Subject is the general area of investigation or thought, whereas topic is one narrow aspect of that subject. Here again the techniques for generating ideas will prove helpful. As you brainstorm, freewrite, ask questions, list, cluster, research, and discuss with others, you may come up with narrow aspects of the general subject; but if not, go through the process again, this time starting with the subject you are interested in. For instance, "racist language" is a general subject about which lengthy scholarly treatises, magazine and newspaper articles, and even books have been written. A suitable topic on that subject would explore one narrow aspect of that broad subject, as Zine Magubane does in "Why 'Nappy' is Offensive" at the end of this chapter.

WRITING THE FIRST DRAFT

The first draft will likely be your unpolished first effort to create the entire essay, to put all of your ideas about your topic into an organized, coherent whole. Fashion a title that best reflects what you plan to do in the paper. Then begin with a paragraph that introduces your topic by providing a context or background for it and that leads to a **thesis statement.** In the body of your paper, the paragraphs between your introductory and concluding paragraphs, construct **fully developed paragraphs,** each of which is focused on one specific topic—often stated in a **topic sentence**—that is related to your thesis. Bring your paper to an end by writing an appropriate **conclusion.**

Draft Your Title.   The title is the first thing that your readers see. In the draft stage, do the best you can to create a working title. You will almost surely change your title as your paper goes through various drafts, and you may even want to wait until you have written a draft or two before you create your title. However, many writers find it helpful to have a title in mind as one more aid in focusing the direction of the paper. If you knew nothing but the title of Zine Magubane's essay later in this chapter, "Why 'Nappy' is Offensive," you have a really good idea of what her paper is about. On the other hand, a colorful title may serve to capture or reflect what the paper is about but in an intriguing way. For instance, student Nate Hayes's paper (Chapter 6) arguing against human cloning is entitled "Hello, Dolly," a reference to the first cloned animal, a sheep named Dolly, but also a fun play on the title of the musical *Hello, Dolly.*

Draft Your Introduction.   After your title, your audience reads the first paragraph of your paper. This paragraph serves the important function of introducing the subject of your paper and leading to the specific aspect of that subject that the paper focuses on. Writers are often advised to begin with a general statement that serves to intrigue readers or catch their attention. That general sentence leads to more specific sentences, which in turn lead to an even more specific one, the thesis statement. The first paragraph not only introduces readers to the specific focus of the paper but also sets the tone, prepares readers for what is to follow, and engages their interest. As with your title, you may not be satisfied with your introduction in the first draft or two.

Because one of the tasks of the introduction is to entice readers or capture their attention, think about appropriate ways to achieve that goal in your own introduction. You might try a memorable or catchy statement, a colorful example or anecdote, a startling fact, or similar approach. For instance, here are the first several sentences of the introduction to Nate's paper "Hello, Dolly":

> Little Bo Peep has lost her sheep, but now she can clone a whole new flock! When Dr. Ian Wilmut and his team successfully cloned Dolly the sheep, the world was mystified, amazed, and scared. Immediately, members of the shocked public began to imagine worst case scenarios of reincarnated Hitlers and Dahmers.

The references to Little Bo Peep, Dolly the sheep, and Adolf Hitler and Jeffrey Dahmer all serve as lures to intrigue readers. Nate goes on with his introduction in this way:

> The medical field, however, relished the possibilities of cloning in curing patients with debilitating or terminal illnesses. The controversy over human cloning is part of the larger debate about the potential capabilities of scientists to alter or enhance the biological makeup of humans. This debate over how far "homo sapiens [should] be allowed to go" has grown increasingly heated with developments such as the successful cloning of sheep (Pethokoukis 559).

After his initial startling and colorful language, Nate becomes more focused on his real topic, the possibilities of human cloning as an answer to crippling and deadly illnesses. Note his use of MLA style to cite his source for the quotation and paraphrase in the last sentence.

Draft Your Thesis Statement.
Remember that your thesis indicates the central idea of your paper, suggests the direction you will take with that idea, states your position on a topic, or asks a question that you will answer in the course of your paper. Nate's opening sentences in the previous examples lead him to this position statement: *To many people, human cloning makes sense as the next major breakthrough in medical science, but until the troubling issues associated with the procedure are resolved, human cloning must not be allowed to happen.* From his introductory sentences to his increasingly more focused sentences and finally his thesis, readers know what to expect in the rest of his paper: details of the "troubling issues" to argue his position in opposition to attempts at human cloning at this time.

Another example is Zine Magubane's introduction to "Why 'Nappy' is Offensive." It is shorter than the student illustration above but it leads quickly and clearly to a statement of what the essay is about:

> When Don Imus called the Rutgers University basketball team a bunch of "nappy-headed ho's" he brought to the fore the degree to which black women's hair has served as a visible marker of our political and social marginalization. "Nappy," a historically derogatory term used to describe hair that is short and tightly coiled, is a preeminent example of how social and cultural ideas are transmitted through bodies. Since African women first arrived on American shores, the bends and twists of our hair have became markers of our subhuman status and convenient rationales for denying us our rightful claims to citizenship.

Reading this paragraph tells you immediately that Magubane is going to explain why the term "nappy" exemplifies social and cultural derogation and degradation of African American women. You can expect to read in the rest of the paper why the kind of hair referred to as "nappy" serves as "markers " and "rationales" for the treatment of African women and is therefore offensive.

Not every kind of writing requires a thesis, but most do, especially the kinds of writing that you will do for your college courses. Not every thesis needs to be stated explicitly, either, but there must almost always be some clearly implied central point to your writing. Further, you want to state your thesis early in your paper so that your readers know fairly quickly what your central purpose is. Often a thesis statement works best in the first paragraph. Your thesis might even need two sentences to completely state it, especially for longer papers. In the draft stage, you may not know the exact wording of your thesis but you will want to have a good idea of what it includes. As with a working title, a working thesis helps focus your thoughts as you draft your essay. As you work through drafts of your paper, you will very likely be refining and polishing your thesis. An ideal thesis statement will indicate the specific topic of the paper, suggest how you will approach it, and may even hint at how you will support or develop it.

Develop an Effective Strategy. When you are satisfied that you have a clear understanding of your purpose, your audience, your topic, and your thesis, it is time to plan the rest of your first draft. How will you organize your essay? What strategies will you use to develop and support your thesis? It is helpful in both your own writing and in evaluating the writing of others to be familiar with common kinds of writing and the strategies writers use for organizing and developing their ideas. If you understand what strategies are available to a writer and what elements make those strategies work, you can better evaluate how well a selection is written.

Writers use many different **strategies** or **rhetorical methods** to organize and develop their ideas, depending on their purposes and their audience. Whether they pursue persuasive, expository, or expressive purposes, writers must be focused and clear if they want to engage their readers. They can achieve clarity or coherence with good organization and logical development of ideas. Writers seldom use any one method exclusively or even think about any particular pattern or mode of development. Instead, they first decide what their purpose for writing is, and then they use whatever combination of patterns best achieves their purpose.

In your college courses, you will often be given written assignments. No matter what the course, whether it is art history, communications, science, anthropology, or business, the instructor may require a paper on a subject relevant to the course. Furthermore, students are very likely to encounter essay questions on exams, for instructors in courses across the curriculum seem to agree that one of the best tests of understanding is to ask students to write in some detail on quizzes or exams about important course material. Whether it is biology or English, students may be asked to argue a position on a controversial issue. An art professor may ask students to write a description of a painting, or a math professor may test understanding by asking students to explain in writing how to solve a problem. Whatever a writer's purpose, some fairly standard models can help to organize written work. But remember: seldom will a writer use just one of these rhetorical modes in isolation; they are almost always used in combinations of two or more. The important consideration is how a writer can best organize and develop the material for the best effect, that best suits the purpose of the assignment.

- **Argument/Persuasion.** Argument is a mode of persuasion in which the goal is either to convince readers of the validity of the writer's position (**argument**) or move readers to accept the author's view and even act on it (persuasion). In argument, writers set forth an assertion (often called a **proposition**) about a debatable topic and offer proof intended to convince readers that the assertion is a valid or true one. In persuasion, a writer goes a step further and offers a course of action, with the ultimate goal of making readers take action. The supporting evidence or proof must be so convincing that readers cannot help but agree with the validity of the author's position. The reasoning process must be so logical that readers inevitably draw the same conclusions that the author does from the evidence. Many of the readings in this textbook are arguments, including some that are paired because their authors hold differing viewpoints on an issue. For instance, on the issue of cloning, James D. Watson in "All for the Good" differs in opinion from Ian Wilmut in "Dolly's False Legacy" (Chapter 20). Joshua Green in "Deadly Compromise" (Chapter 14) lays out the arguments both for and against capital punishment and takes the position that both are wrong, while John O'Sullivan in "Deadly Stakes: The Debate Over Capital Punishment" looks at arguments in opposition to capital punishment to make his case in favor of it (Chapter 14). You will find readings whose primary purpose is argument or persuasion located throughout the textbook. For a fuller discussion of argumentation, see Chapter 5.
- **Cause–Effect Analysis.** A writer who wants to explain why something happened or show what happened as a result of something—or perhaps both—is doing cause and effect analysis. This type of analysis is used frequently in news broadcasts and magazine and newspaper articles to explain phenomena, such as the chain of events that led to a particular action, the effects of a particular event or crisis, or both causes and effects of a specific situation. Cause and effect analysis is also used frequently to argue. A writer might use the strategy of causal analysis in arguing that offering sex education in schools or making contraceptives readily available to high school students would be more effective in reducing the number of teenage pregnancies than prohibiting explicit sex scenes on prime time television. The writer would have to sort out possible causes to explain the high rate of teenage pregnancies, determine which likely are most responsible and which are contributing factors, and then conjecture likely results if the recommendation were followed. Many argumentative essays use causal analysis to develop their argument. Indeed, any argument on the effects of an activity—viewing television, playing video games, listening to violent music—of necessity is a

causal analysis. Sissela Bok undertakes a causal analysis in her look at opposing sides on the issue of media violence in "Aggression: The Impact of Media Violence" (Chapter 9). Similarly, Philip G. Zimbardo uses causal analysis in "Revisiting the Stanford Prison Experiment: A Lesson in the Power of Situation" (Chapter 14) when he explains the results of his experiment to determine the effects of anonymity on power, especially when good people are placed in a bad situation. (Chapter 12)

- **Comparison–Contrast.** Another strategy for developing ideas is to show similarities and differences between two elements. Comparison and contrast can be useful in an argument piece in which the writer supports one of two possible choices and needs to explain reasons for that choice. In an expository essay—that is, one with the purpose of explaining something—comparison and contrast can be useful to demonstrate a thorough understanding of the subject. Comparing or contrasting usually promotes one of two purposes: to show each of two subjects distinctly by considering both side by side or to evaluate or judge two things. An analogy is a useful kind of comparison when seeking to explain a complicated or unfamiliar subject by showing its similarities to a less complicated or more familiar subject. An example of a writer using comparison–contrast to make a point is Joshua Foer, whose essay "Enter Right, Exit Left" in Chapter 3 compares the political attitudes of his graduating class in 2004 to what they were when they began as college freshmen in 2000.

- **Classification–Division.** Classification is the process of sorting information and ideas into categories or groups; division is the act of breaking information, ideas, or concepts into parts in order to better understand them. A writer may use classification to explain how a particular class of people, things, or ideas can be separated into groups and labeled according to common characteristics that distinguish them from other groups. A writer may use division to make a large, complex subject easier to understand by dividing it into smaller, more manageable parts. Thus, Murray Weidenbaum in "Dispelling the Myths about the Global Economy" (Chapter 26) looks at the negative connotations of "globalization" by identifying ten different components of that negative image and examining each one in terms of why he feels it is false.

- **Definition.** Writers often need to define as they inform or argue. Definition is the process of making clear a precise meaning or significance. In definition, a writer conveys the essential characteristics of something by distinguishing it from all other things in its class. You are familiar with dictionary definitions of words. Writers employ a similar technique to clarify or to explain, but usually in more detail than dictionaries give. In addition to providing brief definitions of terms, a writer may provide an extended definition, that is, take the meaning of a word beyond its dictionary definition or beyond the limits of a simple definition. An extended definition may go for a paragraph or two or even for the length of an entire essay. A writer using abstract terms or concepts unfamiliar to an audience will find the extended definition a useful tool, as Deborah Tannen does in "We Need a Higher Quality Outrage" in Chapter 3 when she defines the term "agonism." Howard Moody, in "Sacred Rite or Civil Right?" (Chapter 15), draws distinctions between the state's definition and the church's definition of marriage. These definitions are key components in Moody's argument and help him achieve his central purpose.

- **Exemplification.** Examples and illustrations are crucial to writing, no matter what the primary purpose. Without examples, writing stays at the general or abstract level and leaves readers only vaguely understanding what the writer means. Examples make meaning clear and help make writing more interesting, livelier, and more engaging than an essay without details. Examples may be brief and numerous or extended and limited in number, and they may take the form of narratives. Most of the readings in this textbook contain examples of one kind or another. Much of Zine Magubane's "Why 'Nappy' is Offensive" later in this chapter and Jean Kilbourne's "Advertising's Influence on Media Content" in Chapter 9 consist of examples that both illustrate and argue their theses. It would be difficult to find an effective piece of writing that does not use examples of some sort.

- **Narration.** Narration is the re-creation of an experience for a specific purpose. It may be a brief anecdote, a story, or a case history. Writers use narration for a variety of purposes: to explain, to illustrate a particular point, to report information, to entertain, or to persuade. Often a narrative is only one part of a written work, but occasionally it may be the entire means of development. Journalists are accustomed to asking themselves a series of questions when they write their stories to ensure that they give complete narratives: What happened? To whom did it happen? When did it happen? Where did it happen? Why did it happen? How did it happen; that is, under what circumstances or in what way did it happen? Narration is often combined with description. In making his argument that Americans should donate to world charities that aid impoverished children, Peter Singer in "The Singer Solution to World Poverty" narrates hypothetical examples in order to forcefully and vividly persuade readers to act (Chapter 13).

- **Description.** Description depicts in words a person, place, or thing by appealing to the senses, that is, by evoking through words certain sights, smells, sounds, or tactile sensations. Description is an almost indispensable part of writing; it is certainly inextricably linked with narration. As with narration and all other kinds of writing, description has a purpose. The purpose of description may be objective—to convey information without bias—or it may be subjective—to express feelings, impressions, or attitudes about a person, place, or thing. Almost all of the readings in this book have description in one form or another, and often description goes hand in hand with narration. A good example of this combination is the excerpt titled "Serving in Florida" from Barbara Ehrenreich's book *Nickel and Dimed* in Chapter 24.

Keep in mind that these various rhetorical methods—ways of organizing and developing ideas—are almost never used in isolation. Seldom will you find a piece of writing that does not combine two or more of these strategies, and they are all equally useful depending on your purpose for writing, the audience you are writing to, and the context you are writing in. You will notice as you read the essays in this textbook that all of the writers employ a variety of strategies to achieve their purpose.

Draft the Body of Your Paper.   The body of your paper will consist of a number of paragraphs that explain, defend, or develop your thesis. Each paragraph must contain key ideas, supporting evidence, detailed explanation, or other information that directly advances your purpose. A typical paragraph focuses on one topic related to the thesis of the paper, has a topic sentence that expresses that single topic, contains perhaps seven to ten supporting sentences, and has a concluding sentence that leads to the next paragraph.

- **Topic sentence.** Each of the paragraphs in the body of the paper should have a topic sentence. Remember that the thesis statement answers the question, "What is this essay about?" In the same way, the topic sentence answers the question, "What is this paragraph about?" If your topic sentence is not clearly stated, it should be clearly implied.
- **Supporting sentences.** Sentences in the paragraph should be organized logically, should support only the topic of that paragraph, and should lead clearly and smoothly from one to another. They are used to support the topic sentence, that is, to explain it, illustrate it, or amplify or expand on it. Paragraphs contain details related to and supportive of the focus of the paragraph. They include a mix of both general and specific or detailed statements.
- **Concluding sentence(s).** The final sentence or sentences summarize the connections between the sentences and bring the paragraph to closure. Sometimes the final sentence points to the subject of the next paragraph.
- **Transition.** Provide effective transition to move from thought to thought and point to point as well as from sentence to sentence and paragraph to paragraph. In any kind of writing, you want to strive to be as coherent as possible, and you go a long way in achieving that goal when you provide clear markers to help your readers follow the development of your paper and see connections between ideas and points. We have many tools with which to link or show the connection between thoughts and ideas. Repeating key words, using pronouns to refer to nouns, and using transitional words all help achieve clarity or coherence. The following are just a few examples of the many words we have to make transitions clear:
  - **To show addition:** furthermore, in addition, also, again, too, as well as, another
  - **To show consequence:** therefore, as a result, because, consequently, thus, then, hence, so that, for this reason, since

- **To show contrast:** on the other hand, however, in contrast, instead, conversely, on the contrary, but, yet, compared to
- **To show similarity:** likewise, similarly, in the same way, moreover, analogous to
- **To illustrate:** for example, such as, in particular, to illustrate, for instance, for one thing, to explain, namely, that is, in this case
- **To show time relationship:** later, earlier, afterward, before, next, eventually, at length, before long, meanwhile, subsequently
- **To make a concession:** although, even though, still, of course, while it may be true, in spite of, at any rate
- **To emphasize:** importantly, unquestionably, without a doubt, of prime importance, certainly, undeniably
- **Summary:** in brief, in summary, in essence, in other words, to conclude, generally, in any event, on the whole, as I have shown

Draft Your Concluding Paragraph.   This final paragraph brings the paper to a satisfying conclusion. You may not be ready to write your conclusion when you write the first draft of your paper because the conclusion should come logically from all that has gone before. Sometimes you need to write several drafts before you can write your conclusion. When you are ready to write it, you have a number of approaches to choose from. Sometimes writers simply restate their introductions, but try to be more imaginative. You don't have to restate major points, as they should be clear in readers' minds, but referring to them or highlighting them lends emphasis to what you have written and stresses its significance. Try to leave your readers with something to think about: stress the importance of what you have written, suggest a course of action, or point to questions raised by your paper that need further study or exploration. You might refer back to your introduction by mentioning a detail or image from it or end with an amusing anecdote or humorous or striking comment.

Here is the conclusion from Nate's paper, "Hello, Dolly":

> There are just far too many unanswered questions, and who knows how many remain unasked? It is not easy to anticipate all the possible ramifications for mankind of human cloning. The bottom line is that ethical, psychological, social, and religion questions need to be explored, discussed, and resolved before research in genetic engineering that aims to create new life or significantly alter existing life can be allowed to continue.

Nate reiterates his position and suggests several things that must be done before he would change his mind about scientists pursuing human cloning. Zine Magubane, on the other hand, reinforces her central point, as stated in her thesis, by summarizing her key reasons "Why 'Nappy' is Offensive":

> For African-American women, the personal has always been political. What grows out of our head can mean the difference between being a citizen and being a subject; being enslaved or free; alive or dead. As Don Imus found out this week,

300 years of a tangled and painful racial history cannot be washed away with a simple apology.

No matter what strategy you choose for concluding your paper, readers should feel that they have come to a satisfactory end.

REVISING AND EDITING YOUR PAPER

Writers use many techniques to make the revision process meaningful. You truly want to revise, not simply rewrite, your paper, so leave some time between drafts to give yourself a fresh perspective on what you have written. Obviously that means not starting any writing project at the last minute. You will find that it works to your advantage to begin writing as soon as possible after getting an assignment. The more time you have to draft and revise, the more satisfied you are likely to be with your final effort.

When revising, read each sentence and paragraph carefully. Try reading your paper out loud and listen to how it sounds, or read it to someone else to get feedback from a (presumably) objective audience. Rewrite passages that sound awkward or seem to lead nowhere, move things around if the paper seems disorganized, and look for ways to improve the development of every point you make. If you have trouble with certain grammatical structures or misspell the same words all the time, make a conscientious effort to look for those trouble spots. Although the most important aspect of your writing is your content—what you say, how well you say it, and how well you present it—you also want to pay attention to sentence-level skills. Errors at this level distract your reader from what you are saying, and too many such errors weaken your effectiveness as a writer.

It is not uncommon for successful writers to produce several drafts before they are satisfied with their work. As you revise and write new drafts, apply the self-evaluation questions below to help you in the process.

Self-evaluation.   Apply the same questions to your own writing that you ask when evaluating the writing of others, as detailed in Chapter 1 on critical reading. Ask yourself if you have a clearly stated central idea, if your paragraphs are fully developed with specific and detailed statements, if your overall organizing pattern is clear, if your writing is understandable and intelligent, and if the language you have used is appropriate and idiomatic. Here is the list again, modified to suit an evaluation of your own work:

- Does your title accurately reflect what the essay is about? Is it catchy, intriguing, or engaging? Your title is the first thing that your audience will read, so
- Does your introduction give enough information to get your readers easily into the essay?
- Do you achieve your stated or implied purpose?

- Is your essay organized?
- Is your thesis or main idea thoroughly explained, developed, or argued?
- Have you supplied enough details, examples, or other evidence to fully support or illustrate the thesis?
- If it is an argument or persuasion essay, is the evidence convincing? Is the argument logical and reasonable? Have you avoided fallacies in the logic of your argument?
- If the purpose of the essay is to describe, have you conveyed the essence of the thing with appropriately vivid words?
- Can you anticipate questions that your readers might have or challenges they might make about any of your assertions? If so, can you revise your paper to address those potential questions or challenges?
- Does your conclusion bring your paper to a satisfactory closure?
- Is your writing clear?
- Have you used colorful, engaging, and/or lively language?
- Is your tone appropriate for your subject and audience?
- How are sentence-level skills? Have you constructed effective sentences that are varied in structure and length? Are your words spelled correctly and are sentences punctuated according to standard conventions?

PROOFREADING

After you have revised your paper to the best of your ability, write the final draft. Most instructors require papers to be typewritten or done on a computer, but follow whatever guidelines your instructor sets for written assignments. See Appendix 2 for formatting guidelines, unless your instructor provides different ones for you. Leave time to proofread your final version and make any last minute corrections, preferably on the word processor but, if necessary, write them neatly in ink. At this final stage, you are looking for careless or previously undiscovered errors that you can fix easily. If you have given yourself time to write your several drafts, edit, and revise, the proofreading stage should just be a final check of work well done.

EXERCISE

The student paper below is five paragraphs and approximately 800 words long. The assignment was to select a historical document and assess its relevance to some aspect of today's culture. Josanne selected the November 19, 1863, address by President Abraham Lincoln at Gettysburg and wrote her essay on its relevance to today's battle against terrorism. As you read the essay, note what you think are strengths and weaknesses of it and be prepared to discuss your responses in class

Begley 1

Josanne Begley

Professor Schilling

English 101-8

9 June 2008

Josanne's introduction begins with a general statement and becomes more specific as she moves toward her thesis. Josanne frames her thesis in the form of a question.

The Gettysburg Address and the War Against Terrorism
Time alters everything in the physical world:
people are born and die, structures are built
and destroyed, civilizations rise and fall. But
does it follow that the passage of time alters
the relevance of the ideas of great thinkers and
leaders of the past? Can the words of a speech
that is over 140 years old have any significance
to today's world? What can the "Gettysburg Address"
possibly say to a nation at war with terrorism?

The paragraph focuses on trials that America has survived, connecting the Civil War with the war on terrorism.

Ever since the American founders established a
nation based on the principle that all men and women
are created equal and are entitled to be free, its
enemies have tried its ability to survive. At war
internally, the United States even put itself to the
test during the Civil War over the issue of slavery.
Many people gave their lives in that long fight to
preserve the freedom for all people that is a hallmark
of this country. More recently, terrorists put America
to the test when they used its own airplanes as
flying bombs and crashed three of them into the World
Trade Center and the Pentagon, along with another one
that was diverted into a field in Pennsylvania. That
trial, too, was not without sacrifices.

Josanne discusses the Gettysburg Address and quotes a passage whose words she will refer to later.

After a bloody battle at Gettysburg during the
Civil War, President Abraham Lincoln delivered his
famous address to dedicate a cemetery at the site
of the battle. The Confederacy was fighting for the
right to own and use slaves, but President Lincoln

Begley 2

knew that slavery went against the principles of
freedom and equality that the nation was built
upon. In his speech, Lincoln charged the people of
the Union to carry on the fight for which so many
lives had already been given:

> The world will little note nor long
> remember what we say here, but it can
> never forget what they did here. It is for
> us the living, rather, to be dedicated
> here to the unfinished work which they
> who fought here have thus far so nobly
> advanced. It is rather for us to be here
> dedicated to the great task remaining
> before us—that from these honored dead we
> take increased devotion to that cause for
> which they gave the last full measure of
> devotion—that we here highly resolve that
> these dead shall not have died in vain.

Lincoln realized that those who gave their lives
at the battle of Gettysburg died for a cause they
believed in, and his speech to those assembled for
the dedication of the cemetery reiterated the need
for the living to carry on the battle with renewed
and even stronger commitment.

Note how the first sentence makes the transition into the new paragraph and shifts the focus to the war on terrorism. Josanne contrasts the Civil War with the war on terrorism but then highlights the relevance of Lincoln's words at Gettysburg to the events of September 11.

After the terrorist attacks on September 11,
2001, America is once again fighting for freedom,
this time not only for the right of each human
being to live his or her life as he or she sees fit
but also to live that life without the constant
fear of a terrorist attack. Obviously the war
against terrorism is different from the Civil War.
This war has a nebulous and widespread enemy; there

Begley 3

is no one specific country to target but rather persons and their followers whose goal it is to destroy the United States. The war on terrorism has already gone beyond the number of years it took to fight the Civil War and is likely to be protracted for many more years. The goal of this war—eradicating terrorism—is not easy to achieve, but that does not mean that the country will not fight for it. We must not and will not let the thousands of people who lost their lives on that eleventh day of September to "have died in vain." As buildings were burning and crumbling into rubble, brave police officers and courageous firemen "gave the last full measure of devotion" as they tried to save the lives of innocent people trapped in those buildings. Hearing the horrendous news about the attacks in New York and the Pentagon, people on another hijacked plane rallied together and saved untold numbers of lives by giving up their own. Like the dead at Gettysburg, these people in New York, Washington, D.C., and Pennsylvania died heroic deaths.

Josanne's conclusion answers the question posed in her thesis and continues to emphasize the relevance of Lincoln's words to today's battle.

      Lincoln's words at Gettysburg do indeed have strong relevance for us today. As a nation, we "can never forget" what those who died on September 11, 2001, did. We must commit ourselves "to the task remaining before us." We must complete "the unfinished work" of preserving our basic liberties and of eliminating terrorism. We must resolve, as Lincoln put it to his audience over 140 years ago, "that this nation under God shall have a new birth of freedom, and that government of the people, by the people, for the people shall not perish from the earth."

WHY 'NAPPY' IS OFFENSIVE

ZINE MAGUBANE

Zine Magubane is an associate professor of sociology and African diaspora studies at Boston College and author of Bringing the Empire Home: Race, Class, and Gender in Britain and Colonial South Africa *(2003). This piece appeared in the April 12, 2007, issue of the* Boston Globe. *The incident that sparked this essay was the live on-air remarks by white radio "shock jock" Don Imus on his show early in April 2007 as he watched clips of the Rutgers women's basketball team playing a game.*

When Don Imus called the Rutgers University basketball team a bunch of "nappy-headed ho's" he brought to the fore the degree to which black women's hair has served as a visible marker of our political and social marginalization. "Nappy," a historically derogatory term used to describe hair that is short and tightly coiled, is a preeminent example of how social and cultural ideas are transmitted through bodies. Since African women first arrived on American shores, the bends and twists of our hair have became markers of our subhuman status and convenient rationales for denying us our rightful claims to citizenship.

Establishing the upper and lower limits of humanity was of particular interest to Enlightenment era thinkers, who struggled to balance the ideals of the French Revolution and the Declaration of Independence with the fact of slavery. The 1789 *Declaration of the Rights of Man and Citizen* did not discriminate on the basis of race or sex and had the potential to be applied universally. It was precisely because an appeal to natural rights could only be countered by proof of natural inequality that hair texture, one of the most obvious indicators of physical differences between the races, was seized upon. Nappy hair was demonstrable proof of the fact that neither human physiology nor human nature was uniform and, therefore, that social inequalities could be justified.

Saartjie Baartman, a South African "bushwoman," was exhibited like a circus freak in the Shows of London between 1810 and 1815. The leading French anatomist of the day, George Cuvier, speculated that Baartman might be the "missing link" between the human and animal worlds because of her "peculiar features" including her "enormous buttocks" and "short, curling hair." In *Notes on the State of Virginia,* Thomas Jefferson reflected on why it would be impossible to incorporate blacks into the body politic after emancipation. He concluded it was because of the differences "both physical and moral," chief among them the absence of long, flowing hair.

4   For a runaway slave, the kink in her hair could mean the difference between freedom in the North and enslavement or worse if she were to be caught and returned to her master. Miscegenation meant that some slaves had skin as light as whites and the rule of thumb was that hair was a more reliable indicator than skin of a person's racial heritage. Thus, runaway slaves often shaved their heads in order to get rid of any evidence of their ancestry and posters advertising for fugitive slaves often warned slave catchers to be on the lookout for runaways with shaved heads: "They might pass for white."

In the late 1960s, after the FBI declared Angela Davis one of the country's 10 most wanted criminals, thousands of other law-abiding, Afro-wearing African-American women became targets of state repression—accosted, harassed, and arrested by police, the FBI, and immigration agents. The "wanted" posters that featured Davis, her huge Afro framing her face like a halo, appeared in post offices and government buildings all over America, not to mention on television and in *Life* magazine. Her "nappy hair" served not only to structure popular opinions about her as a dangerous criminal, but also made it possible to deny the rights of due process and habeas corpus to any young black woman, simply on the basis of her hairstyle.

For African-American women, the personal has always been political. What grows out of our head can mean the difference between being a citizen and being a subject; being enslaved or free; alive or dead. As Don Imus found out this week, 300 years of a tangled and painful racial history cannot be washed away with a simple apology.

PERSONAL RESPONSE

What other racial or ethnic features might "serve as visible political and social markers"? Have you ever felt personally "marked" because of a specific feature of your body?

QUESTIONS FOR CLASS AND SMALL-GROUP DISCUSSION

1. Assess the effectiveness of Magubane's writing strategies. For instance, how effective do you find her opening? Does she have a clearly stated thesis? Is the essay organized? Does she use transitional words or phrases to move her paper from point to point? Does the conclusion bring the piece to a satisfactory end?

2. Discuss the use that Magubane makes of examples. How do they support her thesis?

3. What do you understand Magubane to mean when she writes: "For African-American women, the personal has always been the political" (paragraph 6)?

4. Overall, how effective do you find the essay? Are you persuaded that "nappy" is indeed an offensive term?

Writing a Summary

Students often must write both informal exercises and formal papers based on readings in their textbooks. In writing assignments for the course using this textbook, for instance, you will find frequent use for information or ideas discussed in the readings. For formal writing assignments, you may be instructed to choose among the writing topics that end each chapter in Parts 2–5, or you may be asked to suggest your own topic for a paper on a reading or readings. You may choose to argue in favor of or against a position another author takes; you may use information from one or more of the readings to write an essay suggested by a particular chapter; you may decide to compare and contrast two or more essays in a chapter or explain various perspectives on an issue. At some point, you may want to use some of the readings from this or another textbook in combination with other print and Internet resources in a research paper.

This and the next three chapters introduce several specific types of assignments that you may be asked to write and provide guidelines for writing them. This chapter focuses on the summary, Chapter 4 on writing a critique, Chapter 5 on writing an argument, and Chapter 6 on writing a synthesis with documentation. In all of these assignments, you may be called on to paraphrase, quote, and document material on which you are writing. The guidelines for paraphrasing, quoting, and documenting sources are explained in Chapter 6. All illustrations of handling source material follow MLA (Modern Language Association) documentation style. If your instructor prefers that you use APA (American Psychological Society) documentation style, see Chapter 7 for guidelines.

WRITING A SUMMARY

Summarizing produces an objective restatement of a written passage in your own words in a much shorter version than the original. The purpose of a summary is to highlight both the central idea or ideas and the major points of a work. A summary does not attempt to restate the entire reading. You might summarize an entire book in the space of a paragraph or perhaps even a sentence, although you will not do full justice to a lengthy work that way.

Many reasons call for summarizing. Your instructor may ask you to write a summary of an essay, or a passage from one, to gauge your understanding. Such an assignment may be informal, something that you write in class as a quiz or an ungraded journal entry, or you may be assigned a formal summary, a longer piece that you write out of class in detail and with care. Many kinds of writing include summaries as part of the development of their main ideas. For instance, if you are asked to report on an individual or group research project for a science class, you will probably summarize your purpose, methodology, data, and conclusions. If you write an argumentative paper, you may need to summarize either opposing viewpoints or your own supporting evidence. A research paper often includes summaries of information from source materials, and the research process itself necessitates summarizing portions of what you read. Reviews of books or articles almost always include summaries of the works under discussion, and essay questions on an examination often require summaries of information or data. Across the curriculum, no matter what course you are taking, you will probably be asked to summarize.

Summaries serve useful purposes. Professors summarize as they lecture in order to convey information in a condensed way when a detailed review would take far too much time. Textbook chapters often present summaries of chapter contents as part of chapter introductions (as in Parts 2–5 of this textbook). In this textbook, some of the questions for small-group and class discussion following the readings ask you to summarize major points or portions of readings, in order to facilitate your understanding of the text. That process, in turn, enhances the quality of your classroom experience and develops your abilities to follow the discussion intelligently and to make useful contributions to the discussion yourself. Your instructor may ask you to write a summary of a piece you have read as a formal assignment. Summarizing is also an excellent strategy to enhance your own study habits. After reading an assignment for any of your courses, try to write a summary of the reading. If you cannot put into your own words the major ideas of what you have just read, you may need to go back and reread the material.

Outside the classroom and the academic environment, summaries routinely give brief introductions, overviews, and conclusions of subjects at hand. In business, industry, law, medicine, scientific research, government, or any other field, both managers and workers often need quick summaries to familiarize themselves with the high points or essence of information. Knowing how to summarize accurately is a skill that you will find useful in both your academic writing and in your profession or job.

A Summary Is Not a Substitute for Analysis.   Do not mistakenly assume that putting another person's words into your own words is an analysis. Instead, **a summary is a brief, concise, objective restatement of the important elements of a piece of writing of any length,** from a paragraph to an entire book. A summary may be brief, as in a one-paragraph abstract that precedes a report or long paper and gives a very short overview of it, or it may be several paragraphs or even pages in length, depending on the length of the writing or writings being summarized. You may summarize as an informal exercise for your own purposes or as a formal assignment that you hand in to your instructor for evaluation.

Abstract.   An abstract, like all summaries, is a condensed, objective restatement of the essential points of a text. Its distinguishing characteristic is its brevity. Abstracts are usually quite short, perhaps 100 to 200 words, whereas summaries may be much longer, depending on the length of what is being summarized. As with all summaries, an abstract helps readers determine quickly if an article or book will be of interest or use. It can also serve as a brief guide to the key points before reading an article or as an aid in recalling the contents of the piece after reading it. Below is an example of an abstract of Henry Jenkins' "Art Form for the Digital Age" (Chapter 8). This abstract provides a broad overview of Jenkins' article, including his major points and conclusions. In his essay, he discusses or develops each of these components at length, providing examples and supporting evidence where necessary. You can see how an abstract, like summaries of other lengths, is useful for getting a quick overview of a report or essay.

Formal and Informal Summaries.   Informal summaries are primarily for personal use and are usually not handed in for evaluation by an instructor. Formal

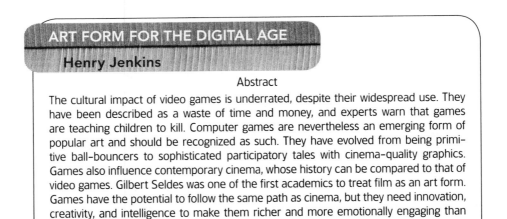

ART FORM FOR THE DIGITAL AGE

Henry Jenkins

Abstract

The cultural impact of video games is underrated, despite their widespread use. They have been described as a waste of time and money, and experts warn that games are teaching children to kill. Computer games are nevertheless an emerging form of popular art and should be recognized as such. They have evolved from being primitive ball-bouncers to sophisticated participatory tales with cinema-quality graphics. Games also influence contemporary cinema, whose history can be compared to that of video games. Gilbert Seldes was one of the first academics to treat film as an art form. Games have the potential to follow the same path as cinema, but they need innovation, creativity, and intelligence to make them richer and more emotionally engaging than they are now.

summaries are those that others will read and are sometimes graded assignments. In either case, the process for writing a summary is virtually the same. For an example of an informal summary that would help a student prepare for a class discussion or recall key elements of an article, see the summary of Joe Saltzman's "What's in a Name? More than You Think," located in the discussion that follows that reading in Chapter 1. An example of a formal summary follows Joshua Foer's "Enter Right, Exit Left," later in this chapter. The summaries of both Saltzman's and Foer's articles underscore the need for a close, critical reading of the text to fairly represent what a writer says.

The trick in summarizing accurately is knowing what is important, and therefore must be included, and what is secondary, and therefore should be omitted. Here you see the usefulness of the guidelines for critical reading. When you read critically, you identify the main idea or thesis of the selection, and you highlight or in some way mark major points. A summary must include the main idea of what you are summarizing, and it should include major points, and only major points. Thus, if you learn to read critically, you can write a summary.

Although the process is the same for both an assignment that you will hand in to your instructor and a summary for your own use, a formal summary requires the kind of care that you give to longer writing assignments. The following directions will help you prepare and draft your formal summary:

1. Begin by carefully reading the work. Make a mental note of its thesis or main idea but do not write anything in the margins yet. If you try to highlight for a summary on your first reading, you might end up underlining or noting too many things. Wait until you have read the entire selection through once before writing anything.

2. After your first reading, write in your own words the thesis or central idea as you understand it. Then go back to the article, locate the thesis or main idea, underline it, and compare it with the sentence you wrote. If your sentence differs from the sentence(s) you underlined, rephrase your own sentence.

3. Next, read the article again, this time looking for major points of development or illustration of the thesis. As you reread, make marginal notes and underline, circle, or in some way mark the key supporting points or major ideas in the development of the thesis.

4. After you have finished reading, look at your notes and state in one sentence, in your own words, the thesis and each major point. Do not include details or minor supporting evidence unless leaving them out would misrepresent or unfairly represent what you are summarizing. If the writing you are summarizing comes to any important conclusions, note them as well in one sentence in your own words.

5. If you are still unclear about which are major and which are minor points, give the piece another reading. The more you read it, the better you understand its purpose, method of development, and major points.

Now you are ready to write your summary.

6. In your opening sentence, state the author's full name, the title of the work, and the thesis or main idea. Write in complete sentences, whether your summary is 100 words or 500 words long.

7. Use the author's last name when referring to what he or she says in the article or when quoting the author directly.

8. Use attributive tags throughout; that is, use words and phrases that attribute or point to your source. Such tags serve the purpose of reminding your readers who you are quoting or summarizing. They may take the form of the author's last name or pronouns referring to the author, credentials of the author, published source of the material, or other information that identifies the author (for example, "Foer, writing from his position as a senior about to graduate," a recent article on the *New York Times* Op-Ed page, or "he argues").

9. Do not use the exact words of the author unless you use quotation marks around those words. The summary must use your own wording. Use direct quotations sparingly, and only for a significant word, phrase, or sentence, and make sure that anything you put in quotation marks uses the exact wording of the article.

GUIDELINES FOR WRITING A SUMMARY

- On your first reading, mentally note the thesis or central idea of the work or passage you are summarizing without writing anything down.
- After your first reading, write down your understanding of the thesis, locate the thesis in the work, underline it, check what you have written against it, and adjust your own sentence if necessary.
- Now reread the work, noting key points, either in the margin, by highlighting, or on a separate piece of paper.
- When you have finished your second reading, once again write in your own words a one-sentence summary of the thesis or central idea. Use the author's name and title of the reading in that sentence.
- Write in your own words a one-sentence summary of each major point the author has used to develop, illustrate, or support the thesis or central idea. State only essential details related to each major point.
- Do not include minor points unless you believe their omission would give an unfair representation of what you are summarizing.
- Where appropriate, write in your own words a one-sentence summary of any conclusion from the piece.
- Use attributive tags throughout your summary.
- Keep your summary short, succinct, and focused on the central idea and major points of the piece you are summarizing.
- Edit for grammar, punctuation, and spelling before handing in your assignment.

10. Use present tense to describe or explain what the author has written ("Foer explains" or "Foer concludes").

11. Provide clear transitions from point to point, just as you would in a longer assignment, and write in clear, coherent language.

12. Edit what you have written before turning it in to your instructor.

ILLUSTRATION: MAKING MARGINAL NOTES AND SUMMARIZING

Joshua Foer's "Enter Right, Exit Left" is reprinted here, along with examples of the kinds of marginal notes a student might make after a first reading of the essay when preparing to write a formal summary of an essay. The notes highlight the central idea and major points of the selection, so that when the student is ready to write a summary, he or she will already have marked the important points to include. Following the essay, the chapter presents questions for discussion and a sample summary of the essay.

ENTER RIGHT, EXIT LEFT

Joshua Foer

Joshua Foer was a senior at Yale University and about to graduate when he wrote this piece for the May 23, 2004, issue of the New York Times.

Opening paragraphs contrast his parents' generation with his own.

Thirty-eight years ago, John Kerry delivered a graduation speech on behalf of his Yale class that was sharply critical of the conflict in Vietnam. In many ways, his words that day set the tone for the radicalism that would define the Yale campus for generations to come.

Thesis: His generation's attitudes have changed as world has changed.

For my parents' generation, which went to school in the 1960's and 70's, college was often a radicalizing experience. For the Yale class of 2004—which I graduate with tomorrow—it has been the opposite. The world has changed significantly since we entered college four years ago; over that time, our attitudes have changed, too.

9/11 was his generation's first national trauma, whereas his parents' generation had experienced many traumas.

On 9/11, we were barely a week into our sophomore year. Because the terrorist attacks were the first national trauma my generation experienced, I believe they had a more profound effect on our still malleable political psyches than they had on our parents and grandparents, who had lived through national traumas before.

His generation supported Iraqi war.

4   What do I base this on? Consider this: One of the most under-reported statistics about the war in Iraq is my generation's overwhelming support for it—not just in its early stages but well into last year. While the conventional wisdom holds that young Americans tend to be more liberal than older Americans, that wasn't the case this time. According to a CNN/USA Today/Gallup poll taken in October [2003], a majority of 18- to 29-year-olds thought the war worthwhile, the same percentage as in the population at large. The same survey found that President Bush had a 9 percent higher approval rating among people under 30 than he did among older respondents. Of my 11 junior-year suite-mates, a racially and geographically diverse group of Democrats, only three opposed the war in Iraq. Across the Yale campus, similar sentiments reigned. During our junior year, when the national debate over Iraq was at its height, one of the most visible student political organizations on campus was the Yale College Students for Democracy, a group of hawkish liberals and neo-conservatives who supported the war. The biggest campus-wide "Support Our Troops" rally was at least as well attended as any antiwar protest.

Certainly the 9/11 attacks left a deep imprint on our political conscience, but my generation was probably predisposed to these more hawkish views long before the planes crashed into the Twin Towers and the Pentagon.

Class of 2004 had faith in government.

The class of 2004 grew up at a time when it was easy to have faith in the goodness of our government. Vietnam, Watergate and even Iran-contra were not a part of our direct political memory. For my generation, abuse of power meant sexual indiscretions in the Oval Office—not shifting rationales for war. While President Bush's claims about weapons of mass destruction and links between Iraq and Al Qaeda may have revived memories of the Gulf of Tonkin for some of our parents, my generation wasn't inclined toward incredulousness. After all, according to that same poll, 50 percent of those surveyed under 30 said they trusted government to do the right thing; for Americans older than us, that number was 36 percent.

Believed America was a force for the good.

Many of us in the class of 2004 grew up in the 1990's believing that America was a force for good in the world. We became conscious of international affairs at a time when the American military was intervening to stop genocide in the Balkans, fighting to distribute food to starving people in Somalia, and protecting democracy in Haiti. Even if these ventures

Now young people are rethinking their trust in the government: disillusioned by inaccurate claims about weapons of mass destruction and prisoner abuse in Iraq.

Young people's support for the Administration and the war is not as strong as it once was.

Still an open question whether today's generation of young people will remain liberal or return to being more conservative than their parents' generation.

weren't always successful, they were at least apparently selfless. Many of us reached the conclusion that the United States was wrong not when it intervened in the affairs of others, but when it sat on its hands, as it did in the case of Rwanda. It was only natural that we would apply that same logic to Iraq.

8   But that logic may not hold. As conditions in Iraq have grown more chaotic, many of us who supported the war are re-evaluating our positions. Over the last year, we've been forced to relearn the lessons of our parents' generation, and it has been a deeply disillusioning experience. The revelation that our government exaggerated claims about weapons of mass destruction has taught us that you can't always trust authority. The photos of Abu Ghraib and flag-draped coffins have taught us the cost of our untempered idealism about spreading our values.

According to a poll released last month by the Harvard University Institute of Politics, college students are no longer more supportive of President Bush than the population at large, and their support for the war has dropped sharply from 65 percent a year ago to 49 percent last month. But the most notable change, which suggests just how deeply young people have been affected by recent events, is that the percentage of students who describe themselves as liberal has increased significantly over the last year—from 36 percent to 44 percent.

Do these numbers indicate a profound rethinking of our political orientation or are they just a blip? It's possible, I guess, that my generation will remain liberal on social issues (like gay marriage) and conservative when it comes to foreign affairs and national security. It's even possible that we will be the first generation in a long time to be more conservative than our parents. I imagine, though, that we'll have to wait until our 10th reunion to find out.

PERSONAL RESPONSE

Where do you position yourself politically? Do you find yourself more or less radical, more or less conservative, than your parents' generation?

QUESTIONS FOR CLASS OR SMALL-GROUP DISCUSSION

1. Analyze the rhetorical effectiveness of Foer's essay. How well does the title reflect the content? What organizing principle does Foer use? What supporting proof or examples does he use to develop or explain his thesis?

2. Discuss the events that Foer says have had the most impact on his generation and their effects on young people's political views by considering what effect they have had on you. Would you name other events that have had an equal or greater impact than those he cites?

3. Foer says that it is possible that his generation "will be the first generation in a long time to be more conservative than [their] parents" (paragraph 9). What is your viewpoint on that statement? Do you find your friends and classmates to be conservative on some issues and liberal on others?

4. Foer comments that his generation grew up "believing that America was a force for good in the world" (paragraph 8). To what degree did/do you share that view of America? Has your opinion of America's involvement in international affairs changed in any way by developments in recent years?

Summary of Joshua Foer's "Enter Right, Exit Left"

In his essay "Enter Right, Exit Left," Joshua Foer explains the change from conservative to liberal in the attitude of many of his generation of undergraduate college students toward the American government and its foreign policies. Many in his generation were more conservative politically than their parents, he says, because they grew up believing in the goodness of the American government and its position as a positive world force. Many in his generation supported the administration and the war in Iraq. However, Foer asserts that revelations about the absence of proof that there were weapons of mass destruction in Iraq and the prisoner abuse in Abu Ghraib have led to a drop in their support of the administration, a drop in their support for the war, and an increase in the number declaring themselves liberal. Foer concludes by stating that it remains to be seen whether those shifts are temporary or permanent.

EXERCISE

Read Deborah Tannen's "We Need a Higher Quality of Outrage" and then summarize it, following the guidelines for writing a summary outlined previously. Your instructor will tell you whether you are to hand in your summary. Prepare for class discussion by considering your responses to the questions that follow the essay.

WE NEED A HIGHER QUALITY OUTRAGE

Deborah Tannen

Deborah Tannen is professor of sociolinguistics at Georgetown University. Author of many scholarly articles and books on subjects in her field, she is probably best known for her general-audience books beginning with You Just Don't Understand: Women and Men in Conversation *(1990), which first gained her international attention. Her other books include* Talking from 9 to 5: Women and Men at Work *(1994);* The Argument Culture: Stopping America's War on Words *(1999);* I Only Say this because I Love You: Talking to Your Parents, Partner, Sibs and Kids when You're All Adults *(2002); and* You're Wearing That?: Mothers and Daughters in Conversation *(2006). This essay first appeared in the* Christian Science Monitor *on October 20, 2004.*

We need to ratchet up the level of opposition in our public and private discourse.

This statement may seem surprising, coming from someone who wrote a book, *The Argument Culture,* claiming that the rise of opposition is endangering our civic life. Why do I now say we need more? The key is what I call "agonism:" ritualized opposition, a knee-jerk, automatic use of warlike formats.

Agonism obliterates and obfuscates real opposition. When there's a ruckus in the street outside your home, you fling open the window to see what's happening. But if there's a row outside every night, you shut the window and try to block it out. That's what's happening in our public discourse. With all the shouting, we have less, rather than more, genuine opposition—the kind that is the bedrock on which democracy rests.

4   Agonism grows out of our conviction that opposition is the best, if not the only, path to truth. In this view, the best way to explore an idea is a debate that requires opponents to marshal facts and arguments for one side, and ignore, ridicule, or otherwise undermine facts and arguments that support the other side.

Many journalists prize two types of agonism: One is the valuing of attack over other modes of inquiry, such as analyzing, integrating, or simply informing. The other is a seemingly laudable search for "balance," which results in reporting accusations without examining their validity.

Legitimate opposition is quashed when dissension from public policy is branded "hate speech" or unpatriotic. True hate speech stirs passions against members of a group precisely because of their membership in that group. Expressing passionate opposition to—even hatred for—the policies of elected officials is a legitimate, necessary form of engagement in public life. Candidates and individuals may differ—indeed, must differ—on public policy, such as whether invading Iraq enhanced or hampered American security. But questioning the patriotism of those who believe the invasion was a mistake quashes legitimate debate.

We can know others' policies, but we cannot know their motives. Accusing opponents of venal motives makes it easy to dismiss valid criticism. One can decry the fact that many of the contracts for rebuilding Iraq were awarded to Halliburton without claiming that the war was undertaken in order to enrich the company the vice president once led. One can argue that having received medals for heroic deeds in the Vietnam war does not equip John Kerry to execute the war in Iraq without seeking to discredit not only his, but all, Purple Hearts. One can argue that the president is using the Sept. 11 attacks to bolster his pubic profile without going so far as to claim (as does a message circulating on the Internet) that he played a role in authorizing those attacks. And one can validly defend the way the war was conducted without accusing one's critics of undermining the war effort.

8   Agonism leads to the conviction that fights are riveting to watch. Together with ever-diminishing budgets and corporate demands for ever-greater profits, this conviction tempts TV producers to quickly assemble shows by finding a spokesperson for each side—the more extreme, the better—and letting them slug it out. This format leaves no forum for the middle ground, where most viewers are. The result is that the extremes define the issues, problems seem insoluble, and citizens become alienated from the political process.

A single-minded devotion to "balance" also creates the illusion of equivalence where there is none. For example, as shown repeatedly by journalist Ross Gelbspan as well as in a recent article by Maxwell and Jules Boykoff in the academic journal *Global Environmental Change,* news coverage of global warming actually ends up being biased because news reports of scientists' mounting concern typically also feature prominently one of the few "greenhouse skeptics" who declare the concern bogus. This "balanced" two-sides approach gives the impression that scientists are evenly divided, whereas in fact the vast majority agree that the dangers of global climate change are potentially grave.

Take, too, the current bemoaning of negativity in the presidential campaign. Given the devotion to "balance," reports tend to juxtapose negative statements from both sides. But negativity comes in many forms. Attacks on an opponent's character distract attention from the issues that will be decided in the election. Attacks on an opponent's proposed and past policies are appropriate; we need more of such attention to policy.

The preoccupation with balance plays a role here, too. If the goal is only ensuring balance, then journalists can feel their work is done when they have reported accusations flung from each side, abnegating the responsibility to examine the validity of the attacks.

12   Ironically, while the press is busy gauging who's ahead and who's behind in the contest, significant opposition is left out. Martin Walker, of United Press International, notes that when President Bush addressed the United Nations last month, newspapers in every country other than our own—including our British allies and papers such as the French *Le Figaro,* which supported the invasion of Iraq—reported the event as a duel, with President Bush on one side and UN Secretary-General Kofi Annan or the international community on the other. The American press, whether they were supportive or critical of the president's speech, ignored the oppositional context and reported on his speech alone.

This downplaying of genuine opposition is mirrored in our private conversations. In many European countries, heated political discussions are commonplace and enjoyed; most Americans regard such conversations as unseemly arguments, so they avoid talking politics—especially with anyone whose views differ, or are unknown, lest they inadvertently spark a conflict or offend someone who disagrees.

As a result, we aren't forced to articulate—and therefore examine—the logic of our views, nor are we exposed to the views of those with whom we disagree. And if young people don't hear adults having intense, animated political discussions, the impression that politics has no relevance to their lives is reinforced. Surely this contributes to the woefully low voter turnout among young Americans.

The Yugoslavian-born poet Charles Simic has said, "There are moments in life when true invective is called for, when it becomes an absolute necessity, out of a deep sense of justice, to denounce, mock, vituperate, lash out, in the strongest possible language."

16   We have come to such a moment. Leaving aside invective, vituperation, and mockery, I believe that we need space for peaceful yet passionate outrage. The challenges we face are monumental. Among them are the spread of nuclear weapons, the burgeoning number of individuals and groups who see the United States as a threat, and the question of how far to compromise our liberties and protections in the interest of security.

On the domestic side, the challenges include the impending insolvency of Medicare and social security, the rising number of working Americans with no health insurance, and the question of whether the checks and balances provided by the three branches of government should be strengthened or weakened.

In the face of challenges of these proportions, we can no longer afford to have voices of true opposition muted by the agonistic din.

PERSONAL RESPONSE

Tannen suggests that young Americans have "the impression that politics has no relevance to their lives" (paragraph 14). Is this statement true of you personally? Of your friends? How important do you believe that politics are?

QUESTIONS FOR CLASS OR SMALL-GROUP DISCUSSION

1. What do you understand to be the difference between "agonism" and "real opposition" (paragraph 3)? To what extent do you agree with this distinction?

2. Explain in your own words the two types of agonism that Tannen believes "journalists prize" (paragraph 5). State in your own words the effect Tannen believes they have on public discourse and then discuss whether you agree with her.

3. Discuss what forms you think "peaceful yet passionate outrage" might take on the global and domestic challenges Tannen names in paragraphs 16 and 17. Are you convinced by what she says in the essay that "true opposition" on these subjects has been "muted by the agonistic din" (paragraph 18)?

CHAPTER 4

Writing a Critique

THE CONNECTION BETWEEN READING CRITICALLY AND WRITING A CRITIQUE

Recall the guidelines for reading critically outlined in Chapter 1: The final step is to evaluate what you have read. A critique is the written form of an evaluation of a passage or an entire work. Reading critically is the biggest aid to writing a critique; applying the guidelines for reading critically is a crucial part of preparing to write a critique. You will need to understand not only the purpose of the piece and its central idea but also the main points the writer makes. Reading critically enriches your understanding of a work and its components, enabling you to focus your critique. So the first step in writing a critique is to read critically and, in the process, to determine your opinion of the piece. Apply the guidelines detailed in Chapter 1, but especially look for the following: thesis and purpose of the writing, who the likely intended audience is, key ideas or supporting evidence for the thesis, the author's use of language, how well the piece is organized, and how successfully the piece has achieved its stated or implied goal.

You may need to read the piece several times before you are clear on your own viewpoint and therefore prepared to write.

WRITING A CRITIQUE

When you write a critique, your goal is to make a formal analysis of and response to a piece of writing, whether a selected passage or an entire essay. Your purpose encompasses both explaining and evaluating a piece of writing. *A critique differs from a summary, which is an objective restatement in your own words of the original material. When you summarize, you leave out your personal or subjective viewpoint. In a critique, you begin objectively but then add your own subjective response to the work.*

Prewriting

Determine Your Position. To convince an audience that your analysis and response are reasonable or valid, you must convey your views confidently. Thus, before you even begin writing your critique, you must have a clear idea of your own viewpoint on the work. A firm conviction of your own position will help persuade an audience that your critique is sensible and fair. How do you arrive at your position? You do so by carefully reading and rereading the piece you are to critique, by thinking seriously about what the piece says and how it says it, and by assessing how persuaded you are as a reader by what the author has said. This stage in the writing process is crucial for helping you formulate and make concrete the points you want to make in the formal assignment.

As with other kinds of writing, any number of tools for generating writing ideas can be used to help you arrive at your position when writing a critique. The following suggestions are variations on those mentioned in Chapter 2, but here they are worded specifically to help you discover your response to a piece of writing that you are to critique.

- **Freewriting.** As soon as you have read or reread the work, write for ten minutes on any impressions of any aspect of the piece that occur to you. Write down everything that comes to mind, no matter how jumbled. When your time is up, select a phrase or word that seems important to your purpose, no matter how vaguely, and write a sentence with the phrase or word in it. Put that sentence at the top of another blank piece of paper and repeat the process of writing for ten minutes without thinking very deeply or long about what you are writing. If you do this several times, you should end up with a fairly good idea of the position you want to take in the analysis/ assessment part of your paper.

- **Listing.** Another way to discover your viewpoint is to simply list terms or phrases describing your response to the piece you are critiquing. Then study your list and group related ideas together. Do you see a pattern? Does one dominant viewpoint emerge from these groupings? If so, write a statement reflecting that pattern or viewpoint. That should give you a sense of your position when it comes to writing your assessment of and response to the work.

- **Asking Questions.** Asking questions is a very useful tool for generating ideas, perhaps most useful when thinking about and drafting your response to a piece of writing. See the discussion on analysis that follows for a number of useful questions to ask when assessing the success of a writer's argument, language, evidence, and logic. These questions will help you arrive at your overall response to the work and discover your own position in relation to that of the writer whose work you are critiquing. However, because the response section of a critique expresses your personal, subjective reaction to the work, you will want to ask additional questions:
    - Do you agree with the writer's position on the subject? Why or why not?
    - What reasons can you give for supporting or disagreeing with the writer?
    - Are you convinced by the writer's logic, evidence, and language? Why or why not?

If you are not convinced, can you give other evidence to counter the arguments or evidence of the writer? You do not need to go into great detail in the response section of your paper, but you do need to explain your reasons for your response. Give careful thought, then, to not only what you think of the piece of writing but also why you think that way. What specific elements of the work influence your reaction to the work? As with freewriting and listing, write your questions and answers. Review what you have written and consider whether you have left anything unasked or unanswered.

Drafting Your Critique

When you are satisfied with your prewriting activities and feel that you have generated enough ideas to write your critique confidently, you are ready to write your first draft. As with all writing assignments, you will likely write several drafts of a paper before you reach the final version. As you write your first draft, keep in mind the following notes about verb tense and handling source material.

- **Verb Tense.** Whenever you write about or refer to another person's work, use the present tense: "Robert Sollod **argues** . . ." or "Sollod **asserts** that. . . ." Use the past tense only to refer to something that happened before the time span of the essay: "Sollod **says** that this omission is not a new development, recalling that his own undergraduate career over thirty years earlier **lacked** any real information on religion and spirituality."
- **Handling Quotations and Paraphrases.** When writing a critique, you will often want to quote a passage directly or paraphrase it. In either case, you must cite the page number where the original appears and use attributive tags (words that identify the source) to give credit to the source. Full details about handling source material appear in Chapter 6, with further examples in Chapter 7, but here are examples from the student paper that follows "The Hollow Curriculum":

Kari quotes part of a sentence in this way:

> Sollod continues by warning that a lack of religious studies has resulted in "the loss of ethics, a sense of decency, moderation, and fair play in American society" (45).

She attributes the material to Sollod, uses quotation marks around words that she has taken directly from the source, and gives the page number where the material appears in parenthesis after the closing quotation mark but before the period. **Kari's sources are listed alphabetically at the end of her paper** in a section labeled "Works Cited." Because it is alphabetical by author (or title if no author is named), readers know that the parenthetical number refers to the specific page in the work by Sollod where the quoted words appear.

Here Kari quotes material but leaves some of the words out:

> This wide-ranging analysis enables Sollod to reach his large and somewhat diverse audience. He bases much of his reasoning upon

the idea that "religious and spiritually based concepts . . . are the backbone upon which entire cultures have been based" (43).

The **three spaced periods (ellipsis points)** indicate where words appear in the original.

In this next example, **Kari paraphrases (puts in her own words)** some of Sollod's main points, which are made in the order in which Kari paraphrases them. In this case, she must still give a page number, even when they are not Sollod's exact words:

His proposed solution includes a curriculum assessment of current course offerings in religion and spirituality, active leadership of faculty and administrators across the university to initiate curriculum change, and the involvement of students in the form of debates and committees (45).

Note that Kari uses the author's name (or a pronoun when the antecedent is clear) throughout the paper whenever she refers to his work. When she quotes from a second source, as she does with the Beckman piece listed in her Works Cited list, she makes it absolutely clear in her paper that she is referring to that source:

In fact, as Joanne Beckman of Duke University explains . . .

One of your primary obligations in any writing that incorporates the words or ideas of other authors is fairness to those you borrow from. Along with that is the obligation to be as clear and accurate as possible for your readers. Quoting and paraphrasing your sources and using attributive tags helps you realize those obligations.

The following section lists the components of a formal critique and gives directions for writing each of those components. In general, a written critique includes these components: (1) an introduction; (2) an objective, concise summary of the work or passage; (3) an objective analysis of the author's presentation; (4) a subjective response detailing your opinion of the author's views; and (5) a conclusion.

Introduction.   The first paragraph of your critique should name the author and title of the work that you are critiquing. Do not neglect this information, as it immediately tells readers the subject of your critique. Then give a very brief overview of the piece in two to four sentences. Your intent in the introduction is not to summarize the piece but to tell readers its purpose. Generally, stating the thesis or central idea of the piece along with a highlight or two and/or its major conclusion(s) will be enough to convey its essence and provide background for the rest of your paper. Finally, your introduction should state your own thesis. In one sentence, indicate your assessment of the passage or work that you examined. Your thesis statement should be worded to reveal your position to readers before they begin reading the body of your paper.

Summary.   The first section in the body of your critique should offer an objective summary of the piece. This summary states the original author's purpose and includes key ideas and major points. Where appropriate, include direct quotations that are particularly important to the development of the piece. Do not write anything evaluative or subjective at this point. Your purpose here is to give a fair and accurate summary of the intent and main points of the work you are analyzing.

Analysis.   Once you have summarized the work by stating its purpose and key points, begin to analyze the work. Your goal is to examine how well the author has achieved the purpose and consider the validity or significance of the author's information. Do not try to look at every point the author makes; rather, limit your focus to several important aspects of the piece. Remain as objective as possible in this section, saving your personal opinion of the author's position for the response section of your critique. Different purposes for writing—persuasive, expository, and expressive—require application of different criteria to judge a writer's success in achieving the intended purpose. In general, however, certain considerations help in the assessment of any piece of writing. Questions about validity, accuracy, significance, and fairness help you to evaluate any author's success or failure.

Assess Persuasive Writing.   Recall that in Chapter 2 argumentative writing is defined as a mode of persuasion in which the goal is either to convince readers of the validity of the writer's position (argument) or to move readers to accept the author's view and perhaps even act on it (persuasion). This means that the writer must supply evidence or proof to support his or her position in such a way as to convince readers that the position is valid, whether they agree with the position or not. If the purpose is to persuade, the supporting evidence or proof must be so convincing that readers adopt the position themselves. Chapter 5 is devoted to a fuller discussion of writing an argument, so you may want to look at that chapter. In any event, when assessing the success of another writer's argument, you should gauge how well that writer has used the standard strategies for argumentation. Furthermore, pay attention to the writer's use of language. Finally, assess the validity of the argument by examining the evidence the writer presents to support his position and the logic of his conclusions.

Look Closely at a Writer's Language.   In particular, make sure that the writer defines any words or terms that may be unclear, abstract, or ambiguous. Ask yourself if the writer's language seems intended to intimidate or confuse readers or if the writer attempts to manipulate readers by relying on emotionally loaded words. Does the writer make sarcastic remarks or personal attacks? Ultimately, examine a writer's evidence, to evaluate credibility and fairness. Good writers do not rely on manipulative language, unclear terms, or loaded or sarcastic words to achieve their purposes.

Examine a Writer's Use of Appeals.   Appeals are persuasive strategies that support claims or assertion or that respond to opposing arguments. They call upon logic, ethical considerations, or emotion to convince. An appeal to reason or logic uses statistics, facts, credible authority, expert testimony, or verifiable evidence to support claims in a reasoned, nonemotional way. Karen Sternheimer in "Do Video Games Kill?" (Chapter 8) relies on statistics to counter the claim that there is a causal relation between video games and the impulse to commit murder. Ethical appeals call upon shared values or beliefs to sway readers or motivate them to act. Paul Hawken, in "A Declaration of Sustainability" (Chapter 22) calls upon shared beliefs and the common good to urge individuals to become socially responsible to ultimately ensure the future of mankind. Emotional appeals use language that is heavily charged to evoke feelings of pity, awe, sympathy, or shock, for instance, rather than intellectual responses not tied to the feelings. Both Joe Saltzman in "What's in a Name" (Chapter 1) and Charles Krauthammer in "The War and the Words" (Chapter 1) discuss ways that reporters can sway emotions by the words they choose to describe the war in Iraq. A balance of these three kinds of appeals makes the best arguments. As you examine a writing for the appeals used, determine how balanced they are. If a writer relies heavily on one kind of appeal to the exclusion of the others, especially if the main appeal is to emotion, the argument is probably weak.

Evaluating a Writer's Evidence.   A writer should support any generalizations or claims with ample, relevant evidence. As a critical reader, consider the kinds of evidence used and the value or significance of that evidence. Evidence may take many forms, including hard fact, personal observation, surveys, experiments, and even personal experience. In evaluating evidence, ask how well the writer provides a context or explanation for the evidence used. Consider whether the writer establishes the significance of the evidence and how it is relevant to the thesis or central point. For instance, factual evidence may be supplied in the form of statistics, facts, examples, or appeals to authorities. Statistics can be manipulated to conform to the needs of the person using them, so make sure that they are based on a large and representative sample, that the method of gathering the statistics yields accurate results, and that the statistics come from reliable sources. Look closely at statements of facts, as well; they should give accurate, complete, and trustworthy information. Examples are specific instances or illustrations that reveal a whole type, and they should give believable, relevant, reliable, and representative support for an author's thesis. Finally, authorities are people who have the training or experience needed to make trustworthy and reliable observations on matters relating to their areas of expertise. In completing a critique, make sure, as far as possible, that the piece under study appeals to believable and credible authorities.

Judge a Writer's Logic.   Argumentative or persuasive writing must portray a logical, reasonable, and accurate reasoning process supplemented by relevant, sensible supporting proofs. You will be in a good position to evaluate a writer's reasoning process if you are mindful of any pitfalls that undermine the success of the argument. Evaluating the writer's logic is part of the process of critiquing a work. ***For a fuller discussion and more examples of common flaws or fallacies, see the section on assessing evidence in Chapter 5.*** The following list is a summary of some of these flaws in logic that you should look for when writing your critique:

- **Hasty or faulty generalization.** The drawing of a broad conclusion on the basis of very little evidence. Example: Assuming that all rock musicians use hard drugs before performances because of the highly publicized behavior of one or two musicians is an example of faulty generalization.

- **Oversimplification.** Offering a solution or an explanation that is too simple for the problem or issue being argued. This fault in logic overlooks the complexity of an issue. Example: Arguing that the crime rate will go down if we just outlaw handguns overlooks such important considerations as crimes committed with weapons other than handguns and the likely probability that the criminal underworld would continue to have access to guns, illegal or not.

- **Stereotyping.** A form of generalization or oversimplification in which an entire group is narrowly labeled or perceived on the basis of a few in the group. Example: Arguing that women are not suited for combat because women are weaker than men is a stereotype based on the fact that the average woman is weaker than the average man. Not all women are weaker than men.

- **False analogy.** Falsely claiming that, because something resembles something else in one way, it resembles it in all ways. Example: Arguing that antiabortionists cannot favor the death penalty because they view abortion as murder is a false analogy.

- *Non sequitur.* Drawing inferences or conclusions that do not follow logically from available evidence. Example: Reminding a child who will not eat her food of all the starving children in the world is a line of reasoning that does not follow: if the child eats her food, will that lessen the starvation of other children? If the child does not eat the food, can the food itself somehow aid those starving children?

- *Ad hominem* **arguments.** Attacking the character of the arguer rather than the argument itself. Example: Arguing that because someone has been in prison, you shouldn't believe anything she says.

- **Circular reasoning or begging the question.** Making a claim that simply rephrases another claim in other words. It assumes as proof the very claim it is meant to support. Example: A parent replying "because I said so" when a child asks why he must do something.

- **Emotionally charged language.** Relying on language guaranteed to appeal to their audiences on an emotional rather than an intellectual level. Example: Invoking images of dirty homeless children in rags living on dangerous streets and eating scraps of garbage when arguing for increased funds for child services is an appeal to the emotions. This appeal is all right to use sparingly, but it becomes a fault in logic when the argument is based entirely on such language.

- **Either-or reasoning.** Admitting only two sides to an issue and asserting that the writer's is the only possible correct one. Example: Arguing that if you do not support your country's involvement in war as I do, you are not patriotic. The implication is that "either you are for your country or you are against it and the right way is my way."

- **Red herring.** Diverting the audience's attention from the main issue at hand to an irrelevant issue. Example: Calling attention to the suffering of

---

WRITING A CRITIQUE: PREPARATION AND EVALUATION

First, read the text critically by

- determining the main point, the chief purpose, and the intended audience;
- identifying arguments that support or develop the main point;
- locating evidence used to support the arguments; and
- determining any underlying biases or unexamined assumptions.

Then evaluate the text by asking

- Has the author clearly stated or implied a thesis, main idea, or position?
- Has the author written to a clearly identifiable audience?
- What rhetorical strategies in the development and organization of the essay does the writer use? Is the development appropriate to the purpose? Is the essay logically and clearly organized?
- If the writing is an argument, does the author use verifiable facts or convincing evidence? If the essay seeks to explain, define, describe, or accomplish some other purpose, has the writer supplied enough details to clearly achieve the stated or implied purpose?
- Are language and word choice accurate, imaginative, correct, and/or appropriate?
- Does the text leave any unanswered questions? When quoting exactly or paraphrasing your source, follow the guidelines for documenting sources.

---

a victim's family when arguing for the death penalty shifts focus away from the relevant reasons for capital punishment.

- *Post hoc, ergo propter hoc* **reasoning.** Assuming that something happened simply because it followed something else without evidence of a causal relationship. Example: Arguing that an airline is faulty because of flight delays at an airport assumes that the airline caused the delays, when a more important factor might be weather conditions that prevented airplanes from flying.

Response.   In this part of your critique, express your own position relative to that of the writer of the piece and give reasons why you believe as you do. You may find yourself in total agreement or absolutely opposed to the author's position, or you may place yourself somewhere in between. You may agree with some points the author makes but disagree with others. No matter what position you take, you must state your viewpoint clearly and provide reasons for your position. These reasons may be closely linked to your assessment of key elements of the paper, as laid out in your assessment section, or they may spring from ideas that you generated in your prewriting activities.

Conclusion.   The final paragraph of your critique should reiterate in several sentences your overall assessment of the piece, the conclusions you have drawn from your analysis, and your personal response to the work. This section is not the place to introduce new material; rather, it is an opportunity to provide an overall summary of your paper. You want your readers to feel that you have given them a thorough and thoughtful analysis of the work under consideration, and that you have brought your comments to a satisfying close.

GUIDELINES FOR WRITING A CRITIQUE

- **Begin with an Introduction.** The introduction familiarizes readers with the work under discussion, provides a context for the piece, and states your thesis.
- **Summarize main points.** The summary tells readers what major points the writer makes to support her position.
- **Analyze how well the writer has achieved her purpose.** The analysis tells readers what aspects of the work you have examined, depending on the kind of writing you are considering. In general, assess the overall presentation of evidence, judging its validity, accuracy, significance, and fairness.
- **Explain your response to the piece.** The response section tells readers your personal viewpoint by explaining the extent to which you agree or disagree with the author.
- **Conclude with your observations of the overall effectiveness** of the piece and your personal views on the subject. The conclusion summarizes for readers the results of your analysis and your overall judgment of the piece.

EXERCISE

Read Robert N. Sollod's "The Hollow Curriculum" and the sample critique that follows. Prepare for class discussion by answering the questions for response and discussion after the essay and considering how your response to the piece compares to that of the student writer Kari Kolb.

THE HOLLOW CURRICULUM

ROBERT N. SOLLOD

Robert N. Sollod is a professor of clinical psychology at Cleveland State University. He is author of many articles on spirituality, psychology, and related topics, and co-author of a textbook, Beneath the Mask: Introduction to Theories of Personality *(2003). Sollod was a member of the Task Force on Religious Issues in Graduate Education and Training for the American Psychological Association when he wrote this essay for the* Chronicle of Higher Education, *a professional publication for faculty, staff, and administrators in colleges and universities.*

The past decade in academe has seen widespread controversy over curricular reform. We have explored many of the deeply rooted, core assumptions that have guided past decisions about which subjects should be emphasized in the curriculum and how they should be approached. Yet I have found myself repeatedly disappointed by the lack of significant discussion concerning the place of religion and spirituality in colleges' curricula and in the lives of educated persons.

I do not mean to suggest that universities should indoctrinate students with specific viewpoints or approaches to life; that is not their proper function. But American universities now largely ignore religion and spirituality, rather than considering what aspects of religious and spiritual teachings should enter the curriculum and how those subjects should be taught. The curricula that most undergraduates study do little to rectify the fact that many Americans are ignorant of religious and spiritual teachings, of their significance in the history of this and other civilizations, and of their significance in contemporary society. Omitting this major facet of human experience and thought contributes to a continuing shallowness and imbalance in much of university life today.

Let us take the current discussions of multiculturalism as one example. It is hardly arguable that an educated person should approach life with knowledge of several cultures or patterns of experience. Appreciation and understanding of human diversity are worthy educational ideals. Should such an appreciation exclude the religious and spiritually based concepts of reality that are the backbone upon which entire cultures have been based?

4   Multiculturalism that does not include appreciation of the deepest visions of reality reminds me of the travelogues that I saw in the cinema as a child—full of details of quaint and somewhat mysterious behavior that evoked some superficial empathy but no real, in-depth understanding. Implicit in a multicultural approach that ignores spiritual factors is a kind of critical and patronizing attitude. It assumes that we can understand and evaluate the experiences of other cultures without comprehension of their deepest beliefs.

Incomprehensibly, traditionalists who oppose adding multicultural content to the curriculum also ignore the religious and theological bases of the Western civilization that they seek to defend. Today's advocates of Western traditionalism focus, for the most part, on conveying a type of rationalism that is only a single strain in Western thought. Their approach does not demonstrate sufficient awareness of the contributions of Western religions and spirituality to philosophy and literature, to moral and legal codes, to the development of governmental and political institutions, and to the mores of our society.

Nor is the lack of attention to religion and spirituality new. I recall taking undergraduate philosophy classes in the 1960s in which Plato and Socrates were taught without reference to the fact that they were contemplative mystics who believed in immortality and reincarnation. Everything that I learned in my formal undergraduate education about Christianity came through studying a little Thomas Aquinas in a philosophy course, and even there we focused more on the logical sequence of his arguments than on the fundamentals of the Christian doctrine that he espoused. I recall that Dostoyevsky was presented as an existentialist with hardly a nod given to the fervent Christian beliefs so clearly apparent in his writings. I even recall my professors referring to their Christian colleagues, somewhat disparagingly, as "Christers." I learned about mystical and spiritual interpretations of Shakespeare's sonnets and plays many years after taking college English courses.

We can see the significance of omitting teaching about religion and spirituality in the discipline of psychology and, in particular, in my own field of clinical psychology. I am a member of the Task Force on Religious Issues in Graduate Education and Training in Division 36 of the American Psychological Association, a panel chaired by Edward Shafranske of Pepperdine University. In this work, I have discovered that graduate programs generally do not require students to learn anything about the role of religion in people's lives.

8   Almost no courses are available to teach psychologists how to deal with the religious values or concerns expressed by their clients. Nor are such courses required or generally available at the undergraduate level for psychology majors. Allusions to religion and spirituality often are completely missing in textbooks on introductory psychology, personality theory, concepts of psychotherapy, and developmental psychology.

Recent attempts to add a multicultural perspective to clinical training almost completely ignore the role of religion and spirituality as core elements of many racial, ethnic, and national identities. Prayer is widely practiced, yet poorly understood and rarely studied by psychologists. When presented, religious ideas are usually found in case histories of patients manifesting severe psychopathology.

Yet spiritual and mystical experiences are not unusual in our culture. And research has shown that religion is an important factor in the lives of many Americans; some studies have suggested that a client's religious identification may affect the psychotherapeutic relationship, as well as the course and outcome of therapy. Some patterns of religious commitment have been found to be associated with high levels of mental health and ego strength. A small number of psychologists are beginning to actively challenge the field's inertia and indifference by researching and writing on topics related to religion and spirituality. Their efforts have not as yet, however, markedly affected the climate or curricula in most psychology departments.

Is it any wonder that religion for the typical psychotherapist is a mysterious and taboo topic? It should not be surprising that therapists are not equipped even to ask the appropriate questions regarding a person's religious or spiritual life—much less deal with psychological aspects of spiritual crises.

12   Or consider the field of political science. Our scholars and policy makers have been unable to predict or understand the major social and political movements that produced upheavals around the world during the last decade. That is at least partly because many significant events—the remarkable rise of Islamic fundamentalism, the victory of Afghanistan over the Soviet Union, the unanticipated velvet revolutions in Eastern Europe and in the Soviet Union, and the continuing conflicts in Cyprus, Israel, Lebanon, Northern Ireland, Pakistan, Sri Lanka, Tibet, and Yugoslavia—can hardly be appreciated without a deep understanding of the religious views of those involved. The tender wisdom of our contemporary political scientists cannot seem to comprehend the deep spirituality inherent in many of today's important social movements.

Far from being an anachronism, religious conviction has proved to be a more potent contemporary force than most, if not all, secular ideologies. Too often, however, people with strong religious sentiments are simply dismissed as "zealots" or "fanatics"—whether they be Jewish settlers on the West Bank, Iranian demonstrators, Russian Baptists, Shiite leaders, antiabortion activists, or evangelical Christians.

Most sadly, the continuing neglect of spirituality and religion by colleges and universities also results in a kind of segregation of the life of the spirit from the life of the mind in American culture. This situation is far from the ideals of Thoreau, Emerson, or William James. Spirituality in our society too often represents a retreat from the world of intellectual discourse, and spiritual pursuits are often cloaked in a reflexive anti-intellectualism, which mirrors the view in academe of spirituality as an irrational cultural residue. Students with spiritual interests and concerns learn that the university will not validate or feed their interests. They learn either to suppress their spiritual life or to split their spiritual life apart from their formal education.

Much has been written about the loss of ethics, a sense of decency, moderation, and fair play in American society. I would submit that much of this loss is a result of the increasing ignorance, in circles of presumably educated people, of religious and spiritual world views. It is difficult to imagine, for example, how ethical issues can be intelligently approached and discussed or how wise ethical decisions can be reached without either knowledge or reference to those religious and spiritual principles that underlie our legal system and moral codes.

16   Our colleges and universities should reclaim one of their earliest purposes—to educate and inform students concerning the spiritual and religious underpinnings of thought and society. To the extent that such education is lacking, our colleges and universities are presenting a narrow and fragmented view of human experience.

Both core curricula and more advanced courses in the humanities and social sciences should be evaluated for their coverage of religious topics. Active leadership at the university, college, and departmental levels is needed to encourage and carry out needed additions and changes in course content. Campus organizations should develop forums and committees to examine the issue, exchange information, and develop specific proposals.

National debate and discussion about the best way to educate students concerning religion and spirituality are long overdue.

PERSONAL RESPONSE

Describe the degree to which you are spiritual or religious. How important is religion in your life?

QUESTIONS FOR CLASS OR SMALL-GROUP DISCUSSION

1. Sollod gives examples of how an understanding of religion and spirituality would help someone trained in his field, psychology, and how it would help political scientists. In what other disciplines or fields do you think

such training would be important? Explain how it would enhance the understanding of people trained in those fields.

2. Discuss whether you agree with Sollod that religion and spirituality have a place in the college curriculum.

3. Sollod calls for campus organizations to develop forums and committees to examine the place of religion and spirituality on the college campus and to develop specific proposals on the issue (paragraph 18). Conduct your own class forum or create a class committee to consider the issues that Sollod raises. Where do people learn about spirituality? How do you think a person could benefit from learning about religion and spirituality in college courses?

SAMPLE STUDENT PAPER: CRITIQUE

Kolb 1

Kari Kolb

Dr. Aaron

English 150-420

January 2008

A Critique of "The Hollow Curriculum"

In his essay "The Hollow Curriculum," Robert Sollod addresses the controversial subject of religion in the public school system, particularly at the college level. Sollod believes that by failing to acknowledge religious histories and teachings, universities contribute to the declining morality of society. He recommends an evaluation of course offerings in terms of ways in which courses on religion or spirituality can be integrated into higher education curriculum. Such a project would involve not only university faculty and administrators but also American citizens nationwide. While it may be true that recent years have seen a moral or ethical decline in

Kolb 2

the general public, Sollod's assertion
that this decline is a result of religious
ignorance is not only unfounded but also
untrue.

Sollod begins his piece by noting the
lack of religious and spiritual emphasis
in the national curriculum and in the lives
of most Americans (43). Noting that much of
multicultural appreciation depends on a full
understanding of others' cultures, Sollod
points out that many other cultures are built
on a foundation of religious and spiritual
beliefs and suggests that all-inclusive
religious studies would enrich the lives and
careers of college students (43-44). Sollod
continues by warning that a lack of religious
studies has resulted in "the loss of ethics,
a sense of decency, moderation, and fair
play in American society" (45). His proposed
solution includes a curriculum assessment
of current course offerings in religion and
spirituality, active leadership of faculty
and administrators across the university
to initiate curriculum change, and the
involvement of students in the form of debates
and committees (45).

Sollod has a solid sense of his audience,
made up primarily of faculty and staff in
higher education. By implication, what he
proposes is of interest to students as well.
Sollod draws readers into his argument
with a series of questions and then offers
information in a simple yet authoritative
manner. He provides detailed examples,
explaining how religious understanding would

Kolb 3

enhance all areas of study, ranging from
the broad fields of political science and
psychology to the ideas of Shakespeare and
Socrates. This wide-ranging analysis enables
Sollod to reach his large and somewhat diverse
audience. He bases much of his reasoning upon
the idea that "religious and spiritually based
concepts . . . are the backbone upon which
entire cultures have been based" (43), a point
that informs his argument throughout. Sollod's
valid argument is made even more credible when
he extends it to include familiar examples,
such as conflicts in the former Soviet Union,
Ireland, and the Middle East. At times, Sollod
relies on emotional appeals, seen most often in
his occasional use of loaded words and phrases
such as "continuing shallowness and imbalance"
(43) and "mysterious and taboo" (44). In
general, though, he makes a fair and logical
argument, and he concludes with a rational
solution to what he sees as a serious problem.

   Sollod is correct when he states that the
college curriculum would be greatly enhanced
by the addition of courses in religion and
spirituality or the incorporation of such
material in traditional courses. Such courses
would provide a solid grounding for most
professions and promote a greater cultural
understanding in general. However, Sollod
exaggerates in his statement that the loss of
ethics in American society is "a result of the
increasing ignorance, in circles of presumably
educated people, of religious and spiritual
world views" (45). Here, Sollod makes an

inaccurate generalization, with no evidence
or clear reasoning to back up his position.
On the contrary, statistics show that in the
past thirty years, religion has not only
sustained itself, but it has also diversified.
According to a recent survey, "Some 375 ethnic
or multiethnic religious groups have already
formed in the United States in the last three
decades. Sociologists of religion believe
the numbers will only increase in the coming
years" (Beckman). These religious groups
are not only the creations of immigrants,
but they also reflect America's growing
diversity. In fact, as Joanne Beckman of
Duke University explains, almost half of
the baby boomer generation has dropped out
of their traditional churches and are "just
as willing to sample Eastern religions, New
Age spiritualism, or quasi-religious self-
help groups. . . . [F]or [these] seekers,
spirituality is a means of individual
expression, self-discovery, inner healing, and
personal growth." Although the deterioration
of moral values is a frustrating problem in
our society, it cannot, as Sollod suggests,
be attributed entirely to a lack of religious
appreciation and diversity.

"The Hollow Curriculum" endorses a
controversial proposal that has prompted much
deliberation: the addition of, or increase
in, religious and spiritual studies in our
national curriculum. Although Sollod does well
in arguing his position on the subject, he
assumes, without proof, that much of

Kolb 5

university life is shallow and that
university curricula is unbalanced. Further,
he makes a hasty generalization when he
places the blame of America's ethical undoing
on the lack of "knowledge or reference to
those religious and spiritual principles that
underline our legal system and moral codes"
(45). In this generalization, he neglects
to recognize the growing religious and
spiritual diversity of the American people.
This omission weakens the foundation of
his argument-that an increase in religious
studies will benefit all areas of life-by
overlooking evidence showing that, despite
an increase in spiritual awareness, the loss
of ethics remains a problem in our society.
Sollod thus undermines his own position and
leaves his readers, though inspired by his
zeal, understandably skeptical.

Works Cited

Beckman, Joanne. "Religion in Post-
    World War II in America." <u>Divining</u>
    <u>America.</u> September 2005. <u>The National</u>
    <u>Humanities Center.</u> 17 Sept. 2008 http://
    nationalhumanitiescenter.org/tserve/
    twenty/tkeyinfo/trelww2.htm
Sollod, Robert. "The Hollow Curriculum."
    <u>Perspectives on Contemporary Issues:</u>
    <u>Readings Across the Curriculum 5th ed.,</u> ed.
    Katherine Anne Ackley. Boston: Wadsworth
    Cengage Learning, 2009. 66-69.

> ### EXERCISE
>
> Read Earl Ofari Hutchinson's "Trash Rap Makes Imus Possible" and prepare for class discussion by answering the questions for response and discussion after the essay and/or writing a critique of the essay. Your instructor may want you to hand in your work or use it for class discussion.

TRASH RAP MAKES IMUS POSSIBLE

EARL OFARI HUTCHINSON

Earl Ofari Hutchinson is a journalist, political analyst, broadcaster, and author. Among his nine books on race, politics, and social issues are Blacks and Reds: Race and Class in Conflict, 1919–1990 *(1995);* Betrayed: A History of Presidential Failure to Protect Black Lives *(1996);* The Assassination of the Black Male Image *(1997);* A Colored Man's Journey Through 20th Century Segregated America *(2000);* The Emerging Black GOP Majority *(2006); and* The Latino Challenge to Black America: Towards a Conversation between African Americans and Hispanics *(2007). This piece appeared on the op-ed page of the* Philadelphia Inquirer *on April 12, 2007. Don Imus (title and paragraph 2) referred to members of the Rutgers Women's basketball team as "nappy-headed hos" (most of the press, including the* LA Times, *spell it with the e: "hoes") while on the air during his radio/MSNBC talk show in April 2007. The public outcry over his language resulted in his suspension from MSNBC and subsequent firing by CBS.*

"Can U Control Yo Hoe"—so asks the high priest of gangster rap, Snoop Dogg, on his CD *R&G: (Rhythm and Gangsta): The Masterpiece.*

In "Housewife" on his CD *2001,* Dr. Dre says, "Naw, 'hoe' is short for honey."

Rapper Beanie Sigel says, "Watch Your Bitches" on his 2001 album *The Reason.*

And 50 Cent commands: "Bitch choose with me" on his 2003 track "P.I.M.P."

Just a light sampling of how gangster rappers, some black filmmakers, and comedians routinely reduce young black women to "stuff," "bitches" and "hoes." Their contempt reinforces the slut image of black women and sends the message that violence, mistreatment and verbal abuse of black women are socially acceptable. Despite lawsuits, protests and boycotts by women's groups, gangster-themed films and rap music continue to soar in popularity. Hollywood and music companies rake in small fortunes off them, and so do a few rappers.

Now enter shock-jock Don Imus, the latest white guy to be transformed into a racially and gender-incorrect punching bag for his Michael Richardsesque epithets against the Rutgers University women's basketball team. He, of course, has been verbally mugged, battered and abused. He is on furlough from his radio show, and MSNBC has canceled the simulcast on TV. Imus has genuflected—no, groveled—to the Rev. Al Sharpton, civil rights leaders, and the Rutgers team, begging forgiveness. Imus certainly deserves the kick in the shins he's getting. Even he admits that he rocketed way past the line of what—even by the raunchy and low-road standards of shock-jockism—is considered acceptable.

But again, Imus is the softest of soft targets. The same can't be said for the black rap shock-jocks. They made Imus possible. They gave him the rapper's bad-housekeeping seal of approval to bash and trash black women. In many ways, their artistic degradation has had even more damaging consequences for young black women. Homicide now ranks as one of the leading causes of death of young black females. A black woman is far more likely to be raped than a white woman and slightly more likely to be the victim of domestic violence than a white woman.

4   Who are the assailants? Not white racist cops or Klan nightriders, but other black males. The media play their own roles, often magnifying and sensationalizing crimes by black men against white women, but ignoring or downplaying crimes against black women. The verbal demeaning of black women has made them the scapegoats for many of the crisis social problems in American society.

What's even more galling is that some blacks cite a litany of excuses, such as poverty, broken homes and abuse, to excuse the sexual abuse and violence (both physical and rhetorical) by top black male artists. These explanations for the misdeeds of rappers and singers are phony and self-serving. The ones who have landed hard on a court docket are anything but hard-core, dysfunctional, poverty types. P. Diddy, who predated R. Kelly as the poster boy for extramusical malevolence, is college-educated and hails from a middle-class home. He typifies the fraud that these artists are up-from-the-ghetto, self-made men.

The daunting puzzle, then, remains why so many blacks storm the barricades in fury against a Richards or an Imus, but are stone silent, or utter only the feeblest of protests, when blacks bash and trash. Or even worse, tacitly condone their verbal abuse. There are two reasons for that.

Blacks have been the ancient target of racial stereotypes, negative typecasting, and mockery. This has made them hypersensitive to any real or perceived racial slight from whites. That's totally understandable, and civil-rights leaders are right to criticize celebrities, politicians and public figures for their racial gaffes, slips or broadsides.

8   The second reason is that blacks fear that if they publicly criticize other blacks for their racial attitudes, such disagreements will be gleefully twisted, mangled and distorted into a fresh round of black-bashing by whites. But that's a lame reason for *not* speaking out, and loudly, against blacks who, either out of ignorance or for profit, or both, routinely commercialize racial and gender trash talk.

Such failure fuels the suspicion that blacks, and especially black leaders, are more than willing to play the race card, and call white people bigots, when it serves their interests, but will circle the wagons and defend any black who comes under fire for bigotry—or anything else, for that matter.

The same standard of racial accountability must apply whether the racial and gender offender is an Imus or a 50 Cent. When it doesn't, that's a double standard, and that always translates into hypocrisy. Imus got his trash-talk pass yanked. Now let's yank it from blacks who do the same or worse.

PERSONAL RESPONSE

Do you listen to and enjoy rap music? If so, explain what you like about it. If not, explain why not.

QUESTIONS FOR CLASS OR SMALL-GROUP DISCUSSION

1. How would you characterize the tone of this essay? Locate and discuss specific words and phrases that convey Hutchinson's attitude toward his subject. For instance, what do you make of this passage: "Imus has genuflected—no, groveled—to the Rev. Al Sharpton" (paragraph 2)? Find other language that is emotionally charged and discuss how it functions in the essay.

2. What issues does Hutchison raise in the matter of the furor over Don Imus's sexist and racist language? What proof or evidence does Hutchinson offer to support the position that he takes on his subject? To what extent are you satisfied with that evidence and the degree of development for his major points?

3. How convinced are you by this essay that "trash talk makes Imus possible" (title)?

Writing an Argument

Much of the writing that you do for your college classes is argumentation. It may not be called that formally, but any writing exercise that asks you to state a position and defend it with evidence that is true or reasonable is a form of argument. Whenever you state your opinion or make an assertion and back it with proof, you are making an argument. As you can see, just about any writing that has a thesis or implicit central idea that requires evidence or proof is a form of argument. Whether you provide evidence to explain, illustrate what you know, inform, prove a point, or persuade, if you take a position on a subject and support or develop it with evidence to demonstrate that it is valid or sound, you are making an argument.

However, oftentimes students are specifically assigned the rhetorical mode of argumentation, a reasoning process that seeks to provide evidence or proof that a proposition is valid or true. An argument sets forth a claim in the form of a thesis statement, refutes the arguments of the opposition—sometimes giving in or conceding to certain points—and presents a coherent, organized set of reasons why the claim is reasonable. To demonstrate that your position is logical or right, you must offer reasons why you believe that way in order to convince your audience. An argument may have several goals or purposes, either singly or in combination, such as to show relationships between things (causal argument), to explain or define something (definition argument), to evaluate something or support a position on it (evaluative argument), to inform (informative argument), or to sway an audience to change a position or take action on something (persuasive argument). Argumentation is a useful tool for developing critical thinking because doing it well requires close analysis of your own ideas as well as those of others. Writing an argument involves the same general procedure as that detailed in Chapter 2 on the writing process: prewriting or planning, drafting, revising, and editing.

NARROWING YOUR FOCUS
AND DISCOVERING YOUR POSITION

All arguments begin with a position, claim, or proposition that is debatable and that has opposing viewpoints. Statements of fact are not debatable; abstract generalizations are too vague. If your position is not debatable, there is no argument. Furthermore, in an argument, your goal is to convince those opposed to your position or who are skeptical of it that yours is valid or true. You might even want to persuade your audience to abandon their position and adopt yours or go beyond that and perform some action. Your first step, then, is to select a controversial subject or issue that you have a strong interest in. That begins the process that will ultimately lead you to the position you want to take on it.

A good starting point for discovering a topic to argue is to make a list of controversial issues currently in the news or being discussed and debated publicly or among your friends or family. *Remember that this is only a starting point.* These general topics are far too broad for a short paper, but they give you a beginning from which to start narrowing your focus. From your list, select the subjects that interest you most or that you feel strongly about and develop a series of questions that you might ask about them. This process of considering a variety of views when contemplating a topic you would like to argue helps you solidify your position. For instance, you might ask the following: Should bilingual education be offered in public schools? Should the electoral college be abolished? Is affirmative action a fair policy? Should gay couples be allowed to marry? While such questions seldom have absolutely right or wrong answers, it is useful to frame your position by saying (or implying), "Yes, bilingual education should be offered in public schools," or, "No, affirmative action is not a fair policy." But making up your mind about how you feel about an issue is only the beginning. You must also convince others that your position is logical, reasonable, or valid. You do that by providing strong evidence or reasons to support your position and by anticipating and addressing the arguments of those who do not agree with you.

Examples.

1. Suppose you are interested in the subject of downloading music from the Internet without paying for it, currently illegal but still being done all over the world. Should those who download music from the Internet be charged with a crime? Should those who wish to download music from the Internet have to pay for that service? People will disagree on how these questions should be answered; thus, they are legitimate subjects for argumentation. Suppose you believe that, no, downloading music from the Internet should not be regarded as a criminal act. What other questions does that position lead to, then? Should downloading music be free and open to anyone who wants to do it? If so, what is the fairest way to treat artists whose music is being downloaded from the Internet? Do they not have the right to profit from the use of their music?

2. Consider the suggestion that the grading system at the college level be abolished. You might wonder: Should the grading system be abolished? Who would benefit from abolishing the grading system? Why should the grading system be abolished? Why should the grading system not be abolished? What would replace the grading system were it abolished? How would abolishing the grading system affect students and instructors? Would it change the dynamics of the learning process?

3. Imagine that the office in charge of programming at your campus wants to bring a controversial person for its speaker series. Suppose you are a student at a private faith-based liberal arts college and the speaker is an avowed atheist, or, suppose you are a state-funded liberal arts university and the speaker is a religious-right fundamentalist. Who would support bringing this speaker to campus? Who would oppose it? What reasons might both those in favor and against bringing the speaker to campus give to support their position? Are there contexts or situations where it might be appropriate and others where it wouldn't? Which side would you support in such a controversy?

The following list of potentially controversial subjects may give you an idea of the kinds of general topics that can be narrowed for an argumentative paper. To this list, add others that appeal to you as potential topics for an argument. Then, select those subjects that you have the strongest interest in or hold opinions about and, taking each in turn, spend some time writing down questions that come to mind about that subject, issues related to it that you are aware of, and/or what your preliminary position on the subject is: What is the controversy? Who is affected by it? Why is it controversial? What is the context or situation? What is your position on that controversy? Why do you believe as you do? What evidence or proof do you have to support your position? What do those opposed to your position argue?

At this stage, you are simply **brainstorming or freewriting** to see what you know about certain self-selected subjects that you would be comfortable with developing into an argument paper. When you have finished, examine the results of your brainstorming session and narrow your list to the one or two that you have the most to say about or feel most strongly about. Brainstorm further on those issues by framing questions about the subject or trying to identify the problem associated with it. Keep in mind that you not only want to find an issue or issues that you have a strong interest in, but you also must consider the implications of the position you take on that issue. How will you convince your audience that your position is reasonable or logical? How can you best defend your position? How can you best meet the arguments of those opposed to you?

You are looking for a topic that poses a question or problem you believe that you know the answer or solution to. This is your position. Once you know your position, you are ready to commit time to thinking about and researching the best evidence or proof to support your position.

POSSIBLE SUBJECTS FOR ARGUMENTATION

Abstinence-only education

Adolescents tried as adults

Advertising images

AIDS treatment or prevention

Airline security

Animal rights

Arts funding

Banning smoking in public places

Bilingual education

Binge drinking

Censorship

Civil rights

College—is it for everyone?

Compensation for organ donors

Controversial speakers on campus

Date rape

Downloading music from the Internet

Drugs and drug abuse

Drunken driving punishment

Eating disorders

Education costs

Electoral college

Eliminating the grading system

Embryo or stem-cell research

English-only movement

The environment

Free agency in sports

Free trade agreements

Gays in the military

Gender issues

Gender roles

Genetic engineering

Government-sponsored child day care

Global warming

Gun control/Gun rights

Hate groups

Homelessness

Home schooling

Human cloning

Human rights

Illegal aliens

Immigration

Inoculation against HPV

Intellectual freedom

Internet: government control

Minimum-wage jobs

Mudslinging in political campaigns

National image of America abroad

National security

Nuclear energy

Nuclear proliferation

Nuclear waste

Ozone layer

Outsourcing

The Patriot Act

Pay inequity

Pollution

Poverty

Publishing images of war

Racial profiling

Regulating toxic emissions

Reparations for slavery

Runaway teens

Same-sex marriages

School prayer

Space exploration

Special interest groups

Standardized exams

Steroids and athletes

Sports violence

Stereotypes in mass media

Sweatshops

Terrorism in America

Tobacco use

Violence in film

Violence in rock lyrics

Violence in schools

Violence on television

Workplace discrimination

Example. Erin was intrigued by an essay she read on advertising images of women, so she began the process of discovering her position by thinking about the very general subject "advertising images." Here are the questions she asked:

- Do advertising images affect behavior? Very likely, or advertisers wouldn't put so much money into advertising.
- Isn't it the purpose of an ad to influence behavior?
- So what if they do affect behavior? What's the harm?
- Such power might influence behavior the wrong way.
- What is the wrong way? Affects self esteem. Makes people feel inadequate. Reduces women to objects.
- What about men? Ads affect them too.
- Some ads set up unrealistic, even impossible-to-attain images of men and women. Young or old, male or female.
- Ads present false images of relationships between men and women. Ads focus a lot on sex and on attacking people's vulnerabilities.
- Who bears responsibility? Advertisers. They need to consider the effects of their ads. What should they do? Modify images that attack and weaken self esteem.
- Topic: advertisers' responsibility for their ads. (Use Kilbourne's essay on harmful images and O'Toole's defense of advertising.)

Her questions, answers, and ideas may look rambling, but they ultimately led her to her topic, which she refined by focusing specifically on ads featuring women that have the potential to affect self-esteem and body image. Her paper appears later in this chapter in the section on sample student papers.

GUIDELINES FOR NARROWING YOUR FOCUS AND DISCOVERING YOUR POSITION

- Make a list of controversial or arguable subjects about which you have an opinion or are strongly interested in.
- Ask questions about each subject from as many angles as you can think of.
- Keep narrowing your focus as often as possible.
- Write down ideas that occur to you as you ask your questions.
- Select one or two topics that seem most promising to you.
- Repeat the brainstorming process by asking more questions and writing more thoughts as they occur. At this stage you are working toward a defensible position on a fairly narrow topic.
- Consider how you might defend your position, how you would counter arguments against it, and what evidence you might need.
- Select the topic that emerges as your strongest and begin the process of thinking about, researching, and writing your paper on that narrow topic.

STRUCTURING AN ARGUMENT

Structuring an argument is similar to structuring most other kinds of writing. Recall that in Chapter 2, the typical essay has certain components: a title, an opening paragraph that introduces the topic by providing a context or background for it and that leads to a **thesis statement;** fully developed paragraphs in the body of the paper that advance, support, illustrate, or otherwise relate to the thesis; and a **conclusion.** Effective arguments follow that pattern, with some additions or variations. In formal argumentation, these parts of your essay might be labeled differently, but they are essentially the same. For instance, a thesis might be called a proposition or position statement but it is still the central idea of the paper. Development might be referred to as offering supporting proof by refuting the opposition, making concessions where necessary, and offering evidence in a logical, well-reasoned well. What follows are various components of a well-organized and developed argument.

Introduction.   The opening of your argument lays the groundwork for the rest of the paper by establishing the tone you will take, providing any clarification or preliminary information necessary and/or giving a statement of your own qualifications for asserting a position on the topic. Here is an opportunity to provide a context for your argument, establish your initial credibility, and connect with your audience. Credibility is the level of trustworthiness your audience perceives in you. If you can convey an impression that you are credible early in your paper, your audience may be more willing to think of you as reliable or trustworthy and therefore be more receptive to your argument. Otherwise, they may dismiss your evidence, question your motive, or simply refuse to accept what you are saying.

Context.   When explaining background or situation, you establish a context within which your audience is to consider your argument. Establishing tone is part of the context as well. You might provide a striking quotation, cite statistics, or define the problem or controversy in terms that everyone agrees on. For instance, in her essay " "We Need a Higher Quality Outrage" (Chapter 3), Deborah Tannen defines a term that is probably unfamiliar to readers by comparing it to a familiar situation, thus establishing a common bond: "Agonism obliterates and obfuscates real opposition. When there's a ruckus in the street outside your home, you fling open the window to see what's happening. But if there's a row outside every night, you shut the window and try to block it out. That's what's happening in our public discourse." Her audience may not understand her first sentence, but the next sentences make her meaning clear with an example that just about everyone can identify or sympathize with. Peter Singer's opening in "The Singer Solution to World Poverty" provides another example of context when he recounts the plot of a film about a Brazilian woman who sells a homeless child to organ peddlers. From there, he moves to his real point when he asks what the difference is between the immoral act of that fictional woman and "an American who already has a TV and upgrades to a better one—knowing that the money could be donated to an organization that would use it to save the lives of kids in need?" He goes on to discuss reasons why moral judgments of the two situations might not be the same, but he establishes a sympathetic bond with readers in his opening that leads smoothly to his focus on the ethics of our actions.

Credibility.   Any number of strategies help to establish credibility in an argument. Beginning with your introduction and continuing throughout your argument, demonstrating to your readers that you are fully informed, reasonable, and fair establishes credibility and makes your audience more receptive to your position. Using trustworthy outside sources to support, explain, defend, or back general statements demonstrates that your position is based on more than just your personal opinion. To show that others, perhaps professionals with more experience than you, have done research or hold similar views reflects well on your own credibility. Furthermore, citing sources or statistics shows that you have done your homework, that you are so familiar with or knowledgeable about your subject that you know what others have to say about it. These things go to your credibility as a writer. Using hard data such as facts or statistics also helps, as does acknowledging and countering viewpoints opposed to yours.

Statement of the Case.   As clearly as possible in your opening paragraph(s), provide a rationale or need for what you are arguing. Provide a context for the argument, give relevant background material, or explain why you believe as you do. Establishing need helps to convey your credibility by showing that you are knowledgeable about your subject. It is also a good strategy for connecting with your audience. In stating the case for the argument, you might explain that it is worth upholding or endorsing because it has some bearing on the lives of readers or the common good of a community or society. You may also want to indicate the degree to which a particular issue or policy is controversial. Take, for instance, Michael Crichton's opening in "Patenting Life" (Chapter 20): "You, or someone you love, may die because of a gene patent that should never have been granted in the first place. Sound far-fetched? Unfortunately, it's only too real." His next sentences elaborate on that opening, but the compelling first few sentences strongly suggest a need to look at the issue of gene patents.

Proposition.   The proposition is an assertion or claim about the issue. It is virtually the same as a thesis or position statement and should be stated clearly near the beginning of the essay. You must make your position clear very early in the argument and then devote the rest of your paper to providing supporting evidence, details, or facts to "prove" that your position is a logical or reasonable one. The strength of your argument will come from your skill at refuting or challenging opposing claims or viewpoints, giving in or conceding on some points, and then presenting your own claims, evidence, or other details that support your position.

Refutation of Opposing Arguments.   It is not enough to find facts or evidence that argue your own position and therefore prove its validity; you must also realize that those opposed to your position will have their own facts or evidence. You must try to project what you think others may say or even try to put yourself into their position. An excellent strategy for argumentation, therefore, is to first look at the claims of others and challenge or dispute them. One of the chief strengths of a good argument is its ability to counter evidence produced by the opposing side. In fact, you must imagine more than one opposing side. Rarely is an issue represented by just two equal and opposing arguments. Often it is represented by multiple viewpoints. Obviously you cannot present every aspect and every position of an issue, but you must demonstrate that you are aware of the major viewpoints on your subject and that the position you have taken is a reasonable one. The preparatory step of anticipating or imagining the opposing position(s) will be a huge help in developing your own argument. Ask yourself what you think will be the strategy of those opposed to your position and how you can best address that opposition and counter it with your own logical reasoning. Ignoring an opposing opinion is a major fault in argumentation because it suggests that you have not explored enough aspects of the topic to warrant the position you are taking. For more on refutation, see the section on anticipating the opposition in the section on strategies for effective argumentation later.

Concessions to Opposing Arguments.   Oftentimes, some of what those opposed to your position argue is valid or irrefutable. A very effective, necessary, and wise strategy is to make concessions to the opposition. It helps establish your reliability as a fair-minded person. The act of acknowledging limitations or exceptions to your own argument and accepting them actually strengthens your argument. It indicates your commitment to your position despite its flaws, or suggests that, even flawed, your position is stronger than the positions of those opposed to it. It is best to make these concessions or acknowledgements early in your paper rather than later. For

GUIDELINES: STRUCTURE OF AN ARGUMENT

- **Introduction**—Familiarizes audience with subject, provides background or context, conveys your credibility, and establishes tone.
- **Statement of the case**—Provides rationale or need for the argument.
- **Proposition**—Asserts a position or claim that will be supported, demonstrated, or proved in the course of the paper.
- **Refutation of opposing arguments**—Mentions and counters potential evidence or objections of opposing arguments.
- **Concession**—Acknowledges validity of some opposing arguments or evidence.
- **Development of the argument**—Offers convincing, creditable, evidence in support of proposition.
- **Conclusion**—Brings paper to a satisfactory end.

more on making concessions, see the section on conceding to the opposition in the section on strategies for effective argumentation.

Development of Your Argument. In this stage of the process, you present evidence or proof to persuade your audience of the validity of your position. The argument will be most effective if it is organized with the least convincing or least important point first, building to its strongest point. This pattern lends emphasis to the most important points and engages readers in the unfolding process of the argument as the writer moves through increasingly compelling proofs. A successful argument also gives evidence of some sort for every important point. Evidence may include statistics, observations or testimony of experts, personal narratives, or other supporting proof. A writer needs to convince readers by taking them from some initial position on an issue to the writer's position, which readers will share if the argument succeeds. The only way to do this is to provide evidence that convinces readers that the position is a right or valid one.

Conclusion. In the closing paragraph(s) of your paper, you have a final opportunity to convince your audience that the evidence you have presented in the body of your paper successfully demonstrates why your proposition is valid. You may want to summarize your strongest arguments or restate your position. You may want to suggest action, solutions, or resolutions to the conflict. This final part of your paper must leave your audience with a feeling that you have presented them with all the essential information they need to know to make an intelligent assessment of your success at defending your position and possibly persuading them to believe as you do.

STRATEGIES FOR ARGUING EFFECTIVELY

While the previous section outlines the essential structure of an argument, the following comments will also help you write an effective argument.

Know Your Audience. A consideration of who your audience is will help you anticipate the arguments of those opposed to you. Many instructors tell their students to imagine an audience who disagrees with your position. After all, there really is no argument if you address an audience of people who believe exactly as you do. Knowing your audience will help you figure out what strategies you must use to make your position convincing. Imagine that you are addressing an audience who is either indifferent to or opposed to your position. This will help direct the shape of your argument because such an audience will require solid evidence or persuasive illustrations to sway its opinion.

Establish an Appropriate Tone. Tone refers to the writer's attitude toward his or her subject. As a writer of argument, you want your audience to take you seriously, to weigh what you have to say in defense of your position, and, ideally, to not only agree that your reasoning is sound but also to agree with your position. Therefore, try to keep your tone sincere, engaging, and balanced. You do not want to take a hostile, sarcastic, or antagonistic tone because then you risk alienating your audience. If you are too light, flippant, or humorous, your audience might believe you to be insincere or not truly interested in your topic.

Anticipate the Arguments of the Opposition.
As mentioned above, one key aspect of argumentation is refuting arguments of those who hold opposing opinions. How do you anticipate what those opposed to your position believe? Perhaps you are already familiar with opposing positions from your own observations or discussions with others, but a good step in your preparation is to look for written articles that express an opinion or position that you do not share. Read the articles, determine the authors' position, and note the evidence they produce to support their positions. How can you refute them? What evidence of your own contradicts them and supports your own position? Sometimes students find themselves being convinced by the arguments of others and find themselves switching positions. Do not worry if that happens to you. In fact, it will probably aid you in your own argument because you are already familiar with the reasoning of that position and can use the new evidence that persuaded you to find fault with your old position.

Keep in mind that this strategy of refuting an opposing argument does not always require disproving the point. You may also question its credibility, challenge the point, identify faulty logic, or otherwise cast doubt on it. Take care when challenging the opposition that you are on solid ground and can back up your own claims with proof. To attack a point by simply declaring it wrongheaded or insubstantial without having your own solid evidence is to considerably weaken your argument. So look for any of the following ways to challenge the opposition:

- Question the validity of data or evidence: Are statistics accurate? What is the source of data? Does the opposition skew or slant data to fit its own needs?
- Question authority: What are the credentials of authorities cited in arguments? Do their credentials qualify them to have informed opinions on the topic? Do they have questionable motives?
- Challenge the logic of the opposition: What fallacies do you find? What flaws in the reasoning process are there?

Make Concessions.
Sometimes it is necessary to concede a point to the opposition—that is, to acknowledge that the opposition has made a reasonable assertion. Making a concession or two is inevitable in arguments of complex issues. Conceding to the opposition is actually a good strategy as long as you follow such a concession with even stronger evidence that your position is the reasonable one. You agree that the opposition makes a good point, but you follow that agreement with an even more persuasive point.

Follow a Logical Line of Reasoning.
Formal argumentation typically follows one of two common lines of reasoning, **deductive** and **inductive** reasoning. In *deductive* reasoning, you move from a general principle, or shared premise, to a

conclusion about a specific instance. Premises are assumptions that people share, and the conclusion will be implied in the premises or assumptions. The traditional form of deductive reasoning is the **syllogism** which has two **premises** and a conclusion. A premise is defined as an assumption or a proposition on which an argument is based or from which a conclusion is drawn. The premises are often referred to as *major* and *minor*, with the major premise being the general truth and the minor premise a specific instance. The classic syllogism, offered by Aristotle (384–322 BCE), a Greek mathematician and logician, is the following:

> **Major premise**: All men are mortal.
> **Minor premise**: Socrates is a man.
> **Conclusion:** Socrates is mortal.

This simple example of syllogism indicates the basic formula: A is B. C is B. Therefore A is C. Arguments are described as valid when the premises lead logically to the conclusion. If they do not, the argument is invalid. Similarly, an argument is said to be sound if the argument is valid and leads to the conclusion; it is unsound if the argument is valid but does not lead to the conclusion or if the conclusion is valid but the argument is not. Here is another example:

> **Major premise:** Driving while drunk is illegal.
> **Minor premise:** Joe was drunk when he drove home from the party.
> **Conclusion:** Joe committed a crime.

In contrast, *inductive* reasoning moves from a number of specific instances to a general principle. Rather than begin with a shared assumption or generalization, you must provide sufficient data or evidence that the generalization is warranted. Your intent is to show the general pattern by presenting relevant specific instances as evidence. To avoid being accused of overgeneralizing or making a hasty generalization, you must provide enough data, examples, or specific instances to ensure that your audience is satisfied with your conclusion. In contrast to deductive reasoning, which rests on certainties (shared or commonly acknowledged truths), inductive reasoning relies on probability (the likelihood that something is true).

Example:

> **Observation one:** Students entering the classroom have wet hair and damp clothes.
> **Observation two:** Students typically come from outside the building to class.
> **Conclusion:** It must be raining outside.

With induction, you must be very careful that your data do indeed warrant your conclusion. For instance, consider the following example of **hasty generalization:**

> **Observation one:** The daily high temperatures for the last several days have been unusually high.
> **Observation two:** I don't remember it ever being this hot during the summer.
> **Conclusion:** We must be experiencing global warming.

Obviously there is not enough evidence in either of the observations to establish that global warming accounts for the recent high temperatures.

While formal argumentation is useful when arguing in abstract or ideal disciplines, such as mathematics, it is less effective in complex, real-world situations—that is, the kinds of arguments in which you are likely to be engaged. Aristotle himself realized that syllogistic reasoning, which deals in absolutes, was not suited to all arguments and that many arguments depended on an informal logic of probabilities or uncertainties. His study of this system of reasoning was known as **rhetoric,** which he defined as "the faculty of discovering in any particular case all of the available means of persuasion." Formal syllogistic logic typically leads to one correct and incontrovertible conclusion, while informal or rhetorical logic allows for probable or possible conclusions. As in syllogistic logic, the reasoning process must be rational and practical.

The Toulmin Model of Reasoning.

One effective model of informal argumentation, or practical reasoning, is that described by Stephen Toulmin, a twentieth century philosopher, mathematician, and physicist. This method is not as constrictive as formal syllogistic reasoning because it allows for probable causes and reasonable evidence. With this method, an argument is broken down into its individual parts and examined: each stage of the argument leads to the next. Toulmin defined argumentation as a process or logical progression from **data** or **grounds** (evidence or reasons that support a claim), to the **claim** (the proposition, a debatable or controversial assertion, drawn from the data or grounds) based on the **warrant** (the underlying assumption). The *claim* is the point your paper is making, your thesis or arguable position statement. *Data* or *grounds* constitute your proof and demonstrate how you know the claim is true or the basis of your claim. *Warrants* are the underlying assumptions or inferences that are taken for granted and that connect the claim to the data. They are typically unstated or implied and can be based on any of several types of appeals: logic, ethics, emotion, and/or shared values.

This view of argumentation as a logical progression has similarities to formal argumentation but does not rely on inductive or deductive reasoning that leads inevitably to one true conclusion. Rather, it relies on establishing the relationship between data and the claim by offering evidence that supports the warrant and leads to the best possible, the most probable, or the most likely conclusion. In such reasoning, the argument often attempts to defuse opposing arguments with the use of **qualifiers** such as *some, many, most, usually, probably, possibly, might,* or *could.* Qualifiers indicate awareness that the claim is not absolute but reasonable in the specific instance. This step reveals how sure you are of your claim.

The argument should also recognize any **conditions of rebuttal**—that is, exceptions to the rule. Rebuttals address potential opposing arguments, usually by showing flaws in logic or weakness of supporting evidence. An argument will also, if necessary, make **concessions** or acknowledgments that certain opposing arguments cannot be refuted. Often **backing**—additional justification or support for the warrant—is supplied as a secondary argument to justify the warrant. To succeed, an argument following the Toulmin model depends heavily on the strength of its warrants or assumptions, which in turn means having a full awareness of any exceptions, qualifications, or possible reservations.

Use Appeals Effectively. Aristotle maintained that effective persuasion is achieved by a balanced use of three appeals to an audience: *logos* (logic), *ethos* (ethics), and *pathos* (emotion, related to the words pathetic, sympathy, and empathy). Other appeals may be used, such as shared values. In the Toulmin method, appeals support warrants. Thus, a good argument will use sound reasoning or apply inductive or deductive reasoning (logic), it will call upon recognized authority or establish the credibility of its sources (ethics), and it will reach audience members on an affecting, disturbing, touching, or other poignant level (emotion). An argument may also make appeals to the audience on the basis of shared values, such as human dignity, free speech, fairness, and the like.

Logical appeals offer clear, reasonable, well-substantiated proofs, including such things as data, statistics, case studies, or authoritative testimony or evidence, and they acknowledge and refute the claims of the opposition. We see such a logical appeal in Jessica Reaves' "What the Rest of Africa Could Learn about AIDS" (Chapter 21) when she cites statistics that demonstrate Senegal's success in combating and preventing AIDS, in sharp contrast to other African countries.

Ethical appeals are often made in the introduction and conclusion because they are not based on statistics or hard data. Rather, they take advantage of the beliefs or values held by the audience and often help establish context. Barbara Kingsolver's opening series of questions in "A Pure, High Note of Anguish" (Chapter 17) makes a strong ethical appeal to the common pain and shock at the events of the September 11, 2001, terrorist attacks in New York, Washington, D.C., and Pennsylvania, especially during the first confused weeks following the catastrophes when she wrote the essay.

Emotional appeals can be quite effective but must not be overdone, certainly not to the exclusion of logical appeals. Anna Quindlen in "Our Tired, Our Poor, Our Kids" (Chapter 13) makes a strong emotional appeal in her opening paragraph with a striking and startling description: "Six people live here, in a room the size of the master bedroom in a modern suburban house. . . . One woman, five children. The baby was born in a shelter." Her opening touches readers on an emotional level and sets the tone for what she argues in the rest of her article.

Use Analogy. An analogy is a comparison of two things in order to show their similarities. Often the comparison is of a difficult or unfamiliar concept to a simpler or more familiar one, an excellent way to advance your argument. As a strategy in argumentation, you want to make the point that if the situation in the example is true or valid, it will be true or valid in the situation you are arguing. Paul Johnson in "American Idealism and Realpolitik" (Chapter 18) uses an extended analogy when he compares the concept of life without America's taking responsibility for enforcing law abroad to "the bestial existence described in Thomas Hobbes' great work, *Leviathan.*" You must choose your comparisons wisely and avoid making false comparisons: if the argument is weak for your example, it will be weak for the argument you are making.

Assess the Evidence. Reading critically is important in argumentation. You can build your own argument by trying to keep an open mind when analyzing the arguments of those opposed to your position as you read in search of evidence to support your position. What questions should you ask when analyzing the positions of those opposed to you? Consider the following: What is the author's purpose? How well does he or she achieve that purpose? What evidence does the writer give in support of that purpose? How does the author know the evidence is true? What is the argument based on? Has the writer omitted or ignored important evidence? Does the author's argument lead to a logical conclusion? Sometimes something that seems to be logical or reasonable turns out to be false. Are you convinced that the author's sources are trustworthy? What sort of language does the writer use? Is it clear and fair? Does the writer use words that are heavily charged or "loaded" and therefore likely to play on emotions rather than appeal to reason? Does the writer make any of the common fallacies (errors of reasoning) associated with attempts to be logical and fair?

Avoid Common Rhetorical Fallacies. Part of your strategy in writing a good argument is to evaluate your own reasoning process as well as that of other writers, especially those whose works you may use in support of your own argument. A fallacy is a flaw or error in reasoning that makes an argument invalid or, at best, weak. Look for these **common flaws** or **fallacies** in your own writing or in that of any writing you analyze:

- *Ad hominem* **arguments.** This Latin term means "against the man" or "toward the person" and applies to arguments that attack the character of the arguer rather than the argument itself. *Ad hominem* arguments often occur in politics, for instance, when opponents of a candidate refer to personal characteristics or aspects of the candidate's private life as evidence of her or his unsuitability to hold office. **Example:** Arguing that a candidate would not make a good senator because she is a single parent or that a candidate would not be effective as mayor because he is homosexual ignores the more important questions of qualifications for the office, the candidate's stand on issues relevant to the position, the candidate's experience in political office, and similar substantive considerations.

- **Circular reasoning or begging the question.** This error makes a claim that simply rephrases another claim in other words. It assumes as proof the very claim it is meant to support. **Examples:** This sort of logic occurs in statements such as "We do it because that's the way we've always done it," which assumes the validity of a particular way of doing things without questioning or examining its importance or relevance. Another example is stating that your candidate is the best person for an office because he is better than the other candidates.

- **Either–or reasoning.** If a writer admits only two sides to an issue and asserts that his is the only possible correct one, the writer has probably not given full thought to the subject or is unaware of the complexity of the issue. Most arguable topics are probably complex, and few are limited to either one or another right viewpoint. Be wary of a writer who argues that there is only one valid position to take on an issue.

- **Emotionally charged language.** Writers may rely on language guaranteed to appeal to their audiences on an emotional level rather than an intellectual level. Writers do not have to avoid appeals to the emotions entirely, but they should limit their use of such appeals. Arguments on ethical or moral issues such as abortion or capital punishment lend themselves to emotional appeals, but arguments on just about any subject may be charged with emotion. This fallacy can appeal to any number of emotions, such as fear, pity, hatred, sympathy, or compassion. Emotionally charged language also includes **loaded words,** those whose meanings or emotional associations vary from person to person or group to group, and **slanted words,** those whose connotations (suggestive meaning as opposed to actual meaning) are selected for their emotional association. **Examples:** Abstract words are usually loaded, such as democracy, freedom, justice, or loyalty. Words may be slanted to convey a good association, such as those used in advertisements—cool, refreshing, or smooth—or to convey a bad association—sweltering, noisy, or stuffy. In argumentative writing, loaded or slanted language becomes problematic when it is used to deceive or manipulate.

- **False analogy.** A writer may falsely claim that, because something resembles something else in one way, it resembles it in all ways. This warning does not deny that analogy has a place in argument. It can be an extremely useful technique by emphasizing a comparison that furthers an argument, especially for a difficult point. Explaining a difficult concept in terms of a simpler, more familiar one can give helpful support to readers. However, make sure that the analogy is true and holds up under close scrutiny. **Example:** A controversial analogy that is sometimes used is the comparison of America's internment of American citizens of Japanese descent during World War II to Hitler's concentration camps. On some levels the comparison is justified: people in the U.S. internment camps were held against their will in confined areas guarded by armed soldiers, they often lost all of their property, and some were even killed in the camps. On the other hand, they were not starved to death, exterminated, or used as subjects of medical experiments. The analogy is useful for making a point about the unfair treatment of American citizens during wartime, but many would argue that the analogy breaks down on some very important points.

- **Faulty appeal to authority.** Stating that a claim is true because an authority says it is true may be faulty if the authority is not an expert in the area being discussed, the subject is especially controversial with much disagreement over it, or the expert is biased. Such false appeals appear often in advertisement, as when an actor who portrays a lawyer on television appears in an ad for a real-life law firm. Similarly, actors who portray doctors on medical television shows are often used in health and beauty products to present an appearance of authority. The underlying assumption seems to be that audience members will equate the fictional lawyer's or doctor's words with those of an actual lawyer or physician.

- **Hasty generalization.** A writer makes a hasty generalization if she draws a broad conclusion on the basis of very little evidence. Such a writer probably has not explored enough evidence and has jumped too quickly to conclusions. **Examples:** Assuming that all politicians are corrupt because of the bad behavior of one is an example of making a hasty generalization. Condemning all films with violent content because of one film that has received widespread criticism for its graphic violence is another example.

- **Oversimplification.** In oversimplification, the arguer offers a solution that is too simple for the problem or issue being argued. **Example:** For instance, arguing that the problem of homelessness could be solved by giving jobs to homeless people overlooks the complexity of the issue. Such a suggestion does not take into account such matters as drug or alcohol dependency that sometimes accompanies life on the streets or a range of other problems faced by people who have lost their homes and learned to live outdoors.

- *Non sequitur.* This Latin term, meaning "does not follow," refers to inferences or conclusions that do not follow logically from available evidence. Non sequiturs also occur when a person making an argument suddenly shifts course and brings up an entirely new point. **Example:** The following demonstrates a *non sequitur:* "My friend Joan broke her arm during a gymnastics team practice after school. After-school activities are dangerous and should be banned."

- *Post hoc, ergo propter hoc* **reasoning.** This Latin term means "after this, therefore because of this." It applies to reasoning that assumes that *Y* happened to *X* simply because it came after *X*. **Example:** Accusing a rock group of causing the suicide of a fan because the fan listened to the group's music just before committing suicide is an example of such reasoning. Although the music might be a small factor, other factors are more likely to account for the suicide, such as a failed love relationship, feelings of low self-worth, or personal despair for a variety of reasons.

- **Red herring.** A red herring diverts the audience's attention from the main issue at hand to an irrelevant issue. The fallacy is to discuss an issue or topic as if it were the real issue when it is not. Writers of mystery fiction often use red herrings to distract readers from identifying the stories' criminals. That is part of the fun of reading a mystery. But an argumentative writer who tries to use red herrings probably does not have enough relevant supporting evidence or does not recognize the irrelevance of the evidence. **Example:** Arguing against the death penalty on the grounds that innocent people have been executed avoids the issue of why the death penalty is wrong. Citing the execution of innocent people is a red herring.

- **Stereotyping.** Another form of generalization is stereotyping—that is, falsely applying the traits of a few individuals to their entire group or falsely drawing a conclusion about a group on the basis of the behavior or actions of a few in that group. Stereotyping is also oversimplification because it ignores the complexity of humans by reducing them to a few narrow characteristics. Stereotyping produces a false image or impression of a large number of people who have a certain thing in common—most frequently race, ethnicity, gender, or sexual preference—but also such widely differing things as occupation, hair color, speech habits, or educational level. **Example:** Any assertion about an entire group of people on the basis of a few in that group is stereotyping.

STRATEGIES FOR CONSTRUCTING A CONVINCING ARGUMENT

- **Know your audience.** This helps you know what evidence you need to make your argument convincing.
- **Establish appropriate tone.** Your attitude toward your subject is important in making your argument convincing. Using the appropriate tone strengthens your argument.
- **Anticipate the arguments of those opposed to you.** Anticipating and countering others' arguments strengthens your own position.
- **Make concessions where necessary.** Acknowledging truths in the arguments of others reveals that you are aware of those truths but are still committed to your own position. Follow such concessions with your own even stronger evidence, proof, or support.
- **Follow a logical line of reasoning.** Whether formal or informal, inductive or deductive, or some other method recommended by your instructor, your argument must be reasonable and sound.
- **Use appeals effectively.** Appeals to logic, ethics, emotions, or shared values all help develop your argument. Be cautious when appealing to emotions; such appeals are all right in small measure but your main appeals should be to logic and/or ethics.
- **Assess the evidence.** Examine carefully the evidence you use for your argument. Weak or flawed evidence weakens your own argument.
- **Look for flaws in your own and others' reasoning process.** Avoid fallacies or errors in reasoning in your own writing and examine the arguments of others for such flaws.

SAMPLE STUDENT PAPERS

In the following pages you will find two student papers demonstrating effective argumentation. The first is annotated with marginal comments on the student's strategies, while the second is presented without comment as an exercise for classroom use or your own study. In addition to noting their argumentative strategies, pay attention to the ways they use sources to bolster their arguments. **Both students follow MLA style guidelines for handling source material as outlined in Chapters 6 and 7.**

In her introductory women's studies and sociology classes, Rita became interested in the status of women in the work force. She learned about federal legislation that made it illegal to discriminate in the workplace on the basis of sex, among other things. She also knew that when her mother and grandmother were growing up, the women's movement had done much to address inequities in women's lives. So she was surprised by some of the facts that she learned in her classes about women's work force participation and earnings. On the other hand, Rita had often heard people comment that women have now achieved equity, even arguing that there was no longer job discrimination or discrepancies between what men and women earn for the same work. Furthermore, several class-action sex-discrimination lawsuits brought by female employees against large corporations had been in the news recently, with the corporations hotly denying any form of sex discrimination. Therefore, when her English instructor assigned an argumentative paper using source materials, Rita decided to research this controversial subject.

Rita's question was, have women really achieved equality in the work place? Her reading in this area led her to the conclusion that, no, despite everything that has been done to make women equal to men in employment, they have not yet achieved that goal. Although she found that there are differences in not only earnings but also rates of promotion and representation at higher, managerial ranks, she decided to focus her paper on just the issue of the wage gap. The proposition she formulated for her paper is the following: Despite decades of struggling for women's equality in the workplace, the wage gap between men and women remains unacceptably wide.

Rita begins with background information and establishes importance of issue by appealing to the common good. Her proposition states clearly what her position is.

Fleming 1

Rita Fleming

English 102-2

Professor White

19 June 2008

Women in the Workforce: Still Not Equal

Nearly seventy-one million American women, over half of those over the age of 16, are in the civilian labor force, and over half of those women work full time, year round. Many people have the perception that women's large presence in the workforce in combination with federal laws that prohibit job discrimination means that women enjoy equality with men in the workplace.

However, recent class-action sex-discrimination suits brought by women workers against large corporations suggest that millions of

Fleming 2

women feel discriminated against in the workplace. Furthermore, a look at labor statistics compiled by the federal government, such as those from the U.S. Census Bureau, reveals that women on average are still paid significantly less than men. Despite decades of struggling for women's equality in the workplace, the wage gap between men and women remains unacceptably wide.

Rita acknowledges the opposition, makes concessions, and reaffirms her position.

Some argue that workplace inequity has disappeared as a result of federal legislation that makes discrimination in employment illegal. It is true that efforts to correct disparities between men's and women's wages have a long history. Executive Orders have been legislated to fight discrimination in employment, beginning in 1961 with President John F. Kennedy's Executive Order 10925 creating a President's Committee on Equal Employment Opportunity prohibiting discrimination on the basis of sex, race, religious belief, or national origin. The Equal Pay Act of 1963 prohibits paying women less than men working in the same establishment and performing the same jobs, and Title VII of the 1964 Civil Rights Act prohibits job discrimination on the basis of not only race, color, religion, and national origin but also sex. It is also true that when the Equal Pay Act was signed, women working full-time, year round made only 59 cents on average for every dollar a man made and that the figure had increased to 82 cents by 2005 (Brunner). Yes, women have made gains over the past forty years, but is 82 cents for every dollar a man makes acceptable? If women are truly equal to men in this society, why are

their average earnings not equal? Finally, if
there is true pay equity in the workplace, why
does the number of workplace suits charging
discrimination of all kinds, including wage
inequities, continue to rise ("Class Action Suits
in the Workplace" 84)?

Rita offers explanations for the inequity by citing data supporting her position.

    There are many reasons for this inequity.
One reason is that most women work in service
and clerical jobs, including such occupations as
secretaries, teachers, cashiers, and nurses. For
instance, in 2006, 92.3% of registered nurses and
82.2% of elementary and middle school teachers
were women (BLS). In 2006, 97.7% of preschool and
kindergarten teachers, 97.1% of dental hygienist,
and 97.3% of secretaries were (BLS). In 1999, 97.3%
of preschool and kindergarten teachers as well
as dental assistants were female, and 96.7% of
secretaries were (Weinberg 11). Women also tend to
work at jobs that pay less than the jobs that men
typically work at. Eitzen and Zinn point out that,
as the economy shifted in recent times from being
manufacturing-based to being more service oriented,
a dual labor market emerged. In a dual labor
market, there are two main types of jobs, primary
and secondary. Primary jobs are usually stable,
full-time jobs with high wages, good benefits, and
the opportunity to move up the promotion ladder,
whereas secondary jobs are the opposite. Secondary
occupations are unstable, normally part time, with
few benefits and little opportunity for advancement
(218). Unfortunately, large corporations have been
eliminating many primary jobs and creating new,
secondary jobs to take their places, and it is

Fleming 4

mostly women who are hired to fill these secondary
positions.

*Continues
to explain,
backing
assertions with
supporting
proof.*

   The term "occupational segregation" is used
to describe the phenomenon of women workers being
clustered in secondary or low-paying jobs (Andersen
and Collins 238). This segregation is particularly
startling when you consider such statistics as
the following: "Since 1980, women have taken 80
percent of the new jobs created in the economy,
but the overall degree of gender segregation has
not changed much since 1900" (Andersen and Collins
236). Fully 60% of women workers are in clerical and
service occupations, while only 30% are managers
and professionals ("USA" 68). In the very few
occupations where the median earnings for women
are at least 95% of those for men, only Fleming 4
one—meeting and convention planners—employs a
higher percentage of female workers than male
(Weinberg 13). Women are simply not crossing over
into traditionally male-dominated occupations at
a very high rate. This does not mean that women
do not have opportunities or are not educated. It
could mean, however, that the workplace is still
plagued by old, outdated stereotypes about gender-
based occupations.

*As she offers
more reason
to account for
the wage gap,
Rita reinforces
her position
that the gap is
unacceptable.*

   Another explanation for the wage gap is that
women earn less because of the differences in years
of experience on the job. Collectively, women earn
less because they haven't worked as many years as
men have in certain professions (Robinson 183-84).
Women often drop out of the job market to have
their families, for instance, while men stay at
their jobs when they have families. Yet another

Fleming 5

<u>reason</u> for the wage gap, offered by Borgna Brunner,
is that older women may be working largely in
jobs that are "still subject to the attitudes and
conditions of the past." Brunner points out: "In
contrast, the rates for young women coming of
age in the 1990s reflect women's social and legal
advances. In 1997, for example, women under 25
working full-time earned 92.1% of men's salaries
compared to older women (25-54), who earned 74.4% of
what men made." This is great news for young women
but a dismal reality for the significantly large
number of working women who fall into the 25-54 age
group.

> *Rita ends with strongest argument, that the wage gap cannot be explained by the usual means.*

    <u>Reasons to account for the persistence of
a wage gap are many, but sometimes there is
no explanation at all</u>. Analysts have tried to
determine why, as the U.S. Census Bureau figures
for 1999 reveal, "Men earn more than women at
each education level," taking into account all
year-round, full-time workers over age 25 (Day
and Newburger 4). Surprisingly, the wage gap is
greater than one might expect at the professional
level: female professionals (doctors, lawyers,
dentists) make substantially less than what male
professionals make. Female physicians and surgeons
aged 35-54, for instance, earned 69% of what male
physicians and surgeons made (Weinberg 21). How
can such a wage gap be explained? The reality is,
according to the *Women's International Network
News*, "Between one-third and one-half of the
wage difference between men and women cannot be
explained by differences in experience, education,
or other legitimate qualifications" ("USA" 68).

Fleming 6

Even the U. S. Census Bureau concludes: "There is a substantial gap in median earnings between men and women that is unexplained, even after controlling for work experience . . . education, and occupation" (Weinberg 21). Given this statement, it is likely that the most unfair reason of all to explain why women are paid less than men for the same or equal work is simply discrimination. This situation is intolerable.

What can be done to correct the wage differential between men's and women's earnings? Laws have failed to produce ideal results, but they have done much to further women's chances in the workplace and they give women legal recourse when they feel that discrimination has taken place. Therefore, better vigilance and stricter enforcement of existing laws should help in the battle for equal wages. Young women should be encouraged to train for primary jobs, while those who work in secondary jobs should lobby their legislators or form support groups to work for better wages and benefits. Working women can join or support the efforts of such organizations as 9to5, the National Association of Working Women. Women's position in the workforce has gradually improved over time, but given the statistics revealing gross differences between their wages and those of men, much remains to be done.

Rita suggests actions to address the problem she has substantiated in her paper.

Works Cited

Rita follows MLA style guidelines for documenting sources.

Andersen, Margaret L., and Patricia Hill Collins, ed. Race, Class and Gender: An Anthology, 3rd ed. Belmont, CA: Wadsworth, 1998.

Brunner, Borgna. "The Wage Gap: A History of Pay Inequity and the Equal Pay Act." Infoplease March

Fleming 7

2005. 14 Oct. 2008 <http://www.infoplease.com/spot/
    equalpayact1.html>

"Class Action Suits in the Workplace are on the Rise."
    HR Focus April 2007: 84-85.

Day, Jennifer Cheeseman and Eric C. Newburger. The
    Big Payoff: Educational Attainment and Synthetic
    Estimates of Work-Life Earnings. United States
    Census Bureau, July 2002. 15 Oct. 2008 <http://
    www.census.gov/prod/2002pubs/ p23-210.pdf>

Eitzen, Stanley D., and Maxine Baca Zinn. Social
    Problems. 7th ed. Needham Heights, MA: Allyn and
    Bacon, 1997.

"101 Facts on the Status of Working Women."
    Business and Professional Women October 2007.
    12 October 2008 <http://www.bpwusa.org/files/
    public/101FactsOct07.pdf>

Robinson, Derek. "Differences in Occupational
    Earnings by Sex." In Women, Gender, and Work, ed.
    Martha Fetherolf Loutfi. Geneva: International
    Labor Office, 2001

United States. Department of Labor Bureau of Labor
    Statistics (BLS) Women in the Labor Force: A
    Databook (2006 Edition). 20 Nov. 2006. 12 Oct. 2008
    <http://www.bls.gov/cps/wlf-databook2006.htm.>

Weinberg, Daniel H. Evidence from Census 2000 about
    Earnings by Detailed Occupation for Men and Women.
    United States Census Bureau, May 2004. 15 Oct. 2008
    <http://www.census.gov/prod/2004pubs/censr-15.pdf>

EXERCISE

Read the student paper that follows and evaluate its success as an argument. What is Erin's thesis? What strategies does she use for developing her argument? Does she acknowledge the opposition, refute it, and/or make concessions? Are her own reasons valid or sound? Is she guilty of any fallacies? Are you convinced that her position is valid or reasonable?

Anderson 1

Erin D. Anderson

Dr. Mitchell

English 150-2 24

February 2008

Ads and Attitudes:

Advertisers' Responsibility for the Images They Produce

Flipping through the latest issue of a popular fashion magazine, a high-school freshman encounters in-your-face color advertisements on literally every second or third page, displaying pop superstars in their favorite brand of makeup and models flaunting their Barbie-doll physiques in the latest styles. At the same time, a middle-aged housewife changes the channel from a commercial about super-mom to an infomercial claiming that she, too, can have great abs if she calls now. Both the impact of advertising on culture and the accountability required of those publicizing the messages reflected in advertisements are the topics of much debate. Although the overall purpose of advertising is to promote and sell a product to the population in order to make a profit, advertisers must also take responsibility for the powerful images that their advertisements portray and the sometimes-unattainable standards that they endorse.

In addition to creating a market for products, advertisements have the unparalleled power to define what is popular and accepted in a society, therefore creating images in the minds of those who are subjected to the advertisements. Advertisers

Anderson 2

seek to create a universal ideal about the world
behind the products, thus developing a correlation
between the product and the new and better world.
In splashing their ads with image after image
of stunning blondes with swarms of men at their
beck and call, advertisers imply that a female
consumer can attain this fantasy if she can pass
this silent test of physical attractiveness (with
help from the advertised product, of course). They
hope that through appeals to the internal desires
of people to be or have what is popular, the
consumers will rush out and buy their products or
risk not living up to society's standard. Although
this tactic may lead to increased sales for the
advertiser, which is what he/she has set out to do,
it raises questions as to the appropriateness of an
advertising strategy that can so seriously distort
a person's view of himself or herself.

Jean Kilbourne reflects on this ability of
ads to "sell values, images, and concepts of
success and worth, love and sexuality, popularity
and normalcy" in her essay entitled "Beauty and
the Beast of Advertising" (8). She contends that
when magazine ads, television commercials, and
other means of advertising continue to reinforce
the same types of images, stereotypes result,
and these stereotypes can have negative effects
on consumers (9). One detrimental stereotype that
Kilbourne traces back to advertising is the
view of women as sex objects. She sees that women
are constantly confronted with images of outward

Anderson 3

perfection and are taught that if they are not
the thin, long-legged, forever radiant beauties
of these idealistic ads, their "desirability and
lovability" suffer (9). This leads not only to
feelings of dissatisfaction and shame, but also
to more serious problems such as eating disorders
or obsession over weight. Although Kilbourne's
essay focuses on the images in advertising that
negatively affect females, males in society can
also be influenced by advertisements. One must
merely think of all the ads he/she has seen in his
or her lifetime showing a rugged cowboy without
a care in the world pushing a certain brand of
deodorant or cigarettes in order to understand the
scope of these images.

In light of the tremendous power of
advertisements, one is compelled to conclude
that something must be done to monitor the
images entering our society via ads; thus, the
responsibility of the advertisers themselves
comes into question. John O'Toole, president
of the American Association of Advertising
Agencies, defines the purpose and scope of
advertising and defends the methods advertisers
use to sell products in his aptly titled piece
"What Advertising Isn't." O'Toole contends that
advertising is "salesmanship [. . .] functioning
in the paid space and time of mass media" (292). He
points out that advertising, unlike other forms of
communication, is not meant to cover all sides of
the story; instead, it presents products in their

Anderson 4

most favorable light (294). He also asserts that in
order to get a full understanding about a product
and its benefits, one should look to all relevant
sources, including unbiased reports in newspapers
or magazines and opinions of others (293).

Another argument employed by O'Toole in
support of advertisers is that ads simply reflect
the values of society (293). One of these societal
values includes the consumers' desire to see
themselves in the place of these flawless images
on billboards and in magazines. However, the
near impossibility of attaining this standard
even further causes self-image problems. It is
evident that there are additional elements at
work that factor into the values and expectations
of a culture, such as other media forms, family
influences, job and peer pressures. Moreover,
each person is responsible for the way he or she
interprets advertisements, and he or she must
recognize attempts to alter a belief and refuse to
allow this to happen.

While it is true that ads are not the sole
cause of the self-image problem, constant subjection
to such unrealistic concepts of beauty, success,
and popularity in advertising can contribute to an
already vulnerable sense of self. For this reason,
it is the responsibility of advertisers to realize
this vulnerability and modify the images they are
presenting to the masses in such a way as to begin
displaying a representative image of today's women
and men. This shift would cause more of America to
relate to the people being shown and would be a

Anderson 5

welcome respite from the artificiality in many of
today's advertisements.

Advertising, an undeniable force in
contemporary American society, not only markets
products themselves but also creates a sense
of what one should have, look like, and/or
be. The extraordinary power of advertising to
influence self-concept leads one to question the
responsibility of advertisers to convey fair
images. Only after advertisers modify their
strategies to accommodate the physical realities of
today's population, thereby further connecting with
their audience, can advertising images really reach
their optimum effectiveness for society as a whole.

Works Cited

Kilbourne, Jean. "Beauty and the Beast of
Advertising." Media & Values Winter 1989: 8-10.

O'Toole, John. "What Advertising Isn't." In
Perspectives on Contemporary Issues: Readings
Across the Disciplines, 3rd ed. ed. Katherine Anne
Ackley. Boston: Heinle Cengage Learning, 2003.
292-297.

ILLUSTRATION: COMPARING ARGUMENTS

EXERCISE

Read the two essays that follow and then compare them in terms of their authors'
success at writing a convincing argument, keeping in mind the guidelines for successful argumentation outlined above. What strategies do the writers use to advance their
arguments? Is either of the essays more logical or convincing than the other, or are
they equally persuasive?

HPV VACCINE TEXAS TYRANNY

MIKE ADAMS

Counterthink Cartoons are NewsTarget.com parodies or satirical commentary on various matters that the owners of the website believe to be of public concern. This cartoon and commentary were posted on Wednesday, February 7, 2007, by Mike Adams and Dan Berger. The link to the NewsTarget website is http://www.NewsTarget.com.

Commentary by Mike Adams, the creator of this cartoon:

On Friday, Feb. 2, Texas governor Rick Perry issued an executive order that bypassed the will of the people and the entire Texas legislature, mandating the vaccination of young girls with the HPV vaccine sold by Merck—the same drug company that reportedly gave thousands to Perry's campaign efforts. The vaccine is absolutely worthless as a medical treatment according to top docs in the alternative health field, and in my opinion, the so-called "science" supporting the vaccine as the only prevention for cervical cancer is an outright fraud.

But the story gets even more interesting when you start connecting the dots. A key Merck lobbyist, a man named Mike Toomey, actually served as the governor's chief of staff. In other words, a former top power person for the governor now works for Merck, the drug company that gave money to the campaign of the governor who essentially used dictatorial power to mandate, without any public debate whatsoever, the mass vaccination of young girls with a drug that will earn tens of millions of dollars in profits for Merck. Sound suspicious? It should.

The "dirty money connection" seems obvious to many readers who have been following this story, including one who posted, *"Only a man, Rick Perry especially, would sign an executive order, bypassing legislation, to inject girls with chemicals made by one of his contributors even though most parents have never seen sufficient information about this vaccine. Perry should be impeached as a threat to the*

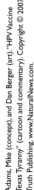

Adams, Mike (concept), and Dan Berger (art). "HPV Vaccine Texas Tyranny" (cartoon and commentary). Copyright © 2007 Truth Publishing. www.NaturalNews.com.

safety of our children." (See http://blogs.chron.com/texaspolitics/archives/2007/02/
lawmakers_resci.html)

4   ***The humanitarian cover story.***   Drug companies are experts at framing their
profit pursuits as public health initiatives. "We have to protect the little girls!" they
insist, but what's really going on behind closed doors is a far less altruistic push—
the push for profits. Requiring millions of young girls to get these new vaccines
just happens to generate enormous profits for Merck. But Merck officials, and even
the governor of Texas, would have you believe that has nothing to do with this.
Apparently, the fact that Merck will earn obscene profits from this initiative never
entered their minds.

   Nonsense. If Merck really wants to help these teenage girls, **why don't they
pledge to give away all their vaccines free of charge?** In fact, if they're such a humanitarian organization, why don't they give away all their drugs, and release third
world countries from patent protection at the same time? The answer, of course,
is because **this is all about money, not public health.** If Merck was really about
"patients first," they should convert to a 501(c)3 non-profit, stop paying their CEOs
$10+ million salaries, and give all their drugs away for free as a gift to humankind,
shouldn't they?

   That will never happen, of course, because it really is about the money. The
sick care industry is a for-profit industry, and the more people drug companies can
target as being sick today—or even possibly someday being sick at some future date
that "justifies" treatment right now—the more money they can sock away in the
bank. When it comes to money, it seems drug companies will stop at nothing to
get more of it, including influencing state officials to mandate vaccine consumption
policies that have nothing whatsoever to do with evidence-based medicine or genuine compassion for the health and lives of human beings.

   What's happening in Texas right now is a form of **medical tyranny,** and it's
only the beginning of what may prove to be a monumental battle between personal
freedoms vs. the corporate-controlled State.

8   ***We must stop the medical tyranny.***   If we let Texas get away with this medical
tyranny, forcing all young girls to undergo these HPV vaccinations even against
their parents' wishes, more states will follow suit. Merck is right now lobbying hard
to pass similar measures in over twenty other states, and if we don't put a stop to
the Texas situation, Merck will feel emboldened and likely urge other governors to
make the same declarations in their states, calling it a "public health" measure but
actually pocketing the profits from massive sales of these vaccines.

   What can you do?   I say we fight the tyranny by exposing it. You can **take action
to spread the word on this issue.** POST this cartoon to your website and LINK
to our articles on this topic. We give you full permission to reprint this cartoon
and forward it to your friends. Expose this medical madness before we all end up
prisoners under a system of medical tyranny that turns the bodies of teenage girls

into profit centers for Big Pharma! And unlike Merck, we don't care about the intellectual property royalties on this comic. Make as many copies as you want. Print up T-shirts. Add it to your book. Use it as you wish, and you don't owe me a dime. Why? Because I actually do care about my fellow human beings and I'm here to help stop the medical madness sweeping America today.

Speak up now or surrender your health freedoms forever.   You see, if we don't stand up to this kind of medical tyranny, it will only get worse. This debate is not merely about one vaccine, it's about surrendering your health freedom to a medical system that is owned and controlled by Big Pharma. Drug companies practically run the FDA, the EPA and even control the FTC (when was the last time the FTC investigated and prosecuted drug company monopolies?). Drug companies influence the DEA to keep their own drugs legal while the exact same "street" drugs are illegal. They own our elected officials, almost all of which accepted at least some money from drug companies in their last election campaign. Drug companies also own the mainstream media by propping up television networks, cable networks, newspapers, magazines and websites with literally billions of dollars in advertising. On top of that, drug companies heavily influence the medical journals and medical schools, and have effectively limited the entire conventional medical industry to a "drugs and surgery" approach to health, practically censoring nutritional knowledge out of existence.

Given this environment, is anyone supposed to believe we will see anything resembling honest debate or genuine science about this HPV vaccine? The entire industry, including drug companies, doctors, medical journals and the mainstream media, is twisting the facts to create the illusion that these vaccines are both safe and effective when, in reality, they are probably neither. Nor are they necessary. Cervical cancer is prevented in a hundred other ways, including adequate sunlight exposure and vitamin D consumption, supplementation with probiotics, adequate intake of selenium and zinc, increased consumption of trace minerals and iodine, regular physical exercise and many other safe, natural, non-patented strategies.

12   America is being hoodwinked over the HPV vaccine. To call this anything resembling genuine public health policy is an absolute joke. **It's really just a grand moneymaking scheme that exploits the bodies of young girls, marketed to look like compassionate health care.** Supporters of this policy are shameless, ignorant and devious in framing their nonsensical arguments using carefully-chosen words and phrases that make them seem like they're delivering a cancer cure from God. But in reality, mandatory HPV vaccines are a deal with the devil.

Consider this: With all the drugs being prescribed, all the toxic chemicals being consumed, and all the diseases now ravaging America—a country with the highest rates of degenerative disease in the world—does anybody really think that injecting one more drug is the answer? You'd have to be crazy to think so.

PERSONAL RESPONSE

What do you think of the cartoon?

QUESTIONS FOR CLASS OR SMALL-GROUP DISCUSSION

1. Comment on the cartoon as a persuasive tool.
2. What strategies does Adams use to advance his argument? What evidence does he give to support his position? Does he make any unsupported claims?
3. Comment on Adams' tone and language. Discuss their appropriateness, given the context of the cartoon and commentary and their intended audience.
4. What actions does Adams call for? Are you persuaded to act?

THE HPV DEBATE NEEDS AN INJECTION OF REALITY

ARTHUR ALLEN

Arthur Allen, a Washington-based writer and journalist, is the author of Vaccine: The Controversial Story of Medicine's Greatest Lifesaver *(2007). He has written about the subject of vaccines for such publications as the* New York Times, *the* Washington Post, *and the* Atlantic Monthly. *This article appeared in the April 7, 2007, issue of the* Washington Post.

The recommendation was that all children be given a vaccine for a carcinogenic virus whose spread is associated, in many minds, with sinful activities. Here's what some leading pediatricians had to say about it: "We are notably poor soothsayers in predicting which child will be put at high risk by future behavior. Pediatricians must initiate, then, an insurance policy for young patients that matures in adulthood."

That statement was made in 1992. Its authors were Neal Halsey and Caroline Breese Hall of the American Academy of Pediatrics' infectious-disease committee. They called for universal vaccination of newborns and adolescents against hepatitis B, a disease that, in the United States, spreads mainly through sex and shared hypodermic needles. Halsey and Hall were pushing universal vaccination because earlier programs to immunize at-risk groups—drug users, prostitutes, prisoners, gay males—had been a miserable failure.

The choice to vaccinate infants was controversial, but the virus is a deadly one. In the early 1990s, about 250,000 Americans were infected with hepatitis B each year. About a fifth would become chronic carriers and suffer, in some cases, scarring of the liver. About 6,000 died each year of liver cancer associated with hepatitis B.

And although children represented a small percentage of those infected, they were more likely to become chronic hepatitis B carriers.

4   There was controversy in the medical community over the hepatitis B vaccination program, but it was implemented, in that pre-Internet era, with minimal public fretting. Nearly every state now requires the vaccination for entry to primary school.

Now there are questions about mandatory vaccination of girls for the human papilloma virus, which can cause cervical cancer. This vaccine offers similar, if slightly less dramatic, hope to a large population of neglected Americans. But politically, it's a very different story this time. A powerful movement has sprung up to oppose mandatory HPV immunization. Much of this resistance is, I believe, misguided. Yet I have my own reservations about mandating the HPV vaccine at this time.

The results of the hepatitis B vaccination program that began in the 1990s have been dramatic. In the Morbidity and Mortality Weekly Report of March 16, the Centers for Disease Control and Prevention reported that the number of new cases had fallen to about 50,000 in 2005. New infections were most reduced in the vaccinated groups—98 percent among elementary-school children and young teenagers, and 90 percent among 15- to 24-year-olds.

Similarly, in trials completed last year, the HPV vaccine was shown to prevent 70 percent of the growths that lead to cervical cancer, which strikes 14,000 American women each year, killing one-fourth of them. The 20,000 women who received the vaccine in trials by Merck, the manufacturer, experienced no major side effects. By preventing precancerous growths, the vaccine also can reduce the need for extra gynecological visits and painful procedures.

8   This all sounds good. It helps explain why liberal groups such as Women in Government accepted funding from Merck this year to help the drug firm lobby state legislatures to make the HPV vaccine mandatory for sixth-grade girls.

So what's wrong with ordering parents to get their children immunized by a product that has the power, like the hepatitis B vaccine, to help prevent a deadly disease? Plenty, according to the many activists who have whipped up a firestorm on the issue in places from California to Maryland and the District, where the city council last week took the first step toward requiring HPV vaccination. (Virginia acted this year to require the immunizations but made it fairly easy for parents to opt out.)

In my view, the fact that HPV is sexually transmitted is no reason to keep children from being vaccinated against it. Immunizing infants against hepatitis B has clearly shown that public health campaigns can prevent disease without causing moral turpitude. In any case, HPV's spread is not linked to risky sexual behavior. The virus is as common as influenza: About 80 percent of women will be exposed to it at some point.

When the CDC led a drive to enforce mandatory vaccination against measles in the 1970s, it discovered that immunization rates increased by as much as 20 percent. The parents who had their kids vaccinated only when their schools required it often had been unaware of the vaccine, unable to afford it, or too overwhelmed to get their children to a clinic. Those who strongly opposed the vaccination could usually opt out under state laws. The same would be true of the HPV vaccine.

12   Most cervical cancers can be prevented with regular pap smear tests, which find precancerous growths that can be excised. Most of the women who get cervical cancer haven't had the test done in at least three years. It stands to reason that, without a mandatory vaccination, many of the girls who don't get vaccinated will belong to the same groups that fall through the cracks of the patchy U.S. healthcare system.

During a recent radio interview about this issue, I was dismayed to hear callers claim that proposed HPV mandates would make their children "guinea pigs" in a contemporary Tuskegee—a reference to the notorious experiments in which black men with syphilis were studied but not given penicillin. I responded by asking whether it was better to be neglected by the medical mainstream than to be enrolled in a measure that covers all girls—rich, poor, black, white, Hispanic and Asian.

Sadly, as long as the HPV vaccine is not required, the people who need it most probably won't get it. "Those who are well-informed with good families, parents involved with their children, will go ahead," said Hall, who is with the University of Rochester Medical Center in New York. "Those who are not as well informed or involved in the care of their children will not get the vaccine."

So why, given all these arguments, do I think that requiring HPV vaccination for school-age girls is a mistake at the present time? The most obvious reason is that when a vaccine is mandated, it must be available for free to those who can't afford it. But state health officials are already struggling to provide for existing mandated vaccines such as DTP (diphtheria, tetanus and pertussis), MMR (measles, mumps and rubella) and chickenpox. They simply don't have the money to buy the HPV immunization for girls whose families can't afford it.

16   Second, the vaccine, while promising, has no track record. Merck's hepatitis B vaccine was licensed in 1986, which allowed plenty of time to observe its efficacy and safety before it became mandatory—and forestalled the "guinea pig" argument. While the hepatitis B vaccine proved quite safe, there's no guarantee that the HPV immunization won't provoke a rare side effect.

But there is a third, less tangible reason for holding off—one that has to do with the kind of public perceptions that are essential to successful vaccination programs and are magnified in this era of instant blogging.

With only Merck and a few activists pushing the HPV vaccine, it lacks credibility. This has opened the door to critics of immunization in general, who are gaining support among people who fear an HPV-vaccine mandate.

Our rickety pediatric vaccination system is a three-legged stool whose stability relies on the participation of drug companies, which need a profit incentive; the government, which buys about half of all childhood vaccines; and parents, who are called on to submit their children to vaccination not only to protect them but to diminish the spread of disease.

20   In failing to include two legs of the system, those pushing for immediate mandatory vaccination are risking its collapse. The HPV vaccine may do great things, but we shouldn't rush it.

PERSONAL RESPONSE

Where do you position yourself on the issue of mandatory HPV vaccinations?

QUESTIONS FOR CLASS OR SMALL-GROUP DISCUSSION

1. How effective do you find Allen's opening paragraphs about the hepatitis B vaccine? Why does he start with that subject when his main focus is on the HPV vaccine?
2. Where does Allen make concessions in his argument?
3. What do you think of Allen's answers to the question he asks at the beginning of paragraph 15?
4. Comment on the effectiveness of Allen's metaphor in the closing paragraphs.

CHAPTER 6

Synthesizing Material and Documenting Sources Using MLA Style

WRITING A SYNTHESIS

A synthesis draws conclusions from, makes observations on, or shows connections between two or more sources. In writing a synthesis, you attempt to make sense of the ideas of two or more sources by extracting information that is relevant to your purpose. The ability to synthesize is an important skill, for people are continuously bombarded with a dizzying variety of information and opinions that need sorting out and assessment. To understand your own thinking on a subject, it is always useful to know what others have to say about it. You can see the importance of reading and thinking critically when synthesizing the ideas of others. The sources for a synthesis may be essays, books, editorials, lectures, movies, group discussions, or any of the myriad forms of communication that inform academic and personal lives. At minimum, you will be required in a synthesis to reflect on the ideas of two writers or other sources, assess them, make connections between them, and arrive at your own conclusions on the basis of your analysis. Often you will work with more than two sources; certainly you will do so in a research paper.

Your purpose for writing a synthesis will be determined by the nature of your assignment, although syntheses are most commonly used to either explain or argue. Perhaps you want to explain how something works or show the causes or effects of a particular event. You may argue a particular point, using the arguments of others as supporting evidence or as subjects for disagreement in your own argument. You may want to compare or contrast the positions of other writers for the purpose of stating your own opinion on the subject. When you write a research paper, you most certainly must synthesize the ideas and words of others. Whether your synthesis paper is a report or an argument, you must sort through and make sense of what your sources say. Sometimes you will want to read many sources to find out what a number of people have to say about a particular subject in order to discover your own position on it.

Synthesis, then, involves not only understanding what others have to say on a given subject but also making connections between them, analyzing their arguments or examples, and/or drawing conclusions from them. These are processes you routinely employ in both your everyday life and in your courses whenever you consider the words, ideas, or opinions of two or more people or writers on a topic. Beginning with Chapter 8, each chapter in Parts 2–5 ends with a list of suggestions for writing. Many of the topics require that you synthesize material in the readings in that chapter. These topics ask you to argue, to compare and contrast, to explore reasons, to explain something, to describe, or to report on something, using at least two of the essays in the chapter.

In all cases, no matter what your purpose for writing the synthesis, you will need to state your own central idea or **thesis** early in your paper. In preparation for

---

GUIDELINES FOR WRITING A SYNTHESIS

- **Determine your purpose for writing by asking yourself what you want to do in your essay.** Without a clear purpose, your synthesis will be a loosely organized, incoherent jumble of words. Although your purpose is often governed by the way in which the assignment is worded, make sure you understand exactly what you intend to do.

- **Consider how best to accomplish your purpose.** Will you argue, explain, compare and contrast, illustrate, show causes and effects, describe, or narrate? How will you use your sources to accomplish your purpose?

- **Read each source carefully and understand its central purpose and major points.** If you are unclear about the meaning of an essay, reread it carefully, noting passages that give you trouble. Discuss these passages with a classmate or with your instructor if you still lack a clear understanding.

- **Write a one-sentence statement of the central idea or thesis and a brief summary of each source you will use in your paper.** This process will help clarify your understanding of your sources and assist you in formulating your own central idea. These statements or summaries can then be incorporated appropriately into your synthesis.

- **Write a one-sentence statement of your own thesis or central purpose for writing the synthesis.** This statement should be a complete sentence, usually in the first paragraph of your essay. The thesis statement helps you focus your thoughts as you plan your essay by limiting the nature and scope of what you intend to accomplish. It also is a crucial aid to your readers, because it is essentially a succinct summary of what you intend to do.

- **Develop or illustrate your thesis by incorporating the ideas of your sources into the body of your paper, either by paraphrasing or directly quoting.** Part of your purpose in writing a synthesis is to demonstrate familiarity with your sources and to draw on them in your own essay. This goal requires that you make reference to key ideas of the sources.

- **Document your sources.** Keep in mind the guidelines for documenting all borrowed material.

writing your essay, you will complete a very helpful step if you locate the central idea or thesis of each of the works under analysis and summarize their main points. The summary is itself a kind of synthesis, in that you locate the key ideas in an essay, state them in your own words, and then put the ideas back together again in a shortened form. This process helps you understand what the authors believe and why they believe it. Furthermore, your own readers benefit from a summary of the central idea or chief points of the articles you are assessing. As you write your essay, you will not only be explaining your own view, opinion, or position, but you also will be using the ideas or words of the authors whose works you are synthesizing. These will have to be documented, using the appropriate formatting for documenting sources illustrated in this chapter.

In-Text Citations, Paraphrasing, and Quoting.   No matter what your purpose or pattern of development, if you draw on the writing of someone else, you must be fair to the author of the material you borrow. If you paraphrase an author's words or, occasionally, quote them exactly as they appear in the original text, you must cite your source. In any case, when you are using the ideas or words of another, you must give credit to your source. In academic writing, credit is given by naming the author of the borrowed material, its title, the place and date of publication, and the page number or numbers where the information is located.

The rest of this chapter introduces some basic skills needed to incorporate the words and ideas of others into your own written work. It begins with a discussion of documenting sources, goes on to provide guidelines and examples for paraphrasing and quoting, illustrates some useful tools for handling source material and integrating source materials, and ends with directions for documenting sources from collections of essays, such as this textbook. The guidelines in this chapter follow MLA (Modern Language Association) documentation style. (*Note:* If your instructor prefers that you use APA style or gives you a choice of styles, guidelines for APA documentation style appear in Chapter 7) MLA style is used primarily in the humanities disciplines, such as English and philosophy, whereas other disciplines have their own guidelines. If you learn the skills necessary for paraphrasing, quoting, and documenting the material located in this textbook, you will be prepared to incorporate library and Internet resources, as well as other materials, into long, complex research papers. For more discussion of MLA style, with sample works-cited entries for a broad range of both print and nonprint sources, including the Internet, see Chapter 7.

IN-TEXT CITATIONS USING MLA STYLE

The MLA style of documentation requires that you give a brief reference to the source of any borrowed material in a parenthetical note that follows the material. This parenthetical note contains only the last name of the authority and the page number or numbers on which the material appears or only the page number or numbers if you mention the author's name in the text.

The parenthetical citation is placed within the sentence, after the quotation or paraphrase, and before the period. If punctuation appears at the end of the words you are quoting, ignore a comma, period, or semicolon but include a question mark or exclamation mark. In all cases, the period for your sentence follows the parenthetical citation.

The name or title that appears in the parenthetical citation in your text corresponds to an entry in the Works Cited page at the end of your paper. This entry contains complete bibliographic information about the work you reference, including the full name of the author, the complete title, the place of publication, and the date of publication.

Treat World Wide Web sources as you do printed works. Because many web sources do not have page numbers, omit page numbers. Some authorities recommend naming the title of Internet source material in the text and placing the author's name in the parentheses, or repeating the author's name in the parentheses, even if it is used in the text.

Illustration: In-text Citations. The following examples show formats for citing sources in the text of your paper. The "works cited" format for many of the references illustrated here can be found in the section "Creating a Works Cited Page" in Chapter 7.

- **Book or article with one author.** Name the author followed by the page number: (Sollod 15)
- **Book or article with two or three authors.** Name authors followed by the page number: (Barrett and Rowe 78) (Fletcher, Miller, and Caplan 78)
- **Book or article with more than three authors.** Name just the first author followed by "et al." (Latin for "and others") and then the page number: (Smith et al. 29)

Note: Reproduce the names in the order in which they appear on the title page. If they are not listed alphabetically, do not change their order.

- **Article or other publication with no author named.** Give a short title followed by the page number: ("Teaching" 10)

Note: If you cite two anonymous articles beginning with the same word, use the full title of each to distinguish one from the other: ("Classrooms without Walls" 45) ("Classrooms in the 21st Century" 96)

- **Two works by the same author.** Give the author's name followed by a comma, a short title and the page number: (Heilbrun, *Hamlet's Mother* 123) (Heilbrun, *Writing a Woman's Life* 35)
- **Works by people with the same last name.** If your list of cited works has works by authors with the same last name, include the first name of the author in the parenthetical citation and then the page number or numbers: (Gregory Smith 16)

GUIDELINES FOR DOCUMENTING SOURCES

- Provide a citation every time you paraphrase or quote directly from a source.
- Give the citation in parentheses following the quotation or paraphrase.
- In the parentheses, give the author's last name and the page number or numbers from which you took the words or ideas. Do not put any punctuation between the author's last name and the page number.
- If you name the author as you introduce the words or ideas, the parentheses will include only the page number or numbers.
- At the end of your paper, provide an alphabetical list of the authors you quoted or paraphrased and give complete bibliographic information, including not only author and title but also where you found the material. This element is the "Works Cited" page.

PARAPHRASING

Paraphrasing is similar to summarizing in that you restate in your own words something someone else has written, but a paraphrase restates everything in the passage rather than highlighting just the key points. Summaries give useful presentations of the major points or ideas of long passages or entire works, whereas paraphrases are most useful in clarifying or emphasizing the main points of short passages.

To paraphrase, express the ideas of the author in your own words, being careful not to use phrases or key words of the original. Paraphrases are sometimes as long as the original passages, though often they are slightly shorter. The purpose of paraphrasing is to convey the essence of a sentence or passage in an accurate, fair manner and without the distraction of quotation marks. If your paraphrase repeats the exact words of the original, then you are quoting, and you must put quotation marks around those words. A paper will be more interesting and more readable if you paraphrase more often than you quote. Think of your own response when you

---

GUIDELINES FOR PARAPHRASING

- Restate in your own words the important ideas or essence of a passage.
- Do not repeat more than two or three exact words of any part of the original, unless you enclose them in quotation marks.
- If you must repeat a phrase, clause, or sentence exactly as it appears in the original, put quotation marks around those words.
- Keep the paraphrase about the same length as the original source.
- Give the source of the paraphrased information either in your text or in parentheses immediately after the paraphrase.
- Try to paraphrase rather than quote as often as possible, saving direct quotations for truly remarkable language, startling or unusual information, or otherwise original or crucial wording.

read something that contains quotations. Perhaps, like many readers, you will read with interest a paraphrase or short quotation, but you may skip over or skim quickly long passages set off by quotation marks. Readers generally are more interested in the ideas of the author than in his skill at quoting other authors.

Illustration: Paraphrasing.   This section provides examples of paraphrases using selected passages from the sources indicated.

1. **Source:** Graff, Gerald. *Beyond the Culture Wars: How Teaching the Conflicts Can Revitalize American Education.* New York: W.W. Norton, 1992.

   > **Original** (page 118): But the most familiar representation of the sentimental image of the course as a scene of conflict-free community is the one presented on untold numbers of college catalog covers: A small, intimate class is sprawled informally on the gently sloping campus greensward, shady trees overhead and ivy-covered buildings in the background. Ringed in a casual semicircle, the students gaze with rapt attention at a teacher who is reading aloud from a small book—a volume of poetry, we inevitably assume, probably Keats or Dickinson or Whitman. The classroom, in these images, is a garden occupying a redemptive space inside the bureaucratic and professional machine.
   >
   > **Paraphrase:** Gerald Graff notes that many colleges project a common sentimental image of campus life as an idyllic community set among ivy-covered buildings and characterized by small classes, attentive students, and poetry-reading instructors. The classroom becomes a haven from conflict and stress (118).

2. **Source:** Dahl, Ronald. "Burned Out and Bored." *Newsweek* 15 Dec. 1997: 8.

   > **Original** (page 8): What really worries me is the intensity of the stimulation. I watch my eleven-year-old daughter's face as she absorbs the powerful onslaught of arousing visuals and gory special effects. Although my son is prohibited from playing violent video games, I have seen some of his third-grade friends at an arcade inflicting blood-splattering, dismembering blows upon on-screen opponents in distressingly realistic games. . . . Why do children immersed in this much excitement seem starved for more? That was, I realized, the point.

COMMENT

Even when you put material into your own words, you must cite the source and give a page number where the paraphrased material is located.

> **COMMENT**
>
> When it is clear that you are paraphrasing from the same source in two or more con-secutive sentences *and* you have named the author or source in the first sentence, you need give only one parenthetical citation at the end of the series of sentences.

Paraphrase: Dahl believes that the over-stimulation of today's youth has resulted in a generation with a previously unprecedented threshold for excitement. It takes increasingly more violent, more shock-ing, and more thrilling events to stimulate young people (8).

3. **Source:** Camarota, Steven A. "The High Cost of Cheap Labor: Illegal Immigration and the Federal Budget." Center for Immigration Studies. August 2004 <http://www.cis.org/articles/2004/fiscalexec.html>

Original: Our findings show that many of the preconceived notions about the fiscal impact of illegal households turn out to be inaccurate. In terms of welfare use, receipt of cash assistance programs tends to be very low, while Medicaid use, though significant, is still less than for other households. Only use of food assistance programs is significantly higher than that of the rest of the population. Also, contrary to the perceptions that illegal aliens don't pay payroll taxes, we estimate that more than half of illegals work "on the books." On average, illegal households pay more than $4,200 a year in all forms of federal taxes. Unfortunately, they impose costs of $6,950 per household.

Paraphrase: According to a 2004 study by the Center for Im-migration Studies of the impact of illegal immigration on the federal budget, many of the notions about illegal immigrants are incorrect. Al-though they do receive more food aid than the general population, they receive less welfare and Medicaid benefits. Furthermore, most illegal immigrants pay federal taxes (Camarota).

> **COMMENT**
>
> For Internet or other electronic sources without pagination, many instructors recom-mend that you repeat the author's name in parentheses after all paraphrases and di-rect quotations, even if the name is already included in the text.

QUOTING

When you want to include the words of another writer, but it is not appropriate to either paraphrase or summarize, you will want to quote. Quoting requires that you repeat the exact words of another, placing quotation marks before and after the material being quoted. A crucial guideline requires that you copy the words exactly as they appear in the original text. To omit words or approximate the original within quotation marks is sloppy or careless handling of your source material.

Be selective in the material you choose to quote directly, however. You should usually paraphrase the words of another, restating them in your own language, rather than relying on exactly copying the words. How do you know when to quote rather than paraphrase? You should quote only words, phrases, or sentences that are particularly striking or that must be reproduced exactly because you cannot convey them in your own words without weakening their effect or changing their intent. Quote passages or parts of passages that are original, dramatically worded, or in some way essential to your paper. Otherwise, rely on paraphrasing to refer to the ideas of others. In either case, document your source by identifying the original source and the location of your information within that source.

Illustration: Quoting.   This section provides examples of quotations using selected passages from Gerald Graff's "Ships in the Night." The source for all examples in this section is the following:

> **Source:** Graff, Gerald. *Beyond the Culture Wars: How Teaching the Conflicts Can Revitalize American Education.* New York: W.W. Norton, 1992.

> **1. Original** (page 106): To some of us these days, the moral of these stories would be that students have become cynical relativists who care less about convictions than about grades and careers.
>
> **Quotation:** Gerald Graff suggests that "students have become cynical relativists who care less about convictions than about grades and careers" (106).

GUIDELINES FOR QUOTING

- Be selective: Quote directly only words, phrases, or sentences that are particularly striking and whose beauty, originality, or drama would be lost in a paraphrase.
- Quote directly passages that are so succinct that paraphrasing them would be more complicated or take more words than a direct quotation would require.
- Enclose the exact words you are quoting between quotation marks.
- Do not change one word of the original unless you indicate with brackets, ellipses, or other conventions that you have done so.
- Provide the source of your quoted material either in your text or in parentheses following the material.

> **COMMENTS**
>
> - Place double quotation marks before and after words taken directly from the original.
> - When the quoted material is an integral part of your sentence, especially when preceded by the word "that," do not capitalize the first letter of the first word.
> - Where possible, name the author whose ideas or words you are quoting or paraphrasing.
> - In parentheses after the quotation, give the page number in the source where the quotation is located (hence the phrase "parenthetical citation"). This example contains only the page number because the author's name is mentioned in the text. If the text had not given the author's name, it would be included in the parenthetical citation.

2. **Original** (page 118): The more fundamental question we should be asking in most cases is not how *much time* teachers are spending in the classroom but *under what conditions.*

   Quotation: Gerald Graff believes that "[t]he more fundamental question [. . .] is not *how much* time teachers are spending in the classroom but *under what conditions*" (118).

3. **Original** (page 109): Among the factors that make academic culture more confusing today than in the past is not only that there is more controversy but that there is even controversy about what can legitimately be considered controversial. Traditionalists are often angry that there should even be a debate over the canon, while revisionists are often angry that there should even be a debate over "political correctness," or the relevance of ideology and politics to their subjects.

   Quotation: In discussing the factors that confuse people about college curricula today, Gerald Graff notes: "Traditionalists are often angry that there should even be a debate over the canon, while revisionists are often angry that there should even be a debate over 'political correctness' [. . .]" (109).

> **COMMENTS**
>
> - When a quotation preceded by *that* forms an integral part of your sentence, do not capitalize the first word in the quotation, even when it is capitalized in the original. In this example, because the *t* in *the* is capitalized in the original, the bracket around the lower-cased *t* in the quotation indicates that the letter has been changed. Use the ellipsis (three spaced periods) to indicate the omission of text from the original.
> - If some text is italicized in the original, you must italicize it in your quotation.
> - Use brackets around ellipsis points to indicate that they are your addition.

> **COMMENTS**
>
> - If your direct quotation is preceded by introductory text and a colon or comma, capitalize the first letter of the first word of the quotation.
> - If you quote something that appears in quotation marks in the original source, use single marks within the double quotes.
> - If your quotation appears to be a complete sentence but the actual sentence you quote continues in the original, you must use the ellipsis at the end of your quotation to indicate that.
> - If an ellipsis comes at the end of a quotation, the closing quotation mark follows the third period, with no space between the period and quotation mark. The parenthetical citation follows as usual.

Combination of Paraphrase and Direct Quotation. The following example illustrates how one can combine paraphrasing and quoting for a balanced handling of source material.

> **4. Original** (page 118): But the most familiar representation of the sentimental image of the course as a scene of conflict-free community is the one presented on untold numbers of college catalog covers: A small, intimate class is sprawled informally on the gently sloping campus greensward, shady trees overhead and ivy-covered buildings in the background. Ringed in a casual semicircle, the students gaze with rapt attention at a teacher who is reading aloud from a small book—a volume of poetry, we inevitably assume, probably Keats or Dickinson or Whitman. The classroom, in these images, is a garden occupying a redemptive space inside the bureaucratic and professional *machine.*
>
> **Paraphrase and Quotation:** Gerald Graff thinks that colleges project an image different from the realities of academic life. College catalog covers, he says, foster "the sentimental image of the course as a scene of conflict-free community" when they portray students sitting outside on a sunny day, mesmerized by the instructor who stands before them, reading someone's words of insight or wisdom. According to him, the classroom becomes "a garden occupying a redemptive space inside the bureaucratic and professional machine" (118).

Here are two more examples of correctly handled direct quotations:

> **5.** Jack Santino in "Rock and Roll as Music; Rock and Roll as Culture" maintains that "[s]uch things as suicide, drugs, sex, and violence *are* teenage concerns" and that, "while artists have a responsibility not to glamorize them, that does not mean these themes should not be explored" (196).

> **COMMENTS**
>
> Notice the difference between examples 5 and 6. The first integrates the quoted material into the sentence with the word *that,* so the first words in each of the quoted passages do not require a capital first letter. In the second example, the quotation is introduced and set off as a separate sentence, so the first word after the quotation mark begins with a capital letter.

6. In "Rock and Roll as Music; Rock and Roll as Culture," Jack Santino observes: "Furthermore, such things as suicide, drugs, sex, and violence *are* teenage concerns. While artists have a responsibility not to glamorize them, that does not mean these themes should not be explored" (196).

INTEGRATING SOURCE MATERIALS INTO YOUR PAPER

When quoting or paraphrasing material, pay special attention to your treatment of source materials. Authors have developed many ways of skillfully integrating the words and ideas of other people with their own words. Your paper should not read as if you simply cut out the words of someone else and pasted them in your paper. You can achieve smooth integration of source materials into your text if you keep the following suggestions in mind:

- **Mention the cited author's name in the text of your paper to signal the beginning of a paraphrase or quotation.** The first time you mention the name, give both first and last names. After the first mention, give only the last name:

  Robert Sollod points out in "The Hollow Curriculum" that colleges would not think of excluding courses on multiculturalism from today's curriculum, given the importance of "appreciation and understanding of human diversity." **Sollod** asks: "Should such an appreciation exclude the religious and spiritually based concepts of reality that are the backbone upon which entire cultures have been based?" (A60).

- **Mention the source if no author is named.** This practice gives credit to the source while providing an introduction to the borrowed material:

> **CAUTION**
>
> Never incorporate a quotation without in some way introducing or commenting on it. A quotation that is not introduced or followed by some concluding comment, referred to as a "bald" or "dropped" quotation, detracts from the smooth flow of your paper.

A *U.S. News & World Report* **article** notes that, although no genes determine what occupation one will go into, groups of genes produce certain tendencies—risk-taking, for instance—that might predispose one to select a particular kind of work ("How Genes Shape Personality" 64).

- **Give citations for all borrowed material.** State the authority's name, use quotation marks as appropriate, give the source and page number in a parenthetical citation, give some sort of general information, and/or use a pronoun to refer to the authority mentioned in the previous sentence. *Do not rely on one parenthetical citation at the end of several sentences or an entire paragraph:*

    Regna Lee Wood has also researched the use of phonics in teaching children to read. **She** believes that the horrible failure of our schools began years ago. Wood notes that "it all began in 1929 and 1930 when hundreds of primary teachers, guided by college reading professors, stopped teaching beginners to read by "matching sounds with letters that spell sounds" (52). **She** adds that since 1950, when most reading teachers switched to teaching children to sight words rather than sound them by syllable, "fifty million children with poor sight memories have reached the fourth grade still unable to read" (52).

- **Vary introductory phrases and clauses.** Avoid excessive reliance on such standard introductory clauses as "Smith says," or "Jones writes." For instance, vary your verbs and/or provide explanatory information about sources, as in the following examples:

    Michael Liu notes the following:
    Professor Xavier argues this point convincingly:
    According to Dr. Carroll, chief of staff at a major health center:
    As Marcia Smith points out,

- **The first mention of an authority in your text (as opposed to the parenthetical citation) should include the author's first name as well as last name.** The second and subsequent references should give the last name only (never the first name alone).

    First use of author's name in your paper: Susan Jaspers correctly observes that . . .
    Second and subsequent mentions of that author: Jaspers contends elsewhere that . . .

- **Combine quotations and paraphrases.** A combination provides a smoother style than quoting directly all of the time:

    W.H. Hanson's 2008 survey of college students reveals that today's generation of young people differs from those he surveyed in 2003. Hanson discovered that today's college students "are living through a period of profound demographic, economic, global, and technological change." Since these students of the 00s see themselves living in a "deeply troubled nation," they have only guarded optimism about the future (32–33).

- **For long quotations (more than four typed lines), set the quoted material off from the text (referred to as a block quotation).** Write your introduction to the quotation, generally followed by a colon. Then begin a new line indented ten spaces from the left margin, and type the quotation, double spaced as usual.

- **Do not add quotation marks for block quotations indented and set off from the text.** If quotation marks appear in the original, use double quotation marks, not single. If you quote a single paragraph or part of one, do not indent the first line any more than the rest of the quotation.

- **For block quotations, place the parenthetical citation after the final punctuation of the quotation.** See the following example of a block quotation:

> In her article exploring the kind of workforce required by a high-tech economy, Joanne Jacobs suggests that many of today's high school graduates lack crucial skills necessary for jobs in the rapidly growing technical and computer industries. For instance, a number of corporations agreed on the following prerequisites for telecommunications jobs:
>
> - Technical reading skills (familiarity with circuit diagrams, online documentation, and specialized reference materials).
> - Advanced mathematical skills (understanding of binary, octal, and hexadecimal number systems as well as mathematical logic systems).
> - Design knowledge (ability to use computer-aided design to produce drawings) (39–40).

USING ELLIPSIS POINTS, BRACKETS, SINGLE QUOTATION MARKS, AND "QTD. IN"

This section offers some additional guidelines on the mechanics of handling source materials and incorporating them into your paper.

Ellipsis Points.

- **If you want to omit original words, phrases, or sentences from your quotation of source material, use ellipsis points to indicate the omission.** Ellipsis points consist of three spaced periods, with spaces before, between, and after the periods. In quotations, ellipses are most frequently used within sentences, almost never at the beginning, but sometimes at the end. In every case, the quoted material must form a grammatically complete sentence, either by itself or in combination with your own words.

MLA style calls for the use of brackets around ellipsis points to distinguish between your ellipses and the spaced periods that sometimes occur in works. In that case, leave a space before the second and third periods but no space before the first or after the third. Use an ellipsis mark to indicate that you have left words out of an otherwise direct quotation:

> **Original:** The momentous occurrences of an era—from war and economics to politics and inventions—give meaning to lives of the individuals who live through them.
>
> **Quotation with ellipses in the middle:** Arthur Levine argues, "The momentous occurrences of an era [. . .] give meaning to lives of the individuals who live through them" (26).

Use ellipsis marks at the end of a quotation only if you have dropped some words from the end of the final sentence quoted. In that case, include four periods. When the ellipsis coincides with the end of your own sentence, leave a space before the first bracket, and immediately follow the last bracket with the sentence period and the closing quotation mark.

> **Quotation with ellipses at the end:** You know the old saying, "Eat, drink, and be merry [. . .]."

If a parenthetical reference follows the ellipsis at the end of your sentence, leave a space before the first bracket, and immediately follow the last bracket with the closing quotation mark, a space, the parenthetical reference, and the sentence period.

> According to recent studies, "Statistics show that Chinese women's status has improved [. . .]" (*Chinese Women* 46).

- **Ellipsis points are not necessary** if you are quoting a fragment of a sentence, that is, a few words or a subordinate clause, because context will clearly indicate the omission of some of the original sentence.

> Sociobiologists add that social and nurturing experiences can "intensify, diminish, or modify" personality traits (Wood and Wood 272).

Brackets.

- **The *MLA Handbook for Writers of Research Papers*, 6th ed., says that "[u]nless indicated in brackets or parentheses . . . , changes must not be made in the spelling, capitalization, or interior punctuation of the source" (3.7.1).** Although you should look for ways to integrate source material into your text that avoid overuse of brackets, the following guidelines apply when changing source material is unavoidable.
- **If you want to change a word or phrase to conform to your own sentence or add words to make your sentence grammatically correct, use brackets to indicate the change.** The brackets enclose only the changed portion of the original.

Original: They were additional casualties of our time of plague, demoralized reminders that although this country holds only two percent of the world's population, it consumes 65 percent of the world's supply of hard drugs.

Quotation: According to Pete Hamill in his essay "Crack and the Box," America "holds only two percent of the world's population, [yet] it consumes 65 percent of the world's supply of hard drugs" (267).

Original: In a miasma of Walt Disney images, Bambi burning, and Snow White asleep, the most memorable is "Cinderella."

Quotation: Louise Bernikow recalls spending Saturday afternoons at the theatre when she was growing up "[i]n a miasma of Walt Disney images, [. . .]the most memorable [of which] is 'Cinderella'" (17).

Note: This example illustrates the use not only of brackets but also of ellipsis points and single and double quotation marks.

- **Use brackets if you add some explanatory information or editorial comment, or use them to indicate that you have changed the capitalization in the quoted material.**

  Original: Marriage is another dying institution [. . .]. "If we live together," the attitude goes, "why should I commit myself? Why should I assume responsibility?"

  Quotation: Even the perspective toward marriage carries the attitude, "'[W]hy should I commit myself? Why should I assume responsibility?'" (Barrett and Rowe 346).

  Original: Then, magically, the fairy godmother appears. She comes from nowhere, summoned, we suppose, by Cinderella's wishes.

  Quotation: Louise Bernikow points out that "[s]he [the fairy godmother] comes from nowhere, summoned [. . .] by Cinderella's wishes" (19).

- **The Latin word *sic* (meaning "thus") in brackets indicates that an error occurs in the original source of a passage you are quoting.** Because you are not at liberty to change words when quoting word for word, reproduce the error but use [*sic*] to indicate that the error is not yours.

  Original: Thrills have less to do with speed then changes in speed.

  Quotation: Dahl makes this observation: "Thrills have less to do with speed then [*sic*] changes in speed" (18).

Single Quotation Marks.

- **If you quote text that itself appears in quotation marks in the original, use single marks within the double that enclose your own quotation.**

  Original: This set me pondering the obvious question: "How can it be so hard for kids to find something to do when there's never been such a range of stimulating entertainment available to them?"

  Quotation: Dahl is led to ask this question: "'How can it be so hard for kids to find something to do when there's never been such a range of stimulating entertainment available to them?'" (18–19).

- **Occasionally you will have to quote something that is already a quotation within a quotation,** where the original contains single quotation marks within double quotes. In that case, use double quotation marks within single within double:

  > **Original:** In my interviews with the chief witness, he swears he heard Smith say: "'It wasn't me! I didn't do it!'"
  > **Quotation:** Johnson records an interview with a chief witness in the case. Smith is said to have proclaimed, ""It wasn't me! I didn't do it!'"" (23).

Qtd. in.

- **If you quote or paraphrase material that is already quoted, use the abbreviation "qtd." with the word "in."** Use "qtd. in" whenever you quote or paraphrase the published account of someone else's words or ideas. The works cited list will include not the original source of the material you quoted or paraphrased but rather the indirect source, the one where you found the material. You will likely be using the single quotation marks within the double because you are quoting what someone else has quoted.

  > **Original:** Printed in bold letters at the entrance of the show is a startling claim by Degas' fellow painter Auguste Renoir: "If Degas had died at 50, he would have been remembered as an excellent painter, no more; it is after his 50th year that his work broadened out and that he really becomes Degas."
  > **Quotation:** Impressionist painter Auguste Renoir observed of Degas: "'If Degas had died at 50, he would have been remembered as an excellent painter, no more; it is after his 50th year that his work broadened out and that he really becomes Degas'" (qtd. in Benfey).
  > **Original:** Teen suicide is nearly four times more common today than it was a few decades ago, says Dr. Janice Grossman, a suicide expert.
  > **Quotation:** According to Dr. Janice Grossman, an expert on suicide, "Teen suicide is nearly four times more common today than it was a few decades ago" (qtd. in Arenofsky).

GUIDELINES FOR INTEGRATING SOURCE MATERIALS INTO YOUR PAPER

- Avoid "bald" or "dropped" quotations by introducing all direct quotations.
- Use the author's name, where appropriate, to signal the beginning of a paraphrase or quotation.
- Cite sources for all borrowed material.
- Name a source, if the article does not list an author's name.
- Vary the way you introduce source material.
- Try combining direct quotations and paraphrases in the same sentence.
- Become familiar with appropriate uses of ellipsis points, brackets, single quotation marks, and "qtd. in."

DOCUMENTING SOURCES IN A COLLECTION OF ESSAYS

You have been reading about and looking at examples of one important component of source documentation: in-text citations. The other component is the alphabetical list, appearing on a separate page at the end of your paper, of all the works you quoted from or paraphrased. This is the list of works cited. Each entry in the list begins with the author's name, last name first, followed by the title of the article, book, or other source and information about its place and date of publication. The author's name (or title of the work, if it is published anonymously) in the text's parenthetical citation refers to one item in this list at the end of the paper.

You will find more discussion of documenting sources in Chapter 7, but the brief treatment here gives useful guidelines for short papers using materials reprinted in a collection of essays, such as this textbook. Although the examples in this section illustrate how to document materials reprinted in the third edition of this textbook, the guidelines apply to any collection of essays. Because *Perspectives on Contemporary Issues* is a collection of other people's works, not the editor's, you will probably not have occasion to use the words or ideas of Ackley herself. However, because you are not reading the essays in their original source, you must indicate that you have read them in her book.

You may prefer an acceptable alternative to constructing a separate page of works cited. Cite bibliographic information about the source parenthetically in your text, just as you do for author and page numbers. If you are writing about one of the readings from this book, or even two or three of them, your instructor may prefer that you provide information that would otherwise appear on a "Works Cited" page in parenthetical citations.

> A fairly simple difference distinguishes a formal "Works Cited" page from parenthetical citations of full publication details: The former is more appropriate when the sources are not the focus or subject of the paper but rather provide supporting or illustrative material, as in a synthesis or research paper. The latter is more appropriate when the source is the focus of the paper, its main subject, as in a summary or critique. See the example at the end of this chapter.

Citing One Source.   Suppose your paper quotes or paraphrases a statement from Zine Magubane's essay "Why 'Nappy' is Offensive." After you write either the exact words of Magubane or your paraphrase of her words, put a parenthesis, then give her last name and the page number where you read the words *with no punctuation between them,* and then close the parenthesis: (Magubane 43). Do not write the word "page" or "pages" nor insert a comma between the author's name and the number of the page. If Magubane's piece is the only one you use in your paper, write "Work Cited" (note the singular form of "Work") at the end of your paper and enter complete bibliographic information for the article:

```
                        Work Cited
Magubane, Zine. "Why 'Nappy' is Offensive." In
      Perspectives on Contemporary Issues: Readings
      Across the Disciplines. 5th ed. ed. Katherine
      Anne Ackley. Boston: Wadsworth Cengage
      Learning, 2009. 43-44.
```

Citing Two or More Sources.   If you draw material from two or more essays from Ackley (or from any collection of essays), you do not need to repeat the full information for the collection with the citation for each essay. Instead, list the collection by the editor's name, giving full bibliographic information. Then list separately each article you use by author and title, but after each essay title, give only the collection editor's name and the inclusive page numbers of the essay. You may, if you wish, follow the model for citing one source.

For example, suppose you write a paper on using the power of words and images to affect perception. In your essay, you use information or words from several essays in this textbook. Here is how your "Works Cited" page might look:

```
                        Works Cited
Ackley, Katherine Anne, ed. Perspectives on
      Contemporary Issues: Readings Across the
      Disciplines. 5th ed. Boston: Wadsworth
      Cengage Learning, 2009.
Krauthammer, Charles. "The War and the Words."
      Ackley 14-15.
Magubane, Zine. "Why 'Nappy' is Offensive."
      Ackley 43-44.
Saltzman, Joe. "What's in a Name? More than You
      Think." Ackley 8-11.
```

You may also do your "Works Cited" page this way:

```
                        Works Cited

Krauthammer, Charles. "The War and the Words." In
        Perspectives on Contemporary Issues: Readings
        Across the Disciplines, 5th ed. ed. Katherine
        Anne Ackley. Boston: Wadsworth Cengage
        Learning, 2009. 14-15.

Magubane, Zine. "Why 'Nappy' is Offensive." In
        Perspectives on Contemporary Issues: Readings
        Across the Disciplines, 5th ed. ed. Katherine
        Anne Ackley. Boston: Wadsworth Cengage
        Learning, 2009. 43-44.

Saltzman, Joe. "What's in a Name? More than You
        Think." In Perspectives on Contemporary Issues:
        Readings Across the Disciplines, 5th ed. ed.
        Katherine Anne Ackley. Boston: Wadsworth
        Cengage Learning, 2009. 8-11.
```

Parenthetical Documentation of Source Material. When a single reading is the primary focus of your paper (or it concentrates on two or three readings)—that is, the paper deals with limited primary sources, as opposed to secondary source materials that provide illustration or supporting evidence—you can provide full bibliographic information parenthetically the first time you mention each source. Then you do not have to construct a separate Works Cited page. This technique may be convenient when your paper focuses on just one work; for instance, if you were to write a formal summary or critique of one reading or a paper on one or two works of literature. At the first mention of the source, provide full publication information in a parenthetical citation:

```
According to Jennifer McLune in "Hip-Hop's Betrayal
    of Black Women" (in Katherine Anne Ackley,
    ed. [Boston: Wadsworth Cengage Learning, 2009]
    247-251), hip-hop music demeans and exploits
    black women.
```

Notice that the author's name and the title of the work are mentioned in the text of the paper and not in the parenthetical citation. Brackets indicate parentheses within parentheses. After this first documentation of full publication information, parenthetical citations will give only author and page number or just page number.

STUDENT PAPERS DEMONSTRATING SYNTHESIS WITH IN-TEXT CITATIONS USING MLA STYLE

Following are two examples of student papers that synthesize material from several sources and follow MLA guidelines for paraphrasing and quoting. The first, Nate Hayes's "Hello Dolly," uses sources located in this textbook. The marginal comments call attention to various strategies of writing an effective synthesis. Note that a "Works Cited" list appears on a separate page at the end. The works-cited page gives full bibliographic information for each source. Notice that works are listed alphabetically and that each citation conforms in punctuation and spacing to the MLA style of documentation (Chapter 7). The second, Barbara Novak's "The Shock-Proof Generation," uses sources from a previous edition as well as an outside source.

Note that MLA formatting guidelines call for the author's last name to appear in the running head before the page number, even on the first page. Note also that the student's name, class, instructor's name, and date appear on the left-hand side above the title of the paper. MLA style recommends using the day/month/year format for the date. For more on using MLA style in writing that uses sources, including guidelines for formatting the works cited list, see Chapter 7.

Hayes 1

Nate Hayes

English 102-2

Professor Fay

1 March 2008

Hello, Dolly

Little Bo Peep has lost her sheep, but
now she can clone a whole new flock! When Dr.
Ian Wilmut and his team successfully cloned
Dolly the sheep, the world was mystified,
amazed, and scared. Immediately, members of
the shocked public began to imagine worst case
scenarios of reincarnated Hitlers and Dahmers.

The medical field, however, relished the
possibilities of cloning in curing patients
with debilitating or terminal illnesses. The
controversy over human cloning is part of the
larger debate about the potential capabilities
of scientists to alter or enhance the
biological makeup of humans. This debate over
how far "homo sapiens [should] be allowed to go"
has grown increasingly heated with developments
such as the successful cloning of sheep
(Pethokoukis 559). To many people, human cloning
makes sense as the next major breakthrough in
medical science, but until the troubling issues
associated with the procedure are resolved,
human cloning must not be allowed to happen.

Scientists, politicians, and the general
public all have mixed feelings about the
developments in medical science. Even people
like Ian Wilmut, the Scottish embryologist
whose team of researchers was responsible
for cloning Dolly, and James D. Watson,

The opening paragraph introduces readers to the controversial issue that is the subject of the paper.

Nate's thesis is a straightforward declarative sentence that makes his position on the subject clear.

Nate briefly indicates the views of two scientists holding differing opinions on the subject of the paper.

Only page numbers are given in the citation because the author's name is mentioned in the text. Note that last names only are used because Nate has already given their full names.

Nate uses single quotation marks within the double because the word superpersons is in quotation marks in Watson's article.

Nate continues to draw on Wilmut's comments because Nate shares his viewpoint.

Nobel-Prize-winning co-discoverer of the double helix configuration of DNA, hold different views on the issue. Despite his previous work on cloning, Wilmut is very cautious, especially about whole-being cloning. He raises a number of questions about the wisdom of carrying on full speed with cloning research, suggesting: "Even if the technique were perfected, however, we must ask ourselves what practical value whole-being cloning might have" (564). On the other hand, Watson urges: "You should never put off doing something useful for fear of evil that may never arise" (563). Although he does not directly address the issue of cloning in his article "All for the Good," Watson touches on the subject when he states his strong support of research on germ-line genetic manipulations in pursuit of what he calls "'superpersons'" or "gene-bettered children" (563). The controversy has divided people and spurred ongoing discussions—or arguments—about the extent to which human genetic makeup should be modified or amended.

The populations that might benefit most if human cloning were to become a reality are infertile couples, homosexual couples, or single people wanting children. In commenting on this possible use for cloning, Wilmut suggests that having an identical version of yourself or someone you love would be unsettling and difficult to handle emotionally (565). Cloning has even been suggested as a possibility for grieving parents to replace—or bring back to life—a child who has died tragically or violently by using cells to clone a new, identical person. On this point, Wilmut wonders how

Hayes 3

Nate expresses his own views on the points that Wilmut raises in opposition to human cloning.

the cloned child would feel when he learns that he exists to replace another child. Wilmut's cautious approach to the issue of cloning is sensible. Many potential problems associated with human cloning need close examination. For instance, it is commonly believed that an infant would be exactly the same as the parent it is cloned from. This cannot be true. The infant would look the same, of course, but mentally and emotionally he or she would be an entirely new person. This new child would have feelings, thoughts, and experiences completely different from those of the person he or she was cloned from. The same would be true in the case of cloning a child that had died. Even were the parents to attempt replicating an environment identical to that of the original child, it would be an impossible task. Furthermore, a clone would surely have problems with individuality. How could a carbon copy of another human being feel unique? Cloning thus poses the risk of serious psychological harm.

An alternative to cloning a whole person is to clone an entity for making spare human parts. The idea is that a brainless clone might be produced that could supply crucial body parts, such as a heart, a liver, kidneys, and eyes. However, this possibility still lies in the realm of science fiction. No one has figured out how to do such a thing in the first place, let alone suggest ways to deal with all the potential problems of dealing

Nate mentions an alternative use of cloning but rejects that as well.

Hayes 4

with such a creature. Such a step is obviously not the best use of human cloning.

Nate suggests a possible alternative to human cloning, stem-cell research, but notes that it is controversial as well.

A potentially beneficial use of genetic manipulation lies in stem cell research. Stem cells are those that have not yet specialized. Scientists believe that such cells could be isolated and grown into healthy tissue that could then be used in humans to cure just about any ailment known to humans. Research in this area holds far more promise than research into cloning whole humans, although this research has its detractors and critics also. As James Pethokoukis reports, "[G]enetic engineering might be able to alter mankind in some astounding ways," and such potential has many people worried (560).

Author's full name is given because this is the first mention of his name in the text of the paper, even though it is mentioned parenthetically in paragraph 1.

There are just far too many unanswered questions, and who knows how many remain unasked? It is not easy to anticipate all the possible ramifications for mankind of human cloning. The bottom line is that ethical, psychological, social, and religion questions need to be explored, discussed, and resolved before research in genetic engineering that aims to create new life or significantly alter existing life can be allowed to continue.

Nate's conclusion rephrases and emphasizes his thesis statement.

Works Cited

Ackley, Katherine Anne, ed. *Perspectives on Contemporary Issues: Readings Across the Disciplines*. 4th ed. Boston: Wadsworth Cengage Learning, 2006.

Pethokoukis, James. "Our Biotech Bodies, Ourselves." Ackley 559-561.

Watson, James D. "All for the Good." Ackley 561-563.

Wilmut, Ian. "Dolly's False Legacy." Ackley 564-566.

Although the student paper below was written several years ago, it illustrates the incorporation of sources into a paper. Assess the essay using the criteria for critical reading and examine the ways in which it handles source materials. Keep in mind the marginal comments on Nate Hayes's paper above, and refer to the guidelines for handling source material that follow the essay for more information.

Note also that Barb Novak's assignment was to write an essay identifying what she saw as the defining political and/or social events for young college-age students at the time that she was attending college. Your instructor may ask you to write a similar essay, citing the events that you feel have defined and shaped today's generation of young college students and drawing on several of the readings in this textbook.

Novak 1

Barbara Novak

English 150-2

24 May 2008

The Shock-Proof Generation

Arthur Levine, an education faculty member at Harvard, believes that "every college generation is defined by the social events of its age" (26). To confirm his belief Levine questioned university students about "what social or political events most influenced their generation" (26). While the Great Depression influenced those who grew up after World War I, those born after World War II were affected by the assassination of John F. Kennedy. Students surveyed in 1979 rallied around Vietnam and Watergate, and those questioned in 1993 remembered the explosion of the Challenger. What modern political or social events have the youth of today been influenced by?

Novak 2

Psychiatric professor Ronald Dahl might suggest that the events that have the greatest impact on today's youth will be more stunning and dramatic than ever. While observing his own young children and their friends, Professor Dahl could not help but notice that despite "ever-greater stimulation, their young faces were looking disappointed and bored" (19). Dahl believes that the over-stimulation of today's youth has resulted in a generation with a previously unprecedented threshold for excitement. Consequently, it takes increasingly shocking, violent, or thrilling events to stimulate young people. Consistent with their insatiable appetite for excitement, the upcoming generation, described by Dahl as "burned out and bored," will be influenced by political and social events that are more violent, thrilling, or fast-paced than those remembered by previous generations.

The widely publicized tragedy at Columbine High School is one example of a political and social event shocking enough to influence the current generation of young Americans. Two high school students, Eric Harris and Dylan Klebold, entered their own school on April 20, 1999, and executed a carefully planned rampage of terror. Fifteen members of the school community were killed before the young men took their own lives (Pellegrini). The violence carried out that day by Harris and Klebold reached a climactic point high enough to actually have a shocking effect on modern over-stimulated youth. Therefore, the calamity that occurred at

Novak 3

Columbine High School will be an occurrence indicated by most of today's youth as an event that defines their generation.

Dahl writes: "What really worries me is the intensity of the stimulation. I watch my eleven-year old daughter's face as she absorbs the powerful onslaught of arousing visuals and gory special effects in movies" (19). Over-exposure to such violence, whether in video games, television, movies, or music lyrics, leads to de-sensitization of the viewer. Prior to, as well as after, the events in Littleton there were numerous school shootings; however, the impact of these paled in comparison to that of Columbine. If an increase in exposure to violence creates youth who are increasingly tolerant of violence, it can be inferred that the power of the events at Columbine was greater than that of other school shootings because it was phenomenally more violent. If Dahl's beliefs regarding today's youth are correct, the social and political events that define this generation will become increasingly violent simply because it will take more violence to obtain a reaction.

Dahl also poses the following question: "Why do [small] children immersed in this much excitement seem starved for more? That was, I realized, the point. I discovered during my own reckless adolescence that what

Novak 4

creates exhilaration is not going fast, but
going faster [. . .]. Thrills have less to
do with speed than changes in speed" (19). The
unthinkable actions carried out by Eric Harris and
Dylan Klebold were attempts to create exhilaration
by changing the speed of a normal day at Columbine
High School. Unfortunately, Harris and Klebold were
raised in a world of "ever-greater stimulation"
(Dahl 19). Therefore, the efforts necessary to create
exhilaration were nearly as enormous as the impact
of the shooting.

Recognizing the tragedy at Columbine High
School as an event that will define a generation
allows it to be examined as an indicator of the
problems that exist within that age group. The
future of our nation lies upon the shoulders of the
young. It is crucial to be aware of the immense
effects of the violent and negative images that
bombard this group on a daily basis. Realizing the
over-stimulation that is occurring among young
Americans will help not only to prevent another
tragedy like Columbine, but it will also ensure
that the next generation will have the ability to
successfully handle the problems of the future.

Works Cited

Ackley, Katherine Anne, ed. *Perspectives on Contemporary
        Issues: Readings Across the Disciplines*. 3rd ed.
        Boston: Wadsworth Cengage Learning, 2003.

Dahl, Ronald. "Burned Out and Bored." Ackley 18-20.

Levine, Arthur. "The Making of a Generation." Ackley
        26-33.

Novak 5

Pellegrini, Frank. "Colorado Shootings: Now,

the Aftermath." *Time* 21 Apr. 99. 20 Sept.

2001 <http://www.time.com/time/nation/

article/0,8599,23427,00.html>

CHAPTER 7

Writing a Research Paper

No matter what course you are asked to write a paper using sources for, your goal is the same: to skillfully support a carefully formulated thesis with documented evidence. Writing such a paper can seem both overwhelming and exciting, especially if you have never written one before. This chapter presents a brief overview of the key steps in discovering a topic, researching it, and writing a paper incorporating the sources you have used. Keep in mind the discussion in Chapter 6 on paraphrasing, quoting, and documenting sources. A research paper is likely to be much longer than a writing assignment generated from readings in this book, but otherwise little difference separates the processes of using materials from this textbook and using materials from other sources in terms of accuracy and fairness to your sources. Furthermore, the process of writing a research paper is not much different from the process of writing any other paper, as explained in Chapter 2. To do your best work, you will go through the prewriting, drafting, revising, editing, and proofreading stages.

DEFINING YOUR PURPOSE

Your instructor will tell you whether your purpose in the research paper is to argue, explain, analyze, or come to some conclusion about something. Many instructors prefer that students write argumentative papers. In that case, you will make a judgment about your topic on the basis of what you find in your research. Recall the discussion in Chapter 5 on writing an argument. The same guidelines apply whether you are writing a researched argument or one without sources. You will begin your research with an idea of what your position is, then research your subject extensively, arrive at an informed opinion, and finally defend that position by presenting evidence that seems valid (that is, logical and convincing) to you. If you want to go a step further and convince your audience to adopt your position or to act on suggestions you propose, then your purpose is persuasion. The subjects for argumentative papers are virtually unlimited, but they often include controversial issues, such as those addressed in this textbook, topics on which people hold widely varying opinions.

On the other hand, some instructors direct students to explain or analyze something in their research papers. An informative paper does not necessarily address a controversial subject. If you are to write an explanatory paper, you will gather information about your topic and present it in such a way that your reader fully understands it. You will explain, describe, illustrate, or narrate something in full detail, such as what a black hole is, how photosynthesis works, the circumstances surrounding a historical event, significant events in the life of a famous person, and the like.

Audience.   Having a clear sense of your audience will direct your research and help you write your paper. If you are writing an argument, the most useful audience to address is one that is opposed to your position or, at best, uncertain about where they stand on the issue. A good argument seeks to persuade or convince an audience, so anticipating readers who are not already convinced will help sharpen your argument. If your purpose is to explain, illustrate, or analyze, your audience is likely to be informed in general about the particular subject of your paper but not in great depth. Unless instructed otherwise, assume an intelligent audience of non-specialists who are interested in learning more about the topic of your paper. Imagining this audience will keep you from having to define or explain every term or concept and give you room for interesting, informative, and/or intriguing material about the topic.

DISCOVERING A TOPIC

Once you know your purpose and audience, the next step in writing a research paper is to find a subject that you will be comfortable working with for many weeks and then narrow it to a specific topic. Some instructors assign topics, but most leave the choice to students. The freedom to choose your own research paper topic can be intimidating because so much depends on selecting the right topic. You want a topic that not only holds your interest but that also offers you an opportunity to investigate it in depth.

The process of discovering what you will write about involves first determining the broad subject you are particularly interested in pursuing. Once you have settled on the subject, you will need to narrow it to one specific aspect of that subject. For many research paper assignments, that topic will have to be arguable, one that requires you to investigate from several angles and arrive at and defend your own position. This position will be worded in the form of a hypothesis or thesis, stated most often as a declarative statement but sometimes as a question. Discovering your final topic takes time, so do some serious thinking about this important step as soon as the paper is assigned. You will be reshaping, narrowing, and refining your topic for much of the research process, so you do not want to switch subjects halfway through.

Any or all of the suggestions for generating ideas in the prewriting stage that are discussed in Chapter 2 would be useful when trying to discover a topic for your research paper. Brainstorming, making lists, clustering, even researching in a preliminary way and talking with others can be of use. Asking questions, thinking about your personal interests or personal opinion, considering commonly held opinions, and thinking about controversial topics can all be quite helpful in the process of discovering a research topic.

Asking Questions.   One of the best ways to approach the research project is to ask questions about a subject that interests you and that seems worth investigating. As you read through the suggestions for discovering a topic that follow, think in terms of questions that you might ask about the initial subjects you come up with. Try to think in terms of questions that can be answered in a research paper as opposed to a short essay. As you narrow your field of potential topics, look for those about which you can ask questions whose answers are neither too broad nor too narrow. You want the topic that you ultimately select to be challenging enough that your paper will be interesting to you as well as to your audience. Avoid topics about which questions are unanswerable or highly speculative. Your goal in the research process will be to arrive at an answer, insofar as that is possible, to your question.

Any of the topics listed as possible subjects of argumentation in Chapter 5 are appropriate for researched writing. Here are examples of questions that one might ask about various argumentative subjects when trying to generate ideas for a research paper:

- Under what conditions, if any, is censorship justifiable?
- Should research into human cloning continue?
- Do advertising images of women set up impossible standards of femininity?
- What is the appropriate punishment for steroid use in athletes?
- Which plays a more prominent role in determining behavior, genes or environment?
- What role does phonics education play in the teaching of reading?
- How dangerous is secondhand smoke?
- Should cities be allowed to ban smoking in public places such as bars, restaurants, and private clubs?
- Should sex education be taught by parents or by schools?
- Was King Arthur a real person?
- What is the best strategy for combating terrorism?
- Are restrictions on freedom of speech necessary in time of war?
- How far should Homeland Security go to protect Americans from terrorists?
- Is there still a "glass ceiling" for women in the work force?
- Should the government provide child day care for all workers?
- Does watching too much television have a harmful effect on preschool children?
- What factors affect academic success in females versus males?
- Should the electoral college be abolished?
- Does America need an official language?

- Is hormone replacement therapy a safe choice for women?
- Do women do better academically in all-female schools?
- Should prostitution be legalized?
- Should there be a formal apology from the government for slavery?
- Should there be reparations for slavery, as there has been for Japanese interned in camps during WWII?
- Should grades be abolished?
- Should the HPV vaccination be mandatory?
- What should be done about illegal immigrants in the United States?

Generating Topics from Personal Interest.   One way to find a topic for your research paper is to begin with subjects you already know well, are interested in, or think you would like to improve your knowledge of. Begin by writing down such things as hobbies, sports, issues in your major, contemporary social issues, or topics in classes you are taking. Consider topics that attracted your interest in high school or in previous college classes, any reading you have already done on subjects that appeal to you, or the kinds of things that capture your attention when you watch television news, read news magazines or newspapers, or select nonfiction books for leisure-time reading.

Generating Topics from Personal Opinions.   Virtually any topic can be turned into an argument, but opinions are always subject to debate. Therefore, one way to generate a research paper topic is to begin with your own strongly held opinions.

Caution: Avoid a topic that is based entirely on opinion. Evaluative statements are especially good for argumentative papers because they are likely to have differing opinions. Once you say that something is the best, the most significant, the most important, or the greatest, for instance, you have put yourself in the position of defending that statement. You will have to establish your criteria for making your judgment and defend your choice against what others might think. Here are some ideas for this particular approach:

- The most influential person in the twentieth century (or in America, in the world, in a particular field such as education, government, politics, arts, entertainment, or the like)
- The most significant battle in the Civil War (or World War I, World War II, the Korean War, the Vietnam War, the Gulf War)
- The greatest basketball (or football, tennis, soccer, baseball) player (either now playing or of all time)
- The greatest or worst president
- The best movie, book, or album of all time
- The business or industry with the greatest impact on American life in the last decade (or last twenty years, last fifty years, or century)

Because your conclusion on any of these or similar topics is your opinion, you need to establish criteria for your conclusion, clearly describe the process you used to make it, and explain the logical basis for that process.

Generating Topics from Commonly Held Opinions.   Another possibility for a research paper topic is to take a commonly held opinion (though not necessarily one that you share), especially one based on stereotyped assumptions about a group or class of people, and explore the validity of that belief. Your goal is to determine whether the commonly held opinion is a valid, partially valid, or invalid position. Even if you cannot arrive at a definitive evaluation of the validity of the statement, you can still present the evidence you find and explain why your research does not reach a conclusion. Here are examples of commonly held beliefs:

- Watching violence on television produces violent behavior.
- People who were abused as children often grow up to be abusers themselves.
- Men naturally perform mechanical tasks better than women do.
- Women naturally perform better at nurturing children than men do.
- Young people do not have much hope for a bright future.
- Women are more emotional than men.
- People stay on welfare because they are too lazy to work.
- Homosexuals could become "straight" if they wanted to.
- Homeless people could get off the streets if they really tried.

When determining the validity of a commonly held opinion or belief, your research focuses on gathering evidence without bias. Although you may want to interview people about their opinions on a particular belief, the basis of your conclusion must rest on clearly reliable evidence.

Generating Topics from Controversy.   Yet another way to discover a topic you find intriguing enough to commit many hours of time to is to think of controversial issues that always generate heated debate. These topics may be frequently discussed in newspapers, news magazines, and on television news programs and talk shows. They may be issues on which candidates for public office, from local county board members to state and federal officials, are pressed to take stands. Here are some examples of controversial statements:

- Affirmative action laws are unfair to white males and should be repealed.
- Media coverage of celebrity trials should be banned.
- Birth parents should always have a legal right to take back children they have given up for adoption.
- Children whose parents are on welfare should be placed in state-run orphanages.
- Women should be barred from participating in combat duty.
- Graphic violence in the movies (or in video games or MTV videos) poses a serious threat to the nation's moral values.
- The federal government should stop funding projects in the arts and the humanities.
- The federal government should provide unlimited funds to support research to find a cure for AIDS.

- Children who commit murder should be tried as adults no matter what their age.
- Illegal aliens should be forced to return to their country of origin.

Narrowing Your Subject to a Specific Topic. Most research paper assignments are short enough that you simply must narrow your focus to avoid a too shallow or too hopelessly general treatment of your topic. Keep in mind the distinction between **subject** and **topic**: Subject is the general area under investigation, whereas topic is the narrow aspect of that subject that you are investigating. For example, Jack the Ripper is a subject, but entire books have been written on the notorious 1888 murders in the Whitechapel area of London. A suitable topic on the subject would be to explore the controversy surrounding the alleged links of the Duke of Clarence with the murders, taking a position in favor of the theory most plausible to you.

One way to get a sense of how a general topic can be narrowed is to look at the table of contents of a book on a subject that interests you. Notice the chapter headings, which are themselves subtopics of the broad subject. Chapters themselves are often further subdivided. You want to find a topic that is narrow enough that you can fully explore it without leaving unanswered questions, yet broad enough that you can say enough about it in a reasonably long paper.

To narrow your subject to a topic, take a general subject and go through the brainstorming process again, this time listing everything that comes to mind about that particular subject. What subtopics does your subject have? What questions can you ask about your general subject? How might you narrow your focus on that subject? Ultimately, you want to generate an idea that gives focus to your preliminary library search.

FORMING A PRELIMINARY THESIS AND A WORKING BIBLIOGRAPHY

No matter what your purpose or who your audience is, you will have one central idea, most often articulated early in the paper in the form of a single thesis statement. You will take a position on your topic and defend or illustrate it convincingly with evidence from your source materials.

When you believe that you have narrowed your topic sufficiently, you are ready to form your preliminary thesis. This is the position that you believe you want to take on your topic, based on your early thinking about and narrowing down of a subject. Your preliminary or working thesis can be in the form of either a question or a statement. In much the same way as your final thesis gives direction and focus to your paper, your preliminary thesis gives you direction and focus in the research process. As you review potential sources and read about your topic, you may find yourself changing your preliminary thesis for any number of reasons. Perhaps your topic is too narrow or too new and you simply cannot find enough sources with which to write a fair and balanced research paper. Or you may discover that your topic is too broad to cover in a research paper and that you need to narrow your focus even more.

A common reason for changing a preliminary thesis is that, once you actually start reading sources, you discover that you want to change your initial position. You may discover that you were wrong in your assumption or opinion about your topic and that you are persuaded to change your position. Part of the pleasure in researching a topic is discovering new ideas or information, so it makes sense that your early views on your topic may shift as you learn more about it. More than likely, your final thesis will differ in some way from your preliminary thesis.

With your preliminary thesis in mind, you are ready to start the actual research process. First, you need to locate potential sources. A working bibliography is a list of the sources you **might** use in your research paper, those that look particularly promising during a preliminary search. At this point, you will not have had time to read or even carefully skim all potential sources, let alone imagine how they fit together to support your working thesis. Your goal is to find the sources that bear most directly on your topic and select from them the most useful ones to read carefully, taking notes as you read. One obvious place to start looking for sources is the library; another source is the Internet.

GUIDELINES FOR DEVELOPING A WORKING BIBLIOGRAPHY

- List sources that sound promising for your research, recording titles and locations as you discover them.
- If the source is a library book, record the title, author, and call number.
- If the source is an article from your library, write the title of the piece, the name of its author, the title of the magazine or journal where it appears, the date of the issue, and the inclusive pages numbers. You will need all this information to find the article.
- For other sources in the library, such as videotapes, audiotapes, government documents, or pamphlets, write down as much information as you can find to help locate them. Write the location of any source, such as a special collection, government document, stack, periodical, and so on.
- For an Internet site, record the URL (Uniform Resource Locator), the name of the site, the name of its creator or author, if available, and the date the site was created, if available. If you use the source in your paper, you will add the date that you accessed the material in the works cited entry, so include that as well.
- You may want to retrieve the full text files of Internet sites that seem promising as you discover them to ensure their availability when you are ready to begin reading and taking notes.

USING THE LIBRARY

Your library has a good number of valuable resources to help you in your search for materials on your research topic. While the Internet has made searching for reference materials easy and quick, libraries house books, periodicals, and other materials that you can hold, leaf through, check out, and read. Furthermore, many libraries have special collections on specific subjects and offer databases that are inaccessible from the Internet. Increasingly, libraries are working to connect their own digital resources stored in databases to Internet search engines. In the meantime, do not overlook the potential for excellent sources available on your own campus or through your university library's online catalog. Your library may have print copies of sources that you cannot find on the Internet.

Online Catalog.   Begin your library search for sources on your general subject or topic (if you have sufficiently narrowed your focus) by reviewing the online catalog for titles of potential sources. The catalog cross-references sources by name of author, by title, and by subject matter. In this searching stage, you probably will not know titles of works or authors, so you will begin by looking under subject headings for titles that sound relevant to your research subject. The catalog gives titles of books, audio-visual materials, and government documents housed in the library. Jot down the titles and call numbers of materials that look promising and then locate them. One advantage of using your library is that you can physically examine a book, flip through its table of contents, check its index, read the author's credentials, and skim some of the text. If it seems to suit your purpose, you can check it out and take it home with you.

Indexes.   In addition to books and other materials listed in the catalog of the library, you should look into both general and specialized indexes for additional titles of sources. These resources are usually located in the reference room. Here are titles of some **general indexes:**

- *Bibliographic Index* lists by subject bibliographies that appear in books, pamphlets, and periodical articles.
- *Biography Index* lists articles and books on important people; it also lists the people included in the index by profession or occupation.
- *Essay and General Literature Index* focuses on material in the social sciences and humanities, organized according to author, subject, and title. It lists periodical articles, individual essays, and book chapters on particular subjects.
- *Monthly Catalog of United States Government Publications* indexes all government-generated materials.
- *General Science Index* is arranged by subject and lists articles in general science periodicals.
- *Periodical Abstracts* provides abstracts of articles from over 1,600 periodicals, covering the humanities, social sciences, general science, and general interest. It is updated monthly and is available in electronic format.
- *Reader's Guide to Periodical Literature* is a standard reference tool for locating articles in popular magazines. Organized by both subject and author, it

provides titles of articles, authors, names of publications, and dates of publication. It publishes supplements every two weeks, so you can find very recent articles. It is also available in electronic format.

Specialized indexes.   List articles on particular subjects or areas that appear in professional journals, written by and published for specialists in those areas. Indexes cover specific areas of interest in the humanities, fine arts, social sciences, and natural and applied sciences. A look at just a few of the titles of specialized indexes gives you an idea of the resources available in your library's reference room:

- *Art Index* collects titles of articles on archaeology, art history, architecture, and the fine arts.
- *Biological Abstracts* gives brief summaries of articles on biology and biomedicine.
- *Business Index* is a good source for current material on business topics.
- *The Directory of Online Databases* provides a current listing of databases in all fields.
- *Historical Abstracts* contains abstracts of articles on world history.
- *Humanities Index* lists titles of periodical articles on a broad range of topics in the social sciences and humanities.
- *MLA International Bibliography of Books and Articles on the Modern Languages and Literatures* provides titles of articles on languages and literature, arranged by nationality and literary period.
- *Philosopher's Guide to Sources, Research Tools, Professional Life, and Related Fields* is useful for all sorts of information on philosophical topics.
- *Psychological Abstracts* presents abstracts of articles and books in all areas of the social sciences.
- *Political Science: A Guide to Reference and Information Sources* cites current sources on a range of topics in political science.

USING ELECTRONIC SOURCES

Electronic Databases.   Many libraries provide access to electronic indexes or databases, often on CD-ROM, that list books and periodical articles related to particular subject areas. CD-ROMs have a disadvantage that the Internet does not have in that, once it is produced, it cannot be updated. Still, CD-ROMs can be very useful for locating articles for research. You can search these resources by subject, author, title, or keywords. Generally, such a listing provides the full name of the author, the title, and complete bibliographic information (publisher and year for books; title of magazine or journal, month and year of issue, and page numbers for articles).

Often, computer services provide abstracts of articles and sometimes entire texts that you can download and print out or send for via mail or fax for a fee.

Your library may have one of the following frequently-used databases. All are subscription services that require a pass code to access the database:

1. **InfoTrac College Edition** provides a searchable database of some 15 million periodical articles from over 5,000 journals, newspapers, and magazines covering the last twenty years. It is a rich resource of readings on just about any topic you are interested in searching. InfoTrac College Edition offers specialized databases to which your library can subscribe, including *Custom Newspapers*, which contains articles from well-known newspapers like the *Wall Street Journal* and the *New York Times*; Health Reference Center, with articles on topics such as medicine, disease, public health, and other health-related topics; and *General Reference Center*, which has articles from publications of general interest.

2. **EBSCO,** a subscription information service, offers databases similar to InfoTrac, that is, specialized databases with links to periodical articles in such areas as business, education, and health. It also offers full-text databases and provides online access to more that 150 databases and thousands of e-journals.

3. **LexisNexis Academic Universe,** is a subscription information service designed specifically for colleges, universities, and schools. It provides the full text of more than 350 newspapers from the U.S. and abroad, updated daily, and texts of more than 300 magazine and journals and over 600 newsletters. It also supplies broadcast transcripts from the major television and radio networks as well as political transcripts covering Congressional committee hearings, press briefings from the State, Justice, and Defense departments, and presidential news conferences.

Locating Material on the Internet.   Although you do not want to miss the pleasure of going to the library for sources for your research paper, the Internet can be another valuable tool in your search for potential sources. Most colleges and universities make computers readily available to their students, so even if you do not own a computer, you will likely have access to one in your campus library or computing services center. While it cannot replace the library, the Internet does offer resources that a library does not. The same could be said of the library, of course. A fair conclusion notes that each offers excellent but different kinds of materials for the researcher.

To find Internet materials, you can use any of a number of equally good search engines available on the web. Search engines collect many sites in their databanks; they return sites that match the keywords you type to begin your search. Search engines get their information in one of two major ways, either crawler-based technology or human-powered directories, but increasingly they use a combination of both. Crawler-based search engines gather their information automatically by "crawling" or sending "spiders" out to the web, searching the contents of other systems and creating a database of the results. Human-powered directories depend on humans for the listings you get in response to a search; they manually approve material for inclusion in a database. You can find more about these terms and others related to the Internet by going to http://www.Webopedia.com, an online dictionary and search engine for definitions of computer and Internet terms.

Be very careful when searching for sources on the Internet, keeping in mind the guidelines in Chapter 1 on evaluating Internet sources. Begin by choosing your search engine from among the best known or most used; they are likely to be the most reliable. Commercially-backed search engines are usually well maintained and frequently upgraded, thus ensuring reliable results. Chapter 1 has a list of well-known search engines that are quite reliable, and likely to give you the results you seek in your search:

USING OTHER SOURCES

Do not overlook other excellent sources of information, such as personal interviews, surveys, lectures, taped television programs, films, documentaries, and government publications. For example, if you research the human genome project, you will likely find a number of books, periodical articles, and government documents on the subject. A search of the World Wide Web will turn up hundreds of thousands of site matches. You could easily become overwhelmed by the mass of materials available on your subject. Your task is to select the sources that seem most relevant to your project and to narrow your research topic as quickly as possible to avoid wasting time gathering materials you ultimately cannot use. To clarify and focus your own approach to the subject, you may want to interview a biology professor for information about the scientific aspects of the project and a philosophy professor for an opinion on its ethical implications. In addition to such interviews, you may use material from a lecture, a television documentary, a film, or your own survey.

The Difference between Primary and Secondary Sources.   "Primary" refers to original sources, actual data, or first-hand witnesses, such as interviews, surveys, speeches, diaries, letters, unpublished manuscripts, photographs, memoirs or autobiographies, published material written at the time of the event such as newspaper articles, and similar items. They are actual recorded accounts or documentary evidence of events. "Secondary" refers to sources like books and articles that discuss, explain, or interpret events or are seen second-hand. They are written or recorded after the fact and represent processed information, interpretations of, or commentary on events.

For instance, suppose you are interested in the controversy over a film like Mel Gibson's *The Passion of the Christ* (2004). (See a still image from the film in the "Responding to Visuals" section at the end of Chapter 10.) Literally hundreds of articles have been written about the film, ranging from harsh criticism of it to high praise. These articles represent secondary sources, while the film itself is the primary source. For a paper on the film, you would view the movie and undoubtedly include details of it in your paper, but you would also offer the commentary and opinions of others who reacted to, analyzed, and wrote about it.

Another example is student Sam Cox's paper "Proving Their Loyalty During World War I: German Americans Confronted with Anti-German Fervor and

Suspicion." (See introduction and conclusion to his paper later in the chapter.) Sam was interested in the subject of the loyalty of German Americans living in the United States during WWI. To find out, he read numerous newspaper accounts of and by German Americans as reported in two newspapers and written in both German and English. To help him come to his conclusion that German Americans were loyal to America at the time that America was at war with Germany, Sam read dozens of both primary and secondary sources. These are listed together in his works cited page at the end of his paper. A selection of his sources appear later in this chapter, as do his opening paragraphs.

Reporting the Results of a Survey Using Tables and Graphs. Surveys are another good primary source. In a group-written paper, four students were interested in the question of the influence of gender on academic success on their college campus. They prepared a survey which they distributed to classmates. Their paper, "Are Girls Smarter Than Boys? A Study of Academic Success Between the Sexes," reports the results of their findings based on 103 surveys and includes four charts and graphs that represent these findings. One of these is reproduced in the guidelines for putting all of the parts of the paper together. An abstract of their paper appears in that section as well.

CREATING A PRELIMINARY BIBLIOGRAPHY

Once you compile a list of sources to investigate, start locating and evaluating them. If you discover that you cannot use a source, cross it off your list. When you find a source that definitely looks promising for your research topic, record it. Make sure that you record all pertinent bibliographic information about your source, preferably in the form in which it will appear on your works cited page. The section in this chapter entitled "Documenting Sources" lists appropriate formats for various kinds of sources. Note the following sample work cited formats for some common types of sources:

Book with One Author.

```
Conolly-Smith, Peter. Translating America: An
     Immigrant Press Visualizes American Popular
     Culture, 1895-1918. Washington: Smithsonian
     Books, 2004.
```

Journal Article with One Author.

Capozzola, Christopher. "The Only Badge Needed Is
     Your Patriotic Fervor: Vigilance, Coercion,
     and the Law in World War I America." <u>Journal
     of American History</u> 88 (2002): 1354-1382.

Journal Article with Two Authors.

Fabes, Richard A., and Jeremiah Strouse. "Formal
     versus Informal Sources on Sex Education:
     Competing Forces in the Sexual Socialization of
     Adolescents." <u>Adolescence</u> 20 (1985): 250-61.

Journal Article with No Author Named.

"USA: The Facts about Wage Discrimination and Equal
     Pay." <u>Women's International Network News</u> 25.1
     (Winter 1999): 68.

Newspaper Article with Author Named.

Warrick, Pamela. "Questions of Life and Death."
     <u>Los Angeles Times</u> 4 Aug. 1991: E1+.

Magazine Article with Author Named.

> Moody, Howard. "Sacred Rite or Civil Right?" <u>Nation</u>
>
>   5 July 2004: 8.

Magazine Article with No Author Named.

> "Another Challenge to Coffee's Safety." <u>Science</u>
>
>   <u>News</u> 20 Oct. 1990: 253.

Chapter from a Collection of Essays.

> Smiley, Jane. "You Can Never Have Too Many." <u>The</u>
>
>   <u>Barbie Chronicles: A Living Doll Turns Forty.</u>
>
>   Ed. Yona Zeldis McDonough. New York:
>
>   Touchstone/Simon and Schuster, 1999. 189-192.

Government Document.

> United States. Cong. House. Committee on Armed
>
>   Services. <u>Women in the Military: Hearing</u>
>
>   <u>before the Military Personnel and</u>
>
>   <u>Compensation Subcommittee.</u> 101st Cong.,
>
>   2nd sess. 20 Mar. 1990: 14-56.

Internet Website.

> "Americans Have Long Questioned Electoral College."
>
> Web page. <u>Gallup Poll Releases.</u> 16 Nov 2000.
>
> 29 Nov. 2008 <http://www.gallup.com/poll/
>
> releases/pr001116.asp>.

A Translation.

> Witten, Johann. "Letters to Christoph Witten,
>
> 3 December 1914, 5 December 1915, 9 September
>
> 1919, 18 September 1920." <u>News from the Land</u>
>
> <u>of Freedom: German Immigrants Write Home.</u>
>
> Trans. Susan Vogel. Eds. Walter Kamphoefner,
>
> Wolfgang Helbich, and Ulrike Sommer. Ithaca:
>
> Cornell UP, 1991. 278-83.

Following the formatting guidelines for the works cited page will save time later in the process when you put your paper in its final form. As you record information in the proper format, alphabetize your list, placing new items in the appropriate alphabetical position. Then, when you need to assemble the works cited page, just move the list to the file where you store your paper (or keep the list in the same file). As you evaluate sources to determine whether they are appropriate for your paper, delete those that you decide not to pursue further. Here is how a list of the works on the previous sample bibliography entries would look in a computer file:

> "Americans Have Long Questioned Electoral
>
> College." <u>Gallup Poll Releases.</u> 16 Nov.
>
> 2000. 29 Nov. 2008, <http://www.gallup
>
> .com/poll/releases/pr001116.asp>.

"Another Challenge to Coffee's Safety."
Science News 20 Oct. 1990: 253.

Capozzola, Christopher. "The Only Badge
Needed Is Your Patriotic Fervor:
Vigilance, Coercion, and the Law in
World War I America." Journal of
American History 88 (2002): 1354-
1382.

Conolly-Smith, Peter. Translating America: An
Immigrant Press Visualizes American
Popular Culture, 1895-1918. Washington:
Smithsonian Books, 2004.

Fabes, Richard A., and Jeremiah Strouse.
"Formal versus Informal Sources on Sex
Education: Competing Forces in the
Sexual Socialization of Adolescents."
Adolescence 20 (1985): 250-61.

Moody, Howard. "Sacred Rite or Civil Right?"
Nation 5 July 2004: 28.

Smiley, Jane. "You Can Never Have Too Many."
The Barbie Chronicles: A Living Doll
Turns Forty. Ed. Yona Zeldis McDonough.
New York: Touchstone/Simon and Schuster,
1999. 189-192.

United States. Cong. House. Committee on
Armed Services. Women in the Military:
Hearing before the Military Personnel
and Compensation Subcommittee. 101st
Cong., 2nd sess. 20 Mar. 1990: 14-56.

"USA: The Facts about Wage Discrimination and
Equal Pay." Women's International
Network News 25.1 (Winter 1999): 68.

Warrick, Pamela. "Questions of Life and
Death." Los Angeles Times 4 Aug.
1991: E1+.

EVALUATING PRINT SOURCES

Before you begin taking notes from any source, carefully assess its reliability. Ideally, your research should rely on unbiased, current, well-documented sources written by people with the authority to discuss the subject. However, you are likely to find a great number of sources that are written from particular perspectives that are out of date or incomplete, that are written by people with no authority whatsoever, or that do not document their own sources. Part of your job as a researcher is to try to discover these aspects of your sources, to reject those that are completely unreliable, and to use with caution sources about which you lack complete confidence. While you may never know for sure how much to trust a particular source, you can check certain things to help in your assessment.

Check for Bias.   Try to find out if the author, publication, organization, or person being interviewed is known to give fair coverage. People, organizations, and publications often promote particular perspectives, which you should recognize and take into account. You need not reject sources outright if you know they take particular positions on subjects, especially controversial issues. However, your own paper should be as unbiased as possible, which requires acknowledgment of the known biases of your sources.

Check the Date of Publication.   In general, an increasingly recent publication or update of a website provides an increasingly reliable source. For many subjects, current information is crucial to accurate analysis. If you are researching issues such as global warming, morality at high governmental levels, or controversial treatments for AIDS victims, for instance, you need the most recent available information. However, if you are examining a historical matter, such as the question of Richard III's guilt in his two young cousins' deaths or whether King Arthur of Britain is an entirely mythical figure, you can rely in part on older materials. You still want to look for the latest theories, information, or opinions on any subject you research, though.

Check the Author's Credentials.   Find out if the author has sufficient education, experience, or expertise to write or speak about your subject. You can do this in a number of ways. Any book usually gives information about an author, from a sentence or two to several paragraphs, either on the dust jacket or at the beginning or end of the book. This information reveals the author's professional status, other books the author has published, and similar information that helps to establish her authority. You can also look up the author in sources like *Contemporary Authors, Current Biography,* and *Who's Who.* Other checks on an author's reliability might review what professionals in other sources say about her or to note how often her name shows up on reference lists or bibliographies on your subject.

Check the Reliability of Your Source.   In evaluating a book, determine whether the publishing house is a respectable one. For a magazine, find out if it is published by a particular interest group. Evaluation of a book could include reading some representative reviews to see how it was received when first published. Both the *Book Review Digest* and *Book Review Index* will help you locate reviews.

Check the Thoroughness of Research and Documentation of Sources.   If your source purports to be scholarly, well-informed, or otherwise reliable, check to see how the evidence was gathered. Determine whether the source reports original research or other people's work and what facts or data support its conclusions. Look for references either at the ends of chapters or in a separate section at the end of a book. Almost all journal articles and scholarly books document sources, whereas few magazine articles and personal accounts do. Also, consider how statistics and other data are used. Statistics are notoriously easy to manipulate, so check how the author uses them and confirm his fair interpretation.

EVALUATING INTERNET SOURCES

As with print sources, you must take care to evaluate any material you locate on the Internet before you use it in your paper. The Internet may pose more difficulty, because its resources may offer fewer clues than a book or journal article might give. However, searching the Internet will turn up many useful sources, such as scholarly projects, reference databases, text files of books, articles in periodicals, and professional sites. You must use your judgment when selecting sources for your research paper. Remember that anyone with some knowledge of the Internet can create a website, so be very cautious about accepting the authority of anything you find on the Internet. In general, personal sites are probably not as reliable as professional sites and those of scholarly projects. Reference databases can be extremely useful tools for locating source materials.

You must apply the same sort of skills that you bring to critical reading when looking at an Internet website, particularly when searching for materials for a class assignment. You must ask a number of questions about the site before accepting and using materials that you locate on the Internet. Some key areas to consider are the authority or credentials of the person or persons responsible for the site, the scope, accuracy, timeliness, and nature of the information at the site, and the presentation of the information at the site. Here is a list of questions that will help you evaluate Internet websites:

- **What can you tell about the site from its URL?** Websites exist for a variety of purposes, including the following: to sell a product, to advocate a position, to influence readers, and to inform. They may be sponsored by individuals for personal reasons, by professionals to impart information, by corporations to sell products, by agencies or groups to influence opinion or advocate a specific position. Knowing what domain the abbreviation at the end of the URL represents can give you your first clue about a website's purpose. The domain is the system for indicating the logical or geographical location of a web page from the Internet. Outside the United States, domains indicate country, such as ca (Canada), uk (United Kingdom), or au (Australia). In the United States, the following are common domains:
  - **Educational** websites exist to provide information about educational institutions, including elementary, secondary, and university levels. Their Internet addresses end in **.edu**.

- **Government** websites provide information about governmental departments, agencies, and policies at all levels of government, including city, county, state, and federal governments. Their Internet addresses end in **.gov**.
- **Organizational** websites advocate the viewpoint of particular groups. The URL for organizational websites typically end in **.org**.
- **Commercial** websites aim to sell products or services. Their URLs usually end in **.com**.
- **Military** websites provide information about the military. Their Internet addresses end in **.mil**.
- **News** websites exist to provide information about current events. Their Internet addresses usually end in **.com**.
- **Personal** websites are constructed by individuals about themselves. The address or personal sites end in various ways, probably most typically **.com**.
- **Entertainment** websites exist to amuse, entertain, and provide information about the entertainment industry. Their Internet addresses usually end in **.com**.
- **Internet service provider** websites exist to provide information about companies and services related to the Internet. Their website addresses end in **.net**.

- **What do you know about the author of the site?** Is the author of the website qualified to give information on the subject? Does the site give information about the author's qualifications? Are the author's credentials, such as academic affiliation, professional association, or publications, easily verified? Because anyone can create a web page, you want to determine whether the author of the website you are looking at is qualified to give the information you are seeking.
- **Is the material on the website presented objectively, or do biases or prejudices reveal themselves?** The language used may be a clue, but probably the best way to discover a particular bias is to look at a great many sites (and other sources) on the same topic. When you understand the complexity of your topic and the variety of viewpoints on it, you should be able to determine whether a site is objective or subjective.
- **Is the information reliable?** Can you verify it? How does it compare with information you have learned from other sources? How well does the website compare with other sites on the same topic? Does the site offer unique information or does it repeat information that you can find at other sites?
- **How thoroughly does the website cover its topic?** Does it provide links to other sites for additional information? Does the site have links to related topics, and do those links work?
- **How accurate is the information?** This may be difficult to assess when you first begin your research, but the more you read about your topic and examine a variety of sources, the better able you will be to evaluate information accuracy.
- **When was the website last updated?** Is the information at the site current?
- **What is your impression of the visual effect of the site?** Are the graphics helpful or distracting, clear or confusing? Are words spelled correctly? Is the page organized well?

ILLUSTRATION: SEEKING PROMISING WEBSITES

Suppose, for example, that student Shawn Ryan is interested in finding information on the Internet for his paper on King Arthur. When he first enters the keywords "Arthurian legend," a search engine returns almost 80,000 matches. Obviously, he cannot look at every match, but he can begin his search by scrolling through the first page of matches, picking a site that sounds promising, and going to that site. The list shows several entries that appear to be newsgroups or personal sites, whereas two will take him to the sites of a scholarly society and a scholarly project associated with a university. Because he is looking for sources for a research paper, as opposed to satisfying general curiosity, Shawn prefers the scholarly sites.

Both of the scholarly sites provide enormously useful information. The entry labeled "Arthurian websites" takes him to the home page of the North American branch of the International Arthurian Society, whose journal, *Arthuriana*, Shawn can read on the web. Furthermore, the site offers manuscripts, reviews, and scholarly essays, including the titles of over two hundred sources listed under the heading "Nonfiction and Research." In addition, the site offers links to other Arthurian sites.

As with print sources, Shawn has to judge the trustworthiness and reliability of an Internet source on the basis of who created the site, the credentials of the authorities, and the kind of information it gives. For instance, he particularly likes the information available at the website for the Camelot Project at the University of Rochester. Shawn determines that this site is a reliable source for several reasons. According to its home page, the Camelot Project aims to create a database of Arthurian texts, bibliographies, and other information. This goal tells Shawn that the site is not devoted to one person's opinions or to an informal collection of materials. Rather, it has a legitimate, scholarly aim, making it a valuable source of relevant materials for his paper. The Camelot Project itself is sponsored by the University of Rochester and the Robbins Library, associations that assure a certain level of reliability and scholarly appropriateness.

Finally, the material at the site is continually updated, the most recent change occurring just one month before Shawn visited the site. Thus, Shawn has found a source that he is confident he can trust and that is sure to lead him to other reliable sources.

QUESTIONS TO ASK WHEN EVALUATING SOURCES

1. Is the publication or site known to be fair, or does it have a bias or slant?
2. Does the source seem one sided, or does it try to cover all perspectives on an issue?
3. Is the information current or outdated?
4. Does the authority have respectable credentials?
5. How reliable is the source?
6. How thoroughly does the source cover its subject?
7. Does the source offer adequate documentation for its information?
8. If the source relies on research data, how was evidence gathered? Are statistics used fairly, or are they misrepresented?

TAKING NOTES

When you find an article, book, pamphlet, website, or other source you believe will be important or informative in your research, take notes from that source. There are several kinds of notes that you will take:

Summary.   A summary produces an objective restatement of a written passage in your own words. A summary is much shorter than the original work. Because its purpose is to highlight the central idea or ideas and major points of a work, make summary notes to record general ideas or main points of a large piece of writing, perhaps several pages, a chapter, or an entire article.

Paraphrase.   A paraphrase is a restatement of the words of someone else in your own words. Use paraphrasing when you want to use another writer's ideas but not the exact words, or to explain difficult material more clearly. Your own version of someone else's words must be almost entirely your own words. When incorporating paraphrased material into your research paper, you must be clear about when the paraphrased material begins and ends.

Direct Quotation.   A direct quotation is a record of the exact words of someone else. You will want to quote directly when the words are unique, colorful, or so well stated that you cannot fairly or accurately paraphrase them. Use direct quotations when you do not want to misrepresent what an author says or when the author makes a statement that you wish to stress or comment on. You may want to quote directly in order to analyze or discuss a particular passage. Use direct quotations sparingly and integrate them smoothly into your paper. Too many direct quotations in your paper will interrupt the flow of your own words.

Recording Source and Page Numbers.   Note-taking is crucial to the success of your paper. You must take accurate and careful notes, reproducing an author's words exactly as they appear if you quote, completely restating the author's words if you paraphrase, and accurately capturing the essence of the material if you summarize. In any case, you will give a citation in your paper, so ***you must record the source and page number for any notes.***

    Caution: When taking notes, some students are tempted to write every detail as it appears in the original, thinking that they will paraphrase the material at some later time. They must then spend valuable time later rephrasing material when they should be concentrating on writing their papers, or else they take the easier route and use the direct quotations. The result may be a paper that is too full of direct quotations and lacking in effective paraphrases. Remember that you should quote directly only language that is particularly well expressed or material that you do not feel you can adequately restate in your own words. Your final paper should have far more paraphrases than direct quotations.

    Where you record your notes does not matter, as long as you develop an efficient system. The important consideration is the accuracy and fairness of your notes. Traditionally, researchers have used 4 × 6 inch cards, because they are large enough to record ideas, summaries, quotations, or major points. When the note taking part of the research ends, the researcher can shuffle the cards about, arranging them in the order that makes sense for the research paper. Some people like the note card system and work well with it, but most now prefer to use a computer as a more convenient way to record and store notes.

A computer can be very helpful for organizing and sorting notes. Most programs allow you to arrange your notes in numerical order. However, make sure to develop a filing system for your notes. If your program lets you create folders, you can keep your notes from different sources under specific headings, each with its own subheadings.

Place the subject heading at the beginning of your notes, and put the page number at the end. **Make sure that your notes clearly identify sources for all information.**

GUIDELINES FOR TAKING NOTES

- **Write both the author's last name and the page number from which the information is taken.** That is all the information you need, as long as you have a bibliography card or file for the source that lists complete bibliographic information.
- **Use subject headings as you take notes.** This labeling system will help you sort and arrange your notes when you write your paper.
- **Record only one idea or several small, related ones in each note.** This practice will help you to organize your notes when you begin writing.
- **Place quotation marks before and after the material taken directly from a source.**
- **Don't rely on memory to determine whether words are identical to the original or paraphrased.**
- **Use notes to summarize.** A note may refer to an entire passage, an article, or a book without giving specific details. Make a note to remind you that the information is a summary.
- **Use notes to record original ideas that occur to you while you are reading.** Make sure you identify your own ideas.

HANDLING SOURCE MATERIAL

Handling source material fairly, accurately, and smoothly is one of your main tasks in writing a successful research paper. More than likely your instructor will evaluate your research project not only on how successfully you argue, explain, examine, or illustrate your topic but also on how skillfully you handle source materials. This means that you must take great care not only when you take notes but also when you transfer those notes into your paper. Always keep in mind—as you are taking notes, when drafting your paper, and when writing its final version—that you must acknowledge the source for all borrowed material. Any information that you take from a source must be properly attributed to its author or, if no author, to its title. At the same time, you must not simply drop material into your text but be mindful of providing smooth integration of your source material into your own text. After all, the text is your work: the thesis of the paper, the overall organization and development, transitions from point to point, general observations, and the conclusions are all yours. Your source materials serve to support, illustrate, develop, or exemplify your own words. This means that the source materials must not interrupt the flow of your words or call attention to themselves. They are an important and integral part of your own paper.

Illustration: Summarizing, Paraphrasing, and Quoting.   Chapter 6 has detailed directions and summary guidelines for both paraphrasing source material and quoting directly. Chapter 6 also discusses some common tools for handling source material: ellipsis points, brackets, single quotation marks, and "qtd. in." Sample research papers located later in this chapter also give examples of the correct handling of source material. Here is another illustration that shows how to handle source material based on this opening paragraph from Ian Wilmut's "Dolly's False Legacy," located in Chapter 20:

> Overlooked in the arguments about the mortality of artificially reproducing life is the fact that, at present, cloning is a very inefficient procedure. The incidence of death among fetuses and offspring produced by cloning is much higher than it is through natural reproduction—roughly 10 times as high as normal before birth and three times as high after birth in our studies at Roslin. Distressing enough for those working with animals, these failure rates surely render unthinkable the notion of applying such treatment to humans.

In the following passage from Nate Hayes' research paper, "A Positive Alternative to Cloning" (see sample pages at the end of this chapter), he combines summary, paraphrase, and direct quotation. Nate begins by summarizing and then paraphrases and quotes from the introductory paragraph:

> One big question has to do with the high failure rate of cloning. Despite having been responsible for the first cloned mammal, Dr. Wilmut is very conservative in his views of the wisdom of carrying on full speed with cloning research because of its unreliability.
>
> In "Dolly's False Legacy," he identifies some of the likely problems a cloned human might have. For instance, Wilmut warns of the inefficiency of cloning, noting the high death rate in fetuses and live births when cloning is used in animal tests. This fact leads him to suggest that "these failure rates surely render unthinkable the notion of applying such treatment to humans" (564).

Nate first identifies the author and title of his source and summarizes a key point of Wilmut's essay. Then he paraphrases the reference to death rates in animals produced by cloning versus those produced naturally. Finally, Nate quotes directly a passage that he believes is forcefully worded.

GUIDELINES FOR HANDLING SOURCE MATERIAL

- **Introduce or provide a context for quoted material.** "Dropped" quotations occur when you fail to integrate quotations smoothly into your text. The abrupt dropping of a quotation disrupts the flow of your text.
- **Name your authority or, when no author is named, use title of the source.** Provide this information either in the text itself or in the parenthetical citation. Rely on standard phrases such as "one writer claims," "according to one expert," and the like to introduce quotations or paraphrases.
- **Use both first and last names of author at the first mention in your text.** After that, use just last name. Always use last name only in parenthetical citations (unless you have sources by two authors with the same last name).
- **Acknowledge source material when you first begin paraphrasing.** Make sure you give some kind of signal to your reader when you begin paraphrasing borrowed material. This is particularly important if you paraphrase more than one sentence from a source. Otherwise, your reader will not know how far back the citation applies.
- **Quote sparingly.** Quote directly only those passages that are vividly or memorably phrased, so that you could not do justice to them by rewording them; that require exact wording for accuracy; or that need the authority of your source to lend credibility to what you are saying.
- **Intermingle source material with our own words.** Avoid a "cut-and-paste" approach to the research process. Remember that source materials serve primarily to support your generalizations. Never run two quotations together without some comment or transitional remark from you.
- **Make sure that direct quotations are exact.** Do not change words unless you use brackets or ellipses to indicate changes. Otherwise, be exact. For instance, if your source says "$2 million," do not write "two million dollars."
- **Make sure that paraphrases are truly your own words.** Do not inadvertently commit plagiarism by failing to paraphrase fairly.

AVOIDING PLAGIARISM

Giving proper credit to your sources is a crucial component of the research process. It is also one of the trickiest aspects of the process, because it requires absolute accuracy in note-taking. Many students have been disheartened by low grades on papers that took weeks to prepare, because they were careless or inaccurate in handling and documenting source materials.

Simply defined, **plagiarism** is borrowing another person's words without giving proper credit. The worst form of plagiarism is deliberately using the words or important ideas of someone else without giving any credit to that source. Handing in a paper someone else has written or copying someone else's paper and pretending it is yours are the most blatant and inexcusable forms of plagiarism, crimes that on some campuses carry penalties like automatic failure in the course or even immediate expulsion from school. Most student plagiarism is not deliberate, but rather results from carelessness either in the research process, when notes are taken, or in the writing process, when notes are incorporated into the student's own text. Even this unintentional plagiarism can result in a failing grade, however, especially if it appears repeatedly in a paper.

Keep the following standards in mind when you take notes on your source materials and when you write your research paper:

- **You commit plagiarism if you use the exact words or ideas of another writer without putting quotation marks around the words or citing a source.** The reader of your paper assumes that words without quotation marks or a source citation are your own words. To use the words of another without proper documentation suggests that you are trying to pass the words off as your own without giving credit to the writer.
- **You commit plagiarism if you use the exact words of another writer without putting quotation marks around those words, even if the paper cites the source of the material.** Readers assume that words followed by a parenthetical citation are paraphrased from the original—that is, that they are your own words and that the general idea was expressed by the author of the source material.
- **You commit plagiarism if you paraphrase by changing only a few words of the original or by using the identical sentence structure of the original, with or without a source.** Again, readers assume that words without quotation marks followed by a parenthetical citation are your own words, not those of someone else. In a paraphrase, the *idea* is that of another; the *words* are your own.
- **You inaccurately handle source material when you use quotation marks around words that are not exactly as they appear in the original.** Readers assume that all words within quotation marks are identical to the original.

Obviously, accuracy and fairness in note-taking are essential standards. Great care must be taken when you read your source materials and again when you transfer your notes to your final paper.

ILLUSTRATION: PLAGIARISM, INACCURATE DOCUMENTATION, AND CORRECT HANDLING OF SOURCE MATERIAL

The passage that follows is from page 8 of Jean Kilbourne's "Beauty and the Beast of Advertising." Complete bibliographic information follows, as it would appear on a bibliography card or list and on the works cited page of a research paper:

Kilbourne, Jean. "Beauty and the Beast of
Advertising." <u>Media & Values</u> Winter 1989: 8-10.

Note that the title of the magazine is correct as written, with the ampersand (&) instead of "and" and with no spaces between the words. Here is the passage:

> "You're a Halston woman from the very beginning," the advertisement proclaims. The model stares provocatively at the viewer, her long blonde hair waving around her face, her bare chest partially covered by two curved bottles that give the illusion of breasts and cleavage.
>
> The average American is accustomed to blue-eyed blondes seductively touting a variety of products. In this case, however, the blonde is about five years old.
>
> Advertising is an over $130 billion a year industry and affects all of us throughout our lives. We are each exposed to over 1,500 ads a day, constituting perhaps the most powerful educational force in society. The average adult will spend 11.2 years of his/her life watching television commercials. But the ads sell a great deal more than products. They sell values, images, and concepts of success and worth, love and sexuality, popularity and normalcy. They tell us who we are and who we should be. Sometimes they sell addictions.

Now look at each of these sentences from a hypothetical research paper using information from the Kilbourne article. The commentary that follows identifies plagiarism, inaccurate handling of the original source material, or correct handling of source material:

1. Advertising is an over $130 billion a year industry and affects us throughout our lives.
   [This is **plagiarism:** Quotation marks are needed around words identical to the original and a source must be cited.]

2. We are each exposed to over 1,500 ads a day (Kilbourne 8).
   [This is **plagiarism:** Quotation marks are needed around words taken directly from the original.]

3. The average American is used to blue-eyed blondes seductively selling a variety of things (Kilbourne 8).
   [This is **plagiarism:** Original words are changed only slightly and the original sentence structure is retained.]

4. Kilbourne's analysis of advertising begins with the following quotation from a popular advertisement: "You're a Halston woman from the very beginning" (8).
   [This is **inaccurate documentation:** Single quotation marks are needed within the double marks to indicate that quotation marks are in the original.]

5. In her analysis of the ways in which advertising uses women's bodies to sell products, Jean Kilbourne argues that ads sell much more than just products. Ads "sell values, images, and concepts of success and worth" (8).
[This is **correct:** The text acknowledges the author and the general idea of the article is adequately summarized. Quotation marks enclose material taken directly from the original.]

Students are sometimes frustrated by these guidelines governing note-taking and plagiarism, arguing that virtually everything in the final paper will be in quotation marks or followed by citations. But keep in mind that your final paper is a synthesis of information you have discovered in your research with your own thoughts on your topic, thoughts that naturally undergo modification, expansion, and/or revision as you read and think about your topic.

Probably half of the paper will be your own words. These words will usually include all of the introductory and concluding paragraphs, all topic sentences and transitional sentences within and between paragraphs, and all introductions to direct quotations. Furthermore, you need give no citation for statements of general or common knowledge, such as facts about well-known historical or current events. If you keep running across the same information in all of your sources, you can assume it is general knowledge.

GUIDELINES FOR AVOIDING PLAGIARISM

- **For direct quotations, write the words exactly as they appear in the original.** Put quotation marks before and after the words. Do not change anything.
- **For paraphrased material, restate the original thought in your own words, using your own writing style.** Do not use the exact sentence pattern of the original, and do not simply rearrange words. You have to retain the central idea of the paraphrased material, but do so in your own words.
- **When using borrowed material in your paper, whether direct quotations or paraphrases, acknowledge the source by naming the author or work as you introduce the material.** Doing so not only tells your reader that you are using borrowed material but also often provides a clear transition from your own words and ideas to the borrowed material that illustrates or expands on your ideas.
- **Provide an in-text citation for any borrowed material.** Give the author's last name if it is not mentioned in the text of the paper, followed by page number(s). If the source material is anonymous, use a shortened version of the title in place of a name.
- **Assemble all sources cited in your paper in an alphabetical list at the end of the paper.** This is your list of works cited, containing only those works actually used in the paper.

DOCUMENTING SOURCES

Follow the Appropriate Style Guidelines. The examples of documentation and sample research papers that appear in this chapter all follow MLA (Modern Language Association) documentation style. That style governs because this textbook is often used in English courses, and English is located within the discipline of the humanities. However, your instructor may permit you to choose the style appropriate to the major field you intend to study. A section later in this chapter provides guidelines for writing a research paper using APA (American Psychological Association) style. That style is probably as commonly used as MLA in undergraduate course papers. In addition to MLA and APA, other frequently used documentation styles are CBE (Council of Biology Editors) and Chicago. Following this summary of the chief differences among those four styles, the chapter lists stylebooks that give additional guidelines.

SUMMARY OF DIFFERENCES AMONG DOCUMENTATION STYLES

- **MLA:** Used by writers in the many areas of the humanities (English, foreign languages, history, and philosophy); requires parenthetical in-text citations of author and page number that refer to an alphabetical list of works cited at the end of the paper.

- **APA:** Used by writers in the behavioral and social sciences (education, psychology, and sociology); requires parenthetical in-text citations of author and date of publication that refer to an alphabetical list of references at the end of the paper.

- **CBE:** Used by writers in technical fields and the sciences (engineering, biology, physics, geography, chemistry, computer science, and mathematics); requires either a name–year format or a citation–sequence format. The name–year format places the author's last name and the year of publication in parentheses, referring to an alphabetical list of references at the end of the paper.

- **Chicago:** Used by some areas of the humanities, notably history, art, music, and theatre; requires a superscript number (e.g., [1]) for each citation, all of which are numbered sequentially throughout the paper; no number is repeated. Numbers correspond either to footnotes at the bottoms of pages or a list of notes at the end of the paper.

    The first note gives complete information about the source, with shortened information for each subsequent reference to that source. A bibliography follows the notes, giving the same information, except for the page number, as in the first citation of each source. The information is also punctuated and arranged differently from the note copy.

Style Guides. To find full details on a particular documentation style, consult the following style guides:

MLA

Gibaldi, Joseph. <u>MLA Handbook for Writers of Research Papers</u>. 6th ed. New York: MLA, 2003.

APA

American Psychological Association. <u>Publication Manual of the American Psychological Association</u>. 5th ed. Washington: APA, 2001.

CBE

CBE Style Manual Committee. <u>Scientific Style and Format: The CBE Manual for Authors, Editors, and Publishers</u>. 7th ed. Chicago: Council of Science Editors, 2006.

Chicago

The Chicago Manual of Style. 15th ed. Chicago: U of Chicago P, 2003.

Turabian Kate L. A Manual for Writers of Term Papers, Theses, and Dissertations. 6th ed. Rev. by John Grossman and Alice Bennet. Chicago: U of
Chicago P, 1996.

Internet Citation Guides.   Many research resources are available on the Internet,
including guides for citing such sources. Your university librarian may have created
a website where you will find the names and URLs of sites that give directions for
citing electronic sources. Keep in mind that Internet sites constantly change. URLs
that were correct when this book was published may no longer be correct, or the
sites may have ceased functioning. However, the ease of changing and updating
Internet sites means that they may have more current information than print guides
offer. If you doubt the reliability and currency of a website, consult with your instructor about the advisability of using the site. Here are a few reliable sites:

> *Columbia Guide to Online Style* (site provides models of both MLA and APA
> formatting): http://www.columbia.edu/cu/cup/cgos2006/basic.html
>
> *Using Modern Language Association (MLA) Format,* Purdue University's Online
> Writing Lab. Provides links to APA guidelines, too: http://owl.english.
> purdue.edu/owl/resource/557/01/
>
> *MLA and APA Citation,* University of Delaware's Writing Center:
> http://www.english.udel.edu/wc/documentation/index.html
>
> *Style Sheet for Citing Resources (Print & Electronic).* UC-Berkeley Library.
> Provides examples and rules for MLA, APA, Chicago, and Turabian:
> http://www.lib.berkeley.edu/Help/guides.html
>
> *Cómo citar recursos electronic* by Assumpció Estivill and Cristobal Urbana,
> Spanish-language guide to citing electronic sources: http://www.ub.es/
> biblio/citae.htm
>
> *How to Cite Electronic Sources,* Library of Congress. Explains how to cite me-
> dia available online, such as films, music, maps, photographs, and texts:
> http://lcweb2.loc.gov/ammem/ndlpedu/start/cite/index.html
>
> *MLA Style,* Modern Language Association of America. Includes list of
> frequently asked questions about MLA style: http://www.mla.org/
> style_faq.html

CITING SOURCES IN THE TEXT

Recall from the discussion in Chapter 6 on documenting sources with in-text citations and the discussion in this chapter on taking notes that a crucial task of the
researcher is to identify accurately sources for all borrowed material. This section
expands the discussion from Chapter 6 with illustrations of treatments for several
types of sources. It also includes guidelines for creating a list of works cited that

incorporates a variety of sources, including electronic sources. These examples follow MLA guidelines as they appear in Joseph Gibaldi's *MLA Handbook for Writers of Research Papers,* 6th edition (New York: MLA, 2003).

In-Text Citations.   Remember that you must name your source for any borrowed material. The parenthetical citation must give enough information to identify the source by directing your reader to the alphabetized list of works cited at the end of your paper. The citation should also give the page number or numbers, if available, on which the material appears.

Author–Page Format.   MLA guidelines call for the author–page format when acknowledging borrowed material in the text of your paper. You must name the author (or source, if no author is named) and give a page number or numbers where the borrowed material appears in the source. The author's name or title that you give in your text directs readers to the correct entry in the works cited list, so the reference must correspond to its entry on that list. Here are some examples:

Book Or Article with One Author.   Author's last name and page number, without punctuation.

   (Sollod 15)

Book Or Article with Two or Three Authors.   Both or all three authors' last names followed by the page number.

   (Barrett and Rowe 78)   (Fletcher, Miller, and Caplan 78)

Note: Reproduce the names in the order in which they appear on the title page. If they are not listed alphabetically, do not change their order.

Book Or Article with More Than Three Authors.   First author's last name followed by et al. and then page number.

   (Smith et al. 29)

Article Or Other Publication with No Author Named.   Short title followed by page number.

   ("Teaching" 10)

Note: When citing any source in a parenthetical reference in your text that appears on your works cited list, use the full title if short or a shortened version. When using a shortened version, begin with the word by which the source is alphabetized. If you cite two anonymous articles beginning with the same word, use the full title of each to distinguish one from the other.

   ("Classrooms without Walls" 45)   ("Classrooms in the 21st Century" 96)

Two Works by the Same Author.   Author's name followed by a comma, a short title, and the page number.

   (Heilbrun, <u>Hamlet's Mother</u> 123)   (Heilbrun, <u>Writing a Woman's Life</u> 35)

Works by People with the Same Last Name.

First and last names of author and page number.

(Gregory Smith 16)

Example: Consider this example of an in-text citation from Erin Anderson's research paper located at the end of this chapter. Erin uses the following source:

> Longley, Lawrence D., and Neal R. Peirce. The Electoral College Primer 2000. New Haven, CT: Yale UP, 1999.

When Erin quotes from that source in her paper, this is how she documents it:

> In The Electoral College Primer 2000, Lawrence D. Longley and Neal R. Peirce explain their opposition to the electoral college system. They assert that in an "advanced democratic nation, where . . . popular choice is the most deeply ingrained of government principles," a voting system where popular votes don't necessarily mean electoral votes is "irrational" (132).

For her second and subsequent references to this source, she does the following:

> Longley and Peirce also explain the "faithless elector" issue. The Constitution nowhere requires the chosen electors to vote for the winner of the popular vote. However, in the history of the electoral college, only nine votes of the over 20,000 cast have been known to go "'against instructions'" (113).

Exceptions to Author–Page Format.

Many papers must accommodate some exceptions to the basic author–page parenthetical citation. For instance, for non-print sources such as an Internet website, a lecture, a telephone conversation, a television documentary, or a recording, name the source in parentheses after the material without giving a page number.

Citing an Entire Work.

You may want to refer to an entire work rather than just part of it. In that case, name the work and the author in the text of your paper, without a parenthetical citation:

> Sir Arthur Conan Doyle's Hound of the Baskervilles features Watson to a much greater degree than do the earlier Holmes stories.

Citing Volume and Page Number of a Multivolume Work.

If you refer to material from more than one volume of a multivolume work, state the volume number, followed by a colon, and then the page number. Do not use the words or abbreviations for *volume* or *page*. The two numbers separated by a colon explicitly indicate volume and page. Your works cited entry will state the number of volumes in the work.

> Edgar Johnson's critical biography of Charles Dickens concludes with a rousing tribute to the author's creative imagination: "[T]he world he [Dickens] created shines with undying life, and the hearts of men still vibrate to his indignant anger, his love, his tears, his glorious laughter, and his triumphant faith in the dignity of man" (2: 1158).

Works Cited Entry.

Johnson, Edgar. <u>Charles Dickens: His Tragedy and Triumph</u>. 2 vols. New York: Simon, 1952.

If you draw material from just one volume of a multivolume work, your works cited entry states which volume, and your in-text citation gives only the page number:

The works of Charles Dickens fervently proclaim "his triumphant faith in the dignity of man" (Johnson 1158).

Works Cited Entry.

Johnson, Edgar. <u>Charles Dickens: His Tragedy and Triumph</u>. Vol. 2. New York: Simon, 1952.

Citing a Work by a Corporate Author or Government Agency.

Cite the author's or agency's name followed by a page reference, just as you would for a book or periodical article. However, if the title of the corporate author is long, put it in the body of the text to avoid an extensive parenthetical reference:

Testifying before a subcommittee of the U.S. House Committee on Public Works and Transportation, a representative of the Environmental Protection Agency argued that pollution from second-hand smoke within buildings is a widespread and dangerous threat (173–174).

Citing Internet Sources.

According to the MLA online guidelines, works on the World Wide Web are cited just like printed works when citing sources in your text. A special consideration with web documents is that they generally do not have fixed page numbers or any kind of section numbering. If your source lacks numbering, MLA says that you have to omit numbers from your parenthetical references. In that case, in your parenthetical citation, give the author's last name, if known (Plonsky), or the title if the original gives no author's name ("Psychology with Style"). If an author incorporates page numbers, section numbers, or paragraph numbers, you may cite the relevant numbers. Give the appropriate abbreviation before the numbers: (Plonsky, pars. 5–6). (*Pars.* is the abbreviation for *paragraphs.*) For a document on the World Wide Web, the page numbers of a printout should normally not be cited, because the pagination may vary in different printouts.

Remember that the purpose of the parenthetical citation is to indicate the location of the quotation or paraphrase in the referenced work and to point to the referenced work in the list of works cited. Whatever entry begins the reference in the works cited list (i.e., author's last name or title of work), that same entry should also appear in the parenthetical reference. A citation for an Internet source should reference the site in the body of the text, if possible, rather than including parenthetical information. For example, here is Erin's Internet source:

Geraghty, Jim. "Do Elections Need New Rules?" Online posting. 22 Nov. 2000. <u>Policy.com News and Events: Daily Briefing</u>. 29 Nov. 2000 <http://www.policy.com/news/dbrief/dbriefarc834.asp>.

In her paper, she documents the source this way:

> Former First Lady Hillary Clinton has given her support for the abolition of the electoral college; in fact, she is reported to have said that she would "be willing to co-sponsor a measure to abolish the electoral college" (Geraghty).

Note: *When mentioning the name of an author for a World Wide Web source in the text rather than in the parenthetical citation, it is sometimes difficult to tell when borrowed material ends, especially when paraphrasing. Some instructors recommend that students repeat the author's name in the parenthetical citation, even when it is mentioned in the text. The same holds true when citing a source that has no author, just a title.*

GUIDELINES FOR IN-TEXT CITATION

- **Name the source for all borrowed material, including both direct quotations and paraphrases,** either in your text or in parentheses following the borrowed material.
- **Give the citation in parentheses at the end of the sentence containing the quotation or paraphrase.**
- **In the parentheses, state the author's last name and the page number or numbers from which you took the words or ideas, with no punctuation between the name and the page number.**
- **For smooth transition to borrowed material, name the author or source as you introduce the words or ideas.** In that case, the parentheses will include only the page number or numbers.
- **At the first mention of an author in your text, use the author's full name.** Thereafter, use the last name only.
- **When citing Internet sources that have no page numbers, use the author's last name in parentheses.** If you mention the author's name in your text, it is helpful to repeat it in the parenthetical citation as well, to indicate where the borrowed material ends.
- **Create a page titled "Works Cited" at the end of your paper that lists all sources quoted or paraphrased in the paper.** Do not include any works that you consulted but did not directly use in your paper.

CREATING A *WORKS CITED* PAGE USING MLA STYLE

The works cited page of a research report lists in alphabetical order all the sources you cite in your paper. It comes at the end of your paper, beginning on a separate page.

Include an entry for every work quoted from, paraphrased, summarized, or otherwise alluded to in your paper. *Do not include on your list of works cited any sources you read but did not use in the paper.* You may want to include a list of useful works that informed your understanding of the topic but that you did not quote or paraphrase from in your final paper; to do so, create a separate page entitled "Works Consulted."

GENERAL GUIDELINES FOR CREATING A *WORKS CITED* LIST

- Begin your list of cited works on a new page after the conclusion of your paper.
- Center the title "Works Cited" one inch from the top of the page.
- Continue the page numbers of the text, with a separate number for each of the works cited pages.
- Alphabetize the list of sources.
- Begin the first line of each entry flush with the left margin. Indent the second and subsequent lines within each entry five spaces.
- Begin with the author's last name, followed by a comma and then the first name. For a source with two or more authors, invert only the first name. List the other name or names in normal order.
- Underline (italicize) the titles of books, journals, magazines, and newspapers. Do not use quotation marks. [Note: MLA guidelines recommend underlining instead of italics because printers are not uniform in the way they reproduce italics. Underlining has therefore become a convention that is understood to represent italics. However, if your instructor approves, and if your printer clearly distinguishes italics from regular print, you may use italics for the titles of books and journals.]
- Double-space within and between all entries.
- Place a period at the end of each entire entry.

The remainder of this section gives guidelines for creating works cited entries for books, periodicals, and electronic sources, supplemented by models for miscellaneous types of entries. The numbers on this list correspond to the numbered illustrations in each section (books, periodicals, electronic sources, miscellaneous) in the following pages:

Print Sources.

1. Book with a single author
2. Article in a collection
3. Collection or anthology
4. Book with two or more authors
5. Two works by the same author
6. Reprint of a book
7. Preface, foreword, introduction, or afterword to a book
8. Edition of a book
9. Multivolume work
10. Article in a journal with continuous pagination
11. Article in a journal with separate pagination
12. Article in a weekly or biweekly magazine

13. Article in a monthly or bimonthly magazine
14. Article in a quarterly magazine
15. Magazine article with no author
16. Newspaper article
17. Periodical article that does not appear on consecutive pages

Creating a Works Cited List for Electronic Sources.

18. Scholarly project
19. Professional site
20. Article in a reference database
21. Online article

Online Sources of Full-text Articles.

22. Article with author named, scholarly journal
23. Article in magazine
24. Article with no author named
25. Article in magazine from personally subscribed service

Miscellaneous Electronic Sources.

26. Personal site
27. Posting to a discussion group
28. E-mail message
29. Government document

Works Cited Formats for Sources Other than Books, Periodicals, and Electronic Sources.

30. Congressional record
31. Government publication
32. Lecture
33. Letter
34. Personal interview
35. Reprint of an article provided by an information service
36. Telephone interview
37. Pamphlet
38. Television or radio program
39. Sound recording
40. Article in a reference book

Books in a Works Cited List. Citations for books have several main parts: author's name, title of book, and publication information, including place of publication, publisher, and date the book was published. Often a book has more than one author or an editor, and often books are collections of a number of essays with individual authors.

The following section provides guidelines for documenting the most common kinds of books that you are likely to come across in your research.

1. **Book with a Single Author**

> Author's name. <u>Title of Book</u>. City of publication: Publisher, date of publication.
> Leonardi, Susan J. <u>Dangerous by Degrees: Women at Oxford and the Somerville College Novelists</u>. New Brunswick: Rutgers UP, 1989.

2. **Article in a Collection**

Name the author, the title of the article, the title of the collection, the editor or coeditors of the collection, publication information, and the **inclusive page numbers** of the entire article. Follow this format:

> Author's name. "Title of Article." <u>Title of Collection</u>. The abbreviation "Ed." Editor's name in normal order. City of publication: Name of

---

GUIDELINES FOR CREATING A *WORKS CITED* LIST FOR BOOKS

- **Begin with the author's last name, followed by a comma, and then the first name, followed by a period.** For a source with two or more authors, invert the first author's name with a comma before and after the first name, then write the word *and* and put the other author's name in normal order.
- **Underline the title of the book.**
- **State the city of publication, the publisher, and the date the book was published:** City: Publisher, date. Note that only the city name is given unless it is not unclear which city it is. For cities like Boston, New York, Los Angeles, and London, for instance, you would not need to add state or country. For a city like Athens, it is necessary to add the state to avoid ambiguity: Athens, OH. Use the same state abbreviation system as for zip codes.
- **Separate each item in an entry by a period:** Author. Title. Publication information and date. Note that each period is followed by two spaces. MLA guidelines acknowledge that most editors require material that is going to be printed to use only one space after a concluding punctuation mark but state that there is nothing wrong with using two unless your instructor requests that you do otherwise.
- **For essays in collections, begin by listing the author of the essay, then the title within quotation marks, the book it appears in, the editor's name, and publication information for the book.** Put the inclusive page numbers of the essay at the end of the entry.
- **Shorten publishers' names and drop such words as *Inc., Co.,* and *Press*.** Abbreviate *University* and *Press* for university presses, as "U of Wisconsin P" for University of Wisconsin Press or "Oxford UP" for Oxford University Press.

publisher, date of publication. Inclusive page numbers on which the article appears.

> Rose-Bond, Sherry, and Scott Bond. "Sherlockiana." <u>Encyclopedia Mysteriosa: Comprehensive Guide to the Art of Detection in Print, Film, Radio, and Television</u>. Ed. William L. DeAndrea. New York: Prentice, 1994. 327–330.

If the edition has two or more editors, use the abbreviation "Eds." followed by both editors' names:

> Spacks, Patricia Meyer. "Sisters." <u>Fetter'd or Free?: British Women Novelists, 1670–1815</u>. Eds. Mary Anne Schofield and Cecilia Macheski. Athens, OH: Ohio UP, 1986. 136–151.

3. Collection or Anthology

Use this format when you cite the ideas of the editor(s) or when you refer to the entire collection. Name the editor, followed by the abbreviation "ed." Treat the rest of the entry as you would for a book.

> Editor's name, ed. <u>Title of Collection</u>. City of publication: Publisher, date of publication.
> Salwak, Dale, ed. <u>The Life and Work of Barbara Pym</u>. Iowa City: U of Iowa P, 1987.

For two or more editors, list the first editor's name in inverted order, followed by a comma, the word *and,* and the second editor's name in normal order.

> Schofield, Mary Anne, and Cecilia Macheski, eds. <u>Fetter'd or Free?: British Women Novelists, 1670–1815</u>. Athens, OH: Ohio UP, 1986.

4. Book with Two or More Authors

List the names of the authors in the same order as they are listed on the title page, even if they are not in alphabetical order.

> First author's name in inverted order, and second author's name in normal order. <u>Name of Book</u>. City of publication: Publisher, date of publication.
> Gilbert, Sandra M., and Susan Gubar. <u>The Madwoman in the Attic: The Woman Writer and the Nineteenth-Century Literary Imagination</u>. New Haven: Yale UP, 1979.

5. Two Works by the Same Author

List the books in alphabetical order by title. For the second and subsequent books by the same author, type three hyphens followed by a period in place of the name.

> Heilbrun, Carolyn. <u>Hamlet's Mother and Other Women</u>. New York: Ballantine, 1990.
> ---. <u>Writing a Woman's Life</u>. New York: Ballantine, 1988.

6.   Reprint of a Book

Follow the same format as for books, but add the date of the first publication after the title.

> Author's name. Title of Book. First date of publication. City of publication of this edition: Publisher, date of publication.
> Symons, Julian. Bloody Murder: From the Detective Story to the Crime Novel: A History. 1972. 1985. London: Pan Macmillan, 1992.

If a different publisher produced earlier editions, you have the option of naming the place of publication and publisher for the other editions as well as for the current one.

> Symons, Julian. Bloody Murder: From the Detective Story to the Crime Novel: A History. London: Faber, 1972. London: Viking, 1985. London: Pan Macmillan, 1992.

7.   Preface, Foreword, Introduction, or Afterword to a Book

If you use material *only* from the preface, foreword, introduction, or afterword of a book, your works cited entry begins with the name of the person who wrote the selection you use, not necessarily with the author of the book (though sometimes they are the same person). You will need to indicate what part of the book you cite (preface, foreword, introduction, or afterword), then name the book and author and give complete bibliographic information. Finally, give the inclusive page numbers of the preface, foreword, introduction, or afterword. Follow this model:

> Author of introduction. Introduction. Title of Book. By author's name in normal order. Place of publication: Publisher, date of publication. Inclusive page numbers on which the introduction appears.
> Green, Richard Lancelyn. Introduction. The Adventures of Sherlock Holmes. By Arthur Conan Doyle. 1892. Oxford: Oxford UP, 1993. xi-xxxv.

8.   Edition of a Book

Use this format for a book prepared for publication by someone other than the author if you refer primarily to the text itself:

> Doyle, Arthur Conan. The Adventures of Sherlock Holmes. Ed. Richard Lancelyn Green. Oxford: Oxford UP, 1994.

If you refer primarily to the work of the editor, for instance, material from the introduction or notes to the text, begin with the editor's name:

> Green, Richard Lancelyn, ed. The Adventures of Sherlock Holmes. By Arthur Conan Doyle. 1892. Oxford: Oxford UP, 1993.

9. **Multivolume Work**

If you draw material from two or more volumes of a work, cite the total number of volumes in the entire work. When you refer to the work in the text of your paper, your parenthetical reference gives the volume number and page number.

> Johnson, Edgar. <u>Charles Dickens: His Tragedy and Triumph</u>. 2 vols. New York: Simon, 1952.

If you refer to only one volume of a multivolume work, state the number of that volume in the works cited entry. Your parenthetical in-text citation supplies page number only, not volume and page.

> Johnson, Edgar. <u>Charles Dickens: His Tragedy and Triumph</u>. Vol. 2. New York: Simon, 1952.

Periodicals in a Works Cited List. Periodicals are magazines or journals that are published frequently and at fixed intervals. Distinguish between journals and magazines by considering audience, subject matter, and frequency of publication. Journals are fairly specialized, are usually written for people in a specific profession, are more technical and research-oriented than magazines, and generally appear much less frequently than magazines, perhaps bimonthly or four times a year. Magazines, on the other hand, are intended for general audiences, are not heavily research-oriented, and usually appear in monthly or even weekly editions. As with books, works cited entries for periodicals have three main divisions: the author's name, the title of the article, and publication information, including the name of

---

GUIDELINES FOR CREATING *WORKS CITED* ENTRIES FOR PERIODICALS

- Place the author's name first, in inverted order, followed by a period.
- If the article is published anonymously, begin the entry with the title. For placing the entries in alphabetical order on the list, ignore *The, A, And,* and numbers at the beginnings of titles.
- State the title of the article, enclosing it in quotation marks, ending with a period.
- State the name of the periodical, underlined, followed by no punctuation.
- Follow periodical title with the date of publication. For publications with a specific day and month named, use this format: day month year. For journals, include volume number and issue number, if given, and enclose the date in parentheses. Abbreviate the names of all months except May, June, and July.
- Follow the date with a colon and the inclusive page numbers of the article.
- Do not use the abbreviations *p.* or *pp.* for pages.
- Separate the main parts of the entry with periods followed by two spaces.

the periodical, the date the article was published, and the inclusive page numbers the article appears on.

10. **Article in a Journal with Continuous Pagination**
     Use this format for journals that continue pagination throughout the year.

> Author's name. "Title of Article." <u>Name of Periodical</u> volume number (date): inclusive page numbers of article.
> Groff, Patrick. "The Maturing of Phonics Instruction." <u>Education Digest</u> 52 (Mar. 1991): 402–408.

11. **Article in a Journal with Separate Pagination**
     Use this format for journals that begin each issue with page 1. Give the issue number as well as the volume number.

> Author's name. "Title of Article." <u>Name of Periodical</u> volume number. Issue number (date): inclusive page numbers of article.
> Annan, Kofi. "Development Without Borders." <u>Harvard International Review</u> 23.2 (Summer 2001): 84.

12. **Article in a Weekly or Biweekly Magazine**

> Author's name. "Title of Article." <u>Name of Magazine</u> complete date, beginning with the day and abbreviating the month, page number(s).
> Bazell, Robert. "Sins and Twins." <u>New Republic</u> 21 Dec. 1987: 17–18.

13. **Article in a Monthly or Bimonthly Magazine**

> Author's name. "Title of Article." <u>Name of Magazine</u> date, including month and year: page number(s).
> Bowden, Mark. "The Lessons of Abu Ghraib." <u>Atlantic Monthly</u> July-Aug. 2004: 33–36.

14. **Article in a Quarterly Magazine**

> Fletcher, John C., Franklin G. Miller, and Arthur L. Caplan. "Facing Up to Bioethical Decisions." <u>Issues in Science and Technology</u> Fall 1994: 75–80.

15. **Magazine Article with No Author**

> "Teaching for Millions." <u>Success</u> Oct. 1992: 10.

16. **Newspaper Article**
     Supply the following, in this order:

     a) author's name, if known;

     b) article title;

     c) name of the newspaper, underlined;

d) city where the newspaper is published, if not included in its name, in brackets after the name;

e) the date, beginning with the day, abbreviating the month, and the year, followed by a colon;

f) page number(s) where the article appears. If the newspaper has more than one section and each section is paginated separately, give both section and page number. If you gather material from a special edition of the newspaper, indicate that fact, as well.

> Kingsolver, Barbara. "A Pure, High Note of Anguish." <u>Los Angeles Times</u> 23 Sept. 2001: M1.

17.   Periodical Article that Does Not Appear on Consecutive Pages
Give only the first page number followed by a plus sign:

> Nye, Joseph S. Jr. "The Decline of America's Soft Power." <u>Foreign Affairs</u> May–June 2004: 16+.

Creating a **Works Cited** *List for Electronic Sources.*   As with other types of sources you cite in your research paper, your works cited entries for electronic sources should provide enough information that your reader can locate them. These sources pose a particular problem that books, periodicals, and other print media do not: They change frequently, with updates, move to new sites, or are even removed from the Internet. References to electronic works require slightly more and certainly different information than print sources require. Supply as much of the following information as is available, in this order:

a) author's name;

b) title of the work;

c) title of the site;

d) date the site was created or updated or the date of the posting;

e) if a posting, name of the listserv, newsgroup, or forum;

f) date that you accessed the material; and

g) URL of the site.

See the guidelines that follow for additional details. Keep in mind that electronic sources are not uniform in the amount of information they provide. A site may not incorporate page numbers, an author's name, reference markers such as paragraph or page breaks, or other conventional print references. You can supply only the information that is available at any particular site. Use common sense: Include as much information as you have available to you.

18.   Scholarly Project

> <u>Virtual London: Monuments and Dust</u>. Co-directors Michael Levenson, David Trotter, and Anthony Wohl. 4 Sept. 2008. U of Virginia. 12 Nov. 2004 <http://www.iath.virginia.edu/mhc>.

19. Professional Site

> The Camelot Project. Ed. Alan Lupack and Barbara Tepa Lupack. 3 Sept. 2004. U of Rochester. 4 Dec. 2008<http://www.lib.rochester. edu/camelot/cphome.stm>.

20. Article in a Reference Database

> "Susan Brownell Anthony." The Columbia Encyclopedia, 6th ed. Columbia UP. 2003. Online. 12 Apr. 2005 <http://www.bartleby. com/65/>.

21. Online Article

> Benfey, Christopher. "Better Late than Ever." Slate 18 Dec. 1996. 28 Nov. 2008 <http://slate.msn.com/Art/96–12–18/Art.asp>.

GUIDELINES FOR CREATING A *WORKS CITED* LIST FOR ELECTRONIC SOURCES

- **State the title of the work, following conventional punctuation rules.** For instance, use quotation marks for titles of poems, articles, or other short works within a scholarly project.
- **Do the same for the title of a posting, that is, the information in the subject line.** (Indicate that the source is an online posting.) If you cite a book, underline the title.
- **Name the author, editor, or compiler, if known, last name first.** Use the abbreviation "ed." following the name of an editor.
- **State the title of the scholarly project, database, periodical, or professional or personal site, underlined.** If the site gives no title, give a description of the site (e.g., Home page, web page, weblog, personal site) but do not underline it or enclose it in quotation marks.
- **Name the editor of the scholarly project or database, if the site gives the information.**
- **Supply any identifying information, such as version, volume, or issue number.**
- **Give the date the electronic publication was created or the date of its latest update.**
- **If you are citing a posting to a newsgroup, discussion group, or forum, give the date of the posting.**
- **For a posting to a discussion list or forum, give the name of the list or forum.**
- **If pages are numbered, give the number range or total number of pages.**
- **Supply the name of any institution or organization sponsoring or associated with the site.**
- **State the date when you accessed the source.**
- **Give the electronic address or URL of the service (not the URL of the article) in angle brackets.**
- **Place a period at the end of the entry.**

Online Sources of Full-text Articles.   Examples 22 to 25 illustrate citations from online services offering full-text articles, such as EBSCO, InfoTrac, Proquest, and Periodicals Abstract. The format remains essentially the same as for other electronic sources:

a) Name of author (if given);

b) title of article;

c) title of journal or magazine; volume and issue number if a journal;

d) date of publication;

e) page number(s) if given or *n. pag* (for no pagination);

f) name of the service, such as EBSCO, Infotrac, or LexisNexis;

g) name of the library or library system and the city and state (if necessary) where it is located;

h) date that you read the material; and

i) URL of the site, if you know it, or simply end with the date of access.

22. Article with Author Named, Scholarly Journal

> Taylor, Susan Lee. "Music Piracy: Differences in the Ethical Perceptions of Business Majors and Music Business Majors." <u>Journal of Education for Business</u> 79.5 (May-June 2004): 306+. Infotrac. 14 Nov 2008 <http://Infotrac-college.thomsonlearning.com>.

23. Article in Magazine

> Murphy, Victoria. "The Enemy Strikes Back." <u>Forbes</u> 24 Nov. 2003: 218. LexisNexis. 6 April 2008 <http://wweb.lexis-nexis.com/>.

24. Article with No Author Named

> "Yelling 'Fire.'" <u>New Republic</u> 3 April 2000: 9. EBSCO. University Lib. Stevens Point, WI. 6 April 2008<http://uwsp.edu/library>.

25. Article in Magazine from Personally Subscribed Service

If you access an article through a service that you subscribe to, such as America Online, give the information as usual, followed by the name of the service, the date you accessed it, and the keyword you used to retrieve the source.

> Kalb, Claudia. "The Life in a Cell; Stem-cell Researchers Find Fresh Hope for Curing Deadly Diseases—Along with New Controversies." <u>Newsweek International</u> 28 June 2004: 50. America Online. 12 October 2008. Keyword: Stem-cell research.

Miscellaneous Electronic Sources.

26. **Personal Site**

> Taylor, Andrew. Home page. 21 Sept. 2008, <http://www.thenet.co.uk/ ~hickafric/ataylor1.html>.

27. **Posting to a Discussion Group**

> Walton, Hilary. "New Pym Biography." Online posting. 2 Feb. 2008. Pym-1. 3 Feb. 2008 <pym-1@onelist.com>.

28. **E-Mail Message**

> Konrad, Lucas. "Antique Fire Trucks." E-mail to author. 11 Nov. 2008.

29. **Government Document**

> United States. Dept. of Labor Bureau of Labor Statistics. <u>Occupational Outlook Handbook, 2004–05</u> Edition. Medical Transcriptionists. Online. 18 Sept.2008, <http://www.bls.gov/oco/ocos271.htm>.

Works Cited *Formats for Sources Other than Books, Periodicals, and Electronic Sources.*

30. **Congressional Record**

> United States. Senate. <u>Transportation Systems for Alaskan Natural Gas</u>. 95th Cong., 1st sess. S-2411.Washington: GPO, 1977.
>
> United States. House. Committee on Public Works and Transportation. Subcommittee on Public Buildings and Grounds. To Prohibit Smoking in Federal Buildings. 103rd Cong., 1st sess. H. R. 881.Washington: GPO, 1993.

31. **Government Publication**

> United States. Dept. of Justice. <u>A Guide to Disability Rights</u>. Washington, DC: DOJ, May 2002.

32. **Lecture**

> Schilling, Brian. "The Role of First Responders in Medical Emergencies." Lecture at Whitko High School, 22 Dec. 2008.

33. **Letter**

> White, Jeremy. Letter to author. 1 Oct. 2008.

34. **Personal Interview**

> Yahi, Mourad. Personal interview. 10 Nov. 2008.

35. Reprint of an Article Provided by an Information Service

> Koop, C. Everett. "Life and Death and the Handicapped Newborn." Law & Medicine (Summer 1989): 101–113. Medical Science of Social Issues Resources Series. Boca Raton: SIRS, 1989. Art. 50.

36. Telephone Interview

> Yahi, Laurel. Telephone interview. 12 Jan. 2008.

37. Pamphlet

> Tweddle, Dominic. The Coppergate Helmet. York, UK: Cultural Resource Management, 1984.

38. Television Or Radio Program

> News program: 60 Minutes. ABC. WPTA, Fort Wayne, IN. 12 Dec. 2008.
>
> Series with episode titles: "Lights Out." ER. NBC. WNBC, Atlanta. 23 Sept. 1999.
>
> Radio program: On the Air, WOWO, Fort Wayne, IN. 12 Apr. 2008.

39. Sound Recording

To cite a compact disc, list first the aspect of the recording you want to emphasize: composer, conductor, or performer. Give that name first, then the title of the recording or selection, the manufacturer, and the year of issue (write *n.d.* if no date appears on the package or disc). If you are not using a compact disc, state the medium, such as audiotape or audiocassette. Do not enclose the name of the medium in italics or quotation marks.

> Uchida, Mitsuko, pianist. Piano Sonatas D, KV. 284, Sonata in B flat, KV. 570, and Rondo in D, KV. 485. By Wolfgang Amadeus Mozart. Philips, 1986.

40. Article in a Reference Book

Treat an entry in an encyclopedia or dictionary as you would an article in a collection, but do not cite the book's editor. If the article is signed, begin with the author's name, followed by the title of the entry; otherwise, begin with the title. For familiar reference books such as standard encyclopedias and dictionaries that are frequently updated and reissued, you need not give publication information. Just list the edition (if stated) and year of publication.

> Watkins, Calvert. "Indo-Europe and the Indo-Europeans." American Heritage Dictionary of the English Language. 3rd ed. 1991.

When citing less familiar books, give full publication information.

> Rose-Bond, Sherry, and Scott Bond. "Sherlockiana." Encyclopedia Mysteriosa: A Comprehensive Guide to the Art of Detection in

<u>Print, Film, Radio, and Television</u>. Ed. William L. DeAndrea. New York: Prentice, 1994. 327–330.

Sample Works Cited Pages.   Here are samples of an alphabetized list of sources. The first is drawn from the examples on the previous pages; the second is a selection of sources from Sam Cox's paper on German American loyalty in WWI, which uses both primary and secondary sources.

Cox 28

Works Cited

Annan, Kofi. "Development Without Borders." <u>Harvard International Review</u> 23.2 (Summer 2001): 84.

Benfey, Christopher. "Better Late than Ever." <u>Slate</u> 18 Dec. 1996. 28 Nov. 2008 <http://slate.msn.com/ Art/96-12-18/Art.asp>.

Bowden, Mark. "The Lessons of Abu Ghraib." <u>Atlantic Monthly</u> July-Aug. 2004:33-36.

Kingsolver, Barbara. "A Pure, High Note of Anguish." <u>Los Angeles Times</u> 23 Sept. 2001: M1.

Leonardi, Susan J. <u>Dangerous by Degrees: Women at Oxford and the Somerville College Novelists</u>. New Brunswick: Rutgers UP, 1989.

Murphy, Victoria. "The Enemy Strikes Back." <u>Forbes</u> 24 Nov. 2003: 218. Online. InfoTrac College Edition. 23 April 2008 <http://Infotrac-college .thomsonlearning.com>.

Nye, Joseph S. Jr. "The Decline of America's Soft Power" <u>Foreign Affairs</u> May-June 2004: 16+.

<u>60 Minutes</u>. ABC. WPTA, Fort Wayne, IN. 12 Dec. 2008.

Spacks, Patricia Meyer. "Sisters." <u>Fetter'd or Free?: British Women Novelists</u>, 1670-1815. Eds. Mary Anne Schofield and Cecilia Macheski. Athens, OH: Ohio UP, 1986. 136-151.

United States. Dept. of Justice. <u>A Guide to Disability Rights</u>. Washington, DC: DOJ, May 2002.

Yahi, Mourad. Personal interview. 10 Nov. 2008.

Cox 29

Works Cited

"The Alarm Against Spies." <u>Literary Digest</u> 21 July
    1917: 13-14.

"Am Dienstag kommen die deutschen Zeitungen unter
    den Arm des Censors." <u>Indianapolis Spottvogel</u>
    14 October 1917: 1.

Brocke, Frank. "'We had to be so careful' A Farmer's
    Recollections of Anti-German Sentiment in World
    War I." <u>History Matters: The U.S. Survey Course
    on the Web</u>. 31 March 2006. 30 Oct. 2008 <http://
    historymatters.gmu.edu/d/3>.

"A Call to German Americans to 'Organize.'"
    <u>Literary Digest</u> 50 9 January 1915: 42-43.

"Deutsche Kundgebung in New York." <u>Indianapolis
    Spottvogel</u> 9 August 1914: 4.

"German-American Loyalty." <u>Literary Digest</u> 50 29 May
    1915: 1262-64.

Heinrichs, Rudolf. "A Family Letter." <u>Atlantic
    Monthly</u> 120 (1917): 739-45.

"Der Kampf für Erhaltung der persönlichen Freiheit
    ist der Kampf der Deutschen in Amerika."
    <u>Indianapolis</u> Spottvogel16 August 1914: 17.

"Malicious Anti-German Attacks." <u>Indianapolis
    Spottvogel</u> 16 August 1914: 9.

Ramsey, Paul. "The War against German-American
    Culture: The Removal of German Language
    Instruction from the Indianapolis Schools,
    1917-1919." <u>Indiana Magazine of History</u> 95.4
    (2002): 285-303.

Witten, Johann. Letters to Christoph Witten, 3
    December 1914, 5 December 1915, 9 September 1919,
    18 September 1920. Trans. Susan Vogel. <u>News from
    the Land of Freedom: German Immigrants Write</u>

```
                                                    Cox 30

    Home. Eds Walter Kamphoefner, Wolfgang Helbich, and
        Ulrike Sommer. Ithaca: Cornell University Press,
        1991. 278-83.
```

ASSEMBLING THE PARTS OF A RESEARCH PAPER

In general, putting a research paper together is not so different from writing any other kind of paper. Following the guidelines explained in Chapter 2 on the writing process, you will have the same components in a longer paper with sources as you do in a shorter one. You will have an introduction, though it is likely to be longer than in other writing assignments. You must have a thesis statement or clearly evident central idea. Your paper as a whole and individual paragraphs within it must be organized and fully developed. Sentences must be crafted grammatically and imaginatively, and your language should be idiomatic, colorful, and clear. You must provide transitions between points within paragraphs and from paragraph to paragraph throughout the paper, and you must have a conclusion that brings the paper to a satisfactory finish. Of course a major difference between the research paper and other papers you will write for your college classes is that research papers incorporate the works of others. Thus, you will have in-text citations for all references to your sources and a works cited list of all sources referenced in your paper. Your instructor may also ask you to include an outline of your paper.

The following sections will take you through the process of putting together your final paper. They address the following components:

- Title page or first page of paper without a separate title page
- Pagination and spacing
- Tables, figures, and illustrations
- Outline page
- Introductory paragraph and body of the paper
- Conclusion
- Works cited page
- The complete research paper

Title Page.   Although MLA style does not require a separate title page, many instructors ask for it. If your instructor requires a title page, follow these guidelines:

- Center your title about one-third to halfway down the page.
- Do not underline your title, enclose it in quotation marks, capitalize every letter, or place a period after it.

- Capitalize the first letter of every important word in the title.
- Underneath the title, about halfway down the page, write your name, centered on the line.
- Drop farther down the page and center on separate lines, double spaced, your instructor's name; the course name, number, and section; and the date.

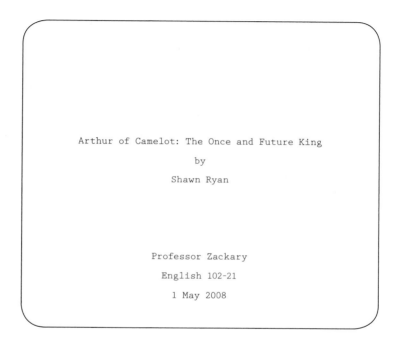

```
Arthur of Camelot: The Once and Future King

                        by

                   Shawn Ryan




             Professor Zackary

              English 102-21

               1 May 2008
```

First Page of a Research Paper with a Separate Title Page. If your instructor requires a separate title page, follow these guidelines for the first text page of your paper:

- Type your last name and the number 1 in the upper right-hand corner, one half inch from the top of the page, flush with the right margin.
- Drop down two inches from the top of the page and center your title, exactly as it appears on your title page.
- Do not underline your title, enclose it in quotation marks, capitalize every letter, or place a period after it.
- Capitalize the first letter of every important word in the title.
- Double-space and begin the body of your paper.

> Ryan 1
>
> Arthur of Camelot: The Once and Future King
>
> North and west the wind blew beneath the
> morning sun, over endless miles of rolling grass
> and far scattered thickets . . . [and] Dragonmount,
> where the dragon had died, and with him, some said,
> the Age of Legend—where prophecy said he would be
> born again. (Jordan 13)

First Page of a Research Paper without a Separate Title Page.   If your instructor does not require a separate title page, follow these guidelines:

- Type your last name and the number 1 in the upper right-hand corner, one-half inch from the top of the page, flush with the right margin.
- Place your name, your instructor's name, the course title and section, and the date in the upper left-hand corner, one inch from the top of the paper and flush with the left margin.
- Double-space between each line.
- Double-space below the date and center your title.
- Do not underline your title, enclose it in quotation marks, capitalize every letter, or place a period after it.
- Capitalize the first letter of every important word in the title.
- Double-space again and begin the body of your paper.

> Hayes 1
>
> Nate Hayes
>
> Professor White
>
> English 102-8
>
> 15 April 2008
>
> A Positive Alternative to Cloning
>
> Since Dr. Ian Wilmut's successful cloning of
> a sheep, the debate over how far medical science
> should be allowed to go has grown increasingly

Hayes 2

heated. Some people are completely opposed to any

kind of experimentation that involves genetic

manipulation or the development of procedures that

some consider should be reserved only for God.

Pagination and Spacing.   The entire paper should be double-spaced, with each page numbered in the upper right-hand corner, one-half inch from the top and flush with the right margin. MLA style requires that pagination begin with page 1 and recommends that you include your last name before the page number.

Tables, Figures, and Illustrations.   Place tables, figures, and illustrations close to the parts of the paper that they relate to. A table is labeled *Table*, given an Arabic number, and captioned. This information is capitalized as you would a title, placed above the table, and typed flush with the left-hand margin on separate lines. Place the name of the source and any additional comments directly below the table, as illustrated here:

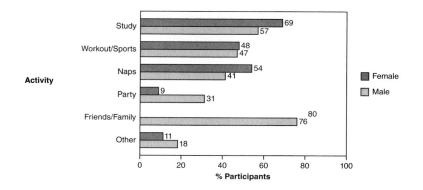

Male vs. Females: Free Time Activities
Survey conducted by Margo Borgen, Morris Boyd, Maicha Chang, and Kelly Kassien, University of Wisconsin–Stevens Point, May 2008.

Visual images such as photographs, charts, maps, and line drawings are labeled *Figure* (usually abbreviated *Fig.*), assigned an Arabic number, and given a title or caption. A label and title or caption are positioned below the illustration and have the same margins as the text. The following illustrates correct handling of a visual image:

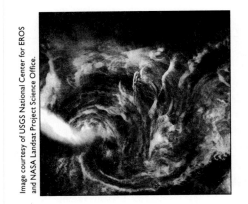

Image courtesy of USGS National Center for EROS and NASA Landsat Project Science Office.

Fig. I   *Whirlpool in the Air: a spinning formation of ice, clouds, and low-lying fog off the eastern coast of Greenland*

Outline Page.   If your instructor requires a formal outline, place it immediately after the title page. Your instructor will tell you how detailed your outline should be, but follow these basic directions in most cases:

- Begin your outline with the thesis statement of your paper.
- Double-space between all lines of the outline.
- Use uppercase roman numerals (I, II, III) for each major division of your outline and capital letters (A, B, C) for each subdivision under each major division.
- If you find it necessary to further subdivide, use Arabic numerals (1, 2, 3) under capital letters and lowercase letters (a, b, c) under Arabic numerals.
- Do not number the outline page unless it runs to two or more pages. If your outline is two or more pages long, number all pages after the first in lower-case roman numerals (ii, iii, iv), placed in the upper right-hand corner, one-half inch from the top of the page and flush with the right margin.
- End with a statement summarizing your conclusion.

Here are outline pages from two student papers, the first with a fairly brief outline, the second with more detail.

Outline

<u>Thesis:</u> An examination of some of the research on Arthurian legend suggests that the evidence supports the theory that a man like Arthur did exist.

I.   The birth of Arthur

    A.   The legend

    B.   Evidence of Tintagel

II.   The places and people most important to Arthur

    A.   Camelot

    B.   Glastonbury Abbey

    C.   Lancelot and Perceval

III.   Arthur's impact on society

    A.   His image

    B.   The difference between the man and the legend

<u>Conclusion</u>: Arthur's existence as a man is indeterminable, but Arthur's presence in the minds and hearts of people everywhere gives credence to his existence as a leader of nations.

Outline

<u>Thesis</u>: Parents, educators, and reading experts disagree on the issue of whether phonics instruction is beneficial to beginning readers.

I.   Introduction

    A.   Rudolph Flesch's observations

    B.   National Assessment of Education Progress reports

II.   Background

    A.   Introduction to phonics

　　　　B.　Failure of schools to teach reading

　　　　C.　Regna Lee Wood

　III.　Phonics instruction

　　　　A.　How phonics works

　　　　B.　Problems associated with the teaching of
　　　　　　phonics

　　　　C.　Factors associated with teaching phonics

　　　　　　1.　Direct

　　　　　　2.　Systemic

　　　　　　3.　Intensive

　IV.　Negative effects of phonics instruction

　　　　A.　Lack of information and knowledge

　　　　B.　Hooked on Phonics

　　V.　Positive effects of phonics instruction

　　　　A.　Present-day improvements over early
　　　　　　techniques

　　　　B.　Myths about phonics dispelled

　　　　C.　Andrew Schuster's story

　VI.　Jeanne Sternlicht Chall's research

　　　　A.　History of research

　　　　B.　The Great Debate

Conclusion: The debate over the benefits of phonics

remains unresolved.

Introductory Paragraphs and Body of the Paper.　　As for any other kind of writing assignment, begin with an introduction that provides background information that clearly portrays the topic of your paper or the direction your argument will take, or that in some way sets the stage for what follows. State your thesis or central idea early in the paper. If your topic is controversial, explain the nature of the controversy. Once you have introduced your topic sufficiently, begin developing your argument. Here are the opening pages, with marginal notes, of Nate Hayes' paper, which he expanded from his synthesis paper with his instructor's permission (See "Hello Dolly" in Chapter 6). Following that are the opening paragraphs from Sam Cox's paper "Proving Their Loyalty During World War I: German-Americans Confronted with Anti-German Fervor and Suspicion," which uses both primary and secondary sources.

Nate's introduction provides a context for his topic and states the nature of the controversy over cloning and stem-cell research.

Complete bibliographic information for the Pethokoukis source is given on Nate's works cited page.

Nate's thesis states his position: he is opposed to further research on cloning but believes that stem-cell research should continue. Readers can expect to see a development in the rest of the paper of each of these points as well as supporting evidence from various authorities in support of his position.

Hayes 1

Nate Hayes

Professor White

English 102-8

15 April 2008

A Positive Alternative to Cloning

Since Dr. Ian Wilmut's successful cloning of a sheep, the debate over how far medical science should be allowed to go has grown increasingly heated. A very promising development lies in stem cell research, which could lead to developments that could "alter mankind in some astounding ways" (Pethokoukis 560). Such potential has many people worried about the extent to which human genetic makeup should be modified or amended. Some people are completely opposed to any kind of experimentation that involves genetic manipulation or the development of procedures that some consider should be reserved only for God. Scientists and medical researchers, though, are excited about the potential for previously unimaginable achievements in the prevention and cure of debilitating or fatal diseases. The controversy centers on the questions of how far science should go and who should control the technology. A review of the arguments for and against stem-cell research leads me to conclude that, although there needs to be a long, serious national debate on the subject, scientists should stop short of cloning humans but be allowed to continue their research on stem cells.

What exactly is cloning? According to the National Bioethics Advisory Commission (NBAC), the

Nate provides the acronym for the long name of the advisory commission and then uses it whenever he quotes from the commission again. Nate gives only the page number because he has mentioned the name of the source in his text. The ellipses points (three spaced periods) indicate that he has omitted some words from the original sentence.

Nate is using general knowledge here and does not need to document his statements.

Nate combines a direct quotation and a paraphrase. The parenthetical citation tells the source and the page number on which the quoted and paraphrased material is found.

Paragraph 3 is phrased entirely in Nate's own words. He has done enough reading on his topic to understand some of the questions and to supply his own responses to them. The paragraph consists of general knowledge that Nate has acquired and thus does not require any documentation.

Hayes 2

word "in its most simple and strict sense . . ." refers to a precise genetic copy of a molecule, cell, plant, animal or human being" (13). This technique of cloning used by Dr. Wilmut's team to create Dolly is called somatic cell nuclear transplantation. Sex cells contain only one set of 23 chromosomes, whereas body cells house two sets for a total of 46. When the parent's sperm fertilizes the egg, 46 chromosomes establish a human. During nuclear transfer cloning, the fertilization step is skipped because "the nucleus is removed from an egg and replaced with the diploid nucleus of a somatic [body] cell" (NBAC 15). Therefore, there is only one true parent, and the clone will be the exact genetic copy of that parent.

The controversy over cloning involves both ethical and religious issues. Should humans "play God"? What if the process were used to create exact copies of evil people? What potential dreadful side effects might develop in cloned humans? What possible reasons can there be for wanting to clone humans? The suggested uses for cloned humans usually focus on replacing loved ones who have died, particularly young children who have died tragically, either from illness or accident. The idea is that cloning the dead child would in effect replace the child that died. However, that new child would be a real person, with thoughts and feelings unique to him or her. The new child would only look like the dead child and have identical genetic material. He or she would grow up in an entirely different environment, even if the parents attempted to recreate the identical

Nate does not need to give a citation at the end of the first sentence in paragraph 4 because he has named his authority, and his second sentence clearly indicates that he is still paraphrasing from that same authority. The parenthetical citation gives the page number.

Hayes 3

conditions in which the dead child was nurtured. It would simply be impossible to recreate those conditions. Furthermore, would the child not be damaged psychologically if she knew that she was replacing another child? There are simply too many unexplored questions associated with cloning.

One big question has to do with the high failure rate of cloning. Despite having been responsible for the first cloned mammal, Dr. Wilmut is very conservative in his views of the wisdom of carrying on full speed with cloning research because of its unreliability. In "Dolly's False Legacy," he identifies some of the likely problems a cloned human might have. For instance, Wilmut warns of the inefficiency of cloning, noting the high death rate in fetuses and live births when cloning is used in animal tests. This fact leads him to suggest that "these failure rates surely render unthinkable the notion of applying such treatment to humans" (564). Indeed, one of the chief difficulties with cloning is its high failure rate. Rick Weiss cites one example of this difficulty in his article "Failure in Monkeys Hints at Human Cloning Snags": "Despite having tried 135 times, researchers in Oregon have 'utterly failed' to clone a single monkey"

Nate introduces his direct quotation. The colon is used because both the introductory statement and the quotation are complete sentences.

(2). These failures are particularly significant because of the genetic similarity between monkeys and humans. The implications for success in cloning humans is dismal indeed, much to the delight of those who disapprove of it.

As with human cloning, research on stem cells is riddled with controversy. Here, though, the controversy is aimed at research on embryonic

The information about James D. Watson establishes his credentials. Nate's combination of both paraphrase and direct quotations serve to smoothly integrate source material into his text.

Hayes 4

stem cells as opposed to adult stem cell research: "Hailed by some as a cure for deadly disease, derided by others as the destruction of human life, embryonic stem cells are at the center of a heated debate over science, religion and politics around the globe" (Kalb 50). Embryonic stem cells are those that have not yet specialized. Scientists believe that such cells could be isolated and grown into "healthy replacement tissue" that could then be used in humans to cure just about any ailment known to humans (Lemonick 89). The healthy tissue would be surgically implanted into the body, replacing or repairing damaged tissue. Research in this area holds great promises.

James D. Watson, Nobel-Prize-winning co-discoverer of the double helix configuration of DNA, is a strong supporter of research on germ-line genetic manipulations in pursuit of what he calls "'superpersons'" or "gene-bettered children" (563).

This word is in both single and double quotation marks because it is in quotation marks in the original article.

Cox 1

Sam Cox

Professor Aaron

Humanities 310-01

12 April 2008

Proving Their Loyalty During World War I:

German-Americans Confronted with Anti-German

Fervor and Suspicion

In May 1915, a <u>Milwaukee Abendpost</u> editorial

voiced the unsettling feelings that German-Americans

Cox 2

were experiencing in the early months of the
First World War and that would intensify as the
war dragged on. Supportive of the Fatherland in
the European conflict, German-Americans found
themselves at odds with an English-speaking
majority and Anglo-oriented government. After the
United States entered the war on the side of the
Triple Entente, many German-Americans were faced
with the agonizing choice of whom to support. A
review of the Indianapolis Telegraph und Tribüne
and the Indianapolis Spottvogel leads to the
conclusion that German-Americans unwaveringly
supported their new homeland in the war in nearly
all instances.

Nevertheless, the loyalty and trustworthiness
of German-Americans was questioned by many in
the public. The government implemented certain
measures intended to track the activity of the
German population in the United States and censor
their publications. German culture came under
popular and official attack throughout the country
as German-Americans experienced intense pressure
to Americanize. German-Americans responded by
trying to prove their loyalty to the United States.
They participated in Liberty Loan war bond drives
and discontinued the use of the German language.
As a result, the influence of Germans on American
life faded after World War I. German-Americans were
forced to decide whether their loyalties lay with
Germany, the land of their heritage, or with the
United States, their adopted homeland and enemy
of Germany. Finding their loyalty questioned all
around them, German-Americans sacrificed their
culture, language, and unique identity in the

Cox 3

face of overwhelming pressure to become true
Americans and prove their dedication to their
new homeland.

Conclusion.   Recall from Chapter 2 that the conclusion brings the paper to a satisfying end, no matter what its length. Whether the assignment is a 500-word essay or a 5,000-word research paper, readers should not be left with unanswered questions and should have a sense that the writer has fully explained, argued, developed, or illustrated the central idea or thesis. A good conclusion forcefully reiterates the introduction, reinforces the writer's connection with the audience, looks to the future, reemphasizes the central argument, or suggests a course of action. Here is the conclusion to Sam Cox's paper. Notice how his conclusion reinforces points made in the opening paragraphs above but does so without repeating them word for word.

German-Americans bore an unfounded attack on
their language and culture during World War I.
Efforts to wipe out their language, their cultural
establishments, their newspapers, and their ethnic
identity were so powerful in that era of suspicion,
threats, and violence, that most German-Americans
succumbed to the unyielding pressure. They changed
the names of clubs, shut down newspapers, bought
Liberty Bonds, and stopped speaking German. Done
willingly but often reluctantly, these actions
demonstrated their loyalty to their new homeland
during the time when their loyalty was demanded
most. Despite their deep affection for their
old Fatherland and the knowledge that they were
surrendering much of their cultural identity,

German-Americans wanted to prove that they were
steadfast patriots of their new homeland of freedom
and prosperity.

Works Cited Page.   The works cited pages for Nate Hayes' research paper on
stem-cell research illustrate how to cite some of the most common sources used in
undergraduate research papers, including books, essays in a collection, and periodical articles from online full-text sources.

Hayes 14

Works Cited

Ackley, Katherine Anne, ed. <u>Perspectives on
    Contemporary Issues: Readings Across the
    Disciplines</u>, 4th ed. Boston: Wadsworth Cengage
    Learning, 2006.

Cherfas, Jeremy. <u>Man-Made Life</u>. New York: Pantheon
    Books, 1982.

Kalb, Claudia. "The Life in a Cell: Stem-cell
    Researchers Find Fresh Hope for Curing Deadly
    Diseases—Along with New Controversies." <u>Newsweek
    International</u> 28 June 2004: 50. America Online.
    22 Nov. 2008. Keyword: Stem-cell research.

Lemonick, Michale D. "Tomorrow's Tissue Factor."
    <u>Time</u> 11 Jan. 1999: 89. Online. InfoTrac College
    Edition. 22 Nov. 2008 <http://Infotrac-college
    .thomsonlearning.com>.

Merzer, Martin. "A Human Clone Won't Be Carbon
    Copy, Experts Say." <u>Houston Chronicle</u> 28 Dec.
    1998: 8. 14 Nov. 2008. EBSCO. University Library.
    Stevens Point, WI <http://library.uwsp.edu>.

Hayes 15

National Bioethics Advisory Commission (NBAC).

Cloning Human Beings. Rockville, MD: NBAC, 1997.

Pethokoukis, James. "Our Biotech Bodies, Ourselves."

Ackley 559-561.

Watson, James D. "All for the Good." Ackley 561-563.

Weiss, Rick. "Failure in Monkeys Hints at Human

Cloning Snags." Washington Post 29 Jan. 1999:

A02. Online. 14 Nov. 2008. EBSCO. University

Library. Stevens Point, WI <http://library.uwsp.

edu>.

---. "Human Embryo Cloned, Korean Researchers Say."

Denver Post 17 Dec. 1998: A01. 14 Nov. 2008.

EBSCO. University Library. Stevens Point, WI

<http://library.uwsp.edu>.

Wilmut, Ian. "Dolly's False Legacy." Ackley 564-566.

STUDENT RESEARCH PAPER USING MLA STYLE

The following student research paper implements MLA style guidelines for incorporating and documenting source material as explained in Chapters 6 and 7.

Anderson 1

Erin D. Anderson

Professor Heather A. Schilling

English 150-2

12 June 2008

The Electoral College: Time for a Change

The electoral college system, which has been in

place for over 200 years, is one of the most widely

debated of all governmental policies; in fact,

over 850 proposals for its change or abolishment
have been offered in Congress (Vile 109). However,
only two of these reforms have ever been enacted.
Questions are once again being raised concerning
whether another alternative would better suit
modern America or if reform would do more harm
than good. People have many contrasting opinions
about the popular direct voting proposal, which
would abolish the Electoral College altogether.
In light of the year 2000 election, which placed
in the White House a candidate who had half a
million fewer popular votes than his opponent, the
electoral college system should be abolished.

The electoral college system has its origins in
the Constitutional Convention that took place in
Philadelphia in 1787. The Framers themselves were
ambivalent when it came to how the President should
be elected, which made the process of determining
how to choose the President a complicated one.
In fact, Pennsylvania delegate James Wilson
declared that the presidential selection issue was
"'the most difficult of all [. . .]'" of those
discussed, one that "'has greatly divided the
house, and will also divide people out of doors'"
(qtd. in Sayre and Parris 23). Proposals were made
for election by Congress, election by the people,
and election by state governments (Sayre and Parris
23). However, as the issue remained unsolved and
the end of the Convention was nearing, the Brearly
Committee on Unfinished Parts suggested the
electoral college system.

The following very brief summary of this
system was adapted from Shlomo Slonim's "Electoral

Anderson 3

College": Instead of a direct popular election, this system provided for indirect election of the President through a college of electors, in which each state receives a number of electoral votes based on its total number of Senators and Representatives. On the first Tuesday in November of election years, the general population technically casts ballots for the electors that represent their choice for President and Vice President. The electors themselves are individuals "pledged to support a particular candidate's election in the electoral college" (543)

Popular vote totals are used to determine which party slate will become that state's electors. On the Monday following the second Wednesday in December, the electors meet in their respective state capitals and cast their ballots for President and Vice President. A majority of the 538 electoral votes is needed in order to be selected or the matter is put up to vote in the House of Representatives. Under this system, "Popular will is expressed state by state, rather than by a national referendum" (Slonin 543-544). An added feature of the electoral college system is the winner-takes-all unit rule system.

Although the Constitution leaves the choice of how the states' electoral votes are cast up to the states themselves, every state except Maine and Nebraska has chosen over time to award all of a state's electoral votes to the winner of the popular vote (Cronin xii).

Michael Glennon proposes in his comprehensive guide to the electoral college that the debate

Anderson 4

by the Framers of the Constitution about
presidential selection was rooted in a disagreement
on two essential issues: first, the extent and
view of democracy to be used in determining the
winner, and second, the degree of federalism to be
considered (6). These two issues continue to lie at
the center of the debate. On one hand are those who
desire the abolishment of the electoral college;
in their view, direct democracy, where the will
of the people is directly translated into policy,
is the key principal. On the other hand, those
who support the Electoral College as it is believe
that federalism is of ultimate importance and that
democracy is still supported through the electoral
college, but in a different way.

Many people vehemently argue in support of
the electoral college system. As explained in
William C. Kimberling's The Electoral College,
the main arguments center on two requirements
that are placed on candidates in order to be
chosen President. First, winning a majority in
the electoral college means that the candidate
has "*sufficient* popular vote to [. . .] govern,"
even if his/her support is not the majority of the
voting population. Secondly, the votes the winner
has secured must be "sufficiently *distributed* across
the country" (7). According to Kimberling, these two
requirements together ensure that whoever is chosen
will be able to handle governing the nation (7).

A second strong argument used in support of the
Electoral College is that it promotes the important
Constitutional concept of federalism. Judith A.
Best, distinguished professor of political science

Anderson 5

at State University of New York at Cortland,
refers to federalism as one of the two essential
principles of the "constitutional solar system
[. . .] around which everything else [. . .]
rotates" (65). She believes that this federal
principal, based on state-by-state victories and
therefore, electoral votes, provides for a better
overall assessment of the strengths and weaknesses
of the competing candidates than a direct popular
vote would because it ensures that the winning
candidate has "broad, cross-national support"
(67). This requirement of broad support promotes
the pulling together of "coalitions of states
and regions," rather than the candidate's having
support just from specific regions of the country
(Kimberling 12).

In response to those who claim that the
electoral college is undemocratic, Best points
out that "politics and mathematics are two very
different disciplines" (18). Those who support
abolishing the electoral college in favor of direct
election claim that numbers themselves determine
who the President should be. However, Best believes
that in a political decision as important as
electing a President, the "will of the people"
is not necessarily the same as the "will of the
majority" (19). She points out that one of the basic
principals of the Constitution is majority rule
with minority consent; in her view, the Electoral
College better provides for the minority.

However, over time many have expressed
opposition to the indirect and complex electoral
college system. Their main criticism is the

possibility of a "minority President," that is, one
elected without the majority of the popular vote
but with a majority of the electoral votes.

Other criticisms leveled against the electoral
college system include the "so-called faithless
electors," the winner-takes-all unit rule, and the
possibility of decreased voter turnout (Kimberling
9). In addition, critics say that the electoral
college does not accurately reflect the national
popular will and that rural states are over
represented in the current system because each state
receives two electoral votes regardless of size plus
those attributed to population (Kimberling 9).

In The Electoral College Primer 2000, Lawrence
D. Longley and Neal R. Peirce explain their
opposition to the electoral college system. They
assert that in an "advanced democratic nation,
where [. . .] popular choice is the most deeply
ingrained of government principles," a voting
system where popular votes don't necessarily mean
electoral votes is "irrational" (132). In addition,
they point out that even if a direct popular vote
were to choose a candidate who proved less than
ideal in the long run, the candidate would still be
the choice of the people (132). Longley and Peirce
also explain the "faithless elector" issue. The
Constitution nowhere requires the chosen electors
to vote for the winner of the popular vote.
However, in the history of the Electoral College,
only nine votes of the over 20,000 cast have been
known to go "'against instructions'" (113).

Critics of the electoral college system see the
2000 election as a prime example of the minority

Anderson 7

President criticism. The election of governor George Bush by the Electoral College despite Vice President Al Gore's winning the popular vote (50,996,582 to Bush's 50,456,062) is seen by many as a problem. Because of the complicated nature of the electoral college system and what many see as its drawbacks, several reform proposals have been brought to Congress. These proposals generally fall into four categories: the district system, the proportional system, the automatic plan, and the direct popular election. Wisconsin's Role in Electing the President describes the four main Electoral College alternatives. The district system would eliminate the unit rule and provide that two of each state's electoral votes would be determined by popular vote, while the rest would be allocated on a district-by-district basis. The proportional system would divide the state's electoral votes in "direct proportion to the popular vote" of the state. The automatic plan would simply eliminate the role of the actual elector and provide that the electoral votes would automatically be signed to the winner of the popular election. Finally, direct popular election would abolish the Electoral College altogether, instead requiring a "nationwide popular vote," with the winner receiving at least 40% of the votes (Watchke 12).

The direct voting alternative is by far the most popular proposal alternative. However, this alternative has its own set of pros and cons which must be evaluated before making a judgment about which presidential election system should be in place.

Proponents of a direct voting system have several arguments as to why a direct popular vote would be preferable to the electoral college system. They argue that it provide an increased and more direct democracy for the people, an increased authority for the President, and a simpler, one-person-one-vote system that would eliminate the intermediate electoral college in the Presidential selection procedure. In addition, they feel that the electoral college system is out of date because America is faced with a different set of circumstances and challenges than when it was created.

Those in favor of direct election believe this system is the only way to achieve a true democracy. Former First Lady Hillary Clinton has expressed her belief that abolition of the electoral college is important in a democracy; in fact, she said that she would "be willing to co-sponsor a measure to abolish the electoral college" (Geraghty). Another argument is that a popular vote would give more authority to the President because the vote totals would be a direct communication of the will of the people, rather than an indirect translation that takes electoral votes into account (Sayre and Parris 69). Thirdly, in the words of Yale Law School professor Akhil Amar, the Electoral College is a "brilliant 18th-century device that cleverly solved [. . .] 18th-century problems." However, he sees that "'[a]s we approach the 21st century, we confront a different cluster of problems, and our constitutional machinery [. . .] does not look so brilliant'" (qtd. in Sung). Finally, those in

Anderson 9

defense of direct election often cite public
opinion surveys that reflect popular support
for abolishment of the electoral college. One
such survey, conducted by the trusted Gallup
Organization and released on November 16, 2000,
revealed that 61% of Americans would like to see
direct popular vote in place of the electoral
college system ("Americans Have Long Questioned").

Direct voting also seems to have its drawbacks,
however. Its opponents claim that direct election
would lead to manipulation in campaigns,
jeopardize the two-party system with a multitude of
candidates, cause even more runoffs and recounts,
and sacrifice the federalist system currently in
place.

Curtis Gans, director of the Committee for the
Study of the American Electorate, suggests that a
direct popular vote system would greatly change the
way campaigns are run. With such a system, where
the goal is to win over the masses rather than
focus on groups of states all around the nation, he
believes even more of the election funds would go
toward mass television advertising, leading to the
"'handing [of the] American presidential campaign
to whatever media adviser could outslick the
other'" (qtd. in Sung). This, in turn, would lead
to increased "'opponent bashing,'" a factor that
already has been leading citizens to "'tune out
politics'" (qtd. in Sung).

According to Wallace Sayre and Judith Parris,
direct elections, especially those including
a popular vote runoff provision, would tend to
"encourage a multitude of minor party candidacies"

Anderson 10

because, depending on the proposal, these minor party candidates would not need to win entire states in order to receive part of the vote (73). They believe, therefore, that many candidates would tend to run as "spoilers," with the goal of forcing a runoff. In order to protect the two-party system, which is an important basis of American government, they insist that the electoral college system must stay in place.

Judith Best reflects on the increase in recounts and runoffs that she feels would follow from a direct voting system: "If the advocates of direct nonfederal election stuck with a majority requirement for victory, nearly every general election would be turned into a national primary followed by a runoff election" (57). She believes that with the lifting of the state division, focusing only on the national vote, "a recount of every ballot box in the country" could be necessary, because recounts and challenges in one state would no longer be limited in scope, but could demand a national result questioning (57).

Thomas Cronin brings up an important point that makes one question whether the current system should be abolished. He argues that while there are some imperfections in the electoral college system, no one can be sure of the effects of abandoning it in place of a direct vote (viii). President John F. Kennedy himself opposed abolishment, explaining that "'[i]f it is proposed to change the balance of power of one of the elements of the [governmental] solar system, it is necessary to consider the others'" (qtd. in Glennon 76). Therefore, because

Anderson 11

changes would undoubtedly have a holistic effect on the intricate political system, it is necessary to carefully weigh this decision.

After weighing arguments for both the current electoral college system and the direct voting alternative, Cronin's position makes the most sense. Although the electoral college system may be complex and does have its imperfections, there is no way of knowing just what other effects and problems may result from its abolishment. Even in light of the 2000 presidential election, in which President George W. Bush did not win the majority of the popular vote, I see the electoral college system as a way to moderate the will of the people in general with the good of the government. Furthermore, a very strong argument is that the system ensures that the candidate who is victorious has proven that he or she has secured enough voter support to warrant the presidential office. It is very important that the winner has both a sufficient popular vote and a sufficient distribution of votes across the country, a fact that he or she demonstrates by securing enough states' electoral votes to win the election.

However, the current electoral college system could better represent the population in general. Adopting the relatively small change that Maine and Nebraska have made to their system, which selects two electoral votes a popular vote and determines the remainder of the electoral votes by Congressional district, would help to improve the system. This would not be such an extreme change as abolishing the electoral college altogether,

yet it would represent the popular vote more
closely because of the district divisions. Thus,
the benefits of the current electoral college
would almost entirely remain in place, while those
who want the election to more closely reflect the
popular will would also be appeased.

The 2000 presidential election was an anomalous
one, and the extremely close margins of support,
both in the popular vote and the Electoral College
count, caused an increase in discussion about the
electoral college system. One even sees divisions
among party lines regarding support for or
opposition against this system. However, one must
note that the conflict in the 2000 election was not
completely rooted in the Electoral College itself.
Many believe that the recounts and challenges
would still have taken place even with a system of
direct election.

In conclusion, Michael Glennon's comment in
When No Majority Rules seems particularly apt when
he reflects on the essential dilemma in electing
America's President: "Just as Winston Churchill
concluded about democracy, the electoral college is
probably the worst possible method of choosing the
President—except for all the others" (3). Indeed,
there is no perfect solution that will satisfy
both those desiring to elect a president by popular
vote and those who support the electoral college.
However, weighing both the pros and cons in the
arguments over the current system, it is clear
that the electoral college should be kept in place,
though modified slightly to better represent the
people. Such a compromise would reflect what was

Anderson 13

at the very heart of the Constitution when it was
established over two centuries ago and what will
carry this country and its citizens through the
coming centuries.

Works Cited

"Americans Have Long Questioned Electoral College."
    Gallup Poll Releases. 16 Nov 2000. 29 Nov. 2008
    <http://www.gallup.com/poll/releases/ pr001116.
    asp>.

Best, Judith A. The Choice of the People?: Debating
    the Electoral College. Lanham, MD: Rowman &
    Littlefield, 1996.

Cronin, Thomas E. "The Electoral College
    Controversy." Foreword. Best vii-xxv.

Geraghty, Jim. "Do Elections Need New Rules?"
    Policy.com News and Events: Daily Briefing.
    22 Nov. 2000. 29 Nov. 2008 <http://www.policy.com/
    news/dbrief/dbriefarc834.asp>.

Glennon, Michael J. When No Majority Rules: The
    Electoral College and Presidential Succession.
    Washington, D.C.: Congressional Quarterly, 1992.

Kimberling, William C. The Electoral College.
    Washington, D.C.: National Clearinghouse on
    Election Administration, Federal Election
    Commission, May 1992.

Longley, Lawrence D., and Neal R. Peirce. The
    Electoral College Primer 2000. New Haven, CT:
    Yale UP, 1999.

Power, Max S. "Logic and Legitimacy: On
    Understanding the Electoral College Controversy."
    Ed. Donald R. Matthews. Perspectives on
    Presidential Selection. Washington, D.C.:
    Brookings, 1973. 204-237.

Anderson 14

Sayre, Wallace S., and Judith H. Parris. <u>Voting</u>
<u>for President: The Electoral College and the</u>
<u>American Political System</u>. Washington, D.C.:
Brookings, 1972.

Slonim, Shlomo. "Electoral College." <u>Encyclopedia</u>
<u>of the American Presidency</u>. Eds. Leonard W. Levy
and Louis Fisher. New York: Simon & Schuster,
1994. 542-547.

Sung, Ellen. "Time to Reform the Electoral College?"
<u>Policy.com News and Events: Daily Briefing</u>.
31 July 2000. 21 Nov. 2008. ⟨http://www.policy.com/
news/dbrief/dbriefarc770.asp⟩.

Vile, John R. "Electoral College Reform."
<u>Encyclopedia of Constitutional Amendments,</u>
<u>Proposed Amendments, and Amending Issues, 1789-</u>
<u>1995</u>. Santa Barbara, CA: ABC-CLIO, 1996. 109-112.

Watchke, Gary. <u>Wisconsin's Role in Electing the</u>
<u>President</u>. Madison, WI: Wisconsin Legislative
Reference Bureau, Mar. 2000.

WRITING A RESEARCH PAPER USING APA STYLE

The documentation style of the American Psychological Association (APA), also referred to as the *author–date system,* is used widely in the behavioral and social sciences. It differs from that of the Modern Language Association (MLA), used primarily in the humanities, in some significant ways. APA style cites sources in parenthetical notes in the sentences to which they refer, as does MLA style, but the contents of the notes differ. In the APA system, the year of publication is given in the parenthetical note, and page numbers are given only for quotations, not for paraphrases. Finally, sources are listed at the end of the paper on a page called *References* rather than *Works Cited,* and formatting for that page is quite different from formatting in MLA style. This section gives general guidelines for both parenthetical citations and composing a references page using APA style. The guidelines are accompanied by sample pages from a student research paper using APA documentation style. For complete guidelines on APA Style, consult the following book:

American Psychological Association. *Publication Manual of the American Psychological Association*. 5th ed. Washington: APA, 2001.

For the latest updates on APA Style, go to the official website of the American Psychological Association, located at http://www.APA.org.

PARENTHETICAL CITATIONS USING APA STYLE

- For a quotation, include the author's last name, a comma, the year the work was published, another comma, and the page number, preceded by the abbreviation *p.* or *pp.:*

  Many experts agree that "it is much easier and more comfortable to teach as one learned" (Chall, 1989, p. 21).

- If the source has two authors, name them both, and separate their names with an ampersand (&):

  President Truman and his advisors were aware that the use of the bomb was no longer required to prevent an invasion of Japan by the Soviets (Alperovitz & Messer, 1991, 1992).

- Omit from the parenthetical citation any information given in the text:

  Samuel E. Wood and Ellen R. Green Wood (1993a) note that sociobiologists believe that social and nurturing experiences can "intensify, diminish, or modify" personality traits (p. 272).

- If the author's name is given in the text, follow it with the year of publication in parentheses:

  Nancy Paulu (1988) believes that children who are taught phonics get off to a better start than those who are not taught phonics.

- For works with three to five authors, name all of the authors the first time you refer to the work, but give only the last name of the first author followed by "et al." in subsequent citations. For a work with six or more authors, give only the first author's last name, followed by "et al." for all citations, including the first.
- If the author's name is repeated in the same paragraph, it is not necessary to repeat the year. However, if the author is cited in another paragraph, give the year of the work again.

- For summaries and paraphrases, give author and year but not the page number where the information appears:

    > Minnesota scientists have concluded that this data shows that genes are more influential than nurture on most personality traits (Bazell, 1987).

- If the source names no author, cite a short form of the title:

    > The twins were both born with musical abilities, but their unique experiences determined whether they acted on this ability ("How Genes Shape Personality," 1987).

Note: The first letter of each word in the short title is capitalized, but in the references list, only the first letter of the first word is capitalized.

- If you use two or more sources by the same author and they were published in the same year, add lowercase letters to refer to their order on the references page:

    > Wood and Wood (1993a) observe that . . .
    >
    > Other authorities (Wood & Wood, 1993b) agree, pointing out that . . .

- If one of your sources quotes or refers to another, and you want to use the second source in your paper, use the words *cited in*, followed by the source you read and the year the source was published. If you quote directly, give the page number of the source you read on which the quotation appeared:

    > Gerald McClearn, a psychologist and twin researcher at Pennsylvania State University, explained personality development realistically when he said: "'A gene can produce a nudge in one direction or another, but it does not directly control behavior. It doesn't take away a person's free will'" (cited in "How Genes Shape Personality," 1987, p. 62).

- To cite electronic material, indicate the page, chapter, figure, table, or equation at the appropriate point in the text. Give page number(s) for quotations. If the source does not provide page numbers, use paragraph number if available, preceded by the paragraph symbol or the abbreviation *para*. If neither page number or paragraph number is visible, cite the heading and the number of the paragraph so that the reader can locate the material at the website:

    > (Merriwether, 2004, p. 27)
    > (Johnson, 1999, para. 3)
    > (Shaw, 2003, conclusion section, para. 1)

Abstract.   Papers written in APA style often have an abstract, which succinctly summarizes its important points, instead of an outline. Here is the abstract of the paper of a group of students who surveyed classmates on various study and leisure-time patterns to discover if sex has an influence on academic achievement:

Abstract

Can differences in academic achievement be explained on the basis of biological sex? We hypothesized that sex is not the dominating factor influencing the success of University of Wisconsin-Stevens Point (UWSP) students. We conducted a survey of 108 college students, investigating their pastimes, study habits, work schedules and housing status in addition to their grade point averages (GPA). The data showed a small difference in GPAs with respect to sex but not large enough for sex alone to be the deciding factor. Our hypothesis that sex alone does not account for academic success was proved. We found that other factors, such as length of time spent studying, the number of hours of work per week, and time spent partying all play significant roles as well.

SAMPLE PAGES FROM A STUDENT RESEARCH PAPER USING APA STYLE

Here are the opening pages of a student research paper illustrating in-text citations using APA style.

```
Cory L. Vandertie                          Phonics 1

Professor Kathy Mitchell

English 102

19 April 2008
```

In papers written in APA style, provide a shortened version of the title as a running head, in the upper right-hand corner of the page along with the page number. If your instructor requires a separate title page, the title page is numbered 1.

The introductory paragraphs provide background for the research topic.

Cory read about the Flesch book in Groff's book, hence "cited in."

Write the author's full name the first time it is mentioned.

Although only the first letter of the first word in the title of a work is capitalized in the references list, in your paper you must capitalize as you would other titles.

Phonics 2

The Phonics Controversy

In recent years, school officials, teachers, and parents have been wrestling with the issue of how best to teach reading, with the controversy often centering on the conflict over the effectiveness of phonics in such instruction. Rudolph Flesch, in his best-selling 1955 book *Why Johnny Can't Read,* was one of the first educators to advocate the use of phonics in reading classes. His book not only brought national attention to the reading problems of America's children but also endorsed the use of phonics to overcome those problems (cited in Groff, 1989). Neither the problem of children's inability to read effectively nor the effectiveness of phonics instruction has been satisfactorily addressed in the 50 years since Flesch's book, however. Over a decade ago, Regna Lee Wood (1992) warned about declining literacy rates. In "That's Right—They're Wrong: Decline in Reading Ability Due to Abandonment of Phonics," she points out that in 1930, only 3 million Americans could not read, but in 1990, 30 to 35 million U.S. citizens could not read and were considered to be truly illiterate. In 2000, the National Assessment of Educational Progress (NAEP) reported that "more than a third (37 percent) of America's fourth grade children (roughly 10 million kids) could not read at even a basic level" and of those 10 million, "up to 40 percent will eventually drop out of high school" (cited in Stephenson, 2002). Statistics such as these have created tension among educators as they debate how to improve reading skills.

This is a paraphrase, so no page number need be given.

Although there are two works by Regna Lee Wood on Cory's list of references, the date of publication indicates the specific work being cited.

Cory asks a question as his thesis, reflecting the controversy over teaching phonics. He will answer the question in the course of the paper.

Give the page number on which a direct quotation appears in the source.

The year of Groff's publication has already been mentioned in this paragraph, so it is not repeated here.

Phonics 3

The declining literacy rate is an alarming indicator that something must be done differently in our schools. Wood (1998) discovered that 70 percent of U.S. high school students cannot read ninth-grade assignments and that 30 percent of U.S. twelfth graders cannot read at a fourth-grade level. Educators and parents who are concerned about this dramatic increase in the illiteracy rate and the inability of the majority of students to read at their own grade levels cannot refuse to explore all possible explanations for the failure of our schools to teach reading adequately. One avenue for exploration that may prove fruitful is the phonics controversy. Parents, teachers, and reading experts familiar with phonics all differ sharply in their views, compounding the dilemma of whether phonics instruction should be included in American schools. What role *does* phonics education play in the teaching of reading?

More than 450 years ago, phonics instruction was introduced to help young readers learn more about the relationship between letters and sound (Groff, 1989).Some researchers think that phonics has been used to teach reading since the time of ancient Greeks. Chall (1989) describes the method "as a tool for helping beginners identify words accurately so that they can read texts with comprehension earlier and more efficiently" (p. 4). Groff agrees that phonics instruction can be very useful for the development of children's word recognition skills. The problem is how to convince parents and teachers of the benefits of phonics. Wood (1992) believes that the horrible

Phonics 4

failure of our schools to teach children to read skillfully began years ago. She writes that "[the failure of schools to teach reading] began in 1929 and 1930 when hundreds of primary teachers, guided by college reading professors, stopped teaching beginners to read by matching sounds with letters that spell sounds" (p. 52).

Phonics is not the entire answer to the question of how best to teach children to read, however. Most reading experts agree that "the most the application of phonics can do is help children produce the approximate pronunciation of words" (Groff, 1989, p. 6). Roberts (1989), writing for Parents magazine, reports that phonics may not help all children learn to pronounce words. He explains that anyone who has a visual or auditory handicap will find it harder to read using phonics. For instance, Roberts points out that a child who has suffered from an ear infection that caused temporary hearing loss at an early age may find it difficult to learn to read by using phonics because of missing out on experiencing sound discrimination.

* * * * *

In conclusion, many experts believe that we have the ability and the knowledge to educate our schoolchildren more effectively by using phonics. But while both traditional and experimental evidence supports the use of phonics, the debate continues.

Educators who are not familiar with phonics instruction must be enlightened, perhaps with in-service workshops from experts on phonics

---

The brackets indicate that Cory has added his own words to the direct quotation.

For a smooth transition and to avoid too many parenthetical interruptions, mention author and source in text whenever you can.

Phonics 5

instruction. Parents, too, may need to be
convinced.

    Reading experts must be willing to work
together to resolve some of the issues in the
phonics debate, perhaps by putting together a
combination of approaches to the teaching of
reading that includes phonics. The bottom line is
that we all must work to find a solution to the
appalling rate of adult illiteracy in this country
and the unsettling inability of students to read
at their own grade levels. We must find solutions
to these problems, or we risk jeopardizing not only
our children's futures but our own.

APA STYLE REFERENCES LIST

- Bibliographic entries for all works cited in a paper are listed in alphabetical order on a page entitled *References*.
- After the first line of each entry, use a hanging indentation of 5 spaces.
- Give the last names and only the initials of the first and middle names of authors.
- The year of publication, in parentheses, follows the author's name.
- For a book, capitalize only proper nouns and the first word of the title and subtitle; underline the title.
- If a book is edited, place the abbreviation "Ed." or "Eds." in parentheses after the name(s) of the editor(s).
- If a citation names two or more authors, each name is reversed and an ampersand (&), not the word *and,* is placed before the last name.
- For an article, book chapter title, or title of an essay in a collection, capitalize as for a book title and do not use quotation marks or underlining.
- Capitalize the first letters of all important words in the name of the periodical and underline it.
- Use the abbreviations "p." and "pp." for inclusive page numbers of articles in magazines and journals, except when volume and issue number are given. If volume number is given for a periodical, place it after name of the periodical

and underline it. If an issue number is also given, place it in parentheses after the volume number but do not underline it:

> Hamby, A. L. (1991, Spring). An American Democrat: A reevaluation of the personality of Harry S Truman. Political Science Quarterly, 106, pp. 33–55.
>
> Stephenson, F. (2002, Aug.). The phonics revival. Florida Trend, 45 (4), pp. 10–24.

- If two or more works by the same author appear on the references list, put them in chronological order. Repeat the author's name each time, followed by the date in parentheses.
- If you cite two works of one author published in the same year, alphabetize them by title, and give each entry a lowercase letter: (1996a), (1996b).
- Words like "university" and "press" are spelled out, not abbreviated.

Below are two reference lists, one from Cory's paper on phonics and the other from the group project of four students who used a survey for their primary source and supplemented with several secondary sources retrieved from the Internet.

Phonics 14

References

Carbo, M. (1987, February). Reading styles research: What works isn't always phonics. Phi Delta Kappan, 68, 431-435.

Chall, J. S. (1989). The role of phonics in teaching reading. Washington, DC: U.S. Department of Education, Office of Educational Research and Improvement.

Groff, P. (1977). Phonics: Why and how. Morristown, NJ: General Learning.

Groff, P. (1989). Modern phonics instruction. Washington, DC: U.S. Department of Education, Office of Educational Research and Improvement.

Johnson, D. (1999). Critical issue: Addressing the literacy needs of emergent and early readers. [Electronic version.] 2 Feb. 2005. North Central Regional Educational Laboratory.http://www

Phonics 15

.ncrel.org/sdrs/areas/issues/content/cntareas/

reading/1i100.html.

Mesmer, H. E. & Griffith, P. (2005, Dec.) Everybody's

selling it—but just what is explicit, systematic

phonics instruction? Reading Teacher, 59 (4),

pp. 366-376.

Roberts, F. (1989, January). Does phonics cure

reading problems? Parents, p. 49.

Stephenson, F. (2002, August). The phonics revival.

Florida Trend, 45 (4), pp. 10-24.

Weaver, C. (1991, April). Weighing the claims about

phonics first. Education Digest, pp. 19-22.

Wood, R. L. (1992, September 14). That's right—

they're wrong: Decline in reading ability due

to abandonment of phonics. National Review,

pp. 49-52.

Wood, R. L. (1998). Time for a '2 By 1' Core

Curriculum. Oklahoma City: Oklahoma Council of

Public Affairs.

References

Burke, P. (1989 June). Gender identity, sex, and

school performance. Social Psychology. Quarterly.

Retrieved 2006 April 21, from http://links.jstor

.org

Duckworth, A.L. & Seligman, M.E.P. (2006 February).

Self-discipline gives girls the edge: gender

in self-discipline, grades and achievement

test scores. <u>Journal of Education Psychology</u>.
Retrieved 2006 April 21, from http://www.web105
.epnet.com

Pajares, F. (2002). Gender and perceived self-
efficacy in self-regulated learning. <u>Theory into
Practice</u>. Retrieved 2006 April 21, from http://
relayweb.hwwilsonweb.com

Wang, Y., Arboldea, A., Shelly II, M.C., Whalen,
D. F. (2004). The influence of residence hall
community on academic success of male and female
undergraduate students. <u>Journal of College &
University Student Housing</u>. Retrieved 2006
April 21, from http://www.web110.epnet.com

PART • TWO

The Arts, Media Studies, and Popular Culture

CHAPTER

8

Music and Video Games

People's opinions about what expressive forms can be considered works of art change and evolve over time. Henry Jenkins' "Art Form for the Digital Age," written in 2000 when video games were beginning to get creative in the scope and range of what they offered players, argues that video games are a legitimate art form that must be taken seriously. He writes that they play an important part in "shaping the aesthetic sensibility of the 21st century." As you read what he has to say in defense of his proposition, consider the video games that you, your friends, or your kids play. Does Jenkins make a compelling case for viewing them as art?

Certainly video games are treated seriously by young people, particularly boys, and many writers have explored the larger issues of whether video games have value and how to account for the fact that they are a "gendered" phenomenon. Critics of video games question whether they have any "redeeming social value" and explore how we account for their wild popularity with boys but girls' almost indifferent attitude toward them. These subjects are treated in greater length in this book in Chapter 15 on gender and sex roles and Chapter 23 on marketing and consumerism, but for an intriguing commentary on the effects of playing violent video games on young people in this chapter, read Karen Sternheimer's "Do Video Games Kill?" An academic whose article was published in a sociological journal, Sternheimer argues that blaming youth violence on video games is unfair and inaccurate. Citing newspaper articles and studies done following some high profile school shootings in the late nineties, she argues that much more than playing violent video games is to blame for the deviant behavior of a few white middle-class males who murdered their classmates.

While video games are a very recent development in games—and popular culture—music has been an integral part of humans' lives from their earliest existence. Song and instrumental music have spoken to, soothed, excited, and otherwise influenced humans of virtually all cultures and time periods in a seemingly endless variety of styles, subject matter, and methods of delivery. Each new musician, composer, or singer hopes to create a style uniquely his or her own, often acknowledging the influence of a previous form or artist. Sometimes a wholly new form of musical expression is created, from which generations of musicians and music lovers in turn take their inspiration.

The subject of the effect of certain lyrics in contemporary rock, hip-hop, and gangsta rap music generates heated debate, with defenders of the music just as convinced of their legitimacy as their detractors. Like violent video games, sexually explicit and violently graphic music lyrics come under frequent and vocal attack from those who believe they have devastating effects on certain groups of people. Cathleen Rountree and Jennifer McLune hold opposing viewpoints on the subject of hip-hop music, which is often the target of criticism. Rountree's "In Defense of Hip-Hop" calls for a sympathetic understanding of the hip-hop culture. She believes that hip-hop has been a scapegoat and urges readers not to blame hip-hop artists for the violent and misogynistic content of their music because "they're simply reflecting their surrounding environment." In contrast, McLune asserts in "Hip-Hop's Betrayal of Black Women" that "women, too, are raised in this environment of poverty and violence, but have yet to produce the same negative and hateful representation of black men that male rappers are capable of making against women." As you read those two essays, think about your reaction to and understanding of hip-hop and gangsta rap music. With which writer are you more sympathetic? Is one more persuasive than the other?

ART FORM FOR THE DIGITAL AGE

HENRY JENKINS

Henry Jenkins is Director of Comparative Media Studies and Professor of Literature at the Massachusetts Institute of Technology. Among his publications are dozens of periodical articles and nine books, beginning in 1992 with What Made Pistachio Nuts?: Early Sound Comedy and the Vaudeville Aesthetic *and* Textual Poachers: Television Fans and Participatory Culture. *Among his other books are* Classical Hollywood Comedy *(1994), co-edited with Kristine Brunovska Karnick;* From Barbie to Mortal Kombat: Gender and Computer Games *(1998), co-edited with Justine Cassell;* Hop On Pop: The Politics and Pleasures of Popular Culture *(2003), co-edited with Tara McPherson and Jane Shattuc;* Rethinking Media Change: The Aesthetics of Transition *(2003), co-edited with David Thorburn;* Convergence Culture: Where Old and New Media Collide *(2006); and* Fans, Bloggers and Gamers: Exploring Participatory Culture *(2006). This article was first published in the September 2000 issue of* Technology Review.

Video games shape our culture. It's time we took them seriously.

Last year, Americans bought over 215 million computer and video games. That's more than two games per household. The video game industry made almost as much money from gross domestic income as Hollywood. So are video games a massive drain on our income, time and energy? A new form of "cultural pollution," as one U.S. senator described them? The "nightmare before Christmas," in the words of another? Are games teaching our children to kill, as countless op-ed pieces have warned?

No. Computer games are art—a popular art, an emerging art, a largely unrecognized art, but art nevertheless.

4   Over the past 25 years, games have progressed from the primitive two-paddles-and-a-ball Pong to the sophistication of Final Fantasy, a participatory story with cinema-quality graphics that unfolds over nearly 100 hours of play. The computer game has been a killer app for the home PC, increasing consumer demand for vivid graphics, rapid processing, greater memory and better sound. The release this fall of the Sony Playstation 2, coupled with the announcement of next-generation consoles by Nintendo and Microsoft, signals a dramatic increase in the resources available to game designers.

Games increasingly influence contemporary cinema, helping to define the frenetic pace and model the multi-directional plotting of *Run Lola Run,* providing the role-playing metaphor for *Being John Malkovich* and encouraging a fascination with the slippery line between reality and digital illusion in *The Matrix.* At high schools and colleges across the country, students discuss games with the same passions with which earlier generations debated the merits of the New American Cinema. Media studies programs report a growing number of their students want to be game designers rather than filmmakers.

The time has come to take games seriously as an important new popular art shaping the aesthetic sensibility of the 21st century. I will admit that discussing the art of video games conjures up comic images: tuxedo-clad and jewel-bedecked patrons admiring the latest Streetfighter, middle-aged academics pontificating on the impact of Cubism on Tetris, bleeps and zaps disrupting our silent contemplation at the Guggenheim. Such images tell us more about our contemporary notion of art—as arid and stuffy, as the property of an educated and economic elite, as cut off from everyday experience—than they tell us about games.

New York's Whitney Museum found itself at the center of controversy about digital art when it recently included web artists in its prestigious biannual show. Critics didn't believe the computer could adequately express the human spirit. But they're misguided. The computer is simply a tool, one that offers artists new resources and opportunities for reaching the public; it is human creativity that makes art. Still, one can only imagine how the critics would have responded to the idea that something as playful, unpretentious and widely popular as a computer game might be considered art.

8   In 1925, leading literary and arts critic Gilbert Seldes took a radical approach to the aesthetics of popular culture in a treatise titled *The Seven Lively Arts.* Adopting what was then a controversial position, Seldes argued that America's primary contributions to artistic expression had come through emerging forms of popular culture such as jazz, the Broadway musical, the Hollywood cinema and the comic strip. While these arts have gained cultural respectability over the past 75 years, each was disreputable when Seldes staked out his position.

Readers then were skeptical of Seldes' claims about cinema in particular for many of the same reasons that contemporary critics dismiss games—they were suspicious of cinema's commercial motivations and technological origins, concerned about Hollywood's appeals to violence and eroticism, and insistent that cinema had not yet produced works of lasting value. Seldes, on the other hand, argued that cinema's popularity demanded that we reassess its aesthetic qualities.

Cinema and other popular arts were to be celebrated, Seldes said, because they were so deeply imbedded in everyday life, because they were democratic arts embraced by average citizens. Through streamlined styling and syncopated rhythms, they captured the vitality of contemporary urban experience. They took the very machinery of the industrial age, which many felt dehumanizing, and found within it the resources for expressing individual visions, for reasserting basic human needs, desires and fantasies. And these new forms were still open to experimentation and discovery. They were, in Seldes' words, "lively arts."

Games represent a new lively art, one as appropriate for the digital age as those earlier media were for the machine age. They open up new aesthetic experiences and transform the computer screen into a realm of experimentation and innovation that is broadly accessible. And games have been embraced by a public that has otherwise been unimpressed by much of what passes for digital art. Much as the salon arts of the 1920s seemed sterile alongside the vitality and inventiveness of popular culture, contemporary efforts to create interactive narrative through modernist hypertext or avant-garde installation art seem lifeless and pretentious alongside the creativity that game designers bring to their craft.

12   Much of what Seldes told us about the silent cinema seems remarkably apt for thinking about games. Silent cinema, he argued, was an art of expressive movement. He valued the speed and dynamism of D.W. Griffith's last-minute races to the rescue, the physical grace of Chaplin's pratfalls and the ingenuity of Buster Keaton's engineering feats. Games also depend upon an art of expressive movement, with characters defined through their distinctive ways of propelling themselves through space, and successful products structured around a succession of spectacular stunts and predicaments. Will future generations look back on Lara Croft doing battle with a pack of snarling wolves as the 21st-century equivalent of Lillian Gish making her way across the ice floes in *Way Down East?* The art of silent cinema was also an art of atmospheric design. To watch a silent masterpiece like Fritz Lang's Metropolis is to be drawn into a world where meaning is carried by the placement of shadows, the movement of machinery and the organization of space. If anything, game designers have pushed beyond cinema in terms of developing expressive and fantastic environments that convey a powerful sense of mood, provoke our curiosity and amusement, and motivate us to explore.

Seldes wrote at a moment when cinema was maturing as an expressive medium and filmmakers were striving to enhance the emotional experience of going to the movies—making a move from mere spectacle towards character and consequence. It remains to be seen whether games can make a similar transition. Contemporary games can pump us full of adrenaline, they can make us laugh, but they have not yet provoked us to tears. And many have argued that, since games don't have characters of human complexity or stories that stress the consequences of our actions, they cannot achieve the status of true art. Here, we must be careful not to confuse the current transitional state of an emerging medium with its full potential. As I visit game companies, I see some of the industry's best minds struggling with this question and see strong evidence that the games released over the next few years will bring us closer and closer to the quality of characterization we have come to expect from other forms of popular narrative.

In the March 6 [2000] issue of *Newsweek,* senior editor Jack Kroll argued that audiences will probably never be able to care as deeply about pixels on the computer screen as they care about characters in films: "Moviemakers don't have to simulate human beings; they are right there, to be recorded and orchestrated . . . The top-heavy titillation of Tomb Raider's Lara Croft falls flat next to the face of Sharon Stone. . . ." Yet countless viewers cry when Bambi's mother dies, and World War II veterans can tell you they felt real lust for *Esquire*'s Vargas girls. We have learned to care as much about creatures of pigment as we care about images of real people. Why should pixels be different?

In the end, games may not take the same path as cinema. Game designers will almost certainly develop their own aesthetic principles as they confront the challenge of balancing our competing desires for storytelling and interactivity. It remains to be seen whether games can provide players the freedom they want and still provide an emotionally satisfying and thematically meaningful shape to the experience. Some of the best games—Tetris comes to mind—have nothing to do with storytelling. For all we know, the future art of games may look more like architecture or dance than cinema.

16   Such questions warrant close and passionate engagement not only within the game industry or academia, but also by the press and around the dinner table. Even Kroll's grumpy dismissal of games has sparked heated discussion and forced designers to refine their own grasp of the medium's distinctive features. Imagine what a more robust form of criticism could contribute. We need critics who know games the way Pauline Kael knew movies and who write about them with an equal degree of wit and wisdom.

When *The Seven Lively Arts* was published, silent cinema was still an experimental form, each work stretching the medium in new directions. Early film critics played vital functions in documenting innovations and speculating about their potential. Computer games are in a similar phase. We have not had time to codify what experienced game designers know, and we have certainly not yet established a canon of great works that might serve as exemplars. There have been real creative accomplishments in games, but we haven't really sorted out what they are and why they matter.

But games do matter, because they spark the imaginations of our children, taking them on epic quests to strange new worlds. Games matter because our children no longer have access to real-world play spaces at a time when we've paved over the vacant lots to make room for more condos and the streets make parents nervous. If children are going to have opportunities for exploratory play, play that encourages cognitive development and fosters problem-solving skills, they will do so in the virtual environments of games. Multi-player games create opportunities for leadership, competition, teamwork and collaboration—for nerdy kids, not just for high school football players. Games matter because they form the digital equivalent of the Head Start program, getting kids excited about what computers can do.

The problem with most contemporary games isn't that they are violent but that they are banal, formulaic and predictable. Thoughtful criticism can marshal support for innovation and experimentation in the industry, much as good film criticism helps focus attention on neglected independent films. Thoughtful criticism could even contribute to our debates about game violence. So far, the censors and culture warriors have gotten more or less a free ride because we almost take for granted that games are culturally worthless. We should instead look at games as an emerging art form—one that does not simply simulate violence but increasingly offers new ways to understand violence—and talk about how to strike a balance between this form of expression and social responsibility. Moreover, game criticism may provide a means of holding the game industry more accountable for its choices. In the wake of the Columbine shootings, game designers are struggling with their ethical responsibilities as never before, searching for ways of appealing to empowerment fantasies that don't require exploding heads and gushing organs. A serious public discussion of this medium might constructively influence these debates, helping identify and evaluate alternatives as they emerge.

20   As the art of games matures, progress will be driven by the most creative and forward-thinking minds in the industry, those who know that games can be more than they have been, those who recognize the potential of reaching a broader public, of having a greater cultural impact, of generating more diverse and ethically responsible content and of creating richer and more emotionally engaging stories. But without the support of an informed public and the perspective of thoughtful critics, game developers may never realize that potential.

PERSONAL RESPONSE

Do you find video games aesthetically appealing in any way? If you play video games, explain their appeal, and if you do not play them, explain why not.

QUESTIONS FOR CLASS OR SMALL-GROUP DISCUSSION

1. Jenkins begins by stating, "Video games shape our culture." How does he support that statement? Do you agree with Jenkins on the importance of video games in "shaping the aesthetic sensibility of the 21st century" (paragraph 7)?

2. In paragraph 5, Jenkins gives examples of video games that illustrate his observation that they have progressed over time from a primitive state to sophistication. What criteria does he use to make that judgment? What examples of currently popular video games can you name that illustrate his point? If you do not believe that they have continued to evolve, give examples that disprove his point.

3. What is Jenkins' argumentative strategy? That is, what is his proposition? What is his supporting evidence? Does he acknowledge opposing viewpoints or make any concessions? Does he urge action? How persuasive do you find the essay?

4. Explain Gilbert Seldes' approach to popular culture (paragraph 9 and following) and assess its applicability to the question of video games as a legitimate art form.

5. In several places, Jenkins states that certain things in the development of video games "remain to be seen" (paragraphs 14 and 16). He also writes in his concluding paragraph of the potential of video games. In your opinion, have video games achieved any of the potential that Jenkins believed they had in 2000? You might first consider whether that is or should be the goal of video games.

DO VIDEO GAMES KILL?

KAREN STERNHEIMER

Karen Sternheimer, whose work focuses on youth and popular culture, teaches in the sociology department at the University of Southern California and is author of Kids These Days: Facts and Fictions About Today's Youth *(2006) and* It's Not the Media: The Truth About Pop Culture's Influence on Children *(2003). Her commentary has been published in several newspapers and she has appeared on numerous television and radio programs. This article appeared in the Winter 2007 issue of* Contexts, *the journal of the American Sociological Association.*

As soon as it was released in 1993, a video game called *Doom* became a target for critics. Not the first, but certainly one of the most popular first-person shooter games, *Doom* galvanized fears that such games would teach kids to kill. In the years after its release, *Doom* helped video gaming grow into a multibillion dollar industry, surpassing Hollywood box-office revenues and further fanning public anxieties.

Then came the school shootings in Paducah, Kentucky; Springfield, Oregon; and Littleton, Colorado. In all three cases, press accounts emphasized that the shooters loved *Doom*, making it appear that the critics' predictions about video games were coming true.

But in the ten years following *Doom*'s release, homicide arrest rates fell by 77 percent among juveniles. School shootings remain extremely rare; even during the 1990s, when fears of school violence were high, students had less than a 7 in 10 million chance of being killed at school.

4   During that time, video games became a major part of many young people's lives, few of whom will ever become violent, let alone kill. So why is the video game explanation so popular?

Contemporary Folk Devils

In 2000 the FBI issued a report on school rampage shootings, finding that their rarity prohibits the construction of a useful profile of a "typical" shooter. In the absence of a simple explanation, the public symbolically linked these rare and complex events to the shooters' alleged interest in video games, finding in them a catchall explanation for what seemed unexplainable—the white, middle-class school shooter. However, the concern about video games is out of proportion to their actual threat.

Politicians and other moral crusaders frequently create "folk devils," individuals or groups defined as evil and immoral. Folk devils allow us to channel our blame and fear, offering a clear course of action to remedy what many believe to be a growing problem. Video games, those who play them, and those who create them have become contemporary folk devils because they seem to pose a threat to children.

Such games have come to represent a variety of social anxieties: about youth violence, new computer technology, and the apparent decline in the ability of adults to control what young people do and know. Panics about youth and popular culture have emerged with the appearance of many new technologies. Over the past century, politicians have complained that cars, radio, movies, rock music, and even comic books caused youth immorality and crime, calling for control and sometimes censorship.

8   Acting on concerns like these, politicians often engage in battles characterized as between good and evil. The unlikely team of Senators Joseph Lieberman, Sam Brownback, Hillary Rodham Clinton, and Rick Santorum introduced a bill in March 2005 that called for $90 million to fund studies on media effects. Lieberman commented, "America is a media-rich society, but despite the flood of information, we still lack perhaps the most important piece of information—what effect are media having on our children?" Regardless of whether any legislation passes, the senators position themselves as protecting children and benefit from the moral panic they help to create.

Constructing Culpability

Politicians are not the only ones who blame video games. Since 1997, 199 newspaper articles have focused on video games as a central explanation for the Paducah, Springfield, and Littleton shootings. This helped to create a groundswell of fear that schools were no longer safe and that rampage shootings could happen wherever there were video games. The shootings legitimated existing concerns about the new medium and about young people in general. Headlines such as "Virtual Realities Spur School Massacres" (*Denver Post*, July 27, 1999), "Days of Doom" (*Pittsburgh Post-Gazette*, May 14, 1999), "Bloodlust Video Games Put Kids in the Crosshairs" (*Denver Post*, May 30, 1999), and "All Those Who Deny Any Linkage between Violence in Entertainment and Violence in Real Life, Think Again" (*New York Times*, April 26, 1999) insist that video games are the culprit.

These headlines all appeared immediately after the Littleton shooting, which had the highest death toll and inspired most (176) of the news stories alleging a video game connection.

Across the country, the press attributed much of the blame to video games specifically, and to Hollywood more generally. The *Pittsburgh Post-Gazette* article "Days of Doom" noted that "eighteen people have now died at the hands of avid *Doom* players." The *New York Times* article noted above began, "By producing increasingly violent media, the entertainment industry has for decades engaged in a lucrative dance with the devil," evoking imagery of a fight against evil. It went on to construct video games as a central link: "The two boys apparently responsible for the massacre in Littleton, Colo., last week were, among many other things, accomplished players of the ultraviolent video game *Doom*. And Michale Carneal, the

14-year-old boy who opened fire on a prayer group in a Paducah, Ky., school foyer in 1997, was also known to be a video-game expert."

12   Just as many stories insisted that video games deserved at least partial blame, editorial pages around the country made the connection as well:

> President Bill Clinton is right. He said this shooting was no isolated incident, that Kinkel and other teens accused of killing teachers and fellow students reflect a changing culture of violence on television and in movies and video games. (*Cleveland Plain Dealer*, May 30, 1998)
>
> The campaign to make Hollywood more responsible . . . should proceed full speed ahead. (*Boston Herald*, April 9, 2000)
>
> Make no mistake, Hollywood is contributing to a culture that feeds on and breeds violence. . . . When entertainment companies craft the most shocking video games and movies they can, peddle their virulent wares to an impressionable audience with abandon, then shrug off responsibility for our culture of violence, they deserve censure. (*St. Louis Post-Dispatch*, April 12, 2000)

The video game connection took precedence in all these news reports. Some stories mentioned other explanations, such as the shooters' social rejection, feelings of alienation at school, and depression, but these were treated mostly as minor factors compared with video games. Reporters gave these other reasons far less attention than violent video games, and frequently discussed them at the end of the articles.

The news reports typically introduce experts early in the stories who support the video game explanation. David Grossman, a former army lieutenant described as a professor of "killology," has claimed that video games are "murder simulators" and serve as an equivalent to military training. Among the 199 newspaper articles published, 17 of them mentioned or quoted Grossman. Additionally, an attorney who has filed several lawsuits against video game producers wrote an article for the *Denver Post* insisting that the games are to blame. By contrast, only seven articles identified sociologists as experts. Writers routinely presented alternative explanations as rebuttals but rarely explored them in depth.

Reporting on Research

By focusing so heavily on video games, news reports downplay the broader social contexts. While a handful of articles note the roles that guns, poverty, families, and the organization of schools may play in youth violence in general, when reporters mention research to explain the shooters' behavior, the vast majority of studies cited concern media effects, suggesting that video games are a central cause.

16   Since the early days of radio and movies, investigators have searched for possible effects—typically negative—that different media may have on audiences, especially children. Such research became more intense following the rise in violent crime in the United States between the 1960s and early 1990s, focusing primarily

on television. Several hundred studies asked whether exposure to media violence predicts involvement in actual violence.

Although often accepted as true—one scholar has gone so far as to call the findings about the effects of media violence on behavior a "law"—this body of research has been highly controversial. One such study fostered claims that television had led to more than 10,000 murders in the United States and Canada during the 20th century. This and many other media-effects studies rely on correlation analysis, often finding small but sometimes statistically significant links between exposure to media violence and aggressive behavior.

But such studies do not demonstrate that media violence causes aggressive behavior, only that the two phenomena exist together. Excluding a host of other factors (such as the growing unrest during the civil rights and antiwar movements, and the disappearance of jobs in central cities) may make it seem that a direct link exists between the introduction of television and homicides. In all likelihood any connection is incidental.

It is equally likely that more aggressive people seek out violent entertainment. Aggression includes a broad range of emotions and behaviors, and is not always synonymous with violence. Measures of aggression in media-effects research have varied widely, from observing play between children and inanimate objects to counting the number of speeding tickets a person received. Psychologist Jonathan Freedman reviewed every media-violence study published in English and concluded that "the majority of studies produced evidence that is inconsistent or even contradicts" the claim that exposure to media violence causes real violence.

20   Recently, video games have become a focus of research. Reviews of this growing literature have also been mixed. A 2001 meta-analysis in *Psychological Science* concluded that video games "will increase aggressive behavior," while a similar review published that same year in a different journal found that "it is not possible to determine whether video game violence affects aggressive behavior." A 2005 review found evidence that playing video games improves spatial skills and reaction times, but not that the games increase aggression.

The authors of the *Psychological Science* article advocate the strong-effects hypothesis. Two of their studies were widely reported on in 2000, the year after the Columbine High School shootings, with scant critical analysis. But their research was based on college undergraduates, not troubled teens, and it measured aggression in part by subjects' speed in reading "aggressive" words on a computer screen or blasting opponents with sound after playing a violent video game. These measures do not approximate the conditions the school shooters experienced, nor do they offer much insight as to why they, and not the millions of other players, decided to acquire actual weapons and shoot real people.

Occasionally reporters include challenges like this in stories containing media-effects claims, but news coverage usually refers to this body of research as clear, consistent, and conclusive. "The evidence, say those who study violence in culture, is unassailable: Hundreds of studies in recent decades have revealed a direct correlation between exposure to media violence—now including video games—and increased aggression," said the *New York Times* (April 26, 1999). The *Boston Herald* quoted a clinical psychologist who said, "Studies have already shown that watching television shows with aggressive or violent content makes children more aggressive" (July 30, 2000). The psychologist noted that video game research is newer, but predicted that "in a few years, studies will show that video games increase a child's aggression even more than violent TV shows." News reports do not always use academic sources to assess the conclusiveness of media effects research. A *Pittsburgh Post-Gazette* story included a quote by an attorney, who claimed, "Research on this has been well-established" (May 14, 1999).

It is no accident that media-effects research and individual explanations dominate press attempts to explain the behavior of the school shooters. Although many politicians are happy to take up the cause against video games, popular culture itself suggests an apolitical explanation of violence and discourages a broader examination of structural factors. Focusing on extremely rare and perhaps unpredictable outbursts of violence by young people discourages the public from looking closely at more typical forms of violence against young people, which is usually perpetrated by adults.

24   The biggest problem with media-effects research is that it attempts to decontextualize violence. Poverty, neighborhood instability, unemployment, and even family violence fall by the wayside in most of these studies. Ironically, even mental illness tends to be overlooked in this psychologically oriented research. Young people are seen as passive media consumers, uniquely and uniformly vulnerable to media messages.

Missing Media Studies

News reports of the shootings that focus on video games ignore other research on the meanings that audiences make from media culture. This may be because its qualitative findings are difficult to turn into simple quotations or sound bites. Yet in seeking better understanding of the role of video games in the lives of the shooters and young people more generally, media scholars could have added much to the public debate.

For instance, one study found that British working-class boys boast about how many horror films they have seen as they construct their sense of masculinity by appearing too tough to be scared. Another study examined how younger boys talk about movies and television as a way to manage their anxieties and insecurities regarding their emerging sense of masculinity. Such studies illustrate why violent video games may appeal to many young males.

Media scholars have also examined how and why adults construct concerns about young people and popular culture. One such study concluded that some adults use their condemnation of media as a way to produce cultural distinctions that position them above those who enjoy popular culture. Other researchers have found that people who believe their political knowledge is superior to that of others are more likely to presume that media violence would strongly influence others. They have also found that respondents who enjoy television violence are less likely to believe it has a negative effect.

28   Just as it is too simplistic to assert that video game violence makes players more prone to violence, news coverage alone, however dramatic or repetitive, cannot create consensus among the public that video games cause youth violence. Finger-wagging politicians and other moralizers often alienate as many members of the public as they convert. In an ironic twist, they might even feed the antiauthoritarian appeal that may draw players of all ages to the games.

The lack of consensus does not indicate the absence of a moral panic, but reveals contradictory feelings toward the target group. The intense focus on video games as potential creators of violent killers reflects the hostility that some feel toward popular culture and young people themselves. After adult rampage shootings in the workplace (which happen more often than school shootings), reporters seldom mention whether the shooters played video games. Nor is an entire generation portrayed as potential killers.

Ambivalence about Juvenile Justice

The concern in the late 1990s about video games coincided with a growing ambivalence about the juvenile justice system and young offenders. Fears about juvenile "super-predators," fanned by former Florida Representative Bill McCollom's 1996 warning that we should "brace ourselves" against the coming storm of young killers, made the school shootings appear inevitable. McCollom and other politicians characterized young people as a "new breed," uniquely dangerous and amoral.

These fears were produced partially by the rise in crime during the late 1980s and early 1990s, but also by the so-called echo boom that produced a large generation of teens during the late 1990s. Demographic theories of crime led policymakers to fear that the rise in the number of teen males would bring a parallel rise in crime. In response, virtually every state changed its juvenile justice laws during the decade. They increased penalties, imposed mandatory minimum sentences, blended jurisdiction with criminal courts, and made it easier to transfer juvenile cases to adult criminal courts.

32   So before the first shot was fired in Paducah, politicians warned the public to be on the lookout for killer kids. Rather than being seen as tragic anomalies, these high-profile incidents appeared to support scholarly warnings that all kids posed an increasing threat. Even though juvenile (and adult) crime was in sharp decline by the late nineties, the intense media coverage contributed to the appearance of a new trend.

Blaming video games meant that the shooters were set aside from other violent youth, frequently poor males of color, at whom our get-tough legislation has been targeted. According to the National Center for Juvenile Justice, African-American youth are involved in the juvenile justice system more than twice as often as whites. The video game explanation constructs the white, middle-class shooters as victims of the power of video games, rather than fully culpable criminals. When boys from "good" neighborhoods are violent, they seem to be harbingers of a "new breed" of youth, created by video games rather than by their social circumstances. White, middle-class killers retain their status as children easily influenced by a game, victims of an allegedly dangerous product. African-American boys, apparently, are simply dangerous.

While the news media certainly asked what role the shooters' parents may have played, the press tended to tread lightly on them, particularly the Kinkels of Springfield, Oregon, who were their son's first murder victims. Their middle-class, suburban, or rural environments were given little scrutiny. The white school shooters did more than take the lives of their classmates; their whiteness and middle-class status threatened the idea of the innocence and safety of suburban America.

In an attempt to hold more than just the shooters responsible, the victims' families filed lawsuits against film producers, Internet sites, and video game makers. Around the same time, Congress made it more difficult to sue gun manufacturers for damages. To date, no court has found entertainment producers liable for causing young people to commit acts of violence. In response to a lawsuit following the Paducah shootings, a Kentucky circuit judge ruled that "we are loath to hold that ideas and images can constitute the tools for a criminal act," and that product liability law did not apply because the product did not injure its consumer. The lawsuit was dismissed, as were subsequent suits filed after the other high-profile shootings.

Game Over?

36 Questions about the power of media and the future of the juvenile justice system persist. In March 2005, the U.S. Supreme Court ruled that juvenile executions were unconstitutional. This ruling represents an about-face in the 25-year trend toward toughening penalties for young offenders. While many human rights and children's advocates praised this decision, it was sharply criticized by those who believe that the juvenile justice system is already too lenient. Likewise, critics continue to target video games, as their graphics and plot capabilities grow more complex and at times more disturbing. Meanwhile, youth crime rates continue to decline. If we want to understand why young people, particularly in middle-class or otherwise stable environments, become homicidal, we need to look beyond the games they play. While all forms of media merit critical analysis, so do the supposedly "good" neighborhoods and families that occasionally produce young killers.

Recommended Resources

Ronald Burns and Charles Crawford. "School Shootings, the Media, and Public Fear: Ingredients for a Moral Panic." *Crime, Law, and Social Change* 32 (1999): 147–68. Examines fears about school shootings in the 1990s, paying special attention to the disproportional response compared to the actual threat.

Jonathan L. Freedman. *Media Violence and Its Effect on Aggression: Assessing the Scientific Evidence* (University of Toronto Press, 2002). A thorough analysis of media-effects research, with a critique of methods and interpretation of results.

Erich Goode and Nachman Ben-Yehuda. *Moral Panics: The Social Construction of Deviance* (Blackwell, 1994). A primer on moral panics, with basic definitions as well as several seminal case studies.

40   John Springhall. *Youth, Popular Culture and Moral Panics: Penny Gaffs to Gangsta-Rap, 1830–1996* (St. Martin's, 1998). A history of fears about young people and media.

Franklin E. Zimring. *American Youth Violence* (Oxford University Press, 1998). A comprehensive look at trends in youth crime, juvenile justice, and political discourse about youth violence.

PERSONAL RESPONSE

What is your opinion of violent video games? Are they harmless fun, or do you believe that they may have some effect on behavior? What is your experience with playing such games or watching others play them?

QUESTIONS FOR CLASS OR SMALL-GROUP DISCUSSION

1. Sternheimer mentions the term "folk devils" and suggests that "video games, those who play them, and those who create them have become contemporary folk devils" (paragraph 4). What do you understand her to mean by that term? Can you give examples of other such "folk devils?"

2. What criticisms of media-effects research does Sternheimer make? What do you think of her rationale for those criticisms?

3. Discuss the factors besides video games that may account for aggressive behavior in teenagers, according to Sternheimer.

4. What point does Sternheimer make about poor males of color who get in trouble with the law vs. white middle-class males who kill? Do your own observations confirm or contradict her viewpoint?

5. Analyze the structure of Sternheimer's argument. What is her thesis? Where does she make concessions? What evidence does she supply? How convinced are you by her evidence?

IN DEFENSE OF HIP-HOP

CATHLEEN ROUNTREE

Cathleen Rountree is a film journalist, educator, and author, who holds M.A, BFA, and Ph.D. degrees. Among her nine books are The Writer's Mentor: A Guide to Putting Passion on Paper *(2002),* The Movie Lovers' Club *(2006), and a five-volume series documenting women's life stages. She lectures frequently on such subjects as artists*

*and the creative process, women's issues, men's issues, and childhood
and adolescent issues. This piece appeared in the May 19, 2007, issue
of the* Santa Cruz Sentinel. *You can visit her on the blog* Women in
World Cinema *at www.womeninworldcinema.org.*

Long under fire from stalwart social regulators, such as the likes of Tipper Gore, members of Congress and those bastions of self-righteousness found on cable news broadcasts, hip-hop music frequently assumes the central role of scapegoat when violent words and deeds erupt among the young—and sometimes the old, as we saw with the Don Imus escapade in April.

Yes, those sleazy words, "nappy-headed hos," that Slimy Imus regurgitated during his live radio broadcast in reference to the Rutgers University women's basketball team, inadvertently returned social critics [including Al Sharpton] to the comfort zone of blaming hip-hop for all that ails contemporary pop culture. The fact that Imus used hip-hop as an excuse for his long-standing and well-documented proclivity for racial epithets seemed especially smarmy.

It was comedian Flip Wilson's cross-dressing character Geraldine who immortalized the excuse: "The Devil made me do it!" Now, it often seems, in many circles hip-hop equals Satan: "Hip-Hop made me do it." If the music is sometimes violent, misogynistic, or materialistic, don't blame hip-hop artists, for they're simply reflecting their surrounding environment.

4   What elicits my ire is the person who condemns hip-hop without having a basic understanding of it, something I myself had once been guilty of. But, about four years ago, I watched "Tupac Resurrection," a documentary about the life and [as yet unsolved] murder of rap artist Tupac Shakur. The two-hour screening time was for me an epiphany and an entirely new world opened up: a world of beats, words, images, insights, raw expressions that were positively transporting. Like any new convert, I explored, studied, listened to, read about, fell in love with, even proselytized, an art form about which I, too, had once been critical. In fact, it became such a valued part of my life that I eagerly devoted a unit to it in a course I teach at UC Santa Cruz on the Arts in a Multicultural Society.

What had changed? Through "Tupac Resurrection" I found the humanity and powerful social commentary inherent in the entire lexicon of hip-hop culture, and, believe me, it is a unique, fully animated, communicative and consequential culture. The best of hip-hop culture is, in addition to artistic, both political and spiritual, and makes people think. Indeed, hip-hop culture serves as a crossover culture—from music to music videos to movies, from black to white, from urban to suburban, from youth to middle-aged, from deprived to privileged, from street smart to public enemy, from authenticity to false personas and negative stereotypes, from sistahs to "bitches and hos," from bros to "pimps," from freedom to incarceration, from life-affirming to nihilistic, from community to isolation, from politically engaged to apathetic, from principled to morally corrupt, from life to death.

This summer "The Hip Hop Project," a film produced by Bruce Willis and Queen Latifah, beats its way to movie theaters. "The Hip Hop Project" is the compelling story of Kazi, a formerly homeless teenager who inspired a group of

New York City teens to transform their life stories into powerful works of art, using hip-hop as a vehicle for self-development and personal discovery.

Kazi challenges these young people to write music about real issues affecting their lives as they strive to overcome daunting obstacles to produce a collaborative album. Russell Simmons, hip-hop mogul and longtime supporter of the project, partners with Bruce Willis to donate a recording studio to the Hip Hop Project. After four years of collaboration, the group produces a powerful and thought-provoking CD filled with moving personal narratives and sharp social commentaries. In contrast to all the negative attention focused on hip-hop and rap music, this is a story of hope, healing and the realization of dreams. It should be required viewing for both Don Imus and Al Sharpton.

PERSONAL RESPONSE QUESTION

Do you listen to and enjoy hip-hop? If so, explain its appeal. If not, explain what kind(s) of music you do listen to and enjoy.

QUESTIONS FOR CLASS OR SMALL-GROUP DISCUSSION

1. In what way (s) does Rountree defend hip-hop music (title)?
2. How might blaming "hip-hop artists for all that ails contemporary pop culture" be a "comfort zone" (paragraph 2)? What do you think are the "ails" of pop culture that Rountree has in mind?
3. In paragraph 5, Rountree asserts the ways that she believes the hip-hop culture has an inherent "humanity and powerful social commentary." What do you understand her to mean by that and to what extent do you agree with her?
4. If you have seen either the documentary of Tupak Shakur's life (paragraph 4) or *The Hip-Hop Project* (paragraph 6), explain your assessment of or reaction to it. If you have seen any films or documentaries similar to those that Rountree mentions, what image of the hip-hop culture did they convey?
5. Rountree maintains that the hip-hop culture is a "cross-over culture" (paragraph 5). How doe she define cross-over culture, and to what extent do you agree with her?

HIP-HOP'S BETRAYAL OF BLACK WOMEN

JENNIFER MCLUNE

Jennifer McLune is a librarian, activist, and writer living in Washington, D.C. This piece appeared in ZMagazine Online *in the July/August 2006 issue. According to its mission statement, it is "dedicated to resisting injustice, defending against repression, and*

*creating liberty. It sees the racial, gender, class, and political dimen-
sions of personal life as fundamental to understanding and improving
contemporary circumstances; and it aims to assist activist efforts for a
better future." You can view* Z *at www.zmagsite.zmag.org.*

Kevin Powell in Notes of a HipHop Head writes, "Indeed, like rock and roll, hip-hop sometimes makes you think we men don't like women much at all, except to objectify them as trophy pieces or, as contemporary vernacular mandates, as baby mommas, chickenheads, or bitches.

"But just as it was unfair to demonize men of color in the 1960s solely as wild-eyed radicals when what they wanted, amidst their fury, was a little freedom and a little power, today it is wrong to categorically dismiss hip-hop without taking into serious consideration the socioeconomic conditions (and the many record labels that eagerly exploit and benefit from the ignorance of many of these young artists) that have led to the current state of affairs. Or, to paraphrase the late Tupac Shakur, we were given this world, we did not make it."

Powell's "socio-economic" explanation for the sexism in hip-hop is a way to silence feminist critiques of the culture. It is to make an understanding of the misogynistic objectification of black women in hip-hop so elusive that we can't grasp it long enough to wring the neck of its power over us. His argument completely ignores the fact that women, too, are raised in this environment of poverty and violence, but have yet to produce the same negative and hateful representation of black men that male rappers are capable of making against women.

4   Powell's understanding also lends itself to elitist assumption that somehow poverty breeds sexism, or at least should excuse it. Yet we all know that wealthy white boys can create the same hateful and violent music as poor black boys. As long as the boys can agree that their common enemy is female and that their power resides in their penis, women must not hesitate to name the war they have declared on us.

Hip-hop owes its success to the ideology of woman-hating. It creates, perpetuates, and reaps the rewards of objectification. Sexism and homophobia saturate hip-hop culture and any deviation from these forms of bigotry is made marginal to its most dominant and lucrative expressions. Few artists dare to embody equality and respect between the sexes through their music. Those who do have to fight to be heard above the dominant chorus of misogyny.

The most well known artists who represent an underground and conscious force in hip-hop—like Common, The Roots, Talib Kweli, and others—remain inconsistent, apologetic, and even eager to join the mainstream player's club. Even though fans like me support them because of their moments of decency toward women, they often want to remain on the fence by either playing down their consciousness or by offering props to misogynistic rappers. Most so-called conscious artists appear to care more about their own acceptance by mainstream artists than wanting to make positive changes in the culture.

The Roots, for example, have backed Jay-Z on both his Unplugged release and Fade to Black tours. They've publicly declared their admiration for him and have signed on to his new "indie" hip-hop imprint Def Jam Left to produce their next album. Yet Jay-Z is one of the most notoriously sexist and materialistic rappers of his generation.

8   Hip-hop artists like Talib Kweli and Common market themselves as conscious alternatives, yet they remain passive in the face of unrelenting woman-hating bravado from mainstream artists. They are willing to lament in abstract terms the state of hip-hop, but refuse to name names—unless it's to reassure their mainstream brethren that they have nothing but love for their music.

Talib Kweli has been praised for his song "Black Girl Pain," but clearly he's clueless to how painful it is for a black girl to hear his boy Jay-Z rap, "I pimp hard on a trick, look Fuck if your leg broke bitch, hop up on your good foot."

The misogyny in hip-hop is also given a pass because some of its participants are women. But female hip-hop artists remain marginalized within the industry and culture—except when they are trotted out to defend hip-hop against feminist criticism. But the truth is, all kinds of patriarchal institutions, organizations, and movements have women in their ranks in search of power and meaning. The token presence of individual women changes nothing if women as a group are still scapegoated and degraded.

Unlike men, women in hip-hop don't speak in a collective voice in defense of themselves. The pressure on women to be hyper-feminine and hyper-sexual for the pleasure of men, and the constant threat of being called a bitch, a ho—or worse, a dyke—as a result of being strong, honest, and self-possessed, are real within hip-hop culture and the black community at large. Unless women agree to compromise their truth, self-respect, and unity with other women and instead play dutiful daughter to the phallus that represents hip-hop culture, they will be either targeted, slandered, or ignored altogether. As a result, female rappers are often just as male-identified, violent, materialistic, and ignorant as their male peers.

12   Hip-hop artist Eve, who describes herself as "a pit bull in a skirt," makes an appearance in the Sporty Thieves video for "Pigeons," one of the most hateful misogynistic anthems in hip-hop. Her appearance displays her unity not with the women branded "pigeons," but with the men who label them. This is a heartbreaking example of how hip-hop encourages men to act collectively in the interest of male privilege while dividing women into opposing camps of good and bad or worthy and unworthy of respect.

Lip-service protest against sexism in hip-hop culture is a sly form of public relations to ensure that nobody's money, power, or respect is ever really threatened. Real respect and equality might interfere with hip-hop's commercial appeal. We are asked to dialogue about and ultimately celebrate our "progress"—always predicated on a few rappers and moguls getting rich. Angry young black women are expected to be satisfied with a mere mention that some hip-hop music is sexist and that this sexism of a few rappers is actually, as Powell calls it, "the ghetto blues, urban folk art, a cry out for help." My questions then are: "Whose blues? Whose art? Why won't anybody help the women who are raped in endless rotation by the gaze of the hip-hop camera?"

They expect us to deal with hip-hop's pervasive woman-hating simply by alluding to it, essentially excusing and even celebrating its misogyny, its arrogance, its ignorance. What this angry black woman wants to hear from the apologists is that black women are black people too. That any attack on the women in our community is an attack on us all and that we will no longer be duped by genocidal tendencies in black-face. I want to hear these apologists declare that any black man who makes music perpetuating the hatred of women will be named, shunned, and destroyed, financially and socially, like the traitor of our community he is. That until hip-hop does right by black women, everything hip-hop ever does will fail.

If we accept Powell's explanation for why hip-hop is the way it is—which amounts to an argument for why we should continue to consume and celebrate it— then ultimately we are accepting ourselves as victims who know only how to imitate our victimization while absolving the handful of black folk who benefit from its tragic results. I choose to challenge hip-hop by refusing to reward its commercial aspirations with my money and my attention.

16   I'm tired of the ridiculous excuses and justifications for the unjustifiable pillaring of black women and girls in hip-hop. Are black women the guilty parties behind black men's experience of racism and poverty? Are black women acceptable scapegoats when black men suffer oppression? If black women experience double the oppression as both blacks and women in a racist, patriarchal culture, it is our anger at men and white folks that needs to be heard.

The black men who make excuses for the ideology of woman-hating in hip-hop remind me of those who, a generation ago, supported the attacks on black female writers who went public about the reality of patriarchy in our community. The fact that these black female writers did not create incest, domestic violence, rape, and other patriarchal conditions in the black community did not shield them from being skewered by black men who had their feelings hurt by the exposure of their male privilege and domination of black women. Black women's literature and activism that challenges sexism is often attacked by black men (and many male-identified women) who abhor domination when they are on the losing end, but want to protect it when they think it offers them a good deal.

Black women writers and activists were called traitors for refusing to be silent about the misogynistic order of things and yet women-hating rappers are made heroes by the so-called masses. To be sure, hip-hop is not about keeping it real. Hip-hop lies about the ugly reality that black women were condemned for revealing. Hip-hop is a manipulative narrative that sells because it gets men hard. It is a narrative in which, as a Wu Tang Clan video shows, black women are presented as dancing cave "chicks" in bikinis who get clubbed over the head; or where gang rapes are put to a phat beat; or where working class black women are compared to shit-eating birds.

As a black woman who views sexism as just as much the enemy of my people as racism, I can't buy the apologies and excuses for hip-hop. I will not accept the notion that my sisters deserve to be degraded and humiliated because of the frustrations of black men—all while we suppress our own frustrations, angers, and fears in an effort to be sexy and accommodating. Although Kevin Powell blames the negatives in hip-hop on everything but hip-hop culture itself, he ultimately concludes, "What hip-hop has spawned is a way of winning on our own terms, of us making something out of nothing."

20   If the terms for winning are the objectification of black women and girls, I wonder if any females were at the table when the deal went down. Did we agree to be dehumanized, vilified, made invisible? Rather than pretending to explain away the sexism of hip-hop culture, why doesn't Powell just come clean—in the end it doesn't matter how women are treated. Sexism is the winning ticket to mainstream acceptability and Powell, like Russell Simmons and others, knows this. It's obvious that if these are the winning terms for our creativity, black women are ultimately the losers. And that's exactly how these self-proclaimed players, thugs, and hip-hop intellectuals want us—on our backs and pledging allegiance to the hip-hop nation.

If we were to condemn woman-hating as an enemy of our community, hip-hop would be forced to look at itself and change radically and consistently. Then it would no longer be marketable in the way that these hip-hop intellectuals celebrate. As things stand, it's all about the Benjamins on every level of the culture and black women are being thugged and rubbed all the way to the bank.

PERSONAL RESPONSE

Write in response to McLune's statement in paragraph 5 that "[h]ip-hop owes its success to the ideology of woman hating."

QUESTIONS FOR CLASS OR SMALL-GROUP DISCUSSION

1. How well do you think that McLune explains her title? In what ways is hip-hop a betrayal of black women, according to her?
2. Explain in your own words McLune's argument against Kevin Powell's explanation for the "misogynistic objectification of black women in hip-hop" (paragraph 3).
3. McLune writes: "Few artists dare to embody equality and respect between the sexes through their music" (paragraph 5). What do you think of her assessment of those few artists she names who "represent an underground and conscious force in hip-hop" (paragraph 6)? Can you name similar artists who resist using sexist and homophobic lyrics?
4. To what extent do you agree with McLune's comments on female hip-hop artists (paragraphs 10–12)?
5. Discuss your opinion of what McLune calls for apologists of Black hip-hop music and the artists themselves to do.

○ PERSPECTIVES ON MUSIC AND VIDEO GAMES ○
Suggested Writing Topics

1. Argue your position on Henry Jenkins's opening statement in "Art Form for the Digital Age" that video games shape our culture and should be taken seriously.

2. Henry Jenkins in "Art Form for the Digital Age writes: "It remains to be seen whether games can provide players the freedom they want and still provide an emotionally satisfying and thematically meaningful shape to the experience" (paragraph 16). Using the example of a specific video game (or more than one, if you like), argue whether you believe that games today have achieved that goal.

3. Argue in support of or against the statement that video games have "a socially redeeming value."

4. Rock, hip-hop, rap, and other musical groups have long been able to whip a crowd into an almost hysterical frenzy during their performances. If you have ever seen or experienced such a phenomenon, describe what happened and explore why you think music has that kind of control over people's emotions.

5. Refute or support this statement in Jennifer McLune's "Hip-Hop's Betrayal of Black Women": "Sexism and homophobia saturate hip-hop culture and any deviation from these forms of bigotry is made marginal to its most dominant and lucrative expressions" (paragraph 5). Use examples from song lyrics to support your position.

6. Argue in support of or against Cathleen Rountree's assertion that hip-hop is "a unique, fully animated, communicative and consequential culture" (paragraph 5).

7. Do a detailed analysis of the lyrics of a hip-hop, rap, or other song that you are familiar with. What images do they portray? What message, if any, do they send? How do the lyrics work to make the song artistically good?

8. Analyze the lyrics of a song that you believe to be socially responsible or that comments on a current social issue.

9. Analyze your involvement with a video game that you find particularly compelling.

10. Drawing on any of the readings in this chapter, argue in support of or against the statement that music or video games influence violent behavior in individuals.

Research Topics

1. Henry Jenkins in "Art Form for the Digital Age" notes that a leading critic in the 1920s argued that the important contributions to America's artistic expression came from popular culture, especially "jazz, the Broadway musical, the Hollywood cinema and the comic strip" (paragraph 9). Select one of those forms and research its development as a culturally respectable medium Consider questions like the following: How long did it take for the form to gain legitimacy? What was the nature of early criticism of it? What contributions does the form make to culture? What are

the chief characteristics of its evolution from its primitive beginnings to sophistication?

2. Argue in support of or against the view that rock or hip-hop music is violent or that it is a menace to society.

3. Research the development of hip-hop or gangsta rap music, taking into consideration Jennifer McLune's "Hip-Hop's Betrayal of Black Women" and Cathleen Rountree's "In Defense of Hip-Hop."

4. Research the subject of the influence of violent video games on behavior, drawing on Karen Sternheimer's "Do Video Games Kill?" Note the list of resources that she mentions at the end of her article. You may want to consider doing an analysis of newspaper coverage of more recent school shootings, using an approach similar to Sternheimer's.

5. Research the phenomenon of the physiological and psychological effects of music. Look not only for information about scientific research on the subject but also for comments or criticisms of people skeptical of such research. Weigh the evidence and arrive at your own opinion on the subject.

6. Research a particular musician, musical group, or entertainer from the 1950s, 1960s, or 1970s. Find out the performer's history, the audience he or she appealed to, what distinguished him or her from others, and what his or her influence seems to have been on popular culture. Formulate your own assessment of the entertainer's significance and make that your thesis or central idea.

7. Research a particular kind of music, such as hip-hop, rap, "grunge," alternative, blues, jazz, or salsa for the purpose of identifying its chief characteristics, the way it differs from and is influenced by other kinds of music, and its artistic merit or social significance. Include opposing viewpoints and argue your own position on its merits or significance.

8. Examine allegations of racism, sexism, and/or homophobia leveled against a particular video game, song, musician, or group and draw your own conclusions about the fairness, appropriateness, and/or accuracy of those allegations.

9. Research the history of a popular hand-held video game, including among other things marketing strategy, target audience, responses of users, and longevity of the game.

10. Research the latest studies and opinion pieces on the cultural impact of video games and draw your own conclusions about their importance in shaping culture.

Responding to Visuals

Musicians The Game (left) and 50 Cent (right) perform during the taping of the Vibe Awards in Santa Monica, California, November 15, 2004.

1. What do the performers' facial expressions reveal about how they feel about performing?
2. What do the clothes and jewelry of the performers reveal about them? How do the two performers contrast?
3. How does the background function, especially the blurred graffiti on the wall?
4. Vibe awards are presented to outstanding performers in urban music. What impression of urban music might someone who is unfamiliar with it get from this photograph?

RESPONDING TO VISUALS

© Steve Skjold/Alamy

Youth Express Leader and member, ages 19 and 13, shooting at a Point Blank video game with red and blue replica 45 caliber plastic pistols in St. Paul, Minnesota.

1. What is the implied message of this photograph? What details of the image contribute to your understanding of that message?
2. What do the looks on the two young men's faces suggest about their enjoyment of the video game?
3. What is the effect of the photographer's perspective? Might a change in perspective alter the implied message of the image?
4. How would the image change were the two young people white or some other ethnic group? Does their age have an effect on your perception of the image?

CHAPTER

9

Media Studies

Media studies is a broad subject area that examines the effect of the media on individuals and society. It encompasses all sorts of media—film, television, newspapers, magazines, radio, and the Internet—and looks at the ways that these media influence our opinions, thoughts, behavior, and attitudes. While the subjects of the other chapters in Part 2 are also "media," those chapters look at issues relating to specific media; this chapter considers broader issues relating to "the media" as a whole or several kinds of media. Media analysts often serve as watchdogs against threats to freedom of speech and thought. They concern themselves with social issues such as media violence, censorship in the media, biased reporting, discrimination in programming, and the way in which the media shape social and political discourse. They analyze the power of the media and the power behind the media.

A look at the goals and purposes of university media studies programs gives an idea of what is involved in "media studies." Such programs examine the social, cultural, political, ethical, aesthetic, legal, and economic effects of the media and are interested in the variety of contexts in which the media have influence in those areas. They cite in their rationales for their programs the proliferation of media, the interconnectedness of media on a global level, and the pervasiveness of media in our lives. Furthermore, large numbers of groups, agencies, and organizations identify themselves as "media watchers" and many are media activists. You will find both conservative and liberal, extremists and moderates on such a list.

One particular aspect of popular culture that media analysts have long been interested in is violence in the media and its influence on people, especially young people. The first reading in this chapter provides an overview of the issue by one of the most well-known contributors in the debate over the role media violence plays in forming children's characters and values. An excerpt from her book *Mayhem: Violence as Public Entertainment* (1998), Sissela Bok's "Aggression: The Impact of Media Violence" discusses a topic that is often quite volatile. As you read what she has to say, consider your own position on this controversial issue.

Media watchers know that which news stories are reported and how they are reported—what gets emphasized and what gets left out—can shape or destroy someone's reputation or bring an issue to the public's attention. Peter H. Gibbon's "The End of Admiration: The Media and the Loss of Heroes" focuses on the subject of the role that journalists play in building or destroying the reputations of public figures. He suggests that journalists, by encouraging cynicism and celebrity worship, discourage hero worship and idealism. He believes that, with the media's central bias toward bad news, journalists have made it difficult if not impossible for Americans to have heroes. Consider his words carefully as you read his essay. Is he on target with his critique, or does he over-generalize or ignore positive examples to prove his point? Can you supply examples to either support or refute his argument?

For a different perspective on journalists, David Wallis in "The Wrong Lesson: Teaching College Reporters to be Meek" calls attention to censorship of certain articles in campus newspapers at several colleges and argues that preventing student journalists from printing objectionable stories teaches them to be poor journalists. As you read his commentary, think about your own school newspaper, either on the campus where you are currently a student or on another campus that you have experience with. Were student journalists prevented from printing any articles that administrators felt were at odds with school policy? Or were they at liberty to print all articles they considered newsworthy?

Another issue of concern to media analysts is commercial media's dependence on advertising and their need to make a profit. Jean Kilbourne in "Advertising's Influence on Media Content" argues that advertising has a big influence not only on audiences but also on the media itself. She explains two major ways in which that influence is exerted and gives examples to support her allegations. Kilbourne would argue that the power advertisers hold over commercial media produces a biased media. As you read her examples and her analyses of the influence of advertisers on various kinds of media, see if you can think of other examples to either support or refute what she claims.

AGGRESSION: THE IMPACT OF MEDIA VIOLENCE

Sissela Bok

Born in Sweden and educated in Switzerland, France, and the United States, Sissela Bok earned a Ph.D. in philosophy from Harvard University. She has been a professor of philosophy at Brandeis University and is currently a Distinguished Fellow at the Harvard Center for Population and Development Studies. Widely known for her writings on topics in bioethics, applied ethics, biography and autobiography, and public affairs, her books include Lying: Moral Choice in Public and Private Life *(1978);* Secrets: On the Ethics of Concealment and Revelation *(1983);* A Strategy for Peace: Human Values and the Threat of War *(1989);* Alva Myrdal: A Daughter's Memoir *(1991);* Common Values *(1995); and* Mayhem: Violence as Public Entertainment *(1998), from which the following is taken.*

Even if media violence were linked to no other debilitating effects, it would remain at the center of public debate so long as the widespread belief persists that it glamorizes aggressive conduct, removes inhibitions toward such conduct, arouses viewers, and invites imitation. It is only natural that the links of media violence to aggression should be of special concern to families and communities. Whereas increased fear, desensitization, and appetite primarily affect the viewers themselves, aggression directly injures others and represents a more clear-cut violation of standards of behavior. From the point of view of public policy, therefore, curbing aggression has priority over alleviating subtler psychological and moral damage.

Public concern about a possible link between media violence and societal violence has further intensified in the past decade, as violent crime reached a peak in the early 1990s, yet has shown no sign of downturn, even after crime rates began dropping in 1992. Media coverage of violence, far from declining, has escalated since then, devoting ever more attention to celebrity homicides and copycat crimes. The latter, explicitly modeled on videos or films and sometimes carried out with meticulous fidelity to detail, are never more relentlessly covered in the media than when they are committed by children and adolescents. Undocumented claims that violent copycat crimes are mounting in number contribute further to the ominous sense of threat that these crimes generate. Their dramatic nature drains away the public's attention from other, more mundane forms of aggression that are much more commonplace, and from . . . other . . . harmful effects of media violence.

Media analyst Ken Auletta reports that, in 1992, a mother in France sued the head of a state TV channel that carried the American series *MacGyver,* claiming that her son was accidentally injured as a result of having copied MacGyver's recipe for making a bomb. At the time, Auletta predicted that similar lawsuits were bound to become a weapon against media violence in America's litigious culture. By 1996, novelist John Grisham had sparked a debate about director Oliver Stone's film *Natural Born Killers,* which is reputedly linked to more copycat assaults and murders than any other movie to date. Grisham wrote in protest against the film after learning that a friend of his, Bill Savage, had been killed by nineteen-year-old Sarah Edmondson and her boyfriend Benjamin Darras, eighteen: after repeated viewings of Stone's film on video, the two had gone on a killing spree with the film's murderous, gleeful heroes expressly in mind. Characterizing the film as "a horrific movie that glamorized casual mayhem and bloodlust," Grisham proposed legal action:

> Think of a film as a product, something created and brought to market, not too dissimilar from breast implants. Though the law has yet to declare movies to be products, it is only a small step away. If something goes wrong with the product, either by design or defect, and injury ensues, then its makers are held responsible. . . . It will take only one large verdict against the like of Oliver Stone, and his production company, and perhaps the screenwriter, and the studio itself, and then the party will be over. The verdict will come from the heartland, far away from Southern California, in some small courtroom with no cameras. A jury will finally say enough is enough; that the demons placed in Sarah Edmondson's mind were not solely of her own making.

4   As a producer of books made into lucrative movies—themselves hardly devoid of violence—and as a veteran of contract negotiations within the entertainment industry, Grisham may have become accustomed to thinking of films in industry terms as "products." As a seasoned courtroom lawyer, he may have found the analogy between such products and breast implants useful for invoking product liability

to pin personal responsibility on movie producers and directors for the lethal consequences that their work might help unleash.

Oliver Stone retorted that Grisham was drawing "upon the superstition about the magical power of pictures to conjure up the undead spectre of censorship." In dismissing concerns about the "magical power of pictures" as merely superstitious, Stone sidestepped the larger question of responsibility fully as much as Grisham had sidestepped that of causation when he attributed liability to filmmakers for anything that "goes wrong" with their products so that "injury ensues." Because aggression is the most prominent effect associated with media violence in the public's mind, it is natural that it should also remain the primary focus of scholars in the field. The "aggressor effect" has been studied both to identify the short term, immediate impact on viewers after exposure to TV violence, and the long-term influences. . . . There is near-unanimity by now among investigators that exposure to media violence contributes to lowering barriers to aggression among some viewers. This lowering of barriers may be assisted by the failure of empathy that comes with growing desensitization, and intensified to the extent that viewers develop an appetite for violence—something that may lead to still greater desire for violent programs and, in turn, even greater desensitization.

When it comes to viewing violent pornography, levels of aggression toward women have been shown to go up among male subjects who view sexualized violence against women. "In explicit depictions of sexual violence," a report by the American Psychological Association's Commission on Youth and Violence concludes after surveying available research data, "it is the message about violence more than the sexual nature of the materials that appears to affect the attitudes of adolescents about rape and violence toward women." Psychologist Edward Donnerstein and colleagues have shown that if investigators tell subjects that aggression is legitimate, then show them violent pornography, their aggression toward women increases. In slasher films, the speed and ease with which "one's feelings can be transformed from sensuality into viciousness may surprise even those quite conversant with the links between sexual and violent urges."

Viewers who become accustomed to seeing violence as an acceptable, common, attractive way of dealing with problems find it easier to identify with aggressors and to suppress any sense of pity or respect for victims of violence. Media violence has been found to have stronger effects of this kind when carried out by heroic, impressive, or otherwise exciting figures, especially when they are shown as invulnerable and are rewarded or not punished for what they do. The same is true when the violence is shown as justifiable, when viewers identify with the aggressors rather than with their victims, when violence is routinely resorted to, and when the programs have links to how viewers perceive their own environment.

8   While the consensus that such influences exist grows among investigators as research accumulates, there is no consensus whatsoever about the size of the correlations involved. Most investigators agree that it will always be difficult to disentangle the precise effects of exposure to media violence from the many other factors contributing to societal violence. No reputable scholar accepts the view expressed by 21 percent of the American public in 1995, blaming television more than any

other factor for teenage violence. Such tentative estimates as have been made, suggest that the media account for between 5 and 15 percent of societal violence. Even these estimates are rarely specific enough to indicate whether what is at issue is all violent crime, or such crimes along with bullying and aggression more generally.

One frequently cited investigator proposes a dramatically higher and more specific estimate than others. Psychiatrist Brandon S. Centerwall has concluded from large-scale epidemiological studies of "white homicide" in the United States, Canada, and South Africa in the period from 1945 to 1974, that it escalated in these societies within ten to fifteen years of the introduction of television, and that one can therefore deduce that television has brought a doubling of violent societal crime:

> Of course, there are many factors other than television that influence the amount of violent crime. Every violent act is the result of a variety of forces coming together—poverty, crime, alcohol and drug abuse, stress—of which childhood TV exposure is just one. Nevertheless, the evidence indicates that if hypothetically, television technology had never been developed, there would today be 10,000 fewer homicides each year in the United States, 70,000 fewer rapes, and 700,000 fewer injurious assaults. Violent crime would be half of what it now is.

Centerwall's study, published in 1989, includes controls for such variables as firearm possession and economic growth. But his conclusions have been criticized for not taking into account other factors, such as population changes during the time period studied, that might also play a role in changing crime rates. Shifts in policy and length of prison terms clearly affect these levels as well. By now, the decline in levels of violent crime in the United States since Centerwall's study was conducted, even though television viewing did not decline ten to fifteen years before, does not square with his extrapolations. As for "white homicide" in South Africa under apartheid, each year brings more severe challenges to official statistics from that period.

Even the lower estimates, however, of around 5 to 10 percent of violence as correlated with television exposure, point to substantial numbers of violent crimes in a population as large as America's. But if such estimates are to be used in discussions of policy decisions, more research will be needed to distinguish between the effects of television in general and those of particular types of violent programming, and to indicate specifically what sorts of images increase the aggressor effect and by what means; and throughout to be clearer about the nature of the aggressive acts studied.

12   Media representatives naturally request proof of such effects before they are asked to undertake substantial changes in programming. In considering possible remedies for a problem, inquiring into the reasons for claims about risks is entirely appropriate. It is clearly valid to scrutinize the research designs, sampling methods, and possible biases of studies supporting such claims, and to ask about the reasoning leading from particular research findings to conclusions. But to ask for some demonstrable pinpointing of just when and how exposure to media violence affects levels of aggression sets a dangerously high threshold for establishing risk factors.

We may never be able to trace, retrospectively, the specific set of television programs that contributed to a particular person's aggressive conduct. The same is true when it comes to the links between tobacco smoking and cancer, between drunk driving and automobile accidents, and many other risk factors presenting public health hazards. Only recently have scientists identified the specific channels through which tobacco generates its carcinogenic effects. Both precise causative mechanisms and documented occurrences in individuals remain elusive. Too often, media representatives formulate their requests in what appear to be strictly polemical terms, raising dismissive questions familiar from debates over the effects of tobacco: "How can anyone definitively pinpoint the link between media violence and acts of real-life violence?

If not, how can we know if exposure to media violence constitutes a risk factor in the first place?" Yet the difficulty in carrying out such pinpointing has not stood in the way of discussing and promoting efforts to curtail cigarette smoking and drunk driving. It is not clear, therefore, why a similar difficulty should block such efforts when it comes to media violence. The perspective of "probabilistic causation" . . . is crucial to public debate about the risk factors in media violence. The television industry has already been persuaded to curtail the glamorization of smoking and drunk driving on its programs, despite the lack of conclusive documentation of the correlation between TV viewing and higher incidence of such conduct. Why should the industry not take analogous precautions with respect to violent programming?

Americans have special reasons to inquire into the causes of societal violence. While we are in no sense uniquely violent, we need to ask about all possible reasons why our levels of violent crime are higher than in all other stable industrialized democracies. Our homicide rate would be higher still if we did not imprison more of our citizens than any society in the world, and if emergency medical care had not improved so greatly in recent decades that a larger proportion of shooting victims survive than in the past. Even so, we have seen an unprecedented rise not only in child and adolescent violence, but in levels of rape, child abuse, domestic violence, and every other form of assault.

16   Although America's homicide rate has declined in the 1990s, the rates for suicide, rape, and murder involving children and adolescents in many regions have too rarely followed suit. For Americans aged 15 to 35 years, homicide is the second leading cause of death, and for young African Americans, 15 to 24 years, it is *the* leading cause of death. In the decade following the mid-1980s, the rate of murder committed by teenagers 14 to 17 more than doubled. The rates of injury suffered by small children are skyrocketing, with the number of seriously injured children nearly quadrupling from 1986 to 1993; and a proportion of these injuries are inflicted by children upon one another. Even homicides by children, once next to unknown, have escalated in recent decades.

America may be the only society on earth to have experienced what has been called an "epidemic of children killing children," which is ravaging some of its communities today. As in any epidemic, it is urgent to ask what it is that makes so many capable of such violence, victimizes so many others, and causes countless more to live in fear. Whatever role the media are found to play in this respect, to be sure, is but part of the problem. Obviously, not even the total elimination of media violence would wipe out the problem of violence in the United States or any other society. The same can be said for the proliferation and easy access to guns, or for poverty, drug addiction, and other risk factors. As Dr. Deborah Prothrow-Stith puts it, "It's not an either or. It's not guns or media or parents or poverty."

We have all witnessed the four effects that I have discussed . . .—fearfulness, numbing, appetite, and aggressive impulses—in the context of many influences apart from the media. Maturing involves learning to resist the dominion that these effects can gain over us; and to strive, instead, for greater resilience, empathy, self control, and respect for self and others. The process of maturation and growth in these respects is never completed for any of us; but it is most easily thwarted in childhood, before it has had chance to take root. Such learning calls for nurturing and education at first; then for increasing autonomy in making personal decisions about how best to confront the realities of violence.

Today, the sights and sounds of violence on the screen affect this learning process from infancy on, in many homes. The television screen is the lens through which most children learn about violence. Through the magnifying power of this lens, their everyday life becomes suffused by images of shootings, family violence, gang warfare, kidnappings, and everything else that contributes to violence in our society. It shapes their experiences long before they have had the opportunity to consent to such shaping or developed the ability to cope adequately with this knowledge. The basic nurturing and protection to prevent the impairment of this ability ought to be the birthright of every child.

PERSONAL RESPONSE

Has this essay in any way changed your views on the question of how media violence affects young people? Select a statement or passage that especially interests you, either positively or negatively, and discuss your response to it.

QUESTIONS FOR CLASS OR SMALL-GROUP DISCUSSION

1. Summarize the viewpoints of both John Grisham and Oliver Stone on the matter of "copycat" killings. What does Bok think that both men sidestep in their arguments? What do you think of Grisham's and Stone's arguments? Do you agree with either one? Do you think that Bok is correct in her comments on their arguments?

2. Explain what you understand Bok to mean by the term "'aggressor effect'" (paragraph 6). What do investigators have to say about violent pornography and the aggressor effect?

3. What is your response to this statement: "No reputable scholar accepts the view expressed by 21 percent of the American public in 1995, blaming television more than any other factor for teenage violence" (paragraph 9)? What does Bok have to say about the studies conducted by Brandon S. Centerwall?

4. Bok notes the difficulty of showing the precise causal relationships between tobacco smoking and cancer and between drunken driving and automobile accidents, even though most people seem to accept that smoking causes cancer and that drunk driving is a chief cause of automobile accidents. What do you think of her application of the "'probabilistic causation'" factor to the matter of media violence? That is, how valid do you find her logic? Are you convinced that even though we cannot precisely pinpoint the direct causes of societal violence, we can still discuss and propose "efforts to curtail" the "risk factors in media violence" (paragraph 15)?

5. What, according to Bok, might be the effects on children of early and ongoing exposure to media violence? Are you persuaded by her argument that research on the causal links between exposure to media violence and violent behavior must continue?

THE END OF ADMIRATION: THE MEDIA AND THE LOSS OF HEROES

Peter H. Gibbon

Peter H. Gibbon is a research associate at Harvard University's Graduate School of Education. He has done extensive research on the educational systems of Japan, China, and Germany and is co-author, with Peter J. Gomes, of A Call to Heroism: Renewing America's Vision of Greatness *(2002), about the disappearance of public heroes in American society. His articles have appeared in magazines such as* Newsweek *and* Time *and in a number of newspapers, including the* New York Times, Los Angeles Times, Philadelphia Inquirer, *and* Washington Post. *He has also made guest appearances on many television and radio programs. This piece, based on a talk he delivered at a seminar on the history of journalism hosted by Hillsdale College, appeared in the May 1999 issue of* Imprimis.

I travel around the country talking to Americans about the loss of public heroes. I point out that New York City's Hall of Fame for Great Americans attracts only a few thousand visitors each year, while Cleveland's Rock and Roll Hall of Fame draws over one million.

I describe a 25-foot stained glass window in the Cathedral of St. John the Divine—dedicated in the 1920s to four athletes who exemplified good character and sportsmanship—and I offer a quick list of titles of contemporary books on sports: *Shark Attack,* on the short and bitter career of college coaches; *Meat on the Hoof,* about the mercenary world of professional football; *Personal Fouls,* on the mistreatment of college athletes; *The Courts of Babylon,* on the venality of the women's professional tennis circuit; and *Public Heroes, Private Felons,* on college athletes who break the law.

I contrast two westerns: *High Noon,* which won four Academy Awards in 1959, and *Unforgiven,* which was voted "Best Picture" in 1992. The hero of *High Noon,* Will Kane, is a U.S. marshal. The hero of *Unforgiven,* Will Munny, is a reformed killer and alcoholic reduced to pig farming.

4   I mention that our best-selling postage stamps feature Elvis Presley and Marilyn Monroe and that our most popular TV show was, until it left the air recently, *Seinfeld.*

I remind my audiences that Thomas Jefferson is now thought of as the president with the slave mistress and Mozart as the careless genius who liked to talk dirty.

I add that a recent biography of Mother Teresa is titled *The Missionary Position.*

I offer some reasons for the disappearance of public heroes. Athletes have given up on being team players and role models. Popular culture is often irreverent, sometimes deviant. Revisionist historians present an unforgiving, skewed picture of the past. Biographers are increasingly hostile toward their subjects. Social scientists stridently assert that human beings are not autonomous but are conditioned by genes and environment.

8   Hovering in the background are secularism, which suggests that human beings are self-sufficient and do not need God, and modernism—a complex artistic and literary movement that repudiates structure, form, and conventional values.

Finally, in an age of instant communication, in which there is little time for reflection, accuracy, balance or integrity—the media creates the impression that sleaze is everywhere, that nothing is sacred, that no one is noble, and that there are no heroes.

Nothing to Admire

Radio, television, and computers offer news with such speed that newspaper and magazine circulation has plummeted, and readers have smaller vocabularies. I recently wrote an op-ed piece syndicated in several newspapers. My title, *"Nil Admirari,"* which means "nothing to admire," came from the Roman lyric poet Horace.

None of the newspapers used the title, and one editor reminded me that newspaper stories are now aimed at a sixth-grade reading level.

12   In the Age of Information, the image reigns. There are 81 television sets for every 100 Americans. In the typical household, the television is on six hours a day. Television has become our chief source of local and national news, and broadcast journalists have become more prominent and more powerful than columnists. There used to be three channels. Now, there are over one hundred. When we weary of television channels, we can turn to countless radio stations, videotapes, and web pages.

This explosion of information means we now have a vast menu of choices that allows us to be transported to many different worlds and provides us with educational opportunities undreamed of thirty years ago. It also means that we spend more time in front of television and computer screens and less time reading to our children. It is no wonder that our children have shorter attention spans and smaller vocabularies.

A Wired World

Along with this vast menu of choices is the absence of gatekeepers. As parents, we need to realize that there are dangers that come with too many choices and too few guides. We need to remind ourselves that their well-being depends not only on nutrition, sunlight, and exercise; on friendship, work, and love; but also on *how they see the world*. Subtly and powerfully, the media helps shape their world view.

The media has a liberal bias, but its *central* bias is toward bad news. Accidents, crimes, conflict, and scandal are interesting. Normality is boring. The prevalence of bad news and the power of the image encourage children—and us—to overestimate the chance of an accident, the risk of disease, the rate of violence, the frequency of marital infidelity. The average policeman, for example, never fires a gun in action, and most Americans are monogamous.

16   In a wired world with no restraint, the media can misinform us. It can also make us suspicious, fearful, and cynical. It can lead us to lose faith in our nation, repudiate our past, question our leaders, and cease to believe in progress.

We know the worst about everyone instantly. Over and over again, we see clips of George Bush vomiting, Dan Quayle misspelling "potato," Gerald Ford tripping.

No longer do we want our child to grow up and become president. We harbor dark suspicions about the personal conduct of scoutmasters, priests, and coaches. We think army sergeants harass their subordinates. We have trouble calling any public figure a hero. A wired world becomes a world without heroes, a world of *nil admirari*, with no one to admire.

Americans tell pollsters the country is in moral and spiritual decline. In the midst of peace and prosperity, with equality increasing and health improving, we are sour. With our military powerful and our culture ascendant, pessimism prevails.

Crusaders or Rogues?

20   Should we blame journalists? It is certainly tempting. Just as we blame teachers for the poor performance of students, so we can blame reporters for the nation's malaise.

But just as teachers are not responsible for poverty and disintegrating families, journalists are not responsible for satellites, fiber optic cables, transistors, and microprocessors—the inventions that make possible instant information. Journalists did not cause the sexual revolution. They did not invent celebrity worship or gossip. Nor did they create leaders who misbehave and let us down.

At the same time, in the world of *nil admirari*, journalists are not innocent, and they know it. Roger Rosenblatt, a veteran of the *Washington Post, Time, Life,* and the *New York Times Magazine,* says, "My trade of journalism is sodden these days with practitioners who seem incapable of admiring others or anything." In his memoir, former presidential press secretary and ABC News senior editor Pierre Salinger writes, "No reporter can be famous unless they have brought someone down." And *New Yorker* writer Adam Gopnik comments, "The reporter used to gain status by dining with his subjects; now he gains status by dining on them."

Journalists can also be greedy. Eager for money, some reporters accept handsome speaking fees from organizations they are supposed to be covering. Some are dishonest, making up quotations, even inventing stories. No longer content with anonymity, many reporters seek celebrity, roaming the talk shows and becoming masters of the sound bite. They write autobiographies and give interviews to other journalists.

24   Just as our president is enamored of Hollywood, so are our journalists. Larry King recently spent a full hour interviewing singer Madonna. *Sixty Minutes* devoted much of a show to "bad boy" actor Sean Penn. Actors, supermodels, and musicians are no longer just entertainers. They are treated like philosopher–kings, telling us how to live. In a recent interview, actress Sharon Stone, star of *Basic Instinct,* advises parents to make condoms available to their teenagers.

Aggressive and anxious for ratings, television news shows feature hosts and guests who come armed with hardened opinions. Many are quick to judge and prone to offer easy solutions for complex problems. "Talking heads" argue, yell, interrupt, and rarely make concessions.

But in the world of *nil admirari,* journalists are now reviled more often than revered.

In the 1980s, muckraker Steven Brill skewered lawyers. In his new magazine, *Brill's Content,* he lambastes journalists. In *Right in the Old Gazoo,* former Wyoming Senator Alan Simpson accuses journalists of becoming "lazy, complacent, sloppy, self-serving, self-aggrandizing, cynical and arrogant beyond belief." In *Breaking the News,* writer James Fallows comments that while movies once portrayed journalists as crusaders, they are now portrayed as rogues "more loathsome than . . . lawyers, politicians, and business moguls."

28   How much of this is new?

Since the founding of America, reporters have been harsh critics of public figures. George Washington did not like reading in pamphlets that the essence of his education had been "gambling, reveling, horse racing and horse whipping." Thomas Jefferson did not relish the label "effeminate." Abraham Lincoln did not appreciate being portrayed by cartoonists as a baboon.

Throughout our history, reporters have also received harsh criticism. Just after the Civil War, abolitionist Harriet Beecher Stowe claimed the press had become so vicious that no respectable American man would ever again run for president. In 1870, the British critic and poet Matthew Arnold toured America and concluded, "If one were searching for the best means . . . to kill in a whole nation . . . the feeling for what is elevated, one could not do better than take the American newspaper." At the turn of the century, novelist Henry James condemned what he called the "impudence [and] the shamelessness of the newspaper and the interviewer." In the early decades of the 20th century, "yellow journalism," "muckraking," and "debunking" became household words to describe newspaper stories that exaggerated and distorted events to make them more sensational.

Nor is the media's fascination with celebrities new. When silent screen idol Rudolph Valentino and educational reformer Charles William Eliot died within a day of each other in 1926, high-minded Americans complained that the press devoted too many columns to a celebrity and too few to a hero of education. Between 1925 and 1947, millions of Americans listened to Walter Winchell's radio program, *The Lucky Strike Hour* and read his column in the *New York Mirror*. Winchell hung out at the Stork Club, collecting gossip about celebrities and politicians from tipsters. He urged all newspaper offices to post these words on their walls: "Talk of virtue and your readers will become bored. Hint of gossip and you will secure perfect attention."

32   In short, media critics have always called reporters cynical. Reporters have always collected gossip and featured celebrities. And high-minded Americans have always warned that journalists could lower the nation's moral tone.

An Empire of Information

From the outset, thoughtful critics conceded that journalists had an obligation to inform and expose. But those same critics were afraid that reporters would eliminate privacy and slander leaders; that by repeating gossip and emphasizing crime and corruption, newspapers would coarsen citizens; and that journalists would become more influential than ministers, novelists, professors, and politicians. They were right.

Journalists *have* become more powerful than ministers, novelists, professors, and politicians. They preside over an empire of information unimaginable to our ancestors—an empire that reaches small villages in India and can change governments in China; an empire characterized by staggering choice, variety, and technological sophistication.

An empire of information ruled by the modern media *has* eliminated privacy. With recorders and cameras, reporters freely enter dugouts, locker rooms, board rooms, hotel rooms. There are neither secrets nor taboos. Some listen in on private telephone conversations and sift through garbage for incriminating documents.

36   Early critics were also right to worry that journalists could contribute to a decline in taste and judgment, could destroy the feeling for the elevated, could eliminate appetite for the admirable. The empire they have created is slick, quick, hard-hitting, entertaining, and inescapable. It makes us more knowledgeable, but it also leaves us overwhelmed, convinced that the world is a sleazy place, and mistrustful of authority and institutions. It all but extinguishes our belief in heroism.

Hope for the Future

Are there reasons to be hopeful about the future of America and the future of the media?

I believe there are. Intent on exposing our faults, we forget what we do well. America is much better and healthier than the country portrayed in the media and in pessimistic opinion polls. The American people are basically hardworking, ideal-istic, compassionate, and religious.

American journalism is still biased, but it is slowly becoming more balanced. We have the *Washington Times* as well as the *Washington Post, U.S. News & World Report* as well as *Newsweek, National Review* as well as the *Nation*, the *Wall Street Journal* as well as the *New York Times*. We have prominent conservative and liberal commentators.

40   In the late 1990s, newspaper and television journalists have become more self-critical. Some recognize the need to become less cynical, less greedy, less celebrity oriented, less combative; and a few recognize the need to report the normal and the good rather than only the sensational and the deviant.

Reporters, editors, and publishers are influential, but they are not all-powerful. In America, the consumer is king. We choose our sources of information just as we purchase cars and potato chips. When CNN interrupted its coverage of the Lorena Bobbitt trial to report on the Chernobyl nuclear disaster, the number of angry callers caused the network's switchboard to crash. Reporters could be more courageous and less concerned with profits, but American citizens could be more high-minded.

In the Age of Information, journalists and citizens face the same challenges. We need to study the past so as not to become arrogant, to remember the good so as not to become cynical, and to recognize America's strengths so as not to dwell on her weaknesses. We need to be honest and realistic without losing our capacity for admi-ration—and to be able to embrace complexity without losing our faith in the heroic.

PERSONAL RESPONSE

Gibbon states that "we have trouble calling any public figure a hero" (paragraph 16). Are there public figures whom you admire as heroes, and if so, what makes them heroic? If you cannot think of any public hero whom you would regard as a hero, explore reasons why this is so.

QUESTIONS FOR CLASS OR SMALL-GROUP DISCUSSION

1. Assess the effectiveness of the series of contrasts Gibbon makes in the first six paragraphs. Then discuss the explanations he gives to account for them in the next several paragraphs. Do you accept his explanations? Are there any that you would challenge?

2. Gibbon alleges that journalists can be greedy and dishonest, seeking ce-lebrity status for themselves (paragraphs 24 and 25). To what extent do you agree with Gibbon? Can you name journalists who either support or refute his claims?

3. In paragraph 34, Gibbon briefly summarizes both positive and negative views of journalists over time, with emphasis on the negative. He concludes

that those who feared the worst "were right." To what extent do you agree with Gibbon that the worst fears of critics of journalists have been realized?

4. To what extent do you agree with Gibbon in this passage from paragraph 37: "The empire they created is slick, quick, hard-hitting, entertaining, and inescapable. It makes us more knowledgeable, but it also leaves us overwhelmed, convinced that the world is a sleazy place, and mistrustful of authority and institutions. It all but extinguishes our belief in heroism"? Do you think he is wrong or unfair in any part of this passage?

THE WRONG LESSON: TEACHING COLLEGE REPORTERS TO BE MEEK

David Wallis

David Wallis is the founder of Featurewell.com, a Web-based syndicate that markets articles by more than 1,000 prominent journalists. Wallis is also the editor of the book Killed: Great Journalism Too Hot to Print *(2004), a collection of provocative articles that were killed by leading publications mostly because they might have attracted lawsuits or offended; and* Killed Cartoons: Casualties of the War on Free Expression *(2007). This article appeared in the August–September 2004 issue of* Reason.

When staffers at Baylor University's newspaper published an editorial earlier this year that supported same-sex marriage and likened discrimination against gays to religious intolerance, the president of the Baptist school in Waco, Texas, did not turn the other cheek. Instead, Robert B. Sloan issued a veiled threat to the paper's editors. "Espousing in a Baylor publication a view that is so out of touch with traditional Christian teachings," he seethed in the next edition of the *Baylor Lariat*, "comes dangerously close to violating University policy."

A board of faculty advisers promised that the *Lariat* would "avoid this error" in the future. Explaining that the editors would not be punished for their sins, a board member said, "It was a teachable moment." Teachable indeed. But what was the lesson?

Forget for the moment that Baylor is a private university not subject to First Amendment limitations and that the school owns the newspaper. At a crucial moment in their development, Baylor journalists-in-training learned to shut up, fall in line, and stop questioning authority. That's bad for liberty, whether or not it was an infringement of liberty in itself.

4   Judging by the consistently tame questioning of America's political leaders and the prevalence of "have a nice day" journalism that features countless stories on dogs with 12-inch tongues and cats that can use a toilet just like a human being,

deference and inoffensiveness are lessons that have been taken to heart by many in the mainstream media.

The Baylor case is no isolated incident. Many school administrators, faced with student editors who boldly test the boundaries, react like the commissars at the old Soviet *Pravda*. In recent months, Barton County Community College in Kansas fired its paper's media adviser after she resisted an order not to run a letter criticizing the school's basketball coach. La Roche College, a Catholic school in Pittsburgh, confiscated 900 copies of the *La Roche Courier* in which a columnist dared to suggest that "condoms and other forms of contraception could eliminate unwanted babies out of wedlock." And Long Island University in New York changed the locks on its student newspaper offices and suspended its editor for rigorous reporting that revealed the failing grades of a former student government president who had mysteriously resigned.

Deplorable in itself, a repressive atmosphere on campus can breed a pernicious self-censorship. Chris Carroll, director of student media at Vanderbilt University and a former president of College Media Advisers, an organization that monitors collegiate censorship, worries that young journalists are increasingly "submissive." He cites a troubling case at his own university: "I had a freshman who was on something that I think could have been a story, [concerning] our current chancellor, with some of his affiliations with corporate boards outside the school. He kept digging and learning more and more and more, and he talked to the chancellor, who scared the living shit out of him. . . . He said, 'You know I'm here on financial aid; these people can sue me, ruin me, ruin my family,' and he quit the paper. He's gone."

If colleges discourage young reporters from investigating powerful interests while in school, how can society expect them to probe political corruption once they graduate? When students cower rather than proclaim their opinions on campus, how can we expect them to stand up for what they believe off campus?

8   There's a simple, market-driven tactic to convince schools not to strangle free speech. Parents who value the First Amendment should steer away from colleges that censor their students. Hitting offending colleges in the endowment would provide dictatorial administrators with a valuable lesson, one they would not soon forget.

PERSONAL RESPONSE

Describe your own school's attitude toward the student newspaper, either at your current school or at one that you have previously attended.

QUESTIONS FOR CLASS OR SMALL-GROUP DISCUSSION

1. What, for Wallis, seems to be the "right lesson" to teach college reporters? Do you agree with him?

2. How does Wallis define liberty and what actions of college administrators represent a denial of that liberty? To what extent does his implied definition reflect your own?

3. Where does Wallis use loaded language? How does that language work to advance, support, or argue his position?

4. Discuss whether you believe that student newspapers should be free to print anything they like, excluding libelous, false, or inaccurate stories.

ADVERTISING'S INFLUENCE ON MEDIA CONTENT

JEAN KILBOURNE

Jean Kilbourne is a social theorist who has lectured for many years on advertising images of women and on alcohol and liquor advertisements. A widely published writer and speaker who has twice been named Lecturer of the Year by the National Association of Campus Activities, she is perhaps best known for her award-winning documentaries on advertising images, Killing Us Softly, Slim Hopes, *and* Pack of Lies. *This piece is an excerpt from Chapter 1 of Kilbourne's latest book,* Can't Buy My Love: How Advertising Changes the Way We Think and Feel *(2000) (hard cover title:* Deadly Persuasion: Why Women and Girls Must Fight the Addictive Power of Advertising*). You can find additional resources and other information at Kilbourne's website: www.jeankilbourne.com.*

Advertising's influence on media content is exerted in two major ways: via the suppression of information that would harm or "offend the sponsor" and via the inclusion of editorial content that is advertiser-friendly, that creates an environment in which the ads look good. The line between advertising and editorial content is blurred by "advertorials" (advertising disguised as editorial copy) "product placement" in television programs and feature films, and the widespread use of "video news releases," corporate public-relations puff pieces aired by local television stations as genuine news. Up to 85 percent of the news we get is bought and paid for by corporations eager to gain positive publicity.

Although people have become used to news reporters popping up in commercials and movies (as Joan Lunden and Linda Ellerbee did in television commercials for Vaseline and Maxwell House coffee, respectively, and as almost everyone at CNN did in the movie *Contact*), many were shocked in late 1997 when retired newsman David Brinkley became the pitchman for agribusiness giant Archer Daniels Midland, a company that has been convicted of price fixing on an international scale.

In 1998 Nike's sponsorship of CBS's Olympic coverage was rewarded when the correspondents delivered the news wearing jackets emblazoned with Nike's symbolic swoosh. The president of CBS News vehemently denied that this sponsorship had anything to do with the thwarting of a follow-up to a hard-hitting investigative piece on Nike for *48 Hours*. The editor of *The San Francisco Examiner* likewise denied that Nike's co-sponsorship of their big annual promotion was in any way related to the decision to kill a column by a reporter that was highly critical of Nike.

4   In 1996 Chrysler Corporation set off a furor by demanding in writing that magazines notify it in advance about "any and all editorial content that encompasses sexual, political, social issues or any editorial that might be construed as provocative or offensive." According to Chrysler spokesman Mike Aberlich, placing an ad is like buying a house: "You decide the neighborhood you want to be in." Fear of losing the lucrative Chrysler account led *Esquire* to kill a long story with a gay theme, already in page proofs, by accomplished author David Leavitt. Will Blythe, the magazine's literary editor, promptly quit, saying in his letter of resignation that "in effect, we're taking marching orders (albeit, indirectly) from advertisers." Of course, had Blythe not gone public, the public would never have known what happened. When we don't get the story, we don't know what we're missing.

In reaction to the Chrysler letter, the American Society of Magazine Editors and Magazine Publishers of America issued a joint statement in the fall of 1997 calling for editorial integrity and barring magazines from giving advertisers a preview of stories, photos, or tables of contents for upcoming issues. This is to their credit, of course, but it won't protect us from similar phenomena occurring: According to an article in the *Columbia Journalism Review,* in 1997 a major advertiser (unnamed in the article) warned all three newsweeklies—*Time, Newsweek,* and *U.S. News & World Report*—that it would award all of its advertising to the magazine that portrayed its company's industry in the most favorable light during the upcoming quarter.

More often than not, self-censorship by magazine editors and television producers makes such overt pressure by corporations unnecessary. According to Kurt Andersen, the former editor of *New York* magazine, "Because I worked closely and happily with the publisher at *New York,* I was aware who the big advertisers were. My antennae were turned on, and I read copy thinking, 'Is this going to cause Calvin Klein or Bergdorf big problems.'" No doubt this is what ran through the minds of the CBS executives who canceled Ed Asner's series after two large corporate advertisers—Vidal Sassoon and Kimberly-Clark—withdrew their sponsorship because of Asner's association with Medical Aid for El Salvador.

Sometimes the self-censorship involves an entire industry rather than a specific company or corporation. For example, several radio stations in the Midwest not only refused to play a commercial advocating vegetarianism in which country singer k.d. lang appeared as a spokesperson, but also banned lang's songs from the air. Clearly this kind of thinking has more serious consequences than an occasional editorial omission or favorable mention—it warps a worldview and distorts the editorial content we read and the programs we listen to and watch.

8   Nowhere is this more obvious than in most women's and girls' magazines, where there is a very fine line, if any, between advertising and editorial content. Most of these magazines gladly provide a climate in which ads for diet and beauty products will be looked at with interest, even with desperation. And they suffer consequences from advertisers if they fail to provide such a climate.

Gloria Steinem provides a striking example of this in her article "Sex, Lies & Advertising," in which she discusses an award-winning story on Soviet women that was featured on the cover of the November 1980 issue of *Ms.* In those days, *Ms.*, like every other woman's magazine, depended on advertising. Following that story, *Ms.* lost all hope of ever getting Revlon ads. Why? Because the Soviet women on the cover weren't wearing makeup.

More recently, the editor of *New Woman* magazine in Australia resigned after advertisers complained about the publication's use of a heavyset cover girl, even though letters had poured in from grateful readers. According to *Advertising Age International,* her departure "made clear the influence wielded by advertisers who remain convinced that only thin models spur sales of beauty products." One prevalent form of censorship in the mass media is the almost complete invisibility, the eradication, of real women's faces and bodies.

No wonder women's magazines so often have covers that feature luscious cakes and pies juxtaposed with articles about diets. "85 Ways to Lose Weight," *Woman's Day* tells us—but probably one of them isn't the "10-minute ice cream pie" on the cover. This is an invitation to pathology, fueling the paradoxical obsession with food and weight control that is one of the hallmarks of eating disorders.

12   It can be shocking to look at the front and back covers of magazines. Often there are ironic juxtapositions. A typical woman's magazine has a photo of some rich food on the front cover, a cheesecake covered with luscious cherries or a huge slice of apple pie with ice cream melting on top. On the back cover, there is usually a cigarette ad, often one implying that smoking will keep women thin. Inside the magazine are recipes, more photos of fattening foods, articles about dieting—and lots of advertising featuring very thin models. There usually also is at least one article about an uncommon disease or trivial health hazard, which can seem very ironic in light of the truly dangerous product being glamorized on the back cover.

In February 1999, *Family Circle* featured on its front cover a luscious photo of "gingham mini-cakes," while promoting articles entitled "New! Lose-Weight, Stay-Young Diet," "Super Foods That Act Like Medicine," and "The Healing Power of Love." On the back cover was an ad for Virginia Slims cigarettes. The same week, *For Women First* featured a chocolate cake on its cover along with one article entitled "Accelerate Fat Loss" and another promising "Breakthrough Cures" for varicose veins, cellulite, PMS, stress, tiredness, and dry skin. On the back cover, an ad for Doral cigarettes said, "Imagine getting more." *The Ladies' Home Journal* that same month offered on its cover "The Best Chocolate Cake You Ever Ate," along with its antidote, "Want to Lose 10 lbs? Re-program Your Body." Concern for their readers' health was reflected in two articles highlighted on the cover, "12 Symptoms You Must Not Ignore" and "De-Stressors for Really Crazy Workdays"—and then undermined by the ad for Basic cigarettes on the back cover (which added to the general confusion by picturing the pack surrounded by chocolate candies).

The diseases and health hazards warned about in the women's magazines are often ridiculous. *Woman's Day* once offered a "Special Report on Deadly Appliances," which warned us about how our appliances, such as toasters, coffeemakers, baby monitors, and nightlights, can suddenly burst into flame. Lest we think this is not a serious problem, the article tells us that in 1993, the last year for which figures were available, 80 people died and 370 were injured by these killer appliances.

I don't wish to minimize any death or injury. However, on the back cover of this issue of *Woman's Day* is an advertisement for cigarettes, a product that kills over four hundred thousand people, year in and year out.

The January 1995 issue of *Redbook* warns us on the cover about all sorts of pressing problems from frizzy hair to "erotic accidents" and promotes an article entitled "If Only They'd Caught It Sooner: The Tests Even Healthy Women Need." On the back cover, as always, an ad for Virginia Slims. Needless to say, being set afire from smoking in bed (one of the leading causes of fire deaths) does not make it into the "erotic accidents" article.

16   An informal survey of popular women's magazines in 1996 found cover stories on some of the following health issues: skin cancer, Pap smears, leukemia, how breast cancer can be fought with a positive attitude, how breast cancer can be held off with aspirin, and the possibility that dry-cleaned clothes can cause cancer. There were cigarette ads on the back covers of all these magazines—and not a single mention inside of lung cancer and heart disease caused by smoking. In spite of increasing coverage of tobacco issues in the late 1990s, the silence in women's magazines has continued, in America and throughout the world. In my own research, I continue to find scanty coverage of smoking dangers, no feature stories on lung cancer or on smoking's role in causing many other cancers and heart disease . . . and hundreds of cigarette ads.

Dr. Holly Atkinson, a health writer for *New Woman* between 1985 and 1990, recalled that she was barred from covering smoking-related issues, and that her editor struck any reference to cigarettes in articles on topics ranging from wrinkles to cancer. When Atkinson confronted the editor, a shouting match ensued. "Holly, who do you think supports this magazine?" demanded the editor. As Helen Gurley Brown, former editor of *Cosmopolitan*, said: "Having come from the advertising world myself, I think, 'Who needs somebody you're paying millions of dollars a year to come back and bite you on the ankle?'"

It is not just women's magazines that tailor their articles to match their ads. The July 1995 issue of *Life* magazine warns us of the dangers our children face, including drugs, and asks, "How can we keep our children safe?" On the back cover is a Marlboro ad. Our children are far more likely to die from tobacco-related diseases than from any other cause, but cigarettes are not mentioned in the article.

Americans rely on the media for our health information. But this information is altered, distorted, even censored on behalf of the advertisers—advertisers for alcohol, cigarettes, junk food, diet products. We get most of our information from people who are likely to be thinking, "Is this going to cause Philip Morris or Anheuser-Busch big problems?" Of course, in recent years there has been front-page coverage of the liability suits against the tobacco industry and much discussion about antismoking legislation. However, there is still very little information about the health consequences of smoking, especially in women's magazines. The Partnership for a Drug-Free America, made up primarily of media companies dependent on advertising, basically refuses to warn children against the dangers of alcohol and tobacco. The government is spending $195 million in 1999 on a national media campaign to dissuade adolescents from using illicit drugs, but not a penny of the appropriated tax dollars is going to warn about the dangers of smoking or drinking.

20 No wonder most people still don't understand that these heavily advertised drugs pose a much greater threat to our young people and kill far more Americans than all illicit drugs combined. Thirty percent of Americans still don't know that smoking shortens life expectancy, and almost 60 percent don't know it causes emphysema. There is still so much ignorance that, when I was invited recently to give a talk on tobacco advertising to students at a progressive private school outside Boston, the person extending the invitation said she was also going to invite someone from the tobacco industry to represent "the other side." I was tempted to ask her if she felt equally compelled to have a batterer on hand during a discussion of domestic violence.

The influence of these huge and powerful corporations on the media leads to a pernicious kind of censorship. The problem is exacerbated by the fact that many of these corporations own and control the media. In 1996 the Seagram Company ran a whiskey ad on an NBC affiliate in Texas, thus breaking the decades-old tradition of liquor ads not being carried on television. Although network television is leery of running liquor ads for fear of offending their beer advertisers, *Advertising Age* reported that Seagram might have a "winning card to play," since the company owns 50 percent of both the USA Network and the Sci-Fi Channel. Although both have a ban on hard-liquor advertising, a top executive for USA Network said, "If Seagram came to us with a hard-liquor ad, we'd have to look at it."

Today, Time Warner, Sony, Viacom, Disney, Bertelsmann, and News Corporation together control most publishing, music, television, film, and theme-park entertainment throughout the developed world. It is estimated that by the end of the millennium these companies will own 90 percent of the world's information, from newspapers to computer software to film to television to popular music. We may be able to change the channel, but we won't be able to change the message.

Almost everywhere we look these days, anywhere in the world, there is a message from one of these conglomerates. An ad in *Advertising Age* shows a huge picture of the earth and the headline, "Do you see the trillion dollar market?" The triumph of democracy is becoming the triumph of consumerism, as the global village is reduced to a "trillion dollar market."

24 "Why 6,000,000 women who used to carry a little red book now carry a little red lipstick," says an ad for *Allure*, an American beauty magazine, featuring a Chinese woman in a military uniform wearing bright red lipstick. The copy continues, "When nail polish becomes political, and fashion becomes philosophy, *Allure* magazine will be there." In the world of advertising the political is only personal. Six million women carrying a book of political ideas might be a movement, even a revolution. The same women, carrying lipstick, are simply red-lipped consumers. Advertisers are adept at appropriating dissent and rebellion, slickly packaging it, and then selling it right back to us.

Although the conglomerates are transnational, the culture they sell is American. Not the American culture of the past, which exported writers like Ernest

Hemingway and Edgar Allan Poe, musical greats like Louis Armstrong and Marian Anderson, plays by Eugene O'Neill and Tennessee Williams, and Broadway musicals like *West Side Story.* These exports celebrated democracy, freedom, and vitality as the American way of life.

Today we export a popular culture that promotes escapism, consumerism, violence, and greed. Half the planet lusts for Cindy Crawford, lines up for blockbuster films like *Die Hard 2* with a minimum of dialogue and a maximum of violence (which travels well, needing no translation), and dances to the monotonous beat of the Backstreet Boys. *Baywatch,* a moronic television series starring Ken and Barbie, has been seen by more people in the world than any other television show in history. And at the heart of all this "entertainment" is advertising. As Simon Anholt, an English consultant specializing in global brand development, said, "The world's most powerful brand is the U.S. This is because it has Hollywood, the world's best advertising agency. For nearly a century, Hollywood has been pumping out two-hour cinema ads for Brand U.S.A., which audiences around the world flock to see." When a group of German advertising agencies placed an ad in *Advertising Age* that said, "Let's make America great again," they left no doubt about what they had in mind. The ad featured cola, jeans, burgers, cigarettes, and alcohol—an advertiser's idea of what makes America great.

Some people might wonder what's wrong with this. On the most obvious level, as multinational chains replace local stores, local products, and local character, we end up in a world in which everything looks the same and everyone is Gapped and Starbucked. Shopping malls kill vibrant downtown centers locally and create a universe of uniformity internationally. Worse, we end up in a world ruled by, in John Maynard Keynes's phrase, the values of the casino. On this deeper level, rampant commercialism undermines our physical and psychological health, our environment, and our civic life and creates a toxic society. Advertising corrupts us and, I will argue, promotes a dissociative state that exploits trauma and can lead to addiction. To add insult to injury, it then co-opts our attempts at resistance and rebellion.

28   Although it is virtually impossible to measure the influence of advertising on a culture, we can learn something by looking at cultures only recently exposed to it. In 1980 the Gwich'in tribe of Alaska got television, and therefore massive advertising, for the first time. Satellite dishes, video games, and VCRs were not far behind. Before this, the Gwich'in lived much the way their ancestors had for a thousand generations. Within ten years, the young members of the tribe were so drawn by television they no longer had time to learn ancient hunting methods, their parents' language, or their oral history. Legends told around campfires could not compete with *Beverly Hills 90210.* Beaded moccasins gave way to Nike sneakers, sled dogs to gas-powered skimobiles, and "tundra tea" to Folger's instant coffee.

Human beings used to be influenced primarily by the stories of our particular tribe or community, not by stories that are mass-produced and market-driven. As George Gerbner, one of the world's most respected researchers on the influence of the media, said, "For the first time in human history, most of the stories about people, life, and values are told not by parents, schools, churches, or others in the community who have something to tell, but by a group of distant conglomerates that have something to sell." The stories that most influence our children these days are the stories told by advertisers.

PERSONAL RESPONSE

What is your initial response to what Kilbourne tells readers that she will argue in the rest of her book: "Advertising corrupts us and, I will argue, promotes a dissociative state that exploits trauma and can lead to addiction. To add insult to injury, it then co-opts our attempts at resistance and rebellion" (paragraph 27)? Are you skeptical or intrigued?

QUESTIONS FOR CLASS OR SMALL-GROUP DISCUSSION

1. What is your opinion on the matter of whether corporations should have the right to review editorial content of publications they advertise in and whether magazines should practice self-censorship? Is it just good business, or is it more than that, as Kilbourne claims? Do you think Kilbourne overreacts when she writes that this practice "warps a worldview and distorts the editorial content we read and the programs we listen to and watch" (paragraph 7)?

2. State in your own words the issues that Kilbourne is most concerned about in her allegations against women's and girls' magazines. To what extent do you agree with her? Although she cites many examples, can you provide others that either support or refute her arguments?

3. Summarize Kilbourne's point about alcohol and tobacco advertising. Is her argument valid? To what extent do you agree with her?

4. Kilbourne alleges that America exports "a popular culture that promotes escapism, consumerism, violence, and greed" (paragraph 26). To what extent do you agree with her? Can you provide examples that either support or refute this view?

5. Without having read the rest of the book that this excerpt comes from *(Can't Buy My Love: How Advertising Changes the Way We Think and Feel)*, are you inclined to think that Kilbourne is right in her criticism of advertising, or do you find her argument in this excerpt unconvincing?

○ PERSPECTIVES ON MEDIA STUDIES ○

Suggested Writing Topics

1. Advertisers contend that they do not create problems but simply reflect the values of society. Explain your position on the subject of how much responsibility advertisers should bear for the images they produce in their advertisements.

2. Define the word "hero" and use a person you admire to illustrate the meaning of the word.

3. With Peter H. Gibbon's "The End of Admiration: The Media and the Loss of Heroes" in mind, argue either in support of or against the statement that America no longer has heroes.

4. Survey a selection of magazines aimed at a specific audience—girls, women, boys, men—in terms of the kind of analysis Jean Kilbourne does in "Advertising's Influence on Media Content." Explain what you find and whether your conclusions agree with or differ from hers.

5. Use examples of well-known advertisements to explore the question of whether advertisers underestimate the intelligence of consumers.

6. With Sissela Bok's "Aggression: The Impact of Media Violence" in mind, write an essay on the subject of the sexual or violent content of any entertainment medium, such as Hollywood film or television programs. How is sex or violence handled? Is there too much? Is it too graphic? How is it portrayed, and what is its relevance to the plot? Are sex and violence linked?

7. Listen to two radio talk shows, one liberal and one conservative, and compare the two. Or, do the same for two television programs or two books. What subjects do they discuss? How do their approaches differ? Do you find yourself persuaded by one over the other? Why?

8. Select a news item in the headlines this week and follow the media's coverage of it, mixing media if possible. For instance, you could track the story as reported on an Internet site, on a national news program, and in a newspaper, or as it is handled by several different Internet sites, television programs, or newspapers. What conclusions can you draw about the media's handling of the story? Do you detect any bias in reporting it?

9. Write a paper in response to the central argument of any of the essays in this chapter.

10. Imagine that you are preparing to give a talk to a group of children about the possible dangers of exposure to media violence. Write an essay to that group as audience and include details, facts, or references to studies that you think would make an impression on them.

Research Topics

1. Research the subject of advertising ethics by locating articles and books representing the opinions of both those who are critical of advertisements and those who defend them. Argue your own position on the subject, supporting it with relevant source materials.

2. Research images of a specific group in advertising. For instance, you could focus on images of women, as Jean Kilbourne has done in "Advertising's Influence on Media Content," and locate additional research and opposing

viewpoints. Consider, also, the topics of advertising images of men, advertisements that encourage destructive behavior, or advertisements aimed at children.

3. Take as your starting point any of the accusations that Jean Kilbourne makes in "Advertising's Influence on Media Content" about corporate sponsors, self-censorship, alcohol or tobacco advertisements, or conflicting messages in women's magazines. Locate sources, do some preliminary reading, and narrow your focus on one aspect of the broader topic.

4. Research the question of whether allegations that the media have a liberal bias are true. Is it simply a perception, or can such bias, if it exists, be documented?

5. Select a news story that got a great deal of media coverage and research how it was reported in a variety of media sources. Compare the handling of the news item by the different sources. What conclusions can you draw on whether there is bias in reporting the story?

6. Research any of the issues raised by Sissela Bok's article, perhaps including her book, *Mayhem: Violence as Public Entertainment,* as one of your sources. For instance, you may want to read more about the effects of violent entertainment on children's moral and psychological development, the debate between protecting children and preserving First Amendment rights, or the measures taken by other nations to control media violence without censorship. Formulate your own position on the issue, and support it with references from your source materials.

7. Explain your own perspective on some aspect of popular culture, taking into account the views expressed by any of the writers in this chapter. Focus on a specific issue about which you have formed an opinion after reading their views, refer to the other writers as a way of providing the context for your own essay, supplement those readings with additional research, and then explain in detail your own position. For instance, examine one form of popular entertainment, such as rock videos, popular music, television shows, advertising, or movies, for the ways in which it promotes or fosters an attitude of acceptance of violence.

RESPONDING TO VISUALS

"I like it. It's dumb without trying to be clever."

1. What are the implications of this cartoon about consumers?
2. What aspects of advertising and consumers does the cartoon make fun of?
3. What does the cartoon imply about the role of advertisements?

RESPONDING TO VISUALS

Camel cigarette ad featuring movie star John Wayne, who died of cancer in 1979.

1. How does the ad make use of the fame of Hollywood film actor John Wayne?
2. In what ways does this advertisement use sex to sell its product?
3. What appeals to authority does the advertisement make?
4. What details of the advertisement do you think are most persuasive?

CHAPTER

10

Film and Television

Makers of Hollywood films, television shows, Broadway productions, and other products of the entertainment industry hope to tap into or even create trends that will have widespread appeal and thus result in huge profits. Because of its high visibility, ready availability, and ease of access to all age groups, the entertainment industry has always been closely scrutinized and subject to attack by its critics. Popular Hollywood films and television programs are particularly prime targets for both criticism and praise. Hollywood watchdogs and film critics pay attention not only to the craft of film production but also to the content of films. Indeed, the current ratings system evolved in response to alarm at the exposure of young viewers to graphic sex and violence, sometimes unwittingly, before such guidelines were in place. In recent years, many people have been sharply critical of films and television programs for what they see as irresponsible depiction of shocking images, excessive violence, and unnecessarily graphic sex. Defenders have been just as heated in their responses.

Television has been the target of suspicion, attack, and ridicule from the time it was invented. At first, people thought "the tube" would never replace the radio, especially when its early live-only broadcasts included inevitable comical errors. Once the problems were resolved and television broadcasting became increasingly sophisticated in both technology and programming, television became a commonplace medium. Television programs now number in the thousands, with not only cable access but also computer-controlled satellite dishes bringing a dizzying array of viewing choices into people's homes. Many families own not only two or three (or more) televisions but also at least both a DVD and a CD player. With the seemingly endless demand for television shows from viewers, network producers and local station managers are always looking for programs that will attract viewers and draw sponsors.

One of the oldest debates about television programming has to do with its depiction of violence. Mike Males, in "Stop Blaming Kids and TV," expresses his opinion on whether television violence causes violent and criminal behavior. While many people argue that television violence has enormous influence on children and bears large responsibility for the high U.S. homicide rate, Males argues that television does not cause violent behavior. He cites numerous studies as well as his own personal observations from working with youths to support his firm belief that critics are wrongheaded to blame teens and mass media for problems such as youth violence, excessive teenaged drinking, and increased rates of smoking among teenagers. He argues that there are other, more plausible causes of these problems. Where do you stand on this issue?

Another area of television programming that researchers have begun to investigate is reality shows. These programs follow real people over time behaving in unscripted situations, such as surviving on a faraway and exotic island, selecting a potential mate from a group of 25 hopefuls, having a new home built for them, or competing to be the top singer or dancer in the nation. A couple of dozen such shows air during the regular television season and even more in the summer. The concept is not new: in the 1950s, for instance, *Queen for a Day* was an early variation, where contestants were selected to tell their sad stories and the winner was the one who garnered the loudest audience applause. But the proliferation of such programs is a twenty-first century phenomenon. In "Getting Real with Reality TV," Cynthia M. Frisby discusses research that helps explain why audiences view such television programs. After defining the social comparison theory developed in the 1950s, Frisby explains the results of a survey that she and others conducted to determine how that theory applies to reality show viewers. As you read her article, think about your own viewing habits, particularly if you watch reality television shows.

The other two articles in this chapter discuss the subject of films. In "Creating Reel Change," Donovan Jacobs is interested in the positive effects of certain television and Hollywood films, especially documentaries, that deal with important social issues and that hope to influence audiences to take action in the interest of whatever cause the film is about. In contrast to so many critics of Hollywood films who believe that they promote antisocial behavior, Jacobs focuses on films that provide examples of pro-social behavior. As you read his article, see if you have viewed any of the films he mentions and, if so, consider whether you responded in the way that companies who produce such films and documentaries hope viewers will respond.

Louise Bernikow has an entirely different interest in mind, the portrayal of women's roles in movies. She is critical of a certain type of Hollywood film as well as the fairy tales the films are based on. Her essay, "Cinderella: Saturday Afternoon at the Movies," is a feminist analysis of a specific fairy tale and the Disney movie version that she remembers from her childhood. The essay is a classic example of the kind of critique of popular culture that many writers were making during the 1970s and 1980s. Although the film she refers to was produced years ago, it is still in circulation, and the fairy tale she recalls is very likely familiar to you as well.

STOP BLAMING KIDS AND TV

MIKE MALES

Mike Males, senior researcher for the Justice Policy Institute and sociology instructor at the University of California, Santa Cruz, is author of several books: The Scapegoat Generation: America's War on Adolescents *(1996);* Framing Youth: Ten Myths about the Next Generation *(1998);* Smoked: Why Joe Camel is Still Smiling *(1999);* Juvenile Injustice: America's "Youth Violence" Hoax *(2000); and* Kids & Guns: How Politicians, Experts and the Press Fabricate Fear of Youth *(2001). This essay first appeared in the October 1997 issue of the* Progressive.

"Children have never been very good at listening to their elders," James Baldwin wrote in *Nobody Knows My Name*. "But they have never failed to imitate them." This basic truth has all but disappeared as the public increasingly treats teenagers as a robot-like population under sway of an exploitative media. White House officials lecture film, music, Internet, fashion, and pop-culture moguls and accuse them of programming kids to smoke, drink, shoot up, have sex, and kill.

So do conservatives, led by William Bennett and Dan Quayle. Professional organizations are also into media-bashing. In its famous report on youth risks, the Carnegie Corporation devoted a full chapter to media influences.

Progressives are no exception. *Mother Jones* claims it has "proof that TV makes kids violent." And the Institute of Alternative Media emphasizes, "the average American child will witness. . . . 200,000 acts of (TV) violence" by the time that child graduates from high school.

4   None of these varied interests note that during the eighteen years between a child's birth and graduation from high school, there will be fifteen million cases of *real* violence in American homes grave enough to require hospital emergency treatment. These assaults will cause ten million serious injuries and 40,000 deaths to children.

In October 1996, the Department of Health and Human Services reported 565,000 serious injuries that abusive parents inflicted on children and youths in 1993. The number is up four-fold since 1986.

The Department of Health report disappeared from the news in one day. It elicited virtually no comment from the White House, Republicans, or law enforcement officials. Nor from Carnegie scholars, whose 150-page study, "Great Transitions: Preparing Adolescents for a New Century," devotes two sentences to household violence. The left press took no particular interest in the story, either.

All sides seem to agree that fictional violence, sex on the screen, Joe Camel, beer-drinking frogs, or naked bodies on the Internet pose a bigger threat to children than do actual beatings, rape, or parental addictions. This, in turn, upholds the Clinton doctrine that youth behavior is the problem, and curbing young people's rights the answer.

8   Claims that TV causes violence bear little relation to real behavior. Japanese and European kids behold media as graphically brutal as that which appears on American screens, but seventeen-year-olds in those countries commit murder at rates lower than those of American seventy-year-olds.

Likewise, youths in different parts of the United States are exposed to the same media but display drastically different violence levels. TV violence does not account for the fact that the murder rate among black teens in Washington, D.C., is twenty-five times higher than that of white teens living a few Metro stops away. It doesn't explain why, nationally, murder doubled among nonwhite and Latino youth over the last decade, but declined among white Anglo teens. Furthermore, contrary to the TV brainwashing theory, Anglo sixteen-year-olds have lower violent-crime rates than black sixty-year-olds, Latino forty-year-olds, and Anglo thirty-year-olds. Men, women, whites, Latino, blacks, Asians, teens, young adults, middle-agers, and senior citizens in Fresno County—California's poorest urban area—display murder and violent-crime rates double those of their counterparts in Ventura County, the state's richest.

Confounding every theory, America's biggest explosion in felony violent crime is not street crime among minorities or teens of any color, but domestic violence among aging, mostly white baby boomers. Should we arm Junior with a V-chip to protect him from Mom and Dad?

In practical terms, media-violence theories are not about kids, but about race and class: If TV accounts for any meaningful fraction of murder levels among poorer, nonwhite youth, why doesn't it have the same effect on white kids? Are minorities inherently programmable?

12   The newest target is Channel One, legitimately criticized by the Unplug Campaign—a watchdog sponsored by the Center for Commercial-Free Public Education—as a corporate marketing ploy packaged as educational TV. But then the Unplug Campaign gives credence to claims that "commercials control kids" by "harvesting minds," as Roy Fox of the University of Missouri says. These claims imply that teens are uniquely open to media brainwashing.

Other misleading claims come from Johns Hopkins University media analyst Mark Crispin Miller. In his critique of Channel One in the May edition of *Extra!*, Miller invoked such hackneyed phrases as the "inevitable rebelliousness of adolescent boys," the "hormones raging," and the "defiant boorish behavior" of "young men." Despite the popularity of these stereotypes, there is no basis in fact for such anti-youth bias.

A 1988 study in the *Journal of Youth and Adolescence* by psychology professors Grayson Holmbeck and John Hill concluded: "Adolescents are *not* in turmoil, *not* deeply disturbed, *not* at the mercy of their impulses, *not* resistant to parental values, and *not* rebellious."

In the November 1992 *Journal of the American Academy of Child and Adolescent Psychiatry,* Northwestern University psychiatry professor Daniel Offer reviewed 150 studies and concluded, in his article "Debunking the Myths of Adolescence," that "the effects of pubertal hormones are neither potent nor pervasive."

16   If anything, Channel One and other mainstream media reinforce young people's conformity to—not defiance of—adult values. Miller's unsubstantiated claims that student consumerism, bad behaviors, and mental or biological imbalances are compelled by media ads and images could be made with equal force about the behaviors of his own age group. Binge drinking, drug abuse, and violence against children by adults over the age of thirty are rising rapidly.

The barrage of sexually seductive liquor ads, fashion images, and anti-youth rhetoric, by conventional logic, must be influencing those hormonally unstable middle-agers.

I worked for a dozen years in youth programs in Montana and California. When problems arose, they usually crossed generations. I saw violent kids with dads or uncles in jail for assault. I saw middle-schoolers molested in childhood by mom's boyfriend. I saw budding teen alcoholics hoisting forty-ouncers alongside forty-year old sots. I also saw again and again how kids start to smoke. In countless trailers and small apartments dense with blue haze, children roamed the rugs as grownups puffed. Mom and seventh-grade daughter swapped Dorals while bemoaning the evils of men. A junior-high basketball center slept outside before a big game because a dozen elders—from her non-inhaling sixteen-year-old brother to her grandma—were all chain smokers. Two years later, she'd given up and joined the party.

As a rule, teen smoking mimicked adult smoking by gender, race, locale, era, and household. I could discern no pop-culture puppetry. My survey of 400 Los Angeles middle-schoolers for a 1994 *Journal of School Health* article found children of smoking parents three times more likely to smoke by age fifteen than children of nonsmokers. Parents were the most influential but not the only adults kids emulated. Nor did youngsters copy elders slavishly. Youths often picked slightly different habits (like chewing tobacco, or their own brands).

20   In 1989, the Centers for Disease Control lamented, "75 percent of all teenage smokers come from homes where parents smoke." You don't hear such candor from today's put-politics-first health agencies. Centers for Disease Control tobacco chieftain Michael Eriksen informed me that his agency doesn't make an issue of parental smoking. Nor do anti-smoking groups. Asked Kathy Mulvey, research director of INFACT: "Why make enemies of fifty million adult smokers" when advertising creates the real "appeal of tobacco to youth?"

Do ads hook kids on cigarettes? Studies of the effects of the Joe Camel logo show only that a larger fraction of teen smokers than veteran adult smokers choose the Camel brand. When asked, some researchers admit they cannot demonstrate that advertising causes kids to smoke who would not otherwise. And that's the real issue. In fact, surveys found smoking declining among teens (especially the youngest) during Joe's advent from 1985 to 1990.

The University of California's Stanton Glantz, whose exposure of 10,000 tobacco documents enraged the industry, found corporate perfidy far shrewder than camels and cowboys.

"As the tobacco industry knows well," Glantz reported, "kids want to be like adults." An industry marketing document advises: "To reach young smokers, present the cigarette as one of the initiations into adult life . . . the basic symbols of growing up."

24   The biggest predictor of whether a teen will become a smoker, a drunk, or a druggie is whether or not the child grows up amid adult addicts. Three-fourths of murdered kids are killed by adults. Suicide and murder rates among white teenagers resemble those of white adults, and suicide and murder rates among black teens track those of black adults. And as far as teen pregnancy goes, for minor mothers, four-fifths of the fathers are adults over eighteen, and half are adults over twenty.

The inescapable conclusion is this: If you want to change juvenile behavior, change adult behavior. But instead of focusing on adults, almost everyone points a finger at kids—and at the TV culture that supposedly addicts them.

Groups like Mothers Against Drunk Driving charge, for instance, that Budweiser's frogs entice teens to drink. Yet the 1995 National Household Survey found teen alcohol use declining. "Youths aren't buying the cute and flashy beer images," an in-depth *USA Today* survey found. Most teens found the ads amusing, but they did not consume Bud as a result.

By squabbling over frogs, political interests can sidestep the impolitic tragedy that adults over the age of twenty-one cause 90 percent of America's 16,000 alcohol related traffic deaths every year. Clinton and drug-policy chief Barry McCaffrey ignore federal reports that show a skyrocketing toll of booze and drug-related casualties among adults in their thirties and forties—the age group that is parenting most American teens. But both officials get favorable press attention by blaming alcohol ads and heroin chic for corrupting our kids.

28   Progressive reformers who insist kids are so malleable that beer frogs and Joe Camel and Ace Ventura push them to evil are not so different from those on the Christian right who claim that *Our Bodies, Ourselves* promotes teen sex and that the group Rage Against the Machine persuades pubescents to roll down Rodeo Drive with a shotgun.

America's increasingly marginalized young deserve better than grownup escapism.

Millions of children and teenagers face real destitution, drug abuse, and violence in their homes. Yet these profound menaces continue to lurk in the background, even as the frogs, V-chips, and Mighty Morphins take center stage.

PERSONAL RESPONSE

Are you surprised by Males' defense of young people? Have you heard similar arguments before, or is his approach different from what you are used to hearing about television and its influence on young people?

QUESTIONS FOR CLASS OR SMALL-GROUP DISCUSSION

1. Males opens his essay with a quotation from James Baldwin and the following statement: "This basic truth has all but disappeared as the public increasingly treats teenagers as a robot-like population under sway of an exploitative media" (paragraph 1). State the "basic truth" that Males believes the quotation suggests. Then consider what Males seems to mean when he says that teenagers are treated "as a robot-like population." Do you agree with him on that point?

2. Males writes: "In practical terms, media-violence theories are not about kids, but about race and class" (paragraph 10). Are you persuaded by the evidence that Males presents to support this assertion? Can you add further proof or offer a counterargument?

3. Respond to this statement in paragraph 24: "If you want to change juvenile behavior, change adult behavior." Do you agree with Males?

4. How persuaded are you by Males's argument? Do you think that his personal observations strengthen or weaken his argument? What do you think about his use of loaded language and sarcasm? How would you assess the strengths and weaknesses of his argument overall?

GETTING REAL WITH REALITY TV

CYNTHIA M. FRISBY

Cynthia M. Frisby is associate professor of advertising at the University of Missouri School of Journalism, Columbia, and co-editor of Journalism Across Cultures. *Her research interests include identifying the sources of American viewers' fascination with reality TV and the effects of idealized images on perceptions of body esteem among African American women. This essay appeared in the September 2004 issue of* USA Today *magazine.*

Every year, television networks vie to create cutting edge programming. New shows promise more drama, suspense, and laughter while pushing the envelope of what is morally and socially acceptable, funny, thrilling, and, of course, entertaining. Fitting all these criteria—at least according to the soaring ratings—is reality based television.

Reality TV is a genre of programming in which the everyday routines of "real life" people (as opposed to fictional characters played by actors) are followed closely by the cameras. Viewers cannot seem to help but become involved in the captivating plotlines and day-to-day drama depicted daily on their screens. Apparently, people simply take pleasure in watching other people's lives while those under scrutiny enjoy being on television enough to go on for free.

There are three major categories within the reality genre: game shows (e.g., "Survivor"), dating shows (e.g., "The Bachelor"), and talent shows (e.g., "American Idol"). While reality programming breeds fiercely during the regular season, in summer there is an even greater glut since such programs are cheap to produce and, if they fail to draw ratings, they quickly can be flushed away and replaced with something else.

4   It is becoming increasingly difficult to avoid contact with reality TV these days. In offices, hair salons, health clubs, restaurants, and bars, the general public is discussing what happened on television the night before—and it is not the world news they are dissecting. Rather, the hot topic may be what happened on "The Apprentice." Then again, it might be a "did-you-see" conversation concerning "The Bachelor" or "For Love or Money."

Shows such as "The Apprentice," "Survivor," "Fear Factor," "The Amazing Race," "American Idol," "American Girl," "Big Brother," "Extreme Makeover" "Temptation Island," "Cheaters," "The Simple Life," "Queer Eye for the Straight Guy," "The Bachelor," and "The Bachelorette" have reached out and grabbed today's American television viewer. During the 2003–04 season, 10 reality shows ranked among the top 25 prime-time programs in the audience-composition index for adults 18–49 with incomes of $75,000 or more. Nielsen ratings indicate that more than 18,000,000 viewers have been captivated by television programs that take ordinary people and place them in situations that have them competing in ongoing contests while being filmed 24 hours a day. What is it about these shows that attracts millions of loyal viewers week after week? Is it blatant voyeurism, or can their success be explained as a harmless desire for entertainment?

From "Survivor" to "Elimidate" to "Average Joe," to "Joe Millionaire." it seems that reality TV succeeds because it plays off of real-life concerns—looking for love, competing to win a job or big prize, or becoming a millionaire—situations (or dreams) that most people can relate to. However, as these shows become more pervasive, their grip on "reality" seems to be growing more tenuous.

"It's refreshing to see everyday people getting some of the spotlight, rather than just seeing movie stars all the time," maintains CBS News associate Presley Weir. According to CBS, the same element of being human that encourages people to gossip about the lives of their friends, family, and even total strangers is what fosters an audience for reality television. Much like a car crash on the side of the freeway, glimpses into the interior workings of other human beings is often shocking, yet impossible to turn away from. It was this theory that produced MTV's "The Real World," often referred to as "the forerunner of reality television shows." Seven strangers are selected to live together, and viewers watch to find out what happens when individuals with different backgrounds and points of view are left in close quarters.

Media Gratification

8   Researchers frequently refer to at least six gratifications of media use: information (also known as surveillance or "knowledge["]), escape, passing time, entertainment, social viewing/status enhancement, and relaxation. Although the names or labels for these gratifications may change, various studies confirm that they hold up in and across all situations. So what type of gratifications do viewers receive from reality TV?

Actually, individuals compare themselves with others for a variety of reasons, including to: determine relative standing on an issue or related ability; emulate behaviors; determine norms; lift spirits or feel better about life and personal situations; and evaluate emotions, personality, and self-worth.

Those made with others who are superior to or better off than oneself are referred to as upward comparisons. Individuals engaging in upward comparison may learn from others, be inspired by their examples, and become highly motivated to achieve similar goals. Upward comparisons, research suggests, are invoked when a person is motivated to change or overcome difficulties. Self-improvement is the main effect of an upward comparison because the targets serve as role models, teaching and motivating individuals to achieve or overcome similar problems.

On the other hand, when a social comparison involves a target who is inferior, incompetent, or less fortunate, it is referred to as a downward comparison. Its basic principle is that people feel better about their own situation and enhance their subjective well-being when they make comparisons with others who are worse off. Supposedly, downward comparisons help individuals cope with personal problems by allowing them to see themselves and their difficulties in a more positive light by realizing there are others who face more difficult circumstances.

12   A social comparison does not mean that the individual has to give careful, elaborate, conscious thought about the comparison, but implies that there has to be, to some degree, an attempt to identify or look for similarities or differences between the other and self on some particular dimension. There are theorists who might argue that, for a comparison to be considered a comparison, the individual must be aware of the comparison and come into direct contact with the other person. However, psychologists have discovered that social comparisons do not require conscious or direct personal contact because fictional characters illustrated in the media can represent meaningful standards of comparison.

Data on social comparisons and media use suggest that everyday encounters with media images may provide viewers with information that encourages them to engage in an automatic, spontaneous social comparison. This ultimately affects mood and other aspects of subjective well-being. People just might not be able to articulate consciously the comparison process or consciously register its effects (i.e., self-enhancement, self-improvement, etc.).

Reality TV allows audiences to laugh, cry, and live vicariously through so-called everyday, ordinary people who have opportunities to experience things that, until the moment they are broadcast, most individuals only dream about. Viewers may tune into these shows: because they contain elements the audience would like to experience themselves; to laugh at the mistakes of others and/or celebrate successes; or to feel better about themselves because they are at least not as "bad as the people on television."

Exposure to tragic events or bad news invites social comparison among viewers. It is believed that reality audiences may be encouraged to compare and contrast their own situation with those of the reality show stars, and that this comparison process eventually could produce a form of self-satisfaction.

16   In real-life, everyday situations, it would be extremely difficult to avoid making some type of comparison. Frequently, people may compare themselves with others in their immediate environment or in the mass media in order to judge their own personal worth.

We contacted 110 people and asked them to complete a uses and gratifications survey on reality television with two goals in mind: to demonstrate that social comparisons may be elicited by certain television content and to explore if viewers use reality television's content and images as a source for social comparison.

Of the respondents, 78.2% reported being regular viewers of reality television programs. A list of 37 reality shows was presented to the participants. They were asked to check those that they watch on a regular basis, and indicate on a scale of 1–5—number 1 signifying "liked a lot" and number five meaning "extreme dislike"—whether they liked or disliked each of the 37 programs. This paper-and-pencil test also asked respondents to identify the extent to which they considered themselves a "regular viewer of reality television." For purposes of conceptualization, a regular viewer was defined as "one who watches the show every week, and/or records episodes to avoid missing weekly broadcasts."

Data was obtained on other television viewing preferences by asking respondents to indicate how regularly they watch programs like news magazines, talk shows, reality programs, daytime serials, and other offerings and to identify the gratifications obtained from watching reality television.

20   To better understand the cognitive responses made when exposed to media content, a content analysis of the thoughts generated while watching reality TV was conducted. The researcher coded any and all thoughts that contained expressions of, or alluded to, social comparisons that participants "appeared to have" made spontaneously.

Participants were told that they later would see a segment of reality TV and encouraged to view that segment as if they were watching the program at home. While viewing the segment, participants were asked to record all their thoughts, and were given ample space to do so.

Data show that, of all the responses made concerning reality programming, most expressed some type of comparison between themselves and the reality show's stars. We conducted a content analysis of the thoughts and responses provided by the participants and found that, for the most part, men and women, as well as regular viewers and nonviewers, did not differ in terms of how they responded to people on reality shows.

We then compared mood ratings obtained prior to viewing the reality show with those from immediately following exposure to the program. Analysis clearly indicated that regular viewers and nonviewers alike experienced a significant mood enhancement after exposure to reality television.

Captivating Audiences

24 We know that reality television can captivate millions of viewers at any given time on any given day. Research has begun to document how people engage in automatic, spontaneous social comparisons when confronted by certain media images, particularly those of reality TV. We also know that one major effect of exposure to reality television is to feel better about one's own life circumstances, abilities, and talents. Reality TV also serves as a much-needed distraction from the ongoing parade of tragic world events. It allows viewers an outlet by watching others overcome hardships, escape danger, live in a rainforest, land a dream job, learn to survive in Corporate America, and yes, even find love.

Whether the aim is money, love, becoming a rock star, creative expression, or just a chance to be seen on TV, the effect on audiences is the same. People like knowing that there are others who are going through the same life experiences that they are and often make the same mistakes. Despite the shifting desires of society and the fickleness of television audiences, the human need to compare and relate has provided a market for this genre.

So, while viewers realize they are not America's Next Top Model, may not have a chance at becoming the next American Idol, or even an All American Girl, they do enjoy the fact that, through a vicarious social comparison process, they can fall in love, win $1,000,000, or get the office snitch fired.

PERSONAL RESPONSE

Do you watch any reality television shows? If so, explain their appeal. If not, explain why they do not appeal to you.

QUESTIONS FOR CLASS OR SMALL-GROUP DISCUSSION

1. What function do the opening paragraphs serve? What is Frisby's thesis? How well organized and developed do you find her essay?

2. Explain in your own words what the social comparison theory is (paragraph 9) and how it applies in general to viewers of reality television programs, according to Frisby.

3. How do the terms "upward comparison" (paragraph 11) and "downward comparison" specifically apply to viewers who watch reality television shows, according to Frisby?

4. Summarize the results of the uses and gratifications survey (paragraph 18) that Frisby and colleagues conducted.

5. Do you think Frisby's observations accurately describe the people you know who view reality television programs?

CREATING REEL CHANGE

Donovan Jacobs

Donovan Jacobs, a story development consultant based in Los Angeles, has been script consultant for many motion picture production companies and television networks, including Warner Brothers, ABC, and Touchstone Pictures. He specializes in the development of family movies for television. He contributed a chapter to a book by Act One: Training for Hollywood called Behind the Screen: Hollywood Insiders on Faith, Film and Culture *(2005). This piece was written for the November 2006 issue of* Sojourners.

Movie and television directors, producers, and writers interested in saying something of substance to their audiences have often been confronted with a quote generally attributed to former studio head Jack Warner: "If you want to send a message, call Western Union." Despite this adage's implication that films and TV programs should avoid the political and stick to entertaining (and make their studios and networks gobs of money), a number of movies and TV shows over the years have dealt with vital issues and encouraged pro-social behavior.

Now—whether because of, or in response to, opportunities offered by newer media such as the Internet and cable television—a variety of untraditional film and documentary makers seek to do more than portray positive action on the screen. These companies and artists want to motivate their audiences to get better informed on their issues, volunteer to help the subjects of the movie or program, and even advocate for legislation that offers protection to victims and tries to right the wrongs portrayed.

Probably the most publicized of these filmmakers is former eBay president Jeff Skoll, who through his company Participant Productions has committed an estimated $100 million to co-financing and producing a slate of theatrical releases. These movies include *An Inconvenient Truth,* Al Gore's documentary on global warming released earlier this year, and the current *Fast Food Nation,* about a marketing expert's odyssey to discover how his hamburger chain really makes its meat.

4   Participant's distinctiveness thus far hasn't been marked in Hollywood's traditional measures of achievement (four of the company's movies were nominated for Oscars in 2005 but have had mixed success at the box office). Rather, its chief innovation is creation of Internet-based campaigns for each film that allow viewers to join with established organizations to both make personal changes and call for social action in response to the movie's themes.

It's difficult to measure the success of these campaigns. Participant's October 2005 release of *North Country* (about a pioneering female coal miner harassed by male co-workers) was timed to allow audiences to support the National Organization for Women and other feminist groups in efforts to renew the federal Violence Against Women Act (VAWA). North Country only grossed $18 million, meaning about 2 million people saw it in theaters. But if even a small percentage of that number demanded approval of the act, the film may have contributed to the bill's passage in January 2006.

The TV industry has long been criticized for shying away from socially significant topics. But in recent years, the rise of cable television has allowed newer networks to present programs on controversial and vital issues of interest to their targeted audiences.

MTV, which has a reputation for offensive and sexually explicit programs, has also aired documentaries (many starring music and entertainment celebrities) intended to inform and inspire its teen and young adult audiences regarding issues—including discrimination and sexual health—that often escape mainstream media attention. Last summer, MTV announced plans for a special to feature hip-hop star Jay-Z and his efforts to raise awareness of the lack of safe drinking water in several countries during his September international concert tour. MTV's Web site will offer ways for viewers to contribute to building "Play-Pumps," playground carousels that pump fresh water as kids spin them.

8   Lifetime Television has gained solid ratings with its heavily female viewership for a series of issue-based movies and miniseries, including *A Girl Like Me: The Gwen Araujo Story,* about a Latina mother who first opposes then supports her son's determination to live as a woman. Premiering last June, the movie was followed by public service announcements offering suggestions for encouraging tolerance and ending discrimination against transgender persons.

Lifetime's public affairs office has emerged as a lobbying force in Washington, D.C., credited by Rep. Carolyn Maloney with assisting in the passage of legislation involving women's issues such as quick DNA testing of rape kits and video voyeurism (the latter the subject of a 2004 Lifetime movie).

Many of the most vibrant movies and documentaries committed to advocacy come from less prominent filmmakers who use technologies such as DVDs and Web sites not only to inform supporters, but to distribute their work to much wider audiences than otherwise possible. Brave New Films, a Los Angeles-based company run by veteran television producer Robert Greenwald, has focused on creating documentaries (such as last year's *Wal-Mart: The High Cost of Low Price*) that premiere in theaters and then are shown in public DVD screenings with discussion sessions after the film.

The company's current release, *Iraq for Sale: The War Profiteers*, deals with corporations, including Halliburton and Blackwater, that collect billions in taxpayer funds while allegedly delivering shoddy services that endanger U.S. troops and Iraqi citizens. Brave New Films arranged screenings of the movie for thousands of groups in July, devoting each day of a particular week to different audiences and the causes supported by co-sponsoring groups. The timing of these screenings shortly before the 2006 elections was no accident: One of the moviemakers' goals was to aid "get out the vote" drives across the country.

12   The filmmakers also hope to generate support for two proposed bills. One would form a congressional investigative entity to root out corruption and expose wrongdoers, modeled after the World War II-era "Truman Committee." The other legislation is the Honest Leadership and Accountability in Contracting Act of 2006, which defines and demands stiff penalties for war profiteering.

The Social Action goals of the three 20-something filmmakers behind the DVD documentary *Invisible Children* are equally ambitious. After graduating from film school, Jason Russell convinced childhood friends Bobby Bailey and Laren Poole to travel with him to Africa in 2003 to make a movie. The trio stumbled upon the story of thousands of children in northern Uganda, many of them orphans in refugee camps, who must hide in the countryside and in basements each night to avoid abduction by the Lord's Resistance Army, a rebel force that turns its victims into child soldiers and maims or kills those who resist.

Invisible Children seems amateurish and silly in spots, but the film's irreverence may make its heavy subject matter more appealing to the thousands of groups (mainly high school and college students) who have attended screenings around the United States. The movie's Web site features stories of young people inspired by the documentary to raise thousands of dollars to fund educational programs set up by the filmmakers in Uganda. This school year, more than 600 Ugandan teenagers will have their schooling paid for by American student fundraisers and the sale of native bracelets through the Web site. Natalia Angelo, a spokesperson for the filmmakers, told *Sojourners* that one of the most gratifying aspects of the movie's success has been the opportunity to spotlight stories of altruism and sacrifice by teens and young adults, which counters the prevailing myth of the supposed selfishness and materialism of American youth.

The short movies available through the New York-based Media That Matters Film Festival may seem small in scope, but they still convey a strong sense of urgency regarding the subjects they explore. The 16 documentaries and fictional films in the festival are first screened on the Internet and then made available on DVD each fall to educators across the country, along with teachers' guides that can be downloaded from the festival Web site.

16   Internet links and information in the guides provide sources of detailed information and opportunities for volunteerism and advocacy relating to the movies' broad range of themes. The festival is also affiliated with MediaRights, an organization that helps non-profits and advocacy groups learn to use documentaries to reach out to potential supporters and create change.

One of the shorts in the festival is *In the Morning,* a prizewinning fictional movie based on the true story of an honor killing in Turkey, where a rape victim was murdered by her brother to prevent her from bringing further "shame" on the family. Filmmaker Danielle Lurie stresses that honor killings, which occur primarily in the Middle East, are not linked to Islam—the basis for the killings is tribal. Lurie hopes the movie—which, thanks to the Internet, can be seen in Turkey and throughout the world—might help persuade the young boys often chosen by their fathers to commit the murders (because they tend to get shorter sentences) to not kill their sisters.

Lurie might be echoing everyone from a Hollywood producer like Jeff Skoll to her fellow young filmmakers when she says, "I would be naive to say that any single film on its own could make a difference, but my hope is that a movie, along with other films and educational tools, could create enough awareness that those in positions of power could effect change." Increasingly, it looks like these and other movies are placing the audience in those positions of power.

PERSONAL RESPONSE

Write about a film that has made a difference to you, perhaps one that made you aware of a problem you didn't know about before or moved you to act or think differently.

QUESTIONS FOR CLASS OR SMALL-GROUP DISCUSSION

1. What, according to Jacobs, have nontraditional films and documentaries done to "promote pro-social behavior" (paragraph 2)?

2. How convincing do you find Jacobs' examples and explanations of how they support his thesis?

3. Discuss the range of topics covered by the films that Jacobs mentions. If you have seen any of them, what did you think of them? If you haven't seen any of them, which might you be interested in viewing, based on Jacobs' comments about them?

4. Discuss additional topics that you think would make good subjects for the kinds of films that Jacobs is writing about.

CINDERELLA: SATURDAY AFTERNOON AT THE MOVIES

LOUISE BERNIKOW

Louise Bernikow's work has centered on women's culture. Her personal essays reflecting on women's psychology, women's friendships, and the ties between women are collected in Among Women *(1980), from which this piece is taken. Her other books include the following:* Let's Have Lunch: Games of Sex and Power *(1981);* Alone in America: The Search for Happiness *(1986);* The Women in Our Lives: Cinderella, Scarlett, Virginia, and Me *(1989);* The American Women's Almanac: An Inspiring and Irreverent Women's History *(1997);* Bark if You Love Me: A Woman-Meets-Dog Story *(2001); and* Dreaming in Libro: How a Good Dog Tamed a Bad Woman *(2007).*

No, Cinderella, said the stepmother,
you have no clothes and cannot dance.
That's the way with stepmothers.
  (Anne Sexton, "Cinderella")

Turn and peep, turn and peep,
No blood is in the shoe,
The shoe is not too small for her,
The true bride rides with you.
  (Grimms' Cinderella)

I begin with a memory of movies and mother, a dark theatre and a Saturday afternoon. In a miasma of Walt Disney images, Bambi burning and Snow White asleep, the most memorable is "Cinderella." I carry her story with me for the rest of my life. It is a story about women alone together and they are each other's enemies. This is more powerful as a lesson than the ball, the Prince, or the glass slipper. The echoes of "Cinderella" in other fairy tales, in myth and literature, are about how awful women are to each other. The girl onscreen, as I squirm in my seat, needs to be saved. A man will come and save her. Some day my Prince will come. Women will not save her; they will thwart her. There is a magical fairy godmother who does help her, but this, for me, has no relation to life, for the fairy is not real, and the bad women are. The magical good fairy is a saccharine fluff.

There are two worlds in the Cinderella cartoon, one of women, one of men. The women are close by and hostile, the men distant and glittering. Stepsisters and stepmother are three in one, a female battalion allied against Cinderella. The daughters are just like their mother. All women are alike. Lines of connection, energy fields, attach sisters to mother, leaving Cinderella in exile from the female community at home.

Father is far off. On film, neither he nor the Prince has much character. Father is her only tie, her actual blood tie, but the connection does her no good. Daddy is

King in this world; I cannot keep Daddy and King apart in my memory. My own father was as far off, as full of authority, as surrounded by heraldry, the trumpets of fantasy, to me, to my mother. King Daddy.

4   The Prince is rich and handsome. Rich matters more than handsome. The girl among the cinders, dressed in rags, will escape—I am on her side, I want her to escape, get away from the cinders and the awful women—because the Prince will lift her out. The world of the Prince is the world of the ball, music, fine clothes, and good feeling. Were everything to be right at home, were the women to be good to one another and have fun together, it would not be sufficient. The object is the ball, the Prince, the big house, the servants. Class mobility is at stake. Aspiration is being titillated.

To win the Prince, to be saved, requires being pretty. All the women care about this. Being pretty is the ticket, and because Cinderella is pretty, the stepmother and stepsisters want to keep her out of the running. There is no other enterprise. Cinderella does not turn up her nose and hide in a corner reading a book. Being pretty, getting to the ball, winning the Prince is the common ground among the women. What we have in common is what keeps us apart.

Cinderella must be lonely. Why, I wonder, doesn't she have a friend? Why doesn't she go to school? Why doesn't her father tell the awful women to stop? A hurt and lonely girl, with only a prince to provide another kind of feeling. Why doesn't she run away? Why can't the situation be changed? It is as though the house they live in is the only world, there is no other landscape. Women are always in the house, being awful to each other.

Magic. Cinderella has a fairy godmother who likes her and wants her to be happy. She gives the girl beautiful clothes. She doesn't have to instruct Cinderella or give her advice about how to waltz or how to lift her skirt or even give her directions to the palace. Only the clothes and the accoutrements—and a prohibition about coming home at midnight. A powerful woman who wants Cinderella to be pretty and successful in the social world. I know, at whatever age it is that I watch this story unfold, that the mother beside me is not the woman on the screen. Her feelings on such matters are, at best, mixed up. She is not so powerful.

8   I am stirred and confused by the contrast between bad and good women and the way it all seems to revolve around the issue of being pretty. Some women are hostile and thwarting, others enabling and powerful. The stepmother hates Cinderella's prettiness; the fairy godmother adorns it. I look sideways at my mother, trying to decide which kind of woman she is, where she stands on the business of pretty. Often, she braids my hair and settles me into polka dot, parades me before my beaming father. It is good to be pretty. Yet, onscreen, it is bad to be pretty—Cinderella is punished for it. In the enterprise of pretty, other women are your allies and your enemies. They are not disinterested. The heat around the issue of pretty, the urgency and intensity of it, is located among the women, not the men, at whom it is supposedly aimed. Luckily, we move on to the ball and the lost slipper.

This is one of the oldest and most often-told stories, varying significantly from one version to another, one country to another, one period to another. What appears on movie theatre screens or television on Saturday afternoons comes from as far away as China, as long ago as four hundred years. Each teller, each culture along the way, retained some archetypal patterns and transformed others, emphasized some parts of the story, eradicated others. Disney took his version of Cinderella from one written down by a Frenchman named Perrault in the seventeenth century. Perrault's is a "civilized" version, cleaned up, dressed up, and given several pointed "lessons" on top of the original material.

Many of the details about fashionability that we now associate with the story come from Perrault. His has the atmosphere of Coco Chanel's dressing rooms, is modern and glamorous. He concocted a froufrou, aimed at an aristocratic audience and airily decorated with things French. He named one of the sisters Charlotte and set the action in a world of full-length looking glasses and inlaid floors. He invented a couturière called Mademoiselle de Poche to create costumes for the ball, linens and ruffles, velvet suits and headdresses. Disney dropped the French touches.

Perrault's story is set in a world of women with their eyes on men. Even before the King's ball is announced, the stepmother and stepsisters are preoccupied with how they look. They are obsessed with their mirrors, straining to see what men would see. Once the ball is on the horizon, they starve themselves for days so that their shapes shall be, when laced into Mademoiselle de Poche's creations, as extremely slender as those in our own fashion magazines. The ball—and the prospects it implies—intensifies the hostility toward Cinderella. They have been envious. Now, they must keep the pretty girl out of competition. Most of the action of Perrault's story is taken up with the business of the ball.

12   Cinderella is a sniveling, self-pitying girl. Forbidden to go to the ball, she does not object but, instead, dutifully helps her stepsisters adorn themselves. She has no will, initiates no action. Then, magically, the fairy godmother appears. She comes from nowhere, summoned, we suppose, by Cinderella's wishes. Unlike the fairy godmother in other versions of the story, Perrault's and Disney's character has no connection to anything real, has no meaning, except to enable Cinderella to overcome the opposition of the women in her home, wear beautiful clothes, and get to the ball. Cinderella stammers, unable to say what she wants—for she is passive, suffering, and good, which comes across as relatively unconscious. The fairy divines Cinderella's desire and equips her with pumpkin/coach, mice/horses, rats/coachmen, lizards/footmen, clothes, and dancing shoes. She adds the famous prohibition that Cinderella return by midnight or everything will be undone.

These details of the fairy godmother's magic—the pumpkin, image of All Hallows' Eve; midnight, the witching hour; mice, rats, and lizards originated with Perrault. They are specific reminders of an actual and ancient female magic, witchcraft. Since Perrault wrote his story in the seventeenth century, it is not surprising to find echoes of this magic, which was enormously real to Perrault's audience.

Thousands had been burned at the stake for practicing witchcraft, most of them women. A witch was a woman with enormous power, a woman who might change the natural world. She was "uncivilized" and in opposition to the world of the King, the court, polite society. She had to be controlled. Perrault's story attempts to control the elements of witchcraft just as various kings' governments had, in the not too recent past, controlled what they believed to be an epidemic of witchcraft.

Perrault controls female power by trivializing it. The witchcraft in this story is innocent, ridiculous, silly, and playful. It is meant to entertain children.

The prohibition that Cinderella return by midnight is also related to witchcraft. She must avoid the witching hour, with its overtones of sexual abandon. The fairy godmother acts in this capacity in a way that is familiar to mothers and daughters—she controls the girl, warns her against darkness, uses her authority to enforce restraint, prevent excess, particularly excess associated with the ball, the world of men, sexuality.

16   Cinderella's dancing shoes are glass slippers. Perrault mistranslated the fur slipper in the version that came to him, substituting *verre* for *vire* and coming up glass. No pedant came along to correct the mistake, for the glass slipper is immensely appropriate to the story in its modern form and the values it embodies. Call it dainty or fragile, the slipper is quintessentially the stereotype of femininity. I wonder how Cinderella danced in it.

The rags-to-riches moment holds people's imagination long after the details of the story have disappeared. It appeals to everyone's desire for magic, for change that comes without effort, for speedy escape from a bad place—bad feelings. We all want to go to the ball, want life to be full of good feeling and feeling good. But Cinderella's transformation points to a particular and limited kind of good feeling—from ugly to beautiful, raggedy to glamorous. The object of her transformation is not actually pleasure (she does not then walk around her house feeling better) but transportation to the ball with all the right equipment for captivating the Prince.

Transformed, Cinderella goes to the ball, which is the larger world, the kingdom ruled by kings and fathers. The stepmother has no power in that world and does not even appear. This part of the story focuses on men, who are good to Cinderella as forcefully as women have been bad to her. Perrault embellishes Cinderella's appearance in a way that would have been congenial to the French court. In fact, she seems to have gone to the French court. The story is suffused with perfume and "fashionability." The Prince is taken with Cinderella and gives her some candy— "citrons and oranges," according to the text. How French. She, forever good, shares the candy with her stepsisters, who do not, of course, know who she is.

Cinderella has a wonderful time. As readers, hearers, watchers, we have a wonderful time along with her. More than the music and the dancing, the aura of sensual pleasure, everyone's good time comes from the idea that Cinderella is a "knockout." This is exciting. Perrault's word for what happens is that the people are *étonnés*, which means stunned. Cinderella is a showstopper, so "dazzling" that "the King himself, old as he was, could not help watching her." He remarks on this to his Queen, whose reactions we are not told. Being "stunning" is being powerful. This is the way women have impact, the story tells us. This is female power in the world outside the home, in contrast to her former powerlessness, which was within the home, which was another country. This tells me why women spend so much time trying to turn themselves into knockouts—because, in Cinderella and in other stories, it *works*.

20   Presumably, Cinderella's giddiness over her own triumph at the ball makes her forget her godmother's command and almost miss her midnight deadline. Lest we

lose the idea that all men adore Cinderella, Perrault adds a courtier at the end of the story, as the search for the missing Cinderella is carried out, and has him, too, say how attractive Cinderella is. She fulfills, then, the masculine idea of what is beautiful in a woman. She is the woman men want women to be.

Cinderella flees at midnight and loses her shoe. Perrault plays this part down, but Disney has a visual festival with the glinting glass slipper on the staircase and the trumpet-accompanied quest to find its owner. Perrault's Prince sends a messenger to find the shoe's owner, which puts the action at some distance, but Disney gives us a prince in all his splendor.

Cinderella is a heroine and in the world of fairy tales what the heroine wins is marriage to the Prince. Like any classic romance, wafted by perfume and fancy clothes, the young girl is lifted from a lowly powerless situation (from loneliness and depression, too) by a powerful man. He has no character, not even a handsome face, but simply represents the things that princes represent, the power of the kingdom.

Opposition to achieving this triumph comes from the women in the house; help comes from daydream and fantasy. The only proper activity for women to engage in is primping. What is expected of them is that they wait "in the right way" to be discovered.

24   Cinderella obeys the rules. Her reward is to be claimed by the Prince. The lesson of Cinderella in these versions is that a girl who knows and keeps her place will be rewarded with male favor.

Like a saint, she shows neither anger nor resentment toward the women who treated her so badly. In fact, she takes her stepsisters along to the castle, where she marries each off to a nobleman. Now everyone will be happy. Now there will be no conflict, no envy, no degradation. If each woman has a prince or nobleman, she will be content and the soft humming of satisfaction will fill the air. Women otherwise cannot be alone together.

This is the sort of story that poisoned Madame Bovary's imagination. In Flaubert's novel, a woman married to a country doctor, with aspirations for a larger life, goes to a ball where a princely character pays her some attention. The ball and the Prince, seen by Emma Bovary as possibilities for changing everyday life, haunted her uneasy sleep. The ball was over. Wait as she might for its return, for a second invitation, all she got was a false prince—a lover who did not lift her from the ordinariness of her life—and then despair.

The romance depends on aspiration. The Prince must be able to give the heroine something she cannot get for herself or from other women. He must represent a valuable and scarce commodity, for the women must believe there is only one, not enough to go around, and must set themselves to keeping other women from getting it. In "Cinderella," like other fairy tales and other romances, the world of the Prince represents both actual and psychological riches.

28   Perrault's Cinderella is the daughter of a gentleman, turned into a peasant within the household. She has been declassed by female interlopers, reduced to the status of servant, for she belongs to her father's class only precariously. One of the ways women exercise their power, the story tells us, is by degrading other women. Cinderella will be saved from her female-inflicted degradation first by another

female, the fairy godmother, who puts her on the road to her ultimate salvation. At the end of the story, she is restored to her class position, or, better, raised to an even higher position by the Prince.

Her fall from class is represented not only by her tattered clothes, but by the work she is forced to do. She is the household "drudge" and housework is the image of her degradation. Her work has no value in the story; it is the invisible, repetitious labor that keeps things going and makes it possible for the sisters and stepmother to devote themselves to *their* work, which is indolence on the one hand and trying to be beautiful for men on the other. Historically, indolence has been revered as the mark of a lady. What is "feminine" and "ladylike" is far removed from the world of work. Or the world of self-satisfying work. A man prides himself on having a wife who does not work; it increases his value in the eyes of other men; it means he provides well; it enforces conventional bourgeois "masculinity." A lady has long fingernails, neither the typewriter nor the kitchen floor has cracked them. She has porcelain skin; neither the rough outdoors nor perspiration has cracked that. Out of the same set of values comes the famous glass slipper.

The stepmother's class position is as precarious as Cinderella's is. The story does not tell, but we can imagine that whether she was married before to a poorer man or one equally a gentleman, her status and security are now tied to the man she has married and the ones she can arrange for her daughters. History, experience, and literature are full of landless, propertyless women trying to secure marriage to stand as a bulwark against poverty, displacement, and exile, both actual and psychological. The actual situation bears emphasis. The economic reality behind the fairy tale and the competition among the women for the favor of the Prince is a world in which women have no financial lives of their own. They cannot own businesses or inherit property. The kingdom is not theirs. In order to survive, a woman must have a husband. It is in the interest of her daughters' future—and her own—that the stepmother works to prevent competition from Cinderella. She is not evil. Within the confines of her world and the value systems of that world, she is quite nice to her own daughters, only cruel to Cinderella.

Still, the stepmother is an archetypal figure in fairy tales, always a thwarter, often a destroyer of children. Psychologists, and Bruno Bettelheim in particular, have a psychological explanation for this. The "bad" stepmother, Bettelheim points out, usually coexists with the "good" mother, representing two aspects of a real mother as experienced by a child. The stepmother is shaped by the child's unacceptable anger against her own mother. But there are real facts of life at work in these stepmother stories, too, especially as they describe what can happen among women at home. To a man's second wife, the daughter of the first marriage is a constant reminder of the first wife. The second wife is continually confronted with that memory and with the understanding that wives are replaceable, as they frequently and actually were in a world where women died young in childbirth, and men remarried, moved on.

32   A woman marries a man who has a daughter and comes to his household, where the daughter's strongest connection is to her father; the stepmother's strongest connection is to the husband. The Eternal Triangle appears, husband/father at the center, mediating the relationship, stepmother and daughter as antagonists,

competing for the husband/father's attention and whatever he may represent. Anxious, each in her own way and equally displaced, they face each other with enmity. The masculine imagination takes prideful pleasure in the story, placing, as it does, husband/father at center stage, making him King, arbiter of a world of women. . . .

I am writing an essay about Cinderella, spending mornings at the typewriter, afternoons in libraries, interpreting information on index cards of various colors and sheets of yellow paper. I discover something bizarre woven in the story as we now know it: that the story took root in ancient China. The remnants of that culture, especially of the ancient practice of foot-binding, are in the story, in the value of the small foot, in the use of the shoe to represent the potential bride. I see, then, the historical truth behind the terrible moment at the end of "Cinderella."

The Prince brings the slipper to the house of Cinderella's father. First one stepsister, then the other attempts to slip her foot into it, but each foot is too large. The first stepsister's toe is too large. The stepmother hands her daughter a knife and says, "Cut off the toe. When you are Queen you won't have to walk anymore." The second stepsister's heel is too large and her mother repeats the gesture and the advice.

Mutilation. Blood in the shoe, blood on the knife, blood on the floor and unbearable pain, borne, covered, masked by the smile. It is too familiar, frightening in its familiarity. The mother tells the daughter to mutilate herself in the interests of winning the Prince. She will not have to walk. Again, indolence enshrined. As mothers, in fact, did in China until the twentieth century—among the upper classes as unquestioned custom and among peasants as great sacrifice and gamble.

36   It began when the girl was between five and seven years old. The bandages were so tight, the girl might scream. Her mother pulled them tighter and might have tried to soothe her. Tighter. At night, in agony, the girl loosens them. She is punished, her hands tied to a post to prevent unlacing. The bones crack. The pain is constant. Tighter. She cannot walk. Tighter. By her adolescence, the girl has learned to bind her feet herself and the pain has lessened. She has, as a reward, special shoes, embroidered and decorated, for her tiny feet.

I translate the actual foot-binding, the ritual interaction of mother and daughter, to metaphor. A black mother straightens her daughter's hair with a hot iron, singeing the scalp, pulling and tugging. The daughter screams. My mother buys me a girdle when I am fifteen years old because she doesn't like the jiggle. She slaps my face when I begin to menstruate, telling me later that it is an ancient Russian custom and she does not know its origin. I sleep with buttons taped to my cheeks to make dimples and with hard metallic curlers in my hair. Tighter. I hold myself tighter, as my mother has taught me to do.

Is the impulse to cripple a girl peculiar to China between the eleventh and twentieth centuries? The lotus foot was the size of a doll's and the woman could not walk without support. Her foot was four inches long and two inches wide. A doll. A girlchild. Crippled, indolent, and bound. This is what it meant to be beautiful. And desired. This women did and do to each other. Pain in the foot is pain in every part of the body. A mother is about to bind her daughter's feet. She knows the pain in her own memory. She says: "A daughter's pretty legs are achieved through the shedding of tears."

This women did to each other.
This women do.
Or refuse to do.

. . . .

PERSONAL RESPONSE

Select a film for children that you recall from your childhood and discuss what you remember most about it. Do you think it has the same kinds of messages that Bernikow finds in "Cinderella"?

QUESTIONS FOR CLASS OR SMALL-GROUP DISCUSSION

1. Discuss whether you agree with Bernikow's interpretation that "Cinderella" is chiefly "about how awful women are to each other" (paragraph 1).

2. Discuss whether you think it is true that "rich matters more than handsome" (paragraph 4) for men in today's society, whereas being pretty is most important for women (paragraph 5).

3. Do you agree that females' power resides in their being "stunning" (paragraph 19), whereas other kinds of power in women are feared? Discuss your own perceptions of powerful women: Do you view power in women differently from or the same as the way you see it in men?

4. Bernikow sees a parallel between the stepsisters in "Cinderella" cutting off parts of their feet to win the Prince and the practice of foot-binding in China, and she interprets foot-binding as a metaphor for other interactions between mothers and daughters (paragraphs 33–38). To what extent do you agree with her in this interpretation? Do women today go through painful rituals to make themselves appealing to men? Do men go through painful rituals in order to appeal to women?

5. Can you name any current books or recent Hollywood films that have the same sorts of messages that Bernikow sees in "Cinderella"? What other fairy tales or children's stories reinforce Bernikow's point about female rivalry and male power? What would happen if you reversed the sex roles in "Cinderella"?

○ PERSPECTIVES ON FILM AND TELEVISION ○

Suggested Writing Topics

1. Like advertisers, producers of television shows argue that they do not create problems but simply reflect the values of society. Explain your position on the subject of how much responsibility television producers should bear for the images they produce in their advertisements.

2. Write an analysis of a popular television show. Your analysis can be either positive or negative, depending on your own feelings about the show. You may criticize a ridiculous, boring, or poorly acted show, for instance, or you may praise a brilliant, hilarious, or wonderfully acted one.

3. Do an analysis of any fairy tale or children's film for its depiction of female and male sex roles. Do you find stereotyped assumptions about masculinity and femininity? In what ways do you think the fairy tale or film reinforces or shapes cultural definitions of masculinity and femininity?

4. Explore the positive and negative aspects of a particular type of television programming, such as situation comedies, medical dramas, or soap operas.

5. Assess the quality of today's films by using examples of a film or films you have seen recently. Consider, for instance, evaluating the values endorsed by the film(s).

6. Write a position paper on the topic of sexually explicit and graphically violent Hollywood films by selecting one film for close analysis and two or three others to use as examples to support your position.

7. Explore the effects on you, either positive or negative, of a movie or television program that you saw when you were growing up.

8. If you are a fan of reality shows on television, choose one that you particularly like and explain why it appeals to you. If you do not like reality shows, pick one that you particularly dislike and explain why you do not like it.

9. Examine portrayals of any of the following in several television programs: the American family, women, men, a particular ethnic group, or a particular age group.

10. Write a letter to the president of one of the major television networks in which you express your views on the nature and quality of its programming for children.

11. Write a letter to either or both the sponsors and the producer of a television program you find particularly violent, mindless, or vulgar, explaining your complaint and what you would like to see changed.

12. Write a letter to the sponsors or producer of a television program you find intellectually stimulating, educational, or informative, praising the program and pointing out its best features.

Research Topics

1. Select a particular genre of film, such as comedy, western, romance, fantasy, or action, and research observations of various film historians, film critics, and other film commentators about the films in that genre. One approach is to assess the historical development of the genre and its current state. As you do your preliminary reading, look for a controversial

issue on which to focus your research. Then draw your own conclusions after you thoroughly research your subject.

2. Select a particular type of television program, such as reality TV, news program, talk show, children's entertainment, drama, or situation comedy and research what critics say about such programming currently and historically. Is there a program that represents the best of the type? The worst of the type?

3. Film or television critics and commentators sometimes use the term "golden age" to refer to a period in the past when a particular type of film or program reached its peak of excellence. Select a medium—film or television—and a genre—comedy, drama, or another of your choice— and research what characterizes "golden age" for the type and which program(s) or film(s) represent the type. If possible, view representative programs or films and include your responses to them in your research paper.

4. Much has been written about certain images in films or on television, such as the portrayal of women, of minorities, and of class issues. Select a particular image or theme to research for its representation in films or on television. Choose a specific period (films/programs from this year or last year, or films/programs from a previous decade, for instance) and narrow your focus as much as possible. This task will become more manageable once you begin searching for sources and discover the nature of articles, books, and other materials on the general subject.

5. Research a recent film that generated controversy, or view any of the films mentioned in Donovan Jacobs's "Creating Reel Change." View the film yourself and read what critics and other authorities on the subject of film have to say about this particular one.

6. Research the Television Violence Act. Find out what it is and what critics, behaviorists, and media experts say about its potential effectiveness. Then explain your own opinion of the effectiveness of such an act.

7. In 1961, Newton N. Minow coined the term *vast wasteland* for what he saw as television's empty content and anti-intellectualism. Argue either that television remains a vast wasteland or that the phrase is unfair to television. Base your position on research into the views of experts or others who have published opinions on the subject. Include the results of studies or any other relevant data you find.

8. Research any of the subjects relevant to this chapter that are suggested by the titles of books that Mike Males has written: *The Scapegoat Generation: America's War on Adolescents* (1996); *Framing Youth: Ten Myths About the Next Generation* (1998); *Smoked: Why Joe Camel is Still Smiling* (1999); *Juvenile Injustice: America's "Youth Violence" Hoax* (2000); or *Kids & Guns: How Politicians, Experts and the Press Fabricate Fear of Youth* (2001). Refer to one or more of these books in your paper.

RESPONDING TO VISUALS

A still image from director Mel Gibson's film The Passion of the Christ.

1. What is your emotional response to this image? What details of the image contribute to your response to it?

2. Characterize the graphic violence represented by the picture. Do you see any paradox in people's accepting this kind of violence while ordinarily condemning violence in films?

3. Comment on the perspective from which the image is viewed. What is the effect of the close-up of Jesus' upper body?

RESPONDING TO VISUALS

© Spots Illustrations/Jupiter Images

Illustration of family watching three different TVs.

1. Why do you think the faces of the family lack features? What do the glasses add to the image of the family members?
2. What do the positions of their bodies and their demeanor indicate about the family members?
3. What does the illustration suggest about the artist's attitude toward television viewing? Why are there three television sets?
4. What comment on television viewing does the illustration makes?

CHAPTER

11

The Arts

Humans have always used a variety of creative ways in which to express themselves imaginatively through such forms as storytelling, drawing, painting, sculpture, and music. Researchers have discovered paintings in prehistoric caves that provide evidence of the earliest humans' compulsion to tell stories or depict significant aspects of their lives through pictures, while people today argue that videogames, Internet websites, and other digital forms are the latest developments in mankind's quest to express itself aesthetically.

Literature has long been regarded as a significant art form. Indeed, some would claim that imaginative writing, whether it be a short story, a novel, a poem, or some other form of creative expression, is just as crucial to the nurturing of the human soul as are visual arts and music. Certainly Michael Chabon in "Solitude and the Fortresses of Youth" believes this is so. He uses personal experience to explain why he believes young people should not be unduly punished for writing violent material.

The force of his own imagination, he writes, was "nourished, stoked and liberated" by everything he read, including stories depicting "human beings in the most extreme situations and states of emotion—horror stories; accounts of madness and despair." Elsewhere in this textbook, in the section on the natural sciences, several people whose chief interests are science and scientific writing explore the nature of human intelligence as measured by an ability to create metaphor and to think in imaginative ways. Whatever its form, imagination and creativity are clearly important components of human identity. As you read Chabon's essay, think about the degree to which you would describe yourself as creative and consider whether you agree with his point about censorship and the arts.

Andrew D. Arnold looks at the subject of graphic comics as a form of literature that he wishes to see legitimized. In "Comix Poetics," he explains his belief that comics achieve "the same artistic ambitions as poetry." Serious comic artists, he maintains, have much in common with traditional poets and should be given the credit they are due. As you read his essay, consider whether you accept his argument. Are you convinced that graphic literature operates with the same imaginative principles as poetry, or do you think that Arnold is stretching the comparison too far?

As you will see, the essays in this chapter raise some intriguing questions, such as, how do artists benefit society? Would society lose its soul without artists? How would society—or you personally—change without art? Discussing an artistic expression that does not use words or paper, Barbara Ehrenreich explains in "Dance, Dance, Revolution" some of the historical development of dance and argues for its importance in our lives. As you read her essay, consider your life without dance or music to dance to. How important are music and dance to you? Can you envision your life without them?

Many strong supporters of the arts believe that society would be lost without it. Daniel E. Gawthrop makes very clear in "The National Endowment for Football—We're Fighting the Wrong Battle" his belief that the arts have great social importance. Writing to an audience of like-minded individuals, he suggests that the decrease in arts funding begun by Congress can be offset if arts educators convince the public that arts is as important a social element as, say, football. He argues that no amount of government funding can convince people arts are important and that the most important task is sharing how the arts enrich all lives. His goal is a lofty one, so as you read, consider how possible you think it is for him and his colleagues to reach that goal.

The subject of art and artists is so vast that these few readings serve only to indicate the breadth and depth of possible related topics and issues. Despite the persistence of art throughout time, the role of the artist in society and the relative value of art often are frequently debated topics. Tastes change and differ from generation to generation and individual to individual, as do values and beliefs about what is important to sustain and nurture a society and the standards by which people judge the merits of works of art. Determining what makes an artwork "good" or "bad" is often a subjective response to the art rather than a conscious application of objective standards. Do you have trouble determining whether a new movie, painting, or song is a good or bad one? How do you judge such works? As you consider the points made by the writers in this section, also think about the kinds of creative art that appeal to you, including what imaginative writing you like to read and perhaps write yourself. Think about the role that all of these forms of expression play in humans' lives: How might their absence affect humanity? Do you think your life would be impoverished without art, music, and literature? Why or why not?

SOLITUDE AND THE FORTRESSES OF YOUTH

Michael Chabon

Michael Chabon has written numerous articles, stories, novels, screenplays, and teleplays, including the screenplay for the second Spiderman *movie. His collections of short stories include* A Model World and Other Stories *(1991) and* Werewolves in their Youth: Stories *(1999). His novels include* The Mysteries of Pittsburg *(1988);* Wonder Boys *(1995);* The Amazing Adventures of Kavalier & Clay *(2000), which won the Pulitzer Prize for fiction in 2001; and* The Yiddish Policemen's Union *(2007). This essay was published in the April 13, 2004, issue of the* New York Times.

Earlier this month my local paper, the *San Francisco Chronicle*, reported that a college student had been expelled from art school here for submitting a story "rife with gruesome details about sexual torture, dismemberment and bloodlust" to his creative writing class. The instructor, a poet named Jan Richman, subsequently found herself out of a job. The university chose not to explain its failure to renew Ms. Richman's contract, but she intimated that she was being punished for having set the tone for the class by assigning a well-regarded if disturbing short story by the MacArthur winning novelist David Foster Wallace, "Girl with Curious Hair." Ms. Richman had been troubled enough by the student's work to report it to her superiors in the first place, in spite of the fact that it was not, according to the *Chronicle*, "the first serial killer story she had read in her six semesters on the faculty at the Academy of Art University."

Homicide inspectors were called in; a criminal profiler went to work on the student.

The officers found no evidence of wrong doing. The unnamed student had made no threat; his behavior was not considered suspicious. In the end, no criminal charges were brought.

4   In this regard, the San Francisco case differs from other incidents in California, and around the country, in which students, unlucky enough to have as literary precursor the Columbine mass-murderer Dylan Klebold, have found themselves expelled, even prosecuted and convicted on criminal charges, because of the violence depicted in their stories and poems. The threat posed by these prosecutions to civil liberties, to the First Amendment rights of our young people, is grave enough. But as a writer, a parent and a former teenager, I see the workings of something more iniquitous: not merely the denial of teenagers' rights in the name of their own protection, but the denial of their humanity in the name of preserving their innocence.

It is in the nature of a teenager to want to destroy. The destructive impulse is universal among children of all ages, rises to a peak of vividness, ingenuity and fascination in adolescence, and thereafter never entirely goes away. Violence and hatred, and the fear of our own inability to control them in ourselves, are a fundamental part of our birthright, along with altruism, creativity, tenderness, pity and love. It therefore requires an immense act of hypocrisy to stigmatize our young adults and teenagers as agents of deviance and disorder. It requires a policy of dishonesty about and blindness to our own histories, as a species, as a nation, and as individuals who were troubled as teenagers, and who will always be troubled, by the same dark impulses. It also requires that favorite tool of the hypocritical, dishonest and fearful: the suppression of constitutional rights.

We justly celebrate the ideals enshrined in the Bill of Rights, but it is also a profoundly disillusioned document, in the best sense of that adjective. It stipulates all the worst impulses of humanity: toward repression, brutality, intolerance and fear. It couples an unbridled faith in the individual human being, redeemed time and again by his or her singular capacity for tenderness, pity and all the rest, with a profound disenchantment about groups of human beings acting as governments, court systems, armies, state religions and bureaucracies, unchecked by the sting of individual conscience and only belatedly if ever capable of anything resembling redemption.

In this light the Bill of Rights can be read as a classic expression of the teenage spirit: a powerful imagination reacting to a history of overwhelming institutional repression, hypocrisy, chicanery and weakness. It is a document written by men who, like teenagers, knew their enemy intimately, and saw in themselves all the potential they possessed to one day become him. We tend to view idealism and cynicism as opposites, when in fact neither possesses any merit or power unless tempered by, fused with, the other. The Bill of Rights is the fruit of that kind of fusion; so is the teenage imagination.

8   The imagination of teenagers is often—I'm tempted to say always—the only sure capital they possess apart from the love of their parents, which is a force far beyond their capacity to comprehend or control. During my own adolescence, my imagination, the kingdom inside my own skull, was my sole source of refuge, my fortress of solitude, at times my prison. But a fortress requires a constant line of supply; those who take refuge in attics and cellars require the unceasing aid of confederates; prisoners need advocates, escape plans, or simply a window that gives onto the sky.

Like all teenagers, I provisioned my garrison with art: books, movies, music, comic books, television, role-playing games. My secret confederates were the works of Monty Python, H. P. Lovecraft, the cartoonist Vaughan Bodé, and the Ramones, among many others; they kept me watered and fed. They baked files into cakes and, on occasion, for a wondrous moment, made the walls of my prison disappear. Given their nature as human creations, as artifacts and devices of human nature, some of the provisions I consumed were bound to be of a dark, violent, even bloody and horrifying nature; otherwise I would not have cared for them. Tales and displays of violence, blood and horror rang true, answered a need, on some deep, angry level that maybe only those with scant power or capital, regardless of their age, can understand.

It was not long before I began to write: stories, poems, snatches of autobiographical jazz. Often I imitated the work of my confederates: stories of human beings in the most extreme situations and states of emotion—horror stories; accounts of madness and despair. In part—let's say in large part, if that's what it takes to entitle the writings of teenagers to unqualified protection under the First Amendment—this was about expression. I was writing what I felt, what I believed, wished for, raged against, hoped and dreaded. But the main reason I wrote stories—and the reason that I keep on writing them today—was not to express myself. I started to write because once it had been nourished, stoked and liberated by those secret confederates, I could not hold back the force of my imagination. I had been freed, and I felt that it was now up to me to do the same for somebody else, somewhere, trapped in his or her own lonely tower.

We don't want teenagers to write violent poems, horrifying stories, explicit lyrics and rhymes; they're ugly, in precisely the way that we are ugly, and out of protectiveness and hypocrisy, even out of pity and love and tenderness, we try to force young people to be innocent of everything but the effects of that ugliness. And so we censor the art they consume and produce, and prosecute and suspend and expel them, and when, once in a great while, a teenager reaches for an easy gun and shoots somebody or himself, we tell ourselves that if we had only censored his journals and curtailed his music and video games, that awful burst of final ugliness could surely have been prevented. As if art caused the ugliness, when of course all it can ever do is reflect and, perhaps, attempt to explain it.

12   Let teenagers languish, therefore, in their sense of isolation, without outlet or nourishment, bereft of the only thing that makes it all bearable: knowing that somebody else has felt the way that you feel, has faced it, run from it, rued it, lamented it and transformed it into art; has been there, and returned, and lived, for the only good reason we have: to tell the tale. How confident we shall be, once we

have done this, of never encountering the ugliness again! How happy our children will be, and how brave, and how safe!

PERSONAL RESPONSE

What do you think of the case that Chabon mentions in his opening paragraphs? In your opinion, should the student have been expelled for writing his gruesome story? If the teacher's termination was, indeed, a punishment for assigning a violent but disturbing story, as she thinks it was, do you think the punishment just?

QUESTIONS FOR CLASS OR SMALL-GROUP DISCUSSION

1. Explain in your own words what it is that bothers Chabon about the expulsion and/or prosecution of students for writing violent stories and poems. Do you agree with his position on this subject?

2. How do you respond to Chabon's assertion in paragraph 4 that "[i]t is in the nature of a teenager to want to destroy"? Is he correct about that, in your opinion?

3. Explain Chabon's analogy of the Bill of Rights "as a classic expression of the teenage spirit" (paragraph 6). How effective do you find that analogy as a strategy for developing his argument?

4. Comment on Chabon's strategy of using his own experience to further his argument. Does it work to strengthen or weaken the argument?

COMIX POETICS

ANDREW D. ARNOLD

Andrew D. Arnold was a Time.com *columnist from 2002 to 2007. He writes in his final* Time.comix *column that he began doing the column when comics (or, as he prefers, "comix") and graphic novels were just being noticed by the mainstream press. Since then, the genre has gained a large audience of readers and is being taken somewhat seriously by critics and academics. His columns have also appeared in the weekly print magazine,* Time. *This article was published in the March/April 2007 edition of* World Literature Today, *a publication of the University of Oklahoma.*

The debate over comics' qualifications as art has been crushed, like an icky spider, under a pile of masterful books. Art Spiegelman's *Maus*, Chris Ware's *Jimmy Corrigan: The Smartest Kid on Earth*, and Marjane Satrapi's *Persepolis* are just a few of the ever-growing list of important works of graphical literature that prove comic art can carry as much truth, beauty, mystery, emotion, and smart entertainment as any of the other, more traditional, media of expression. Even the Ivory Tower has admitted "graphic novels" (an imperfect term that describes any book-length comic work, including nonfiction) onto course lists. So now we can turn our attention to more interesting comparative questions. For example, can comics create poetry like the works of Shakespeare, T. S. Eliot, or Aleksandr Pushkin?

In short, no, but not from lack of merit or ability. While comics have a similar delivery as poetry—books, paper, words, etc.—the language, syntax, and meaning of comics spring primarily through the relationship between images rather than words. This is not just a different ballgame but a different sport. However, this does not exclude comics from achieving the same artistic ambitions as poetry. Practically since their inception, comics have shown their ability to achieve powerful artistry through the inspired use of condensed, musical, and highly structured language. So, herewith a brief survey of some comic art that rivals the work of many a fine traditional poet.

Early on, during the explosion of newspaper strips in the early twentieth century, creators had the rare kind of artistic freedom that comes from a total lack of rules or precedent. As a result, some of the wildest feats of artistic imagination in the history of the medium occurred at its inception. Perhaps no pioneering comics artist came as close to poetic perfection as George Herriman (1880–1944), author of *Krazy Kat,* which appeared in newspapers from 1913 until the author's death. Like few others, Herriman developed his own "voice" both in his written and visual language to create a work beloved by some of the most highly regarded artists and intellectuals of the time. Gilbert Seldes, cultural essayist par excellence, praised it in his now-classic 1924 book *The Seven Lively Arts* as "the most amusing and fantastic and satisfactory work of art produced in America to-day."

4 Herriman used the core dynamic of his three principal characters—lovesick Krazy Kat, brick-throwing Ignatz Mouse, and dutiful Offica Pup—like a sonnet form, endlessly rifling on the characters' relationships to get at something profoundly tragic and funny about life. One full-page Sunday strip from 1937 exemplifies the many beauties of Krazy Kat. Over the course of several panels, Krazy seeks seclusion under a tree and begins writing in a diary. Little hearts bubble out of its pages as she does so. She speaks to herself in the oddball patois that is one of the strip's hallmarks. "I are alone," she says, "Jetz me . . . an' jetz my dee-dee diary." She puts the diary under a rock and incants over it, "Now beck into sigglution, witch only these kobbil rocks, this blue bin butch-the moon an' the dokk, dokk night know. An' they won't tell-you is illone." The final panel, stretching the width of the page, shows all the other characters reading the book after she has left. In a single page, Herriman creates not a traditional poem but its comic-art equivalent. It has playfulness about both the language ("dee dee diary," "dokk, dokk night") and the images (the background changes from panel to panel though the foreground remains consistent). It also examines great themes like love (those little hearts) and existentialism ("you is illone"). But the essence of the work, called the "gag" panel in this context but akin to a sonnet's final couplet, appears at the end. Herriman bursts the illusion of aloneness and privacy, emphasizing our existence in a community. And it's funny, too. Most important, he communicates this through a wordless image. Impossible in any other medium, here we see an example of cartoon poetry in its purest form.

The comic-book craze that began with the introduction of Superman in 1938 did about as much harm as good for the medium. While massively popularizing the comics' language, cheap comic books also commodified it, leading to a stultification of the form as a mode of personal expression. It wouldn't begin to develop its full potential until the 1960s, when a group of West Coast cartoonists began independently publishing comic books and selling them "underground" in head shops and record stores. Robert Crumb became the most famous member of this movement. Though he would go on to become comics' most brilliant polytechnic, constantly changing styles and subjects, his early work remains his most popular and the closest to what can be called comic poetry. "Freakout Funnies Presents I'm a Ding Dong Daddy," a two-pager that appeared in the premier issue of Zap in 1967, exemplifies the psychedelicized free-form style of the underground era. Wordless except for the onomatopoeia of "Snap!" "Bonk!" and "Pow!" it depicts a big-footed young man having an epiphany on the street. Ecstatic, his mind blown, he runs around hitting his head against the wall, eventually working himself up into such a cosmic frenzy that he explodes into stars. Captured in a thought bubble, the stars dissolve to emptiness as our man from the beginning returns to a state of ignorance. Like the best linguistic poetry, "Ding Dong Daddy" uses the comics language of the past (superhero and gag comics) in radically new ways to express something profound about the culture of its time.

The comics didn't begin to emerge from the "underground" until the 1980s. *Raw,* a magazine edited by Art Spiegelman and Francoise Mouly, became one of the main factors in the shift. Emphasizing works closer to self-aware "art" than salacious entertainment, Raw asserted itself as comics for grown-ups rather than merely "adults." Among the many brilliant pieces to have appeared in its pages, Richard McGuire's "Here" (1989) stands out as one of the most influential works of comics poetry ever published. Its method of using comics to split time into multiple layers that can be read simultaneously still has the shock of the new. It begins as a pregnant woman stands in her living room and announces to her husband, "Honey, I think it's time." Fixing the "camera" to the same location, McGuire begins jumping back and forth in time by generations, then centuries, then millennia, exploring the past and future of a single location in space. He does this in six pages by setting smaller panels inside larger ones, which are all labeled with a year, so one begins to read multiple timelines simultaneously, each with its own narrative. Using similarities of composition, movement, and language, McGuire ties it all together into a fluid comment on the nature of time using a form unique to comics.

The youngest comic-book poet of this survey, Anders Nilsen (b. 1973), has been gaining a major reputation among the comixcenti for his simple, enigmatic, and memorable work. One of his most interesting recent pieces appeared in the excellent biannual anthology series *Mome,* published by Fantagraphics books. . . . The fall 2005 issue included Nilsen's short work "Event." The design couldn't be simpler. Page 1 contains a single gray square with a black border, the size of a postage stamp, accompanying the text, "What you said you would do." On page. . . [2] a slightly smaller square broken into quadrants of different hues sits over the text "Your reasons for not doing it: stated." Page 3 contains a larger, dun-colored square over the word "Unstated." It continues like this, using squares of varying sizes and quantities to represent time, people, events, and consequences affected by and resulting from this original, unnamed inaction. A comics poem with a twist ending, the last panel switches its core geometry to feature red concentric circles over the label "Anxiety experienced every time you think back to this experience for the rest of your life." While lines like that will not win over any old-school poets, as a whole the work reads as a fascinatingly clever minimalist visual poem. The words and pictures are totally dependent on each other to convey the meaning of the work, which reads as a compressed, playful examination of regret. In sum, it is a graphic poem.

8   Culturally, at least, serious-minded comic artists have much in common with traditional poets. You could describe each the same way: an underappreciated author who spends years working on a thin volume to be published by a barely surviving independent press for a small, cultlike audience. Until recently, the difference could be measured in the level of respect accorded one over the other, at least in the United States. Comic artists, regardless of their subject matter, have traditionally hovered in the artistic hierarchy somewhere above pornographers but below children's book authors. But that seems to be changing. There are more comic poets today than at any time before, thanks to the comic medium's explosive growth in the last five years. Like traditional poets who work at the cutting edge of the English language, these artists create the pathways that others will follow.

PERSONAL RESPONSE

Do you read the kinds of comics that Arnold writes about here? If so, explain their appeal; if not, explain why you do not read them.

QUESTIONS FOR CLASS OR SMALL-GROUP DISCUSSION

1. Analyze the structure and development of this essay. What is Arnold's thesis? How well organized is it? What strategy does he use to prove his thesis?

2. Arnold writes in paragraph 5 that the comic book craze "did about as much harm as good for the medium." What do you understand him to mean by that statement?

3. Summarize the contributions, according to Arnold, to the comic art genre of each of the examples he names.

4. Are you convinced by Arnold's examples that comics "achieve the same artistic ambitions as poetry" (paragraph 2)? To what extent do you agree with him that comics qualify as art?

DANCE, DANCE, REVOLUTION

Barbara Ehrenreich

Barbara Ehrenreich's articles appear in a variety of popular magazines and newspapers, including Time, *the* Progressive, Ms., *and the* New York Times, *among many others. Her books include* Witches,

Midwives, and Nurses: A History of Women Healers *(with Deir-dre English) (1973);* Hearts of Men: American Dreams and the Flight from Commitment *(1984);* For Her Own Good: 150 Years of the Experts' Advice to Women *(with Deirdre English) (1989);* Blood Rites: Origins and History of the Passions of War *(1997);* Fear of Falling: The Inner Life of the Middle Class *(2000);* Nickel and Dimed: On (Not) Getting by in America *(2001);* Global Woman, *a collection of essays co-edited with Arlie Russell Hochschild (2002);* Bait and Switch: The (Futile) Pursuit of the American Dream *(2005); and* Dancing in the Streets: A History of Collective Joy *(2007). This article appeared in the* New York Times *on June 3, 2007.*

Compared with most of the issues that the venerable civil liberties lawyer Norman Siegel takes up, this one may seem like the ultimate in urban frivolity: Late last month, he joined hundreds of hip-hoppers, salsa dancers, Lindy Hoppers and techno-heads boogying along Fifth Avenue to protest New York City's 80-year-old restrictions on dancing in bars.

But disputes over who can dance, how and where, are at least as old as civilization, and arise from the longstanding conflict between the forces of order and hierarchy on the one hand, and the deep human craving for free-spirited joy on the other.

New York's cabaret laws limit dancing to licensed venues. They date back to the Harlem Renaissance, which had created the unsettling prospect of interracial dancing.

4   For decades, no one paid much attention to the laws until Mayor Rudolph Giuliani, bent on turning Manhattan into a giant mall/food court, decided to get tough. Today, the city far more famous for its night life than its Sunday services has only about 170 venues where it is legal to get up and dance—hence last month's danced protest, as well as an earlier one in February.

Dust-ups over dancing have become a regular feature of urban life. Dance clubs all over the country have faced the threat of shutdowns because the dancing sometimes spills over into the streets. While neighbors annoyed by sleepless nights or the suspicion of illegal drug use may be justified in their concerns, conflict over public dancing has a long history—one that goes all the way back to the ancient Mediterranean world.

The Greeks danced to worship their gods—especially Dionysus, the god of ecstasy. But then the far more strait-laced Romans cracked down viciously on Dionysian worship in 186 B.C., even going on to ban dancing schools for Roman children a few decades later. The early Christians incorporated dance into their liturgy, despite church leaders' worries about immodesty. But at the end of the fourth century, the archbishop of Constantinople issued the stern pronouncement: "For where there is a dance, there is also the Devil."

The Catholic Church did not succeed in prohibiting dancing within churches until the late Middle Ages, and in doing so perhaps inadvertently set off the dance "manias" that swept Belgium, Germany and Italy starting in the 14th century. Long attributed to some form of toxin—ergot or spider venom—the manias drove thousands of people to the streets day and night, mocking and menacing the priests who tried to stop them.

8   In northern Europe, Calvinism brought a hasty death to the old public forms of dancing, along with the costuming, masking and feasting that had usually accompanied them. All that survived, outside of vestiges of "folk dancing," were the elites' tame, indoor ballroom dances, fraught, as in today's "Dancing With the Stars," with anxiety over a possible misstep. When Europeans fanned out across the globe in the 18th and 19th centuries, the colonizers made it a priority to crush the danced rituals of indigenous people, which were seen as savagery, devil worship and prelude to rebellion.

To the secular opponents of public dancing, it is always a noxious source of disorder and, in New York's case, noise. But hardly anyone talks about what is lost when the music stops and the traditional venues close. Facing what he saw as an epidemic of melancholy, or what we would now call depression, the 17th-century English writer Robert Burton placed much of the blame on the Calvinist hostility to "dancing, singing, masking, mumming and stage plays." In fact, in some cultures, ecstatic dance has been routinely employed as a cure for emotional disorders. Banning dancing may not cause depression, but it removes an ancient cure for it.

The need for public, celebratory dance seems to be hardwired into us. Rock art from around the world depicts stick figures dancing in lines and circles at least as far back as 10,000 years ago. According to some anthropologists, dance helped bond prehistoric people together in the large groups that were necessary for collective defense against marauding predators, both animals and human. While language also serves to forge community, it doesn't come close to possessing the emotional urgency of dance. Without dance, we risk loneliness and anomie.

Dancing to music is not only mood-lifting and community-building; it's also a uniquely human capability. No other animals, not even chimpanzees, can keep together in time to music. Yes, we can live without it, as most of us do most of the time, but why not reclaim our distinctively human heritage as creatures who can generate our own communal pleasures out of music and dance?

12   This is why New Yorkers—as well as all Americans faced with anti-dance restrictions—should stand up and take action; and the best way to do so is by high stepping into the streets.

PERSONAL RESPONSE

Ehrenreich comments that "the need for public, celebratory dance seems to be hardwired into us" (parargraph 10). Does your own attitude about dance support that comment? Do your observations of others support it? Can you "live without [music]" (paragraph 11)?

QUESTIONS FOR CLASS OR SMALL-GROUP DISCUSSION

1. What is the issue that Ehrenreich writes about here? What action does she call for?

2. Summarize the long history of the conflict over public dancing. Can you think of other examples of that conflict?

3. Ehrenreich notes that "hardly anyone talks about what is lost when the music stops and the traditional venues close" (paragraph 9). What, according to her, is lost? Do you agree with her?

4. What value does Ehrenreich believe dance has? To what extent do you agree with her?

THE NATIONAL ENDOWMENT FOR FOOTBALL—WE'RE FIGHTING THE WRONG BATTLE

Daniel E. Gawthrop

Daniel E. Gawthrop is a composer who has received over a hundred commissions to write original music. He is also an announcer/producer for public radio station WETA, Washington, D.C., and has served as a music critic for the Washington Post. *He has twice served on National Endowment for the Arts (NEA) grants panels. In addition to his work as a composer, Gawthrop has been active as a broadcaster, clinician and adjudicator, organist, conductor, teacher and writer, including a period as music critic for the* Washington Post. *This selection first appeared in* Choral Journal, *the official publication of the American Choral Directors Association, in October 1997.*

Why isn't there a National Endowment for Football? Why does the idea make you giggle? Probably because there is no need for an "NEF," since large numbers of people already believe in the importance of football games in their lives and are perfectly willing to support gridiron activities of all kinds. They buy tickets to games in large numbers, watch games on television in vastly larger numbers, play games themselves with their friends and children, and happily, even insistently, support football in the public schools.

When I was in high school, I thought football was terminally stupid. Years later my wife taught me first to understand and later to enjoy the game, and these days I could even be considered a fan. This experience, while not terribly profound, has nonetheless enriched my life in some measure, and I am grateful for it. The enrichment provided by the arts in my life, in dramatic contrast, has been quite profound and far more formative on my character.

This got me thinking: what if we were able to convince a substantial portion of our fellow citizens that the arts deserve a place in their lives at least as significant as, say, football? Could we then not look forward to their buying tickets to arts events in large numbers, watching concerts and ballets and plays on television in vastly larger numbers, playing instruments and singing (and painting and writing and acting) themselves, with their friends and children, and happily, even insistently, supporting the arts in the public schools? At that point the funding problem would be pretty well solved, and there would be no need to beg for alms from Congress year after year, nor any need to risk "governmental control" of the arts.

4   I believe the arts are a critically important component of our culture and that we will all pay a high price if we fail to insist on their remaining in their rightful role as an ennobling and enriching influence in our society. However, I think fighting for public funding (other than for arts education in our public schools, which is critically important) is the wrong battle. By devoting any substantial amount of time and effort to convincing Congress to offer financial support to the arts, we are allowing ourselves to be distracted from a far more important and urgent need.

The real problem is that we live in a society that simply does not value the arts. Until we address and resolve that flaw in our national character, no amount of money, from whatever source, is going to have the desired effect. Meanwhile, if we fight (and even win) a battle for public funding, we are likely to congratulate ourselves for having reached our goal and then relax, without even realizing that our ladder was leaning against the wrong wall all along. If we really want to help people, or if we really want to help the arts, the answer is the same: we must give individuals a reason to value artistic expression. Fail at that, and all else is lost; succeed at that, and funding problems will disappear.

Most National Endowment for the Arts grant money awarded in support of performing ensembles has focused on making artistic experiences available to as wide an audience as possible. On its surface this seems both reasonable and public-spirited; unfortunately, it rather misses the point. One old saw maintains, "If nobody wants to come, no one will make them." We need to be asking ourselves two related questions: First, why would we wish to experience this exhibit, play, concert, or other artistic event, and second, how can we evoke the same desires in someone else, someone who has not yet caught the vision? Once we have found a way to convert our society into avid arts enthusiasts, it will take over the funding process, quite voluntarily, without government involvement.

The bottom line here is that no amount of government-supported art is going to change the fundamental character of our society. While we're busy fighting for federal money, we're failing to do the things that will make that fundamental change. It should he noted that during the period when federal funding for the NEA was increasing each year, audiences (especially young audiences) were dwindling and music programs in the public schools were disappearing. If the goal of federal funding was to increase public awareness and involvement with the arts, it failed conclusively, even spectacularly. That's why I think government funding is a red herring.

8   I say, let's quit worrying about "sending a message to the rest of the world" and get on with the important task we urgently need to complete: converting the heathen. Let's eliminate the self-flagellation over the fact that European arts presentations all rely on government funding and get busy turning out a generation of Americans who understand and appreciate the arts as much as they appreciate the Dallas Cowboys and their cheerleaders. Let's quit trying to get the government to throw money at the arts to spare us the unpleasant necessity of rolling up our sleeves and getting personally involved in the big job of sharing what we understand (and what our fellow citizens don't) about the importance of the arts in everyone's lives.

We need to change the focus of our attention from a distant, unconcerned Congress to local communities, and start changing people, one at a time, by the strength of our examples and our convictions. We need to quit demanding leadership from Washington, from the very folks who got us where we are now, and start exhibiting some leadership of our own. After all, the real arts experts won't be found in think tanks: they're too busy teaching in our public schools, directing our church and community choirs, writing poems and music and books, and sketching and painting and so forth.

The people in our towns and villages who don't (yet) share our vision and understanding are not going to be converted by an NEA grant. We need to invite them, often and fervently, to our concerts and recitals. When they get there, they must be asked to do something: clap in time, sing along, jingle their keys and coins to accompany some rhythmic piece, or any of a thousand other clever ways of getting them involved that you will think of and the government won't.

Involvement will bring them back. Once they're coming back, we need to find ways to encourage their own artistic expressions, however simple, because once they've tasted that, you'll never be able to take it away from them again: they'll become your fans, supporters, singers, board members, volunteer committee members, and more. Before you know it, your community will be supporting the arts in hundreds of ways that are not only better suited to your needs than anything the NEA can provide, but which also create side-effects and ripples throughout the community that will amplify and multiply your original investment.

12   My wife remembers being taken to local symphony concerts as a very young child. Her father took her home at intermission and returned for the second half of the program. A few years of this kind of exposure turned her into an avid listener who was eager to be allowed to stay for the entire concert.

There were no federal grants in those days to bring symphony players into her school, and if there had been, they would not have had the same effect as those repeated exposures, which also carried the psychological impact of her parents' physical presence and obvious sincere interest. It led to instrumental training in elementary school and high school, to playing in a major symphony orchestra, and to a lifelong commitment to support arts institutions of all kinds. That's the progression we need to make our goal.

Bringing a few musicians, or even an entire orchestra, into a school once or twice a year, however worthwhile, simply cannot be expected to create this effect for more than a very few students. Unless they're singing every day, being exposed to musical masterworks regularly, and playing instruments from an early age, the occasional appearance of a few musicians in their midst will be treated as a mystical event with no relevance.

I heard a story about a fellow who walked into an art museum and stopped in front of a painting so valuable there was a guard permanently posted beside it. The man glanced casually at the painting and mumbled, "I don't see what's so hot about that." Overhearing this, the guard smiled and replied, "Ah, but don't you wish you did?"

16   If people in your community don't see what's so hot about the arts, an NEA grant won't fix it. Government money won't fix it. You must fix it.

PERSONAL RESPONSE

Gawthrop says that the arts have had a profound formative influence on his life. What would you identify as the most formative influence on your life?

QUESTIONS FOR CLASS OR SMALL-GROUP DISCUSSION

1. How does Gawthrop's title reflect his content? What relationship does it have with his proposition or claim?

2. To what extent do you agree with Gawthrop that "the arts are a critically important component of our culture" (paragraph 4).

3. Describe your community's level of involvement in promoting the arts.

4. What actions does Gawthrop tell his audience of other arts professionals that they need to take to achieve their goal of "turning out a generation of Americans who understand and appreciate the arts as much as they appreciate the Dallas Cowboys" (paragraph 9)? Do you think his goal is realistic? Is it possible to "change the fundamental character of our society" (paragraph 8)?

○ PERSPECTIVES ON THE ARTS ○
Suggested Writing Topics

1. Argue your position on the subject of violence in any of the creative arts— poetry, drama, short story, novel, dance, the visual arts. Is the expulsion of students or firing of teachers, as described in Michael Chabon's "Solitude and the Fortresses of Youth" justified in uncertain and dangerous times?

2. If you have found that a particular form of creative art is a way to express yourself or use your imagination, as Michael Chabon in "Solitude and the Fortresses of Youth" did with writing, explain what that art is and how it enables you to find self-expression.

3. One of the oldest forms of art is personal decoration. The body is still being used as a surface for symbolic expression by some young people, who use such techniques as branding, piercing, and tattooing. Defend or attack these practices by considering their relative artistic or creative merits.

4. Write an argumentative essay defending the central place of art in education.

5. Daniel E. Gawthrop writes in "The National Endowment for Football—We're Fighting the Wrong Battle" that "we must give individuals a reason to value artistic expression." Devise a plan for realizing that goal.

6. Drawing on at least two of the selections in this chapter, explain your viewpoint on the importance of art. Be sure to defend your position by supplying evidence not only from the essays but also from your own observations.

7. Interview a group of your friends and acquaintances for their opinions of the place of an artist's private beliefs and behavior in judging the artist's work. Then report the results of your survey in an essay that synthesizes the comments of the people whom you survey.

8. Who do you think are today's most creative people? You might highlight a particular group of people (artists, musicians) or a particular person. Give supporting evidence to substantiate your viewpoint.

9. Define *excellence* in relation to a specific art form (for instance, a painting, a novel, a poem, a dance, a song, or a film) by stating the criteria you use for judging that abstract quality and by giving examples you believe best illustrate it.

10. Select a work of art in any medium—painting, music, graphic literature, the theatre, dance, literature—and analyze its importance as a work of art, including what it means to you personally.

11. Answer the question: In what ways do the arts—music, art, drama, literature—contribute to the culture of a people?

12. Explore the question of what makes some art live for all time and other art disappear. What makes a "timeless" work of art? Select a particular painting as an example and explain, in as much detail as possible, why you believe as you do.

13. Define *art* (an admittedly abstract term but one that people never tire of wrestling with), and explain what you think is gained by a culture's interest in and support of art and what you think would be lost without it. As an alternative, argue that nothing is gained by a culture's art and that little or nothing would be lost without it. Make sure you explain why you feel as you do on this subject.

Research Topics

1. Select an issue or question related to the broad subject of the role of the artist in society to research and then argue your position on that issue. For instance, what is the connection between artists' moral nature and their work? Do you think that an artist's private morality should (or does) influence the way his or her work is perceived? What is the connection between

an artist's public life and private behavior? Consider whether evidence of immorality affects or alters in any way the quality of a person's work.

2. In recent years, some people have been highly critical of what they see as obscenity or immorality in contemporary art. The works of Robert Mapplethorpe, for instance, were the object of such widespread, heated public debate that the National Endowment for the Arts was threatened with funding cuts because of similar projects it had supported with grants. Research the issue of censorship in the arts, and write an opinion paper on the subject. Consider: Does society have a moral obligation to limit what people can say, do, or use in their art, or do First Amendment rights extend to any subject or medium an artist wants to use?

3. The discoveries of prehistoric cave drawings that are fairly sophisticated in technique and meaning have led some art historians to suggest that art did not necessarily develop progressively, as has been commonly believed. Research this topic by reading about some of the prehistoric cave drawings that have been discovered and the theories of art historians about their importance. Then weigh the evidence and arrive at your own opinion about the nature and purpose of prehistoric art or its place in the historical development of art.

4. Research the role of the arts in strengthening students' abilities in other subject areas.

5. Research the contributions to art of a well-known artist or performer. Although you will want to provide a brief biographical sketch, your paper should focus on assessing the particular way(s) the artist had an effect on not only his or her own specialty but also "the arts" in general.

6. Research the history of a particular dance form. You may want to use as one of your sources Barbara Ehrenreich's book *Dancing in the Streets: A History of Collective Joy.*

7. In "Dance, Dance, Revolution," Barbara Ehrenreich refers to "the dance 'manias' that swept Belgium, Germany, and Italy starting in the 14th century" (paragraph 7). Research the subject of dance manias during that period.

8. Andrew D. Arnold writes in "Comix Poetics" that "some of the wildest feats of artistic imagination in the history of the medium occurred at [the] inception" of newspaper strips (paragraph 3). Research that historical period and write a paper defending that statement. You will probably want to include the artists that Arnold mentions, George Herriman and Gilbert Seldes.

RESPONDING TO VISUALS

Henderson Advertising for the South Carolina Ballet

"The new ballet will have quite an effect on you."

1. What is the purpose of this advertisement?
2. Does the stance of the mechanic strike you as amusing or odd?
3. How do the mechanic and his environment function in relation to what the advertisement is promoting?
4. What is the target audience of the advertisement? How effectively do you think it reaches that audience?

RESPONDING TO VISUALS

Cover illustration of Superman comic book from DC Comics.

1. Analyze the cover by discussing how the artist conveys action, how Superman is represented, what he is doing, and where the action takes place. What story does the picture tell?

2. Why do you think that comic books and graphic novels are so popular? If you read graphic novels or comic books, explain why they appeal to you.

3. Do you think that graphic literature and/or comic books should be taught as legitimate forms of literature in schools?

PART · THREE

Social and Behavioral Sciences

CHAPTER 12

Education

Education is a complex and crucially important subject. Without education, people face obstacles to participating fully in society. Because of its importance, education is also the subject of controversy. People are divided on issues such as what material and activities are appropriate for the classroom, what methods of delivering material work best, how much homework ought to be required of students, and what skills and knowledge students must demonstrate to go on to subsequent educational levels. Periodically, philosophies of education change, curricula are restructured, classrooms are transformed, and instructors learn new approaches to teaching their subject matter. As a student who has gone through many years of education, beginning in the primary grades, you are uniquely positioned to comment on this subject. You have been immersed in education and are presumably currently enrolled in at least one class, the course for which you are using this textbook. In the essays in this chapter, writers express their strong opinions on the subject of education and criticize certain aspects of the educational system in America, so you are likely to find yourself either nodding your head in agreement or shaking your head in disagreement with what they say.

The first essay in this chapter, Alex Kingsbury's "The Measure of Learning," addresses the issue of how to measure student learning at the college level. Reporting on the recommendations of the U.S. Commission on Higher Education, Kingsbury notes that the government wants colleges and universities to be accountable for student learning, in the way that K-12 schools have been since the No Child Left Behind Act of 2001. He also asks a question that will be of interest to you: "What should a student learn in college?" As you read the article, consider what you have learned in your education so far. Think about what you expect from your college by the time you graduate and whether it should be held accountable for producing certain measurable outcomes in exchange for your investment of time and money.

Next, Judy Blume recounts her experiences with banned books as a child and her sometimes painful experience of having her own books banned, attacked, censored, and vilified. In "Censorship: A Personal View," which is her introduction to a collection of stories by writers who have been censored, Blume explains how she "found [her]self at the eye of a storm." She also asks the question, "What is censorship?" You might think that there is an obvious definition, but she maintains that if you ask a dozen people, you will get a dozen different definitions. So as you read her essay, ask yourself what you consider censorship to be. You also may be interested to note if you have read any of the titles that she mentions which have been banned from the classroom or school libraries.

Following Blume's thoughts on censorship and what to do about it, David Brooks' "One Nation, Enriched by Biblical Wisdom," addresses the controversial issue of religion in public schools. The question of whether students should be allowed to pray in schools or recite the Pledge of Allegiance, specifically the phrase "one nation, under God," has caused much debate for decades. The furor over school prayer has resulted in lawsuits seeking to block schools from allowing public prayer or recitation of God's name. One such case went to the United States Supreme Court, and Brooks' commentary for the *New York Times* appeared the day before the Court began to hear arguments in the *Elk Grove United School District v. Newdow* case. He makes an intriguing point about the issue by looking at it by way of a book about the civil rights movement.

Finally, in a short but pointed essay by a well-known historian, public television host, and biographer, "No Time to Read?" reminds us of the importance of reading books. David McCullough urgently and fervently advises his audience to "read for pleasure. Read what you like and all that you like. Read literally to your heart's content." For him, books are our most important source of education.

As you read these selections, think about your own education, the courses you have taken, your classroom activities, the teachers who have taught you, and your own reading habits. Where do you find yourself agreeing with the authors, and where do you disagree? Are your experiences similar to or different from what they describe? What is your own philosophy of education? How important do you believe education is to your well-being and sense of self? How important is reading to you?

THE MEASURE OF LEARNING

ALEX KINGSBURY

Alex Kingsbury is an education writer for U.S. News & World Report. *He is a graduate of the George Washington University and the Columbia University Graduate School of Journalism. This report was published in the March 12, 2007, edition of* U.S. News & World Report.

In his autobiography, *The Education of Henry Adams,* the grandson of the sixth president delivered the American school system one of its most memorable intellectual smackdowns. His treatise on the value of experiential learning concluded that his alma mater, Harvard University, "as far as it educated at all . . . sent young men into the world with all they needed to make respectable citizens. Leaders of men it never tried to make." His schooling, replete with drunken revelry and privileged classmates, didn't prepare him for a world of radical change: the birth of radio, X-rays, automobiles. "[Harvard] taught little," he said, "and that little, ill."

Today's undergraduate education, of course, is far more than just the canon of classics that Adams studied. And with heavy investments in technology, it's hard to argue that colleges don't prepare students for the job market or the emerging digital world. But the question remains: What should a student learn in college? And whatever that is, which colleges teach it most effectively? With the average cost of private college soaring—and with studies consistently showing American students falling behind their peers internationally—it's a question being asked more and more. And it's one that colleges are at a loss to fully answer. "Every college tries to do what it says in the brochures: 'to help students reach their full potential,'" says Derek Bok, former Harvard president and the author of *Our Underachieving Colleges*. But, he says, "most schools don't know what that means. Nor do they know who is failing to achieve that full potential."

It's called "value added," an elusive measurement of the thinking skills and the body of knowledge that students acquire between their freshman and senior years. In other words, how much smarter are students when they leave college than when they got there? Trying to quantify that value—and assessing how effective each of the nation's 4,200 colleges is at delivering it—is at the heart of one of the most ambitious and controversial higher-education reforms in recent history.

4   Later this month, U.S. Secretary of Education Margaret Spellings will meet with college leaders to discuss the findings of her Commission on the Future of Higher Education and its plan to assess college learning through one or a number of standardized tests. "For years the colleges in this country have said, 'We're the best in the world; give us money and leave us alone,'" says Charles Miller, the chairman of the commission. "The higher-ed community needs to fess up to the public's concerns."

Along with the parents footing the bills, the federal government has a vested interest in knowing how the nation's colleges are doing their jobs. Although the government provides only 10 percent of the funding for all K-12 schools, it is responsible for 24 percent of all money spent on higher education. Despite this inflow of public money, colleges have largely escaped the accountability movement that has been shaping policy and curricula in the early grades.

One Size

Not surprisingly, colleges abhor the idea of government-imposed testing, insisting that they are reforming themselves and that government oversight is not the answer in any case. A one-size-fits-all solution is grossly impractical, they argue, given the variety of American colleges, and it undermines the prized independence of the institutions, widely regarded as among the finest in the world. "No one wants standardized No Child Left Behind-style testing in colleges—not parents, not students, not colleges," says David Ward, president of the American Council of Education. Adds Lloyd Thacker, author of *College Unranked: Ending the College Admissions Frenzy,* "The danger is that the soul of education will be crushed in the rush to quantify the unquantifiable."

A combination of factors has prompted the government to rethink its historically hands-off policy toward higher education. They include a staggeringly high dropout rate, a perceived decline in international competitiveness, and sky-high tuitions. Nationwide, only 63 percent of entering freshmen will graduate from college within six years—and fewer than 50 percent of black and Hispanic freshmen will. And while degree holders have far greater earning power than non-degree holders, the students who incur debt only to drop out are often worse off than if they had never attended college in the first place.

8   And debts they have. A year of tuition at Harvard cost Henry Adams $75, or nearly $1,750 in today's dollars. Now, four years at a public in-state, four-year college costs $65,400, up more than 27 percent in the past five years. Four years at a private school costs more than $133,000. In the past 30 years, the average constant-dollar cost of a degree from a private school has more than doubled. So it's hardly surprising that college students with loans graduate with an average of $19,000 in debt.

Yet an expensive degree does not necessarily a literate citizen make. In 2003, the government surveyed college graduates to test how well they could read texts and draw inferences. Only 31 percent were able to complete these basic tasks at a proficient level, down from 40 percent a decade earlier. Fewer than half of all college students, other studies show, graduate with broad proficiency in math and reading. And, according to Bok, evidence suggests that several groups of college students, particularly blacks and Hispanics, consistently under-perform levels expected of them given their SAT scores and high school grades.

It is just these sorts of reports that have triggered the government's demands for greater accountability. "It was always assumed that higher education knew what it was doing," says John Simpson, president of the University at Buffalo-SUNY. "Now, the government wants provable results."

There are currently two major tools used to measure student learning in college. The Collegiate Learning Assessment, administered to freshmen and seniors, measures critical thinking and analytical reasoning. About 120 schools use it—though nearly all keep the results confidential. Hundreds of schools also administer the National Survey of Student Engagement, which tracks how much time students spend on educational and other activities—a proxy for value added. Colleges have also made efforts to monitor student satisfaction, faculty effectiveness, and best classroom practices. The problem is, schools largely keep these results from the public.

12   Many graduate programs require standardized tests for admission, from the Graduate Record Exam to the more specialized tests for law, medicine, and business. So demonstrating a college's effectiveness could be as simple a matter as tabulating its graduates' pass rates on those exams. But many colleges have no way to determine if their graduates take these exams or how well they score. Nor, colleges argue, can they easily and comprehensively monitor starting salary, graduate school acceptance, or years spent in debt. This is despite the prodigious data-gathering capabilities of the fundraisers in the alumni office.

Should a philosophy major be proficient in calculus? Should a physics major be able to conjugate French verbs? A study of hundreds of students at the University of Washington suggests that measuring success within disciplines might be the way forward instead. "We found that learning outcomes were highly dependent on a student's major," says Catharine Beyer, who has compiled the results of that research into a book to be published this spring. "A chemistry student will learn something very different about writing than a philosophy major. That's why standardized tests across institutions are too simplistic to determine what learning takes place."

Others contend that a myopic focus on testing is simply the wrong way to think about learning. Peter Ewell, vice president at the National Center for Higher Education Management Systems, says that alternative assessments, like portfolios of student work or senior-year capstone projects, can be effective yardsticks for gauging progress. Ball State University in Muncie, Ind., for instance, requires that all students must pass a writing test in order to graduate; in two hours, students must produce a three-page expository essay. In several majors, including architecture and education, students must maintain an electronic portfolio of their work.

In the next five years, Ball State will also give all students the opportunity to participate in an "immersive learning project," in which they solve a real-world problem. One recent class, for example, produced a DVD about the American legal system for the local Hispanic communities. "The limitation of the Spellings commission is that they only think about universities in terms of the classroom," says Jo Ann Gora, Ball State's president. "We see our educational mission in much broader terms, including community involvement that is not easy to quantify with a test."

16   To a large degree, schools already are held accountable for their performance. It happens through the accreditation process, in which an independent panel reviews the operation of an institution and gives its official blessing. When the process started, there were fewer colleges and far fewer federal dollars at stake. But now, with federal student loans contingent on a school's credentials, a loss of accreditation could put a college out of business. Thus, accreditors are reluctant to fail schools, preferring instead to issue warnings and encourage improvement. Accreditors meeting in Washington recently also confessed that some were reluctant to shutter schools that are "failing in the numerical sense" because those institutions were serving students who otherwise might not have options.

Freeze

But if the feds have their way, that sort of attitude may change. The Department of Education recently made an example out of the American Academy for Liberal Education, a minor accrediting agency, by freezing its authority for six months for—among other things—failing to clearly measure student achievement. It was an indication of how quickly the government is moving to implement the recommendations of the commission. "We're not just going to sit around and study this," says Cheryl Oldham, the commission's executive director. "We're going to begin to correct the problems."

Another key resource for evaluating schools is, of course, college rankings—the Best Colleges list by *U.S. News* in particular. College rankings have been blamed for all manner of ills, from runaway tuition costs to unhealthy adolescent stress. But chief among critics' complaints is that *U.S. News* relies more on "inputs" such as SAT scores and the high school class ranks of admittees than "outputs" of the sort that Spellings wants to measure.

"*U.S. News* rankings heavily weight the wealth of a school, through things like spending per student, rather than how much a student learns," says Kevin Carey, a researcher at the nonpartisan think tank Education Sector.

20   Unless colleges release them, *U.S. News* does not have access to such data. But if such measures were incorporated, the rankings could change. Florida, for example, makes data about student learning public, often with surprising results. The average student at the University of Florida, for example, has SAT scores a full 100 points higher than those at Florida International University. There are fewer full-time faculty members at FIU, and only 4 percent of alumni donate money back to the school, compared with 18 percent of University of Florida grads. Those are just two reasons that the University of Florida ranks higher than FIU in the *U.S. News* list. Yet the average earnings of FIU grads—only one measure, to be sure—are significantly higher than those of their University of Florida counterparts.

The state of Texas also requires its public colleges to release more data. In a recent report, the state announced that the tiny University of Texas of the Permian Basin in Odessa far outperformed the larger UT campuses in El Paso and Dallas on the Collegiate Learning Assessment. What's more, Permian Basin also had a greater percentage of students either employed or enrolled in a graduate program within a year after graduation for every year between 2001 and 2004, when compared with its counterparts in El Paso and Dallas.

These are the sorts of statistics students should consider when looking at colleges, guidance counselors say. In their absence, students look elsewhere for comparisons—to campus luxuries like room service or Jacuzzis, for instance, or to the success of a school's sports teams. "Students will choose a college because of its party reputation or its campus facilities or how many times it's been on ESPN, because they don't have a lot of other meaningful information to base their choice on," says Steve Goodman, an educational consultant and college counselor. The irony is that it's often easier to find statistics about a college football running back than it is to find, say, the college's expected graduation rate for black males from middle-class households.

Spellings, for her part, sees outcomes as inseparable from the college search process. She envisions a database on the Web where people can shop for a school the way they shop for a new car—an analogy that incenses academics to no end. (These critics also point out that the Department of Education already maintains such a website, though it is far from user-friendly.)

Acting Now

24   Some schools are already taking the hint. The University of North Carolina recently announced that it was considering requiring the Collegiate Learning Assessment. The Kentucky and Wisconsin governments require that state schools prove learning outcomes. In Texas, in addition to the testing it already mandates, Gov. Rick Perry has proposed a college exit exam. The Arizona State University system has moved to give individual deans more power to require learning assessments. And businesses are lining up to provide the tools to do it. "Employers, governments, and parents want to know what they are paying for," says Catherine Burdt of the educational research firm Eduventures. As the college going population includes more part-time and older students, studies show, the demand for measuring learning outcomes will only increase.

In a few weeks, colleges will hear how Spellings intends to move forward. Colleges, meanwhile, continue to search for that elusive value-added measure, which, however flawed, can lead to better teaching.

"We should not be afraid of a culture of self-scrutiny on campus, but only the faculty can create a culture of learning," says Bok, who is wary of a federally imposed solution. "Those who say it's impossible to quantify a college education are not being honest or they are dissembling. All the things you learn can't be counted, but some can. We need to get more schools interested in examining their own successes and shortcomings."

That might be something Spellings could support—provided that the colleges publish the results.

PERSONAL RESPONSE

How satisfied are you with the college you have chosen to attend? Has it met your expectations so far? If so, how? If not, it what way(s) has it failed?

QUESTIONS FOR CLASS OR SMALL-GROUP DISCUSSION

1. Kingsbury asks, "What should a student learn in college?" (paragraph 2). How would you answer that question?

2. Explain in your own words what "one of the most ambitious and controversial higher-education reforms in recent history" is (paragraph 3). Why is it controversial? Why are colleges and universities concerned by the recommendations of the Commission on the Future of Higher Education?

3. Discuss whether you think colleges and universities should be held accountable in the same way as K-12 schools are.

4. Kingsbury mentions two tools to measure learning that are currently used by many colleges but whose results are not made public (paragraph 11). Do you think such data should be made public? What do you think of the requirements that Ball State University has in place for measuring student learning (paragraphs 14–15)?

5. Discuss your definition of a successful college education. What do you think would be the best measure of what students achieve in their years at college?

CENSORSHIP: A PERSONAL VIEW

Judy Blume

Judy Blume's novels have sold over seventy-five million copies and have been translated into over twenty languages worldwide. Hers are also among the most frequently banned or challenged books in America

*because of her frank treatment of issues relating to children and young
adults. Among her more than two dozen novels are* Are You There,
God? It's Me, Margaret *(1970);* It's Not the End of the World
(1972); Tales of a Fourth Grade Nothing *(1974);* Forever *(1975);*
Wifey *(1978);* Summer Sisters *(1998); and* Double Fudge *(2002).
Blume is founder of the charitable and educational foundation, the
Kids Fund. Because of her experiences with censorship, she edited*
Places I Never Meant To Be: Original Stories by Censored Writ-
ers *(1999), a collection of short stories by authors who have been cen-
sored or banned. The introduction to that collection is reprinted here.*

When I was growing up I'd heard that if a movie or book was "Banned in Boston"
everybody wanted to see it or read it right away. My older brother, for example,
went to see such a movie—*The Outlaw,* starring Jane Russell—and I wasn't supposed to tell my mother. I begged him to share what he saw, but he wouldn't. I was
intensely curious about the adult world and hated the secrets my parents, and now
my brother, kept from me.

A few years later, when I was in fifth grade, my mother was reading a novel
called *A Rage to Live,* by John O'Hara, and for the first time (and, as it turned out,
the only time) in my life, she told me I was never to look at that book, at least not
until I was *much* older. Once I knew my mother didn't want me to read it, I figured
it must be really interesting!

So, you can imagine how surprised and delighted I was when, as a junior in
high school, I found John O'Hara's name on my reading list. Not a specific title
by John O'Hara, but *any* title. I didn't waste a minute. I went down to the public
library in Elizabeth, New Jersey, that afternoon—a place where I'd spent so many
happy hours as a young child, I'd pasted a card pocket on the inside back cover of
each book I owned—and looked for *A Rage to Live.* But I couldn't find it. When
I asked, the librarian told me *that* book was *restricted.* It was kept in a locked closet,
and I couldn't take it out without written permission from my parents.

Aside from my mother's one moment of fear, neither of my parents had ever
told me what I could or could not read. They encouraged me to read widely. There
were no "Young Adult" novels then. Serious books about teenagers were published
as adult novels. It was my mother who handed me *To Kill a Mockingbird* and Anne
Frank's *Diary of a Young Girl* when they were first published.

By the time I was twelve I was browsing in the bookshelves flanking the
fireplace in our living room where, in my quest to make sense of the world, I
discovered J.D. Salinger's *The Catcher in the Rye,* fell in love with the romantic trag-
edies of Thomas Hardy and the Brontë sisters, and overidentified with "Marjorie
Morningstar."

But at the Elizabeth Public Library the librarian didn't care. "Get permission
in writing," she told me. When I realized she was not going to let me check out *A
Rage to Live,* I was angry. I felt betrayed and held her responsible. It never occurred
to me that it might not have been her choice.

At home I complained to my family, and that evening my aunt, the principal
of an elementary school, brought me her copy of *A Rage to Live.* I stayed up half

the night reading the forbidden book. Yes, it was sexy, but the characters and their story were what kept me turning the pages. Finally, my curiosity (about that book, anyway) was satisfied. Instead of leading me astray, as my mother must have feared, it led me to read everything else I could find by the author.

8   All of which brings me to the question *What is censorship?* If you ask a dozen people you'll get twelve different answers. When I actually looked up the word in *The Concise Columbia Encyclopedia* I found this definition: "[The] official restriction of any expression believed to threaten the political, social, or moral order." My thesaurus lists the following words that can be used in place of *ban* (as in book banning): *Forbid. Prohibit. Restrict.* But what do these words mean to writers and the stories they choose to tell? And what do they mean to readers and the books they choose to read?

I began to write when I was in my mid-twenties. By then I was married with two small children and desperately in need of creative work. I wrote *Are You There God? It's Me, Margaret* right out of my own experiences and feelings when I was in sixth grade. Controversy wasn't on my mind. I wanted only to write what I knew to be true. I wanted to write the best, the most honest books I could, the kinds of books I would have liked to read when I was younger. If someone had told me then I would become one of the most banned writers in America, I'd have laughed.

When *Margaret* was published in 1970 I gave three copies to my children's elementary school but the books never reached the shelves. The male principal decided on his own that they were inappropriate for elementary school readers because of the discussion of menstruation (never mind how many fifth- and sixth-grade girls already had their periods). Then one night the phone rang and a woman asked if I was the one who had written that book. When I replied that I was, she called me a communist and hung up. I never did figure out if she equated communism with menstruation or religion.

In that decade I wrote thirteen other books: eleven for young readers, one for teenagers, and one for adults. My publishers were protective of me during those years and didn't necessarily share negative comments about my work. They believed if I didn't know some individuals were upset by my books, I wouldn't be intimidated.

12   Of course, they couldn't keep the occasional anecdote from reaching me: the mother who admitted she'd cut two pages out of *Then Again, Maybe I Won't* rather than allow her almost thirteen-year-old son to read about wet dreams. Or the young librarian who'd been instructed by her male principal to keep *Deenie* off the shelf because in the book, Deenie masturbates. "It would be different if it were about a boy," he'd told her. "That would be normal."

The stories go on and on but really, I wasn't that concerned. There was no organized effort to ban my books or any other books, none that I knew of, anyway. The seventies were a good decade for writers and readers. Many of us came of age during those years, writing from our hearts and guts, finding editors and publishers who believed in us, who willingly took risks to help us find our audience. We were free to write about real kids in the real world. Kids with feelings and emotions, kids with real families, kids like we once were. And young readers gobbled up our books, hungry for characters with whom they could identify, including my own daughter and son, who had become avid readers. No mother could have been more proud to see the tradition of family reading passed on to the next generation.

Then, almost overnight, following the presidential election of 1980, the censors crawled out of the woodwork, organized and determined. Not only would they decide what *their* children could read but what *all* children could read. It was the beginning of the decade that wouldn't go away, that still won't go away almost twenty years later. Suddenly books were seen as dangerous to young minds. Thinking was seen as dangerous, unless those thoughts were approved by groups like the Moral Majority, who believed with certainty they knew what was best for everyone.

So now we had individual parents running into schools, waving books, demanding their removal—books they hadn't read except for certain passages. Most often their objections had to do with language, sexuality, and something called "lack of moral tone."

16   Those who were most active in trying to ban books came from the "religious right" but the impulse to censor spread like a contagious disease. Other parents, confused and uncertain, were happy to jump on the bandwagon. Book banning satisfied their need to feel in control of their children's lives. Those who censored were easily frightened. They were afraid of exposing their children to ideas different from their own. Afraid to answer children's questions or talk with them about sensitive subjects. And they were suspicious. They believed if kids liked a book, it must be dangerous.

Too few schools had policies in place enabling them to deal with challenged materials. So what happened? The domino effect. School administrators sent down the word: Anything that could be seen as controversial had to go. Often books were quietly removed from school libraries and classrooms or, if seen as potential troublemakers, were never purchased in the first place. These decisions were based not on what was best for the students, but what would not offend the censors.

I found myself at the center of the storm. My books were being challenged daily, often placed on *restricted* shelves (shades of Elizabeth, New Jersey, in 1955) and sometimes removed. A friend was handed a pamphlet outside a supermarket urging parents to rid their schools and libraries of Judy Blume books. Never once did the pamphlet suggest the books actually be read. Of course I wasn't the only target. Across the country, the Sex Police and the Language Police were thumbing through books at record speed, looking for illustrations, words or phrases that, taken out of context, could be used as evidence against them.

Puberty became a dirty word, as if children who didn't read about it wouldn't know about it, and if they didn't know about it, it would never happen.

20   The Moral Tone Brigade attacked *Blubber* (a story of victimization in the classroom) with a vengeance because, as they saw it, in this book evil goes unpunished. As if kids need to be hit over the head, as if they don't get it without having the message spelled out for them.

I had letters from angry parents accusing me of ruining Christmas because of a chapter *Superfudge* called "Santa Who?" Some sent lists showing me how easily I could have substituted one word for another: meanie for bitch; darn for damn;

nasty for ass. More words taken out of context. A teacher wrote to say she blacked out offending words and passages with a felt-tip marker. Perhaps most shocking of all was a letter from a nine-year-old addressed to *Jew*dy Blume telling me I had no right to write about Jewish angels in *Starring Sally J. Freedman as Herself.*

My worst moment came when I was working with my editor on the manuscript of *Tiger Eyes* (the story of a fifteen-year-old girl, Davey, whose beloved father dies suddenly and violently). When we came to the scene in which Davey allows herself to *feel* again after months of numbness following her father's death, I saw that a few lines alluding to masturbation had been circled. My editor put down his pencil and faced me. "We want this book to reach as many readers as possible, don't we?" he asked.

I felt my face grow hot, my stomach clench. This was the same editor who had worked with me on *Are You There God? It's Me, Margaret; Then Again, Maybe I Won't; Deenie; Blubber; Forever*—always encouraging, always supportive. The scene was psychologically sound, he assured me, and delicately handled. But it also spelled trouble. I got the message. If you leave in those lines, the censors will come after this book. Librarians and teachers won't buy it. Book clubs won't take it. Everyone is too scared. The political climate has changed.

24   I tried to make a case for why that brief moment in Davey's life was important. He asked me *how* important? Important enough to keep the book from reaching its audience? I willed myself not to give in to the tears of frustration and disappointment I felt coming. I thought about the ways a writer brings a character to life on the page, the same way an artist brings a face to life on canvas—through a series of brush strokes, each detail adding to the others, until we see the essence of the person. I floundered, uncertain. Ultimately, not strong enough or brave enough to defy the editor I trusted and respected, I caved in and took out those lines. I still remember how alone I felt at that moment.

What effect does this climate have on a writer? *Chilling.* It's easy to become discouraged, to second-guess everything you write. There seemed to be no one to stand up to the censors. No group as organized as they were; none I knew of, anyway. I've never forgiven myself for caving in to editorial pressure based on fear, for playing into the hands of the censors. I knew then it was all over for me unless I took a stand. So I began to speak out about my experiences. And once I did, I found that I wasn't as alone as I'd thought.

My life changed when I learned about the National Coalition Against Censorship (NCAC) and met Leanne Katz, the tiny dynamo who was its first and long-time director. Leanne's intelligence, her wit, her strong commitment to the First Amendment and helping those who were out on a limb trying to defend it, made her my hero. Every day she worked with the teachers, librarians, parents and students caught in the cross fire. Many put themselves and their jobs on the line fighting for what they believed in.

In Panama City, Florida, junior high school teacher Gloria Pipkin's award-winning English program was targeted by the censors for using Young Adult literature that was *depressing, vulgar and immoral,* specifically *I Am the Cheese,* by Robert Cormier, and *About David,* by Susan Beth Pfeffer.

28   A year later, when a new book selection policy was introduced forbidding vulgar, obscene and sexually related materials, the school superintendent zealously applied it to remove more than sixty-five books, many of them classics, from the curriculum and classroom libraries. They included *To Kill a Mockingbird, The Red Badge of Courage, The Great Gatsby, Wuthering Heights,* and *Of Mice and Men.* Also banned were Shakespeare's *Hamlet, King Lear, The Merchant of Venice* and *Twelfth Night.*

      Gloria Pipkin fought a five-year battle, jeopardizing her job and personal safety (she and the reporter covering the story received death threats) to help reinstate the books. Eventually, the professional isolation as well as the watered-down curriculum led her to resign. She remains without a teaching position.

      Claudia Johnson, Florida State University professor and parent, also defended classic books by Aristophanes and Chaucer against a censor who condemned them for promoting "women's lib and pornography." She went on to fight other battles—in defense of John Steinbeck's *Of Mice and Men,* and a student performance of Lorraine Hansberry's *A Raisin in the Sun.*

      English teacher Cecilia Lacks was fired by a high school in St. Louis for permitting her creative writing students to express themselves in the language they heard and used outside of school everyday. In the court case that followed, many of her students testified on their teacher's behalf. Though she won her case, the decision was eventually reversed and at this time Lacks is still without a job.

32   Colorado English teacher Alfred Wilder was fired for teaching a classic film about fascism, Bernardo Bertolucci's *1900.*

      And in Rib Lake, Wisconsin, guidance counselor Mike Dishnow was fired for writing critically of the Board of Education's decision to ban my book *Forever* from the junior high school library. Ultimately he won a court settlement, but by then his life had been turned upside down.

      And these are just a few examples.

      This obsession with banning books continues as we approach the year 2000. Today it is not only Sex, Swear Words and Lack of Moral Tone—it is Evil, which, according to the censors, can be found lurking everywhere. Stories about Halloween, witches, and devils are . . . [all] suspect for promoting Satanism. *Romeo and Juliet* is under fire for promoting suicide; Madeleine L'Engle's *A Wrinkle in Time,* for promoting New Age-ism. If the censors had their way it would be good-bye to Shakespeare as well as science fiction. There's not an *ism* you can think of that's not bringing some book to the battlefield.

36   What I worry about most is the loss to young people. If no one speaks out for them, if they don't speak out for themselves, all they'll get for required reading will be the most bland books available. And instead of finding the information they need at the library, instead of finding the novels that illuminate life, they win find only those materials to which nobody could possibly object.

      Some people would like to rate books in schools and libraries the way they rate movies: G, PG, R, X, or even more explicitly. But according to whose standards would the books be rated? I don't know about you but I don't want anyone rating my books or the books my children or grandchildren choose to read. We can make our own decisions, thank you. Be wary of the censors' code words—*family friendly;*

family values; excellence in education. As if the rest of us don't want excellence in education, as if we don't have our own family values, as if libraries haven't always been family-friendly places!

And the demands are not all coming from the religious right. No . . . the urge to decide not only what's right for their kids but for all kids has caught on with others across the political spectrum. Each year *Huckleberry Finn* is challenged and sometimes removed from the classroom because, to some, its language, which includes racial epithets, is offensive. Better to acknowledge the language, bring it out in the open, and discuss why the book remains important than to ban it. Teachers and parents can talk with their students and children about any book considered controversial.

I gave a friend's child one of my favorite picture books, James Marshall's *The Stupids Step Out,* and was amazed when she said, "I'm sorry, but we can't accept that book. My children are not permitted to use that word. Ever. It should be changed to 'The Sillies Step Out.'" I may not agree, but I have to respect this woman's right to keep that book from her child as long as she isn't trying to keep it from other people's children. Still, I can't help lamenting the lack of humor in her decision. *The Stupids Step Out* is a very funny book. Instead of banning it from her home, I wish she could have used it as an opportunity to talk with her child about why she felt the way she did, about why she never wanted to hear her child call anyone stupid. Even very young children can understand. So many adults are exhausting themselves worrying about other people corrupting their children with books, they're turning kids off to reading instead of turning them on.

40   In this age of censorship I mourn the loss of books that will never be written, I mourn the voices that will be silenced—writers' voices, teachers' voices, students' voices—and all because of fear. How many have resorted to self-censorship? How many are saying to themselves, "Nope . . . can't write about that. Can't teach that book. Can't have that book in our collection. Can't let my student write that editorial in the school paper."

PERSONAL RESPONSE

Describe an experience that you have had with being forbidden to read, watch, or listen to something because it was considered inappropriate. How did it make you feel? What was it like to finally read, watch, or listen to it?

QUESTIONS FOR CLASS OR SMALL-GROUP DISCUSSION

1. Blume asks "What is censorship?" (paragraph 8) and observes that it has different meanings to different people. How do you define "censorship"? Give examples to illustrate your definition.

2. Explain in your own words why Blume's books have been challenged or censored.

3. Discuss your own experience in junior and senior high school with banned or challenged books. Were your librarians and teachers free to choose any books they wanted for the library or classroom?

4. Under what circumstances do you think it justifiable to forbid children or young adults to read something?

5. If you have read any of the novels that Blume mentions as having been challenged, banned, or censored, what did you think of them? What parts of the books do you think drew the attention of censors? Do you agree that the books should be withheld from children or young adults?

ONE NATION, ENRICHED BY BIBLICAL WISDOM

David Brooks

David Brooks is a senior editor at the Weekly Standard, *a contributing editor at* Newsweek *and the* Atlantic Monthly, *and the "Machine Age" columnist for the* New York Times Magazine. *He is also a regular commentator on National Public Radio,* CNN's Late Edition, *and* The News Hour with Jim Lehrer. *He is editor of the anthology* Backward and Upward: The New Conservative Writing *(1996) and author of* Bobos In Paradise: The New Upper Class and How They Got There *(2000) and* On Paradise Drive: How We Live Now (and Always Have) in the Future Tense *(2004). "One Nation, Enriched by Biblical Wisdom" first appeared in the* New York Times *on March 23, 2004.*

Tomorrow the Supreme Court will hear arguments about whether it is constitutional for public school teachers to lead the Pledge of Allegiance, including the phrase "one nation under God," in their classrooms. So tonight's reading assignment is *A Stone of Hope* by David L. Chappell.

A Stone of Hope is actually a history of the civil rights movement, but it's impossible to read the book without doing some fundamental rethinking about the role religion can play in schools and public life.

According to Chappell, there were actually two camps within the civil rights movement. First, there were the mainstream liberals, often white and Northern. These writers and activists tended to have an optimistic view of human nature. Because racism so fundamentally contradicted the American creed, they felt, it would merely take a combination of education, economic development and consciousness-raising to bring out the better angels in people's nature.

4   The second group, which we might today call the religious left, was mostly black and Southern. Its leaders, including Martin Luther King Jr., drew sustenance from a prophetic religious tradition, and took a much darker view of human nature.

King wrote an important essay on Jeremiah, the "rebel prophet" who saw that his nation was in moral decline. King later reminded readers that human beings are capable of "calculated cruelty as no other animal can practice." He and the other leaders in the movement did not believe that education and economic development would fully bring justice, but believed it would take something as strong as a religious upsurge. Because the experiences of the Hebrew prophets had taught them to be pessimistic about humanity, the civil rights leaders knew they had to be spiritually aggressive if they wanted to get anything done.

Chappell argues that the civil rights movement was not a political movement with a religious element. It was a religious movement with a political element.

If you believe that the separation of church and state means that people should not bring their religious values into politics, then, if Chappell is right, you have to say goodbye to the civil rights movement. It would not have succeeded as a secular force.

8 But the more interesting phenomenon limned in Chappell's book is this: King had a more accurate view of political realities than his more secular liberal allies because he could draw on biblical wisdom about human nature. Religion didn't just make civil rights leaders stronger—it made them smarter.

Whether you believe in God or not, the Bible and commentaries on the Bible can be read as instructions about what human beings are like and how they are likely to behave. Moreover, this biblical wisdom is deeper and more accurate than the wisdom offered by the secular social sciences, which often treat human beings as soulless utility-maximizers, or as members of this or that demographic group or class. Whether the topic is welfare, education, the regulation of biotechnology or even the war on terrorism, biblical wisdom may offer something that secular thinking does not—not pat answers, but a way to think about things.

For example, it's been painful to watch thoroughly secularized Europeans try to grapple with Al Qaeda. The bombers declare, "You want life, and we want death"—a (fanatical) religious statement par excellence. But thoroughly secularized listeners lack the mental equipment to even begin to understand that statement. They struggle desperately to convert Al Qaeda into a political phenomenon: the bombers must be expressing some grievance. This is the path to permanent bewilderment.

The lesson I draw from all this is that prayer should not be permitted in public schools, but maybe theology should be mandatory. Students should be introduced to the prophets, to the Old and New Testaments, to the Koran, to a few of the commentators who argue about these texts.

12 From this perspective, what gets recited in the pledge is the least important issue before us. Understanding what the phrase "one nation under God" might mean—that's the important thing. That's not proselytizing; it's citizenship.

PERSONAL RESPONSE

Do you believe that public-school children should be allowed to repeat the Pledge of Allegiance? Explain your answer.

QUESTIONS FOR CLASS OR SMALL-GROUP DISCUSSION

1. Analyze the use that Brooks makes of David L. Chappell's book, *A Stone of Hope*. How does Brooks use his references to that book to forward his argument?

2. Given the constraints of writing a newspaper column (limited space, short paragraphs), how convincingly do you think that Brooks argues his central position on the issue of prayers and reciting the Pledge of Allegiance in public schools?

3. Discuss your response to this sentence in paragraph 11: "The lesson I draw from all this is that prayer should not be permitted in public schools, but maybe theology should be mandatory." Do you think that theology should be mandatory in public schools? What would be gained by it?

4. Explain what you think Brooks means in his closing paragraph when he says that "what gets recited in the pledge is the least important issue before us." Why is "understanding what the phrase 'one nation under God' might mean" more important, according to Brooks?

NO TIME TO READ?

David McCullough

David McCullough is a biographer, historian, lecturer, and teacher. He holds twenty-one honorary degrees and has received many awards for his writing, including Pulitzer Prizes for his widely acclaimed biographies Truman *(1992) and* John Adams *(2001). His other books include* The Path Between the Seas *(1977), chronicling the building of the Panama Canal;* Mornings on Horseback *(1981), on the life of the young Theodore Roosevelt;* Brave Companions *(1992), essays on heroic figures of the past and present;* The Great Bridge: The Epic Story of Building the Brooklyn Bridge *(2001); and* 1776 *(2005). McCullough is also well known to viewers of PBS as the host of* The American Experience *and numerous PBS documentaries. "No Time to Read?" appeared in the April 18, 2000, issue of* Family Circle.

Once upon a time in the dead of winter in the Dakota territory, Theodore Roosevelt took off in a makeshift boat down the Little Missouri River in pursuit of a couple of thieves who had stolen his prized rowboat. After several days on the river, he caught up and got the draw on them with his trusty Winchester, at which point they surrendered. Then Roosevelt set off in a borrowed wagon to haul the thieves cross-country to justice. They headed across the snow-covered wastes of the Badlands to the railhead at Dickinson, and Roosevelt walked the whole way, the entire 40 miles.

It was an astonishing feat, what might be called a defining moment in Roosevelt's eventful life. But what makes it especially memorable is that during that time, he managed to read all of *Anna Karenina.*

I often think of that when I hear people say that they haven't time to read.

4   Reportedly, the average American does have time to watch 28 hours of television every week, or approximately four hours a day. The average person, I'm told, reads at a rate of 250 words per minute. So, based on these statistics, were the average American to spend those four hours a day with a book instead of watching television, he or she could, in a week, read: the complete poems of T. S. Eliot; two plays by Thornton Wilder, including *Our Town;* the complete poems of Maya Angelou; Faulkner's *The Sound and the Fury; The Great Gatsby;* and The Book of Psalms.

That's all in one week.

But a week is a long time by today's standards, when information is available at the touch of a finger. Information has become an industry, a commodity to be packaged, promoted and marketed incessantly. The tools for "accessing" data grow ever more wondrous and ubiquitous and essential if we're to keep in step, we've come to believe. All hail the web, the Internet, the Information Highway.

We're being sold the idea that information is learning, and we're being sold a bill of goods.

8   Information isn't learning. It isn't wisdom. It isn't common sense necessarily. It isn't kindness. Or good judgment. Or imagination. Or a sense of humor. Or courage. Information doesn't tell us right from wrong.

Knowing the area of the state of Connecticut in square miles, or the date on which the United Nations Charter was signed, or the jumping capacity of a flea may be useful, but it isn't learning of itself.

The greatest of all avenues to learning—to wisdom, adventure, pleasure, insight, to understanding human nature, understanding ourselves and our world and our place in it—is in reading books.

Read for life, all your life. Nothing ever invented provides such sustenance, such infinite reward for time spent, as a good book.

12   Read for pleasure. Read what you like, and all you like. Read literally to your heart's content. Let one book lead to another. They nearly always do.

Take up a great author, new or old, and read everything he or she has written. Read about places you've never been. Read biography, history. Read books that changed history: Tom Paine's *Common Sense;* the autobiography of Frederick Douglass; Rachel Carson's *Silent Spring.*

Read those books you know you're supposed to have read and imagine as dreary. A classic may be defined as a book that stays long in print, and a book stays long in print only because it is exceptional. Why exclude the exceptional from your experience?

Go back and read again the books written supposedly for children, especially if you think they are only for children. My first choice would be *The Wind in the Willows.* There's much, very much, you can learn in the company of Toad, Rat and Mole.

16   And when you read a book you love—a book you feel has enlarged the experience of being alive, a book that "lights the fire"—then spread the word.

To carry a book with you wherever you go is old advice and good advice. John Adams urged his son, John Quincy, to carry a volume of poetry. "You'll never be alone," he said, "with a poet in your pocket."

PERSONAL RESPONSE

Do you read books for pleasure during your leisure time? If so, what do you like to read? If not, why not?

QUESTIONS FOR CLASS OR SMALL-GROUP DISCUSSION

1. How effective do you find McCullough's opening anecdote about Theodore Roosevelt?

2. Do you agree with McCullough that, on the "idea that information is learning, [. . .] we're being sold a bill of goods" (paragraph 6)? Do you agree with him that "[i]nformation isn't learning" (paragraph 7)?

3. Discuss the extent to which you agree with McCullough's implication that people would have time to read books if they just took the time.

4. Have you read any of the books or any works by the authors that McCullough names? What authors have you heard about whose books you would like to read (paragraph 12)? What books do you "know you're supposed to have read and imagine as dreary" (paragraph 13)? Which of the books for children, besides *The Wind in the Willows*, do you think McCullough may have in mind when he says to read the "books written supposedly for children" (paragraph 14)?

○ PERSPECTIVES ON EDUCATION ○

Suggested Writing Topics

1. With Judy Blume's "Censorship: A Personal View" in mind, define "censorship," using your own experience with a banned, censored, forbidden, or challenged book.

2. Read one or more of the books that Judy Blume mentions in "Censorship: A Personal View" and write an essay explaining why you think it was challenged, censored or banned and whether you agree that it should have been.

3. Explain what you see as the role of parents in children's education.

4. Define *education*, using specific examples to illustrate general or abstract statements. You may want to focus specifically on higher education, as discussed in Alex Kingsbury's "The Measure of Learning."

5. Distinguish among the words *education, knowledge,* and *wisdom*. How are they similar? How are they different? Would a standardized test measure any of them?

6. Read David L. Chappell's *A Stone of Hope,* as discussed in David Brooks' "One Nation, Enriched by Biblical Wisdom" and analyze it in terms of Brooks' remark: [B]ut it's impossible to read the book without doing some fundamental rethinking about the role religion can play in schools and public life."

7. Argue in support of or against this statement from David McCullough's "No Time to Read?": "The greatest of all avenues to learning [. . .] is in reading books" (paragraph 9).

8. Write a paper about a book that had a profound effect on you. Explain briefly what the book is and what it is about, but focus on aspects of it that affected you. Perhaps it moved you emotionally as no other book has or it directed you on a specific path in life. Or, write about a teacher who made an impression and had a significant effect on you. What made that teacher so important to you? Try to explain not only physical characteristics but, more importantly, personality features and admirable qualities. If a particular incident was especially significant in your relationship, narrate what happened.

9. Some people argue that not everyone deserves to go to college and that admitting average or mediocre students into colleges has debased American higher education. Argue in support of or against that position.

10. Assume the role of a student member of the curriculum task force for a department or unit at your university such as business, foreign languages, education, mathematics, computer science, history, music, physics, or your major area, if you have declared one. Your committee has been asked to consider adding a multicultural component to the required courses for the major without dropping any of the courses already required. What recommendations for or against such an addition would you make

11. Imagine that the number of students admitted to college directly after high school has been limited to the upper 33 percent of all graduating seniors and that you do not meet the requirements for admission to college. Under special circumstances, students who fall below the 33 percent mark may be admitted. In a letter to the admissions officer at the college of your choice, argue that you should be admitted despite your class ranking and give reasons why you would make a good student.

Research Topics

1. Research the subject of governmental plans to measure learning in institutions of higher education with a standardized test and argue your position on the subject.

2. Research opinions for and against requiring students to write an essay as part of their qualifications for a degree, as Ball State University now does. (See Alex Kingsbury's "The Measure of Learning.") Arrive at your own viewpoint based on your research and argue your position.

3. Read one of the books that Judy Blume mentions in "Censorship: A Personal View" and research the controversy surrounding it. Explain the arguments both for and against banning or censoring the book and then argue your own position.

4. Research the tracking systems used in many schools. Find opinions supporting and opposing such systems, consider their advantages and disadvantages, and arrive at your own conclusion based on your reading.

5. Research the Supreme Court case of *Elk Grove United School District v. Newdow*, analyze the arguments on both sides, and come to your own conclusion about the phrase "under God" in the Pledge of Allegiance.

6. Spend some time searching the Internet or going through your library's catalog of books and periodicals on the subject of education. You will find a very large number of subtopics under that broad heading. Select a seemingly controversial subtopic that interests you. Keep searching until you have narrowed your focus to one specific aspect of the subject that is suitable for your research project.

7. Research the conflict of traditional versus revisionist curriculum. Interview educators and read periodical articles from the last several years on *political correctness*, defenses for or against *the canon*, or related topics.

8. Both Brooks and McCullough find fault with the electronic media. Research the subject of the role of television or of the Internet in American popular culture in relationship to the reading habits of Americans.

9. Research the controversy over prayer in public schools and explain your own position on the topic.

RESPONDING TO VISUALS

© H. Armstrong Roberts/CORBIS

Boring class, circa 1950s.

1. What do you think the photographer wanted to convey with this picture?
2. Although the caption describes the photograph as that of a boring class, what other emotions do the facial expressions of the students suggest? What does their body language reveal about how they view this particular classroom experience?
3. If you had not been told the date that the photograph was taken, what aspects of the classroom and students would give you clues that it is not recent?
4. Why do you think the teacher is not shown in the photograph?

RESPONDING TO VISUALS

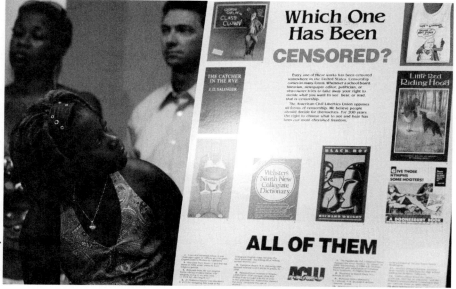

Noel Ingram looks at a display showing books that have been banned at different times by schools, during a news conference in Miami, Wednesday, June 21, 2006, held by the American Civil Liberties Union after the organization filed a lawsuit asking that a federal judge halt the Miami-Dade school board from removing a series of children's books, including one on Cuba. Her mother had joined the lawsuit.

1. What is the effect of showing the young girl peering at the poster? Would the impact of the image be changed were she not in the photograph?

2. Why do you think that the books represented on the poster have been banned? Do you recognize any of them?

3. If you have read any of the books represented on the poster, what did you think of it?

4. Do you think books should be banned for school-aged children? If so, who should make the decision about which books to ban: parents, the administration, or teachers? What if one group believes a book should be banned while another defends it as literature and finds it acceptable?

CHAPTER 13

Poverty and Homelessness

Once largely ignored, the issues of poverty, homelessness, and welfare have prompted heated discussion in recent years. At the community level, social workers and staff members at shelters for the homeless and impoverished struggle to meet the needs of desperate people, while at the state and federal levels, legislators argue over whether to cut welfare funding. The numbers of people in poverty, especially women and children, continue to rise. Many families whose incomes provide just enough for basic necessities, such as shelter and food, are only a paycheck or two away from living on the streets. Worse, a growing number of the nation's poor actually work full-time. Compounding the difficulty of these issues are certain attitudes toward or stereotyped beliefs about people on welfare or living on the streets. Charges of laziness and fraud are often leveled at welfare recipients, despite studies that demonstrate that the vast majority of people on welfare want to work and live independent lives.

The essays in this chapter examine some of the issues associated with poverty and homelessness. First, Anna Quindlen in "Our Tired, Our Poor, Our Kids" looks at the plight of homeless mothers and children in America. She points out some of the effects of homelessness on children, emphasizes the importance of affordable housing, and touches on the effects of welfare reform on homelessness. Closely related to Quindlen's opinion piece is an editorial published in *America* magazine. "Still Hungry, Still Homeless" comments on the rise of poverty and homelessness in the United States, notes the increase in requests for emergency housing and food, and, like Quindlen, mentions the effect of welfare reform on this serious social problem.

Following these two readings on homelessness and hunger in America is a classic essay by one of the best-known writers of the twentieth century. From the collection of his essays, *Nobody Knows My Name,* James Baldwin's "Fifth Avenue, Uptown" was originally published in 1960. A forceful and moving depiction of life in the ghetto in New York City at that time, it touches on the issue of disadvantaged, poorly served minorities and the seeming impossibility of getting out of the ghetto. Speaking from his perspective of having grown up there, Baldwin writes with the authority that only comes from inside knowledge and close personal experience. His voice articulated a strong rallying cry for the Civil Rights movement of the 1960s. As you read his essay, consider whether his observations of almost fifty years ago are still relevant today.

Finally, in "The Singer Solution to World Poverty," Peter Singer broadens the focus of the chapter to world poverty while addressing his essay to the American middle class. Using the logic of his training as a utilitarian philosopher, Singer offers a hypothetical ethical scenario to raise readers' awareness of what he sees as their moral responsibility to donate to world aid funds for poor and starving children.

As you read these essays, think about your own attitudes toward welfare, homelessness, and poverty. These are tough social problems that just about every society must face, but especially so in countries with large urban areas and great gaps between the rich and the poor. Do the Quindlen essay and the *America* editorial in any way reinforce or change your attitudes about these issues? Are you moved by James Baldwin's description of the ghetto? Does Singer persuade you to donate to charities?

OUR TIRED, OUR POOR, OUR KIDS

ANNA QUINDLEN

Anna Quindlen is a novelist, social critic, and journalist who began her career at the New York Post *and then became deputy metropolitan editor of the* New York Times. *In 1986, she began her syndicated column "Life in the Thirties" and a few years later "Public and Private," for which she won a Pulitzer Prize in 1992. Currently she contributes* Newsweek's *prestigious back-page column, "The Last Word," every other week. Her columns are collected in* Living Out Loud *(1988);* Thinking Out Loud *(1992); and* Loud and Clear *(2004). She has written the following novels:* Object Lessons *(1991);* One True Thing *(1994);* Black and Blue *(1998);* Blessings *(2003); and* Being Perfect *(2004). Among her nonfiction books are* How Reading Changed My Life *(1998);* A Short Guide to a Happy Life *(2000); and* Imagining London: A Tour of the World's Greatest Fictional City *(2004). This essay appeared in the March 12, 2001, issue of* Newsweek.

Six people live here, in a room the size of the master bedroom in a modest suburban house. Trundles, bunk beds, dressers side by side stacked with toys, clothes, boxes, in tidy claustrophobic clutter. One woman, five children. The baby was born in a shelter. The older kids can't wait to get out of this one. Everyone gets up at 6 A.M., the little ones to go to day care, the others to school. Their mother goes out to look for an apartment when she's not going to drug-treatment meetings. "For what they pay for me to stay in a shelter I could have lived in the Hamptons," Sharanda says.

Here is the parallel universe that has flourished while the more fortunate were rewarding themselves for the stock split with SUVs and home additions. There is a boom market in homelessness. But these are not the men on the streets of San Francisco holding out cardboard signs to the tourists. They are children, hundreds of thousands of them, twice as likely to repeat a grade or be hospitalized and four times as likely to go hungry as the kids with a roof over their heads. Twenty years ago New York City provided emergency shelter for just under a thousand families a day; last month it had to find spaces for 10,000 children on a given night. Not since the Great Depression have this many babies, toddlers and kids had no place like home.

Three mothers sit in the living room of a temporary residence called Casa Rita in the Bronx and speak of this in the argot of poverty. "The landlord don't call back when they hear you got EARP," says Rosie, EARP being the Emergency Assistance Rehousing Program. "You get priority for Section 8 if you're in a shelter," says Edna, which means federal housing programs will put you higher on the list. Edna has four kids, three in foster care; she arrived at Casa Rita, she says, "with two bags and a baby." Rosie has three; they share a bathroom down the hall with two other families. Sharanda's five range in age from 13 to just over a year. Her eldest was put in the wrong grade when he changed schools. "He's humiliated, living here," his mother says.

4   All three women are anxious to move on, although they appreciate this place, where they can get shelter, get sober and keep their kids at the same time. They remember the Emergency Assistance Unit, the city office that is the gateway to the system, where hundreds of families sit every day surrounded by their bags, where children sleep on benches until they are shuffled off dull-eyed for one night in a shelter or a motel, only to return as supplicants again the next day.

In another world middle-class Americans have embraced new-home starts, the stock market and the Gap. But in the world of these displaced families, problems ignored or fumbled or unforeseen during this great period of prosperity have dovetailed into an enormous subculture of children who think that only rich people have their own bedrooms. Twenty years ago, when the story of the homeless in America became a staple of news reporting, the solution was presented as a simple one: affordable housing. That's still true, now more than ever. Two years ago the National Low Income Housing Coalition calculated that the hourly income necessary to afford the average two-bedroom apartment was around $12. That's more than twice the minimum wage.

The result is that in many cities police officers and teachers cannot afford to live where they work, that in Las Vegas old motels provide housing for casino employees, that in shelters now there is a contingent of working poor who get up off their cots and go off to their jobs. The result is that if you are evicted for falling behind on your rent, if there is a bureaucratic foul-up in your welfare check or the factory in which you work shuts down, the chances of finding another place to live are very small indeed. You're one understanding relative, one paycheck, one second chance from the street. And so are your kids.

So-called welfare reform, which emphasizes cutbacks and make-work, has played a part in all this. A study done in San Diego in 1998 found that a third of homeless families had recently had benefits terminated or reduced, and that most said that was how they had wound up on the street. Drugs, alcohol and domestic abuse also land mothers with kids in the shelter system or lead them to hand their children over to relatives or foster homes. Today the average homeless woman is younger than ever before, may have been in foster care or in shelters herself and so considers a chaotic childhood the norm. Many never finished high school, and have never held a job.

8   Ralph Nunez, who runs the organization Homes for the Homeless, says that all this calls for new attitudes. "People don't like to hear it, but shelters are going to be the low-income housing of the future," he says. "So how do we enrich the experience and use the system to provide job training and education?" Bonnie Stone of Women in Need, which has eight other residences along with Casa Rita, says, "We're pouring everything we've got into the nine months most of them are here—nutrition, treatment, budgeting. By the time they leave, they have a subsidized apartment, day care and, hopefully, some life skills they didn't have before."

But these organizations are rafts in a rising river of need that has roared through this country without most of us ever even knowing. So now you know. There are hundreds of thousands of little nomads in America, sleeping in the back of cars, on floors in welfare offices or in shelters five to a room. What would it mean, to spend your childhood drifting from one strange bed to another, waking in the morning to try to figure out where you'd landed today, without those things that confer security and happiness: a familiar picture on the wall, a certain slant of light through a curtained window? "Give me your tired, your poor," it says on the base of the Statue of Liberty, to welcome foreigners. Oh, but they are already here, the small refugees from the ruin of the American dream, even if you cannot see them.

PERSONAL RESPONSE

What image of the homeless did you have before reading this essay? Has your understanding of them changed in any way now that you have read it? If so, in what way has it changed? If not, explain why.

QUESTIONS FOR CLASS OR SMALL-GROUP DISCUSSION

1. Were you surprised by this statement: "Not since the Great Depression have this many babies, toddlers and kids had no place like home" (paragraph 2)? What effect do you think Quindlen hopes to achieve by mentioning the Great Depression?

2. Explain why, according to Quindlen, there are so many homeless women and children in America. What is the effect of homelessness on children? Are you persuaded of the seriousness of the problem?

3. What does Quindlen mean by the term *working poor* (paragraph 6)?

4. Quindlen uses the term *so-called* to describe welfare reform (paragraph 7). Why do you think she does that? What fault does she find with welfare reform? Do you agree with her?

STILL HUNGRY, STILL HOMELESS

America Magazine Editorial

> America *magazine describes itself as a journal of opinion on current events, historical events, spiritual events, family, books, film, and television for Catholic people. This editorial appeared in the magazine's February 5, 2001, issue.*

One might think that last year's particularly strong economy would have led to a reduction in the number of requests for emergency food and shelter. In fact, however, the year 2000 actually saw a rise in both areas. This was among the sad findings of the United States Conference of Mayors' annual survey of 25 cities around the country, which was released in late December.

Officials in the survey cities estimated that requests for emergency food assistance jumped by 17 percent—the second highest rate of increase since 1992. Over half of the people seeking help were children and their parents: a particularly disturbing finding, given the need for parents to be able to provide adequate and nutritious food for their children. A third of the adults, moreover, were employed. This reflects the fact that minimum wage jobs at $5.50 an hour cannot cover the cost of living for most Americans. Mirroring the conclusions of the mayors' report, Catholic Charities USA found in its own year-end survey that its agencies had seen what it termed "a startling 22 percent increase in the use of their emergency services."

How could this be, in the face of what many politicians have trumpeted as our unprecedented level of prosperity? Ironically, the mayors' report points out that the very strength of the economy has been partly to blame. Seeing that the earnings of middle-class Americans have risen, landlords have been quick to realize that they can charge much higher rents. But for families at the bottom of the economic ladder, whose earnings did not increase, the consequence has been an ever more desperate search for housing within their income range; it is a search that has sometimes ended in homelessness. Even those lucky enough to have Section 8 vouchers have discovered that apartment owners often refuse to accept them, knowing that they can command higher prices than the government's reimbursement rate for the vouchers. Thus, in nearly half the survey cities, the report cites housing costs as a primary reason for the increase in requests for emergency food and shelter.

4   Welfare reform has played its part in this bleak scenario. People leaving Temporary Assistance for Needy Families (T.A.N.F.) may indeed have full-time jobs that pay above the minimum wage and yet still not be making enough to lift them above the poverty line. And all too frequently, they are unaware that despite being employed, they may still be eligible for the food stamps (and Medicaid) that could tide them over from one month to the next. Government agencies are not as aggressive as they should be in promoting these programs among the working poor. True, the number of food assistance facilities has increased, but the strain on their limited resources is so great that half the cities report that these facilities must either send people away or reduce the amount of what they can provide.

The same situation applies to emergency housing requests. Nearly a quarter of them, says the mayors' report, went unmet. Turned-away families in San Antonio, for instance, found themselves obliged to sleep in cars or parks, under bridges or in already doubled- or tripled-up substandard housing. Even when they can be accommodated, in 52 percent of the cities homeless families may have to break up, with older male youths and fathers sent elsewhere.

The outlook for the future is not bright. Almost three-fourths of the survey cities expect a rise in the demand for emergency food. As the officials in Boston put it, "the number of pantries increases every year, and [yet] the requests for assistance have increased by as much as 40 percent." Nor, they add, do they "see any relief in the near future." Again, there as elsewhere, high housing costs, along with low-paying jobs, lead the list of causes for more hunger and homelessness. The answer is implied in the comments of the respondents from Burlington, Vt.: "Without a significant commitment to building a significant number of new and affordable housing units, homelessness will continue to rise." The new secretary-designate of the Department of Housing and Urban Development, Mel Martinez, said at his Senate confirmation hearing that he would try to make more housing available to low-income Americans. We hope that he will act on his words. For many years, however, Congress has shown little interest in this neglected area of American life.

In releasing its annual report in December, Fred Kammer, S.J., president of Catholic Charities USA, spoke of its findings as "a story about . . . escalating need in a land of skyrocketing wealth." He recalled Bill Clinton's promise to "end welfare as we know it." That has happened, but the rise in requests for emergency food and housing calls into question the effectiveness of welfare reform. The real goal, Father Kammer concluded, should be to "end poverty as we know it." Now is the time for Congress to take the strong measures needed to assist the most vulnerable members of society.

PERSONAL RESPONSE

Are you surprised that the numbers of hungry and homeless people in America are rising? Write for a few minutes on your reaction to that fact or to any other part of the essay that caught your attention as you read it.

QUESTIONS FOR CLASS OR SMALL-GROUP DISCUSSION

1. How does the editorial account for the fact that requests for emergency food and shelter continue to rise despite a strong economy (paragraph 1)? That is, what factors account for the high numbers of children and their parents, including employed adults, seeking emergency aid?

2. The editorial comments that "the rise in requests for emergency food and housing calls into question the effectiveness of welfare reform" (paragraph 7). Why has the welfare reform program not worked, according to the editorial? What do you know about the welfare reform program? Do you think it is a good plan, or do you find fault with it, too?

3. Are you persuaded that "now is the time for Congress to take the strong measures needed to assist the most vulnerable members of society" (paragraph 7)? What measures does the editorial suggest would be appropriate? How effective do you think those measures would be?

4. Can you offer any other solutions to the problem of homelessness and poverty in America besides the ones suggested in this article?

FIFTH AVENUE, UPTOWN

JAMES BALDWIN

James Baldwin was one of the best known African American writers of the twentieth century. In both fiction and nonfiction, he became a respected and widely read voice for the Civil Rights movement of the 1960s. Born in Harlem in 1924, he grew up in the ghetto that he describes so vividly in "Fifth Avenue, Uptown," but he left home at seventeen for Greenwich Village. His first novel, the partly autobiographical Go Tell It on the Mountain *(1953), received high critical praise and was followed by several collections of essays:* Notes of a Native Son *(1955);* Nobody Knows My Name *(1963); and* The Fire Next Time *(1963). In 1948, he moved to France, where he lived for most of the rest of his life, returning to America often to lecture and teach. His other works include the novels* Giovanni's Room *(1956);* Another Country *(1961);* Tell Me How Long the Train's Been Gone *(1968);* If Beale Street Could Talk *(1974); and* Just Above My Head *(1979); and collections of essays,* No Name in the Street *(1972) and* The Devil Finds Work *(1976). He died in France in 1987. "Fifth Avenue, Uptown" originally appeared in* Esquire *magazine in 1960 and was later reprinted in* Nobody Knows My Name.

There is a housing project standing now where the house in which we grew up once stood, and one of those stunted city trees is snarling where our doorway used to be. This is on the rehabilitated side of the avenue. The other side of the avenue—for progress takes time—has not been rehabilitated yet and it looks exactly as it looked in the days when we sat with our noses pressed against the windowpane, longing to be allowed to go "across the street." The grocery store which gave us credit is still there, and there can be no doubt that it is still giving credit. The people in the project certainly need it—far more, indeed, than they ever needed the project. The last time I passed by, the Jewish proprietor was still standing among his shelves, looking sadder and heavier but scarcely any older. Farther down the block stands the shoe-repair store in which our shoes were repaired until reparation became impossible and in which, then, we bought all our "new" ones. The Negro proprietor is still in the window, head down, working at the leather.

These two, I imagine, could tell a long tale if they would (perhaps they would be glad to if they could), having watched so many, for so long, struggling in the fishhooks, the barbed wire, of this avenue.

The avenue is elsewhere the renowned and elegant Fifth. The area I am describing, which, in today's gang parlance, would be called "the turf," is bound by Lenox Avenue on the west, the Harlem River on the east, 135th Street on the north, and 130th Street on the south. We never lived beyond these boundaries; this is where we grew up. Walking along 145th Street—for example—familiar as it is, and similar, does not have the same impact because I did not know any of the people on the block. But when I turn east on 131st Street and Lenox Avenue, there is first a soda-pop joint, then a shoeshine "parlor," then a grocery store, then a dry cleaners,' then the houses. All along the street there are people who watched me grow up, people who grew up with me, people I watched grow up along with my brothers and sisters; and, sometimes in my arms, sometimes underfoot, sometimes at my shoulder—or on it—their children, a riot, a forest of children, who include my nieces and nephews.

4   When we reach the end of this long block, we find ourselves on wide, filthy, hostile Fifth Avenue, facing that project which hangs over the avenue like a monument to the folly, and the cowardice, of good intentions. All along the block, for anyone who knows it, are immense human gaps, like craters. These gaps are not created merely by those who have moved away, inevitably into some other ghetto; or by those who have risen, almost always into a greater capacity for self-loathing and self-delusion; or yet by those who, by whatever means—War II, the Korean war, a policeman's gun or billy, a gang war, a brawl, madness, an overdose of heroin, or, simply, unnatural exhaustion—are dead. I am talking about those who are left, and I am talking principally about the young. What are they doing? Well, some, a minority, are fanatical churchgoers, members of the more extreme of the Holy Roller sects. Many, many more are "moslems," by affiliation or sympathy, that is to say that they are united by nothing more—and nothing less—than a hatred of the white world and all its works. They are present, for example, at every Buy Black street-corner meeting—meetings in which the speaker urges his hearers to cease trading with white men and establish a separate economy. Neither the speaker nor his hearers can possibly do this, of course, since Negroes do not own General Motors or RCA or the A & P, nor, indeed, do they own more than a wholly insufficient fraction of anything else in Harlem (those who *do* own anything are more interested in their profits than in their fellows). But these meetings nevertheless keep alive in the participators a certain pride of bitterness without which, however futile this bitterness may be, they could scarcely remain alive at all. Many have given up. They stay home and watch the TV screen, living on the earnings of their parents, cousins, brothers, or uncles, and only leave the house to go to the movies or to the nearest bar. "How're you making it?" one may ask, running into them along the block, or in the bar. "Oh, I'm TV-ing it"; with the saddest, sweetest, most shame-faced of smiles, and from a great distance. This distance one is compelled to respect; anyone who has traveled so far will not easily be dragged again into the world. There are further retreats, of course, than the TV screen or the bar. There are those who are simply sitting on their stoops, "stoned," animated for a moment only, and hideously, by the approach of someone who may lend them the money for a "fix." Or by the approach of someone from whom they can purchase it, one of the shrewd ones, on the way to prison or just coming out.

And the others, who have avoided all of these deaths, get up in the morning and go downtown to meet "the man." They work in the white man's world all day and come home in the evening to this fetid block. They struggle to instill in their children some private sense of honor or dignity which will help the child survive. This means, of course, that they must struggle, stolidly, incessantly, to keep this sense alive in themselves, in spite of the insults, the indifference, and the cruelty they are certain to encounter in their working day. They patiently browbeat the landlord into fixing the heat, the plaster, the plumbing; this demands prodigious patience; nor is patience usually enough. In trying to make their hovels habitable, they are perpetually throwing good money after bad. Such frustration, so long endured, is driving many strong, admirable men and women whose only crime is color to the very gates of paranoia.

One remembers them from another time—playing handball in the playground, going to church, wondering if they were going to be promoted at school. One remembers them going off to war—gladly, to escape this block. One remembers their return. Perhaps one remembers their wedding day. And one sees where the girl is now—vainly looking for salvation from some other embittered, trussed, and struggling boy—and sees the all-but-abandoned children in the streets.

Now I am perfectly aware that there are other slums in which white men are fighting for their lives, and mainly losing. I know that blood is also flowing through those streets and that the human damage there is incalculable. People are continually pointing out to me the wretchedness of white people in order to console me for the wretchedness of blacks. But an itemized account of the American failure does not console me and it should not console anyone else. That hundreds of thousands of white people are living, in effect, no better than the "niggers" is not a fact to be regarded with complacency. The social and moral bankruptcy suggested by this fact is of the bitterest, most terrifying kind.

8 The people, however, who believe that this democratic anguish has some consoling value are always pointing out that So-and-So, white, and So-and-So, black, rose from the slums into the big time. The existence—the public existence—of, say, Frank Sinatra and Sammy Davis, Jr. proves to them that America is still the land of opportunity and that inequalities vanish before the determined will. It proves nothing of the sort. The determined will is rare—at the moment, in this country, it is unspeakably rare—and the inequalities suffered by the many are in no way justified by the rise of a few. A few have always risen—in every country, every era, and in the teeth of regimes which can by no stretch of the imagination be thought of as free. Not all of these people, it is worth remembering, left the world better than they found it. The determined will is rare, but it is not invariably benevolent. Furthermore, the American equation of success with the big times reveals an awful disrespect for human life and human achievement. This equation has placed our cities among the most dangerous in the world and has placed our youth among the most empty and most bewildered. The situation of our youth is not mysterious. Children have never been very good at listening to their elders, but they have never failed to imitate them. They must, they have no other models. That is exactly what our children are doing. They are imitating our immorality, our disrespect for the pain of others.

All other slum dwellers, when the bank account permits it, can move out of the slum and vanish altogether from the eye of persecution. No Negro in this country has ever made that much money and it will be a long time before any Negro does. The Negroes in Harlem, who have no money, spend what they have on such gimcracks as they are sold. These include "wider" TV screens, more "faithful" hi-fi sets, more "powerful" cars, all of which, of course, are obsolete long before they are paid for. Anyone who has ever struggled with poverty knows how extremely expensive it is to be poor; and if one is a member of a captive population, economically speaking, one's feet have simply been placed on the treadmill forever. One is victimized, economically, in a thousand ways—rent, for example, or car insurance. Go shopping one day in Harlem—for anything—and compare Harlem prices and quality with those downtown.

The people who have managed to get off this block have only got as far as a more respectable ghetto. This respectable ghetto does not even have the advantages of the disreputable one—friends, neighbors, a familiar church, and friendly tradesmen; and it is not, moreover, in the nature of any ghetto to remain respectable long. Every Sunday, people who have left the block take the lonely ride back, dragging their increasingly discontented children with them. They spend the day talking, not always with words, about the trouble they've seen and the trouble—one must watch their eyes as they watch their children—they are only too likely to see. For children do not like ghettos. It takes them nearly no time to discover exactly why they are there.

The projects in Harlem are hated. They are hated almost as much as policemen, and this is saying a great deal. And they are hated for the same reason: both reveal, unbearably, the real attitude of the white world, no matter how many liberal speeches are made, no matter how many lofty editorials are written, no matter how many civil-rights commissions are set up.

12   The projects are hideous, of course, there being a law, apparently respected throughout the world, that popular housing shall be as cheerless as a prison. They are lumped all over Harlem, colorless, bleak, high, and revolting. The wide windows look out on Harlem's invincible and indescribable squalor: the Park Avenue railroad tracks, around which, about forty years ago, the present dark community began; the unrehabilitated houses, bowed down, it would seem, under the great weight of frustration and bitterness they contain; the dark, the, ominous schoolhouses from which the child may emerge maimed, blinded, hooked, or enraged for life; and the churches, churches, block upon block of churches, niched in the walls like cannon in the walls of a fortress. Even if the administration of the projects were not so insanely humiliating (for example: one must report raises in salary to the management, which will then eat up the profit by raising one's rent; the management has the right to know who is staying in your apartment; the management can ask you to leave, at their discretion), the projects would still be hated because they are an insult to the meanest intelligence.

Harlem got its first private project, Riverton[1]—which is now, naturally, a slum—about twelve years ago because at that time Negroes were not allowed to live in Stuyvesant Town. Harlem watched Riverton go up, therefore, in the most violent bitterness of spirit, and hated it long before the builders arrived. They began hating it at about the time people began moving out of their condemned houses to

---

[1]The inhabitants of Riverton were much embittered by this description; they have, apparently, forgotten how their project came into being; and have repeatedly informed me that I cannot possibly be referring to Riverton, but to another housing project which is directly across the street. It is quite clear, I think, that I have no interest in accusing any individuals or families of the depredations herein described: but neither can I deny the evidence of my own eyes. Nor do I blame anyone in Harlem for making the best of a dreadful bargain. But anyone who lives in Harlem and imagines that he has not struck this bargain, or that what he takes to his status (in whose eyes?) protects him against the common pain, demoralization, and danger, is simply self deluded. [author's note]

make room for this additional proof of how thoroughly the white world despised them. And they had scarcely moved in, naturally, before they began smashing windows, defacing walls, urinating in the elevators, and fornicating in the playgrounds. Liberals, both white and black, were appalled at the spectacle. I was appalled by the liberal innocence—or cynicism, which comes out in practice as much the same thing. Other people were delighted to be able to point to proof positive that nothing could be done to better the lot of the colored people. They were, and are, right in one respect: that nothing can be done as long as they are treated like colored people. The people in Harlem know they are living there because white people do not think they are good enough to live anywhere else. No amount of "improvement" can sweeten this fact. Whatever money is now being earmarked to improve this, or any other ghetto, might as well be burnt. A ghetto can be improved in one way only: out of existence.

Similarly, the only way to police a ghetto is to be oppressive. None of the Police Commissioner's men, even with the best will in the world, have any way of understanding the lives led by the people they swagger about in twos and threes controlling. Their very presence is an insult, and it would be, even if they spent their entire day feeding gumdrops to children. They represent the force of the white world, and the world's real intentions are, simply, for the world's criminal profit and ease, to keep the black man corraled up here, in his place. The badge, the gun in the holster, and the swinging club make vivid what will happen should his rebellion become overt. Rare, indeed, is the Harlem citizen, from the most circumspect church member to the most shiftless adolescent, who does not have a long tale to tell of police incompetence, injustice, or brutality. I myself have witnessed and endured it more than once. The businessmen and racketeers also have a story. And so do the prostitutes. (And this is not, perhaps, the place to discuss Harlem's very complex attitude toward black policemen, nor the reasons, according to Harlem, that they are nearly all downtown.)

It is hard, on the other hand, to blame the policeman, blank, good-natured, thoughtless, and insuperably innocent, for being such a perfect representative of the people he serves. He, too, believes in good intentions and is astounded and offended when they are not taken for the deed. He has never, himself, done anything for which to be hated—which of us has?—and yet he is facing, daily and nightly, people who would gladly see him dead, and he knows it. There is no way for him not to know it: there are few things under heaven more unnerving than the silent, accumulating contempt and hatred of a people. He moves through Harlem, therefore, like an occupying soldier in a bitterly hostile country; which is precisely what, and where, he is, and is the reason he walks in twos and threes. And he is not the only one who knows why he is always in company: the people who are watching him know why, too. Any street meeting, sacred or secular, which he and his colleagues uneasily cover has as its explicit or implicit burden the cruelty and injustice of the white domination. And these days, of course, in terms increasingly vivid and jubilant, it speaks of the end of that domination. The white policeman standing on a Harlem street corner finds himself at the very center of the revolution now occurring in the world. He is not prepared for it—naturally, nobody is—and, what is possibly much more to the point, he is exposed, as few white people are, to the anguish of the black people around him. Even if he is gifted with the merest mustard grain of imagination, something must seep in. He cannot avoid observing that some of the children, in spite of their color, remind him of children he has known and loved, perhaps even of his own children. He knows that he certainly does not want *his* children living this way. He can retreat from his uneasiness in only one direction: into a callousness which very shortly becomes second nature. He becomes more callous, the population becomes more hostile, the situation grows more tense, and the police force is increased. One day, to everyone's astonishment, someone drops a match in the powder keg and everything blows up. Before the dust has settled or the blood congealed, editorials, speeches, and civil-rights commissions are loud in the land, demanding to know what happened. What happened is that Negroes want to be treated like men.

16   *Negroes want to be treated like men:* a perfectly straightforward statement, containing only seven words. People who have mastered Kant, Hegel, Shakespeare, Marx, Freud, and the Bible find this statement utterly impenetrable. The idea seems to threaten profound, barely conscious assumptions. A kind of panic paralyzes their features, as though they found themselves trapped on the edge of a steep place. I once tried to describe to a very well-known American intellectual the conditions among Negroes in the South. My recital disturbed him and made him indignant; and he asked me in perfect innocence, "Why don't all the Negroes in the South move North?" I tried to explain what *has* happened, unfailingly, whenever a significant body of Negroes move North. They do not escape Jim Crow: they merely encounter another, not-less-deadly variety. They do not move to Chicago, they move to the South Side; they do not move to New York, they move to Harlem. This pressure within the ghetto causes the ghetto walls to expand, and this expansion is always violent. White people hold the line as long as they can, and in as many ways as they can, from verbal intimidation to physical violence. But inevitably the border which has divided the ghetto from the rest of the world falls into the hands of the ghetto. The white people fall back bitterly before the black horde; the landlords make a tidy profit by raising the rent, chopping up the rooms, and all but dispensing with the upkeep; and what has once been a neighborhood turns into a "turf." This is precisely what happened when the Puerto Ricans arrived in their thousands—and the bitterness thus caused is, as I write, being fought out all up and down those streets.

Northerners indulge in an extremely dangerous luxury. They seem to feel that because they fought on the right side during the Civil War, and won, they have earned the right merely to deplore what is going on in the South, without taking any responsibility for it; and that they can ignore what is happening in Northern cities because what is happening in Little Rock or Birmingham is worse. Well, in the first place, it is not possible for anyone who has not endured both to know which is "worse." I know Negroes who prefer the South and white Southerners, because "At least there, you haven't got to play any guessing games!" The guessing games referred to have driven more than one Negro into the narcotics ward, the madhouse, or the river. I know another Negro, a man very dear to me, who says with conviction and with truth, "The spirit of the South is the spirit of America." He was born in the North and did his military training in the South. He did not, as far as I can gather, find the South "worse"; he found it, if anything, all too familiar. In the second place, though, even if Birmingham is worse, no doubt Johannesburg, South Africa, beats it by several miles, and Buchenwald was one of the worst things that ever happened in the entire history of the world. The world has never lacked for horrifying examples; but I do not believe that these examples are meant to be used as justification for our own crimes. This perpetual justification empties the heart of all human feeling. The emptier our hearts become, the greater will be our crimes. Thirdly, the South is not merely an embarrassingly backward region, but a part of this country, and what happens there concerns every one of us.

As far as the color problem is concerned, there is but one difference between the Southern white and the Northerner: the Southerner remembers, historically and in his own psyche, a kind of Eden in which he loved black people and they loved him. Historically, the flaming sword laid across this Eden is the Civil War. Personally, it is the Southerner's sexual coming of age, when, without any warning, unbreakable taboos are set up between himself and his past. Everything, thereafter, is permitted him except the love he remembers and has never ceased to need. The resulting, indescribable torment affects every Southern mind and is the basis of the Southern hysteria.

None of this is true for the Northerner. Negroes represent nothing to him personally, except, perhaps, the dangers of carnality. He never sees Negroes. Southerners see them all the time. Northerners never think about them whereas Southerners are never really thinking of anything else. Negroes are, therefore, ignored in the North and are under surveillance in the South, and suffer hideously in both places. Neither the Southerner nor the Northerner is able to look on the Negro simply as a man. It seems to be indispensable to the national self-esteem that the Negro be considered either as a kind of ward (in which case we are told how many Negroes, comparatively, bought Cadillacs last year and how few, comparatively, were lynched), or as a victim (in which case we are promised that he will never vote in our assemblies or go to school with our kids). They are two sides of the same coin and the South will not change—*cannot* change—until the North changes. The country will not change until it re-examines itself and discovers what it really means by freedom. In the meantime, generations keep being born, bitterness is increased by incompetence, pride, and folly, and the world shrinks around us.

20   It is a terrible, an inexorable, law that one cannot deny the humanity of another without diminishing one's own: in the face of one's victim, one sees oneself. Walk through the streets of Harlem and see what we, this nation, have become.

PERSONAL RESPONSE

Write about the degree to which you can identify with what Baldwin describes here. Is the world he describes completely alien to you or is it familiar?

QUESTIONS FOR CLASS OR SMALL-GROUP DISCUSSION

1. Analyze Baldwin's use of descriptive language. For instance, in paragraph 2, he refers to the proprietors mentioned in paragraph 1 as "struggling in the fishhooks, the barbed wire, of this avenue." What images do the metaphors "fishhooks" and "barbed wire" evoke? Where else do you find effective use of language, either literal or figurative?

2. How relevant to today's young Blacks in Harlem do you think Baldwin's description of them in 1960 is?

3. In your own words, state the contrasts that Baldwin makes between the Northern response to Negroes and the Southern one. Do you think that such views hold true today?

4. Respond to Baldwin's remarks about white people living in slums and his statements that the rise from the slums of a White or a Black person "proves nothing" (paragraph 8).

5. What do you think of Baldwin's observation that "the only way to police a ghetto is to be oppressive" (paragraph 14)?

THE SINGER SOLUTION TO WORLD POVERTY

Peter Singer

Peter Singer, an Australian-born philosopher and bioethicist, is author of the highly influential book Animal Liberation *(1975), which has been translated into two dozen languages. He has served as president of the International Association of Bioethics and as editor of its official journal,* Bioethics. *Among his dozen or so other books are* How Are We to Live?: Ethics in an Age of Self Interest *(1993);* Rethinking Life and Death: The Collapse of Our Traditional Ethics *(1995);* Writings on an Ethical Life *(2000);* The President of Good and Evil *(2004);* The Way We Eat: Why Our Food Choices Matter *(2006); and* Stem Cell Research, *co-edited with Laura Grabel and Lori Gruen (2007). Singer is on the faculty at the Center for Human Values at Princeton University. You can visit his website at www.princeton.edu/~psinger/. This essay appeared in the September 5, 1999, issue of* New York Times Magazine.

In the Brazilian film *Central Station*, Dora is a retired schoolteacher who makes ends meet by sitting at the station writing letters for illiterate people. Suddenly she has an opportunity to pocket $1,000. All she has to do is persuade a homeless nine-year-old boy to follow her to an address she has been given. (She is told he will be adopted by wealthy foreigners.) She delivers the boy, gets the money, spends some of it on a television set, and settles down to enjoy her new acquisition. Her neighbor spoils the fun, however, by telling her that the boy was too old to be adopted—he will be killed and his organs sold for transplantation. Perhaps Dora knew this all along, but after her neighbor's plain speaking, she spends a troubled night. In the morning Dora resolves to take the boy back.

Suppose Dora had told her neighbor that it is a tough world, other people have nice new TVs too, and if selling the kid is the only way she can get one, well, he was only a street kid. She would then have become, in the eyes of the audience, a monster. She redeems herself only by being prepared to bear considerable risks to save the boy.

At the end of the movie, in cinemas in the affluent nations of the world, people who would have been quick to condemn Dora if she had not rescued the boy go home to places far more comfortable than her apartment. In fact, the average family in the United States spends almost one-third of its income on things that are no more necessary to them than Dora's new TV was to her. Going out to nice restaurants, buying new clothes because the old ones are no longer stylish, vacationing at beach resorts—so much of our income is spent on things not essential to the preservation of our lives and health. Donated to one of a number of charitable agencies, that money could mean the difference between life and death for children in need.

All of which raises a question: In the end, what is the ethical distinction between a Brazilian who sells a homeless child to organ peddlers and an American who already has a TV and upgrades to a better one—knowing that the money could be donated to an organization that would use it to save the lives of kids in need?

Of course, there are several differences between the two situations that could support different moral judgments about them. For one thing, to be able to consign a child to death when he is standing right in front of you takes a chilling kind of heartlessness; it is much easier to ignore an appeal for money to help children you will never meet. Yet for a utilitarian philosopher like myself—that is, one who judges whether acts are right or wrong by their consequences—if the upshot of the American's failure to donate the money is that one more kid dies on the streets of a Brazilian city, then it is, in some sense, just as bad as selling the kid to the organ peddlers. But one doesn't need to embrace my utilitarian ethic to see that, at the very least, there is a troubling incongruity in being so quick to condemn Dora for taking the child to the organ peddlers while, at the same time, not regarding the American consumer's behavior as raising a serious moral issue.

In his 1996 book, *Living High and Letting Die,* the New York University philosopher Peter Unger presented an ingenious series of imaginary examples designed to probe our intuitions about whether it is wrong to live well without giving substantial amounts of money to help people who are hungry, malnourished, or dying from easily treatable illnesses like diarrhea. Here's my paraphrase of one of these examples: Bob is close to retirement. He has invested most of his savings in a very rare and valuable old car, a Bugatti, which he has not been able to insure. The Bugatti is his pride and joy. In addition to the pleasure he gets from driving and caring for his car, Bob knows that its rising market value means that he will always be able to sell it and live comfortably after retirement. One day when Bob is out for a drive, he parks the Bugatti near the end of a railway siding and goes for a walk up the track. As he does so, he sees that a runaway train, with no one aboard, is running down the railway track. Looking farther down the track, he sees the small figure of a child very likely to be killed by the runaway train. He can't stop the train and the child is too far away to warn of the danger, but he can throw a switch that will divert the train down the siding where his Bugatti is parked. Then nobody will be killed—but the train will destroy his Bugatti. Thinking of his joy in owning the car and the financial security it represents, Bob decides not to throw the switch. The child is killed. For many years to come, Bob enjoys owning his Bugatti and the financial security it represents.

8   Bob's conduct, most of us will immediately respond, was gravely wrong. Unger agrees. But then he reminds us that we, too, have opportunities to save the lives of children. We can give to organizations like Unicef or Oxfam America. How much would we have to give one of these organizations to have a high probability of saving the life of a child threatened by easily preventable diseases? (I do not believe that children are more worth saving than adults, but since no one can argue that children have brought their poverty on themselves, focusing on them simplifies the issues.) Unger called up some experts and used the information they provided to offer some plausible estimates that include the cost of raising money, administrative expenses, and the cost of delivering aid where it is most needed. By his calculation, $200 in donations would help a sickly two-year-old transform into a healthy six-year-old—offering safe passage through childhood's most dangerous years. To show how practical philosophical argument can be, Unger even tells his readers that they can easily donate funds by using their credit card and calling one of these toll-free numbers: (800) 367–5437 for Unicef; (800) 693–2687 for Oxfam America.

Now you, too, have the information you need to save a child's life. How should you judge yourself if you don't do it? Think again about Bob and his Bugatti. Unlike Dora, Bob did not have to look into the eyes of the child he was sacrificing for his own material comfort. The child was a complete stranger to him and too far away to relate to in an intimate, personal way. Unlike Dora, too, he did not mislead the child or initiate the chain of events imperiling him. In all these respects, Bob's situation resembles that of people able but unwilling to donate to overseas aid and differs from Dora's situation.

If you still think that it was very wrong of Bob not to throw the switch that would have diverted the train and saved the child's life, then it is hard to see how you could deny that it is also very wrong not to send money to one of the organizations listed above. Unless, that is, there is some morally important difference between the two situations that I have overlooked.

Is it the practical uncertainties about whether aid will really reach the people who need it? Nobody who knows the world of overseas aid can doubt that such uncertainties exist. But Unger's figure of $200 to save a child's life was reached after he had made conservative assumptions about the proportion of the money donated that will actually reach its target.

12   One genuine difference between Bob and those who can afford to donate to overseas aid organizations but don't is that only Bob can save the child on the

tracks, whereas there are hundreds of millions of people who can give $200 to overseas aid organizations. The problem is that most of them aren't doing it. Does this mean that it is all right for you not to do it?

Suppose that there were more owners of priceless vintage cars—Carol, Dave, Emma, Fred and so on, down to Ziggy—all in exactly the same situation as Bob, with their own siding and their own switch, all sacrificing the child in order to preserve their own cherished car. Would that make it all right for Bob to do the same? To answer this question affirmatively is to endorse follow-the-crowd ethics—the kind of ethics that led many Germans to look away when the Nazi atrocities were being committed. We do not excuse them because others were behaving no better.

We seem to lack a sound basis for drawing a clear moral line between Bob's situation and that of any reader of this article with $200 to spare who does not donate it to an overseas aid agency. These readers seem to be acting at least as badly as Bob was acting when he chose to let the runaway train hurtle toward the unsuspecting child. In the light of this conclusion, I trust that many readers will reach for the phone and donate that $200. Perhaps you should do it before reading further.

Now that you have distinguished yourself morally from people who put their vintage cars ahead of a child's life, how about treating yourself and your partner to dinner at your favorite restaurant? But wait. The money you will spend at the restaurant could also help save the lives of children overseas! True, you weren't planning to blow $200 tonight, but if you were to give up dining out just for one month, you would easily save that amount. And what is one month's dining out, compared to a child's life? There's the rub. Since there are a lot of desperately needy children in the world, there will always be another child whose life you could save for another $200. Are you therefore obliged to keep giving until you have nothing left? At what point can you stop?

16   Hypothetical examples can easily become farcical. Consider Bob. How far past losing the Bugatti should he go? Imagine that Bob had got his foot stuck in the track of the siding, and if he diverted the train, then before it rammed the car it would also amputate his big toe. Should he still throw the switch? What if it would amputate his foot? His entire leg?

As absurd as the Bugatti scenario gets when pushed to extremes, the point it raises is a serious one: Only when the sacrifices become very significant indeed would most people be prepared to say that Bob does nothing wrong when he decides not to throw the switch. Of course, most people could be wrong; we can't decide moral issues by taking opinion polls. But consider for yourself the level of sacrifice that you would demand of Bob, and then think about how much money you would have to give away in order to make a sacrifice that is roughly equal to that. It's almost certainly much, much more than $200. For most middle-class Americans, it could easily be more like $200,000.

Isn't it counterproductive to ask people to do so much? Don't we run the risk that many will shrug their shoulders and say that mortality, so conceived, is fine for saints but not for them? I accept that we are unlikely to see, in the near or even medium-term future, a world in which it is normal for wealthy Americans to give the bulk of their wealth to strangers. When it comes to praising or blaming people for what they do, we tend to use a standard that is relative to some conception of normal behavior. Comfortably off Americans who give, say, 10 percent of their income to overseas aid organizations are so far ahead of most of their equally comfortable fellow citizens that I wouldn't go out of my way to chastise them for not doing more. Nevertheless, they should be doing much more, and they are in no position to criticize Bob for failing to make the much greater sacrifice of his Bugatti.

At this point various objections may crop up. Someone may say: "If every citizen living in the affluent nations contributed his or her share I wouldn't have to make such a drastic sacrifice, because long before such levels were reached, the resources would have been there to save the lives of all those children dying from lack of food or medical care. So why should I give more than my fair share?" Another, related objection is that the government ought to increase its overseas aid allocations, since that would spread the burden more equitably across all taxpayers.

20   Yet the question of how much we ought to give is a matter to be decided in the real world—and that, sadly, is a world in which we know that most people do not, and in the immediate future will not, give substantial amounts to overseas aid agencies. We know, too, that at least in the next year, the United States government is not going to meet even the very modest United Nations–recommended target of 0.7 percent of gross national product; at a moment it lags far below that, at 0.09 percent, not even half of Japan's 0.22 percent or a tenth of Denmark's 0.97 percent. Thus, we know that the money we can give beyond that theoretical "fair share" is still going to save lives that would otherwise be lost. While the idea that no one need do more than his or her fair share is a powerful one, should it prevail if we know that others are not doing their fair share and that children will die preventable deaths unless we do more than our fair share? That would be taking fairness too far.

Thus, this ground for limiting how much we ought to give also fails. In the world as it is now, I can see no escape from the conclusion that each one of us with wealth surplus to his or her essential needs should be giving most of it to help people suffering from poverty so dire as to be life-threatening. That's right: I'm saying that you shouldn't buy that new car, take that cruise, redecorate the house, or get that pricey new suit. After all, a $1,000 suit could save five children's lives.

So how does my philosophy break down in dollars and cents? An American household with an income of $50,000 spends around $30,000 annually on necessities, according to the Conference Board, a nonprofit economic research organization. Therefore, for a household bringing in $50,000 a year, donations to help the world's poor should be as close as possible to $20,000. The $30,000 required for necessities holds for higher incomes as well. So a household making $100,000 could cut a yearly check for $70,000. Again, the formula is simple: Whatever money you're spending on luxuries, not necessities, should be given away.

Now, evolutionary psychologists tell us that human nature just isn't sufficiently altruistic to make it plausible that many people will sacrifice so much for strangers. On the facts of human nature, they might be right, but they would be wrong to draw a moral conclusion from those facts. If it is the case that we ought to do things that, predictably, most of us won't do, then let's face that fact head-on. Then, if we value the life of a child more than going to fancy restaurants, the next time we dine out we will know that we could have done something better with our money. If that makes living a morally decent life extremely arduous, well, then that is the way things are. If we don't do it, then we should at least know that we are failing to live a morally decent life—not because it is good to wallow in guilt but because knowing where we should be going is the first step toward heading in that direction.

24   When Bob first grasped the dilemma that faced him as he stood by that railway switch, he must have thought how extraordinarily unlucky he was to be placed in a situation in which he must choose between the life of an innocent child and the sacrifice of most of his savings. But he was not unlucky at all. We are all in that situation.

PERSONAL RESPONSE

Do you contribute to charities? If not, are you moved to start doing so after reading this essay? Why do you think more people do not contribute to charities, especially if they could, as Singer argues, help improve life for the world's impoverished children?

QUESTIONS FOR CLASS OR SMALL-GROUP DISCUSSION

1. How effective do you find the opening example from the film *Central Station?*

2. Does it help clarify for you the thesis of Singer's essay? Do you agree with Singer that the failure to donate money to a charity that would save a Brazilian child from starvation is "just as bad as selling the kid to organ peddlers" (paragraph 5)?

3. Comment on the hypothetical scenario from Peter Unger's book that Singer paraphrases in paragraph 7. Do you agree that "Bob's conduct . . . was gravely wrong" and that failure to donate money to charities that would save children's lives is equally wrong (paragraph 8)? How persuasive do you find Singer's discussion of the ethical implications of failing to donate to charities?

4. Discuss your answer to this question: "While the idea that no one need to do more than his or her fair share is a powerful one, should it prevail if we know that others are not doing their fair share and that children will die preventable deaths unless we do more than our fair share?" (paragraph 20).

5. To what extent do you agree with Singer that "we ought to do things that, predictably, most of us won't do" (paragraph 23)? How persuasive do you find Singer's argument to be?

○ PERSPECTIVES ON POVERTY AND HOMELESSNESS ○
Suggested Writing Topics

1. Taking into consideration Anna Quindlen's "Our Tired, Our Poor, Our Children" and the editorial "Still Hungry, Still Homeless," explore the subject of the effects of poverty on self-esteem or other aspects of the well-being of children.

2. Drawing on the readings in this chapter, consider the problems associated with meeting the needs of welfare recipients, impoverished families, or homeless people. What possible solutions are there to the problems? Can you propose additional suggestions for reducing the large numbers of people in poverty or without homes?

3. With Anna Quindlen's "Our Tired, Our Poor, Our Children" and the editorial "Still Hungry, Still Homeless" in mind, write your own opinion piece on the subject of poverty and homelessness in America.

4. Write a letter to James Baldwin or an opinion piece in response to his essay "Fifth Avenue, Uptown."

5. Write an essay showing the relevance of James Baldwin's "Fifth Avenue, Uptown" to the problem of poverty and homelessness today.

6. If you have ever experienced the effects of poverty, too little income, not enough work, or a need to juggle child care with the demands of a job, write an essay describing that experience, how you felt about it, and how you handled it.

7. Create a different hypothetical situation similar to Peter Unger's scenario of Bob and his Bugatti in "The Singer Solution to World Poverty." Detail the moral dilemma of your own scenario and discuss the ethical implications of various responses to the dilemma.

8. Describe your connection with the neighborhood or community you grew up in. When you are ready to begin your career, do you plan to return to the community or do you plan to go someplace completely different?

9. Working in small groups and drawing on the essays in this chapter, create a scenario involving one or more of the following people: a welfare recipient or a homeless person, a welfare caseworker or a staff member at a homeless shelter, a police officer, and either or both a wealthy person and a working-class person with a regular income and a home. Provide a situation, create dialogue, and role-play in an effort to understand the varying perspectives of different people on the issue of welfare or homelessness. Then present your scenario to the rest of your classmates. For an individual writing project, do an analysis of the scenario or fully develop the viewpoint of the person whose role you played.

Research Topics

1. Research your state's policy on welfare, including residency requirements, eligibility for payments, monitoring of recipients, and related issues. Then write a paper outlining your opinion of your state's welfare policy, including any recommendations you would make for changing it.

2. Research the historical development of Harlem, including as one of your sources James Baldwin's "Fifth Avenue, Uptown."

3. From time to time, politicians propose establishing orphanages that would house not only orphaned children but also the children of single parents on welfare or parents deemed unfit to raise their children. Research this subject, and then write a paper in which you argue for or against the establishment of such orphanages. Make sure you consider as many perspectives as possible on this complex issue, including the welfare of the child, the rights of the parent or parents, and society's responsibility to protect children.

4. Research the subject of poverty in America. Focus your research on a particular group, such as children, women, two-parent families, or single-parent families, or target a particular aspect of the subject such as the effects of race, parental education, or employment on poverty.

5. Research an area of public policy on welfare reform, child welfare, homelessness, family welfare, food stamps, job training, or any other issue related to any reading in this chapter.

RESPONDING TO VISUALS

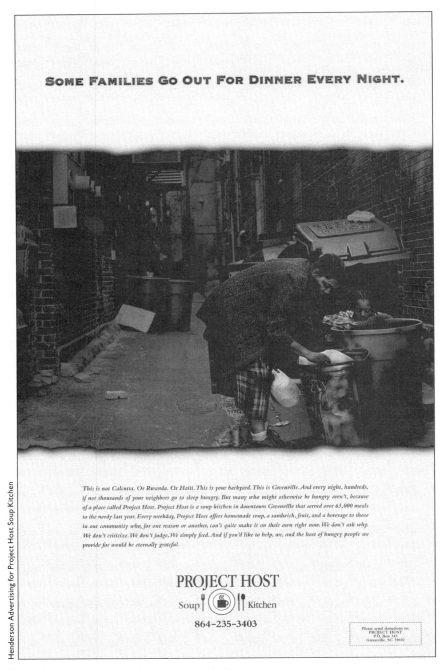

Henderson Advertising for Project Host Soup Kitchen

"Some families go out for dinner every night."

1. What is the point of this public service advertisement?
2. In what ways does the ad engage readers?
3. The text of this advertisement reads: *This is not Calcutta. Or Rwanda. Or Haiti. This is your backyard. This is Greenville. And every night, hundreds, if not thousands of your neighbors go to sleep hungry. But many who might otherwise be hungry aren't, because of a place called Project Host. Project Host is a soup kitchen in downtown Greenville that served over 63,000 meals to the needy last year. Every weekday, Project Host offers homemade soup, a sandwich, fruit, and a beverage to those in our community who, for one reason or another, can't quite make it on their own right now. We don't ask why. We don't criticize. We don't judge. We simply feed. And if you'd like to help, we, and the host of hungry people we provide for would be eternally grateful.* Do you find the text of the advertisement effective?
4. What do you think is the story of the two people in the picture? Why does the photographer place them at the side of the picture instead of the center?

RESPONDING TO VISUALS

A homeless person begging for money.

1. What does the homeless person's body language say about him?
2. What can you tell about the man from the way he is dressed and his facial features? What does the man's sign add to your understanding of him?
3. How does the photographer's perspective affect the way viewers see and respond to the man's situation?
4. Is there any irony in the contrast between the man and the sign behind him?

CHAPTER

14

Criminal Behavior

America has one of the highest rates of violent crime in the world. Although the national crime rate has fallen slightly in recent years, the number of murders and rapes in some areas of the country continues to be alarmingly high. Muggings, armed robbery, and drug trafficking imperil city living. In many large cities, people live in dread and fear, shutting themselves up in their homes at night or arming themselves in case of attack. But crime is not limited to large cities. Small towns have also been shocked and dismayed by violent crimes such as kidnapping, murder, and rape in their own communities. Children have been abducted from their own bedrooms or neighborhoods and discovered later, murdered, or never found again. Even very young children have murdered other children.

The question of what leads a person to commit a crime is of particular interest to many people. Psychologists, social scientists, law enforcement personnel, and others have long tried to account for criminal behavior. The first two articles look at the so-cial conditions that create an environment in which normal, well-adjusted people turn vicious and criminal. In "How People Turn Monstrous," Mark Buchanan raises some intriguing questions about people who do "illegal things in situations where the social context exerts powerful, though perhaps not completely irresistible, forces." Citing the Stanford Prison experiment of Philip Zimbardo and the recent reports of prisoner abuse of Abu Ghraib and Guantánamo prisoners, Buchanan wonders whether it is appropriate to imprison people who behave criminally if they are only doing what others would do in the same situation. As you read his piece, consider whether his logic is sound and whether you agree with him.

Following Buchanan's essay is one by Philip Zimbardo himself. In "Revisiting the Stanford Prison Experiment: A Lesson in the Power of Situation," he summa-rizes the Stanford experiment, tries to account for what happened there, and ex-trapolates lessons that have relevance today to law, criminal justice, and the penal system. He concludes with what he sees as the critical message of his experiment for reducing criminal behavior and modifying the behavior of those in charge of prisoners.

No doubt the worst criminal offense is taking the life of another human being. No matter who the victim, such a crime is reprehensible, but mass murders and the murder of children inevitably lead to renewed debate over the death penalty, as such crimes are particularly heinous. Thus the final two essays in this chapter address the subject of capital punishment. Joshua Green believes that liberals and conservatives are both wrong about the death penalty. In "Deadly Compromise," he details what he sees as flaws in the reasoning of both proponents and opponents of the death penalty and suggests what he thinks should be done to correct the system. Then, John O'Sullivan in "Deadly Stakes: The Debate over Capital Punish-ment" presents his case for the death penalty. Using specific cases of the murders of children in both the United States and Britain as a starting point, he critiques the arguments of those opposed to capital punishment and seeks to persuade his audience that the death penalty is justified. In reading these essays, consider your own position on the death penalty and whether you are persuaded by either or both of their authors.

HOW PEOPLE TURN MONSTROUS

Mark Buchanan

Mark Buchanan, a theoretical physicist, is an associate editor for Com-PlexUs, *a journal on biocomplexity, and the author of* Ubiquity: The Science of History *(2001);* Nexus: Small Worlds and the Groundbreaking Science of Networks *(2002); and, most recently, "The Social Atom: Why the Rich Get Richer, Cheaters Get Caught, and Your Neighbor Usually Looks Like You" (2007). This essay was posted on May 2, 2007, at the* New York Times *blog and can also be found at Buchanan's own blog, www.thesocialatom.blogspot.com.*

It is four years and a few days since CBS News published the first photos documenting the systematic abuse, torture and humiliation of Iraqi prisoners at Abu Ghraib prison. The Bush administration and the American military have worked hard to firmly establish the "few bad apples" explanation of what happened. Eight low-ranking soldiers were convicted, and Staff [Sgt.] Ivan Frederick II, who was found guilty of assault, conspiracy, dereliction of duty and maltreatment of detainees, is now halfway through his eight-year prison sentence.

But there are very good reasons to think that Frederick and the others, however despicable their actions, only did what many of us would have done if placed in the same situation, which puts their guilt in a questionable light. Can someone be guilty just for acting like most ordinary human beings?

In a famous experiment back in the 1970s, Philip Zimbardo and other psychologists at Stanford University put college students into a prison-like setting in the basement of the psychology department. Some of the students played prisoners and others guards, with uniforms, numbers, reflecting sunglasses and so on. The psychologists' aim was to strip away the students' individuality and see what the situation might produce on its own.

4   What happened was truly disconcerting—the guards grew increasingly abusive, and within 36 hours the first prisoner had an emotional breakdown, crying and screaming. The researchers had to stop the experiment after six days. Even normal kids who were professed pacifists were acting sadistically, taking pleasure in inflicting cruel punishments on people they knew to be completely blameless.

These were ordinary American college kids. They weren't monsters, but began acting monstrously because of the situation they were in. What happened was more about social pattern, and its influence, than about the character of individuals.

Emeritus professor at Stanford, Zimbardo has argued in a recent book, "The Lucifer Effect," that what happened in these experiments is also what happened at Abu Ghraib. As he points out, in lots of the photos the soldiers weren't wearing their uniforms; they were anonymous guards who referred to the prisoners with dehumanizing labels such as "detainees" or "terrorists." There was confusion about responsibility and little supervision of the prison at night.

The more the soldiers mistreated the prisoners, the more they saw them as less than human and even more worthy of that abuse. In both the experiments and at Abu Ghraib, most of the abuse took place on the night shift. In both cases, guards stripped prisoners naked to humiliate them and put bags over their heads. In both cases, the abuse involved the forced simulation of sexual behavior among the prisoners.

8   Frederick hooked up wires to hooded detainees, made them stand on boxes and told them they'd be electrocuted if they fell off. He stomped on prisoners['] hands and feet. He and others lined up prisoners against the wall, bags on their heads, and forced them to masturbate. His actions were indeed monstrous.

But when Zimbardo, as an expert witness, interviewed Frederick during his court-martial, these were his impressions:

> He seemed very much to be a normal young American. His psych assessments revealed no sign of any pathology, no sadistic tendencies, and all his psych assessment scores are in the normal range, as is his intelligence. He had been a prison guard at a small minimal security prison where he performed for many years without incident. … there is nothing in his background, temperament, or disposition that could have been a facilitating factor for the abuses he committed at the Abu Ghraib Prison.

If someone chooses to commit an illegal act, freely, of their own will, then they are plainly guilty. Conversely, the same act performed by someone acting without free will, compromised by mental illness, perhaps, or the coercion of others, draws no blame. Far less clear is the proper moral attitude toward people who do illegal things in situations where the social context exerts powerful, though perhaps not completely irresistible, forces.

Can a person be guilty of a crime if almost everyone, except for a few heroic types, would have done the same thing? This is a question for legal theorists, and one likely to arise ever more frequently as modern psychology reveals just how much of our activity is determined not consciously, through free choice, but by forces in the social environment.

12   But the more immediate question is why those who set up the conditions that led to Abu Ghraib, or at least made it likely, haven't also been held responsible. When Frederick arrived at Abu Ghraib, abusive practices, authorized from above, were already commonplace. Prisoners were being stripped, kept hooded and deprived of sleep, put in painful positions and threatened with dogs. On his first day there, Frederick recalled, he saw detainees "naked, handcuffed to their door, some wearing female underclothes."

The conditions cited by Zimbardo, the situational recipe for moral disaster, were already in place.

The conclusion isn't that Frederick and the others didn't do anything wrong, or that they somehow had an excuse for their actions. They could and should have acted better, and Frederick has admitted his own guilt. "I was wrong about what I did," he told the military judge, "and I shouldn't have done it. I knew it was wrong at the time because I knew it was a form of abuse."

But you and I cannot look at Frederick and the other guards as moral monsters, because none of us can know that we'd have acted differently. The evidence suggests that most of us wouldn't have. The coercion of the social context was too powerful.

16   The second conclusion is that those really responsible for the abuse, on a deeper and more systematic level, still should be brought to justice. They're in the upper tiers of the military chain of command and its civilian leadership; they're in the White House.

Today, Frederick will wake up in prison, have his breakfast, take some exercise and face the daily monotony of prison life, something he can expect for the next 1300 days or so. He can be justifiably angry that those responsible for putting him in that setting at Abu Ghraib, where almost anyone would have done the same thing, are today walking around free.

PERSONAL RESPONSE

Buchanan believes that we cannot see Frederick as a "moral monster" because "none of us can know that we'd have acted differently" (paragraph 15). If you have ever done something against your better judgment because of the social context—whether peer pressure, the fact that everyone else was doing it, or any other force that led you to do it—describe what happened. If you haven't personally experienced such a thing, can you imagine yourself ever committing a wrong because of the pressure of the social context?

QUESTIONS FOR CLASS AND SMALL-GROUP DISCUSSION

1. Analyze Buchanan's argument in terms of its logic and validity.
2. How valid do you find his comparison of what happened at Abu Ghraib with the Stanford prison experiment? Can you find any fault with that analogy? Are there other ways to account for Frederick's behavior at Abu Ghraib?
3. How would you answer Buchanan's question: "Can someone be guilty just for acting like most ordinary human beings?" (paragraph 2)? What do you think is "the proper moral attitude toward people who do illegal things in situations where the social context exerts powerful, though perhaps not completely irresistible, forces" (paragraph 11)?
4. Comment on Buchanan's second conclusion, "that those really responsible for the abuse, on a deeper and more systemic level, still should be brought to justice" (paragraph 16).

REVISITING THE STANFORD PRISON EXPERIMENT: A LESSON IN THE POWER OF SITUATION

Philip G. Zimbardo

Philip G. Zimbardo, Professor Emeritus of Psychology at Stanford University, is an internationally recognized scholar, teacher, researcher and author. His 1971 prison experiment at Stanford is a classic study of what happens to essentially good people when they are placed in positions of power in a prison situation. You can read about the experiment, view slides, and consider a number of questions raised by the study at www.prisonexp.org. Zimbardo's books include The Psychology of Attitude Change and Social Influence *(1991);* Violence Workers: Police Torturers and Murderers Reconstruct Brazilian Atrocities *(2002); and* The Lucifer Effect: Understanding How Good People Turn Evil *(2007). This essay was first published in the* Chronicle of Higher Education *on March 30, 2007.*

By the 1970s, psychologists had done a series of studies establishing the social power of groups. They showed, for example, that groups of strangers could persuade people to believe statements that were obviously false. Psychologists had also found that research participants were often willing to obey authority figures even when doing so violated their personal beliefs. The Yale studies by Stanley Milgram in 1963 demonstrated that a majority of ordinary citizens would continually shock an innocent man, even up to near-lethal levels, if commanded to do so by someone acting as an authority. The "authority" figure in this case was merely a high-school biology teacher who wore a lab coat and acted in an official manner. The majority of people shocked their victims over and over again despite increasingly desperate pleas to stop.

In my own work, I wanted to explore the fictional notion from William Golding's *Lord of the Flies* about the power of anonymity to unleash violent behavior. In one experiment from 1969, female students who were made to feel anonymous and given permission for aggression became significantly more hostile than students with their identities intact. Those and a host of other social–psychological studies were showing that human nature was more pliable than previously imagined and more responsive to situational pressures than we cared to acknowledge. In sum, these studies challenged the sacrosanct view that inner determinants of behavior—personality traits, morality, and religious upbringing—directed good people down righteous paths.

Missing from the body of social-science research at the time was the direct confrontation of good versus evil, of good people pitted against the forces inherent in bad situations. It was evident from everyday life that smart people made dumb decisions when they were engaged in mindless groupthink, as in the disastrous Bay of Pigs invasion by the smart guys in President John F. Kennedy's cabinet. It was also clear that smart people surrounding President Richard M. Nixon, like Henry A. Kissinger and Robert S. McNamara, escalated the Vietnam War when they knew, and later admitted, it was not winnable. They were caught up in the mental constraints of cognitive dissonance—the discomfort from holding two conflicting thoughts—and were unable to cut bait even though it was the only rational strategy to save lives and face. Those examples, however, with their different personalities, political agendas, and motives, complicated any simple conceptual attempt to understand what went wrong in these situations.

4   I decided that what was needed was to create a situation in a controlled experimental setting in which we could array on one side a host of variables, such as role-playing, coercive rules, power differentials, anonymity, group dynamics, and dehumanization. On the other side, we lined up a collection of the "best and brightest" of young college men in collective opposition to the might of a dominant system. Thus in 1971 was born the Stanford prison experiment, more akin to Greek drama than to university psychology study. I wanted to know who wins—good people or an evil situation—when they were brought into direct confrontation.

First we established that all 24 participants were physically and mentally healthy, with no history of crime or violence, so as to be sure that initially they were all "good apples." They were paid $15 a day to participate. Each of the student volunteers was randomly assigned to play the role of prisoner or guard in a setting designed to convey a sense of the psychology of imprisonment (in actuality, a mock prison set up in the basement of the Stanford psychology department). Dramatic realism infused the study. Palo Alto police agreed to "arrest" the prisoners and book them, and once at the prison, they were given identity numbers, stripped naked, and deloused. The prisoners wore large smocks with no underclothes and lived in the prison 24/7 for a planned two weeks; three sets of guards each patrolled eight-hour shifts. Throughout the experiment, I served as the prison "superintendent," assisted by two graduate students.

Initially nothing much happened as the students awkwardly tried out their assigned roles in their new uniforms. However, all that changed suddenly on the morning of the second day following a rebellion, when the prisoners barricaded themselves inside the cells by putting their beds against the door. Suddenly the guards perceived the prisoners as "dangerous"; they had to be dealt with harshly to demonstrate who was boss and who was powerless. At first, guard abuses were retaliation for taunts and disobedience. Over time, the guards became ever more abusive, and some even delighted in sadistically tormenting their prisoners. Though physical punishment was restricted, the guards on each shift were free to make up their own rules, and they invented a variety of psychological tactics to demonstrate their dominance over their powerless charges.

Nakedness was a common punishment, as was placing prisoners' heads in nylon stocking caps (to simulate shaved heads); chaining their legs; repeatedly waking them throughout the night for hour-long counts; and forcing them into humiliating "fun and games" activities. Let's go beyond those generalizations to review some of the actual behaviors that were enacted in the prison simulation. They are a lesson in "creative evil," in how certain social settings can transform intelligent young men into perpetrators of psychological abuse.

Prison Log, Night 5

8   The prisoners, who have not broken down emotionally under the incessant stress the guards have been subjecting them to since their aborted rebellion on Day 2, wearily line up against the wall to recite their ID numbers and to demonstrate that they remember all 17 prisoner rules of engagement. It is the 1 a.m. count, the last one of the night before the morning shift comes on at 2 a.m. No matter how well the prisoners do, one of them gets singled out for punishment. They are yelled at, cursed out, and made to say abusive things to each other. "Tell him he's a prick," yells one guard. And each prisoner says that to the next guy in line. Then the sexual harassment that had started to bubble up the night before resumes as the testosterone flows freely in every direction.

"See that hole in the ground? Now do 25 push-ups [expletive] that hole! You hear me!" One after another, the prisoners obey like automatons as the guard shoves them down. After a brief consultation, our toughest guard (nicknamed "John Wayne" by the prisoners) and his sidekick devise a new sexual game. "OK, now pay attention. You three are going to be female camels. Get over here and bend over, touching your hands to the floor." When they do, their naked butts are exposed because they have no underwear beneath their smocks. John Wayne continues with obvious glee, "Now you two, you're male camels. Stand behind the female camels and hump them."

The guards all giggle at this double-entendre. Although their bodies never touch, the helpless prisoners begin to simulate sodomy by making thrusting motions. They are then dismissed back to their cells to get an hour of sleep before the next shift comes on, and the abuse continues.

By Day 5, five of the student prisoners have to be released early because of extreme stress. (Recall that each of them was physically healthy and psychologically stable less than a week before.) Most of those who remain adopt a zombie-like attitude and posture, totally obedient to escalating guard demands.

Terminating the Torment

12   I was forced to terminate the projected two-week-long study after only six days because it was running out of control. Dozens of people had come down to our "little shop of horrors," seen some of the abuse or its effects, and said nothing. A prison chaplain, parents, and friends had visited the prisoners, and psychologists and others on the parole board saw a realistic prison simulation, an experiment in action, but did not challenge me to stop it. The one exception erupted just before the time of the prison-log notation on Night 5.

About halfway through the study, I had invited some psychologists who knew little about the experiment to interview the staff and participants, to get an outsiders' evaluation of how it was going. A former doctoral student of mine, Christina Maslach, a new assistant professor at the University of California at Berkeley, came down late Thursday night to have dinner with me. We had started dating recently and were becoming romantically involved. When she saw the prisoners lined up with bags over their heads, their legs chained, and guards shouting abuses at them while herding them to the toilet, she got upset and refused my suggestion to observe what was happening in this "crucible of human nature." Instead she ran out of the basement, and I followed, berating her for being overly sensitive and not realizing the important lessons taking place here.

"It is terrible what YOU are doing to those boys!" she yelled at me. Christina made evident in that one statement that human beings were suffering, not prisoners, not experimental subjects, not paid volunteers. And further, I was the one who was personally responsible for the horrors she had witnessed (and which she assumed were even worse when no outsider was looking). She also made clear that if this person I had become—the heartless superintendent of the Stanford prison—was the real me, not the caring, generous person she had come to like, she wanted nothing more to do with me.

That powerful jolt of reality snapped me back to my senses. I agreed that we had gone too far, that whatever was to be learned about situational power was already indelibly etched on our videos, data logs, and minds; there was no need to continue. I too had been transformed by my role in that situation to become a person that under any other circumstances I detest—an uncaring, authoritarian boss man. In retrospect, I believe that the main reason I did not end the study sooner resulted from the conflict created in me by my dual roles as principal investigator, and thus guardian of the research ethics of the experiment, and as the prison superintendent, eager to maintain the stability of my prison at all costs. I now realize that there should have been someone with authority above mine, someone in charge of oversight of the experiment, who surely would have blown the whistle earlier.

16   By the time Christina intervened, it was the middle of the night, so I had to make plans to terminate the next morning. The released prisoners and guards had to be called back and many logistics handled before I could say, "The Stanford prison experiment is officially closed." When I went back down to the basement, I witnessed the final scene of depravity, the "camel humping" episode. I was so glad that it would be the last such abuse I would see or be responsible for.

Good Apples in Bad Barrels and Bad Barrel Makers

The situational forces in that "bad barrel" had overwhelmed the goodness of most of those infected by their viral power. It is hard to imagine how a seeming game of "cops and robbers" played by college kids, with a few academics (our research team) watching, could have descended into what became a hellhole for many in that basement. How could a mock prison, an experimental simulation, become "a prison run by psychologists, not by the state," in the words of one suffering prisoner? How is it possible for "good personalities" to be so dominated by a "bad situation"? You had to be there to believe that human character could be so swiftly transformed in a matter of days[—]not only the traits of the students, but of me, a well-seasoned adult. Most of the visitors to our prison also fell under the spell. For example, individual sets of parents observing their son's haggard appearance after a few days of hard labor and long nights of disrupted sleep said they "did not want to make trouble" by taking their kid home or challenging the system. Instead they obeyed our authority and let some of their sons experience full-blown emotional meltdowns later on. We had created a dominating behavioral context whose power insidiously frayed the seemingly impervious values of compassion, fair play, and belief in a just world.

The situation won; humanity lost. Out the window went the moral upbringings of these young men, as well as their middle-class civility. Power ruled, and unrestrained power became an aphrodisiac. Power without surveillance by higher authorities was a poisoned chalice that transformed character in unpredictable directions. I believe that most of us tend to be fascinated with evil not because of its consequences but because evil is a demonstration of power and domination over others.

Current Relevance

Such research is now in an ethical time capsule, since institutional review boards will not allow social scientists to repeat it (although experiments like it have been replicated on several TV shows and in artistic renditions). Nevertheless, the Stanford prison experiment is now more popular then ever in its 36-year history. A Google search of "experiment" reveals it to be fourth among some 132 million hits, and sixth among some 127 million hits on "prison." Some of this recent interest comes from the apparent similarities of the experiment's abuses with the images of depravity in Iraq's Abu Ghraib prison—of nakedness, bagged heads, and sexual humiliation.

20   Among the dozen investigations of the Abu Ghraib abuses, the one chaired by James R. Schlesinger, the former secretary of defense, boldly proclaims that the landmark Stanford study "provides a cautionary tale for all military detention operations." In contrasting the relatively benign environment of the Stanford prison experiment, the report makes evident that "in military detention operations, soldiers work under stressful combat conditions that are far from benign." The implication is that those combat conditions might be expected to generate even more extreme abuses of power than were observed in our mock prison experiment.

However, the Schlesinger report notes that military leaders did not heed that earlier warning in any way. They should have—a psychological perspective is essential to understanding the transformation of human character in response to special situational forces. "The potential for abusive treatment of detainees during the Global War on Terrorism was entirely predictable based on a fundamental understanding of the principles of social psychology coupled with an awareness of numerous known environmental risk factors," the report says. "Findings from the field of social psychology suggest that the conditions of war and the dynamics of detainee operations carry inherent risks for human mistreatment, and therefore must be approached with great caution and careful planning and training." (Unfortunately this vital conclusion is buried in an appendix.)

The Stanford prison experiment is but one of a host of studies in psychology that reveal the extent to which our behavior can be transformed from its usual set point to deviate in unimaginable ways, even to readily accepting a dehumanized conception of others, as "animals," and to accepting spurious rationales for why pain will be good for them.

The implications of this research for law are considerable, as legal scholars are beginning to recognize. The criminal-justice system, for instance, focuses primarily on individual defendants and their "state of mind" and largely ignores situational forces. The Model Penal Code states: "A person is not guilty of an offense unless his liability is based on conduct that includes a voluntary act or the omission to perform an act of which he is physically capable." As my own experiment revealed, and as a great deal of social-psychological research before and since has confirmed, we humans exaggerate the extent to which our actions are voluntary and rationally chosen—or, put differently, we all understate the power of the situation. My claim is not that individuals are incapable of criminal culpability; rather, it is that, like the horrible behavior brought out by my experiment in good, normal young men, the situation and the system creating it also must share in the responsibility for illegal and immoral behavior.

24   If the goals of the criminal system are simply to blame and punish individual perpetrators—to get our pound of flesh—then focusing almost exclusively on the individual defendant makes sense. If, however, the goal is actually to reduce the behavior that we now call "criminal" (and its resultant suffering), and to assign punishments that correspond with culpability, then the criminal-justice system is obligated, much as I was in the Stanford prison experiment, to confront the situation and our role in creating and perpetuating it. It is clear to most reasonable observers that the social experiment of imprisoning society's criminals for long terms is a failure on virtually all levels. By recognizing the situational determinants of behavior, we can move to a more productive public-health model of prevention and intervention, and away from the individualistic medical and religious "sin" model that has never worked since its inception during the Inquisition.

The critical message then is to be sensitive about our vulnerability to subtle but powerful situational forces and, by such awareness, be more able to overcome those forces. Group pressures, authority symbols, dehumanization of others, imposed anonymity, dominant ideologies that enable spurious ends to justify immoral means, lack of surveillance, and other situational forces can work to transform even some of the best of us into Mr. Hyde monsters, without the benefit of Dr. Jekyll's chemical elixir. We must be more aware of how situational variables can influence our behavior. Further, we must also be aware that veiled behind the power of the situation is the greater power of the system, which creates and maintains complicity at the highest military and governmental levels with evil-inducing situations, like those at Abu Ghraib and Guantánamo Bay prisons.

PERSONAL RESPONSE

Describe an example of "mindless group-think" (paragraph 3) that you have either taken part in or witnessed, whether with a small group of friends, at an event such as a concert, or in any other situation where large groups or crowds gathered.

QUESTIONS FOR CLASS OR SMALL-GROUP DISCUSSION

1. On the basis of this brief overview, how would you assess the prison experiment at Stanford? What questions do you have about it? Are you surprised that the "guards" behaved so cruelly and the "prisoners" so obedient and "zombielike" (paragraph 11)?

2. Assess the conclusions that Zimbardo draws about the prison experiment. Do you see any flaws in his conclusions?

3. To what extent do you agree with Zimbardo's application of the lessons from his prison experiment of 1971 to today's criminal justice system?

4. Zimbardo writes in paragraph 4 of "mindless groupthink" and gives examples from the 1960s and 1970s to illustrate what he means about people making "dumb decisions" when they were "caught up in the mental constraints of cognitive dissonance." Can you think of other, more recent examples of such behavior?

DEADLY COMPROMISE

Joshua Green

Joshua Green is a senior editor of the Atlantic *and a contributing editor of the* Washington Monthly. *He has also written for the* New Yorker, *the* New York Times, Playboy, Slate, *and other publications, and he moonlights as a pop music critic for* Westword *in Denver. Previously, he was a staff writer at the* American Prospect *and an editor at the satirical weekly, the* Onion. *This article appeared in the* Washington Monthly *in November 1999.*

In the long-running battle over America's death penalty, two trends have emerged to stoke passions on opposing sides of the debate. An alarming number of men—82—have been freed from death row, or about one for every seven executed. At the same time, the rate of executions has slowed to a trickle as death row inmates languish on average for more than a decade before their sentence is carried out. Two recent examples bear out the problems in our current capital justice system.

In 1978, Robert Alton Harris, a 26-year-old paroled murderer, kidnapped two California teenagers in the parking lot of a fast-food restaurant. He drove to a remote canyon where he killed the two boys, then finished the hamburgers they'd been eating and drove off. Harris was later caught robbing a bank. He confessed to the murders and was sentenced to death in 1979. Yet he managed to delay his execution for 13 years by repeatedly manipulating the appeals system. Harris and his lawyers challenged the quality of his psychiatric evaluation, claimed California's gas chamber was unconstitutional, and argued that the death penalty discriminated against younger killers, males, and those who killed whites. Each of these claims stalled his execution. In a flurry of last-minute appeals, the Supreme Court over-turned four separate stays on the night of Harris' execution before it took the un-precedented step of forbidding lower courts to issue further stays. By the time he was finally put to death in 1992, Harris had managed to get more than 20 appeals.

Like Harris, Aaron Patterson's case centered on a murder confession. He was subsequently sentenced to death for the 1986 stabbing deaths of an elderly Chicago couple. But Patterson is one of Illinois' "Death Row 10," a group facing execution who claim their confessions were beaten out of them by a notorious Chicago police lieutenant since fired for abuse and torture. No physical evidence connects Pat-terson to the murders. The knife was never found. A fingerprint at the scene—not a match—has inexplicably disappeared. The lone witness against him, a teenager who claims police coerced her testimony, has tearfully recanted.

4   While Harris is a metaphor for the conservative case against the current capi-tal justice system, Patterson's case has been seized upon by abolitionists. Both are justified in their outrage. More than 20 years after its reinstatement, the death pen-alty is an unwieldy and ineffective compromise between the roughly 70 percent of Americans who favor capital punishment and the minority who fiercely oppose it. The present system is, quite literally, the worst of both worlds. While an ideological battle has been waged in court, a bottleneck has developed in the nation's prisons. Currently, 3,565 inmates sit on death row, and new arrivals average 300 annually. Yet despite rising numbers of death sentences, executions have never topped 100 in a single year. Everyone is being sentenced to death and no one is dying.

Death Born Again

In the landmark 1972 case of *Furman [v.] Georgia*, the Supreme Court struck down the death penalty on four grounds: it was imposed arbitrarily; used unfairly against minorities and the poor; its infrequent use made it an ineffective deterrent; and lastly, state-sanctioned killing was no longer acceptable behavior. The decision re-sulted in tremendous uncertainty. Each justice filed a separate opinion, an unprec-edented move in 20th century jurisprudence, yielding the longest written decision in Supreme Court history. The length is indicative of the decision's complicated rationale. While the case for abolition earned the five votes necessary, the motiva-tion for each vote varied. This uncertainty left the door open for states to write new death penalty laws that might pass constitutional muster.

Abolition was never very popular. Polls taken in March 1972, shortly before *Furman* was decided, showed a 50 percent approval rating for capital punishment; that number jumped to 57 percent by November. Within the year, 19 state legis-latures passed retooled death penalty statutes they hoped would meet the vague standard of constitutionality hinted at in *Furman*. By the time the Court allowed the modern death penalty by upholding, *Gregg [v.] Georgia* in 1976, 35 states had passed new death penalty laws. They have been in dispute ever since, and the re-sult is today's beleaguered system. Shortly after *Gregg*, the court acceded to death penalty opponents by outlawing mandatory death sentences and instituting com-plex safeguards. This gave rise to a problem that still hampers the courts: Unable to abolish capital punishment in the legislature, defense lawyers have sought to institute a de facto halt to executions by stalling cases in court. The more savvy, like Harris' lawyers, quickly mastered the art of "sandbagging," or using delay tactics to stop an execution. By filing spurious last-minute appeals and repeatedly seeking reversals on obscure technical grounds, activist lawyers (and some judges) could bring the system to its knees. Angered by this end run around the law, conservatives have limited the appeals process at the state and federal levels and expanded the scope of crimes punishable by death. The unfortunate result, as federal prosecutor David Lazarus wrote in this magazine last year ("Mortal Combat," June 1998), is that abolitionists have clogged the courts with endless litigation and slowed the number of actual executions to a trickle. The average delay from sentencing to execution has grown from six years in 1985, to eight years in 1990, to 11 years today.

The Art of Delay

Delays in death penalty cases are caused in part by the tacit acceptance of such maneuvers by liberal judges. The most famous examples are former Supreme Court justices William Brennan, Jr. and Thurgood Marshall, who voted against every death sentence that came before them. Recent limits to federal appeals should eventually block some avenues for delay. But as old methods are thwarted, new ones crop up. Kent Scheidegger, legal director for the conservative Criminal Justice Legal Foundation, cites as an example an increase in the use of "Ford claims"—assertions that a prisoner has gone insane since sentencing and therefore can't be executed under the Eighth Amendment. (This is a particularly savvy ploy, because arguing that insanity occurred after the trial phase means the claim isn't subject to a limit on appeals.)

8   Other recent tools that have been used for manipulation are Marsden and Faretta motions, which a defendant can use to fire his lawyer and represent himself. In a notorious California capital case, the defendant filed numerous such motions, going so far as to sue two court-appointed defenders for $1 million in an effort to delay his sentence. Common sense needn't be a requirement for a claim—a Montana prisoner, who'd held off his execution through two decades of appeals, finally argued that the length of time he'd had to endure on death row was unconstitutional.

Though liberals are commonly faulted for delays, conservatives also slowed the process by making access to court-appointed attorneys more difficult for the poor. In 1995 more than a quarter of California's capital defendants didn't have a lawyer and their cases couldn't begin until one was assigned. And, with conservative anger buttressing support for prosecutors' win-at-all-costs attitude, unscrupulous prosecutors regularly tie up capital cases by fighting defense requests for information.

Innocence Expired

The unfortunate response to dilatory tactics has been to curtail the judicial process by implementing strict time limits. Thirty-six of the 38 death penalty states impose deadlines for presenting new evidence following a conviction. The strictest such law is Virginia's notorious "21-Day Rule," which limits the introduction of new evidence to 21 days after trial. Other states have similar limits that range from 30 days to a year. These laws were intended to establish finality in all criminal cases and most predate the modern death penalty. But they have recently been championed by conservatives as a way to combat delays in execution, despite the obvious risk they carry of killing or imprisoning innocent people.

In recent years, the law's shortcomings have become apparent. Virginia's 21-Day Rule, for example, forbids new DNA evidence from being introduced more than three weeks after trial. And, amazingly, the law doesn't even make provisions for illegally suppressed evidence—such evidence is considered "new" in Virginia and therefore is inadmissible. (A prisoner would instead have to file a federal appeal.) The problem was ably summed up in a defense attorney's testimony before a Virginia legislative committee: "After 21 days, no court in this state, nor any judicial forum afterwards, can save you from execution based on the proof that you are innocent."

12   The circuit court that oversees this system—referred to locally as "the rocket docket"—has succeeded in speeding the processing time of death penalty defendants. Capital cases in Virginia move much more quickly than they do elsewhere. But the results come at a price. One of the most controversial examples is the case of Earl Washington, Jr., a mildly retarded man sentenced to death for the 1982 rape-murder of a Virginia woman. A concerned prosecutor later ordered DNA tests, unavailable at the time, that provided strong evidence Washington is innocent. But because the evidence appeared after the 21-day deadline, Washington had no avenue for appeal. The only recourse for a prisoner with exculpatory evidence is gubernatorial clemency. But governors aren't part of the judiciary and can't order a new trial. And of course they're heavily subject to political pressure. On the last day of his term, Virginia Governor Douglas Wilder commuted Washington's sentence to life in prison. But with no judicial outlet to order a new case, Washington remains in prison.

Such problems are exacerbated by the fact that many prisoners can't find attorneys for post-conviction hearings—in 1995 Congress eliminated the resource centers that once provided them. Without an attorney, the possibility of correcting a mistake like the one in Washington's case all but disappears. State post-conviction review is the first opportunity to present claims of ineffective counsel and the last chance to investigate claims like actual innocence and prosecutorial misconduct. Ironically, the Supreme Court has affirmed that indigent death row inmates have a right to counsel at federal appeals. But without a lawyer at the state level, their claims will doubtless never make it that far.

Fools on the Hill

While state legislatures have failed to improve the system, reforms at the federal level have also been woefully misguided. In the mid-1980s federal judges couldn't find enough qualified lawyers to handle death penalty cases. Attorneys assigned by the court were expensive and didn't necessarily provide competent counsel. So in 1988, at the behest of federal judges, Congress created legal resource centers to process and defend the poor. By most accounts, these centers served their purpose.

But in the tough-on-crime environment of the early '90s, the centers became a political football. Congressman Bob Ingis (R-South Carolina) branded them "think tanks for legal theories that would frustrate the implementation of all death sentences." In 1996, citing fiscal priorities, Congress eliminated federal funding for resource centers—$20 million for 21 centers nationwide. Budget hawks figured they'd won a double victory. They reasoned that by choking off agencies that represent death row inmates they'd rid themselves of an impediment to executions, while saving taxpayers millions in the process.

16   That thinking backfired. A critical function of resource centers—one intended by federal judges—was to keep the appellate system functioning smoothly. With organizational support, full-time lawyers kept tabs on death row cases, filed appeals promptly and steered capital defendants through the complicated legal system. Qualified representation meant indigent defendants didn't require the court's help. The infusion of lawyers trained in capital cases helped offset the costly and often inexperienced court-appointed lawyers who otherwise handled capital cases. Resource centers were a government program that worked. So their elimination had the opposite of the intended effect—it slowed the pace of appeals and increased the likelihood of error.

Other measures were similarly misguided. In 1994, by threatening to block the federal crime bill, congressional Republicans forced passage of the Federal Death Penalty Act, making 54 new crimes death-penalty eligible. The law was largely a symbolic measure—there hadn't been a federal execution in 31 years. Yet death-penalty offenses suddenly came to include drug dealing crimes, conspiracy to commit murder even if no murder was committed, and such rarely committed crimes as murder of a federal poultry inspector. The broadened scope only added to the courts' burden. Federal death sentences soared from 28 the year before the law, to 153 in 1997. Even conservatives thought the law frivolous. "It was an easy way to appear tough," said Scheidegger. "Congress enacted a long string of federal death penalty crimes, most of which are entirely unnecessary, so that they could go back and claim to be tough on the death penalty. It was a rather cynical ploy."

Cynical but costly. Last fall, a judicial conference report determined the average cost of prosecuting a federal death penalty case to be $365,000. The same case cost $218,112 to defend. But if a sentence other than death were sought, the defense costs dropped to $55,772. Factored out for the additional convictions, that's a $73 million price tag on a measure that did little more than let congressmen flex their muscles.

Congress responded to the Oklahoma City bombing with its most ambitious reforms to date. The Antiterrorism and Effective Death Penalty Act of 1996 limited to one the number of appeals a prisoner could file in federal court, barring exceptional circumstances, and placed a one-year time limit on their ability to do so. Conservatives believed this would eliminate sandbagging and streamline the appellate process. "No delay in disposition shall be permissible because of general congestion of the court's calendar," the law read.

20   But like earlier efforts, the Act's aim was largely misdirected—a disingenuous marriage of death penalty and terrorism law that represented a large political compromise. Sponsors touted a connection between terrorists like Timothy McVeigh and speedier laws which, they suggested, would bring criminals to justice. The bill was rushed to passage before the first anniversary of the bombings. But the death penalty "reform" on which the law hinged mainly affected state court cases, where the overwhelming majority of death row inmates are sentenced. Terrorists like McVeigh are prosecuted in federal court.

Problems at the Source

If one source of the problem is in congress, another is at the local level where most death penalty cases originate. Here, too, there is need for reform. The rate and effectiveness with which the death penalty is used varies drastically from states like Ohio, which has executed just one person since reinstatement, to Virginia and Texas, which together have executed 247 people (44 percent of all executions). In recent years, the scrutiny surrounding cases like Aaron Patterson's has made Illinois ground zero for the death penalty debate. The state's 12 exonerations are symptomatic of the problems in the way cases are prosecuted and defended.

Patterson's case illustrates many of these problems. To begin with, he was represented by public defenders and was therefore an easier target. Numerous studies have shown that public defenders often lack the skill, resources, and commitment to defend capital cases properly. Not surprisingly, 90 percent of current death row inmates didn't have a private attorney. As prosecutor David Lazarus has noted, "Clients of the world's great defense attorneys (and even the good ones) don't receive death sentences. Almost without exception, a prerequisite for receiving a death sentence is the inability to hire a lawyer sufficiently talented or motivated to mount a credible defense." Public defenders, he continues, will "substantially increase the probability that a defendant will be convicted of capital murder as opposed to some appropriate lesser offense."

Overzealous prosecutors are another problem. Tenet number one for the career-minded prosecutor is "get tough on crime." While ambitious prosecutors often tout their death penalty convictions, they're far less likely to question whether such convictions are cost effective or necessary. The number of death sentences later reversed suggests that in many cases they're grossly unfair: 40 percent of death row cases are vacated at some point in the appeals process. This can occur ten or even 15 years down the line, at enormous cost to taxpayers and tremendous injustice to defendants. But as a rule, prosecutors don't abandon death penalty cases for fear of appearing soft on crime. Federal judge Alex Kozinski has pointed out that while 80 to 90 percent of all criminal cases end in plea bargains, capital cases almost always go to trial. There is little justification for this discrepancy, given that plea-bargaining death penalty cases would limit costs and nullify the issue of protracted appeals.

24   The tough-on-crime mentality also infects state lawmakers who, like congress, can broaden statutes to include more death penalty crimes. Illinois, which in 1977 had seven crimes that qualified for death, today boasts 19. Often, new additions

are an ill-considered reaction to high-profile crimes like last year's murder of a neighborhood activist in Chicago, which prompted legislators to make killing an activist a death penalty offense. Such moves are well intentioned but only hamper an overburdened system. Prosecutorial excesses also run up costs. While defense lawyers are commonly faulted for delays, prosecutors share the blame. Because of their never-say-die attitude toward upholding convictions, they often drag their feet when exculpatory evidence raises questions of innocence. Prosecutors fought to prevent DNA testing that ultimately freed Ronald Jones, the last man to walk off Illinois' death row. Jones spent nearly two years on death row after tests proved his innocence because prosecutors were unwilling to abandon their case.

In fairness, Illinois has taken steps to address the most serious shortcomings, and other states would do well to follow its lead. Recognizing the need for adequate representation of the poor, the state legislature stepped in to save Illinois' legal resource center when federal funding ended. The result is the Capital Litigation Division of the Illinois State Appellate Defender's Office, essentially a state-funded resource center.

Illinois also joined New York in passing a provision for post-conviction DNA testing. The law acts as a safeguard against mistaken convictions by allowing inmates to petition for DNA analysis of evidence used to convict them. No other state has used DNA to uncover more wrongly convicted defendants than Illinois. Perhaps most noteworthy in the near term is Illinois' activist community. It has played a part in freeing all of the 12 released death row inmates and forced many of the positive changes in the criminal justice system.

Finally, most of the state's major media outlets have given nuanced coverage to death penalty law and have provided detailed reporting on flaws and abuses. This is in marked contrast to the national media, which eagerly covers high-profile exonerations but shies away from stories that don't rise to the level of a *60 Minutes* piece. Consider, for example, the sloppiness of the May 31 *Newsweek* feature on Aaron Patterson and Northwestern University professor David Protess' efforts to free him. "The *Newsweek* article had by my count and my students' count 21 factual errors in three pages," Protess says. "In the entire time that I've been involved in this, I've never seen an article more off-base than that." The author wrote that Patterson "consented to an oral confession," which he did not. She also wrote that the jury "found it hard to believe that Patterson, the son of a Chicago police lieutenant, would be mistreated." In fact, the jury never heard any evidence of physical abuse, thanks to a pretrial ruling. If journalists were to cover the death penalty as thoroughly as they've covered welfare reform, such carelessness would be less common, and the shortcomings of the death penalty system would be a far more prominent public concern.

On the Merits

28   Pragmatism should eclipse the battle between the extremes of liberalism and conservatism that have reigned on the death penalty. Since courts have been unable to speed processing time adequately, the solution is to reduce the number of death sentences handed down. The first step is to provide resources for the system to

function properly, then to enact laws that ensure it does so in a timely manner. Improvements should begin with the resurrection of legal resource centers. Qualified resource center attorneys would prevent prosecutors from running up capital convictions against unprepared or unqualified public defenders. In fact, the motivation for ambitious prosecutors would shift from quantity of convictions to quality. They'd need to be certain of an airtight case before seeking the death penalty, since failing to win a conviction is a political embarrassment. This might even have the secondary effect of removing the stigma attached to settling dubious capital cases.

Resource centers would have a trickle-down effect that would alleviate problems later in the justice cycle: only the most deserving killers would be executed; more convictions would be upheld; having competent lawyers at trial would eliminate the claims of incompetent counsel that delay so many cases today. Cases would proceed more quickly because defendants wouldn't have to wait years for the court to assign them an attorney. And fewer convictions and appeals would curtail the staggering cost to taxpayers.

Even the most conservative estimate of savings is substantial. Federal Judge Kozinski estimates each death penalty case (in state court) costs taxpayers $1 million. If each case were thought of as a million-dollar tax increase, prosecutors would have to be much more discriminating. Cutting the number of death sentences in half would save $150 million each year. To put that figure in perspective, resource centers would need to prevent just 20 cases a year to cover the funding Congress cut for them in 1995. States need to institute minimum qualifications for defense lawyers. Studies show that often it's the worst lawyers, not the worst criminals, who draw death sentences—a fact illustrated in the death penalty case of George McFarland in Texas, whose lawyer repeatedly fell asleep in court ("It's boring," he explained to the *Houston Chronicle*). This reform too would cut time and cost. The Justice Department concluded last fall: "Assuring appropriate resources for the defense at the trial stage minimizes the risk of time-consuming and expensive post-conviction litigation." States could also place time limits on appeals (some already do) to force delay-minded defendants to air their claims early on, rather than withhold them for time-consuming appeals. Appeals could also be bundled and made at one time, rather than sequentially. An exception would of course be made for evidence discovered after conviction. Conservatives, no matter how justified their frustration over delays, should not perpetuate a system that refuses to hear exculpatory evidence. By amending laws like Virginia's 21-Day Rule to allow a judge to rule on credible new evidence, lawmakers would remove a major incentive for delay. The amendment should mirror new programs like one in Illinois that allows post-conviction DNA testing. As a final safeguard, Illinois' attorney general has proposed a board to review capital cases before execution—an idea endorsed by both the state bar association and conservatives like Scheidegger.

None of these improvements will come without political leadership. So politicians sincere about being tough on crime need to be held accountable for the problem. This spring the Texas legislature unanimously passed a bill that would have created an agency to match indigent capital defendants with qualified lawyers. (That Texas, which leads the nation in executions, could pass such a bill unanimously is an indication of how badly it is needed). Nevertheless, Governor Bush vetoed it in June. Undoubtedly, he intended to send a message to voters. But his veto killed a practical, bipartisan agreement that would have hastened justice and likely saved lives. Voters should send their own message right back.

32   The way to repair the "machinery of death" is to shift resources to points earlier in the criminal justice cycle. Only then, with the chance for error greatly diminished, would faster processing be justified. Proponents of capital punishment would have an efficient and equitable system, while opponents could argue abolition purely on its merits. With violent crime at its lowest rate in 25 years, there is no better time for sensible reform.

PERSONAL RESPONSE

Explain whether, after reading this article, you feel that you have a clearer picture of the issues associated with capital punishment.

QUESTIONS FOR CLASS OR SMALL-GROUP DISCUSSION

1. How effective do you find Green's use of examples of death-row cases? How do the opening examples (paragraphs 2 and 3) provide background information for his thesis?

2. What is the "deadly compromise" of the title? What examples does Green use to illustrate the problems inherent in the compromise?

3. Explain what Green means when he says that "reforms at the federal level have . . . been woefully misguided" (paragraph 15).

4. What problems with handling capital crimes does Green find at the state level?

5. What solutions does Green recommend for ending "the battle between the extremes of liberalism and conservativism that have reigned on the death penalty" (paragraph 30)? What do you think of his recommendations? Are you persuaded by his evidence and moved to agree with him?

DEADLY STAKES: THE DEBATE OVER CAPITAL PUNISHMENT

JOHN O'SULLIVAN

John O'Sullivan is editor-in-chief of the National Interest. *He was editor of the* National Review *from 1988 to 1997 and in 1998 was named editor-at-large. His previous posts have included special adviser to Prime Minister Margaret Thatcher, associate editor of the* London Times, *assistant editor of the* London Daily Telegraph, *and editor of*

Policy Review. *He was made a Commander of the British Empire in 1991 and lectures on British and American politics. This opinion piece appeared in* National Review Online *on August 30, 2002.*

By a terrible and macabre coincidence both the American and British peoples have found themselves confronted in the last few days with the chilling evil of child murder—and with the grave dilemma of exactly how to punish and deter it.

Last week a California jury found David Westerfield guilty of the kidnapping and murder of his neighbor's daughter, seven-year-old Danielle Van Dam, while in Britain the entire nation was convulsed for weeks over two missing ten-year-old girls. A nationwide hunt ended when their charred remains were found in a ditch. A school janitor has now been charged with their murders and, in a horrible echo of the "Moors Murders" four decades ago, his girlfriend is suspected of complicity in their deaths. In both cases, it seems that the general public would like to see the death penalty imposed for these and similar crimes. If so, their wishes are almost certain to be thwarted by political elites.

In Britain this elite opposition is quite open. Though polls show that 82 percent of the British would like to see the death penalty restored, the politicians refuse to even to discuss the matter. Their reluctance is reinforced by strong pressure from the European Union that has decreed the death penalty to be incompatible with membership in its civilized ranks. Indeed, EU ambassadors troop annually to the State Department to protest the continued use of capital punishment in the U.S.— and the Secretary of State replies apologetically that this is not really a matter for the federal government. In California, the opposition is more subtle—perhaps because it is carried out in the obscurity of a tortuous appeals process. This is likely to ensure that even if Westerfield is sentenced to death, he will probably die of old age as courts endlessly debate his rights.

4   Since this looks embarrassingly like an undemocratic contempt for majority opinion, opponents of capital punishment realize that they need formidable arguments to justify it. The arguments they use are as follows: that justifying the death penalty on the retributive grounds that the punishment should fit the crime is barbaric; that it does not deter potential murderers as its advocates claim; that there are no other arguments that might justify the state taking a life; that it risks killing the wrongly convicted; and, all in all, that it is a cruel punishment incompatible with a civilized society.

Are these arguments formidable? Well, they are repeated so frequently and in tones of such relentless moral self-congratulation that they doubtless come to seem formidable after a while. But they wilt upon examination. Let us take them in turn: Take retribution. This turns out to be a more complex argument that its opponents may have bargained for. To begin with, far from being cruel or barbaric, retribution is an argument that limits punishment as much as it extends it. We do not cut off hands for parking offenses even though that would undoubtedly halt such offenses overnight. Why? Because we recognize that it would violate retributive norms: It would be excessive in comparison to the crime and therefore cruel.

By the same logic, the death penalty is sometimes the only punishment that seems equal to the horror of a particular crime—a cold-blooded poisoning, say, or the rape and murder of a helpless child, or the mass murders of the Nazis and the Communists. Significantly, such civilized nations as the Danes and the Norwegians, which had abolished the death penalty before the First World War, restored it after 1945 in order to deal equitable justice to the Nazis and their collaborators. Was that an excessive response to millions of murders? Was it cruel, unusual, barbaric, uncivilized? Or a measured and just response to vast historic crimes?

Even abolitionists find it hard to reply to these questions because they differ among themselves about whether or not to stress the cruelty of the death penalty. Sometimes they assert that it is uniquely cruel; sometimes, however, they claim to favor lifetime imprisonment on the grounds that it is actually harsher than a quick trip to God or oblivion. Acting on the same grounds, retentionists can reasonably (and, I think, correctly) maintain that death is more merciful than lifetime incarceration (especially when that incarceration is accompanied by sadistic brutality from other inmates.)

8   But this particular dispute is likely to be moot since, as soon as capital punishment is safely outlawed, the ACLU and its camp-followers will immediately file suit to have the courts declare life without parole to be a cruel and unusual punishment outlawed by the U.S. Constitution. In the British debates of the 1970s over whether or not terrorist murderers should face execution, I well remember being assured by politicians who later served as Northern Ireland ministers that convicted murderers would have to serve their full sentence; for there was simply no legal way of releasing them beforehand. Ho Hum. Those same murderers are now walking the streets of Belfast "on license." The Grim Reaper grants no paroles.

So how about the argument from deterrence? Perhaps the loudest and most confident claim made by abolitionists is that there is "no evidence" that the death penalty is a deterrent to potential murders. If that were so, of course, it would hardly be a decisive point in itself. Mere lack of evidence would not establish the reverse proposition—it would not prove that capital punishment was NOT a deterrent. As it happens, however, this claim of "no evidence" is false.

Last year, a trio of economists from Emory University, Hashem Dezhbakhsh, Paul Rubin, and Joanna Melhop Shepherd, released a study—"Does Capital Punishment Have a Deterrent Effect?"—that concluded on the basis of careful statistical analysis of the recent (i.e. since the restoration of capital punishment in the 1970s) evidence that there was a very significant deterrent effect. Summarizing their conclusions, the statistician Iain Murray of the Statistical Assessment Service in Washington reported that "each execution deters other murders to the extent of saving between eight and twenty-eight innocent lives—with a best-estimate average of eighteen lives saved per execution." On this reasoning, if the 3,527 prisoners now on death row in the U.S. were to be executed, then something like 63,000 lives would be saved! Even if we scale down these estimates sharply, we are left with a very strong argument for capital punishment derived from social concern for the lives of potential victims and the distress of their families. (Mr. Murray is himself an opponent of capital punishment on religious grounds; so he deserves particular credit for his intellectual honesty.)

So, if opponents of the death penalty are to continue to disparage the deterrent argument, they will have to overturn this new research. Mere repetition of past assertions will not be enough. That brings us to what is genuinely the strongest argument of the abolitionists—wrongful execution. For it must certainly be admitted that an innocent man might be wrongly convicted and executed, that we can never entirely eliminate that risk, and that such a miscarriage of justice would be shameful. For that very reason we take extreme measures to avoid it. As a result, only a handful of such miscarriages of justice are known to have happened; none of them has happened since the restoration of capital punishment in the U.S. in 1976; and the science of DNA has now added a further barrier to such terrible mistakes. The recent release of man as a result of DNA evidence, cited by Rod Dreher (in *The Corner*) as justifying his opposition to the death penalty, in reality strengthens the case for it since it makes future errors even less likely than they were before.

12   Even though wrongful executions are exceedingly rare, we know a great deal about them. Yet we hear little or no mention of their exact equivalent on the other side of the argument—namely, murders committed by those who have already committed a murder, served their sentence, and been released to murder again (or who have murdered an inmate or guard in prison). That is curious. For a few years ago there were 820 people in U.S. prisons who were serving time for their second murder of this kind. If the death penalty had been applied after their first murders, their 820 subsequent victims would be alive today. That figure is not a statistical inference but an absolute certainty. Of course, it is intellectually possible for abolitionists to argue that it is better to acquiesce reluctantly in the murder of 820 innocent men than to execute mistakenly one innocent man—but somehow I doubt if that argument, stated so plainly, would convince the democratic majority.

What those 820 murders establish is that, contra the abolitionists, there is another strong argument for capital punishment. It is known technically as the argument from incapacitation (i.e., dead men commit no murders.) And that argument alone is more than adequate justification for capital punishment.

That is perhaps why we never hear of it.

Where, then, does that leave the final, broad conclusion that capital punishment is incompatible with a civilized society? Well, to answer that, we must have some idea of what abolitionists mean by "a civilized society." Do they mean a society that has a written language, at least an oral historical tradition, social institutions that claim a monopoly of force and violence, and similar social inventions? It would seem not since such societies have almost invariably imposed the death penalty, sometimes for crimes much less serious than murder. Indeed, the replacement of private vendettas by state executions is as good a definition of the birth of civil society as political scientists can come up with.

16   Do they then mean a society marked by gentle manners, courtesy, low levels of private violence, and declining crime? If so, that argument too backfires on them. Britain in the 1930s and America in the 1950s were societies that had achieved high levels of social tranquility by comparison with their own pasts and the standards of other advanced societies. Yet they employed the death penalty for serious crimes—indeed, murder trials were among the gripping social entertainments of those days. And as the death penalty was gradually abolished (formal abolition

generally following on a growing reluctance to impose it except in the most terrible cases), so crime and violence rose, and so society became increasingly brutalist in its popular culture—the violence of films and television making the murder trials of the 1930s seem, well, civilized by comparison.

Britain is still in the midst of this perverse experiment that combines official squeamishness with rising levels of violent crime; America began to restore the death penalty in the 1970s—and 20 years later violent crime began to fall.

What the "civilized" argument boils down to in the end, as the late Ernest Van Den Haag used to point out in his intellectual demolitions of the abolitionist case, is the circular logic that capital punishment is incompatible with a civilized society because a civilized society is one that rejects capital punishment. Or, to put the abolitionist case as simply as possible: "People like us don't like capital punishment."

A genuinely civilized society would take a very different view of the evidence cited above. It would pay more attention to the cries of the victims than to its own squeamishness. And it would transfer its compassion from the David Westerfields of this world to the Danielle Van Dams. For if the death penalty would certainly have saved 820 innocent lives, and might arguably save tens of thousands of innocent lives in the future, almost certainly at the cost of no innocent lives at all, then surely a society that shrinks from using it deserves to be called sentimentalist and cruel rather than civilized. And if in addition it ignores majority opinion in order to indulge its refined sensibilities, then it deserves to be called undemocratic too.

20   When next the EU ambassadors come calling at the State Department to complain of executions in Texas, Colin Powell might tell them exactly that.

PERSONAL RESPONSE

Write for a few minutes explaining your views on the death penalty. Has this essay changed your opinion in any way?

QUESTIONS FOR CLASS OR SMALL-GROUP DISCUSSION

1. How does O'Sullivan use the murders of children in both America and Britain to argue his position on capital punishment?

2. State the arguments that opponents of capital punishment typically use to argue their position. What does O'Sullivan have to say about each of those points? How valid or sound do your find his reasoning on each point?

3. Assess the strengths and weaknesses of O'Sullivan's argument. Which is his weakest point? Which is his most persuasive point? Are you convinced to agree with him?

○ PERSPECTIVES ON CRIMINAL BEHAVIOR ○

Suggested Writing Topics

1. Drawing on both "How People Turn Monstrous" By Mark Buchanan and "Revisiting the Stanford Prison Experiment" by Philip G. Zimbardo, write an opinion paper on the subject of "good people pitted against the forces inherent in bad situations" (Zimbardo, paragraph 3).

2. Mark Buchanan writes in "How People Turn Monstrous" that "there are very good reasons to think that [Staff Sgt. Ivan] Frederick [II] and the others, however despicable their actions, only did what many of us would have done if placed in the same situation, which put their guilt in a questionable light" (paragraph 2). Write an essay in response to that statement.

3. Read William Golding's *The Lord of the Flies* and analyze it in light of Philip G. Zimbardo's "Revisiting the Stanford Prison Experiment."

4. Argue for or against capital punishment, taking into account Joshua Green's "Deadly Compromise" and/or John O'Sullivan's "Deadly Stakes: The Debate over Capital Punishment" where appropriate.

5. Select one specific aspect of the problem of crime and violence in America. Write a paper assessing the seriousness of the problem you choose and offering possible solutions, to the degree that you can identify possible solutions.

6. Focusing on crime in your own community, argue for or against the need for improved policing, handling of criminals, or jail or prison facilities.

7. Identify a specific problem in your home town or current community that needs attention, such as bullying in schools, high juvenile crime rate, or high rate of illegal drug sales or abuse, and argue for a solution or specific ways to address the problem.

8. Examine one aspect of inner-city violence, from the perspectives of law-enforcement officers, sociologists, behavioral scientists, educators, and/or social workers.

9. Select one of the readings in the chapter and write a critique of or response to it.

Research Topics

1. Philip G. Zimbardo writes in "Revisiting the Stanford Prison Experiment" that "[t]he social experiment of imprisoning society's criminals for long terms is a failure on virtually all levels." Research the subject of the failure or success of the prison system by identifying one aspect of this broad subject and focusing on it.

2. Research the subject of reform in the penal system and arrive at your own conclusion about the best way to proceed.

3. Research the subject of "the power of anonymity to unleash violent behavior" (Zimbardo, paragraph 2). Besides Zimbardo's Stanford prison experiment, read about Stanley Milgram's experiments at Yale in 1961, which studied students' willingness to commit actions that conflicted with their conscience because they were obeying an authority figure.

4. Whenever a school shooting occurs, people try to find reasons to explain how someone could commit such a crime. Reasons mentioned often include the widespread availability of guns, school cliques, lax parental supervision, bullying in schools, poor school security, lack of religion in schools, the Internet, neo-Nazism, and Satanism, among others. Select one of those subjects or select another reason as a beginning point for research to explain or understand why someone would commit a school shooting, framing your questions and narrowing your focus as you read and discover more about your subject.

5. Research recent statistics on serious crimes such as armed robbery, rape, murder, and assault with a deadly weapon and argue ways to reduce the rates of violent crimes in America.

6. Research the controversy over gun control and arrive at your own position on the subject.

7. Research the social conditions at the root of crime in America.

8. Research the efficacy of capital punishment or life in prison as deterrents.

Responding to Visuals

Protesters call for an end to the death penalty, and in particular a stay of execution for Texas inmate Kenneth Foster, in front of the Supreme Court in Washington on August 29, 2007.

1. Comment on the messages on the placards. What impact do you think the protestors hoped to make with them?
2. Why do you think the photographer selected these protestors for his picture? Does it matter, for instance, that the woman is holding a baby?
3. What is the effect of foregrounding the protestors and placards with the Supreme Court building in the background?
4. How committed to or earnest about their cause do these protesters seem to you? How do you read the looks on their faces?

RESPONDING TO VISUALS

MRA for the Syracuse Partnership To Reduce Juvenile Gun Violence and the Rosamond Gifford Foundation, Photo: © 2001 Chip East

"In a community with guns, everyone's a target."

1. What is the message of this advertisement?
2. What details of the advertisement help convey its message?
3. What is the function of the bullet-ridden stop sign?
4. What audience is the advertisement aimed at? How effectively do you think the ad reaches that audience?

CHAPTER 15

Gender and Sex Roles

Many people use the word *gender* interchangeably with the word sex, but the two have different meanings. Sex is a biological category; a person's sex—whether male or female—is genetically determined. On the other hand, gender refers to the socially constructed set of expectations for behavior based on one's sex. Masculinity and femininity are gender constructs whose definitions vary and change over time and with different cultures or groups within cultures. What is considered appropriate and even desirable behavior for men and women in one culture may be strongly inappropriate in another. Like other cultures, American culture's definitions of masculinity and femininity change with time, shaped by a number of influences, such as parental expectations, peer pressure, and media images. We are born either male or female, and most of us learn to behave in ways consistent with our society's expectations for that sex.

The first two essays look at sexual stereotyping and its effects primarily on males but females as well. First, Megan Rosenfeld's "Reexamining the Plight of Young

Males" argues that researchers should pay more attention to how boys are being raised. Noting that studies of the effects of sexual stereotyping on boys have long been neglected in deference to studies of girls, she quotes a number of authors and researchers who are starting to investigate the conflicting messages that boys get from parents, peers, and popular culture. Next in "The Myth About Boys," David Von Drehle updates Rosenfeld's essay by examining the state of boys today in comparison with the previous decades, especially when he was a boy growing up. As the parent of a ten-year-old boy, he is particularly interested in what psychologists, sociologists, and others project as the future for today's boys. As you read the article, compare and contrast it with what Megan Rosenfeld said about the ways boys were being raised just eight years before this essay was written. How have things changed and how have they stayed the same since then? In addition, try to recall your own childhood, the toys you played with, the games you played, and your playmates. How accurately do Rosenfeld's and Von Drehle's observations match your own experiences or observations?

The focus of the chapter shifts to the subject of marriage with Howard Moody's "Sacred Rite or Civil Right?" Moody asserts that gay marriages show why we need to separate church and state. He gives a historical overview of the roles that both church and state have played in establishing the nature of heterosexual marriage, stressing the differences between the religious definition of marriage and the state's definition. At the heart of his essay is the question of what marriage is, so you may want to think about your own definition of marriage as you read the essay.

The chapter concludes with Whitney Mitchell's "Deconstructing Gender, Sex, and Sexuality as Applied to Identity." Mitchell objects to the way those terms are applied to individuals and believes that they "rob individuals of their dignity as human beings." As you read the essay, consider your feelings about being male or female, recalling especially situations when you were identified on the basis of that characteristic alone.

REEXAMINING THE PLIGHT OF YOUNG MALES

Megan Rosenfeld

Megan Rosenfeld, now a freelance writer, was for many years a Washington Post *staff writer. "Reexamining the Plight of Young Males" first appeared in the* Washington Post *on March 26, 1998.*

Two decades of study about the sexual stereotyping of girls is now inspiring a new subject for gender research: boys. Our boys are in trouble, say a vanguard of researchers, and it's time to pay attention to how we are raising them.

The case begins with numbers. Boy babies die in greater numbers in infancy, and are more fragile as babies than girls. Boys are far more likely than girls to be told they have learning disabilities, to be sent to the principal's office, to be given medication for hyperactivity or attention deficit disorder, to be suspended from high school, to commit crimes, to be diagnosed as schizophrenic or autistic. In adolescence, they kill themselves five times more often than girls do. In adulthood, they are being incarcerated at ever-increasing rates, abandoning families, and becoming more likely to be both the perpetrators and victims of violence.

Some psychologists and educators studying boys argue that because of the way we parent and educate boys, combined with biology and an overlay of popular culture, male children do not fully develop their capacity for emotional depth and complexity. As a result, they are less able than they need to be to navigate the turmoil of adolescence, to develop healthy adult relationships, in some cases to survive at all. While the simple hierarchy of male authority and dominance in our society is becoming obsolete, the men of tomorrow are not being trained for a world in which their traditional survival mechanisms—like physical strength, bluster and bullying—no longer prevail. Meanwhile, traditionally male virtues like courage and determination are too often neglected.

4   "An enormous crisis of men and boys is happening before our eyes without our seeing it. There's been an extraordinary shift in the plate tectonics of gender; everything we ever thought is open for examination," said Barney Brawer, a long-time educator. Brawer is managing the boys component of the Harvard Project on Women's Psychology, Boys' Development, and the Culture of Manhood, which is headed by Carol Gilligan, whose research helped shape the new understanding of girls. For two years the project has held a series of discussions and lectures, sponsored mothers-of-sons support groups, and designed research projects. The public interest in their work has taken the academics by surprise. "It's almost more than we can handle," Brawer said.

A few miles away in Newton, Mass., psychologist William S. Pollack is also worrying about boys and writing a book about them. So are Michael Thompson and Dan Kindlon, also psychologists, and consultants to all-boys schools in the Boston area. Publishers have forked over six-figure advances for these books, due out later this year, hoping to replicate the financial bonanza of Mary Pipher's bestseller on girls, *Reviving Ophelia*.

"We've become very clear about what we want for girls," Brawer said. "We are less clear about what we want for boys."

"Politically Incorrect"

"It's politically incorrect to be a boy," says the mother of an 18-month-old male. Boys are the universal scapegoats, the clumsy clods with smelly feet who care only about sports and mischief. They are seen as "toxic," says Pollack, creatures "who will infect girls with some kind of social cooties." But could it be they are just as much victims of gender stereotyping as girls have been? As their sisters grow up with more options and opportunities than they used to have, boys may be feeling the tightening noose of limited expectations, societal scorn and inadequate role models.

8   "Why is there always a bad boy in every one of my classes, every year, but no bad girls?" a second-grade girl asked Kindlon, who with Thompson is writing a book called *Raising Cain: Protecting the Emotional Life of Boys.* Thompson jokes that the subtitle of the book should really be "how to raise your son so he won't turn out like your husband."

"Our beliefs about maleness, the mythology that surrounds being male, has led many boys to ruin," writes Geoffrey Canada in the newly published *Reaching Up for Manhood: Transforming the Lives of Boys in America.* "The image of male as strong is mixed with the image of male as violent. Male as virile gets confused with male as promiscuous. Male as adventurous equals male as reckless. Male as intelligent often gets mixed with male as arrogant, racist, and sexist."

Said Pollack: "If girls were killing themselves in these numbers we'd recognize this as a public health issue in our society."

A survey on gender by the *Washington Post*, Henry J. Kaiser Family Foundation and Harvard University showed that most parents feel they treat their sons and daughters equally. Still, most parents know that Jack will heedlessly jump off just about anything or pick up a block and make it a gun, while 4-year-old Jill insists on wearing her party dress and wrapping her toy animals in blankets. But while Jill can keep or abandon party dresses as she wishes Jack is often forbidden a toy gun, or he's told repeatedly to sit down and stop running around.

12   A 16-year-old boy in Washington remembers his elementary school as a place without male teachers, where by sixth grade (age 11 or 12) boys were assumed to be the troublemakers. One day a girl sitting next to him made him laugh by sticking a pencil up her nose. When the teacher reprimanded him, the boy blamed his friend and her pencil antics. But the girl denied doing anything—and the teacher believed her and not him. She sent him to sit in the hall for lying. "That kind of thing happened all the time," he said. "It made me not respect teachers very much."

Barb Wilder-Smith is a Boston-area teacher who became interested in researching boys after she gave birth to two of them—and realized she didn't know much about them. Three years ago she took her then 5-year-old to buy a new bike. At the time, his favorite color was pink and he wanted a pink bike. She and her husband were content to let him make his own color choice.

"But the salesman said he couldn't have a pink bike, pink was a girl color, and he had to have a red or blue bike," Wilder-Smith said. "My son looked at him and said, 'That's ridiculous, colors aren't boys or girls, and pink is my favorite color.'"

The boy got his pink bike. But he was teased so much by other children, who called this 5-year-old gay, that he put a sign on his bicycle basket. It read:

I like pink.
I am still a boy.
I have a penis.

Now he is 8, and doesn't let anyone know he likes pink. It was the girls who hassled him about it most mercilessly. Girls who wear blue all the time.

Talking About Differences

16   Considerable trepidation surrounds this new interest in boys. Some parents are afraid that it's about having their boys grow up "to be sweet and nice and good," as Wilder-Smith put it, and will endanger their sons. Feminists of both genders worry that the hard-won changes that benefit girls will be pitted against newly defined needs of boys, and that the old canards about biology being destiny will come back from the near-dead. Some are resentful that attention is being directed toward boys when girls have had only "a nanosecond in the history of educational reform," as Gabrielle Lange wrote in the American Association of University Women magazine "Outlook." Researchers into boys' behavior fear they will be tagged as antifemale, and they tread cautiously into the politically and emotionally loaded field of gender study.

"For 30 years it has been politically unacceptable to talk about [neurological or biological] differences," said Thompson, who has worked as a clinical psychologist with both coed and all-boys schools. But now, he and others note, the scientific community seems more willing to acknowledge that there are differences between males and females. The question is what the significance of these differences is.

Diane F. Halpern, a psychology professor at California State University in San Bernardino, recently surveyed current studies of differences between male and female intelligence. She found that women do better in tasks that test language abilities, fine motor tasks, perceptual speed, decoding nonverbal communication, and speech articulation. Men are superior in "visual working memory," tasks that require moving objects, aiming, fluid reasoning, knowledge of math, science and geography, and general knowledge. At the same time males have more mental retardation, attention deficit disorders, delayed speech, dyslexia, stuttering, learning disabilities and emotional disturbances.

Girls' brains are stronger in the left hemisphere, which is where language is processed, while boys' are more oriented to the right hemisphere, the spatial and physical center. Recent advances in brain study have shown that the two hemispheres are better connected in females, which may eventually explain why the genders show different patterns in cognitive tests.

20   "Boys' early experience of school is being beaten by girls at most things," Thompson said. "The first thing we do in school is make them read and sit still, two things they are generally not as good at."

Boys score better on achievement tests, but girls get better grades—another pattern that inspires all sorts of interpretations. Since boys are bigger risk-takers, perhaps they guess more on tests and by the law of averages get enough right answers. Halpern suggested that since most standardized tests are multiple choice, and female strength tends to be in writing, perhaps they lose out that way. Conversely, since sitting still, neatness and studiousness are rewarded in classroom grades, maybe boys are inadvertently penalized in that arena. It also has been demonstrated repeatedly that scores can change with the right training.

Boys and Learning

Why are so many more boys—six times more—diagnosed with learning disabilities? No one knows for sure, but there are some theories. One is that the standards for diagnosing LD are so loose that disruptive boys are classified to get them to special help and out of the classroom. "The system has shaped the definition rather than the other way around," said Ken Kavale, an expert in learning disabilities who teaches graduate school at the University of Iowa.

Douglas Fuchs, a professor at the Kennedy Center Institute on Education and Learning at Peabody College of Vanderbilt, thinks learning disabilities are over-diagnosed and may be related to early language differences. Millions of boys are now taking Ritalin to treat attention deficit and hyperactivity.

24   No one questions that many boys are legitimately learning disabled—neurologically mis-wired in ways that make traditional learning difficult. But there may be other factors that affect a boy's ability to be successful in school.

Pollack's theory, based on his years of research and clinical practice, is that many boys' problems are rooted in a too-early separation from their mother's nurturing. While boy babies start out with a wider emotional range—more sounds, expressions and wails—parents tend to give them less adoring interaction after about the age of 6 months, he says. Even though boy babies are more physically fragile, he believes that adults tend to think of them as being bigger and tougher, and also to soothe them into quietness rather than try to understand their noise. Boys are so traumatized by this "disruption of their early holding environment" that they harden up and withdraw, which has repercussions for the rest of their lives, Pollack suggests.

Another question is whether we have failed to appreciate the language of boys because so much of it is either violent in imagery or oblique in approach. Wilder-Smith recalled getting a note from one of the 5-year-old boys whose fantasy play-acting she recorded for a year in a Boston school.

"Have a Hindenburg Exploding Life!" the boy Tyler wrote. Wilder-Smith wasn't sure at first if this note was meant affectionately; after she thought about it she realized it was. It just wasn't her kind of language. But she has come to believe that what appears to be violent play or imagery to a woman may be a valuable tool to a boy, his way of conquering fear and his smallness in the universe. Removing that outlet may end up making boys more violent rather than less, she thinks.

28   Barney Brawer likes to use the example of a Vermont farmer working on a broken tractor. His son may spend the day at his side, and yet they may exchange no more than a dozen words. But the son has seen a great deal—perseverance, problem solving (or trying to), engine repair. "We've lost a lot of that kind of communicating," he says.

Boys exhibit different signs of depression, says Pollack, whose book *Real Boys: Rescuing Our Sons from the Myths of Boyhood* will be published later this year. Thus we often fail to recognize them because they are not as evident as the symptoms common to girls—who in adolescence and adulthood are diagnosed with depression at far higher rates than males. "Our view of depression has been feminized," he said. "Boys may have a moody withdrawal rather than tears."

After spending a year observing in a Boston public school, Wilder-Smith is among those who think we may need to reevaluate our attitudes about boy aggression and action. Too often, she suspects, the mothers and female teachers who statistically spend the most time with young boys believe that the key to producing a nonviolent adult is to remove all conflict—toy weapons, wrestling and shoving, imaginary explosions and crashes—from a boy's life.

"I've watched teachers who have the rule with creative writing that there's 'no killing in stories,'" she said. "One boy said, 'But the bad guy! He has to die somehow!' Finally the teacher said the bad guy could die, and allowed him to be run over by a truck. . . . They can't draw it [violence], they can't write about it, they can't act it out."

32   "We do take away a lot of the opportunity to do things boys like to do," said Carol Kennedy, a school principal in Missouri with 34 years' experience in education. "That is be rowdy, run and jump and roll around. We don't allow that." Educator Vivian Gussin Paley once put a running track in her kindergarten classroom. The girls ran around it in laps. The boys chased each other. They all seemed to like it.

Mass media ill-serve both genders, researchers say. Many believe that violence on television encourages aggressive behavior in boys and girls, but they have no conclusive proof of a connection. There is more evidence backed up by teachers that television has encouraged shorter attention spans and a need for artificial excitement. While girls are surrounded by television shows and books in which boys are almost always the protagonist, the hero and the main ingredient, boys rarely get a positive cultural message that it's okay to be afraid or sad, to not be athletic, to have a girl for a friend, or to enjoy writing poetry.

New Pressures

It is no secret that modern life has produced a new style of childhood. But some aspects of contemporary life may exact particular hardships for boys that are rarely acknowledged by those in authority.

For example, divorce in many cases not only removes a boy's primary role model from his daily life, it often brings additional burdens from his mother. He becomes the "man of the family," a role he is generally not prepared to handle. School principals dealing with boys who are sent to their office with behavior problems are finding that many of them are in this situation.

36   "The responsibilities most of our young boys are having placed on them is different than ever before," said principal Kennedy. "Mother is sharing things with that boy that almost makes him a partner rather than a son. . . . We find that even in elementary school, when a boy is taking on the role of being the major babysitter, he is often paying more attention to what happens at home than at school. It's more of a boy problem because a mother can see the boy as head of household, or man of the family, and doesn't tend to do that with a girl."

Unsupervised play is another issue—the lack of it, that is. Researchers like Brawer suspect that while too many hours are being idled away alone, indoors, in front of a television set, too few are being spent outdoors in time-honored games of exploration, mock warfare, fort building, sneaking around, inventing ball games and so forth. Because many parents today are legitimately afraid of criminals and bad drivers careening down neighborhood streets, boys—and girls—are rarely allowed the freedom to investigate and master their home turf in a way that once provided a rehearsal for the real world.

So the questions mount. Brawer, who is writing a dissertation on Attention Deficit and Hyperactivity Disorder, notes that in the 1,700 studies on the subject that he has found, the word "father" is mentioned only three times. "The neurobiological crowd doesn't believe in Freudian language," he said. "But if you look at the conditions under which kids are more or less likely to have problems, the indicators go way down when the father is in the home. This is an area we need to study."

What messages do mothers inadvertently send when they recoil from their son's wish to have a toy gun or his desire to be a ballerina for Halloween? How do fathers restrict a boy's emotional vocabulary when they say "big boys don't cry"? Should some boys, as Thompson and Kindlon suggest, start school at 8 rather than 5 or 6 years of age?

40   "It may still be a man's world, but it's not a boy's," Pollack said. "He's been sat on so long he'll push to keep the dominance. Recognizing boys' pain is the way to change society."

PERSONAL RESPONSE

Select a statement, example, or reference in this essay that particularly impressed you, either favorably or unfavorably, and respond to or explore it.

QUESTIONS FOR CLASS OR SMALL-GROUP DISCUSSION

1. Where does Rosenfeld state her thesis? Are you persuaded that her argument is valid?

2. How effective do you find the anecdote about the little boy wanting a pink bicycle in supporting Rosenfeld's position? What do you think of her other evidence?

3. Do your own experiences and observations bear out Rosenfeld's comment, "As their sisters grow up with more options and opportunities than they used to have, boys may be feeling the tightening noose of limited expectations, society scorn, and inadequate role models" (paragraph 7)? What examples or anecdotes can you provide that support or refute that statement?

4. How effective do you find Rosenfeld's concluding paragraphs, especially her implications about the role of fathers? Can you suggest any answers to the questions she asks in the next-to-last paragraph?

THE MYTH ABOUT BOYS

David Von Drehle

David Von Drehle was for many years a staff writer for the Washington Post *but now writes for* Time *magazine. He is author of the following books:* Among the Lowest of the Dead: Inside Death Row *(1995);* Triangle: The Fire that Changed America *(2003); and, with the political staff of the* Washington Post, Deadlock: The Inside Story of America's Closest Election *(2001). He wrote this article for a cover story for the July 26, 2007, issue of* Time.

My son was born nearly 10 years ago, and I remember telling him that morning that he was one lucky baby. Forget Dr. Spock or Dr. Brazelton—I took my cue from Dr. Pangloss. If this was not the best of all possible worlds, it was certainly the best time and best place to be starting out healthy and free in a land of vast possibilities. In the months and years that followed, however, there came a steady stream of books and essays warning that I had missed something ominous: our little guy had entered a soul-crushing world of anti-boy influences.

There was, for example, Harvard psychologist William Pollack's *Real Boys* (1998), which asserted that contemporary boys are "scared and disconnected," "severely lagging" behind girls in both achievement and self-confidence. The following year, journalist Susan Faludi argued in *Stiffed* that the cold calculus of global economics was emasculating American men. In 2000 philosopher Christina Hoff Sommers blamed off-the-rails feminism for sparking *The War Against Boys*, and two years later writer Elizabeth Gilbert found *The Last American Man* living in a teepee in the Appalachian Mountains. By the time our boy was headed to third grade, magazine editors were grinding out cover headlines like BOY TROUBLE and THE BOY CRISIS, and I was getting worried. The voyage to manhood had come to seem as perilous and flummoxing as the future of Iraq.

It's enough to make people long for the good old days. Sure enough, one of the hot books of the summer is a zestfully nostalgic celebration of boyhood past. *The Dangerous Book for Boys*, by brothers Hal and Conn Iggulden, flits from fossils to tree houses, from secret codes to go-carts, from the Battle of Gettysburg to the last voyage of Robert Falcon Scott. A sensation last year in Britain, the book has been at or near the top of the *New York Times* best-seller list since late spring.

4   *The Dangerous Book*, bound in an Edwardian red cover with marbled endpapers, has many of the timeless qualities of an ideal young man: curiosity, bravery and respectfulness; just enough rogue to leaven the stoic; an appetite for any challenge, from hunting small game to mastering the rules of grammar. It celebrates trial and error, vindicates the noble failure. Rudyard Kipling would have loved it.

These charms alone can't explain the popularity of an amalgam of coin tricks, constellations and homemade magnets, however. Clearly, *The Dangerous Book* has tapped into a larger anxiety about how we're raising young men. This is a subject worth digging into, because it reflects not just on our sons but also on their sisters, on the kind of world these kids might make together—and on the adults who love them, however imperfect we prove to be. With fresh eyes on fresh facts, we might find that an upbeat message to a newborn boy is not so misguided after all.

The Myth of the Boy Crisis

"I don't think anyone will deny that girls are academically superior as a group. Girls are more academically powerful. They make the grades, they run the student activities, they are the valedictorians."

Christina Hoff Sommers, a fellow at the American Enterprise Institute, was explaining how she came to worry deeply about boys. In the book-lined parlor of her suburban Washington home, she ticked through a familiar but disturbing indictment: More boys than girls are in special-education classes. More boys than girls are prescribed mood-managing drugs. This suggests to her (and others) that today's schools are built for girls, and boys are becoming misfits. As a result, more boys than girls drop out of high school. Boys don't read as well as girls. And America's prisons are packed with boys and former boys.

8   Meanwhile, fewer boys than girls take the SAT. Fewer boys than girls apply to college. Fewer boys than girls, in annual surveys of college freshmen, express a passion for learning. And fewer boys than girls are earning college degrees. Even sperm counts are falling. "It's true at every level of society" that boys are stumbling behind, Sommers continued.

Observers of the boy crisis contend that families, schools and popular culture are failing our boys, leaving them restless bundles of anxiety—misfits in the classroom and video-game junkies at home. They suffer from an epidemic of "anomie," as Harvard psychologist William Pollack told me, adrift in a world of change without the help they need to find their way. Even in the youngest grades, test-oriented teachers focus energy on conventional exercises in reading, writing and other seatwork, areas in which girls tend to excel. At the same time, schools are cutting science labs, physical education and recess, where the experiential learning styles of boys come into play. No wonder, the theory goes, our boys get jittery, grow disruptive and eventually tune out. "A boy will get a reputation as hell on wheels that follows him from one teacher to the next, and soon they're coming down on him even before he screws up. So he learns to hate school," says Mike Miller, an elementary school teacher in North Carolina. Miller's principal has ordered every faculty member to read a book this summer titled *Hear Our Cry: Boys in Crisis*.

In short, society treats "boyhood as toxic, as a pathology," says Sommers—who may have been guilty of this herself when she wrote several years ago that the Columbine killers were emblematic of turn-of-the-century boyhood. But she's right that it's not girls who are shooting up their classrooms—and boys are at least five times as likely as girls to die by suicide.

There are statistics to back up every point in that sad litany, but I also found people eager to flay nearly every statistic. For instance: Is it bad that more boys are in special education, or should we be pleased that they are getting extra help from specially trained teachers? And haven't boys always tended to be more restless than girls under the discipline of high school and more likely to wind up in jail? A growing congregation of writers have begun to argue that the trouble with boys is mostly a myth. Sara Mead is one; she was until recently a senior policy analyst at Education Sector, a Washington think tank largely funded by the Gates Foundation. Intrigued by the wave of books and articles about failing boys, Mead crunched some numbers, focusing narrowly on the question of school performance. The former Clinton Administration official concluded that "with a few exceptions, American boys are scoring higher and achieving more than they ever have before."

12   In particular, Mead decided that boys from middle- and upper-income families—especially white families—are doing just fine. "The biggest issue is not a gender gap. It is these gaps for minority and disadvantaged boys," she told me recently in the think tank's conference room. Boys overall are holding their own or even improving on standardized tests, she said; they're just not improving as quickly as girls. And their total numbers in college are rising, albeit not as sharply as the numbers of girls. To Mead, a good-news story about the achievements of girls and young women has been turned into a bad-news story about laggard boys and young men.

The more I probed, the more I realized that the subject of boys is a bog of sociology in which a clever researcher, given a little time, can unearth evidence to support almost any point of view. I also came to the sad realization that this field, like so many others, has been infiltrated by our left-right political noise machine. Our boys have become cannon fodder in the unresolved culture wars waged by their parents and grandparents. On one side, concern for boys is waved off as a mere "backlash against the women's movement," as two writers declared dismissively in the *Washington Post* last year. The opposing side views any divergence from the crisis theme as male-bashing feminism.

Then I came across a new report from the Federal Government: Uncle Sam's annual attempt to paint a broad statistical portrait of the nation's young people. In long rows of little numbers printed on page after page of tables, this report told a different story from that of either the woe bearers or the myth busters.

What the Numbers Say

"America's Children: Key National Indicators of Well-Being, 2007" is the work of many agencies, from the Department of Justice to the Department of Education to the Bureau of the Census and beyond. It gathers a trove of data, and as I made my way through it, I concluded that there's real substance to the boy crisis, and there have been good-faith reasons for sounding an alarm.

16   Statistics collected over two decades show an alarming decline in the performance of America's boys—in some respects, a virtual free fall. Boys were doing poorly in school, abusing drugs, committing violent crimes and engaging in promiscuous sex. Young males lost ground by many behavioral indicators at some point in the 1980s and '90s: sharp plunges on some scales, long erosions on others. I was forced to confront a fact that I had secretly known all along: that teens of 30 years ago—my generation—were the leading edge of an epidemic of thugs, dolts and cads.

No wonder so many writers began calling for change in the late 1990s. Reliable social-science data often lag a couple of years behind the calendar; it takes time to gather and compile a nation's worth of numbers. Stories about social trends that you read today may be describing the reality of 2004 or 2005. The groundbreaking boy books were a response to statistics portraying the worst of a physical, mental and moral health crisis.

There's more to the story, however. That downward slide has leveled off—and in many cases, turned around. Boys today look pretty good compared with their dads and older cousins. By some measures, our boys are doing better than ever.

The juvenile crime rate in 2005 (the most recent year cited in the report) was down by two-thirds from its peak in 1993. Other Justice Department statistics show that the population of juvenile males in prison is only half of its historic high. The number of high school senior boys using illegal drugs has fallen by almost half compared with the number in 1980. And the percentage of high school boys drinking heavily is now the lowest on record. When I was in high school, more than half of all senior boys told researchers they had downed five or more drinks in a row within the previous two weeks—a number that I have no trouble believing. By last year, that figure was fewer than 3 in 10.

20   Today's girls are also doing well by these measures, but their successes in no way diminish the progress of the boys. In fact, together our kids are reversing one of the direst problems of the previous generation: the teen-pregnancy epidemic. According to the new report, fewer than half of all high school boys and girls in 2005 were sexually active. For the boys, that's a decrease of 10 percentage points from the early 1990s. Boys who are having sex report that they are more responsible about it: 7 in 10 are using condoms, compared with about half in 1993. As a result, teen pregnancy and abortion rates are now at their lowest recorded levels.

What about school? Boys in the fourth, eighth and 12th grades all score better—though not dramatically better—on math tests than did the comparable boys of 1990. Reading, however, is a problem. The standardized NAEP test, known as the nation's report card, indicates that by the senior year of high school, boys have fallen nearly 20 points behind their female peers. That's bad, not because girls are ahead but because too many boys are leaving school functionally illiterate. Pollack told me of one study that found even the sons of college-educated parents had a 1 in 4 chance of leaving school without becoming proficient readers. In an economy increasingly geared toward processing information, an inability to read becomes an inability to earn. "You have to be literate in today's world," says Sommers. "We're not going to get away with not teaching boys to read."

Even here, though, there may be grounds for a hopeful outlook. Boys at the fourth- and eighth-grade levels are showing modest improvement in reading and now trail their female classmates by slightly smaller margins than before. If that's a sign of improved teaching and parental focus on reading, then we ought to expect gains in the higher grades soon.

"I think it would be an error not to be optimistic," says Michael Gurian, author of several books about raising boys. "But at the same time there is reason to worry." He sketches the sinking trajectory of undereducated males as blue-collar jobs move to low-wage countries. Though definitive data on the dropout rate are as elusive as Bigfoot, there's little question that a worrisome gap is opening between boys who finish high school and those who don't. Boys with diplomas are now far more likely to go immediately to college than the boys of my era were. Solution: we need more boys with diplomas.

24   And that can be done. A generation of enlightened teaching and robust encouragement has awakened American girls to the need for higher education. Women now outnumber men in college by a ratio of 4 to 3, and admissions officers at liberal-arts colleges are struggling to find enough males to keep their classes close to gender parity. "We've done wonderfully with girls. Now let's do the same for boys," says Gurian. One way to start might be to gear advanced training to male-dominated occupations—already the case in many female-oriented fields. Schoolteachers and librarians (roughly 70% female) must go to college, but firefighters and police officers (pushing 90% male)? Not necessarily. Top executive secretaries are college educated; top carpenters may not be.

About the only scale on which today's boys are faring dramatically worse than the boys of my era is the bathroom scale. When I was in high school in the late 1970s, roughly 1 boy in 20 was obese; today 1 boy in 5 is.

My favorite statistic seemed to sum up all the others: fewer boys today are deadbeats. The percentage of young men between 16 and 19 who neither work nor attend school has fallen by about a quarter since 1984. The greatest gains in this category have been made by black youths. In 1984, 1 out of 3 young black men ages 18 and 19 were neither in school nor working. That proportion has been cut almost in half, to fewer than 1 in 5.

Today's boys may wear their pants too damned baggy and go around with iPod buds in their ears. They know everything about Xbox 360 and nothing about paper routes. I doubt that they slog to school through deep snow as I recall doing back before the globe warmed up. But judging from the numbers, they are pulling themselves up from the handbasket to hell.

So Where Did We Go Right?

28   Unfortunately, it's one thing to observe human behavior—count the crime reports and the teen births and the diplomas awarded and so on—but quite another to explain it. Popular science and the best-seller lists skip eagerly from one theory to the next, lingering with delight on the most provocative if not always the most plausible. A recent paper suggested that falling crime rates can be explained almost entirely by reduced lead exposure in childhood. Which was odd, because last year economist Steven Levitt's best seller *Freakonomics* chalked up the improvement to legalized abortion, which, he theorized, cut the number of unwanted children prone to wind up as criminals.

Or take the teen-pregnancy numbers. It's not enough to credit the virtues of responsibility and better sex education. Something racier is desired. According to some writers, fewer teens are getting pregnant because they've all switched to oral sex. Or maybe the phenomenon is due to a still unexplained decline in sperm counts.

But before we go dizzy on cleverness, let's pull out Occam's razor and consider a simple possibility: maybe our boys are doing better because we're paying them more attention. We're providing for them better; the proportion of children living in poverty is down roughly 2% from a spike in 1993. And we're giving them more time. Parents—both fathers and mothers—are reordering their priorities to focus on caring for their kids. Several studies confirm this. Sociologists at the University of Michigan have tracked a sharp increase in the amount of time men spend with their children since the 1970s. Another long-range survey, reported by University of Maryland researchers, has asked parents since the 1960s to keep detailed diaries of their daily activities. In 1965 child-focused care occupied about 13 hours per week, the vast majority of it done by moms. By 1985 that had dropped to 11 hours per week as moms entered the workforce. The 2005 study found parents spending 20 hours a week focused on their kids—by far the highest number in the history of the survey. Both moms and dads had dramatically shifted their energies toward their kids.

Are there risks of overparenting boys? Sure. And here's where the success of The Dangerous *Book* gets interesting, because it suggests that as parents spend more time with their sons, we may be reconnecting with the fact that the differences between boys and girls need not be threatening and that not all the lore of the past about how to raise boys was wrong.

32   Gregory Hodge is a good example of this return to tradition. He is principal at the Frederick Douglass Academy, a public school in Harlem. His school was one of three recently honored by the Schott Foundation for excellence in educating black male students—the most troubled cohort but also the group making the greatest progress in many areas. Hodge told me that when he arrived at the combination middle school and high school 11 years ago, the academy was already a great success—but the student body was 80% female. The new principal made it his business to recruit more boys. Today, of the academy's 1,450 mostly poor and minority students, half are male. Yet the dropout rate remains virtually zero, and this year (like most years) every member of the senior class graduated and was college-bound. Every one.

Hodge says the secret is to reach boys before they get into trouble—he uses the academy's basketball facilities to lure youngsters still in grade school. Once you have their attention, you must show them a world of possibilities that you genuinely believe they can achieve. "Young people are looking for validation," he says. "You are important. You will be successful. We don't talk about 'if' you go to college. Around here it's 'when' you go to college."

Frederick Douglass Academy students adhere to a strict dress code and accept rigid discipline. Many of them virtually live at the school, even on Saturdays, doing hours of homework, attending required tutorials if they lag behind, participating in dozens of sports and activities, from basketball to lacrosse and ballet to botany. "Everything a private school would offer a rich kid," Hodge explains. But within this highly structured setting, the school recognizes that many boys need room to learn in their own way. "Some of the kids are hardheaded," Hodge says in a gravelly Bronx roar. "That's what makes a boy. They've gotta experiment, learn the hard way that his head won't break concrete. Male students tend to want to find things out for themselves—so why don't you use that as a teacher?

"I once had about 15 boys very close to dropping out," the principal continues. "They weren't into sports. I had to find something for them to get into. Finally I made a recording studio for the little meatheads, and they ran with that. All of them made it through to graduation. I'll try anything—dance, chess, hydroponics, robotics—anything to let these kids know that this is a world they can fit into, where they can be successful."

The Basics of Boyhood

36   Nothing Hodge says is remotely ground-breaking or experimental—and that's precisely the point. Only in recent decades have societies seriously begun to unlock the full potential of girls, but the cultivation of boys has been an obsession for thousands of years. "How shall we find a gentle nature which also has a great spirit?" Socrates asked some 2,500 years ago—essentially the same question parents ask today.

Ours is far from the first society to fear for its sons. Leo Braudy of the University of Southern California, in his 2003 book *From Chivalry to Terrorism,* noted recurring waves of anxiety. Europeans of the 18th century imagined that free trade and the death of feudalism would spell the end of honor and chivalry. Then, with the dawn of the Industrial Age, writers like John Stuart Mill worried that progress itself—with its speed and stress and short attention spans—would cause a sort of "moral effeminacy" and "inaptitude for every kind of struggle." By the end of the 19th century, a manhood malaise permeated the entire Western world: in France it inspired Pierre de Coubertin to create the Olympic movement; in Britain it moved Robert Baden-Powell to found the Boy Scouts; in the U.S. it fueled a passion for the new sport of football and helped make a hero of rough-riding Theodore Roosevelt.

All these reforms shared a common impulse to return to the basics of boyhood—quests, competitions, tribal brotherhoods and self-discovery. There was a recognition that the keys to building a successful boy have remained remarkably consistent, whether a tribal chieftain is preparing a young warrior or a knight is training a squire or a craftsman is guiding an apprentice—or Gregory Hodge is teaching his students. Boys need mentors and structure but also some freedom to experiment. They need a group to belong to and an opponent to confront. As Gurian put it in *The Wonder of Boys,* they must "compete and perform well to feel worthy."

The success of *The Dangerous Book for Boys* is one sign of a society getting in touch with these venerable truths. Nothing in the book suggests that boys are better than girls, nor does the book license destructive aggression. But it does exude the confidence of ages past that boys are to be treasured, not cured. "Is it old-fashioned?" the authors ask themselves about their book. "Well, that depends. Men and boys today are the same as they always were . . . You want to be self-sufficient and find your way by the stars."

A Trip to Boy Heaven

40   If *The Dangerous Book* were a place, it would look like the Falling Creek Camp for Boys in North Carolina—a rustic paradise complete with a rifle range, nearby mountains to climb and a lake complete with swimming dock and rope swing. The choice of activities at the camp is dizzying, from soccer to blacksmithing, from kayaking to watercolors, but no pastime is more popular than building forts of fallen tree limbs and poking at turtles in the creek. Leave your cell phones, laptops and iPods at home.

There I met Margaret Anderson, a pediatric nurse from Nashville and a member of the faculty at Vanderbilt University. She works in the infirmary while her 11-year-old son Gage discovers the woods on multi-day pack trips. "I call this place Boy Heaven," she says.

Falling Creek subscribes to a philosophy of "structured freedom," which is essentially the same philosophy paying dividends among boys at the opposite end of the economic ladder at the Frederick Douglass Academy. It works across the board, says Anderson, and she wishes more of the boys she sees in her busy Nashville practice lived lives of structured freedom too.

"Whether it's urban kids who can't go outside because it's too dangerous or the overscheduled, overparented kids at the other end of the spectrum—I'm worried that boys have lost the chance to play and to explore," Anderson told me. Our society takes a dim view of idle time and casts a skeptical eye on free play—play driven by a boy's curiosity rather than the league schedule or the folks at Nintendo. But listen to Anderson as she lists the virtues of letting boys run themselves occasionally.

44   "When no one's looming over them, they begin making choices of their own," she says. "They discover consequences and learn to take responsibility for themselves and their emotions. They start learning self-discipline, self-confidence, team building. If we don't let kids work through their own problems, we get a generation of whiners."

That made sense to me. As I watched the boys at Falling Creek do things that would scare me to death if my own son were doing them—hammering white-hot pieces of metal, clinging to a zip line two stories above a lake, examining native rattlesnakes—I didn't notice many whining boys. Yates Pharr, director of Falling Creek, seemed to read my mind. "It's the parents who have the anxieties nowadays, far more than the boys," he said. "We've started posting photographs of each day's activity on our website, and still I'll get complaints if we don't have a picture of every camper every day."

Worrying about our boys—reading and writing books about them, wringing our hands over dire trends and especially taking more time to parent them—is paying off. The next step is to let them really blossom, and for that we have to trust them, give them room. The time for fearing our sons, or fearing for their futures, is behind us. The challenge now is to believe in them.

PERSONAL RESPONSE

Explain whether your experience and observation support Von Drehle's comments about how boys are being raised today.

QUESTIONS FOR CLASS OR SMALL-GROUP DISCUSSION

1. How does Von Drehle's opening paragraphs about his sign relate to the rest of the essay?
2. State in your own words what "the myth about boys" is.
3. Von Drehle says of reading "America's Children: Key National Indicators of Well-Being, 2007" that, while "there's real substance to the boy crisis" (paragraph 15), "there's more to the story" (18). What do you understand him to mean by that?
4. In the section labeled "So Where Did We go Right?," what conclusions does Von Drehle reach?

SACRED RITE OR CIVIL RIGHT?

Howard Moody

Howard Moody, minister emeritus of Judson Memorial Church in New York City, is often referred to as the Harriet Tubman of the abortion rights movement. Author of several books, including two with Arlene Carmen on abortion rights and prostitution and a collection of his essays, The God-Man of Galilee: Studies in Christian Living *(1983), he lectures, preaches, and writes often on issues of ethics and social policy. "Sacred Rite or Civil Right?" was first published in the July 5, 2004, issue of the* Nation.

If members of the church that I served for more than three decades were told I would be writing an article in defense of marriage, they wouldn't believe it. My reputation was that when people came to me for counsel about getting married, I tried to talk them out of it. More about that later.

We are now in the midst of a national debate on the nature of marriage, and it promises to be as emotional and polemical as the issues of abortion and homosexuality have been over the past century. What all these debates have in common is that they involved both the laws of the state and the theology of the church. The purpose of this writing is to suggest that the gay-marriage debate is less about the legitimacy of the loving relationship of a same-sex couple than about the relationship of church and state and how they define marriage.

In Western civilization, the faith and beliefs of Christendom played a major role in shaping the laws regarding social relations and moral behavior. Having been nurtured in the Christian faith from childhood and having served a lifetime as an ordained Baptist minister, I feel obligated first to address the religious controversy concerning the nature of marriage. If we look at the history of religious institutions regarding marriage we will find not much unanimity but amazing diversity—it is really a mixed bag. Those who base their position on "tradition" or "what the Bible says" will find anything but clarity. It depends on which "tradition" in what age reading from whose holy scriptures.

4   In the early tradition of the Jewish people, there were multiple wives and not all of them equal. Remember the story of Abraham's wives, Sara and Hagar. Sara couldn't get pregnant, so Hagar presented Abraham with a son. When Sara got angry with Hagar, she forced Abraham to send Hagar and her son Ishmael into the wilderness. In case Christians feel superior about their "tradition" of marriage, I would remind them that their scriptural basis is not as clear about marriage as we might hope. We have Saint Paul's conflicting and condescending words about the institution: "It's better not to marry." Karl Barth called this passage the Magna Carta of the single person. (Maybe we should have taken Saint Paul's advice more seriously. It might have prevented an earlier generation of parents from harassing, cajoling and prodding our young until they were married.) In certain religious branches, the church doesn't recognize the licensed legality of marriage but requires that persons meet certain religious qualifications before the marriage is recognized by the church. For members of the Roman Catholic Church, a "legal divorce" and the right to remarry may not be recognized unless the first marriage has been declared null and void by a decree of the church. It is clear that there is no single religious view of marriage and that history has witnessed some monumental changes in the way "husband and wife" are seen in the relationship of marriage.

In my faith-based understanding, if freedom of choice means anything to individuals (male or female), it means they have several options. They can be single and celibate without being thought of as strange or psychologically unbalanced. They can be single and sexually active without being labeled loose or immoral. Women can be single with child without being thought of as unfit or inadequate. If these choices had been real options, the divorce rate may never have reached nearly 50 percent.

The other, equally significant choice for people to make is that of lifetime commitment to each other and to seal that desire in the vows of a wedding ceremony. That understanding of marriage came out of my community of faith. In my years of ministry I ran a tight ship in regard to the performance of weddings. It wasn't because I didn't believe in marriage (I've been married for sixty years and have two wonderful offspring) but rather my unease about the way marriage was used to force people to marry so they wouldn't be "living in sin."

The failure of the institution can be seen in divorce statistics. I wanted people to know how challenging the promise of those vows was and not to feel this was something they had to do. My first question in premarital counseling was, "Why do you want to get married and spoil a beautiful friendship?" That question often elicited a thoughtful and emotional answer. Though I was miserly in the number of weddings I performed, I always made exceptions when there were couples who had difficulty finding clergy who would officiate. Their difficulty was because they weren't of the same religion, or they had made marital mistakes, or what they couldn't believe. Most of them were "ecclesiastical outlaws," barred from certain sacraments in the church of their choice.

8   The church I served had a number of gay and lesbian couples who had been together for many years, but none of them had asked for public weddings or blessings on their relationship. (There was one commitment ceremony for a gay couple at the end of my tenure.) It was as though they didn't need a piece of paper or a ritual to symbolize their lifelong commitment. They knew if they wanted a religious ceremony, their ministers would officiate and our religious community would joyfully witness.

It was my hope that since the institution of marriage had been used to exclude and demean members of the homosexual community, our church, which was open and affirming, would create with gays and lesbians a new kind of ceremony. It would be an occasion that symbolized, between two people of the same gender, a covenant of intimacy of two people to journey together, breaking new ground in human relationships—an alternative to marriage as we have known it.

However, I can understand why homosexuals want "to be married" in the old fashioned "heterosexual way." After all, most gays and lesbians were born of married parents, raised in a family of siblings; many were nourished in churches and synagogues, taught about a living God before Whom all Her creatures were equally loved. Why wouldn't they conceive their loving relationships in terms of marriage and family and desire that they be confirmed and understood as such? It follows that if these gays and lesbians see their relationship as faith-based, they would want a religious ceremony that seals their intentions to become lifelong partners, lovers and friends, that they would want to be "married."

Even though most religious denominations deny this ceremony to homosexual couples, more and more clergy are, silently and publicly, officiating at religious rituals in which gays and lesbians declare their vows before God and a faith community. One Catholic priest who defied his church's ban said: "We can bless a dog, we can bless a boat, but we can't say a prayer over two people who love each other. You don't have to call it marriage, you can call it a deep and abiding friendship, but you can bless it."

12   We have the right to engage in "religious disobedience" to the regulations of the judicatory that granted us the privilege to officiate at wedding ceremonies, and suffer the consequences. However, when it comes to civil law, it is my contention that the church and its clergy are on much shakier ground in defying the law.

In order to fully understand the conflict that has arisen in this debate over the nature of marriage, it is important to understand the difference between the religious definition of marriage and the state's secular and civil definition. The government's interest is in a legal definition of marriage—a social and voluntary contract between a man and woman in order to protect money, property and children. Marriage is a civil union without benefit of clergy or religious definition. The state is not interested in why two people are "tying the knot," whether it's to gain money, secure a dynasty or raise children. It may be hard for those of us who have a religious or romantic view of marriage to realize that loveless marriages are not that rare. Before the Pill, pregnancy was a frequent motive for getting married. The state doesn't care what the commitment of two people is, whether it's for life or as long as both of you love, whether it's sexually monogamous or an open marriage. There is nothing spiritual, mystical or romantic about the state's license to marry—it's a legal contract.

Thus, George W. Bush is right when he says that "marriage is a sacred institution" when speaking as a Christian, as a member of his Methodist church. But as President of the United States and leader of all Americans, believers and unbelievers, he is wrong. What will surface in this debate as litigation and court decisions multiply is the history of the conflict between the church and the state in defining the nature of marriage. That history will become significant as we move toward a decision on who may be married.

After Christianity became the state religion of the Roman Empire in AD 325, the church maintained absolute control over the regulation of marriage for some 1,000 years. Beginning in the sixteenth century, English kings (especially Henry VIII, who found the inability to get rid of a wife extremely oppressive) and other monarchs in Europe began to wrest control from the church over marital regulations. Ever since, kings, presidents and rulers of all kinds have seen how important the control of marriage is to the regulation of social order. In this nation, the government has always been in charge of marriage.

16   That is why it was not a San Francisco mayor licensing same-sex couples that really threatened the President's religious understanding of marriage but rather the Supreme Judicial Court of Massachusetts; declaring marriage between same-sex couples a constitutional right, that demanded a call for constitutional amendment. I didn't understand how important that was until I read an op-ed piece in the *Boston Globe* by Peter Gomes, professor of Christian morals and the minister of Memorial Church at Harvard University, that reminds us of a seminal piece of our history:

> The Dutch made civil marriage the law of the land in 1590, and the first marriage in New England, that of Edward Winslow to the widow Susannah White, was performed on May 12, 1621, in Plymouth by Governor William Bradford, in exercise of his office as magistrate.
>
> There would be no clergyman in Plymouth until the arrival of the Rev. Ralph Smith in 1629, but even then marriage would continue to be a civil affair, as these first Puritans opposed the English custom of clerical marriage as unscriptural. Not until 1692, when Plymouth Colony was merged into that of Massachusetts Bay, were the Clergy authorized by the new province to solemnize marriages. To this day in the Commonwealth the clergy, including those of the archdiocese, solemnize marriage legally as agents of the Commonwealth and by its civil authority. Chapter 207 of the General Laws of Massachusetts tells us who may perform such ceremonies.

Now even though it is the civil authority of the state that defines the rights and responsibilities of marriage and therefore who can be married, the state is no more infallible than the church in its judgments. It wasn't until the mid-twentieth century that the Supreme Court declared anti-miscegenation laws unconstitutional.

Even after that decision, many mainline churches, where I started my ministry, unofficially discouraged interracial marriages, and many of my colleagues were forbidden to perform such weddings.

The civil law view of marriage has as much historical diversity as the church's own experience because, in part, the church continued to influence the civil law. Although it was the Bible that made "the husband the head of his wife," it was common law that "turned the married pair legally into one person—the husband," as Nancy Cott documents in her book *Public Vows: A History of Marriage and the Nation* (an indispensable resource for anyone seeking to understand the changing nature of marriage in the nation's history). She suggests that "the legal doctrine of marital unity was called coverture . . . [which] meant that the wife could not use legal avenues such as suits or contracts, own assets, or execute legal documents without her husband's collaboration." This view of the wife would not hold water in any court in the land today.

As a matter of fact, even in the religious understanding of President Bush and his followers, allowing same-sex couples the right to marry seems a logical conclusion. If marriage is "the most fundamental institution of civilization" and a major contributor to the social order in our society, why would anyone want to shut out homosexuals from the "glorious attributes" of this "sacred institution"? Obviously, the only reason one can discern is that the opponents believe that gay and lesbian people are not worthy of the benefits and spiritual blessings of "marriage."

At the heart of the controversy raging over same-sex marriage is the religious and constitutional principle of the separation of church and state. All of us can probably agree that there was never a solid wall of separation, riddled as it is with breaches. The evidence of that is seen in the ambiguity of tax-free religious institutions, "in God we trust" printed on our money and "under God" in the Pledge of Allegiance to our country. All of us clergy, who are granted permission by the state to officiate at legal marriage ceremonies, have already compromised the "solid wall" by signing the license issued by the state. I would like to believe that my authority to perform religious ceremonies does not come from the state but derives from the vows of ordination and my commitment to God. I refuse to repeat the words, "by the authority invested in me by the State of New York, I pronounce you husband and wife," but by signing the license, I've become the state's "handmaiden."

20   It seems fitting therefore that we religious folk should now seek to sharpen the difference between ecclesiastical law and civil law as we beseech the state to clarify who can be married by civil law. Further evidence that the issue of church and state is part of the gay-marriage controversy is that two Unitarian ministers have been arrested for solemnizing unions between same-sex couples when no state licenses were involved. Ecclesiastical law may punish those clergy who disobey marital regulations, but the state has no right to invade church practices and criminalize clergy under civil law. There should have been a noisy outcry from all churches, synagogues and mosques at the government's outrageous contravention of the sacred principle of the "free exercise of religion."

I come from a long line of Protestants who believe in "a free church in a free state." In the issue before this nation, the civil law is the determinant of the regulation of marriage, regardless of our religious views, and the Supreme Court will finally decide what the principle of equality means in our Constitution in the third century of our life together as a people. It is likely that the Commonwealth of Massachusetts will probably lead the nation on this matter, as the State of New York led to the Supreme Court decision to allow women reproductive freedom.

So what is marriage? It depends on whom you ask, in what era, in what culture. Like all words or institutions, human definitions, whether religious or secular, change with time and history. When our beloved Constitution was written, blacks, Native Americans and, to some extent, women were quasi-human beings with no rights or privileges, but today they are recognized as persons with full citizenship rights. The definition of marriage has been changing over the centuries in this nation, and it will change yet again as homosexuals are seen as ordinary human beings.

In time, and I believe that time is now, we Americans will see that all the fears foisted on us by religious zealots were not real. Heterosexual marriage will still flourish with its statistical failures. The only difference will be that some homosexual couples will join them and probably account for about the same number of failed relationships. And we will discover that it did not matter whether the couples were joined in a religious ceremony or a secular and civil occasion for the statement of their intentions.

PERSONAL RESPONSE

Explain whether you believe that the issue of how marriage is defined by church and state is relevant to the issue of same-sex marriage.

QUESTIONS FOR CLASS OR SMALL-GROUP DISCUSSION

1. Locate Moody's central purpose and discuss whether you are persuaded that his position is valid.

2. What distinctions does Moody draw between the state's definition of marriage and that of the church?

3. To what extent are you convinced that "the state has no right to invade church practices and criminalize clergy under civil law" (paragraph 20)?

4. How would you answer the question, "So what is marriage?" (paragraph 22)?

DECONSTRUCTING GENDER, SEX, AND SEXUALITY AS APPLIED TO IDENTITY

WHITNEY MITCHELL

Whitney Mitchell of Nashville, Tennessee, received honorable mention in the thirteen-to-seventeen-year-old age category of the 2001 Humanist Essay Contest for Young Women and Men of North

*America for this essay. It was published in the July–August 2002 issue
of the* Humanist, *a social issues–oriented bimonthly that applies the
philosophy of Humanism to current matters of concern.*

By nature, we as humans have a need to identify ourselves and others in broad
and exclusionary/inclusionary terms. But then, "human nature" is actually nothing more than human habit. Every set of standards that we as a society currently
use to identify ourselves is coupled with an opposing set: good versus bad, female
versus male, hetero versus homo. This system of duality in the everyday assessment
of ourselves and those around us holds the power to rob individuals of their dignity
as human beings.

What we must understand is that, just because an individual doesn't fit one set
of standards, the individual doesn't then automatically fit the opposite standards.
Specifically, the female/male binary is constructed as a natural occurrence and pre-
sumed to be unchangeable. However, intersexuality, by definition, offers clear evidence to the contrary. It serves as an opportunity to disprove the concepts of what
is "natural" and to disrupt the hetero-normative systems of sex, gender, and sexuality. It presents the possibility of proving gender to be nothing more than something
abstract and conceptual. Analyzing intersexuality therefore provides greater opportunities for individual liberty and social understanding.

Gender, as it stands, is currently defined by society in the simplest terms of
female and male. However, gender only exists because our society, consciously or
unconsciously, wills it to. What makes a woman is her specific social relation to a
man, and what makes a man is his specific social relation to a woman. To refuse to
be a woman, however, doesn't mean that one becomes a man. It only means that
one refuses one's designated ideological, political, and economic characteristics as
identity and thus refuses gender.

4   Therefore, if the class of "man" were to disappear, if it were no longer used, then
the same would occur with the class of "woman." Gender would no longer be able
to leave anyone behind, condemning them as sick or mentally ill for not fitting our
standards. (Transgender identity and expression are the psychiatric classification
under the Diagnostic Codes 302.3, transvestic fetishism; and 302.85, gender identity disorder.) Identity could exist independently of gender. However, because we
continue to use gender classifications, people who don't identify with such labels are
left in a state of confusion, with no language to use in claiming their own identities.

Our society commonly uses the equation gender = sex. This is a naive and
oversimplified statement. It further categorizes individuals by way of black-and-
white, unrealistic standards. It is difficult for most people to understand that
individuals exist who identify as men with vaginas and women with penises. Therefore gender and sex aren't interchangeable terms. The difference is as simple as
that between the mind and the body. Where gender is a device used for identification
of the mind and emotions, sex is about biology and comfort within one's own body.

Here the concept of gender as changeable and subjective raises questions about
sex reassignment surgery (SRS). However, just as the assumption that gender is the
same as sex is naive, so is the assumption that a change in gender requires a change

in sex as well. An individual born biologically female who, gender-wise, only feels comfortable identifying as male, doesn't necessarily desire SRS in order to become physically male. The individual's body could feel completely comfortable and right despite a discomfort with gender. Therefore the gender that an individual identifies with doesn't always indicate any information regarding the sex of the individual's body. This realization provides an alternative way of seeing individuals independent of society's standards.

By the same token, gender doesn't always indicate any information about an individual's sexuality. The existence of transgendered individuals and transsexual individuals promotes confusion regarding sexuality. Any speculation about the sexual orientation of a trans-individual is as ignorant as the speculation of the sexual orientation of any individual. Just as any individual identifying as male might be attracted to males or females, an individual having had male-to-female SRS may be attracted to males or females. Identification of sexual orientation occurs independently of gender or sex identification, despite whether such identifications change from those assigned at birth. Thus, gender identity is about comfort or discomfort within the established gender roles of society. Sex identity is about comfort within the body. And identification of sexual orientation is more about experiences outside of the self and the body; it isn't about comfort so much as it is about individual desire and attraction.

8   Now that we've clarified the differences between gender, sex, and sexuality, it is obvious why these terms are inefficient for identifying people. They tell us nothing about a person because they are all noninclusive concepts created by humans out of convenience and discomfort. Personally, I've found that the less I use these terms to identify myself, the more comfortable with myself I become and the less I feel the need to identify at all. Thus, not really identifying with any current social role allows for a new liberation uninhibited by the standards of others. As the poet Eileen Myles said: "If we don't define who we are, we are everything. Once we define ourselves, we are nothing."

PERSONAL RESPONSE

Did your parents or care givers treat you differently on the basis of your sex? Were you assigned a "gender identity" that you were comfortable with?

QUESTIONS FOR CLASS OR SMALL-GROUP DISCUSSION

1. What assumptions about the traditional definitions of sex, gender, and sexuality does Mitchell object to?

2. In the conclusion, Mitchell writes that "it is obvious why these terms [gender, sex, and sexuality] are inefficient for identifying people." Is it clear to you? Has Mitchell fully clarified that the differences among those three terms clearly demonstrated their inefficiency for identifying people? Does Mitchell's use of the abstract concept "comfort" to distinguish among those terms help clarify those definitions for you?

3. Do you think it possible for any society, but especially American society, to do away with assigning sex roles? How possible do you think it would be to raise a child not to be conscious of gender? What advantages and disadvantages do you see in having a "genderless" society?

○ PERSPECTIVES ON GENDER AND SEX ROLES ○

Suggested Writing Topics

1. Read any of the books that Megan Rosenfeld mentions in "Reexamining the Plight of Young Males" or that David Von Drehle mentions in "The Myth about Boys" and write a critique of it.

2. Define "marriage," taking into account Howard Moody's article "Sacred Rite or Civil Right?"

3. Write an essay defining and distinguishing among the terms "sex," "gender," and "sexuality," as Whitney Mitchell does in "Deconstructing Sex, Gender, and Sexuality as Applied to Identity."

4. Drawing on two or more of the essays in this chapter, write a reflective essay in which you explore your own concepts of masculinity and femininity (and perhaps androgyny) and the way in which that concept has shaped the way you are today.

5. Consider to what degree you think that sex determines destiny.

6. Conduct an investigative analysis of any of the following for their depiction of female and male sex roles: fairy tales, children's stories, advertising images, music videos, television programs, or film. Do you find stereotyped assumptions about masculinity and femininity? In what ways do you think the subject of your analysis reinforces or shapes cultural definitions of masculinity and femininity?

7. Examine media images for the ways in which gays and lesbians are portrayed. Focus on a particular medium, such as print advertisements, television situation comedies, or film.

8. Explore ways in which you would like to see definitions of masculinity and femininity changed. How do you think relationships between the sexes would be affected if those changes were made?

9. Write a personal narrative recounting an experience in which you felt you were being treated unfairly or differently from persons of the other sex. What was the situation, how did you feel, and what did you do about it?

10. Explain the degree to which you consider gender issues to be important. Do you think too much is made of gender? Does it matter whether definitions of masculinity and femininity are rigid?

11. Argue the case for or against same-sex marriage to an audience of judges sitting on a state's Supreme Court, trying to decide whether to legalize it.

Research Topics

1. Research the history of the contemporary women's movement, the men's movement, or the gay rights movement in America and report on its origins, goals, and influence. You will have to narrow your scope, depending on the time you have for the project and the nature of your purpose.

2. Research the subject of bisexuality, making sure to include differing viewpoints, and then explain your own viewpoint on the topic, supporting your position with relevant source materials.

3. Through research and interviews, write a paper on some aspect of the gay and lesbian experience in America.

4. Research the subject of sex-role stereotyping in books, movies, or other media.

5. Research the shifting views of both the church and the state on marriage. You may want to begin with Nancy Cott's *Public Vows: A History of Marriage and the Nation* that Howard Moody recommends in "Sacred Rite or Civil Right?"

6. Conduct research that seeks to support or refute Megan Rosenfeld's contention that male children "are less able than they need to be to navigate the turmoil of adolescence, to develop healthy adult relationships, in some cases survive at all" ("Reexamining the Plight of Young Males," paragraph 3).

Responding to Visuals

A Marine steadies a child playing with the M60 Maremount machine gun mounted atop an M998 High-mobility Multipurpose Wheeled Vehicle (HMMWV). The vehicle is one of the displays on the pier beside the battleship USS IOWA (BB 61) during Navy Appreciation Week.

1. How do the various components of the photograph contribute to its overall impression? For instance, what is the effect of the position of the American flag?
2. What do the looks on the faces of the man and child contribute to the overall effect?
3. Is there any irony in the contrast between the child and the Marine?

RESPONDING TO VISUALS

© Liz Mangelsdorf/San Francisco Chronicle/CORBIS

These two women, who have been together for 51 years, embrace after their marriage at City Hall. They were the first legally married same-sex couple in San Francisco. Gay marriages were later voided by the California State Supreme Court.

1. What comment does the photographer make by selecting for his subject an older couple who have been together for 51 years?
2. In what way does this photograph get at the heart of the issue of gay marriage?
3. How do the facial expressions and body language of both the married couple and their witnesses reveal the emotional nature of the event?

CHAPTER

16

Race and Ethnicity in America

Racial or ethnic heritage is as important to shaping identity as are sex and social class. One's race or ethnicity can also influence quality of life, educational opportunity, and advancement in employment. American society has a long history of struggling to confront and overcome racism and discrimination on the basis of ethnic heritage. Beginning well before the Civil War, American antislavery groups protested the enslavement of African Americans and worked to abolish slavery in all parts of the country. Other groups besides African Americans have experienced harsh treatment and discrimination solely because of their color or ethnic heritage.

These groups include Chinese men brought to America to help construct a cross-country railroad in the nineteenth century, European immigrants who came to America in large numbers near the end of the nineteenth century in search of better lives than they could expect in their homelands, Japanese men who came in the twentieth century to work at hard labor for money to send home, and Latinos/Latinas and Hispanics migrating north to America. As a result of the heightened awareness of the interplay of race, class, and gender, schools at all levels, from elementary through postgraduate, have incorporated course materials on race, class, and/or gender or created whole courses devoted to those important components of individual identities and histories. The readings in this chapter focus on immigrants and minority groups, particularly African Americans, in a country that still struggles with racial inequities and discrimination.

The chapter begins with the first article in a series by the *Washington Post* on the effects of increases in the numbers of immigrants on American life in the last decade of the twentieth century and in the future. William Booth's "One Nation, Indivisible: Is It History?" contrasts the effects of the first great wave of immigration to America in the period between 1890 and 1920 with the recent second great wave of immigration, as he explores the question of whether America is truly a "melting pot." As you read his article, keep in mind the question posed by its title and consider whether you think, as the writer implies, that the concept of America as a single, indivisible nation is soon to be a matter of history, not fact.

Following Booth's piece, Llewellyn D. Howell in "Ironies of Illegal Immigration" considers several ironies of trying to curb illegal immigration, raising the question of whether such a process is realistically desirable. Noting that immigration is "a complex and dire social problem," Howell wonders whether proposals to regulate and limit it are ignoring the "reality of immigration." Do you agree with the conclusion he reaches, that illegal immigration may in fact be "a good thing"?

Next, Maryann Cusimano Love points out a number of social problems that indicate that America is far from solving its racial problem. In "Race in America: 'We Would Like to Believe We are Over the Problem,'" she takes exception to a statement by a Virginia legislator who believes that "'blacks need to get over' slavery." Finally, Alex Kotlowitz, in "Colorblind," focuses on a specific group, African Americans, in his essay on two towns across the river from one another, "whose only connections are two bridges and a powerful undertow of contrasts." As he researched the circumstances surrounding the death of a black teenager, Kotlowitz discovered a history of racial hostility between the two towns. His interviews with both blacks and whites led him to conclude that only when the members of both groups question their own perspectives can they learn to understand each other. "It's all about perspective," he insists.

ONE NATION, INDIVISIBLE: IS IT HISTORY?

WILLIAM BOOTH

William Booth is a Washington Post *staff writer. This article was the first in a series examining the effects of changing demographics on American life. It appeared in the Sunday, February 22, 1998, issue of the* Washington Post.

At the beginning of this century, as steamers poured into American ports, their steerages filled with European immigrants, a Jew from England named Israel Zangwill penned a play whose story line has long been forgotten, but whose central theme has not. His production was entitled "The Melting Pot" and its message still holds a tremendous power on the national imagination—the promise that all immigrants can be transformed into Americans, a new alloy forged in a crucible of democracy, freedom, and civic responsibility. In 1908, when the play opened in Washington, the United States was in the middle of absorbing the largest influx of immigrants in its history—Irish and Germans, followed by Italians and East Europeans, Catholics and Jews—some eighteen million new citizens between 1890 and 1920.

Today, the United States is experiencing its second great wave of immigration, a movement of people that has profound implications for a society that by tradition pays homage to its immigrant roots at the same time it confronts complex and deeply ingrained ethnic and racial divisions. The immigrants of today come not from Europe but overwhelmingly from the still developing world of Asia and Latin America. They are driving a demographic shift so rapid that within the lifetimes of today's teenagers, no one ethnic group—including whites of European descent—will comprise a majority of the nation's population.

This shift, according to social historians, demographers, and others studying the trends, will severely test the premise of the fabled melting pot, the idea, so central to national identity, that this country can transform people of every color and background into "one America." Just as possible, they say, is that the nation will continue to fracture into many separate, disconnected communities with no shared sense of commonality or purpose. Or perhaps it will evolve into something in between, a pluralistic society that will hold onto some core ideas about citizenship and capitalism, but with little meaningful interaction among groups.

4   The demographic changes raise other questions about political and economic power. Will that power, now held disproportionately by whites, be shared in the new America? What will happen when Hispanics overtake blacks as the nation's single largest minority? "I do not think that most Americans really understand the historic changes happening before their very eyes," said Peter Salins, an

immigration scholar who is provost of the State Universities of New York. "What are we going to become? Who are we? How do the newcomers fit in—and how do the natives handle it—this is the great unknown."

Fear of strangers, of course, is nothing new in American history. The last great immigration wave produced a bitter backlash, epitomized by the Chinese Exclusion Act of 1882 and the return, in the 1920s, of the Ku Klux Klan, which not only targeted blacks, but Catholics, Jews, and immigrants, as well. But despite this strife, many historians argue that there was a greater consensus in the past on what it meant to be an American, a yearning for a common language and culture, and a desire—encouraged, if not coerced by members of the dominant white Protestant culture—to assimilate. Today, they say, there is more emphasis on preserving one's ethnic identity, of finding ways to highlight and defend one's cultural roots.

Difficult to Measure

More often than not, the neighborhoods where Americans live, the politicians and propositions they vote for, the cultures they immerse themselves in, the friends and spouses they have, the churches and schools they attend, and the way they view themselves are defined by ethnicity. The question is whether, in the midst of such change, there is also enough glue to hold Americans together. Black community activist Nathaniel J. Wilcox in Miami says, "Hispanics don't want some of the power, they want all the power." "As we become more and more diverse, there is all this potential to make that reality work for us," said Angela Oh, a Korean American activist who emerged as a powerful voice for Asian immigrants after the Los Angeles riots in 1992. "But yet, you witness this persistence of segregation, the fragmentation, all these fights over resources, this finger-pointing. You would have to be blind not to see it."

It is a phenomenon sometimes difficult to measure, but not observe. Houses of worship remain, as the Rev. Martin Luther King Jr. described it three decades ago, among the most segregated institutions in America, not just by race but also ethnicity. At high school cafeterias, the second and third generation children of immigrants clump together in cliques defined by where their parents or grandparents were born. There are television sit-coms, talk shows, and movies that are considered black or white, Latino or Asian. At a place like the law school of the University of California at Los Angeles, which has about one thousand students, there are separate student associations for blacks, Latinos, and Asians with their own law review journals.

8   It almost goes without saying that today's new arrivals are a source of vitality and energy, especially in the big cities to which many are attracted. Diversity, almost everyone agrees, is good; choice is good; exposure to different cultures and ideas is good. But many scholars worry about the loss of community and shared sense of reality among Americans, what Todd Gitlin, a professor of culture and communications at New York University, calls "the twilight of common dreams." The concern is echoed by many on both the left and the right, and of all ethnicities, but no one seems to know exactly what to do about it.

Academics who examine the census data and probe for meaning in the numbers already speak of a new "demographic balkanization," not only of residential segregation, forced or chosen, but also of a powerful preference to see ourselves through a racial prism, wary of others, and, in many instances, hostile. At a recent school board meeting in East Palo Alto, California, police had to break up a fight between Latinos and blacks, who were arguing over the merits and expense of bilingual education in a school district that has shifted over the past few years from majority African American to majority Hispanic. One parent told reporters that if the Hispanics wanted to learn Spanish they should stay in Mexico.

The demographic shifts are smudging the old lines demarcating two historical, often distinct societies, one black and one white. Reshaped by three decades of rapidly rising immigration, the national story is now far more complicated. Whites currently account for 74 percent of the population, blacks 12 percent, Hispanics 10 percent, and Asians 3 percent. Yet according to data and predictions generated by the U.S. Census Bureau and social scientists poring over the numbers, Hispanics will likely surpass blacks early in the next century. And by the year 2050, demographers predict, Hispanics will account for 25 percent of the population, blacks 14 percent, Asians 8 percent, with whites hovering somewhere around 53 percent. As early as next year, whites will no longer be the majority in California; in Hawaii and New Mexico this is already the case. Soon after, Nevada, Texas, Maryland, and New Jersey are also predicted to become "majority minority" states, entities where no one ethnic group remains the majority.

Effects of 1965 Law

The overwhelming majority of immigrants come from Asia and Latin America—Mexico, the Central American countries, the Philippines, Korea, and Southeast Asia. What triggered this great transformation was a change to immigration law in 1965, when Congress made family reunification the primary criterion for admittance. That new policy, a response to charges that the law favored white Europeans, allowed immigrants already in the United States to bring over their relatives, who in turn could bring over more relatives. As a result, America has been absorbing as many as one million newcomers a year, to the point that now almost one in every ten residents is foreign born. These numbers, relative to the overall population, were slightly higher at the beginning of this century, but the current immigration wave is in many ways very different, and its context inexorably altered, from the last great wave.

12   This time around tensions are sharpened by the changing profile of those who are entering America's borders. Not only are their racial and ethnic backgrounds more varied than in decades past, their place in a modern postindustrial economy has been recast. The newly arrived today can be roughly divided into two camps: those with college degrees and highly specialized skills, and those with almost no education or job training. Some 12 percent of immigrants have graduate degrees, compared to 8 percent of Native Americans. But more than one-third of the immigrants have no high school diploma, double the rate for those born in the United States. Before 1970, immigrants were actually doing better than natives overall, as

measured by education, rate of home ownership, and average income. But those arriving after 1970 are younger, more likely to be underemployed, and live below the poverty level. As a group, they are doing worse than natives. About 6 percent of new arrivals receive some form of welfare, double the rate for U.S.-born citizens. Among some newcomers—Cambodians and Salvadorans, for example—the numbers are even higher.

With large numbers of immigrants arriving from Latin America, and segregating in barrios, there is also evidence of lingering language problems. Consider that in Miami, three-quarters of residents speak a language other than English at home, and 67 percent of those say that they are not fluent in English. In New York City, four of every ten residents speak a language other than English at home, and of these, half said they do not speak English well.

It is clear that not all of America is experiencing the impact of immigration equally. Although even small midwestern cities have seen sharp changes in their racial and ethnic mix in the past two decades, most immigrants continue to cluster into a handful of large, mostly coastal metropolitan areas: Los Angeles, New York, San Francisco, Chicago, Miami, Washington, D.C., and Houston. They are home to more than a quarter of the total U.S. population and more than 60 percent of all foreign-born residents. But as the immigrants arrive, many American-born citizens pour out of these cities in search of new homes in more homogeneous locales. New York and Los Angeles each lost more than one million native-born residents between 1990 and 1995, even as their populations increased by roughly the same numbers with immigrants. To oversimplify, said University of Michigan demographer William Frey, "For every Mexican who comes to Los Angeles, a white native-born leaves."

Most of the people leaving the big cities are white, and they tend to be working class. This is an entirely new kind of "white flight," whereby whites are not just fleeing the city centers for the suburbs but also are leaving the region and often the state. "The Ozzies and Harriets of the 1990s are skipping the suburbs of the big cities and moving to more homogeneous, mostly white smaller towns and smaller cities and rural areas," Frey said. They're headed to Atlanta, Las Vegas, Phoenix, Portland, Denver, Austin, and Orlando, as well as smaller cities in Nevada, Idaho, Colorado, and Washington. Frey and other demographers believe the domestic migrants— black and white—are being "pushed" out, at least in part, by competition with immigrants for jobs and neighborhoods, political clout and lifestyle. Frey sees in this pattern "the emergence of separate Americas, one white and middle-aged, less urban and another intensely urban, young, multicultural, and multiethnic. One America will care deeply about English as the official language and about preserving social security. The other will care about things like retaining affirmative action and bilingual education."

Ethnic Segregation

16   Even within gateway cities that give the outward appearance of being multicultural, there are sharp lines of ethnic segregation. When describing the ethnic diversity of a bellwether megacity such as Los Angeles, many residents speak roaringly of the great mosaic of many peoples. But the social scientists who look at the hard census

data see something more complex. James P. Allen, a cultural geographer at California State University–Northridge, suggests that while Los Angeles, as seen from an airplane, is a tremendously mixed society, on the ground, racial homogeneity and segregation are common. This is not a new phenomenon; there have always been immigrant neighborhoods. Ben Franklin, an early proponent of making English the official language, worried about close-knit German communities. Sen. Daniel Patrick Moynihan (D–N.Y.) described the lingering clannishness of Irish and other immigrant populations in New York in *Beyond the Melting Pot,* a benchmark work from the 1960s that he wrote with Nathan Glazer.

But the persistence of ethnic enclaves and identification does not appear to be going away and may not in a country that is now home to not a few distinct ethnic groups, but to dozens. Hispanics in Los Angeles, to take the dominant group in the nation's second largest city, are more segregated residentially in 1990 than they were ten or twenty years ago, the census tracts show. Moreover, it is possible that what mixing of groups that does occur is only a temporary phenomenon as one ethnic group supplants another in the neighborhood.

If there is deep-seated ethnic segregation, it clearly extends to the American workplace. In many cities, researchers find sustained "ethnic niches" in the labor market. Because jobs are often a matter of whom one knows, the niches were enduring and remarkably resistant to outsiders. In California, for example, Mexican immigrants are employed overwhelmingly as gardeners and domestics, in apparel and furniture manufacturing, and as cooks and food preparers. Koreans open small businesses. Filipinos become nurses and medical technicians. African Americans work in government jobs, an important niche that is increasingly being challenged by Hispanics who want in.

UCLA's Roger Waldinger and others have pointed to the creation, in cities of high immigration, of "dual economies." For the affluent, which includes a disproportionate number of whites, the large labor pool provides them with a ready supply of gardeners, maids, and nannies. For businesses in need of cheap manpower, the same is true. Yet there are fewer "transitional" jobs—the blue-collar work that helped Italian and Irish immigrants move up the economic ladder—to help newcomers or their children on their way to the jobs requiring advanced technical or professional skills that now dominate the upper tier of the economy.

A Rung at a Time

20 Traditionally, immigration scholars have seen the phenomenon of assimilation as a relentless economic progression. The hard-working new arrivals struggle along with a new language and at low-paying jobs in order for their sons and daughters to climb the economic ladder, each generation advancing a rung. There are many cases where this is true. More recently, there is evidence to suggest that economic movement is erratic and that some groups—particularly in high immigration cities—can get "stuck." Among African Americans, for instance, there emerge two distinct patterns. The black middle class is doing demonstrably better—in income, home ownership rates, education—than it was when the demographic transformation (and the civil rights movement) began three decades ago. But for African

Americans at the bottom, research indicates that immigration, particularly of Latinos with limited education, has increased joblessness and frustration.

In Miami, where Cuban immigrants dominate the political landscape, tensions are high between Hispanics and blacks, said Nathaniel J. Wilcox, a community activist there. "The perception in the black community, the reality, is that Hispanics don't want some of the power, they want all the power," Wilcox said. "At least when we were going through this with the whites during the Jim Crow era, at least they'd hire us. But Hispanics won't allow African Americans to even compete. They have this feeling that their community is the only community that counts."

Yet many Hispanics too find themselves in an economic "mobility trap." While the new immigrants are willing to work in low-end jobs, their sons and daughters, growing up in the barrios but exposed to the relentless consumerism of popular culture, have greater expectations, but are disadvantaged because of their impoverished settings, particularly the overwhelmed inner-city schools most immigrant children attend. "One doubts that a truck-driving future will satisfy today's servants and assemblers. And this scenario gets a good deal more pessimistic if the region's economy fails to deliver or simply throws up more bad jobs," writes Waldinger, a professor of sociology and director of center for regional policy studies at the University of California–Los Angeles.

Though there are calls to revive efforts to encourage "Americanization" of the newcomers, many researchers now express doubt that the old assimilation model works. For one thing, there is less of a dominant mainstream to enter. Instead, there are a dozen streams, despite the best efforts by the dominant white society to lump groups together by ethnicity. It is a particularly American phenomenon, many say, to label citizens by their ethnicity. When they lived in El Salvador, for example, they saw themselves as a nationality. When they arrive in the United States, they become Hispanic or Latino. So too with Asians. Koreans and Cambodians find little in common, but when they arrive here they become "Asian," and are counted and courted, encouraged or discriminated against as such. "My family has had trouble understanding that we are now Asians, and not Koreans, or people from Korea or Korean Americans, or just plain Americans," said Arthur Lee, who owns a dry cleaning store in Los Angeles. "Sometimes, we laugh about it. Oh, the Asian students are so smart! The Asians have no interest in politics! Whatever. But we don't know what people are talking about. Who are the Asians?"

24   Many immigrant parents say that while they want their children to advance economically in their new country, they do not want them to become "too American." A common concern among Haitians in South Florida is that their children will adopt the attitudes of the inner city's underclass. Vietnamese parents in New Orleans often try to keep their children immersed in their ethnic enclave and try not to let them assimilate too fast.

Hyphenated Americans

One study of the children of immigrants, conducted six years ago among young Haitians, Cubans, West Indians, Mexicans, and Vietnamese in South Florida and southern California, suggests the parents are not alone in their concerns. Asked by researchers Alejandro Portes and Ruben Rumbauthow how they identified themselves, most chose categories of hyphenated Americans. Few choose "American" as their identity. Then there was this—asked if they believe the United States is the best country in the world, most of the youngsters answered: no.

PERSONAL RESPONSE

Does the fact that many immigrant parents say "they do not want [their children] to become 'too American'" (paragraph 24) surprise you? How important do you consider your race or ethnicity to your identity? Is the neighborhood where you grew up largely composed of a particular racial or ethnic group, or does it have a mixed population?

QUESTIONS FOR CLASS OR SMALL-GROUP DISCUSSION

1. State in your own words what is meant by the terms *melting pot* (paragraphs 1 and 3) and *pluralistic society* (paragraph 3). What does *demographic balkanization* (paragraph 9) mean?

2. How, according to Booth, does the second great wave of immigration differ from the first great wave? What possible effect do social historians and demographers see in this second wave?

3. How has the 1965 immigration law affected American demographics?

4. In what ways, according to Booth, is America still a highly segregated country? Explain whether your own observations and/or experiences support his assertions.

5. Summarize Booth's discussion of terminology for various racial or ethnic groups (paragraphs 23–25). What effect do you think labels or identity markers have on members of those groups?

IRONIES OF ILLEGAL IMMIGRATION

Llewellyn D. Howell

Llewellyn D. Howell, International Affairs Editor of USA Today, *is director and senior research fellow, Asia Pacific Risk Institute, University of Hawaii at Manoa, Honolulu. This article appeared in the July 2006 issue of* USA Today *magazine, a publication of the Society for the Advancement of Education that has no affiliation with the newspaper.*

Pres. George W. Bush's proposal on immigration delivered during his State of the Union address was a political response to a complex and dire social problem. It is social because it has to do with the integration of American society and its continued relatively smooth functioning; dire because there are millions of immigrants in the U.S. who do not have health or automobile insurance or educational support for their children; complex because we not only need these immigrant workers now but, because the economy is doing so well, we will need more of them later. A political response may satisfy some constituent interest groups, but it does not address the reality of immigration.

Let's face the facts on immigration, legal or otherwise. First, the U.S. is going to have more immigrants. America's history is built on regular infusions of new labor, skills, and thinking. Immigrants are an infusion of fresh blood. Simply accommodating ourselves to the process of arriving peoples keeps us in touch with the diversity of cultures that make up the global mosaic.

Second, the country needs more immigrants. This is a paradox in the recovery of the Bush Administration economy. Economic growth over the last year has meant that the attractiveness of the U.S. for immigrants has gone from "push" (escape from Mexico) to "pull" (the U.S. economy inviting them). "Invitation" is presented in the lack of enforcement of immigration laws on U.S. businesses who are employing undocumented workers, despite the facility for requesting verification by the Federal government. The pro-business Bush Administration has an odd track record here.

4   The U.S. population primarily is growing as a result of births in the minority and immigrant communities. We do not like to think about it—as it is a political correctness problem—but there is stratification of labor, mostly along education lines, where the tough jobs in agriculture, manufacturing, and services are taken by those without recourse into the white-collar world of employment. Especially when these low paying jobs do not require language ability, immigrants historically have jumped at these opportunities as a way to get their foot in the door. The U.S.-born unemployed do not think first about having just any job to help plant their feet. They first think about what their wages will be. If you are here illegally, you clearly have a competitive advantage.

It is hard to argue in favor of illegal immigration, but let us at least look at some of the ironies involved in trying to curb it:

- The protectionist policies of the Bush government with regard to the agricultural industry have meant that there are jobs in the fields and processing plants—positions that Americans have not taken, for whatever reason. A part of agricultural competitiveness is that, where mechanization is not possible—picking low-lying fruit and vegetables, food processing, tree and vine trimming—manual labor is necessary. Costs, however, still have to be kept as low as possible to compete in a globalized economy. New immigrants (for the most part, illegals) are taking these jobs at these wages and keeping the U.S. competitively afloat. Were the laborers legal and their wages higher, the Administration would have to be even more protectionist than it is at present.

- If the labor market were not being filled by illegal immigrants crossing the Mexican border, these positions would have to be filled by someone else. If we were to bring more agricultural and service workers into the U.S.

through a regularized process, the resulting body of immigrants would be less Mexican and more Arab, Muslim, South Asian, and African. For those who want an idea of how this would impact American society, take a look at Europe. This is an issue of culture, language, and religion. Author Samuel Huntington (Who Are We?) and others have argued that Mexican culture is not readily compatible with the Anglo-Protestant culture under which the U.S. has prospered. This may be true. but it certainly is more compatible than Iraqi culture.

- If the Mexicans were not coming in illegally, we would have to process— and keep track of—all of them. What would the U.S. Citizenship and Immigration Service (USCIS, the successor agency to the Immigration and Naturalization service under the new Department of Homeland Security) have to look like to process the 500 workers who are sneaking into the country illegally on a daily basis? What would it cost? There roughly are 11,000,000,000 illegal immigrants in the U.S. By any process other than deporting them all, there will be a substantial increase in the size of the government agencies designed to monitor them.

- By making such an issue of illegal immigrants from Mexico, we are discouraging all immigrants about life in the U.S., including those that we need desperately. The issue is plugging up the immigration system for applicants who have math and science skills. Many claim that the education system is being overburdened by the children of illegal immigrants. Yet, such skills have not—at least over the last 20 years—been produced by that same system, forcing us to import our technological capability from India, East Asia, and elsewhere.

Where do these ironies leave us'? We either need the workers or else we have to slow down the economy. We want to limit the size of government, but we will require a bigger government to guard the Mexican border and manage the legal and limited duration immigrant population. We do not want Roman Catholics from just across the border, yet we do not want to import the war between the Shia and Sunni into the country, either. We want residential and medical services, but we do not want to have to pay more for them. In the end, we may have to consider the possibility that illegal immigration may be a good thing.

PERSONAL RESPONSE

Do you think that illegal immigration may be good for the United States?

QUESTIONS FOR CLASS OR SMALL-GROUP DISCUSSION

1. Explain in your own words what you understand by Howell's statement that immigration is "a complex and dire social problem" (paragraph 1). To what extent do you find his observations accurate?

2. What are the "facts on immigration," according to Howell? Do you agree with him on each of the points he makes?

3. Summarize each of the ironies that Howell mentions and comment on each. Do you agree with him?

4. Although Howell says that it is "hard to argue in favor of illegal immigration," is that not what he is doing? What do you think of his concluding sentence, especially of the way he qualifies his statement with the words "may have to," "consider the possibility," and "may be"?

RACE IN AMERICA: "WE WOULD LIKE TO BELIEVE WE ARE OVER THE PROBLEM"

Maryann Cusimano Love

Maryann Cusimano Love is an award-winning educator and children's book author. A professor of international politics at Catholic University, she has also taught courses in globalization, terrorism and security at the Pentagon. As a member of the Council on Foreign Relations, Love has been advising Canadian, Caribbean, and U.S. government and private sector leaders on security issues since 1998. This essay appeared in the Feb. 12, 2007, edition of the Catholic weekly America.

As Senator Barack Obama explores a presidential bid, media headlines across the country ask, "Is America ready for an African-American president?" Between 50 percent and 62 percent of Americans polled answer yes, that race is no longer a barrier in the United States. But that this is considered a newsworthy headline by all the major media outlets and that around 40 percent of those polled answer no suggests otherwise.

A recent controversy in Virginia echoes the issue. A Virginia state legislator, Delegate Frank D. Hargrove Sr., a Republican from a suburb of Richmond, gave a newspaper interview on Martin Luther King Jr. Day in which he said that "blacks need to get over" slavery. He was stating his opposition to a resolution in the Virginia legislature to apologize for slavery and promote racial reconciliation as part of Virginia's activities marking the 400th anniversary of the English settlement at Jamestown in 1607. Officials tout Jamestown's founding as the birthplace of our nation (predating the pilgrims' landing in Plymouth Rock by 13 years), of representative government, of the rule of law and of American entrepreneurism. (Jamestown was settled by the Virginia Company of London in order to bring profits back to shareholders.) But Jamestown was also the birthplace of slavery in our country. Government time and tax money are being spent on the commemoration. One sponsor of the resolution, state Senator Henry Marsh, notes that while "the whole world's attention is on Virginia" because of the Jamestown anniversary, "Virginia can take a leadership role in promoting racial harmony." Delegate Hargrove disagrees. He argues it is "counterproductive to dwell on it," noting that "not a soul today had anything to do with slavery."

Some of Delegate Hargrove's argument is attractive. It lets us all off the hook for the inequities of the past. My Sicilian and Irish great-grandparents emigrated to the United States in the 1900's. By Hargrove's logic, my family is not responsible for slavery or its aftermath, because we were not here when it happened. On the other hand, my husband's family moved from Scotland and Ireland to the Chesapeake Bay region in the 1600's. We know little of the family history, but the name is common in these parts, on both black and white faces. I laugh in the grocery checkout lane with an African-American over our shared name, Love. Did someone in my family tree own someone in your family tree?

4   The flaw in Hargrove's argument is that the inequities of the past persist today. Noting achievements of African-Americans like Senator Obama, we would like to believe we "are over" the race problem. But the statistics paint a more sobering picture. Dr. David Satcher, the 16th surgeon general of the United States, notes that 85,000 African-Americans died in the year 2000 due to inequality in health care. The infant mortality rate of black babies is double the infant mortality rate of white babies in the United States. African-Americans have lower life expectancies than white Americans by six or seven years. Twenty-five percent of black Americans live in poverty. One-third of African-American children live in poverty. Black poverty rates are triple those of whites. Tavis Smiley's book, *Covenant with Black America*, explores many other disturbing inequities that persist in the United States today in housing, education and the criminal justice system. The Hatewatch Web site lists cross burnings and activities of white supremacist groups today, and it is possible to track the hate groups currently active in each state. The Harvard online racial bias tests have shown that millions of Americans harbor racial preconceptions. And 16-year-old Kiri Davis repeated the "doll test" used in the 1954 Brown v. Board of Education case with the same infamous results: 4- and 5-year-old black children in Harlem overwhelmingly said that the black dolls were bad and the white dolls were good and pretty. As past inequities continue into the present, we have a moral responsibility to address them.

To "get over" racial problems in America today, we need to understand them and their roots. But we don't. A recent survey conducted by the University of Connecticut found that more than 19 percent of the 14,000 college students in 50 U.S. universities surveyed believed that Martin Luther King Jr.'s "I Have a Dream" speech was advocating the abolition of slavery. I teach a course at Catholic University on the civil rights movement. Our students, most of them graduates of Catholic elementary and high schools, know little of U.S. or Catholic racial history.

The United States is not alone. Such debates are hallmarks of peace-building efforts in post-conflict societies from South Africa to Colombia. We all face these choices, balancing apologies, reconciliation, redress for past wrongs, with attention to present and future problems.

Delegate Hargrove's suggestion that we "get over" the past by not bringing it up can be tempting because it is easy. Senator Obama's vision of a post-racial politics is inviting because it is hopeful. But we are not there yet, and the only way to get there is to work through the present-day ramifications of our persistent past, not only as individuals ("I don't condone racism") but as communities ("What are we doing to end unacceptable racial inequities?["]).

PERSONAL RESPONSE

What is your response to Delegate Hargrove's statement that "'blacks need to get over slavery'"?

QUESTIONS FOR CLASS OR SMALL-GROUP DISCUSSION

1. State in your own words why Delegate Hargrove is opposed to a resolution in the Virginia legislature to apologize to blacks for slavery. To what extent do you agree that he has a valid point?

2. Summarize the concessions that Love makes to Hargrove's argument.

3. What does Love offer as proof to support her opposition to Hargrove? Do you find her argument valid?

4. What action does Love propose to help America "'get over' racial problems" (paragraph 5)? Can you think of ways to "work through the present-day ramifications of [America's] persistent past" (paragraph 7)?

COLORBLIND

ALEX KOTLOWITZ

Alex Kotlowitz's investigative articles appear regularly in such national magazines as the New Yorker *and the* New York Times Sunday Magazine. *Formerly a staff writer for the* Wall Street Journal, *he is the author of* There are No Children Here: The Story of Two Boys Growing up in the Other America *(1992);* The Other Side of the River: A Story of Two Towns, a Death and America's Dilemma *(1998); and* Never a City So Real: A Walk in Chicago *(2004). This essay appeared in the January 11, 1998, issue of the* New York Times Magazine.

One Christmas day seven years ago, I'd gone over to the Henry Horner Homes in Chicago to visit with Lafeyette and Pharoah, the subjects of my book *There Are No Children Here.* I had brought presents for the boys, as well as a gift for their friend Rickey, who lived on the other side of the housing complex, an area controlled by a rival gang. Lafeyette and Pharoah insisted on walking over with me. It was eerily quiet, since most everyone was inside, and so, bundled from the cold, we strolled toward the other end in silence. As we neared Damen Avenue, a kind of demilitarized zone, a uniformed police officer, a white woman, approached us. She looked first at the two boys, neither of whom reached my shoulder, and then directly at me. "Are you O.K.?" she asked.

About a year later, I was with Pharoah on the city's North Side, shopping for hightops. We were walking down the busy street, my hand on Pharoah's shoulder, when a middle-aged black man approached. He looked at me, and then at Pharoah. "Son," he asked, "are you O.K.?"

Both this white police officer and middle-aged black man seemed certain of what they witnessed. The white woman saw a white man possibly in trouble; the black man saw a black boy possibly in trouble. It's all about perspective—which has everything to do with our personal and collective experiences, which are consistently informed by race. From those experiences, from our histories, we build myths, legends that both guide us and constrain us, legends that include both fact and fiction. This is not to say the truth doesn't matter. It does, in a big way. It's just that getting there may not be easy, in part because everyone is so quick to choose sides, to refute the other's myths and to pass on their own.

4   We'd do well to keep this in mind as we enter the yearlong dialogue on race convened by President Clinton. Yes, conversation is critical, but not without self-reflection, both individually and communally. While myths help us make sense of the incomprehensible, they can also confine us, confuse us, and leave us prey to historical laziness. Moreover, truth is not always easily discernible—and even when it is, the prism, depending on which side of the river you reside on, may create a wholly different illusion. Many whites were quick to believe Susan Smith, the South Carolina mother who claimed that a black man had killed her children. And with the reawakening of the Tawana Brawley case, we learn that, although a grand jury has determined otherwise, many blacks still believe she was brutally raped by a group of white men. We—blacks and whites—need to examine and question our own perspectives. Only then can we grasp each other's myths and grapple with the truths.

In 1992, I came across the story of a sixteen-year-old black boy, Eric McGinnis, whose body had been found a year earlier floating in the St. Joseph River in southwestern Michigan. The river flows between Benton Harbor and St. Joseph, two small towns whose only connections are two bridges and a powerful undertow of contrasts.

St. Joseph is a town of nine thousand and, with its quaint downtown and brick-paved streets, resembles a New England tourist haunt. But for those in Benton Harbor, St. Joseph's most defining characteristic is its racial makeup: It is 95 percent white. Benton Harbor, a town of twelve thousand on the other side of the river, is 92 percent black and dirt poor. For years, the municipality so hurt for money that it could not afford to raze abandoned buildings.

Eric, a high-school sophomore whose passion was dancing, was last seen at the Club, a teenage nightspot in St. Joseph, where weeks earlier he had met and started dating a white girl. The night Eric disappeared, a white man said he caught the boy trying to break into his car and chased him—away from the river, past an off-duty white deputy sheriff. That was the last known moment he was seen alive, and it was then that the myths began.

8   I became obsessed with Eric's death, and so for five years moved in and out of these two communities, searching for answers to both Eric's disappearance and to

matters of race. People would often ask which side of the river I was staying on, wanting to gauge my allegiance. And they would often ask about the secrets of those across the way or, looking for affirmation, repeat myths passed on from one generation to the next.

Once, during an unusually bitter effort by white school-board members to fire Benton Harbor's black superintendent, one black woman asked me: "How do you know how to do this? Do you take lessons? How do you all stick together the way you do?" Of course, we don't. Neither community is as unified or monolithic as the other believes. Indeed, contrary to the impression of those in St. Joseph, the black community itself was deeply divided in its support for the superintendent, who was eventually fired.

On occasion, whites in St. Joseph would regale me with tales of families migrating to Benton Harbor from nearby states for the high welfare benefits. It is, they would tell me, the reason for the town's economic decline. While some single mothers indeed moved to Benton Harbor and other Michigan cities in the early eighties to receive public assistance, the truth is that in the thirties and forties factories recruited blacks from the South, and when those factories shut down, unemployment, particularly among blacks, skyrocketed.

But the question most often asked was: "Why us? Why write about St. Joseph and Benton Harbor?" I would tell them that while the contrasts between the towns seem unusually stark, they are, I believe, typical of how most of us live: physically and spiritually isolated from one another.

12   It's not that I didn't find individuals who crossed the river to spend time with their neighbors. One St. Joseph woman, Amy Johnson, devotes her waking hours to a Benton Harbor community center. And Eric McGinnis himself was among a handful of black teenagers who spent weekend nights at the Club in St. Joseph. Nor is it that I didn't find racial animosity. One St. Joseph resident informed me that Eric got what he deserved: "That nigger came on the wrong side of the bridge," he said. And Benton Harbor's former school superintendent, Sherwin Allen, made no effort to hide his contempt for the white power structure.

What I found in the main, though, were people who would like to do right but don't know where to begin. As was said of the South's politicians during Jim Crow, race diminishes us. It incites us to act as we wouldn't in other arenas: clumsily, cowardly, and sometimes cruelly. We circle the wagons, watching out for our own.

That's what happened in the response to Eric's death. Most everyone in St. Joseph came to believe that Eric, knowing the police were looking for him, tried to swim the river to get home and drowned. Most everyone in Benton Harbor, with equal certitude, believes that Eric was killed—most likely by whites, most likely because he dated a white girl. I was struck by the disparity in perspective, the competing realities, but I was equally taken aback by the distance between the two towns—which, of course, accounts for the myths. Jim Reeves, the police lieutenant, who headed the investigation into Eric's death, once confided that this teenager he'd never met had more impact on him than any other black person.

I'm often asked by whites, with some wonderment, how it is that I'm able to spend so much time in black communities without feeling misunderstood or unwelcomed or threatened. I find it much easier to talk with blacks about race than with fellow whites. While blacks often brave slights silently for fear that if they complain they won't be believed, when asked, they welcome the chance to relate their experiences. Among whites, there's a reluctance—or a lack of opportunity—to engage. Race for them poses no urgency; it does not impose on their daily routines. I once asked Ben Butzbaugh, a St. Joseph commissioner, how he felt the two towns got along. "I think we're pretty fair in this community," he said. "I don't know that I can say I know of any out-and-out racial-type things that occur. I just think people like their own better than others. I think that's pretty universal. Don't you? . . . We're not a bunch of racists. We're not anything America isn't." Butzbaugh proudly pointed to his friendship with Renée Williams, Benton Harbor's new school superintendent. "Renée was in our home three, four, five days a week," he noted. "Nice gal. Put herself through school. We'd talk all the time." Williams used to clean for Butzbaugh's family.

16   As I learned during the years in and out of these towns, the room for day-to-day dialogue doesn't present itself. We become buried in our myths, certain of our truths—and refuse to acknowledge what the historian Allan Nevins calls "the grains of stony reality" embedded in most legends. A quarter-century ago, race was part of everyday public discourse; today it haunts us quietly, though on occasion— the Rodney King beating or the Simpson trial or Eric McGinnis's death—it erupts with jarring urgency. At these moments of crisis, during these squalls, we flail about, trying to find moral ballast. By then it is usually too late. The lines are drawn. Accusations are hurled across the river like cannon fire. And the cease-fires, when they occur, are just that, cease-fires, temporary and fragile. Even the best of people have already chosen sides.

PERSONAL RESPONSE

Describe your feelings as you read this essay and your perspective of the tension between whites and blacks.

QUESTIONS FOR CLASS OR SMALL-GROUP DISCUSSION

1. Locate Kotlowitz's central idea or thesis, and then summarize his viewpoint on that issue. What is your opinion of his viewpoint? Do you agree or disagree with him? To what extent do your own observations or experiences support his conclusions?

2. Discuss your understanding of this statement: "It's all about perspective— which has everything to do with our personal and collective experiences, which are consistently informed by race. From those experiences, from our histories, we build myths, legends that both guide us and constrain us, legends that include both fact and fiction" (paragraph 3). Then explain the extent to which you agree with Kotlowitz.

3. Explain the reference to Jim Crow in paragraph 13, and then respond to Kotlowitz's statement that "race diminishes us. It incites us to act as we wouldn't in other arenas: clumsily, cowardly, and sometimes cruelly."

4. Are you surprised by Kotlowitz's comment in paragraph 15 that he finds it "much easier to talk with blacks about race than with fellow whites"? Does his explanation seem plausible to you? To what extent is your own experience or observation similar to his?

○ PERSPECTIVES ON RACE AND ETHNICITY IN AMERICA ○
Suggested Writing Topics

1. Refer to the comments of at least two writers in this chapter in an essay on some aspect of the subject of stereotyping and prejudice. As you plan your essay, consider the following questions: Where do people get prejudices? What aspects of American culture reinforce and/or perpetuate stereotypes? How can you personally work against stereotyping and prejudice?

2. Explore your position on the issue of a "melting pot" (a society in which minorities are assimilated into the dominant culture) versus pluralism (a society in which ethnic and racial groups maintain separate identities, with no dominant culture). Take into consideration the views of two or more authors in this chapter.

3. Explore the subject of the role that labels play in one's identity, self-esteem, and/or self-concept.

4. Interview at least one other person whose racial or ethnic heritage is different from yours about some of the points raised in at least two of the essays in this chapter. Then write an essay explaining what you learned and how the interview has in any way changed your own views on the issue of racism.

5. Write a reflective essay on your own cultural heritage, explaining your family's background and how you feel about that heritage.

6. Explain the importance of race or ethnicity to your own self-identity. Is it as important as your sex, your job, your socioeconomic level, or your educational level?

7. Alex Kotlowitz writes in "Colorblind": "We—blacks and whites—need to examine and question our own perspectives. Only then can we grasp each other's myths and grapple with the truths" (paragraph 4). Write an essay responding to that statement in which you try to sort out the two perspectives and offer some possible ways for the two groups to begin understanding one another.

8. Write a letter to the editor of the *New York Times Magazine* in which you explain your response to Alex Kotlowitz's viewpoint in "Colorblind," or, referring to his article where relevant, explain your own theory on the conditions that prevent blacks and whites in America from understanding one another's perspectives.

9. Expand on Llewellyn D. Howell's comment in "Ironies of Illegal Immigration" that immigration is a "complex and dire social problem." Taking

each point in turn, explain how immigration is a social problem, what its complexities are, and why the problem is dire. Quote Llewellyn where necessary but do your own analysis of the statement.

10. Argue for or against the statement that racial profiling is necessary in certain circumstances.

11. Argue in support of or opposition to Llewellyn D. Howell's suggestion in "Ironies of Illegal Immigration" that "illegal immigration may be a good thing" (paragraph 10).

12. Explore the role of racial and ethnic diversity in your educational experiences in high school and college. Consider these questions: How diverse are the student populations of schools you have attended? How large a component did multiculturalism play in the curricula of courses you have taken? Have you been satisfied with that aspect of your education?

13. Narrate your first experience with prejudice, discrimination, or bigotry, as either a witness or a victim. Describe in detail the incident and how it made you feel.

14. Explain the effects of racial prejudice on a person or a group of people familiar to you.

15. Write an essay in which you suggest ways for countering prejudice or ethnic and racial hatred in the United States.

Research Topics

1. Research the subject of a public policy like affirmative action, welfare, or bilingual public education as an effective (or ineffective) way to address racial or ethnic inequities in American society.

2. As a starting point for a research project, read Alex Kotlowitz's *There Are No Children Here: The Story of Two Boys Growing Up in the Other America* or *The Other Side of the River: A Story of Two Towns, a Death, and America's Dilemma.* You may decide to find out more about a major point the author makes, or something the author mentions may lead you to a suitable topic. If the book has a bibliography, you have an excellent list of potential resources for your project.

3. Research one aspect of the subject of immigration raised by William Booth in "One Nation, Indivisible: Is It History?"

4. Research and write a paper on one of the following topics related to some of the essays in this chapter: Jim Crow; the influx of Chinese immigrants to America in the nineteenth century; the Chinese Exclusion Act of 1882 and its implications for Japanese immigrants; the Japanese religion Shinto; the internment of people of Japanese ancestry in America during World War II; or the economic, political, or historical relationship of the United States with Puerto Rico, Cuba, Central America, or Mexico.

5. Research the subject of multiculturalism in American education by reading expressions of differing opinions on the subject.

6. Research the subject of whether America is a classless society. Do certain factors such as culture, ethnicity, demographics, nativity, citizenship, mother tongue, religion, skin color, or race play a role in an individual's prospects for social mobility?

7. Select a topic from any of the Suggested Writing Topics and expand it to include library research, Internet research, and/or interviews.

8. Select one of the following groups to whom the U.S. federal government has made reparations and research reasons why those reparations were made: Japanese Americans interned in American prisons camp during World War II or the Sioux Indians whose lands were confiscated in 1877.

RESPONDING TO VISUALS

© William B. Plowman/Getty Images

A friend comforts the Iraqi-born owner, right, of a restaurant burned by apparently racially motivated arson, Plymouth, Massachusetts, September 19, 2001.

1. What emotions does the photograph evoke in you?
2. The restaurant owner had received threatening telephone calls for days be-fore the fire. How does that knowledge affect your understanding of this photograph?
3. Why did the photographer choose this particular moment to take his picture? What does it convey that a picture of the restaurant ruins alone would not?

RESPONDING TO VISUALS

©AP Photo/The Citizen's Voice, Kristen Mullen

Vince Gonzalez, from left, of Scranton, PA; Kevin Gonzalez, 9, of Scranton, PA; Jeanne Brolan from United Neighborhood Centers; Estrella Gonzalez, 6, of Scranton, PA; Charlotte Lewis of Scranton, PA; and Chris Walters of Brooklyn, NY, participate in a rally organized by the Pennsylvania Immigration and Citizenship Coalition in Scranton, PA; Monday, March 12, 2007. The rally was held directly across from the William J. Nealon Federal Building and United States Courthouse during opening day of the first federal trial in the nation to address whether local government can enact ordinances that punish employers and landlords that do business with illegal immigrants.

1. Does the fact that children are being used as part of the protest strengthen or weaken the protest?
2. Do you agree that the two children are "America," as the signs they are holding state?
3. Do you agree that "no one is illegal," as the sign on the right states?
4. Do you believe that children of illegal immigrants should have rights? What about the illegal immigrants themselves? Where do you position yourself on the issue of illegal immigration?

CHAPTER 17

Terrorism and War

Terrorism is a sinister and reprehensible expression of hatred or vengeance. Terrorists, whether individuals or groups, target specific enemies and contrive to cause destruction, create havoc, and in general make a spectacular and grisly statement. Acts of terrorism are not new to this century nor the last, but they do seem to have grown more deadly, more widespread, and increasingly more difficult to combat. Nations, religions, and groups of assorted allegiances and identities have all been victims of numerous violent acts over time.

America is one nation that has experienced terrorism both abroad and at home. For instance, in 1979, militant students in Tehran stormed the U.S. Embassy there and held fifty-two hostages for 444 days. In 1983, a suicide-bomb attack destroyed the U. S. Embassy in Beirut, killing sixty-three. That same year, also in Beirut, Hezbollah suicide bombers claimed responsibility for blowing up U. S. and French military headquarters, killing 241 U. S. and fifty-eight French servicemen. In 1988, Pan Am flight 103, on its way to the United States, exploded over Lockerbie, Scotland, killing 270 people. On American soil, in 1993 a bomb in the underground garage of the World Trade Center killed six and injured more than 1,000 people; in 1995, a truck bomb destroyed a federal building in Oklahoma City, killing 168 and injuring more than 600.

By far the largest acts of terrorism in terms of lives lost and effects on the economy, the way people live, and American society in countless ways have been the September 11, 2001, attacks on the World Trade Center in New York City and the Pentagon in Washington, D.C. Those attacks have had profound effects on America and both its allies and foes. Many countries around the world expressed not only their shock and outrage at the terrorism on American soil but also their deep sympathy for the families, friends, and loved ones of those who lost their lives or were injured in the attacks.

Written less than two weeks after the tragic events of September 11, Barbara Kingsolver's "A Pure, High Note of Anguish" seeks to offer words of consolation by answering questions that her five-year-old asked about the terrorist attacks. As you read her essay, think about how you might answer the questions posed by that child and whether your answers would differ from Kingsolver's. Then, in a speech addressed to people attending a college seminar the year after September 11, Benjamin Netanyahu, former prime minister of Israel and something of an expert on fighting terrorism, offers his observations on America's fight against it. In "Three Key Principles in the War against Terrorism," Netanyahu notes three major ways that he feels America is going to win its battle against terrorism. As you read his words from 2002, consider how successful his predictions have been and whether America still embraces the three principles that Netanyahu identifies.

Next, Ted Koppel in "The Long, Cost-Free War" shares his insights as a columnist and reporter on the government's attempts to prepare "Americans for a struggle that may last decades without simultaneously demoralizing them." He is especially interested in the government's controversial invasions of privacy and treatment of detainees and wonders how Americans will accept the "adjustments" to their liberties that a protracted war against terrorism entails.

Finally, Cathy Young's essay "Terror Then and Now" uses the examples of three European cities—Prague, Dresden, and Vienna—to demonstrate what she calls "the fine line between normality and chaos." Now those cities are bustling, glamorous, and strong; but in the not-so-distant past of the twentieth century, those same cities were marked by chaos and destruction. Young is interested in the lessons the histories of those cities' experiences provide for democratic countries today that are fighting totalitarianism.

A PURE, HIGH NOTE OF ANGUISH

Barbara Kingsolver

Barbara Kingsolver's articles, book reviews, and short stories have appeared in numerous magazines and journals. Her novels include Animal Dreams *(1987);* The Bean Trees *(1988);* Pigs in Heaven *(1993);* The Poisonwood Bible *(1998); and* Prodigal Summer *(2000). Collections of her stories are in* Homeland and Other Stories *(1989), while a collection of her poems appears in* Another America *(1992). Among her nonfiction titles are* High Tide in Tucson: Essays from Now or Never *(1996);* Holding the Line Women in the Great Arizona Mine Strike of 1983 *(1996);* Last Stand: America's Virgin Lands *(2002);* Small Wonder: Essays *(2002); and* Animal, Vegetable, Miracle: A Year of Food Life *(2007). "A Pure, High Note of Anguish" was published on September 23, 2001, in the* Los Angeles Times.

I want to do something to help right now. But I can't give blood (my hematocrit always runs too low), and I'm too far away to give anybody shelter or a drink of water. I can only give words. My verbal hemoglobin never seems to wane, so words are what I'll offer up in this time that asks of us the best citizenship we've ever mustered. I don't mean to say I have a cure. Answers to the main questions of the day—Where was that fourth plane headed? How did they get knives through security?—I don't know any of that. I have some answers, but only to the questions nobody is asking right now but my 5-year old. Why did all those people die when they didn't do anything wrong? Will it happen to me? Is this the worst thing that's ever happened? Who were those children cheering that they showed for just a minute, and why were they glad? Please, will this ever, ever happen to me?

There are so many answers, and none: It is desperately painful to see people die without having done anything to deserve it, and yet this is how lives end nearly always. We get old or we don't, we get cancer, we starve, we are battered, we get on a plane thinking we're going home but never make it. There are blessings and wonders and horrific bad luck and no guarantees. We like to pretend life is different from that, more like a game we can actually win with the right strategy, but it isn't. And, yes, it's the worst thing that's happened, but only this week. Two years ago, an earthquake in Turkey killed 17,000 people in a day, babies and mothers and businessmen, and not one of them did a thing to cause it. The November before that, a hurricane hit Honduras and Nicaragua and killed even more, buried whole villages and erased family lines and even now, people wake up there empty-handed. Which end of the world shall we talk about? Sixty years ago, Japanese airplanes bombed Navy boys who were sleeping on ships in gentle Pacific waters. Three and a half years later, American planes bombed a plaza in Japan where men and women were going to work, where schoolchildren were playing, and more humans died at once than anyone thought possible. Seventy thousand in a minute. Imagine. Then twice that many more, slowly, from the inside.

There are no worst days, it seems. Ten years ago, early on a January morning, bombs rained down from the sky and caused great buildings in the city of Baghdad to fall down—hotels, hospitals, palaces, buildings with mothers and soldiers inside—and here in the place I want to love best, I had to watch people cheering about it. In Baghdad, survivors shook their fists at the sky and said the word "evil." When many lives are lost all at once, people gather together and say words like "heinous" and "honor" and "revenge," presuming to make this awful moment stand apart somehow from the ways people die a little each day from sickness or hunger. They raise up their compatriots' lives to a sacred place—we do this, all of us who are human—thinking our own citizens to be more worthy of grief and less willingly risked than lives on other soil. But broken hearts are not mended in this ceremony, because, really, every life that ends is utterly its own event—and also in some way it's the same as all others, a light going out that ached to burn longer. Even if you never had the chance to love the light that's gone, you miss it. You should. You bear this world and everything that's wrong with it by holding life still precious, each time, and starting over.

4   And those children dancing in the street? That is the hardest question. We would rather discuss trails of evidence and whom to stamp out, even the size and shape of the cage we might put ourselves in to stay safe, than to mention the fact that our nation is not universally beloved; we are also despised. And not just by "The Terrorist," that lone, deranged non-man in a bad photograph whose opinion we can clearly dismiss, but by ordinary people in many lands. Even by little boys— whole towns full of them it looked like—jumping for joy in school shoes and pilled woolen sweaters.

There are a hundred ways to be a good citizen, and one of them is to look finally at the things we don't want to see. In a week of terrifying events, here is one awful, true thing that hasn't much been mentioned: Some people believe our country needed to learn how to hurt in this new way. This is such a large lesson, so hatefully, wrongfully taught, but many people before us have learned honest truths from wrongful deaths. It still may be within our capacity of mercy to say this much is true: We didn't really understand how it felt when citizens were buried alive in Turkey or Nicaragua or Hiroshima. Or that night in Baghdad. And we haven't cared enough for the particular brothers and mothers taken down a limb or a life at a time, for such a span of years that those little, briefly jubilant boys have grown up with twisted hearts. How could we keep raining down bombs and selling weapons, if we had? How can our president still use that word "attack" so casually, like a move in a checker game, now that we have awakened to see that word in our own newspapers, used like this: Attack on America.

Surely, the whole world grieves for us right now. And surely it also hopes we might have learned, from the taste of our own blood, that every war is both won and lost, and that loss is a pure, high note of anguish like a mother singing to any empty bed. The mortal citizens of a planet are praying right now that we will bear in mind, better than ever before, that no kind of bomb ever built will extinguish hatred.

"Will this happen to me?" is the wrong question, I'm sad to say. It always was.

PERSONAL RESPONSE

Write for a few minutes about your emotions when you heard the news of the September 11, 2001, terrorist attacks against the United States.

QUESTIONS FOR CLASS OR SMALL-GROUP DISCUSSION

1. Kingsolver says that she wants "to do something to help" and "can only give words" (paragraph 1). How helpful do you find her words? If you find her words helpful, locate a passage that you find particularly effective. If you do not believe they help, explain why not.

2. Explain the title of the essay. How is it related to Kingsolver's central purpose?

3. What do you think Kingsolver means by her concluding sentence? Why is "'Will this happen to me?'" the "wrong question"?

4. How would you answer the questions that Kingsolver's five-year-old asks (paragraph 1)?

THREE KEY PRINCIPLES IN THE WAR AGAINST TERRORISM

Benjamin Netanyahu

Benjamin Netanyahu, former Prime Minister of Israel, was born in Tel Aviv, grew up in Jerusalem, spent his high school years in the United States, and earned a B.S. in architecture and an M.S. in management studies from M.I.T. In 1979 he organized an international conference against terrorism under the auspices of the Jonathan Institute, a private foundation dedicated to the study of terrorism and named after his brother, who gave his life leading the daring Entebbe rescue mission. Netanyahu served as Israel's Ambassador to the United

Nations from 1986–88, and in 1996 he was elected Prime Minister of Israel. He is author of Terrorism: How the West Can Win *(1986);* A Place Among the Nations *(1992); and* Fighting Terrorism: How Democracies Can Defeat Domestic and International Terrorism *(1995). The following is abridged from a speech delivered at a Hillsdale College seminar in 2002.*

The United States is well on its way to winning the war against terrorism because the United States, under President Bush, has espoused three clear principles.

The first principle is moral clarity. President Bush said in his remarkable speech right after September 11 that there are no good terrorists, only bad terrorists—that terrorism is always evil. In saying this, he was saying that nothing justifies terrorism. It is important to state this point clearly and to elaborate on it, because the main weapon that terrorists use against the West is not bombs or guns, but moral obfuscation: "You're terrorists, because you kill civilians, too. America, Britain, Israel—all are terrorist states." We must harden ourselves against this amoral and debilitating charge.

Terrorism is not defined by the identity of its perpetrator. Nor is it defined by the cause, real or imagined, that its perpetrators espouse. Terrorism is defined by one thing and one thing alone. It is defined by the nature of the act. Terrorists systematically and deliberately attack the innocent. That is a very different thing from the unintentional civilian casualties that often accompany legitimate acts of war.

4   For example, in 1944 the British Air Force set out to bomb the Gestapo headquarters in Copenhagen. The British pilots missed, and instead of hitting the Gestapo they hit a hospital and killed 83 children and four nuns. That was not terrorism. That did not make Britain a terrorist state. That was a terrible but unintentional accident of the kind that accompanies every war. But terrorists don't accidentally kill civilians. The deaths of innocents are not an unintentional byproduct of their strategy. Terrorists deliberately target the innocent. They intentionally cross the lines that define the conventions of war that have been developed, in accordance with basic morality, to try to limit and regulate conflict. They willfully try to kill as many innocent civilians as they can. And this is never justified, regardless of the cause.

Going back to World War II, consider this hypothetical: You're an American officer. You're fighting for the most just cause in history. But you come into a German village—maybe even a village next to a concentration camp—and you line up the women and children in that village and kill them with a machine gun. You have committed an act of terrorism. You have committed a war crime and you will be judged guilty and executed, and properly so. Not even the most just cause can justify terrorism. It is always illegitimate, always criminal.

Allow me to add one other observation—I think an important one—on this point. It is not merely that the goals of terrorists do not justify their means. In addition, the means that terrorists use tell us something about their real goals. We can see this very simply by looking at what happens when terrorists come to power. They don't establish free societies. They don't establish governments that respect human rights. They establish dictatorships that trample human rights. It's the same whether we look at Cuba or at Iran or at Libya or at Afghanistan under the Taliban. Terrorist movements may talk about fighting for democracy and freedom, but if they're in the business of terror, you can bet they plan, when they come to power, to grind human rights into the dust.

So again, terrorism is always criminal, whether practiced by Israel, America, or the Palestinian Authority. The deliberate and systematic assault on innocents is evil. Nor do ratios count. In Afghanistan, when the final tally is over, America will probably have killed a lot more Afghans than the number of Americans slaughtered in New York and Washington. But that doesn't make the Taliban cause just, or America's cause unjust.

8   I think the United States is not and will not be cowed by arguments that try to delegitimize its war against terrorism—arguments that equate terrorism with the unintentional killing of civilians. That's what I mean when I say that President Bush and the American people have moral clarity.

Strategic Clarity

This brings us to the second principle—strategic clarity. I think the United States understands that fighting terrorism doesn't really mean fighting the terrorists. Of course it is necessary and right to go after them. But they are not really the most important target. If you want to fight terrorism—and I've been saying this for over two decades—you don't go out looking for the needle in the haystack. You go after the haystack.

To use a different analogy, if you have kamikaze pilots coming at you, you can shoot down a kamikaze pilot here and there. You can even go after their squadron leader. But you will still have kamikazes coming in. The only way that you can stop the attacks from continuing is to go after the aircraft carrier that is their base. Likewise, if you want to stop terrorism, you have got to go after the regimes that stand behind the terrorists. You have to understand that the terrorists are not floating up in space. They have to take off from a certain place and go back to it. They have to have a location to hatch their grisly plots, and to equip and train themselves. That haven is always the territory of a sovereign state. If you take away the support of that sovereign state, the whole scaffolding of international terrorism will collapse into the dust.

That's exactly what the United States is doing now. It went after the Taliban and Al Qaeda began to crumble. There are remnants in Afghanistan. There is perhaps even a residual terrorist capacity. But when the roots are cut off, the grapes left on the vine wither and die. And this is fairly easy to do, because the whole terror network consists of a half-dozen states with about two dozen terrorist organizations affiliated with them—sometimes working directly for them. If you take care of those states, the rest is easy. And there are only two things you can do with terror-sponsoring states: deter them or dismantle them. That means giving them a choice. This choice was well articulated by the British Prime Minister, speaking to the Taliban: "Surrender terrorism, or surrender power." They didn't surrender terrorism, and out they went. There is no third choice.

12   I think the United States is well on its way to handling two other terrorist regimes. One is practicing terrorism this very moment, inciting radicalism and terror and militancy from the Philippines to Los Angeles. I'm talking about Iran. But the first target will be Saddam Hussein in Iraq. Both of these regimes, if unattended, will succeed—fairly rapidly—in the programs they have launched to develop atomic weapons. And once they possess atomic weapons, these two foundations of the terror network could threaten the world and our civilization with a terror that we cannot even imagine today.

President Bush is absolutely right in boldly naming these two countries and going after them—or in the case of Iran, perhaps, waiting for the implosion of its regime after the collapse of Saddam Hussein. So in addition to the moral clarity to identify all terrorism as illegitimate, the United States is demonstrating strategic clarity in moving to root out the terror-supporting regimes.

Imperative for Victory

Which brings me to the third principle: the imperative for victory. And when I say this, I don't just mean that the United States wants to win. That's obvious. I mean that the United States understands that the only way to defeat terrorism is actually to defeat it. That sounds redundant, but it isn't. There is a very powerful view today, after all—held even by some former Presidents—that says the root cause of terrorism is the deprivation of national rights or civil rights. This deprivation, according to this view, is what's driving terrorism—which is, of course, what the terrorists themselves say. Anyone who knows modern history, however, can enumerate several hundred battles, struggles, conflicts, and wars that were aimed at the achievement of national liberation, independence, or equal and civil rights, and that did not employ terror. Indeed, one has to look very hard to find the use of terrorism in these conflicts.

For example, if we ask what is the worst occupation in history—the very worst—I think most of us would agree that it was the Nazi occupation of Europe. Yet when we look, we're hard pressed to find one example of, say, the French Resistance using terrorism. They had plenty of opportunities, but they never once targeted the wives and children of French collaborators, or even the wives or children of German officers stationed in France. Why didn't they? Because they weren't terrorists. They were democrats. Or take an example closer to home: the struggle of blacks for civil equality in the United States during the 1950s and early 1960s. That struggle never employed terror either, because it also proceeded from a democratic mind-set.

16   The only way to persuade people to obliterate buses full of children, or buildings, or cities—the only way to persuade people to abandon the moral constraints that govern human action, even in war—is to inculcate in their minds the idea that there is a cause higher or more important than morality. That cause could be racial. It could be religious. It could be ethnic. It could be social. But whatever it is, it must be total if it is going to allow people to circumvent morality even to the point of intentionally blowing up children. That kind of thinking proceeds not from a democratic, but from a totalitarian mind-set. That's why, from its inception, terrorism has

been wedded to totalitarianism. From Lenin to Stalin to Hitler, down to the Aya-tollahs, terrorism is bred by totalitarianism. It requires a machine that inculcates hatred from childhood, grinding it into peoples' minds and hearts until they are willing even to blow themselves up for the purpose of murdering innocents.

So the root cause of the kind of systemic terrorism we confront today is totalitarianism, and in order to defeat totalitarianism we have to defeat the totalitarian regimes. That was accomplished through war in the case of Nazi Germany. In the case of the Soviet Union, Ronald Reagan won bloodlessly in the end. But he won. Victory over Nazism and communism were imperative for freedom. And in the case of militant Islamic terrorism, the same spirit is required.

Of course, the United States and its allies are often told that if they fight this war, they'll get hundreds of millions of people angry at them. For instance, many said that if America bombed Afghanistan during Ramadan, tens of thousands of Islamic activists would stream into Afghanistan to help the Taliban. Wrong. The United States bombed Afghanistan during Ramadan, but people who oppose America are streaming out of Afghanistan, not in. And what about all the governments in the area? Are they attacking the United States or are they trying to line up with it? They are trying to line up, because victory breeds victory and defeat breeds defeat. Insofar as the war against terrorism is victorious, it will compress the forces of Islamic militancy and terrorism and make it harder for them to draw recruits.

Antidote: Freedom

With these three principles—moral clarity, strategic clarity and the imperative for victory—the defeat of terrorism is not as distant as many people think. Beyond that, if I had to point to the one thing that is needed in the Arab and Muslim world to ensure that the next century will be better than the last—for them and for us—it would be to promote democracy, a free press, debate and dissent. In the end, the only antidote to terrorism is the antidote to totalitarianism. It is freedom. It is what the American flag represents to me and to billions in the world. It is the key to securing not merely peace of mind, but peace between peoples.

20   This peace is within our power. Now we must show that it is within our will.

PERSONAL RESPONSE

Netanyahu says that "the defeat of terrorism is not as distant as many people think" (paragraph 19). Do you feel confident that terrorism will be defeated soon? Why or why not?

QUESTIONS FOR CLASS OR SMALL-GROUP DISCUSSION

1. To what extent do you agree with Netanyahu's definition of terrorism in his opening paragraphs? Would you add anything to that definition?
2. Netanyahu says that "nothing justifies terrorism" (paragraph 2). Do you agree with him? Explain your answer.

3. Where do you position yourself on Netanyahu's second point, that it is necessary "to root out the terror-supporting regimes" (paragraph 13)? Do you agree with him completely? Why or why not?

4. In his discussion of the third principle, Netanyahu notes that "there is a very powerful view today . . . that says the root cause of terrorism is the deprivation of national rights or civil rights" (paragraph 14). To what extent do you agree with that position? What do you think of the reason that Netanyahu offers as the root cause?

THE LONG, COST-FREE WAR

TED KOPPEL

Ted Koppel is a journalist perhaps best known as the former anchor of ABC's Nightline, *a position he held for twenty-five years. He now contributes a regular op-ed column for the* New York Times, *provides commentary on National Public Radio, serves as managing editor of the Discovery Channel. This essay appeared as an op-ed piece in the November 6, 2006, issue of* The New York Times.

In the operations center at United States Central Command in Tampa, Fla., there is a wall of television screens, one end of the wall quartered so that four live feeds can be seen simultaneously. The signals originate somewhere over Iraq or Afghanistan. The cameras are aboard pilotless drones.

"Predators," some are called, and predators they are. They can be equipped with Hellfire missiles that are remotely fired by operators in Nevada who receive their orders from Centcom in Florida. The enemy, meanwhile, does much of its killing with improvised explosive devices, the most sophisticated of which are designed in Iran.

Such is at least one face of modern warfare, in which combatants exchange mortal blows by remote control, once or even twice removed from the battlefield. The victims are just as dead or mutilated as those in previous wars, but the notion of violence activated from hundreds or even thousands of miles away is telling.

4   The Bush administration is trying to deal with a particularly nettlesome problem: preparing Americans for a struggle that may last decades without simultaneously demoralizing them. Centcom's commander, Gen. John Abizaid, likes to refer to it as the "long war," where "long," means generational, with no end in sight.

To the degree that such a war can be fought at arm's length, with a minimum of friendly casualties, it will be. To the extent that victory can be achieved with a minimum of personal sacrifice, the Bush administration will try to do so.

Senior members of the administration frame that struggle in existential terms. They invoke the nightmarish possibility of a 9/11 on steroids—a terrorist attack using weapons of mass destruction, rattling the very foundations of our society.

The Bush administration uses that frightening image to justify a new worldview, within which even associating with someone who belongs to an organization on the United States terrorist list justifies prosecution here at home.

This practice falls into the category of what Deputy Attorney General Paul J. McNulty calls "preventative prosecution." It's an interesting concept: a form of anticipatory justice. Faced with the possible convergence between terrorism and a weapon of mass destruction, the argument goes, the technicality of waiting for a crime to be committed before it can be punished must give way to preemption.

8   Set aside for a moment the somewhat jarring notion of recalibrating our constitutional protections here at home while our soldiers and diplomats are given the thankless mission of spreading democracy in some of the most inhospitable regions of the Middle East.

There is a whiff of hypocrisy about conjuring up visions of a nuclear or biological holocaust while urging the American public to go about its business and recreation as usual.

We are advised to adjust to the notion of warrantless wiretaps at home, unaccountable C.I.A. prisons overseas and the rendition of suspects to nations that feature prominently on the State Department's list of human rights abusers, because the threats we face are "existential."

But apparently they are not existential enough to warrant any kind of widely shared commitment or sacrifice, like increased taxes or a military draft to meet the Pentagon's growing need for manpower.

12   One can share the Bush administration's perception that the United States confronts real threats that will not be eliminated easily or soon, but still find it impractical and immoral to get on with life as usual while placing the burden solely on the shoulders of the young men and women serving in Iraq and Afghanistan, their families and friends.

We are left with the impression that the grown-ups in Washington would prefer to make the difficult decisions for us without involving the courts, Congress or the press. That is precisely the wrong way to go about winning this war. Back when the United States was widely admired, it was for all that was most cumbersome about our democratic process.

America's efforts to transplant democracy elicit none of that admiration. How can they, when we appear to have lost confidence in fundamental aspects of democracy here at home? What has historically impressed our allies and adversaries has been our often flawed, but ultimately sincere, determination to operate within the law—if not always abroad, then at least within the United States.

Does our system require calibration in the context of the Long War? Perhaps. We cannot, for example, expect to know everything our government does when transparency informs our enemies of what they must not know. That, however, has always been the case. Indeed, there are courts and Congressional committees set up for the express purpose of reconciling the needs for secrecy and for transparency.

16   Furthermore, when officials deem certain crimes (torture, for example) unavoidable in the defense of liberty, those who commit those crimes must still know that they will be held to account before an uncompromised legal system. Congress recently passed a law that ensures exactly the opposite.

It is going to be a long struggle, and we may have to live with whatever adjustments we make to our liberties until the struggle is won, or at least over. Even liberties voluntarily forfeited are not easily retrieved. All the more so for those that are removed surreptitiously.

One might have expected that these issues would feature prominently in the debate leading up to the Congressional elections. They are scarcely mentioned.

Apparently unnerved by the unceasing White House harangue that they are ill suited to waging the war on terrorism, Democrats have largely forfeited the argument that "war," particularly a "long war," may be the wrong prism through which to view the dangers facing the United States.

20   Those who once argued that the task was one for police and intelligence agencies have been mocked into silence. Democrats have given a wide berth to the invasion of privacy, selective suspension of habeas corpus and the mistreatment of detainees, preferring instead to echo the drumbeat of Republican warnings about terrorism in general.

There is a war to be waged. We should be building protective ramparts around our legal system, safeguarding our own freedoms, focusing on our own carefully constructed democracy and leading by example.

It's too bad that we have so little confidence in the most powerful weapon in America's arsenal.

PERSONAL RESPONSE

Do you believe that you are prepared for a decades-long struggle against terrorism (paragraph 4)?

QUESTIONS FOR CLASS OR SMALL-GROUP DISCUSSION

1. How do Koppel's opening paragraphs prepare for and relate to the rest of his article?

2. Koppel writes in paragraph 3 that "the notion of violence activated from hundreds or even thousands of miles away is telling." What do you understand him to mean by that statement?

3. State in your own words what Koppel means when he writes of an "existential" war against terrorism (paragraphs 6, 10, and 11).

4. What do you understand Koppel to mean by his final sentence?

TERROR THEN AND NOW

CATHY YOUNG

Cathy Young (Ekaterina Jung) is a journalist and writer. Born in Russia, she emigrated to the United States with her family in 1980 at the age of 17. She writes a monthly column for Reason *magazine and a weekly one for the* Boston Globe. *Young is author of* Growing Up in Moscow: Memories of a Soviet Girlhood *(1989) and* Cease Fire: Why Women and Men Must Join Forces to Achieve Equality *(1999). This article was published in the November 2006 issue of* Reason.

It wasn't until after I got to Prague on August 12, on a vacation, that I realized I had obliquely witnessed a small skirmish in the War on Terror. "Look at that," my mother said, pointing to the departures screen as we changed planes in Brussels. "The flight to London's been canceled—that's strange."

A few hours later, watching Sky News at our hotel, my family and I learned that all hell had broken loose over a reported plot to bomb U.S.-bound airliners. Had we flown via London, we might have spent our vacation sleeping on the floor at Heathrow airport.

It was ironic that this brush with the international struggle against Islamist terror came as we were on our way to visit three Central European cities that witnessed some of the worst struggles of 20th-century totalitarianism. While those struggles seem almost ancient today, it is fascinating to compare the total conflict of the past with the lower-impact fight that absorbs us now.

4   In the Czech Republic today, the memory of communism and its victims is not what it was when I visited Prague for the first time in 1990, only months after the Velvet Revolution. Back then, most Czechs pretended not to know Russian, which they had been force-fed in the state schools—which created real problems, since most of them also quite genuinely didn't speak English. The hostility toward the Russians was muted but present.

Today, Russian is spoken readily and cheerfully, and the Russians in the Czech Republic are mostly of two varieties: tourists who spend money here, including the nouveau riche who spend quite a lot of it, and guest workers who, after the misery of Russian or Ukrainian provinces, are content with even menial jobs.

Among the Czechs I've spoken with on this and three previous trips in the past five years, none were nostalgic for communism, and all seemed more concerned with the present, with its opportunities and problems, than with the past. Prague, once grim and bare-shelved despite the varied beauty of its architecture, now rivals any other great European city in the abundance of restaurants, souvenir shops, and goods and services; the only major communist relic in everyday life is the lingering tendency to rip off customers in some areas of the service sector. Posters advertising "The Museum of Communism" show a Russian nesting doll with a snarl of pointy teeth.

Yet there are stark reminders that Communist totalitarianism was about murder, not just kitsch. A public art project called "Sculpture Grande '06" is on display in the city; Wenceslas Square is dominated by a genuinely striking piece titled "Kaddish."

8   The sculpture, by Ales Vesely, looks like a combination of a skeleton, a giant emaciated crow and a crown of thorns or barbed wire; it was, the inscription explained, "symbolically placed above the memorial of Jan Palach and Jan Zajic," two students who immolated themselves in 1969 to protest the Soviet invasion of Czechoslovakia and the destruction of the Prague Spring. The modest memorial itself has a granite slab with images of the two young men, an inscription, "In memory of the victims of communism," and a small wooden cross with a barbed-wire wreath.

Our other two major stops, Dresden and Vienna, were full of 20th-century history of a different kind. If World War II and post-World War II memories have a resonance in Vienna, they have a particular poignancy in Dresden, the city firebombed by the Allies in one of the most controversial chapters of "the Good War."

They also have a particular relevance to the global war on terror: Recently, the bombing of Dresden has been cited by some hawks (such as New York Post columnist John Podhoretz) as an example of the kind of resolve on the part of the Allies that the West lacks today in its confrontation with Islamism. The hawks say the resolve to reduce enemy cities to rubble and inflict massive civilian casualties may be a necessary precondition to victory.

Dresden, like no other place in Europe, drives home the full meaning of this argument. The rebuilt city center today is a tiny island of baroque splendor, resurrected out of charred rubble that is still visible on a patch of land by the island's edge, and surrounded by dreary postwar communist-era construction.

12   The destruction of Dresden's fabled cultural treasures was accompanied by the loss of 25,000 to 35,000 lives in a horrific firestorm that engulfed the city. And, while Podhoretz writes that both the leaders and the populations of the Allied nations exhibited "a cold-eyed singleness of purpose that helped break the will and the back of their enemies," the fact is that the Dresden bombing, which had dubious strategic and psychological value, was hugely controversial at the time. Many British and American leaders distanced themselves from the raids, describing them as wanton terror. The bombing of Dresden was also a key factor in postwar attempts to suggest a moral near-parity between the Nazis and the Allies—a dubious strategy to emulate.

In one sense, the prosperity on display in Prague, Dresden, and Vienna demonstrates the distance we've traveled from the horrors of totalitarianism. It's unlikely that Islamist terrorism will prove as physically destructive as the beating Europe took from the right and left hands of modern tyranny.

Yet Dresden and Vienna, at least, are reminders of the fragility of civilization. Before the war, these cities were glittering centers of urban life and culture, much as they are now. Today, walking these same streets amidst the crowds of tourists, the shopping, the dining, the museums, it's hard to imagine that all this vitality and prosperity could be turned into ruin and death. But it was, just six decades ago. Who, relaxing in a Vienna cafe or strolling past the gorgeous Zwinger Palace in Dresden in the mid-1930s, could have imagined the destruction that would follow?

Is radical Islamic terrorism today as great a threat to the West as Nazism and then Communism were in their day? Hitler's and Stalin's empires were vastly more massive and powerful. The power of the Islamist terror network is more spread out and amorphous; this time the bombs could come from within. Yet our responses to Islamist terror in some respects have exceeded our responses to totalitarianism.

16   Returning through Brussels, my parents and I faced new regulations under which no carry-on luggage was allowed on U.S.-bound flights, except for a laptop with no other items in the case and a few essentials in a clear plastic bag. Even the chocolates I had picked up at the duty-free shop at the airport had to be checked at the gate. Back in New York, items that had spilled out of carry-on bags clearly not suited to withstand baggage handling—a pair of sandals, a notebook, what looked like a sandwich in a paper wrap—drifted along on the conveyor belt to nervous laughs from the passengers.

I remembered a comment made a few years ago by the curmudgeonly Arnold Beichman, a scholar and Hoover Institution fellow whom I had gotten to know on my first trip to Prague in 1990. He admitted to a certain nostalgia for the Cold War, at the height of which we did not have to remove our shoes and belts when boarding a plane. Is this a more dangerous world, or a more paranoid one? Or both? None of the "security" measures I saw at the airport inspired a true sense of security, or of anything beyond the appearance of doing something.

But whether of not the London bombing plot had much of a chance of succeeding, the danger is real, and terror could destroy a society just as surely as conventional war. The lessons from Europe's past—the thin line between normality and chaos, the deadliness of totalitarian ideology, the danger of democracies losing sight of their own values while battling an evil empire—remain all too relevant, and the lessons of history offer no easy answers for today.

PERSONAL RESPONSE

Young writes that "the hawks say the resolve to reduce enemy cities to rubble and inflict massive civilian casualties may be a necessary precondition to victory" (paragraph 10). Do you agree with the hawks? Explain your answer.

QUESTIONS FOR CLASS OR SMALL-GROUP DISCUSSION

1. Locate Young's thesis and comment on the effectiveness of the introductory paragraphs.
2. Summarize in your own words the parallels that Young sees between past wars against totalitarianism and communism and today's war on terror. How effective do you find that comparison? In your opinion, do those past conflicts shed light on or provide lessons for the current war?

3. How would you answer the question that Young asks at the beginning of paragraph 15: "Is radical Islamic terrorism today as great a threat to the West as Nazism and then Communism were in their day?"

4. How would you answer the questions that Young asks in paragraph 17: "Is this a more dangerous world, or a more paranoid one? Or both?"

○ PERSPECTIVES ON TERRORISM AND WAR ○

Suggested Writing Topics

1. Explore the effects of the September 11, 2001, terrorist attacks on America. In what ways did they change America?

2. Analyze the responses of people in other nations to the September 11 terrorist attacks.

3. Drawing on Benjamin Netanyahu's "Three Key Principles in the War Against Terrorism," give your own definition of "terrorism" and explain how you believe America ought to fight against it.

4. Write a reflective essay on the nature of heroism and extraordinary sacrifice as demonstrated during the September 11 terrorist attacks or after them.

5. Explain your viewpoint on the issue of how far the state should be allowed to restrict civil liberties for the sake of national security.

6. Write a personal essay explaining your feelings about the September 11 terrorist attacks and/or how you see them affecting you or your generation in the years to come.

7. Answer Cathy Young's question in "Terror Then and Now": "Is this a more dangerous world [than during the Cold War], or a more paranoid one? Or both?"

8. Explore the effects on people of a serious event like a terrorist attack, an automobile accident, an encounter with random violence, or a close brush with death. How does such an event affect their sense of security and the way in which they think about their own lives? Use personal experience or observation to write your essay.

9. Select a statement from any of the readings in this chapter and write an essay in response to it. For instance, Ted Koppel in "The Long, Cost-Free War" says that the government's current practice of invading privacy, holding and mistreating detainees, and suspending *habeas corpus* (paragraph 20) is "precisely the wrong way to go" (paragraph 13). Do you agree or disagree? Elsewhere, he writes: "We should be building protective ramparts around our legal system, safeguarding our own freedoms, focusing on our own carefully constructed democracy and leading by example" (paragraph 21). How do you respond to that?

Research Topics

1. Research the effects of the September 11 terrorist attacks in New York and Washington on the American economy, the American image abroad, or America's role in international politics. All of these topics are broad, so after selecting one, narrow it down further. For instance, you might begin by asking what the economic effects of the attacks were on the airline industry, investment firms, or the stock exchange, and then further narrow your focus as you begin reading on the subject.

2. Research the subject of what led to the events of September 11. What motivated the terrorist attacks? How can one explain why they happened?

3. Research the impact of the events of September 11 and the war on terrorism on Muslim Americans.

4. Research the question of whether there is a double standard in war reporting, especially in the matter of showing prisoner abuse in American detention centers or broadcasting images of coffins returning from war in the Middle East.

5. Research the costs of the war on terrorism and do an analysis of the economics of such a war.

6. Research the role of other nations in coalition-building following the terrorist attacks in New York and Washington.

7. Research the subject of how extremist Muslims contrast with moderate and secularist Muslims. Look at the beliefs and actions of both and identify major areas of difference.

8. Following the terrorist attacks against New York and Washington, the North Atlantic Treaty Organization (NATO) invoked article 5 of its mutual defense treaty. Research the purpose of NATO and assess its role in the aftermath of the September 11 attacks.

9. Research the events that led to the Velvet Revolution (or the Gentle Revolution) in Czechoslovakia and assess whether it has lessons for other countries wanting to overthrow totalitarian rule.

10. Research the "lessons from Europe's past" (paragraph 18, Cathy Young's "Terror Then and Now"), narrow your focus to one specific country or even city (Prague, Dresden, or Vienna for instance), and explain the lessons it provide.

RESPONDING TO VISUALS

© Susan Meiselas/Magnum Photos

Sculpture in a park near the World Trade Center, September 11, 2001.

1. How does the photographer use the sculpture to comment on the terrorist attacks against the twin towers of the World Trade Center? What details combine to make that comment?
2. Would the effect of the picture be different if a human or humans were in it instead of a sculpture?
3. How does the photographer use lines and shapes in the composition of the photograph?

Responding to Visuals

12th March 1946: Commuters boarding a tram in bomb-damaged Dresden, Germany.

1. What is the overall effect of the people boarding a tram amidst the rubble of their damaged city?
2. What image of war does the photograph convey?
3. What is the effect of the buildings that are still standing in the background?

CHAPTER

18

America Abroad
in Political Science

In recent years, international relations have become an extremely important branch of political science, the study of politics, and the workings of the government. America's role as a superpower puts it in the position of being closely scrutinized by leaders, journalists, and ordinary citizens around the world. What America does politically is extremely important to other countries because America's actions are likely to affect them either directly or indirectly in many ways, especially economically and politically. The term *global village,* coined a few decades ago to describe the myriad links among the world's nations, is particularly apt when considering international relations and the perception that other countries have of America. Its political events are reported almost instantaneously around the globe by satellite, and magazines and newspapers also play crucial roles in conveying certain images of America and Americans to other nations.

Other nations pay close attention to American politics and America's foreign policy, as the essays in this chapter indicate. First, Paul Johnson in "American Idealism and Realpolitik" comments on America's role as "the reluctant sheriff of a wild world" and the dilemma it finds itself in as it plays that role. As a nation founded on idealism, America is frequently faced with being both a benign champion of weak and oppressed countries while at the same time having to make practical and sometimes Machiavellian decisions about how to deal with the aggressors against the countries it defends. (Note that "realpolitik" refers to politics or diplomacy based primarily on practical considerations, rather than ideological notions.) Johnson raises some intriguing points about this moral dilemma. Then, although Timothy Garton Ash's "Fortress America" was written before the 2004 presidential election, he makes some telling observations about U. S. foreign policy and how America is perceived abroad. His immediate subject is the 2004 presidential race, but his broader subject is American foreign policy.

An influential aspect of America that has enormous influence on how foreigners perceive it is popular culture. The image of America conveyed abroad as represented by such products as movies, songs, magazines, T-shirts, and celebrities helps perpetuate certain notions about America as a land of glamour, wealth, excess, excitement, and even a kind of innocence. Hollywood has had particular influence in conveying this image. Martha Bayles takes as her subject the way that American popular culture projects a negative image of the country and wonders if that is responsible for the decline in America's reputation around the world. In "Now Showing: The Good, The Bad and the Ugly Americans," she notes that funding for cultural diplomacy was shrinking in America at the same time that Hollywood become very aggressive in its exports abroad. She notes: "American popular culture is no longer a beacon of freedom to huddled masses in closed societies. Instead, it's a glut on the market and . . . our de facto ambassador to the world." As you read her essay, think about what Hollywood suggests to you. Do you think of glamour, of classic films and famous stars, or do you think of cheap sensationalism, escapism, and money-hungry exploiters out to become rich in any way they can? What picture of America do you think today's Hollywood stars, pop recording artists, and other popular culture representatives project?

Finally, in her testimony before the House Committee on Foreign Affairs sub-committee on International Organizations, Human rights, and Oversight, Lisa A. Curtis, senior research fellow at the Heritage Foundation, addresses the topic of the government's efforts to deal with America's image abroad and assesses how well they are working. Curtis elaborates on several of the points raised in Bayles's article and offers a number of solutions to the problem of America's poor image abroad.

AMERICAN IDEALISM AND REALPOLITIK

Paul Johnson

Paul Johnson, eminent British historian and author, has written columns for decades for such British publications as the Spectator, *the* Daily Mail, *and the* Daily Telegraph. *He also contributes to such American publications as* National: The Founding Father Review, *the* Wall Street Journal, *and the* New York Times. *He has written over forty books, primarily on history but also on religion and travel. His most recent are* The Renaissance (A Short History) *(2002);* Napolean *(2002);* George Washington *(2005); and* Creators *(2006). In 2006, Johnson was awarded the Presidential Medal of Freedom. This article was published in the March 12, 2007, issue of* Forbes.

America is the reluctant sheriff of a wild world that sometimes seems mired in wrongdoing. The UN has nothing to offer in the way of enforcing laws and dispensing justice, other than spouting pious oratory and initiating feeble missions that usually do more harm than good. NATO plays a limited role, as in Afghanistan, but tends to reflect the timidity (and cowardice) of Continental Europe. Britain and a few other nations such as Australia are willing to follow America's lead but are too weak to act on their own.

That leaves the U.S. to shoulder the responsibility. Otherwise—what? Is brute force to replace the rule of law in the world because there's no one to enforce it? I wish some of those who constantly criticize America's efforts and the judgment of President Bush would ask themselves this simple question: Would you really like to live in a world where the U.S. sits idly by and lets things happen?

Life in such a world would be like the bestial existence described in Thomas Hobbes' great work, *Leviathan*. If people "live without a common power to keep them all in awe, they are in that condition which is called war, and such a war as is of every man against every man." In that lawless state there will be "continual fear and danger of violent death, and the life of man solitary, poor, nasty, brutish and short."

4   In the 350 years since Hobbes wrote his book nothing essential has changed. For proof, look at the poor people of Sudan, in whose struggle the U.S. has not

been willing to intervene and whose lives are exactly as Hobbes described. The same is true in Somalia, where the U.S. has been indecisive and vacillating. And this was the case in the former Yugoslavia until the U.S., with great misgiving, finally responded to pressure and sent in its forces.

It's fortunate for the world that in areas in which international law doesn't operate and rogue states do as they please, America will sometimes agree to play Leviathan in order to establish law, at the risk of huge financial expense and its soldiers' lives. It does so because it is a country founded on idealism. A majority of Americans have always believed that a society, under God, must come to the rescue of the poor, weak and oppressed if it has the means to do so. The U.S. has applied this idealism systematically to the world as a whole and in many different ways, from the Marshall Plan, which helped raise Europe from ruin in 1948, to declaring war on international terrorism five years ago.

On the Horns of a Dilemma

America is fundamentally and instinctively idealistic. But following these ideals and acting as the world's policeman raises moral issues. We all agree that the sheriff must be righteous, brave and resolute. But should he also, if the situation demands, be cunning, devious and Machiavellian? In short, should America, along with its idealism, also practice realpolitik? And won't these two forces be in constant practical and moral conflict?

It's difficult to exercise authority in large parts of the world and, to use Hobbes' phrase, "keep them all in awe," without a touch of realpolitik. Britain discovered this in the 19th century, just as the Romans had two millennia before. Moreover, as British statesmen such as Benjamin Disraeli and Robert Cecil, Lord Salisbury, found, imperial realpolitik expressed itself principally in two cynical maxims: "Divide and rule" and "My enemy's enemy is my friend." These two maxims are rearing their heads again in the Middle East, and almost unwittingly—and certainly not from any set purpose—the U.S. finds itself following them.

8   U.S. intervention in Iraq has had the inevitable consequence of fueling the Sunni-Shia feud, which has raged in Islam for 1,000 years at varying degrees of intensity. It's now running hotter than ever, and likely to get worse, as more and more of the Middle East is drawn into it. Of course, with the Sunnis fighting the Shia, they have less time and energy to fight the West, and America finds it easier to rule. But this raises moral dilemmas that the U.S. has so far failed to resolve or publicly recognize.

Another situation where realpolitik could come into play is Iran's nuclear power quest. The moment Iran possesses and can deliver nuclear bombs it will use them against Israel, destroying the entire country and its inhabitants. If this danger becomes imminent, Israel has the means—if suitably assisted—to launch a preemptive strike. Should the U.S. provide such assistance and moral encouragement?

China's progress in advanced military technology, especially Star Wars-like rocket defenses, is also giving American strategists problems: How should the U.S. react? The realpolitik answer would be to assist India, China's natural rival and potential antagonist in east and central Asia, to achieve technological parity. But would it be right to do so?

These kinds of questions can arise almost anywhere but do so especially around ruthless totalitarian regimes that are attempting to acquire more military power than is safe to allow them. North Korea is a case in point. It's one thing for the U.S. to make clear that it will defend its allies, such as South Korea and Japan, from nuclear threats. That is straightforward and honorable. But the realpolitik solution would be to assist and encourage China to deal with the problem of a nuclear-armed and aggressive North Korea, the strategy being based on another old maxim: "Set a thief to catch a thief."

12   I don't envy those in Washington whose duty it is to resolve the dilemma between idealism and realpolitik. But they will not go far wrong if they respect the great tripod on which all geopolitical wisdom rests: the rule of law, the consultation of the people and the certitude that, however strong we may be, we are answerable to a higher power.

PERSONAL RESPONSE

How do you answer Johnson's question in paragraph 2: "Would you really like to live in a world where the U.S. sits idly by and lets things happen?"

QUESTIONS FOR CLASS OR SMALL-GROUP DISCUSSION

1. Explain the title. In what ways is America idealistic? In what ways must it practice realpolitik, according to Johnson?
2. Johnson writes that America's idealism conflicts with its role as "the world's policeman," which "raises moral issues" (paragraph 6)? What do you understand him to mean by that?
3. Johnson mentions several examples of the U.S.'s efforts to help other countries and the "practical and moral conflict" that results. Can you provide other, similar examples to illustrate that point?
4. Comment on the effectiveness of Johnson's conclusion.

FORTRESS AMERICA

Timothy Garton Ash

Timothy Garton Ash is a senior fellow at the Hoover Institution Stanford University, and Professor of European Studies and Isaiah Berlin Professorial Fellow at St. Antony's College, Oxford University. He is the author of eight books: Und Willst Du Nicht Mein Brüder Sein . . . Die DDR Heute *(1981);* The Polish Revolution: Solidarity, 1980–82 *(1983);* The Uses of Adversity: Essays on the Fate of

Central Europe *(1989);* The Magic Lantern: The Revolution of 1989 as Witnessed in Warsaw, Budapest, Berlin, and Prague *(1990);* In Europe's Name: Germany and the Divided Continent *(1993);* The File: A Personal History *(1998);* History of the Present: Essays, Sketches, and Dispatches from Europe in the 1990s *(1999); and* Free World: America, Europe and the Surprising Future of the West *(2004). He frequently writes for leading newspapers and magazines and is a regular contributor to the* New York Review of Books. *This essay was first published in the July 22, 2004, issue of the* Guardian.

I have just entered the United States. Since I was on a so-called J-1 visa, this was quite an achievement. First I had to fill in a form asking my host university to send me another form. Armed with that form, I filled in three further forms, including such obviously relevant information as my brother's telephone number, and the names of two people who could verify this information. Then I had to go to Barclays bank to get a special receipt for paying the fee. Then I had to supply a passport photograph 2 inches square in which "the head (measured from the top of the hair to the bottom of the chin) should measure between 1 inch to 1 1/2 inches (25mm to 35mm) with the eye level between 1 1/18 inch to 1 1/2 inches (28mm and 35mm) from the bottom of the photo." Only a few photoshops do these and, once found, Snappy Snaps charged me £24.99 for a double set. Snappy, indeed. The first time you apply, you also have to go for an interview at the embassy.

Finally armed with this precious patent of nobility, I arrived at San Francisco airport, where I was fingerprinted and photographed. Last year, I was taken aside for further investigation, while at the next desk an official of the department of homeland security reduced a girl to a nervous wreck by intrusive questioning about what she would be up to with her American boyfriend. And she, like me, was from Britain, the United States' closest ally. Imagine what it's like if you come from Libya or Iran.

Yes, I know that the United States was attacked by terrorists on September 11, 2001, and some of those terrorists had entered the US on J-1 visas. I understand, obviously, that the country has had to tighten up its security controls. But this is more than just a personal grouse. Heads of leading American universities have publicly complained that such bureaucratic and intrusive procedures are reducing the number of foreign students willing and able to come to study in the US. (I have heard it argued in London that this creates a significant opportunity for British universities.) This raises the larger question of whether the United States' "soft power," its power to attract others and to get them to do what it wants because they find it attractive, has been diminished by the way the Bush administration has reacted to the 9/11 attacks.

4   That, in turn, raises the even larger question of who is winning this "war": al-Qaida or the US?

"God bless America," wrote the poet Philip Larkin, "so large, so friendly and so rich." And American hyperpower, by contrast with the one-dimensional superpower of the Soviet Union, has always depended on having all three dimensions: military, economic and "soft." The soft power of a country is more difficult to measure than its military or economic power, but one yardstick is what I call the "Statue of Liberty test." In this test, countries are rated by the number of people outside who want to get into them, divided by the number of people inside who want to get out. Thus, during the cold war, many people wanted to emigrate from the Soviet Union, while very few wanted to go and live there, whereas hundreds of millions wanted to enter America and very few to leave it. By this rough measure, America still has bags of soft power.

Yet its overall attractiveness surely has been diminished, not just by such bureaucratic procedures, but by Guantánamo, by Iraq, by a certain harsh, militarist, nationalist approach to world affairs, and by a mistaken belief that the "war on terror" can be won mainly, if not solely, by military, intelligence and police means.

If you look at the results of the worldwide survey conducted by the Pew Research Centre, you can see that resentment of America around the world has reached unprecedented levels in the last two years. The Bush administration has imperiled the economic dimension of American power, by running up $500bn trade and budget deficits while increasing military spending to $400bn, and it has largely neglected the third, soft dimension. Meanwhile, even the one in five Americans who possess a passport have become more reluctant to travel outside North America. To give just one small example: American customers of Avis car rentals in Europe are down 40% on 2000 levels. There's a real sense of a "Fortress America."

8 Could the liberal, multilateralist, French-speaking John Kerry, who launches his campaign in earnest at the Democrats' convention in Boston next week, change all this, and restore a Kennedyesque glow to America's image in the world? I find many people in Europe already answer that question with a firm no. Something deeper has changed, they say. Even if America reverts to its previous form, attitudes towards America will not.

But I wouldn't be so sure. Perhaps it's just the effect of sitting here in the Californian sunshine, watching this extraordinary multi-ethnic society working all around me, but I think America's underlying attractions are still all there—damaged by 9/11, diminished by economic competition from booming Asia, but still formidable. If Kerry can summon a spark of charisma, aided by his appealing running mate John Edwards, and if the monstrous ego of Ralph Nader will kindly fall under an appropriately eco-friendly bus, the Democrat has a chance of reminding us that the other America still exists. And much of the world, even the Arab and Muslim world, will respond.

Which is why, if Osama bin Laden is still in a fit state to make political calculations, he must be backing an election victory for George Bush. The object of the terrorist is often to reveal the "true" repressive character of the state against which the terror is directed, and thus win further support for the terrorists' cause. If the United States had just acted in Afghanistan, and then concentrated on hoovering-up the remains of al-Qaida, the United States might clearly be winning the war on terror today. But, as bin Laden must have hoped, the Bush administration overreacted, and thus provided, in Iraq and Guantánamo, recruiting sergeants for al-Qaida of which Osama could only dream.

So in this looking-glass world of backhanded ironies, Republicans are covertly supporting their most extreme opponent, Ralph Nader, because he will take votes from John Kerry, and al-Qaida terrorists will be backing Bush, because he's their best recruiter. But can they do anything to affect the outcome of an American presidential election? Of course they can. A major terrorist attack on the American homeland a few days before November 2 would almost certainly not have the effect that the Madrid pre-election bombing had, sending swing voters to the anti-war opposition.

12   In a recent opinion poll for the *Economist*, handling the war on terror was one of the few areas in which American voters favoured Bush over Kerry. It seems likely there would be a wave of patriotic solidarity with the incumbent. In short, Bush's election chances may depend on the ruthless ingenuity of al-Qaida, while Kerry's election chances may depend on the ability of Bush's department of homeland security to combat it.

PERSONAL RESPONSE

Do you agree that "the Bush administration overreacted" to the September 11 terrorist attacks (paragraph 7)? Explain your answer.

QUESTIONS FOR CLASS OR SMALL-GROUP DISCUSSION

1. What is the purpose of the opening anecdote? How does it relate to Ash's thesis or central point?
2. In what ways does Ash suggest that America is a "fortress" (title)?
3. Explain the references to Guantánamo and Iraq in paragraph 4. What do you think Ash means when he says that America has "a certain harsh, militarist, nationalist approach to world affairs" (paragraph 4)? Do you agree with him?
4. What does Ash mean when he says that al-Qaida terrorists are George W. Bush's "best recruiter" (paragraph 8)? Are you convinced that his point is valid?

NOW SHOWING: THE GOOD, THE BAD AND THE UGLY AMERICANS

Martha Bayles

Martha Bayles teaches humanities at Boston College. She is author of Hole in Our Soul: The Loss of Beauty and Meaning in American Popular Music *(1994), and is currently working on a book about U.S. cultural diplomacy.*

When Benjamin Franklin went to France in 1776, his assignment was to manipulate the French into supporting the American war for independence. This he accomplished with two stratagems: First, he played the balance-of-power game as deftly as any European diplomat; and second, he waged a subtle but effective campaign of what we now call public diplomacy, or the use of information and culture to foster goodwill toward the nation. For Franklin, this meant turning his dumpy self into a symbol. "He knew that America had a unique and powerful meaning for the enlightened reformers of France," writes historian Bernard Bailyn, "and that he himself . . . was the embodiment, the palpable expression, of that meaning." Hence the fur cap and rustic manner that made Franklin a celebrity among the powdered wigs and gilded ornaments of the court of Louis XVI.

Today, as we witness the decline of America's reputation around the world, we're paying far more attention to Franklin's first stratagem than to his second. Indeed, despite a mounting stack of reports recommending drastic changes in the organization and funding of public diplomacy, very little of substance has been done. And most Americans, including many who make it their business to analyze public diplomacy, seem unmindful of the negative impression that America has recently been making on the rest of humanity—via our popular culture.

A striking pattern has emerged since the end of the Cold War. On the one hand, funding for public diplomacy has been cut by more than 30 percent since 1989, the National Science Board reported last year. On the other hand, while Washington was shrinking its funding for cultural diplomacy, Hollywood was aggressively expanding its exports. The Yale Center for the Study of Globalization reports that between 1986 and 2000 the fees generated by the export of filmed and taped entertainment went from $1.68 billion to $8.85 billion—an increase of 427 percent. Foreign box-office revenue has grown faster than domestic, and now approaches a 2-to-1 ratio. The pattern is similar for music, TV and video games.

4   This massive export of popular culture has been accompanied by domestic worries about its increasingly coarse and violent tone—worries that now go beyond the polarized debates of the pre-9/11 culture war. For example, a number of prominent African Americans, such as Bill Stephney, co-founder of the rap group Public Enemy, have raised concerns about the normalization of crime and prostitution in gangsta and "crunk" rap. And in April 2005, the Pew Research Center reported that "roughly six-in-ten [Americans] say they are very concerned over what children see or hear on TV (61%), in music lyrics (61%), video games (60%) and movies (56%)."

These worries now have a global dimension. The 2003 report of the U.S. House of Representatives Advisory Group on Public Diplomacy for the Arab and Muslim World stated that "Arabs and Muslims are . . . bombarded with American sitcoms, violent films, and other entertainment, much of which distorts the perceptions of viewers." The report made clear that what seems innocuous to Americans can cause problems abroad: "A Syrian teacher of English asked us plaintively for help in explaining American family life to her students. She asked, 'Does "Friends" show a typical family?'"

One of the few efforts to measure the impact of popular culture abroad was made by Louisiana State University researchers Melvin and Margaret DeFleur, who in 2003 polled teenagers in 12 countries: Saudi Arabia, Bahrain, South Korea, Mexico, China, Spain, Taiwan, Lebanon, Pakistan, Nigeria, Italy and Argentina. Their conclusion, while tentative, is nonetheless suggestive: "The depiction of Americans in media content as violent, of American women as sexually immoral and of many Americans engaging in criminal acts has brought many of these 1,313 youthful subjects to hold generally negative attitudes toward people who live in the United States."

Popular culture is not a monolith, of course. Along with a lot of junk, the entertainment industry still produces films, musical recordings, even television shows that rise to the level of genuine art. The good (and bad) news is that censorship is a thing of the past, on both the producing and the consuming end of popular culture. Despite attempts by radical clerics in Iraq to clamp down on Western influences, pirated copies of American movies still make it onto the market there. If we go by box office figures, the most popular films in the world are blockbusters like "Harry Potter." But America is also exporting more than enough depictions of profanity, nudity, violence and criminal activity to violate norms of propriety still honored in much of the world.

8 But instead of questioning whether Americans should be super-sizing to others the same cultural diet that is giving us indigestion at home, we still seem to congratulate ourselves that our popular culture now pervades just about every society on Earth, including many that would rather keep it out. Why this disconnect? Partly it is due to an ingrained belief that what's good for show business is good for America's image. During both world wars, the movie studios produced propaganda for the government, in exchange for government aid in opening resistant foreign markets. Beginning in 1939, the recording industry cooperated with the Armed Forces Network to beam jazz to American soldiers overseas, and during the Cold War it helped the Voice of America (VOA) do the same for 30 million listeners behind the Iron Curtain.

In his book, *Cultural Exchange & the Cold War*, veteran foreign service officer Yale Richmond quotes the Russian novelist Vasily Aksyonov, for whom those VOA jazz broadcasts were "America's secret weapon number one." Aksyonov said that "the snatches of music and bits of information made for a kind of golden glow over the horizon . . . the West, the inaccessible but oh so desirable West."

To my knowledge, this passage has not been quoted in defense of Radio Sawa, the flagship of the U.S. government's new fleet of broadcast channels aimed at reaching young, largely Arab audiences. But even if it were, who could imagine such a reverent, yearning listener in the Middle East, South Asia or anywhere else today? The difference is not just between short-wave radio and unlimited broadband, it is also between Duke Ellington and 50 Cent.

During the Cold War, Washington also boosted the commercial export of popular culture, adhering to the view set forth in a 1948 State Department memo: "American motion pictures, as ambassadors of good will—at no cost to the American taxpayers—interpret the American way of life to all the nations of the world, which may be invaluable from a political, cultural, and commercial point of view."

12 And this boosterism continued through the 1960s and '70s, even as movies and rock music became not just unruly but downright adversarial. During the 1970s, the government worked so hard to pry open world markets to American entertainment that UNESCO and the Soviet Union led a backlash against "U.S. cultural

imperialism." In 1967, the VOA began to broadcast rock and soul. And while a provocative figure like Frank Zappa was hardly a favorite at diplomatic receptions, many in the foreign service understood his symbolic importance to dissidents, including Czech playwright (and later president) Vaclev Havel. In general, the U.S. political establishment was content to let America's homegrown counterculture do its subversive thing in Eastern Europe and Russia.

In the 1980s, the mood changed. Under Ronald Reagan appointee Charles Z. Wick, the United States Information Agency (USIA), the autonomous agency set up in 1953 to disseminate information and handle cultural exchange, was more generously funded and invited to play a larger role in policymaking—but at the price of having its autonomy curbed and the firewall between cultural outreach and policy advocacy thinned. It is noteworthy that these changes occurred amid the acrimony of the culture wars. Like the National Endowment for the Arts and public broadcasting, the USIA eventually found itself on Sen. Jesse Helms's list of artsy agencies deserving of the budgetary ax. And while the others managed to survive, the USIA did not. In 1999 it was absorbed into the very different bureaucratic culture of the State Department.

Today we witness the outcome: an unwarranted dismissal of elite-oriented cultural diplomacy, combined with an unquestioned faith in the export of popular culture. These converge in the decision to devote the bulk of post-9/11 funding to Radio Sawa and the other commercial-style broadcast entities, such as al-Hurra (a U.S.-based satellite TV network aimed at Arab listeners) and Radio Farda (which is broadcast in Farsi to Iran). Because the establishment of these new channels has been accompanied by the termination of the VOA's Arabic service, critics have focused largely on their news components. But what benefit is there in Radio Sawa's heavy rotation of songs by sex kitten Britney Spears and foul-mouthed rapper Eminem?

To the charge that the Bush administration is peddling smut and profanity to Arab teens, Radio Sawa's music director, Usama Farag, has stated that all the offensive lyrics are carefully edited out. Yet there is something quaint about the U.S. government's censoring song lyrics in a world where most people have ready access to every product of the American entertainment industry, including the dregs.

16   American popular culture is no longer a beacon of freedom to huddled masses in closed societies. Instead, it's a glut on the market and, absent any countervailing cultural diplomacy, our de facto ambassador to the world. The solution to this problem is far from clear. Censorship is not the answer, because even if it were technologically possible to censor our cultural exports, it would not be politic. The United States must affirm the crucial importance of free speech in a world that has serious doubts about it, and the best way to do this is to show that freedom is self-correcting—that Americans have not only liberty but also a civilization worthy of liberty.

From Franklin's days, U.S. cultural diplomacy has had both an elite and a popular dimension. Needless to say, it has rarely been easy to achieve a perfect balance between the two. What we could do is try harder to convey what the USIA mandate used to call "a full and fair picture of the United States." But to succeed even a little, our new efforts must counter the negative self-portrait we are now exporting. Along with worrying about what popular culture is teaching our children about life, we need also to worry about what it is teaching the world about America.

PERSONAL RESPONSE

What is your opinion of America's pop culture exports, particularly Hollywood films? Do you think they convey a negative image of America?

QUESTIONS FOR CLASS OR SMALL-GROUP DISCUSSION

1. How does the opening paragraph about Franklin relate to the rest of the essay?
2. Bayles writes in paragraph 2 of "the negative impression that America has recently been making on the rest of humanity—via our popular culture." What examples of popular culture can you give that support or refute this statement?
3. State in your own words what you understand Bayles to mean when she writes that we have "an unwarranted dismissal of elite-oriented cultural diplomacy, combined with an unquestioned faith in the export of popular culture" (paragraph 14).
4. Bayles believes that the solution to the problem of the negative image that popular culture gives to people in other countries "is far from clear" (paragraph 16) and concludes that we could "try harder to convey . . . 'a full and fair picture of the United States'" (paragraph 17). Discuss possible solutions to the problem and ways to convey a better, fuller picture of America.

EFFORTS TO DEAL WITH AMERICA'S IMAGE ABROAD: ARE THEY WORKING?

LISA A. CURTIS

Lisa Curtis is a Senior Research Fellow in the Asian Studies Center at The Heritage Foundation whose research focuses on analyzing America's economic, security, and political relationships with India, Pakistan, Sri Lanka, Bangladesh and Nepal. She has served as a professional staff member of the Senate Foreign Relations Committee, as a Senior Adviser in the State Department's South Asia bureau, and as a political analyst on South Asia for the Central Intelligence Agency. The testimony here was delivered to the United States House of Representative Committee on Foreign Affairs' Subcommittee on International Organizations, Human Rights, and Oversight on April 26, 2007.

Mr. Chairman, Members of the Subcommittee, thank you for inviting me here today to discuss U.S. efforts to improve our image abroad. It is an honor to address this Subcommittee on such an important issue and to share my thoughts on how we might improve our public diplomacy efforts in the years to come.[1]

The attacks of September 11, 2001, and their aftermath have renewed Washington's focus on the importance of reaching out to foreign audiences, particularly within the Muslim world, in order to boost support for U.S. values and policies. During the Cold War, U.S. policymakers understood the importance of the tools of public and cultural diplomacy in foreign policy. President Ronald Reagan defined public diplomacy as "Those actions of the U.S. government designed to generate support for U.S. national security objectives."[2]

Recent polls show the image of the U.S. is declining throughout the world and that large majorities of Muslim populations believe the U.S. seeks to undermine Islam as a religion.[3] Defeating terrorist ideology requires that we dispel such negative perceptions of America and that we engage more actively and deliberately with the Muslim world. While we may never change the minds of murderous terrorists who despise America and its democratic ideals, we should reach out to those large segments of Muslim populations that do not support violence against Americans, but who still have mixed feelings about the U.S. and its role in the world.

Efforts to Improve Public Diplomacy

4   Shortly after 9/11, it became clear that merging the United States Information Agency (USIA) into the State Department in 1999 had damaged overall U.S. public diplomacy efforts by cutting valuable resources for programs and undervaluing the mission of public diplomacy in supporting U.S. national security objectives. The Bush Administration has sought to address the shortcomings of U.S. public diplomacy over the last five years, with some positive results. However, much work lies ahead.

---

[1] The Heritage Foundation is a public policy, research, and educational organization operating under Section 501(C)(3). It is privately supported, and receives no funds from any government at any level, nor does it perform any government or other contract work. The Heritage Foundation is the most broadly supported think tank in the United States. During 2006, it had more than 283,000 individual, foundation, and corporate supporters representing every state in the U.S. Its 2006 income came from the following sources: individuals 64%; foundations 19%; corporations 3%; investment income 14%; and publication sales and other 0%. The top five corporate givers provided The Heritage Foundation with 1.3% of its 2006 income. The Heritage Foundation's books are audited annually by the national accounting firm of Deloitte & Touche. A list of major donors is available from The Heritage Foundation upon request. Members of The Heritage Foundation staff testify as individuals discussing their own independent research. The views expressed are their own, and do not reflect an institutional position for The Heritage Foundation or its board of trustees.

[2] Juliana Geran Pilon, *Why America is Such a Hard Sell: Beyond Pride and Prejudice* (Lanham: Rowman and Littlefield Publishers, Inc., 2007), p. 220.

[3] Steven Kull, "Muslim Public Opinion on U.S. Policy, Attacks on Civilians, and Al-Qaeda," worldpublicopinion.org, April 24, 2007.

In the early days following the 9/11 attacks, the Bush Administration responded to the gaps in our public diplomacy strategy by putting in place an Under Secretary for Public Diplomacy, Charlotte Beers, who had spent her career in the private sector as a well-renowned marketing expert. The White House also instituted regular White House-run inter-agency strategic communication meetings. Three years later, as opinion polls showed America's reputation continuing to plummet worldwide—and former Secretary of Defense Rumsfeld asked his famous question about whether America was capturing and eliminating more terrorists than it was creating—the soul-searching to develop a better U.S. public diplomacy campaign continued.

In September 2004, the Office of the Under Secretary for Acquisition, Technology, and Logistics released the "Report of the Defense Science Board Task Force on Strategic Communication." The report concluded that the U.S. needed to transform its strategic communications efforts through a Presidential directive to "connect strategy to structure" and improve interagency coordination. The report called for greater government-private sector collaboration and the creation of an independent, non-profit, and non-partisan Center for Strategic Communication.[4] In April of 2003, The Heritage Foundation released a report titled, "How to Reinvigorate U.S. Public Diplomacy," which included recommendations that the Administration and Congress restore public diplomacy's independent reporting and budget channels that were lost during the USIA/State merger in 1999 and return public diplomacy currently dispersed among other State Department bureaus into one public diplomacy hierarchy.[5]

The Bush Administration has made several attempts since 9/11 to streamline the public diplomacy bureaucracy and tighten strategic communications. Given the myriad and diverse public diplomacy efforts of the U.S. government, however, this has proved to be a far more difficult task than anyone originally expected. In January 2003, President George W. Bush formally established the Office of Global Communications (OGC) to facilitate and coordinate the strategic direction of the White House and individual agency efforts to communicate with foreign audiences.[6] One year ago, President Bush established a new Policy Coordination Committee on Public Diplomacy and Strategic Communication led by the State Department Under Secretary for Public Diplomacy and Public Affairs. This Committee is responsible for coordinating interagency activities, unifying public messaging, ensuring all public diplomacy resources are supporting the messages, and ensuring every agency gives public diplomacy a high priority.

---

[4]Defense Science Board, *Report of the Defense Science Board Task Force on Strategic Communication*, Office of the Under Secretary of Defense for Acquisition, Technology, and Logistics, September 2004, pp. 1–3; 7, 8.

[5]Helle Dale and Steven Johnson, "How to Reinvigorate U.S. Public Diplomacy," *Heritage Foundation Backgrounder No. 1645*, April 23, 2003, at www.heritage.org/Research/NationalSecurity/bg16545.cfm.

[6]General Accounting Office, "U.S. Public Diplomacy: Interagency Coordination Efforts Hampered by the Lack of a National Communication Strategy," April 2005, GAO-05–323.

8   Under Secretary of State for Public Diplomacy and Public Affairs Karen Hughes has moved forward with developing a unified strategic communications apparatus, but progress has been slow, and she will have to persevere in her efforts to corral the disparate efforts. Hughes' office has also had some success in boosting the role of public diplomacy in our overall diplomatic and security policies, but this also has proven to be a bureaucratic challenge.

The most notable progress in developing unified messaging efforts has been in the establishment of a rapid response unit that follows newscasts around the world and offers talking points on breaking international news to rebut negative media stories about the U.S. in the Muslim world and elsewhere. The State Department has also tasked all posts to develop country-specific communications plans, with special focus on 19 posts that are most critical to the efforts to counter terrorist ideology.

Funding for public diplomacy is increasing, and will likely continue to do so as we ramp up public outreach, foreign exchange, and scholarship programs, as well as public diplomacy training for State Department officers. The State Department requested almost $800 million for public diplomacy efforts around the world for fiscal year 2008 and increased public diplomacy spending in the last two years in key regions like the Middle East (25 percent) and in South Asia (nearly 40 percent).[7] The State Department has also revived the Fulbright Scholarship Program, but experts say it will take time to re-establish its effectiveness, since it had been so grossly under-funded throughout the 1990s. The State Department created the Global Cultural Initiative last year to coordinate all government-backed art, music, and literature programs abroad and increased the number of participants in State Department educational and cultural programs to nearly 39,000 this year.[8]

In early January of this year, the State Department held a major conference with over 150 participants, including senior U.S. executives, to discuss how American companies can help improve the U.S. image abroad. The conference represents a significant step in meeting a key recommendation raised by the General Accounting Office in May, 2006, which called on the Secretary of State to develop a strategy to promote the active engagement of the private sector beyond international exchanges.[9] The conference included intensive breakout sessions to generate specific ideas on how the U.S. private sector can get involved in public diplomacy. Recommendations for U.S. businesses with operations overseas included making public diplomacy actions a corporate officer's responsibility; becoming part of the local community through employee volunteerism; greater engagement with responsible non-governmental organizations (NGOs); and creating "circles of influence"

---

[7]Jess T. Ford, "U.S. Public Diplomacy: State Department Efforts Lack Certain Communication Elements and Face Persistent Challenges," testimony Before the House Committee on Appropriations, Subcommittee on Science, the Departments of State, Justice, and Commerce, May 3, 2006, page 2.

[8]Karen Hughes, testimony to the House Appropriations Committee, Subcommittee on State, Foreign Operations, and Related Programs, U.S. House of Representatives, April 19, 2007.

[9]Jess T. Ford, "U.S. Public Diplomacy Efforts."

through relationships with organizations, chambers of commerce, journalists, and local business leaders.[10]

12   During the conference, James E. Murphy, Chief Marketing and Communications Officer of Accenture, reported that U.S. private giving to developing countries exceeds $70 billion annually. This includes gifts from foundations, corporations, private organizations, and individuals. Most of the world is unaware that Americans are providing this level of private and corporate giving to developing countries.

    One example of effective private-public partnership to address the most pressing international problems is the U.S. corporate response to the devastating South Asia earthquake on October 8, 2005. Shortly after the earthquake—which killed over 74,000 people and displaced tens of thousands—U.S. private sector executives from GE, UPS, Pzifer, Xerox, and Citigroup agreed to lead a nationwide effort to raise awareness and resources to help survivors of the earthquake rebuild their lives and communities. The group has raised over $100 million for the earthquake victims.

    The State Department's recent establishment of the Office of Private Sector Outreach to engage and work with businesses, universities, and foundations on public diplomacy issues should also help to identify opportunities and implement various projects that foster cooperation between the U.S. public and private sectors in their overseas missions.

Expanding U.S. Soft Power

While strategic communication is an important element in influencing foreign populations' opinions of America, it is equally important to promote deeper, more frequent cultural engagement, people-to-people exchanges, and targeted development assistance programs to assert America's soft power. In a recent *Washington Post* op-ed, Homeland Security Secretary Michael Chertoff said it well:

16   Moreover, this war cannot be won by arms alone; "soft" power matters. In these ways, our current struggle resembles the Cold War. As with the Cold War, we must respond globally. As with the Cold War, ideas matter as much as armaments. And as with the Cold War, this war requires our patience and resolve.

    The U.S. Agency for International Development (USAID) has become more involved in public diplomacy after the 9/11 Commission reported to Congress that some of the largest recipients of U.S. foreign aid had very strong anti-American sentiment among their populations. Establishing a State-USAID Policy Council and a Public Diplomacy Working Group has helped USAID to establish closer ties with the Department of State to publicize America's humanitarian and development aid initiatives.

    The U.S. response to the South Asia earthquake in the fall of 2005 and its positive impact on Pakistani attitudes toward the U.S. demonstrates that humanitarian assistance can influence popular views of America. I visited Pakistan to attend the International Donors' Conference on November 19, 2005, as a staffer for the Senate

---

[10]U.S. Department of State, "Private Sector Summit on Public Diplomacy: Models for Action," January 9, 2007, pp. 12, 13.

Foreign Relations Committee and saw first-hand the change in the Pakistani population's views of the U.S. because of our rapid and robust humanitarian response
to this monumental disaster. Even our harshest critics admitted that America had
come through for Pakistan at its greatest hour of need. The U.S. Chinook helicop-
ters that rescued survivors and ferried food and shelter materials to the affected
areas became a symbol of America's helping hand.

The U.S. response was well-coordinated among the State Department, Department of Defense (DOD), and USAID. DOD established mobile medical units in
remote areas of the Northwest Frontier Province and makeshift schools in the badly
affected capital of Azad Kashmir, giving the Pakistanis a new perspective on the U.S.
military and demonstrating U.S. interest in the well-being of the Pakistani people.

20   Polling shows that U.S. earthquake relief efforts doubled the percentage of
Pakistanis with favorable views of the U.S. from 23 percent to 46 percent from May
2005 to November 2005. This figure had dropped to 27 percent by 2006, however.
Similarly, the U.S. response to the tsunami disaster had a positive impact on public
opinion of America in Indonesia. Favorable views of the U.S. went from 15 percent
to 38 percent. The point is that providing humanitarian assistance is not only an act
of goodwill, it can reflect positively on the U.S. image in the region where people
are benefiting from the aid.

Engaging with civil society and local religious leaders on issues such as human
rights, political and economic reform, and religion in society also will help build
greater understanding and help defeat misperceptions of the U.S. Twelve years ago
as a Political Officer serving at the U.S. Embassy in Islamabad, I participated in
a USIA-sponsored program to bring together female U.S.-based Islamic scholars
and Pakistani female lawyers, human rights workers, and NGO leaders to discuss
the role of women in Islam. I felt then—and even more so now—that it was one of
the more worthwhile activities I was involved in as a diplomat. The U.S. has an important role to play in facilitating these kinds of open exchanges and in supporting
human rights, democracy, and economic development at the grassroots level. The
State Department should encourage officers' initiation and participation in such
programs on a broad scale.

Recent Polling

We clearly have our work cut out for us. Recent polls tell us that opinions of America have declined markedly—to all-time lows in some countries—over the last few
years. Some of these polls have revealed additional information for consideration.
Recent polling on views of the U.S. role in the world released by the Chicago
Council on Global Affairs, for example, shows that most countries reject the idea
of the U.S. as pre-eminent world leader; however, majorities in these countries still
want the U.S. to participate in international efforts to address world problems. At
the same time, this poll showed that many publics view their country's relations
with the U.S. as improving.

A recent Gallup World Poll, "How Citizens of the U.S. and Predominantly
Muslim Nations View Each Other," shows that Muslims generally admire the West

for its advanced technology and democracy and admire their own societies for their respect for Islam and its teachings and their own family values. In January 2007, 57 percent of Americans reported "not knowing much" or "nothing" about Islam. Although perhaps not the role of the State Department, it seems clear that we as a nation need to learn more about the Muslim faith and get to know and respect its traditions and practices. The Gallup World Poll also concluded that Muslims and Americans generally agreed on the need to control extremism. The polling shows that not only do we need to think about the messages we are sending to the Muslim world, we also need to search for practical ways to engage with it and to build upon our shared values.

Moving Forward

24   The worldwide polls revealing declining support for America are discouraging. But polls change. And with the right public diplomacy strategies and with perseverance, ingenuity, and decisiveness in asserting U.S. soft power, the U.S. can begin to win support from moderate Muslims. Our message needs to be unified and consistent with our actions or it will not be credible. To improve U.S. public diplomacy, we should:

- **Continue to raise the status of public diplomacy as a key element in fighting Islamic extremism and protecting U.S. national security.** Under Secretary Hughes has made progress on this front by empowering Ambassadors to speak more frequently to the media and by including public diplomacy as a key job element in senior State Department officers' evaluations. There has been resistance within the State Department bureaucracy to having officers spend more time on public diplomacy activities, which has led some outside experts to conclude that a separate public diplomacy entity like USIA needs to be re-established. Given Under Secretary Hughes' steady progress in raising the mission of public diplomacy at the State Department, it may be too early to make a decision in this regard. The transformation of the State Department may take some time, but in the end, it may be more beneficial to have a large corps of public diplomacy-savvy diplomats and an integration of U.S. foreign policy and strategic communication.
- **More clearly link the mission of USAID and the role of development and humanitarian assistance to core national security objectives and ensure close coordination between USAID and State Department on programming for aid projects.** The bureaucratic stove piping of resources has often made us our own worst enemy. The establishment of a new Director for U.S. Foreign Assistance at the State Department and new initiatives to address the lack of strategic focus in our assistance programs are steps in the right direction. This bureaucratic reorganization should strengthen, not diminish, the role of U.S. assistance in foreign policy. While officials in Washington will set the aid priorities, they should incorporate input from USAID staff that possess detailed knowledge and insight into civil society

in recipient countries. If we are trying to reach out to these communities and build support for American values and policies, we will have to break down bureaucratic barriers that inhibit efficient communication and operational cooperation between the State Department and USAID. As we seek to promote democratic and economic reform, USAID should play a prominent role in the planning and implementation of projects aimed at reaching all levels of society.

- **Consider establishing a semi-governmental entity to conduct public opinion research in individual countries to allow us to tailor our messages to different audiences and to give U.S. public diplomacy efforts a solid factual foundation.** The Intelligence and Research Bureau of the State Department has conducted limited public polling and there are several credible non-government entities like Zogby International, the Pew Research Center, and WorldPublicOpinion.org that conduct international polls on a regular basis. However, it would be useful to have a semi-governmental agency that would be responsive to government tasking and whose staff could interact closely with government officials.

- **Re-establish the once-popular American libraries in city centers to supplement our efforts to reach people through the internet and electronic media and reinvigorate the book translation program.** Foreign interlocutors have emphasized their positive experiences visiting the libraries in the past and the strong impression these experiences left with them about America. Libraries could help reach audiences that do not have access to the internet and offer a traditional forum for reaching out to the local population. The Bush Administration should also revive USIA's once-robust book translation program, which now operates sporadically and mostly in Spanish. Expanded offerings on U.S. history, economics, and culture should be directed at essential target audiences in Arabic, Urdu, Hindi, Russian, and Chinese and involve private foundations and industry in donating and distributing materials.

- **Revitalize U.S. international broadcasting leadership and recommit resources and funding to Voice of America.** Members of the Broadcasting Board of Governors (BBG) have at times been inefficient in their decision-making and focused more on their own pet projects instead of providing policy guidance to staff directors. Congress should consider making the BBG more of an advisory body and granting executive power to a chairman who would be responsible for strategic planning and implementation of international broadcasting programs. Although the BBG increased America's presence over Arab airwaves by creating Radio Sawa and Al-Hurra TV, it did so by taking resources from the Voice of America. As a result, U.S. programming in South Asia, Africa, and Latin America now lacks content, lively discussion, and airtime.

If we are to isolate and defeat the extremists' hateful and totalitarian ideologies, we will need to focus more U.S. foreign policy attention and resources on soft power strategies that seek to win support from moderate Muslims worldwide. Right now the score is not in our favor. However, with a sustained and focused strategy, and with some patience and perseverance, we should begin to see the fruits of our labor in the years to come.

PERSONAL RESPONSE

Why do you think that America's image abroad has continued to decline despite efforts to improve public diplomacy?

QUESTIONS FOR CLASS OR SMALL-GROUP DISCUSSION

1. State in your own words what the United States government has done since 9/11 to strengthen U. S. public diplomacy, according to Curtis.

2. In paragraph 11, Curtis reports on a major conference to discuss what American companies can do to help improve the image of America abroad, especially "on how the U. S. private sector can get involved in public diplomacy." What suggestions did the participants come up with and how successful do you think they are likely to be?

3. Curtis writes about efforts to "assert America's soft power" (paragraph 15). What do you understand "soft power" to be?

4. Select one of Curtis's suggestions for improving the image of America abroad and discuss whether you agree with her that it could be effective.

○ PERSPECTIVES ON AMERICA ABROAD IN POLITICAL SCIENCE ○

Suggestions for Writing

1. Explain your position on the question of whether America should be responsible for defending weaker countries from oppression.

2. Respond to Paul Johnson's "American Idealism and Realpolitik," either agreeing or disagreeing with him and using examples to support your position.

3. Drawing on Martha Bayles's "Now Showing: The Good, the Bad, and the Ugly Americans" and Lisa A. Curtis's "Efforts to Deal with America's Image Abroad: Are They Working?" explain what you think ordinary American citizens can do to help improve the image of America abroad.

4. Explain the effect that America's wealth, power, commercialism, or any other aspect of its culture has on the way America is perceived by people in other nations.

5. Interview people who have immigrated to America to learn their reasons for coming to this country. Find out what images they had of America

before they came and whether their impressions have changed now that they are living here.

6. If you are familiar with the difficulties a foreigner has had adjusting to life in your own country, tell about that person's experiences. Or, if you have personally experienced life as a foreigner in a country not your own, describe that experience.

7. Explain why you think America's popular culture appeals to people in other countries.

8. Select a recent popular film and analyze the image of America that it projects, or, do a close analysis of a person or object from popular culture that you think represents an aspect of American culture.

9. Analyze an American book or story for the image it projects of America. Try to view the book or story objectively, as if you were a foreigner looking for information about America. What impression do you think a foreigner reading the same book or story would get of America?

Research Topics

1. Research the subject of America's "soft power" in the period following the September 11, 2001, terrorist attacks on American soil.

2. Research the subject of anti-Americanism in countries other than America, whether it exists and, if so, why it exists and how strong it is.

3. Conduct library research to expand on the views expressed by writers in this chapter of the American image abroad. From your research, draw some conclusions about that image. Do you find one particular image or many images? What aspects of America are responsible for the image or images? Does the image of America differ from country to country or even from continent to continent? You should be able to narrow your focus and determine a central idea for your paper after your preliminary search for sources and early review of the materials.

4. Research the subject of U. S. relations with Japan, China, the Soviet Union, the Middle East, or another foreign country that may figure importantly in the future of the United States. On the basis of your research, assess the importance to the United States of strengthening such relations and the potential effects of allowing relations with that country to deteriorate.

5. Research the conditions surrounding America's involvement in Bosnia, Kuwait, or Kosovo. Limit your focus to one aspect of the subject, such as what led to America's involvement, what America's involvement meant to American citizens, or effects on the country of America's intervention. Then argue the extent to which you support that involvement.

6. Martha Bayles in "Now Showing: The Good, the Bad and the Ugly Americans" opens her essay with a reference to Benjamin Franklin's public

diplomacy in France. Research the subject of Franklin's success at diplomacy. What were his goals, what strategies did he use, and determine whether you think they have application to the United States' efforts to improve public diplomacy today.

7. Research the efforts of the U. S. Agency for International Development (USAID) to improve America's image abroad. What has worked and what has failed in achieving that goal?

RESPONDING TO VISUALS

©Reuters/CORBIS

Protesters burn an American flag during demonstrations in the western Pakistani city of Peshawar, October 12, 2001.

1. What is going on in this picture? Select details that convey the overall meaning of the picture.
2. What are the implications of the many cameras and video recorders at this event? Does the rhetorical effectiveness of flag burning depend on its being photographed? Does a gesture such as burning a flag need to be recorded visually in order to be effective? How does capturing the event on film or tape aid its effectiveness as a public expression of protest?
3. How would the meaning of the image change if the photographer had done a close-up of the burning flag, excluding the crowd?

RESPONDING TO VISUALS

© AP Photo/Natacha Pisarenko

A McDonald's sign in part of a poor neighborhood in Caracas is seen Sunday July 6, 2003. Most Venezuelans make the minimum salary per month. Even if two parents are working, it's still not enough to buy the basket of basic goods for the average family of five. Venezuela's economic crisis, the worst in decades, has spared no one—posing the greatest challenge to President Hugo Chavez's grand design of bridging the gap between wealthy and poor in this South American nation.

1. What image of American culture do you think the McDonald's arch represents?
2. To what extent do you think that the symbolic representation of the McDonald's arch is purely American? Can you think of any other icon or symbol that is purely American and that is recognized around the world?
3. What contrast does the photograph suggest between American culture, represented by the McDonald's arch, and the impoverished Venezuelan culture, represented by the poor neighborhood in the photograph?

PART · FOUR

Science and Technology

CHAPTER
19

Digital Technology
and the Internet

Digital technology is constantly changing, with new, ever-faster programs emerging frequently. Although early researchers recognized the potential of computers, no doubt few of them envisioned the staggering capabilities of what they can do or the extent to which they would be so closely and inextricably linked with people's everyday lives. Increasingly sophisticated computers make child's play of activities that just a few years ago were challenging or impossible tasks. Young children today learn skills—sometimes before they enter school—that many of their grandparents will never even try to learn. Indeed, computer technology has advanced at such a rapid rate that its powers seem unlimited, a prospect that fills some with eager anticipation and leaves others feeling intimidated and frightened.

"Cyberspace," a word coined by author William Gibson in his sci-fi novel *Neuromancer*, commonly refers to the nonphysical space and sense of community created by Internet users around the world, the virtual "world" that users inhabit when they are online. People can communicate and share files on the Internet through e-mail and at websites; they can conduct research, shop, play games, and do any number of activities that people have been accustomed to do in physical space. The difference, of course, is that all those activities take place by pressing keys on a keyboard, moving a mouse around, or using a touchpad. Such convenience has changed the way many people conduct their lives, most would say in a positive way. However, the high-tech capabilities of the Internet have also led to problems. The readings in this chapter look at some of those problems as well as the benefits of such technology.

The first two readings focus on Internet websites, with articles on MySpace and Facebook. Cindy Long writes to an audience of educators about the benefits and potential dangers of MySpace, a social networking site founded in 2003, that originally appealed primarily to high school, middle school, and even grade school students, but now is a site used by just about anyone, including politicians, movie stars, and other celebrities. Many schools have blocked students from using MySpace because of its potential as a site for sexual predators to lurk and because some students post questionable content, such as too much personal information or obscene, damaging, or hurtful language. Long's essay cites the opinions of students and teachers on both positive and negative aspects of MySpace.

Next is Michelle Slatalla's *New York Times* "Cyberfamilias" column, a biweekly feature on the influences of the Internet on family life. In "'omg my mom joined facebook!!'" she writes amusingly of her daughter's reaction to her creating an account on Facebook. This social networking website was originally designed for college students with student IDs but has since been opened to anyone with an e-mail address. Slatalla raises the question of whether Facebook should be open to everyone, particularly in light of the age-old problem of the generation gap. Should parents or other adults be privy to young people's online accounts? Does it help or harm parent–child relationships or the rights of young people, for that matter, if adults can read what young people write online?

Next, the focus shifts to look at a large problem for creators of intellectual property, the pirating of copyrighted material such as books, movies, music, television programs, and computer programs, among others. Music downloading was perhaps the first area in which the problem became apparent, and measures were put in place to protect that material. Now, certain technologies make it possible to illegally upload or download films in a matter of seconds; whole books can be scanned without their authors' or publishers' knowledge and made available to anyone with Internet access. A strong advocate for restraints on movie piracy had been the late Jack Valenti, past president of the Motion Picture Association of America. His "Thoughts on the Digital Future of Movies, the Threat of Piracy, the Hope of Redemption" represents his testimony before a Senate Committee hearing on the effects of Internet piracy on the entertainment industry. In it, Valenti spells out the dangers of movie piracy and steps that need to be taken to protect the rights of copyright holders.

The chapter concludes with a look at a relatively new concern in digital technology, aspects of which raise grave concerns for many people, the implantation of a radio frequency identification (RFID) microchip into humans that emits a radio signal with an identification number. The device was originally designed to be linked to medical records for use by heart patients, people with implanted medical devices such has defibrillators, patients who need frequent medical care, and the mentally impaired. Since the FDA approved chip implantation for these uses in 2004, there has been much discussion about the ethics of such chips, particularly concerning privacy. The concern is that the wrong people might gain access to the patient's information or that the information can be used against the patient, such as by an employer or insurance company. Todd Lewan's article "Chips: High Tech Aids or Tracking Tools?" is particularly interested in the privacy issues raised by the relatively new use of RFIDs as human tracking devices and as identification for people in certain high-security positions. He looks at the opinions of both supporters and detractors of their use and identifies a number of the questions that people have about them. As you read his article, consider whether you might agree to having such a device implanted in your body.

I NEED MYSPACE!
Cindy Long

Cindy Long is a Washington, D.C.-based writer who covers education and technology. This essay appeared in the April 2007 issue of NEA Today, *a publication for educators who are members of the National Education Association.*

When Caitlyn McNeill started high school last year, she wished she could take all of her middle school friends with her. Unfortunately, only half of the 16-year-old's friends joined her at Northern High in Owings, Maryland, while the other half went to school in the neighboring town. They still manage to keep in close touch, chatting almost as often as they did when they walked the halls and ate lunch together. The only difference is that now they hang out on MySpace.com, the Web site that has become the 21st century's answer to the 1950s soda shop.

Caitlyn and her friends log on to MySpace to catch up with each other, post bulletins about what's new, and chat about friends, school, weekend plans, and, of course, boys. They decorate their MySpace pages the way they might decorate their bedrooms, complete with colorful, patterned backgrounds and photos; Caitlyn's page is greenish-blue with a star pattern. "It's bright and really cute," she says. Along with posting pictures of themselves and their friends, they link to videos and MP3 files. "My friend has a video from the Fresh Prince of Bel-Air, where Will and Carlton are doing a dance," says Caitlyn. "It's hilarious."

It's all part of the social networking revolution, in which users build personal pages and use those pages to share information, chat online, and keep in touch with others. Hundreds of such sites exist, but MySpace leads the way. It's the third most visited Web site in the United States (behind Yahoo! and Google), averaging 36 million page views a day. Of the millions, many are students. Right now, more than half of American kids online use social networking sites, according to a Pew Internet & American Life Project survey of teenagers.

4　Making connections is what powers the popularity of sites like MySpace, but it can also be cause for concern. News stories abound of online predators stalking young girls and boys by way of their profiles and luring teens, even preteens, into dangerous situations. Some kids post photographs of themselves in less-than-virtuous poses, in barely-there outfits—or worse, in incriminating situations—for all the world to see, including college admissions officers and potential employers. Students have also posted nasty comments about their classmates and teachers. In fact, more than one in three educators surveyed by the National School Boards Association (NSBA)— some 36 percent—said social networking sites have been disruptive at school.

But tell students about the concerns surrounding sites like MySpace, and the common refrain is one adults have been hearing from teenagers since the Stone Age: "You worry too much!" As media-savvy technophiles, they realize some of their peers misuse the Web, but they're asking us to trust that most of them use it safely and responsibly. What's more, research backs up their claims. Most students take steps to protect their privacy, and in some schools, safety and social networking have become part of the curriculum. "Simply blocking access to MySpace at school is not the end of the story," said NSBA Executive Director Anne Bryant. "Students need to be educated about these sites and what the impact of misuse is on themselves as well as others."

Kathy Schrock, who helps educate students on technology issues in Nauset Public Schools on Cape Cod, comes at the problems of social networking with firsthand experience. For an entire year, she had an "imposter page," or fake profile, posted about her on MySpace by five students at a Catholic high school.

"The page they created for me was basically harmless, but it wasn't authentic and I wanted it taken down," says Schrock, the district's administrator for technology, whose "Guide for Educators" is found at www.discoveryschool.com. "I had to call the teacher, who didn't even know about MySpace. I wrote to the school, but the principal wouldn't take care of it. MySpace wouldn't even take it down."

8   That was a year ago. The bogus page has since come down, and MySpace is now quick to remove imposter pages. In fact, its frequently asked questions include, "How do we remove an imposter profile for a teacher/faculty member" and "Someone is pretending to be me—what do I do?"

While high-profile cases involving teenagers creating imposter pages for teachers and classmates have surfaced, Schrock is more concerned about students' safety. Her message to students is simple: if you have a profile, keep it private.

MySpace requires users to be at least 14, and profiles of MySpace users under 16 are automatically set to "private," so only the users they've allowed access can view their profile, send instant messages and e-mails, or add them to their blog list. But kids routinely lie about their ages—either that, or there are a surprising number of high school freshmen and sophomores age 20 or above on MySpace.

Last June, MySpace announced that privacy options would be available to users of all ages and that all users could block others from contacting them, conceal their "online now" status, and prevent others from e-mailing direct links to their images. MySpace users 18 or older can no longer add users under 16 to their friends list unless they already know the person's full name or e-mail address.

12   The new privacy options were announced after a 16-year-old girl tricked her parents into getting her a passport and then flew to the Mideast to be with a man she met on the site. It's one of the most extreme stories—of which there are only a smattering, considering the tens of millions of young people who visit the site regularly.

How often is regularly? "I go on MySpace every chance I get," Caitlyn McNeill says. She's not alone. According to the Pew study, 48 percent of teens visit social networking sites at least once every day.

Most of Caitlyn's MySpace habits align closely with the Pew findings, which show that young people are wise to the dangers posed by social networking sites. Caitlyn and her friends set their profiles to private; Pew found that 66 percent of teens have done the same. Caitlyn uses MySpace to keep in touch with her friends from school and to make plans; Pew found that 91 percent of teens use social networking sites to keep in touch with friends they see a lot, while 72 percent use the site to make plans with those friends. In fact, the tagline of the MySpace site is, "A place for friends."

Caitlyn is also a fairly savvy Internet user. "There are a lot of creeps out there, and I know it," she says. "I don't let anybody add me to their friends list, and I don't accept messages from anybody I haven't met in person. Also, if your profile is set to private, the people at school you don't like can't find out information about you."

16   Sarah Mortimer, who lives in New Hampshire, uses MySpace to keep in touch with friends both near and far. "Since I have switched schools a lot, I am able to keep in touch with kids from my old schools," the 16-year-old says. "It's just really nice to see someone I haven't talked to in, like, 10 years and remember them from my childhood." She has her profile set to private so "rapist killers don't get me," she

says half-jokingly. But her profile also says she lives in Zimbabwe so that anyone searching in her town or ZIP code won't find her.

That's exactly the kind of Internet shrewdness Kim Conner, the computer teacher at Nauset Middle School, is trying to instill among her sixth-, seventh-, and eighth-graders. "One student put up Albert Einstein as his profile photo to help hide his identity," Conner says. "I thought that was rather clever."

Conner has worked social networking safety into the curriculum as a way to "make the kids aware of the different things that can happen when they use the sites without thinking," she says.

As is the case in most districts, Conner and her students can't access MySpace or other social networking sites at school, but she's saved screen shots that she uses to demonstrate how profiles that aren't set to private can reveal identifying details. For example, when kids allow their profiles and instant messages to be open, anyone can read plans they might make online. She uses the following as an example:

> NAUSETGIRL (5:09:55): wotz ^? wnt 2 go out?
> WARRIOR08 (5:09:56): yS, whr do wnt 2 go?
> NAUSETGRIL (5:09:57): How bout the chocl@ Sparrow n Orleans?

20   Suddenly, anyone logged onto the page can see where the girls are meeting.

Conner also uses an example of a profile of a girl who thought she hadn't posted anything identifiable, except for a photo gallery image of her wearing her school's field hockey uniform.

But once students are aware of the dangers and are taught to think carefully about how they use sites like MySpace, Conner believes that the advantages outweigh the disadvantages. "It's really a great way for kids to stay connected outside of school," she says, adding that sometimes students get online and help each other with homework or work on assignments together. But the main benefit of sites like MySpace is that they "allow young people to express themselves, be creative, and show their friends who they really are," says Conner. "It gives them a common venue."

Chris Luty, a senior at Kennedy High School in Silver Spring, Maryland, expresses himself on his MySpace profile with photos, videos, music files, and different fonts and backgrounds. Parents and teachers beware—what kids like Chris might find appealing about their profiles would probably cross the eyes of most adults. On many teen profiles, backgrounds are a blur of vibrant colors, patterns, and clashing, often unreadable fonts, splattered with links and images. But their friends can tell a lot about their sense of humor by the videos they post, or about their musical tastes by the bands they promote.

24   Chris's profile includes an Adam Sandler video and videos of live performances by three of his favorite bands—Godsmack, +44, and Patent Pending. He says that all of his friends on MySpace are people he knows in 'Real life." Otherwise, he says, "I'd have no idea who was sitting behind that keyboard."

Kim Conner acknowledges that there have been problems with abuses of My-Space, but she says she approaches it with "the one bad apple doesn't spoil the whole bushel theory."

"Some really good things can come out of this," Conner says. "It gives all students a way to connect and be together in a safe environment. MySpace can be a very safe and positive thing."

PERSONAL RESPONSE

If you have (or have had) a MySpace or other social network account, write about your experiences with it. If you have never personally had an account, what have you observed of those you know who do have one?

QUESTIONS FOR CLASS OR SMALL-GROUP DISCUSSION

1. Comment on Long's use of examples. For instance, how effective do you find her opening paragraphs? How do they advance the development of her essay? Note other uses of example throughout the essay.

2. Long reports that over a third of the educators surveyed by the National School Boards Association (NSBA) said that "social networking sites have been disruptive at school" (paragraph 4). In what ways might such sites be disruptive? Do you believe they are disruptive?

3. Long quotes NSBA director Anne Bryant as saying that "'students need to be educated'" about sites like MySpace and their potential misuse. What sorts of things do you imagine that such an education would include? What warning or advice would you give a young person interested in such a site?

4. What, according to Long, are the benefits and drawbacks of a social networking account like MySpace? Long notes that Computer Teacher Kim Connor "believes [of sites like MySpace] that the advantages outweigh the disadvantages" (paragraph 21). Do you agree with her?

"OMG MY MOM JOINED FACEBOOK!!"

MICHELLE SLATALLA

Michelle Slatalla, a writer who lives in Northern California, is a regular contributor to the New York Times. *She writes for the "Cyberfamilias" feature, about the changing landscape of family life under the influence of the Net that appears every other week. Slatalla is author of* The Town on Beaver Creek *(2006). This column was published in the* New York Times *on June 7, 2007.*

I have reached a curious point in life. Although I feel like the same precocious know-it-all cynic I always was, I suddenly am surrounded by younger precocious know-it-all cynics whose main purpose appears to be to remind me that I've lost my edge.

Many of these people are teenagers.

Some of them I gave birth to.

4   One was in a breech position.

And the other day, as I drove home with one of my tormenters in the passenger seat, she started laughing at the way I pronounced "Henri Cartier-Bresson."

"Ha ha ha, is that how you think his name sounds?" my daughter said. "Oh, my God. Who told you that?"

It was my college photography professor. Twenty-six years ago.

8   Rather than draw attention to my age, I tried to trick her into thinking of me as someone cool, as we said 26 years ago. "I hope you don't think this gives you the right to make fun of me on your Facebook page," I said.

"My Facebook page?" this person asked incredulously. "My page? Is that what you think Facebook is?"

Suddenly a vague memory from my childhood—the time someone else's mother left her family, wrote a few young adult novels and ended up in a sad apartment complex on the edge of town—welled up, unbidden.

I needed to banish it, along with all evidence of this humiliating conversation. But how?

12   I vowed to fight on her turf.

So last week I joined Facebook, the social network for students that opened its doors last fall to anyone with an e-mail address. The decision not only doubled its active membership to 24 million (more than 50 percent of whom are not students), but it also made it possible for parents like me to peek at our children in their on-line lair.

At Facebook.com, I eyed the home page ("Everyone can join") with suspicion. I doubted Facebook's sincerity. What could a site created by a student who was born three years after I started mispronouncing "Henri Cartier-Bresson" want with me?

Realizing that these were cynical, mocking thoughts cheered me—I felt edgier already—and gave me the courage to join.

16   After I got my Profile page, the first thing I did was to search for other members—my daughter and her friends—to ask them to be my friends.

Shockingly, quite a few of them—the friends, not the daughter—accepted my invitation and gave me access to their Profiles, including their interests, hobbies, school affiliations and in some cases, physical whereabouts.

Meanwhile, my Profile had News Feed to inform me of every development:

Michelle and Paige Ogden are now friends.

20   Michelle is out for a run.

Michelle and Jesse Bendit are now friends.

Michelle is home.

No word from my daughter, though.

24   Out of the blue, I got an invitation to be a friend from one of my neighbors, Ted, who coincidentally had just joined to check out the applications that independent software developers started adding to the site last month. He showed me how to add movie reviews and snippets of music to my Profile.

I invited my friends—my actual friends—to join Facebook. Some did. I sent a "poke" to one to say hello. I wrote on another's "wall." I tagged a photo to make it appear on my friend Tina's Profile. In gratitude, she "poked" me.

Things were going really well, when suddenly something disturbing happened. An instant-message window appeared onscreen to deliver a verdict.

"wayyy creepy," it said. "why did you make one!"

28   Ah, there she was.

"What are you talking about?" I typed innocently.

"im only telling you for your own good," my daughter typed.

"Be my friend," I typed.

32   "You won't get away with this," she typed. "everyone in the whole world thinks its super creepy when adults have facebooks."

"Have facebooks? Is that what you think a Profile page is called?" I typed.

She disconnected.

Feeling as if I had achieved a minor victory in the name of parents of teenagers everywhere, I phoned Michael Wesch, an assistant professor of cultural anthropology at Kansas State University whose research focuses on social networks, to offer him some real-life data to work with.

36   But although he didn't go so far as to say he disapproved of my parenting skills, Professor Wesch reminded me that what Facebook's younger users really are doing is exploring their identities, which they may not want to parade in front of their parents.

"Can't I explore my identity, too?" I asked. "Why does everything fun have to be for them?"

He pointed out that there are a number of other social networks—sober, grown-up places like Linkedin.com (for making business contacts) and Care2.com (for social activists) and Webbiographies.com (for amateur genealogists)—where I could cavort without offending my daughter.

"There is a really good social network for older people, too," Professor Wesch said. "It caters to the older generation with an automatic feed of news that relates to older generations and a number of features tailored to the way people in that generation would interact."

40   "What's it called?" I asked.

"I can't remember the name of it," he said.

"Exactly," I said. "I'm staying where it's fun."

But after receiving a follow-up threat from my daughter ("unfriend paige right now. im serious. i dont care if they request you. say no. i will be soo mad if you dont unfriend paige right now. actually"), I started worrying that allowing parents in would backfire on Facebook.

44   If the presence of people like me alienated Facebook's core younger group, would they flee? And if so, whom would I annoy?

"I can't really comment on your family dynamics," said Brandee Barker, a Facebook spokeswoman. "But I can say that more than 50 percent of Facebook users are outside of college now. As our original demographic gets older, we want to be able to include their social networks."

"Maybe I should lay off my daughter," I said.

"Facebook is all about being a reflection of real-world relationships," she said. "The same thing you're experiencing with your daughter online is a reflection of how you're not a part of her social network in real life."

48   "I thought you weren't going to comment on my family dynamics," I said.

To try to cheer me up, Ms. Barker said, "I'm 36, so I'm O.K. with being friends with my mom on Facebook because I don't think she's weird anymore."

I had only 20 years to wait.

I checked my Profile. My daughter was now my friend. Well, sort of. She had set her privacy settings to grant me only bare-bones access to her profile.

52   She also sent a message: "stop worrying you'll end up writing a young adult novel in an empty apartment because even some extremely old creepsters write real novels"

"I'm glad we're friends," I wrote.

"oh thank god I was starting to worry," she wrote.

I hope she wasn't being cynical.

PERSONAL RESPONSE

Explain whether you believe that parents should have access to their children's social networking accounts.

QUESTIONS FOR CLASS OR SMALL-GROUP DISCUSSION

1. What aspects of this article suggest that it is meant to be amusing? Comment on the tone and language choice, among other things.

2. What does the article say, either implicitly or explicitly, about the generation gap? How would you characterize the author's relationship with her daughter?

3. Slatalla writes that she "started worrying that allowing parents in would backfire on Facebook" (paragraph 43). In what way(s) might it backfire, according to her? Do you think it has backfired?

4. Does the article satisfactorily resolve the issue of whether parents should have access to Facebook, and especially to their own children's profiles? What is your position on that issue?

THOUGHTS ON THE DIGITAL FUTURE OF MOVIES, THE THREAT OF PIRACY, THE HOPE OF REDEMPTION

JACK VALENTI

Jack Valenti was past president and chief executive officer of the Motion Picture Association of America. A former wartime bomber pilot, political consultant, and White House Special Assistant, he is author of four books: The Bitter Taste of Glory *(1971);* A Very Human President *(1975);* Speak Up with Confidence *(2002); and the political novel* Protect and Defend *(1992). This statement was presented to the Permanent Subcommittee on Investigations, a subcommittee of the Senate Committee on Governmental Affairs during a hearing entitled "Privacy & Piracy: The Paradox of Illegal File Sharing on Peer-to-Peer Networks and the Impact of Technology on the Entertainment Industry." Valenti presented his statement at the hearing on September 30, 2003. He died in 2007.*

The Peril of Piracy and the Value of Movies and Intellectual Property to This Nation

It was said that during World War I, French General Foch, later to be Supreme Allied Commander, was engaged in a furious battle with the Germans. He wired military headquarters, "My right is falling back, my left is collapsing, my center cannot hold, I shall attack!"

Some say this version is apocryphal. I choose to believe it is true, because that is precisely the way I feel about the assault on the movie industry by 'file-stealers,' a rapidly growing group whose mantra is "I have the technological power to use as I see fit and I will use it to upload and download movies, no matter who owns them for I don't care about ownership."

To paraphrase Mr. Churchill, I did not become the head of the Motion Picture Association to preside over a decaying industry. I am determined to join with my colleagues in making it plain that we will not allow the movie industry to suffer the pillaging that has been inflicted on the music industry. This Committee understands, I do believe, that the movie industry is under attack. And this Committee would agree, I do believe, that we must counter these attacks NOW with all the resolve and imagination we can summon. To remain mute, inert, to casually attend the theft of our movies would be a blunder too dumb to comprehend.

4   This is not a peculiarly Hollywood problem. It is a national issue that should concern the citizens of this free and loving land. Why? Because the Intellectual Property community is America's greatest trade export and an awesome engine of growth, nourishing the American economy. Intellectual Property (movies, TV programs, home video, books, music, computer software) brings in more international revenues than agriculture, aircraft, automobiles and auto parts—it is also responsible for over five percent of the GDP—it is creating NEW jobs at THREE times the rate of the rest of the economy, at a time when we are suffering some 2 million job losses. The movie industry alone has a surplus balance of trade with every single country in the world. I don't believe any other American enterprise can make that statement—and at a time when this country is bleeding from a $400 billion-plus deficit balance of trade.

The very future of this awesome engine of economic growth is at stake. Happily, our movies draw large crowds to the theaters. But record box-office revenues should not blind anyone to the fact that the movie industry sits on a fragile fiscal bottom. The average film costs over $90 million to make and market. Only one in ten films ever gets this investment returned through theatrical exhibition. Films have to journey through many market venues—premium and basic cable, satellite delivery, home video, network and individual TV stations, international—in order to try to recoup the private risk capital that brings a movie to life.

If a film is kidnapped early in that journey, it's obvious the worth of that film can be fatally depleted long before it can retrieve its investment. Piracy means fewer people buying DVDs, less revenue, and fewer movies being made. Especially hurt will be creative ventures outside the mainstream that involve greater financial risk.

Add to that the fact that in this country almost one million men and women work in some aspect of the movie industry. These are not high-salaried jobs. They are held by ordinary Americans with families to feed, kids to send to college and mortgages to pay. Their jobs, their livelihoods, are put to extreme peril if we bear witness to the slow undoing of one of America's most valuable job-producing industries.

The Onslaught Grows in Force and Speed

8   An outside research group has estimated that 400,000 to 600,000 films are being illegally abducted every day. We know this will increase exponentially in the future. The speed of broadband is nothing compared to the supersonic download speeds being developed right now.

Scientists at CalTech have announced "FAST," an experimental program that can download a DVD quality movie in five seconds! Another experiment at Internet II has dispatched 6.7 gigabytes—more than a typical movie—halfway around the world in one minute! Internet II has conducted new experiments that will make that earlier triumph seem like a slow freight train. These technologies are not decades away. What is experiment today will be in the marketplace a few years from now. Can anyone deny that these huge download speeds brood over our future? Can anyone deny that when one can upload and download movies in seconds or minutes the rush to illegally obtain films will reach the pandemic stage? Can anyone deny the degrading impact this will have on the movie industry? And can anyone deny that limitless stealing of creative works will have a soiling impact on the national economy?

Not only is this piracy endemic in the United States, it flourishes abroad, though most of the pilfering is in the analog format: videocassettes and optical discs, as well as counterfeiting of DVDs. A good part of that thievery springs from organized criminal organizations. We have organized anti-piracy operations throughout the world. We are partnered with local groups in Japan, Great Britain, Germany, France, Italy, in Latin America and other countries where we are every day vigilant, for like virtue we are every day besieged. We estimate that we lose some $3.5 billion annually in analog and optical disc piracy.

We also know that much of the hard-goods pirated products, especially of films in theatrical release, are the result of people illegally camcording movies in theaters, and then distributing them over the Internet. Then they are stamped onto optical disks and sold for pennies on the streets of Asia and Eastern Europe, even before the movie has a chance to open in those countries. It is not pleasant for legitimate dealers and distributors to watch this breakdown in law and ethics.

12   What incentive will companies have to create, nourish and market digital movies online when they are kidnapped and flung around the world? Can high-value legitimate creative works live in an environment of abundant theft unchecked and growing? Will legitimate sites (which I will describe below) stand a chance of success competing against blinding-fast speeds of downloads and all for "free"? How does anyone answer that?

President Kennedy once told a story about a French general in Algeria who ordered his gardener to plant a certain species of tree to line the pebbled drive to his chateau. The gardener, astonished, said, "But mon General, that tree takes fifty years to bloom." To which the General responded, "Ah, we haven't a moment to lose. Plant them today." Precisely the way the movie industry addresses its future—we must plant today the barriers and rebuttals to movie stealing that will go on unchecked tomorrow unless we move with swiftness, resolve and efficiency.

The Dark World of Peer-to-Peer (P2P) So-Called File-Swapping Sites

We know that the infestation of P2P not only threatens the well-being of the copyright industries but consumers and their families as well. As hearings in the House and Senate have conclusively established, downloading KaZaa, Gnutella, Morpheus, Grockster, etc., can lay bare your most private financial and personal information to identity thieves. It can bring into your home and expose your children to pornography of the most vile and depraved character imaginable. Most insidious of all, the pornography finds its way to your children disguised as wholesome material: your son or daughter may "search" for "Harry Potter" or "Britney Spears," and be confronted with files that contain bestiality or child pornography. The pornography distributed through P2P networks is so horrific that the District Attorney from Suffolk County, New York, recently called it the worst his office had ever seen on the Internet. And the most disturbing fact of all is that any 10-year old can easily and swiftly bring down this unwelcome perversion.

Therefore, the business model that current P2P networks celebrate as "the digital democracy" is built on the fetid foundation of pornography and pilfered copyrighted works.

16   I invite members of this Committee to go online to KaZaa and see for yourself the mammoth menu of copyrighted works available FREE, as well as an endless listing of the most throat-choking child porn. It's all there, joyously defiant, enticing all to enter and take whatever you want, risk-free. What a wonderful world we live in!

What would be amusing if it were not so unhelpful are the outcries from critics whose hidden objective is to brutalize and shrink the value of copyright if not totally banish it from the Constitution. They always piously insist they are "opposed to violation of copyright" and then move quickly to defend the right of anyone to use P2P file-swapping sites without regard to who owns the material. Anyone who reads their testimony and dissertations will find, in the words of Horace Walpole, "that they swarm with loose and foolish observations."

The Amazing Internet and How the Movie Industry Wants to Use It

The Internet, without doubt, is the greatest delivery system yet known to this planet. It has the potential to reshape how we communicate, how we buy and how to enlarge the dispatch of knowledge on a scale never before exhibited.

The movie industry is eager to use the Internet to deploy our movies, thousands of titles of every genre, to homes in this country and around the world. We want to give American families additional options for watching movies. They can make their choices easily, as well, when they want to see a movie. All at fair and reasonable prices, a phrase to be defined by the consumer and no one else.

20   Already, the industry is working on VideoOnDemand (VOD), so that everything is instantaneous. The consumer clicks a button and the movie is on the screen.

Now available are sites for legitimate movie viewing such as MovieLink, CinemaNow and others. You can call them up immediately and browse through their catalogue titles available. And it's legitimate, not illegal.

There is only one barrier to expand this immense bounty of movies and other entertainment for consumers. It is a forest thickly crowded with outlaws whose mission in life is to hijack movies and upload them to the Internet; then the feeding begins with illegal downloads. Once we defeat this illegitimacy, the consumers of America will be the cheerful beneficiaries of a never-ending source of high-value entertainment in a lawful environment.

What the Movie Industry is Doing to Baffle Piracy

What is the movie industry doing to find rebuttals to piracy? We are working to address the corrosive effects of piracy by actively and expensively pursuing a comprehensive plan on multiple fronts with every tool we have at our disposal. We have launched an attack on a broad front to go on the offensive against thievery:

(1)   We are trying to educate the public about copyright and explain why it is important to the nation. We have created TV public service announcements (I hope you have seen them), and have joined with colleagues in exhibition who are showing trailers in their theaters. We are in an alliance with Junior Achievement and one million students in grades five through nine, to explain and educate why copyright is central to intellectual property growth, and why filching movies in digital form by uploading and

downloading on the Net is not only just plain wrong, but has a malignant effect on the future of American consumers.

(2)   We have been meeting with a committee representing the nation's universities. These educational institutions are confronted with huge increased costs for large amounts of storage space and bandwidth in their state-of-the-art broadband systems, which are devoured by P2P networks. Most universities are now offering to students a catalogue which outlines that taking movies and music off the Net is an infringement of copyright and carries penalties. These codes of conduct inform students so they are aware that what they might consider to be okay and easy, is a violation of copyright and has to be taken seriously.

(3)   We are investing all our anti-piracy resources to lift the level of law enforcement not only here but in other countries on every continent. In every region of the globe the MPAA has anti-piracy personnel working closely with law enforcement and local governments to keep pirate activity at bay. It's our intention to invest these efforts with more energy and resolve.

(4)   We are embarking on a new project—technological research. We aim to enlist the finest brains of the best in the high-technology field to develop technological measures and means to baffle piracy. At the same time we are continuing to work with the most inventive men and women in the IT and CE sectors. By embracing these innovative scientists, I believe we can extract from this research more than a few counter-measures to put together a technological framework where all our industries can thrive, to the benefit of consumers. We are hopeful, very hopeful.

The Role of the Congress

24   The Congress plays a vital role in establishing legitimacy to the marketplace. Through hearings like this, a forum is provided to explore and probe key issues, and allow debate to take place so that all viewpoints are heard and weighed.

Hearings to date in both chambers have exposed the economic dangers of piracy and its links to organized crime and terrorism. Also the hearings have brought to the ken of the public threats to consumers and the economy by piracy on a swollen scale and pornography easily available to youngsters.

I am sure this Committee understands that in 1998 many meetings took place between all the parties involved in the DMCA [Digital Millennium Copyright Act] legislation. I know very well because I was personally present and active in those meetings. In our conclusions, the ISPs [Internet Service Providers] got what they very much wanted, a safe harbor from liability. The copyright holder was given the tools necessary to identify infringers operating in cyberspace. The ISPs were in agreement with the details of the DMCA because they loved that which benefited them. It is wrong for ISPs to revisit an agreement they approved without hesitation.

Copyright holders have a firm belief that the Congress will never approve any legislation to strip copyright holders of their rights, and will never allow America's greatest trade export to become the victim of theft. This we believe.

PERSONAL RESPONSE

28 What are your views on movie piracy? Do you agree with Valenti that it is a serious problem that needs to be stopped?

QUESTIONS FOR CLASS OR SMALL-GROUP DISCUSSION

1. How effective is Valenti's opening anecdote about General Foch? Is it relevant to his subject and appropriate for his audience?

2. What strategies does Valenti use to convince his audience of the seriousness of the problem of movie piracy? That is, how persuasively does he demonstrate "the perils of piracy" and "the value of movies and intellectual property to this nation"?

3. What do you think of the movie industry's plans to "go on the offensive against thievery" (paragraph 23)? How effective do you think those measures will be in baffling piracy?

4. Where do you position yourself in the debate over movie piracy?

CHIPS: HIGH TECH AIDS OR TRACKING TOOLS?

Todd Lewan

Todd Lewan is an Associated Press National writer and author of The Last Run: A True Story of Rescue and Redemption on the Alaskan Seas *(2005). This article was posted on the AP wire on July 22, 2007, and appeared in newspapers nationwide.*

CityWatcher.com, a provider of surveillance equipment, attracted little notice itself—until a year ago, when two of its employees had glass-encapsulated microchips with miniature antennas embedded in their forearms.

The "chipping" of two workers with RFIDs—radio frequency identification tags as long as two grains of rice, as thick as a toothpick—was merely a way of restricting access to vaults that held sensitive data and images for police departments, a layer of security beyond key cards and clearance codes, the company said.

"To protect high-end secure data, you use more sophisticated techniques," Sean Darks, chief executive of the Cincinnati-based company, said. He compared chip implants to retina scans or fingerprinting. "There's a reader outside the door; you walk up to the reader, put your arm under it, and it opens the door."

4   Innocuous? Maybe.

But the news that Americans had, for the first time, been injected with electronic identifiers to perform their jobs fired up a debate over the proliferation of ever-more-precise tracking technologies and their ability to erode privacy in the digital age.

To some, the microchip was a wondrous invention—a high-tech helper that could increase security at nuclear plants and military bases, help authorities identify wandering Alzheimer's patients, allow consumers to buy their groceries, literally, with the wave of a chipped hand.

To others, the notion of tagging people was Orwellian, a departure from centuries of history and tradition in which people had the right to go and do as they pleased, without being tracked, unless they were harming someone else.

8   Chipping, these critics said, might start with Alzheimer's patients or Army Rangers, but would eventually be suggested for convicts, then parolees, then sex offenders, then illegal aliens—until one day, a majority of Americans, falling into one category or another, would find themselves electronically tagged.

The concept of making all things traceable isn't alien to Americans. Thirty years ago, the first electronic tags were fixed to the ears of cattle, to permit ranchers to track a herd's reproductive and eating habits. In the 1990s, millions of chips were implanted in livestock, fish, dogs, cats, even racehorses.

Microchips are now fixed to car windshields as toll-paying devices, on "contactless" payment cards (Chase's "Blink," or MasterCard's "PayPass"). They're embedded in Michelin tires, library books, passports, work uniforms, luggage, and, unbeknownst to many consumers, on a host of individual items, from Hewlett Packard printers to Sanyo TVs, at Wal-Mart and Best Buy.

But CityWatcher.com employees weren't appliances or pets: They were people made scannable.

12   "It was scary that a government contractor that specialized in putting surveillance cameras on city streets was the first to incorporate this technology in the workplace," says Liz McIntyre, co-author of "Spychips: How Major Corporations and Government Plan to Track Your Every Move with RFID."

Darks, the CityWatcher.com executive, dismissed his critics, noting that he and his employees had volunteered to be chip-injected. Any suggestion that a sinister, Big-Brother-like campaign was afoot, he said, was hogwash.

"You would think that we were going around putting chips in people by force," he told a reporter, "and that's not the case at all."

Yet, within days of the company's announcement, civil libertarians and Christian conservatives joined to excoriate the microchip's implantation in people.

16   RFID, they warned, would soon enable the government to "frisk" citizens electronically—an invisible, undetectable search performed by readers posted at "hotspots" along roadsides and in pedestrian areas. It might even be used to squeal on employees while they worked; time spent at the water cooler, in the bathroom, in a designated smoking area could one day be broadcast, recorded and compiled in off-limits, company databases.

"Ultimately," says Katherine Albrecht, a privacy advocate who specializes in consumer education and RFID technology, "the fear is that the government or your employer might someday say, 'Take a chip or starve.'"

Some Christian critics saw the implants as the fulfillment of a biblical prophecy that describes an age of evil in which humans are forced to take the "Mark of the Beast" on their bodies, to buy or sell anything.

Gary Wohlscheid, president of These Last Days Ministries, a Roman Catholic group in Lowell, Mich., put together a Web site that linked the implantable microchips to the apocalyptic prophecy in the book of Revelation.

20   "The Bible tells us that God's wrath will come to those who take the Mark of the Beast," he says. Those who refuse to accept the Satanic chip "will be saved," Wohlscheid offers in a comforting tone.

In post-9/11 America, electronic surveillance comes in myriad forms: in a gas station's video camera; in a cell phone tucked inside a teen's back pocket; in a radio tag attached to a supermarket shopping cart; in a Porsche automobile equipped with a LoJack anti-theft device.

"We're really on the verge of creating a surveillance society in America, where every movement, every action—some would even claim, our very thoughts—will be tracked, monitored, recorded and correlated," says Barry Steinhardt, director of the Technology and Liberty Program at the American Civil Liberties Union in Washington, D.C.

RFID, in Steinhardt's opinion, "could play a pivotal role in creating that surveillance society."

24   In design, the tag is simple: A medical-grade glass capsule holds a silicon computer chip, a copper antenna and a "capacitor" that transmits data stored on the chip when prompted by an electromagnetic reader.

Implantations are quick, relatively simple procedures. After a local anesthetic is administered, a large-gauge hypodermic needle injects the chip under the skin on the back of the arm, midway between the elbow and the shoulder.

"It feels just like getting a vaccine—a bit of pressure, no specific pain," says John Halamka, an emergency physician at Beth Israel Deaconess Medical Center in Boston.

He got chipped two years ago, "so that if I was ever in an accident, and arrived unconscious or incoherent at an emergency ward, doctors could identify me and access my medical history quickly." (A chipped person's medical profile can be continuously updated, since the information is stored on a database accessed via the Internet.)

28   Halamka thinks of his microchip as another technology with practical value, like his BlackBerry. But it's also clear, he says, that there are consequences to having an implanted identifier.

"My friends have commented to me that I'm 'marked' for life, that I've lost my anonymity. And to be honest, I think they're right."

Indeed, as microchip proponents and detractors readily agree, Americans' mistrust of microchips and technologies like RFID runs deep. Many wonder:

Do the current chips have global positioning transceivers that would allow the government to pinpoint a person's exact location, 24–7? (No; the technology doesn't yet exist.)

32   But could a tech-savvy stalker rig scanners to video cameras and film somebody each time they entered or left the house? (Quite easily, though not cheaply. Currently, readers cost $300 and up.)

How about thieves? Could they make their own readers, aim them at unsuspecting individuals, and surreptitiously pluck people's IDs out of their arms? (Yes. There's even a name for it—"spoofing.")

What's the average lifespan of a microchip? (About 10–15 years.) What if you get tired of it before then—can it be easily, painlessly removed? (Short answer: No.)

Presently, Steinhardt and other privacy advocates view the tagging of identity documents—passports, drivers licenses and the like—as a more pressing threat to Americans' privacy than the chipping of people. Equipping hospitals, doctors' offices, police stations and government agencies with readers will be costly, training staff will take time, and, he says, "people are going to be too squeamish about having an RFID chip inserted into their arms, or wherever."

36   But that wasn't the case in March 2004, when the Baja Beach Club in Barcelona, Spain—a nightclub catering to the body-aware, under-25 crowd—began holding "Implant Nights."

In a white lab coat, with hypodermic in latex-gloved hand, a company chipper wandered through the throng of the clubbers and clubbettes, anesthetizing the arms of consenting party goers, then injecting them with microchips.

The payoff?

Injectees would thereafter be able to breeze past bouncers and entrance lines, magically open doors to VIP lounges, and pay for drinks without cash or credit cards. The ID number on the VIP chip was linked to the user's financial accounts and stored in the club's computers.

40   After being chipped himself, club owner Conrad K. Chase declared that chip implants were hardly a big deal to his patrons, since "almost everybody has piercings, tattoos or silicone."

VIP chipping soon spread to the Baja Beach Club in Rotterdam, Holland, the Bar Soba in Edinburgh, Scotland, and the Amika nightclub in Miami Beach, Fla.

That same year, Mexico's attorney general, Rafael Macedo, made an announcement that thrilled chip proponents and chilled privacy advocates: He and 18 members of his staff had been microchipped as a way to limit access to a sensitive records room, whose door unlocked when a "portal reader" scanned the chips.

But did this make Mexican security airtight?

44   Hardly, says Jonathan Westhues, an independent security researcher in Cambridge, Mass. He concocted an "emulator," a hand-held device that cloned the implantable microchip electronically. With a team of computer-security experts, he demonstrated—on television—how easy it was to snag data off a chip.

Explains Adam Stubblefield, a Johns Hopkins researcher who joined the team: "You pass within a foot of a chipped person, copy the chip's code, then with a push of the button, replay the same ID number to any reader. You essentially assume the person's identity."

The company that makes implantable microchips for humans, VeriChip Corp., of Delray Beach, Fla., concedes the point—even as it markets its radio tag and its portal scanner as imperatives for high-security buildings, such as nuclear power plants.

"To grab information from radio frequency products with a scanning device is not hard to do," Scott Silverman, the company's chief executive, says. However, "the chip itself only contains a unique, 16-digit identification number. The relevant information is stored on a database."

48   Even so, he insists, it's harder to clone a VeriChip than it would be to steal someone's key card and use it to enter secure areas.

VeriChip Corp., whose parent company has been selling radio tags for animals for more than a decade, has sold 7,000 microchips worldwide, of which about 2,000 have been implanted in humans. More than one-tenth of those have been in the U.S., generating "nominal revenues," the company acknowledged in a Securities and Exchange Commission filing in February.

Although in five years VeriChip Corp. has yet to turn a profit, it has been investing heavily—up to $2 million a quarter—to create new markets.

The company's present push: tagging of "high-risk" patients—diabetics and people with heart conditions or Alzheimer's disease.

52   In an emergency, hospital staff could wave a reader over a patient's arm, get an ID number, and then, via the Internet, enter a company database and pull up the person's identity and medical history.

To doctors, a "starter kit"—complete with 10 hypodermic syringes, 10 VeriChips and a reader—costs $1,400. To patients, a microchip implant means a $200, out-of-pocket expense to their physician. Presently, chip implants aren't covered by insurance companies, Medicare or Medicaid.

For almost two years, the company has been offering hospitals free scanners, but acceptance has been limited. According to the company's most recent SEC quarterly filing, 515 hospitals have pledged to take part in the VeriMed network, yet only 100 have actually been equipped and trained to use the system.

Some wonder why they should abandon noninvasive tags such as MedicAlert, a low-tech bracelet that warns paramedics if patients have serious allergies or a chronic medical condition.

56   "Having these things under your skin instead of in your back pocket—it's just not clear to me why it's worth the inconvenience," says Westhues.

Silverman responds that an implanted chip is "guaranteed to be with you. It's not a medical arm bracelet that you can take off if you don't like the way it looks . . ."

In fact, microchips can be removed from the body—but it's not like removing a splinter.

The capsules can migrate around the body or bury themselves deep in the arm. When that happens, a sensor X-ray and monitors are needed to locate the chip, and a plastic surgeon must cut away scar tissue that forms around the chip.

60   The relative permanence is a big reason why Marc Rotenberg, of the Electronic Privacy Information Center, is suspicious about the motives of the company, which charges an annual fee to keep clients' records.

The company charges $20 a year for customers to keep a "one-pager" on its database—a record of blood type, allergies, medications, driver's license data and living-will directives. For $80 a year, it will keep an individual's full medical history.

In recent times, there have been rumors on Wall Street, and elsewhere, of the potential uses for RFID in humans: the chipping of U.S. soldiers, of inmates, or of migrant workers, to name a few.

To date, none of this has happened.

64   But a large-scale chipping plan that was proposed illustrates the stakes, pro and con.

In mid-May, a protest outside the Alzheimer's Community Care Center in West Palm Beach, Fla., drew attention to a two-year study in which 200 Alzheimer's patients, along with their caregivers, were to receive chip implants. Parents, children and elderly people decried the plan, with signs and placards.

"Chipping People Is Wrong" and "People Are Not Pets," the signs read. And: "Stop VeriChip."

Ironically, the media attention sent VeriChip's stock soaring 27 percent in one day.

68   "VeriChip offers technology that is absolutely bursting with potential," wrote blogger Gary E. Sattler, of the AOL site Bloggingstocks, even as he recognized privacy concerns.

Albrecht, the RFID critic who organized the demonstration, raises similar concerns on her AntiChips.com Web site.

"Is it appropriate to use the most vulnerable members of society for invasive medical research? Should the company be allowed to implant microchips into people whose mental impairments mean they cannot give fully informed consent?"

Mary Barnes, the care center's chief executive, counters that both the patients and their legal guardians must consent to the implants before receiving them. And the chips, she says, could be invaluable in identifying lost patients—for instance, if a hurricane strikes Florida.

72   That, of course, assumes that the Internet would be accessible in a killer storm. VeriChip Corp. acknowledged in an SEC filing that its "database may not function properly" in such circumstances.

As the polemic heats up, legislators are increasingly being drawn into the fray. Two states, Wisconsin and North Dakota, recently passed laws prohibiting the forced implantation of microchips in humans. Others—Ohio, Oklahoma, Colorado and Florida—are studying similar legislation.

In May, Oklahoma legislators were debating a bill that would have authorized microchip implants in people imprisoned for violent crimes. Many felt it would be a good way to monitor felons once released from prison.

But other lawmakers raised concerns. Rep. John Wright worried, "Apparently, we're going to permanently put the mark on these people."

76   Rep. Ed Cannaday found the forced microchipping of inmates "invasive . . . We are going down that slippery slope."

In the end, lawmakers sent the bill back to committee for more work.

PERSONAL RESPONSE

Discuss whether you would consider getting an ID chip.

QUESTIONS FOR CLASS OR SMALL-GROUP DISCUSSION

1. This article was written as an Associated Press wire story and published in newspapers across the nation. Assess its effectiveness by considering whether Lewan is impartial and fair in his coverage. Are there aspects of the subject that you think he should have covered but did not?
2. Summarize the arguments for and against chip implants.
3. Several people quoted in the article speak of the potential uses and/or misuses of RFID chips. Discuss ways in which you see such chips being used and explain their relative advantages and disadvantages.
4. How would you answer the question posed by the title? Why?

○ PERSPECTIVES ON DIGITAL TECHNOLOGY AND THE INTERNET ○

Suggested Writing Topics

1. Explore the positive and negative aspects of social networking like My-Space and Facebook and state your conclusions about their suitability for young people.
2. Argue your position on the issue of peer-to-peer technology and file swapping.
3. Argue your position on the issue of radio frequency identification implants.
4. Explain the characteristics of a blog that you particularly like to visit, or follow the postings at one blog for a week and do an analysis of the site. Or, analyze a website that you think is especially well done. Read and write a critical response to *Spychips: How Major Corporations and Government Plan to Track Your Every Move with RFID* by Liz McIntyre and Katherine Albrecht, as mentioned in Todd Lewan's "Chips: High Tech Aids or Tracking Tools?"
5. Drawing on at least one of the readings in this chapter, explore the impact of digital technology on an aspect of contemporary culture.
6. Drawing on at least one of the readings in this chapter, explain how digital technology raises issues for copyright holders.
7. Explain the importance of high-tech digital systems in your life.
8. Write an essay explaining what you see as the benefits and/or dangers of the Internet.
9. Explain the direction that you see digital technology going in over the next decade or two.

Research Topics

1. Research the social impact of networking sites like MySpace and Facebook or video sharing sites like YouTube.

2. Research the economic impact of movie piracy on the entertainment industry.

3. Research the controversy over implanted radio frequency devices, investigate the pros and cons on the issue, and arrive at your own conclusion.

4. Jack Valenti in "Thoughts on the Digital Future of Movies . . ." refers to the "dark world of Peer-to-Peer (P2P) so-called file-swapping sites." Research to either substantiate or refute Valenti's view on the danger that P2P technology and P2P file-swapping sites pose to individuals.

5. Research efforts by the film industry to protect itself from piracy. Which efforts promise to be most effective? Which have proven useless?

6. Research the efforts of rock groups such as Metallica and Pearl Jam to use the Internet to distribute their music while protecting themselves from piracy.

7. Research an area of computer technology that is still in the experimental stages or still being refined.

8. Research the impact of technology in one of the following areas: social networking, medicine, marketing, shopping, entertainment, scholarship/research, American culture, education, or government and politics. You will have to narrow your focus considerably for this subject.

9. Research a problem associated with the Internet such as the availability of pornography for children, the potential dangers of e-mail, the possibility of its use by terrorists, or privacy issues.

RESPONDING TO VISUALS

Online censorship.

1. What comment do you think the picture makes on Internet censorship?
2. Why do you think the photographer chose this perspective rather than focus on a close-up of the screen with the word "censored"?
3. To what extent do you think that certain websites and Internet material should be censored? Have you attended any school where the Internet was censored, or do you know of such schools? Who does the censoring in such institutions? Teachers? Library personnel? Administrators?
4. What effect might censoring the Internet have on students, say those doing research for a class?

RESPONDING TO VISUALS

Tribal boys with a laptop in Australia.

1. What is your reaction to this picture?
2. What is the purpose of the picture?
3. What contrasts in the picture does the photographer emphasize?
4. What do you think the boys are doing with the laptop? Does it matter that we do not know?

BIOETHICS

Bioethics has been a growing area of academic interest for the past thirty years or more. Broadly speaking, it refers to the ethics of biological and health sciences, and its scope encompasses dozens of moral and ethical issues in those areas. Bioethical concerns surround such controversial practices as cloning, cryonics, human genetic engineering, euthanasia, artificial life, transexuality, chip implants inserted into the brains of humans, and genetically modified foods as well as issues concerning organ donation, life support, population control, medical research, and the like. Of great interest to bioethicists has been the mapping of the human genome and what to do with the knowledge that resulted.

Research into the complex structure of the human body since James D. Watson and Francis Crick discovered in 1953 that deoxyribonucleic acid (DNA) molecules arrange themselves in a double helix has made enormous advances. The discovery of this pattern in DNA, a substance that transmits the genetic characteristics from one generation to the next, earned Watson and Crick a Nobel Prize in 1962. Their discovery led other scientists to work on such things as recombinant DNA and gene splicing in the 1970s and eventually to the Human Genome Project, whose goal was to map the entire sequence of human DNA. A genome is the complete set of instructions for making a human being. Each nucleus of the one hundred trillion cells that make up the human body contains this set of instructions, which are written in the language of DNA. This major undertaking by scientists around the world promises to provide medical doctors with the tools to predict the development of human diseases. When the project began in 1988, scientists thought that it would take fifteen years to complete, but the project progressed faster than first predicted and was finished well ahead of schedule.

Now that the human code has been mapped, scientists can begin to better understand how humans grow, what causes human diseases, and what new drugs would combat those diseases by either preventing or curing them. Scientists already are able to identify variations or defects in the genetic makeup of certain cells in human bodies that may result in diseases with genetic origins. Eventually, they will be able to develop tests of an individual's likelihood of developing one of thousands of inherited diseases such as sickle-cell anemia, cystic fibrosis, or muscular dystrophy, and even heart disease or cancer. Because more than 30,000 genes make up the "instruction manual" for the human body, it will take some time before all of them are codified and their functions known. The Human Genome Project raised a number of difficult ethical questions, however, as the essays in this chapter indicate. One of the most controversial steps forward in the potential of scientists to manipulate genes is the capacity to clone living creatures, though gene therapy has other potential uses.

The first two essays, by James D. Watson and Ian Wilmut, respectively, were written for a special *Time* magazine issue on the future of medicine. Wilmut is the Scottish embryologist who cloned the first mammal, the famous sheep Dolly. Watson and Wilmut hold different opinions on just what should and what should not be done with research into human cloning. They raise the ethical and moral questions of human cloning and by implication gene therapy and stem cell research, among other things Then, Michael Crichton in "Patenting Life takes up one of the ethical issues that grew out of the success of the Human Genome Project when he explains why genes are allowed to be patented and how that affects everyone's lives, not just those suffering from particular medical problems. As he raises objections to the patenting of genes and urges support of a House Bill introduced to stop it, consider whether you are persuaded by his arguments that patenting genes is a bad practice.

One highly controversial issue in bioethics is human embryonic stem cell research, in large part because of the techniques used to harvest stem cell lines, which involves either destroying a human embryo or using somatic cell nuclear transfer, often referred to as therapeutic cloning. One of the arguments used by opponents of stem cell research is that it destroys embryonic life and will inevitably lead to human cloning, while supporters argue that the benefits of such research far outweigh the costs. In "Bioethics and the Stem Cell Research Debate," Robyn S. Shapiro gives an overview of the issues involved in the controversy over stem cell research. You will no doubt find as you read the essay that the issue is more complex than you might have thought.

As you read the essays in this chapter, ask yourself the questions that their authors raise: Just how far should science be allowed to go?

ALL FOR THE GOOD

James D. Watson

James D. Watson, with Francis Crick, discovered in 1953 that DNA molecules arrange themselves in a double helix. In 1962, Watson, Crick, and a British biophysicist, Maurice Wilkins, shared the Nobel Prize in medicine for their work on DNA. In 1968 Watson became director of the Cold Springs Harbor Laboratory of Quantitative Biology in New York State. He published The Double Helix, *his best-selling story of the discovery of the structure of DNA, in 1968. His other books include* Genes, Girls and Gamow: After the Double Helix *(2002); with Andrew Berry,* DNA: The Secret of Life *(2003); and* Avoid Boring People: Lessons from a Life in Science *(2007). A recipient of the Presidential Medal of Freedom and author of many scientific papers, Watson directed the Human Genome Project from 1988 to 1992. He wrote this piece for* Time *magazine's January 11, 1999, issue on the future of medicine.*

There is lots of zip in DNA-based biology today. With each passing year it incorporates an ever increasing fraction of the life sciences, ranging from single-cell organisms, like bacteria and yeast, to the complexities of the human brain. All this wonderful biological frenzy was unimaginable when I first entered the world of genetics. In 1948, biology was an all too descriptive discipline near the bottom of science's totem pole, with physics at its top. By then Einstein's turn-of-the-century ideas about the interconversion of matter and energy had been transformed into the powers of the atom. If not held in check, the weapons they made possible might well destroy the very fabric of civilized human life. So physicists of the late 1940s were simultaneously revered for making atoms relevant to society and feared for what their toys could do if they were to fall into the hands of evil.

Such ambivalent feelings are now widely held toward biology. The double helical structure of DNA, initially admired for its intellectual simplicity, today represents to many a double-edged sword that can be used for evil as well as good. No sooner had scientists at Stanford University in 1973 begun rearranging DNA molecules in test tubes (and, equally important, reinserting the novel DNA segments back into living cells) than critics began likening these "recombinant" DNA procedures to the physicist's power to break apart atoms. Might not some of the test-tube-rearranged DNA molecules impart to their host cells disease-causing capacities that, like nuclear weapons, are capable of seriously disrupting human civilization? Soon there were cries from both scientists and nonscientists that such research might best be ruled by stringent regulations—if not laws.

As a result, several years were to pass before the full power of recombinant-DNA technology got into the hands of working scientists, who by then were itching to explore previously unattainable secrets of life. Happily, the proposals to control recombinant-DNA research through legislation never got close to enactment. And when anti-DNA doomsday scenarios failed to materialize, even the modestly restrictive governmental regulations began to wither away. In retrospect, recombinant-DNA may rank as the safest revolutionary technology ever developed. To my knowledge, not one fatality, much less illness, has been caused by a genetically manipulated organism.

4   The moral I draw from this painful episode is this: Never postpone experiments that have clearly defined future benefits for fear of dangers that can't be quantified. Though it may sound at first uncaring, we can react rationally only to real (as opposed to hypothetical) risks. Yet for several years we postponed important experiments on the genetic basis of cancer, for example, because we took much too seriously spurious arguments that the genes at the root of human cancer might themselves be dangerous to work with.

Though most forms of DNA manipulation are now effectively unregulated, one important potential goal remains blocked. Experiments aimed at learning how to insert functional genetic material into human germ cells—sperm and eggs—remain off limits to most of the world's scientists. No governmental body wants to take responsibility for initiating steps that might help redirect the course of future human evolution. These decisions reflect widespread concerns that we, as humans, may not have the wisdom to modify the most precious of all human treasures—our chromosomal "instruction books." Dare we be entrusted with improving upon the results of the several million years of Darwinian natural selection? Are human germ cells Rubicons that geneticists may never cross?

Unlike many of my peers, I'm reluctant to accept such reasoning, again using the argument that you should never put off doing something useful for fear of evil that may never arrive. The first germ-line gene manipulations are unlikely to be attempted for frivolous reasons. Nor does the state of today's science provide the knowledge that would be needed to generate "superpersons" whose far-ranging talents would make those who are genetically unmodified feel redundant and unwanted. Such creations will remain denizens of science fiction, not the real world, far into the future. When they are finally attempted, germ-line genetic manipulations will probably be done to change a death sentence into a life verdict—by creating children who are resistant to a deadly virus, for example, much the way we can already protect plants from viruses by inserting antiviral DNA segments into their genomes.

If appropriate go-ahead signals come, the first resulting gene-bettered children will in no sense threaten human civilization. They will be seen as special only by those in their immediate circles, and are likely to pass as unnoticed in later life as the now grownup "test-tube baby" Louise Brown does today. If they grow up healthily gene-bettered, more such children will follow, and they and those whose lives are enriched by their existence will rejoice that science has again improved human life. If, however, the added genetic material fails to work, better procedures must be developed before more couples commit their psyches toward such inherently unsettling pathways to producing healthy children.

8   Moving forward will not be for the faint of heart. But if the next century witnesses failure, let it be because our science is not yet up to the job, not because we don't have the courage to make less random the sometimes most unfair courses of human evolution.

PERSONAL RESPONSE

Are you as comfortable with the possibility that something might go wrong in "gene-bettered children" as Watson seems to be (paragraph 7)? What is your opinion on that point?

QUESTIONS FOR CLASS OR SMALL-GROUP DISCUSSION

1. How successfully do you believe Watson has defended his position on genetic engineering? What strategies does he use for persuading his audience to agree with him?

2. How effective is the comparison that Watson makes between the public response to physicists' learning how to make the atomic bomb in the 1940s and biologists' ability to do recombinant-DNA procedures in the 1970s? Are you persuaded that the issues are the same? If so, what are their similarities? If not, how do they differ?

3. To what extent do you agree with Watson when he writes: "Never postpone experiments that have clearly defined future benefits for fear of dangers that can't be quantified" (paragraph 4)?

4. Comment on Watson's response to those who believe that humans "may not have the wisdom to modify the most precious of all human treasures— our chromosomal 'instruction book'" (paragraph 5). Do you share his view on this point?

DOLLY'S FALSE LEGACY

Ian Wilmut

Ian Wilmut is the Scottish embryologist whose team of researchers, in 1996, was the first to clone a mammal from fully differentiated adult mammary cells. Wilmut holds a Ph.D. in animal genetic engineering from Darwin College, University of Cambridge, and has been a re-searcher at the Animal Research Breeding Station (now known as the Roslin Institute) in Edinburgh, Scotland, since 1974. He is co-author of The Second Creation: Dolly and the Age of Biological Control *(2000) and* After Dolly: The Uses and Misuses of Human Cloning *(2006) and has been editor of the* Journal of Reproduction Fertility *since 1993. This essay appeared in the January 11, 1999, issue of* Time *magazine.*

Overlooked in the arguments about the morality of artificially reproducing life is the fact that, at present, cloning is a very inefficient procedure. The incidence of death among fetuses and offspring produced by cloning is much higher than it is through natural reproduction—roughly 10 times as high as normal before birth and three times as high after birth in our studies at Roslin. Distressing enough for those working with animals, these failure rates surely render unthinkable the no-tion of applying such treatment to humans.

Even if the technique were perfected, however, we must ask ourselves what practical value whole-being cloning might have. What exactly would be the dif-ference between a "cloned" baby and a child born naturally—and why would we want one?

The cloned child would be a genetically identical twin of the original, and thus physically very similar—far more similar than a natural parent and child. Human personality, however, emerges from both the effects of the genes we inherit (nature) and environmental factors (nurture). The two clones would develop distinct person-alities, just as twins develop unique identities. And because the copy would often be born in a different family, cloned twins would be less alike in personality than natural identical twins.

4   Why "copy" people in the first place? Couples unable to have children might choose to have a copy of one of them rather than accept the intrusion of genes from a donor. My wife and I have two children of our own and an adopted child, but I find it helpful to consider what might have happened in my own marriage if

a copy of me had been made to overcome infertility. My wife and I met in high school. How would she react to a physical copy of the young man she fell in love with? How would any of us find living with ourselves? Surely the older clone—I, in this case—would believe that he understood how the copy should behave and so be even more likely than the average father to impose expectations upon his child. Above all, how would a teenager cope with looking at me, a balding, aging man, and seeing the physical future ahead of him?

Each of us can imagine hypothetical families created by the introduction of a cloned child—a copy of one partner in a homosexual relationship or of a single parent, for example. What is missing in all this is consideration of what's in the interests of the cloned child. Because there is no form of infertility that could be overcome only by cloning, I do not find these proposals acceptable. My concerns are not on religious grounds or on the basis of a perceived intrinsic ethical principle. Rather, my judgment is that it would be difficult for families created in this way to provide an appropriate environment for the child.

Cloning is also suggested as a means of bringing back a relative, usually a child, killed tragically. Any parent can understand that wish, but it must first be recognized that the copy would be a new baby and not the lost child. Herein lies the difficulty, for the grieving parents are seeking not a new baby but a return of the dead one. Since the original would be fondly remembered as having particular talents and interests, would not the parent expect the copy to be the same? It is possible, however, that the copy would develop quite differently. Is it fair to the new child to place it in a family with such unnatural expectations?

What if the lost child was very young? The shorter the life, the fewer the expectations parents might place on the substitute, right? If a baby dies within a few days of birth and there is no reason to think that death was caused by an inherited defect, would it then be acceptable to make a copy? Is it practical to frame legislation that would prevent copying of adults or older children, but allow copying of infants? At what age would a child be too old to be copied in the event of death?

8   Copying is also suggested as a means by which parents can have the child of their dreams. Couples might choose to have a copy of a film star, baseball player or scientist, depending on their interests. But because personality is only partly the result of genetic inheritance, conflict would be sure to arise if the cloned child failed to develop the same interests as the original. What if the copy of Einstein shows no interest in science? Or the football player turns to acting? Success also depends upon fortune. What of the child who does not live up to the hopes and dreams of the parent simply because of bad luck?

Every child should be wanted for itself, as an individual. In making a copy of oneself or some famous person, a parent is deliberately specifying the way he or she wishes that child to develop. In recent years, particularly in the U.S., much importance has been placed on the right of individuals to reproduce in ways that they wish. I suggest that there is a greater need to consider the interests of the child and to reject these proposed uses of cloning.

By contrast, human cloning could, in theory, be used to obtain tissues needed to treat disorders such as Parkinson's disease and diabetes. These diseases are associated with cell types that do not repair or replace themselves, but suitable cells will one day be grown in culture. These uses cannot be justified now; nor are they likely to be in the near future.

Moreover, there is a lot we do not know about the effects of cloning, especially in terms of aging. As we grow older, changes occur in our cells that reduce the number of times they can reproduce. This clock of age is reset by normal reproduction during the production of sperm and eggs; that is why children of each new generation have a full life span. It is not yet known whether aging is reversed during cloning or if the clone's natural life is shortened by the years its parent has already lived. Then there is the problem of the genetic errors that accumulate in our cells. There are systems to seek out and correct such errors during normal reproduction; it is not known if that can occur during cloning. Research with animals is urgently required to measure the life span and determine the cause of death of animals produced by cloning.

12   Important questions also remain on the most appropriate means of controlling the development and use of these techniques. It is taken for granted that the production and sale of drugs will be regulated by governments, but this was not always the case. A hundred years ago, the production and sale of drugs in the U.S. was unregulated. Unscrupulous companies took the opportunity to include in their products substances, like cocaine, that were likely to make the patients feel better even if they offered no treatment for the original condition. After public protest, championed by publications such as the *Ladies' Home Journal,* a federal act was passed in 1906. An enforcement agency, known now as the FDA, was established in 1927. An independent body similar to the FDA is now required to assess all the research on cloning.

There is much still to be learned about the biology associated with cloning. The time required for this research, however, will also provide an opportunity for each society to decide how it wishes the technique to be used. At some point in the future, cloning will have much to contribute to human medicine, but we must use it cautiously.

PERSONAL RESPONSE

Does it surprise you that the man who cloned the first mammal is so cautious about the possibility of cloning humans? What do you think of his caution?

QUESTIONS FOR CLASS OR SMALL-GROUP DISCUSSION

1. Assess the effectiveness of Wilmut's title and his opening paragraph. How do they serve to introduce his subject and the position he takes on it?

2. How persuasive do you find Wilmut's reasons for why people might want to clone themselves or their children? Do any of the possible reasons seem more valid to you than others?

3. Wilmut suggests certain ways that human cloning might be used besides cloning entire humans. What do you think of those uses of the technology?

4. Wilmut states that there are important questions that need to be considered before proceeding with the technology to clone humans. State in your own words what those questions are. To what extent do you agree with him that these questions are weighty enough to postpone research until they are answered?

PATENTING LIFE

Michael Crichton

Michael Crichton is an author, critic, and film producer. While earning his degree from Harvard Medical School, he began writing novels. Among his twenty-five novels are such bestsellers as The Andromeda Strain *(1969),* The Terminal Man *(1972),* The Great Train Robbery *(1975),* Sphere *(1987),* Jurassic Park *(1990), and* Airframe *(1996). He is also creator and co-producer of the long-running television drama* ER. *This essay appeared as an op-ed piece in the February 13, 2007, edition of the* New York Times.

You, or someone you love, may die because of a gene patent that should never have been granted in the first place. Sound far-fetched? Unfortunately, it's only too real.

Gene patents are now used to halt research, prevent medical testing and keep vital information from you and your doctor. Gene patents slow the pace of medical advance on deadly diseases. And they raise costs exorbitantly: a test for breast cancer that could be done for $1,000 now costs $3,000.

Why? Because the holder of the gene patent can charge whatever he wants, and does. Couldn't somebody make a cheaper test? Sure, but the patent holder blocks any competitor's test. He owns the gene. Nobody else can test for it. In fact, you can't even donate your own breast cancer gene to another scientist without permission. The gene may exist in your body, but it's now private property.

4   This bizarre situation has come to pass because of a mistake by an underfinanced and understaffed government agency. The United States Patent Office misinterpreted previous Supreme Court rulings and some years ago began—to the surprise of everyone, including scientists decoding the genome—to issue patents on genes.

Humans share mostly the same genes. The same genes are found in other animals as well. Our genetic makeup represents the common heritage of all life on earth. You can't patent snow, eagles or gravity, and you shouldn't be able to patent genes, either. Yet by now one-fifth of the genes in your body are privately owned.

The results have been disastrous. Ordinarily, we imagine patents promote innovation, but that's because most patents are granted for human inventions. Genes aren't human inventions, they are features of the natural world. As a result these patents can be used to block innovation, and hurt patient care.

For example, Canavan disease is an inherited disorder that affects children starting at 3 months; they cannot crawl or walk, they suffer seizures and eventually become paralyzed and die by adolescence. Formerly there was no test to tell parents if they were at risk. Families enduring the heartbreak of caring for these children engaged a researcher to identify the gene and produce a test. Canavan families around the world donated tissue and money to help this cause.

8   When the gene was identified in 1993, the families got the commitment of a New York hospital to offer a free test to anyone who wanted it. But the researcher's employer, Miami Children's Hospital Research Institute, patented the gene and refused to allow any health care provider to offer the test without paying a royalty. The parents did not believe genes should be patented and so did not put their names on the patent. Consequently, they had no control over the outcome.

In addition, a gene's owner can in some instances also own the mutations of that gene, and these mutations can be markers for disease. Countries that don't have gene patents actually offer better gene testing than we do, because when multiple labs are allowed to do testing, more mutations are discovered, leading to higher-quality tests.

Apologists for gene patents argue that the issue is a tempest in a teapot, that patent licenses are readily available at minimal cost. That's simply untrue. The owner of the genome for Hepatitis C is paid millions by researchers to study this disease. Not surprisingly, many other researchers choose to study something less expensive.

But forget the costs: why should people or companies own a disease in the first place? They didn't invent it. Yet today, more than 20 human pathogens are privately owned, including haemophilus influenza and Hepatitis C. And we've already mentioned that tests for the BRCA genes for breast cancer cost $3,000. Oh, one more thing: if you undergo the test, the company that owns the patent on the gene can keep your tissue and do research on it without asking your permission. Don't like it? Too bad.

12   The plain truth is that gene patents aren't benign and never will be. When SARS was spreading across the globe, medical researchers hesitated to study it—because of patent concerns. There is no clearer indication that gene patents block innovation, inhibit research and put us all at risk.

Even your doctor can't get relevant information. An asthma medication only works in certain patients. Yet its manufacturer has squelched efforts by others to develop genetic tests that would determine on whom it will and will not work. Such commercial considerations interfere with a great dream. For years we've been promised the coming era of personalized medicine—medicine suited to our particular body makeup. Gene patents destroy that dream.

Fortunately, two congressmen want to make the full benefit of the decoded genome available to us all. Last Friday, Xavier Becerra, a Democrat of California, and Dave Weldon, a Republican of Florida, sponsored the Genomic Research and Accessibility Act, to ban the practice of patenting genes found in nature. Mr. Becerra has been careful to say the bill does not hamper invention, but rather promotes it. He's right. This bill will fuel innovation, and return our common genetic heritage to us. It deserves our support.

PERSONAL RESPONSE

Crichton believes that "you shouldn't be able to patent genes" (paragraph 5). Do you agree with him? Explain your answer.

QUESTIONS FOR CLASS OR SMALL-GROUP DISCUSSION

1. What are the negative effects of gene patents, according to Crichton?
2. What do supporters of gene patents argue, according to Crichton? Do you think that Crichton effectively addresses those arguments?
3. How well do you think that Crichton argues his position? What argumentative strategies does he use?
4. Do you believe that Crichton has considered all sides of the issue? If not, what do you think he has overlooked?

BIOETHICS AND THE STEM CELL RESEARCH DEBATE

Robyn S. Shapiro

Robyn Shapiro is Ursula von der Ruhr Professor of Bioethics and Director of the Center for the Study of Bioethics at the Medical College of Wisconsin. She is also a health law partner at Gardner Carton & Douglas LLP in Milwaukee, Wisconsin. She publishes and speaks frequently on ethical issues in science and medicine, especially in relation to the law. This essay was first published in the May–June 2006 issue of Social Education, *the journal of the National Council for Social Studies.*

Since its birth in the 1970s, bioethics—the study of ethical issues in science and medicine—has grown to become a significant academic and service-oriented discipline with its own research centers, conferences, journals, and degree programs. As these issues have moved to the center of public debate, the law has assumed an increasingly important place in the discipline of bioethics.

The growing importance of the law as a forum for the debate and mediation of bioethical issues is apparent on several fronts. In the United States Supreme Court, bioethical issues have been central to key reproductive privacy cases, from the Court's 1973 decision in Roe v. Wade, 410 U.S. 113, to its 2000 decision in Stenberg v. Carkart, 530 U.S. 914, which struck down a controversial Nebraska partial-birth abortion law. In state courts, bioethical considerations inform judges' balancing of patient health care confidentiality with a "duty to warn" of potentially dangerous patient behavior (see, for example, the California Supreme Court's landmark 1976 decision, Tarasoff v. Regents of the University of California, 17 Cal. 3d 425). At both the state and federal levels, bioethical debates help shape end-of-life statutes and court cases, including Cruzan v. Missouri Dept. of Health, 497 U.S.

261 (1990), in which the U.S. Supreme Court upheld the State of Missouri's requirement for clear and convincing evidence that a person in a persistent vegetative state had expressed a wish not to be kept alive by life-sustaining equipment.

Today, embryonic stem cell research stands out as a critically important issue about which we have neither ethical consensus nor clear, comprehensive regulation. The ethical debate centers on the fact that stem cell research involves the destruction of very early human embryos. On the federal level, funding for stem cell research has been limited to research using stem cells derived from a limited number of stem cell "lines." On the state level, approaches range from legislative restrictions on stem cell research to the State of California's plan to provide $3 billion in stem cell research funding through the voter-approved California Institute for Regenerative Medicine.

4   In order for potentially revolutionary stem cell research to progress, scientists' long-term needs must be effectively coordinated with appropriate and effective ethical and legal guidance. This article provides brief scientific background and then discussion of key ethical and legal/regulatory issues that surround embryonic stem cell research.

Background

Embryonic stem cells are precursor cells that have the capacity to divide for indefinite periods of time in culture and to give rise to virtually any type of specialized cells in the body. They are derived from the inner cell mass of a 100-cell blastocyst—a very early embryo, usually only 3–4 days old—long before the cells have started to specialize to create a nervous system, spine and other features that, with further development, would transform the embryo into a fetus. Typically, these cells are derived from embryos that originally were created for infertility treatment purposes through in vitro fertilization, but that are no longer desired or needed by the infertile couple for treatment. The extraction of the stem cells from the blastocyst necessarily requires the destruction of that blastocyst.

Because embryonic stem cells are capable of self-renewal and can differentiate into a wide variety of cell types, potential applications of embryonic stem cell research are far-reaching. For example, embryonic stem cell research holds out great promise to those suffering from Type I diabetes. Type I diabetes is an autoimmune disease characterized by destruction of insulin-producing cells in the pancreas. Some of the current efforts to treat these patients use donated human pancreases for transplantation of islets—clusters of cells on the pancreas that produce insulin—in an effort to restore the insulin-secreting function. Islet transplantation efforts are limited by the small numbers of available donated pancreases, as well as the toxicity of immunosuppressive drug treatments that are required to prevent graft rejection. Use of embryonic stem cells that are instructed to differentiate into pancreatic islet cells has the potential to overcome the shortage of effective material to transplant.

Similarly, embryonic stem cell research offers tremendous potential to those suffering from nervous system diseases that result from loss of nerve cells. Since mature cells cannot divide to replace cells that are lost, therapeutic possibilities do not exist in the absence of a new source of functioning nerve tissue. Conceivably, however, with embryonic stem cell research, nerve cells that make the chemical dopamine could be created for individuals with Parkinson's disease, cells responsible for the production of certain neuro-transmitters could be reconstituted for individuals with Alzheimer's, the motor cells that activate muscles could be replaced for ALS patients, and glia (cells that perform numerous functions within the human nervous system) could be formed for individuals with multiple sclerosis.

8   In addition to these promising therapeutic applications of embryonic stem cell research, such research also could provide new insights into how human beings, organs and tissues develop. It also has the potential to substantially change the development and testing of pharmaceutical products. New medications could be tested initially on cells or tissues developed from embryonic stem cells, and only those drugs initially found to be safe and effective would be tested further on animals and humans.

Ethical Issues

Notwithstanding the promise of embryonic stem cells, several ethical issues have made stem cell research controversial. The most vexing ethical issues surrounding embryonic stem cell research, which focus on the moral status of the very early embryo, arise from the fact that isolating embryonic stem cells requires destruction of the embryo.

Some who condemn embryonic stem cell research believe that the embryo is a full person or human subject, with full rights and interests from the moment of conception. Others take a developmental view of personhood, believing that the embryo only gradually becomes a full human being and that the very early embryo is not entitled to the same moral protections to which it would be entitled at a later developmental stage. Still others hold that while the embryo represents human life, such life is not a "person" at any time prior to birth.

The role of science in deciding the difficult ethical question of the moral status of the very early embryo is unresolved. Key issues in deciding this question include the following:

- How significant is it that at less than 14 days a blastocyst has no neural tissue? Some contend that this fact makes derivation of stem cells from a blastocyst prior to this developmental stage no different than allowing organ donation at the point of brain death.
- Is it ethically significant that until formation of the primitive streak at 14 days, a blastocyst can undergo complete fission to form an identical twin? One commentator contends that since "individuality is a sine qua non for personhood, it seems safe to consider 14 days of normal embryonic development to be the minimum requirement for a human being to emerge."
- Is the argument for the protection of the "potential" for human life affected by scientific assertions that an embryo does not have such potential unless it is implanted in a uterus?

- Is it ethically significant that a blastocyst created by somatic cell nuclear transfer, if implanted, would be extremely unlikely to develop into a human being? As one commentator notes, "cytoplasmic factors would have to act on an adult nucleus to produce the same patterns of gene activation that are critical for early embryonic development."

Legal Issues

12   Federal and state legislatures have begun to grapple with the ethical questions involved in stem cell research, but to date, there is no comprehensive or consistent regulation of stem cell research in the United States. Since 1996, riders to federal appropriations language (known as the "Dickey Amendment") have prohibited use of federal funds for "the creation of a human embryo or embryos for research purposes," as well as "research in which a human embryo or embryos are destroyed, disabled or knowingly subjected to a risk of injury or death greater than allowed for research on fetuses in utero . . ." In January 1999, however, the General Counsel of the Department of Health and Human Services (HHS) determined that federal law does not prohibit public funding of embryonic stem cell research as long as the research to be funded does not include derivation of the stem cells from the embryo (and, therefore, destruction of the embryo). In other words, cells could be derived from embryos destroyed in private labs with private money, and then shipped to federally funded scientists for study.

Following this legal clearance from HHS, the director of the National Institutes of Health (NIH) convened a 13-member working group to draw up guidelines for research using embryonic stem cells. This group's guidelines, which became effective August 2000, state that research involving embryonic stem cells is acceptable as long as

- the stem cells come from spare embryos that were originally created through in vitro fertilization for infertility treatment purposes,
- the embryos have not reached the developmental state at which the mesoderm is formed,
- the researcher is not involved in the infertility treatment for which the embryos were created and has not played any role in the donors' decision to donate the embryos for research,
- there is no directed donation of embryos for the derivation of stem cells for eventual use in transplantation, and
- the stem cells are not added to human or animal eggs or embryos via somatic cell nuclear transfer.

On August 9, 2001, however, President Bush effectively suspended the NIH 2000 guidelines. He announced that federal funding for embryonic stem cell research would be available only under the following conditions:

- the stem cells are derived from stem cell lines existing as of August 9, 2001,
- the lines were derived with proper informed consent of the embryo donors,

- the embryos used were originally created through in vitro fertilization for infertility treatment purposes, and
- there were no financial inducements made to the embryo donors.
- No federal funds may be used for derivation or use of stem cells derived from newly destroyed embryos, creation of human embryos for research purposes, or cloning of human embryos for any purpose.

Many contend that the president's restrictions on federal funding of embryonic stem cell research are inhibiting the ability to unlock the potential of embryonic stem cells. One concern relates to recently discovered chromosomal rearrangements in embryonic stem cells over time, which suggest that the federally approved lines may have limited therapeutic potential. Additional concerns relate to the limited number and the narrow racial diversity of the federally approved stem cell lines.

16   Moreover, in addition to the federal funding restrictions, embryonic stem cell research is also subject to some restrictive state laws. While California is providing government funding for stem cell research through the California Institute for Regenerative Medicine, and New Jersey, Massachusetts, Illinois, Wisconsin, and Texas are considering funding measures, other states—including Iowa, Louisiana, Michigan, Arkansas, Nebraska, North Dakota, South Dakota, and Virginia—have laws that limit embryonic stem cell research.

On the other hand, stem cells, as well as their derivation and their uses, are eligible for federal patent protections. In fact, a number of patents relating to human embryonic stem cells have been filed—the most fundamental of which are the "Thomson" patents, named after the University of Wisconsin researcher who led a group that developed the technique for isolating and growing human embryonic stem cells. Thomson patents relate to the methods of deriving and maintaining human embryonic stem cells in vitro, and the products of those methods. These patents were assigned by the inventors to the Wisconsin Alumni Research Foundation, which exclusively licensed their commercial applications within certain fields of use to Geron Corporation, and made licenses to practice under the patent rights for research purposes available through a non-profit corporation.

Some have questioned the ethical acceptability of patenting embryonic stem cells. For example, one commentator has questioned whether the federal government's opposition to direct federal funding of post-August 2001 stem cell lines is consistent with its sanction of exclusive property rights in such lines, since these patent-protected rights can create "indirect research funding" through rewarding market investments. However, such qualms collide with the United States Supreme Court's declaration that "everything under the sun" isolated or manipulated by humanity may be patented and that patent law is not intended to displace the police powers of the states with respect to safety, health and morality. Ironically, then, the current federal position is to allow sensitive ethical questions on stem cell research to be decided by the marketplace, with private money developing products that receive patent protection without the regulatory oversight that would apply to federally funded research.

Conclusion

Stem cell research has emerged as a potential political issue that could play a role in the 2006 mid-term elections and beyond. In his 2006 State of the Union speech, President Bush called upon Congress "to pass legislation to prohibit the most egregious abuses of medical research," including "human cloning in all its forms." Some commentators have criticized this statement for failing to distinguish between human reproductive cloning, which most experts oppose, and therapeutic cloning, in which cloning techniques are used to produce blastocysts for stem cell extraction, not embryos for implantation. In Congress, there are signs of division in the Republican majority on the question of stem cell research. A bill easing current federal restrictions on stem cell research passed the Republican-controlled House of Representatives in 2005 but stalled in the Senate, which is scheduled to take up the bill sometime in 2006. Several key senators, including Senate Majority Leader Bill Frist (R-Tenn.), have spoken in support of the bill.

20   In the meantime, there is no consensus concerning ethical questions surrounding embryonic stem cell research. Continued careful attention to ethical review of the issues that surround this promising research, and consistent incorporation of such analysis into evolving laws and regulations, will assure the appropriate and effective use of this emerging knowledge.

PERSONAL RESPONSE

What is your position on human embryonic stem cell research?

QUESTIONS FOR CLASS OR SMALL-GROUP DISCUSSION

1. Summarize in your own words the arguments in favor of and those opposed to human embryonic stem cell research.
2. State in your own words the ethical issues issues surrounding the subject of human embryonic stem cell research.
3. Summarize the various legal questions raised in state and federal legislatures surrounding the subject of human embryonic stem cell research.
4. Select and discuss a particular comment, fact, or statement that you find intriguing, argumentative, or in need of explanation or clarification.

○ PERSPECTIVES ON BIOETHICS ○

Suggested Writing Topics

1. Compare and contrast the views of James D. Watson in "All for the Good" and Ian Wilmut in "Dolly's False Legacy" on the subject of human cloning. Whom do you find more persuasive?

2. Drawing on at least two of the essays in this chapter, explain where you stand on one of the questions raised in the readings in this chapter about the implications and dangers of genetics research.

3. Write a response to James D. Watson ("All for the Good"), Ian Wilmut ("Dolly's False Legacy"), or Michael Crichton ("Patenting Life"). Explain where you agree, where you disagree, and where you have real concerns about what the person says. Be sure to state why you believe as you do.

4. Argue your position on any of the issues raised by the essays in this chapter: patenting genes, stem-cell research, physician-assisted suicide, universal health care, access to expensive treatments for self-induced health problems, embryo research, mandatory testing for HIV diseases, compulsory genetic screening for certain risk groups, or brain chip implants.

5. Write an essay on another issue, besides the ones identified by the authors of the articles in this chapter, that needs to be looked at closely. For instance, do you think care must be taken to make the results of genetic research available to everyone while protecting the rights of both researchers who make the discoveries and companies that want to profit from them?

6. Conduct a class forum on the ethical, social, and/or legal problems that are associated with the Human Genome Project, human cloning, stem-cell research, or other genetics research. For a writing project, summarize the views of your classmates, and state your own position on the subject.

7. Interview professionals such as a molecular biologist, an ethics professor, or someone else familiar with genetics research or the Human Genome Project on the ethical, social, and/or legal problems associated with the Human Genome Project or stem-cell research. Draw on the views of the professionals whom you interview as you explain your own position on the subject.

Research Topics

1. Starting with Robyn S. Shapiro's "The Bioethics and the Stem Cell Research Debate," update the state of the controversy over stem cell research by finding out what state and federal laws have been passed since 2006; then state your own position on the subject, given its current ethical and legal status.

2. Research one of the issues suggested by the readings in this chapter: stem cell research, physician-assisted suicide, universal health care, access to expensive treatments for self-induced health problems, embryo research, mandatory testing for HIV diseases, and compulsory genetic screening for certain risk groups or during premarital examinations; or the status of genetic disease and genetic therapy.

3. Research the Human Genome Project, and write a paper in which you elaborate on its main objectives, provide representative views on the controversy surrounding it, and explain your own position and why you believe as you do.

4. Research the Genomic Research and Accessibility Act mentioned by Michael Crichton in "Patenting Life." Find out what conditions led to its proposal, what arguments have been made in support of or against it, whether it has passed the House and gone to the Senate, and/or other aspects of the proposed bill.

5. Research the question: Should scientists create human life. Consider pros and cons and arrive at your own conclusion.

6. Select an issue in the area of neurotechnology, such as implantable brain chips, brain imaging, cochlear implants, lie detection technologies, deep brain stimulators, transcranial magnetic stimulation, brain computer interfaces, forensic neuroscience, and neuromarketing. Research the controversy over the issue and arrive at your own conclusion.

7. Research some aspect of the history and/or practice of eugenics, such as the program of Nazi Germany under Hitler or in the U.S. programs for forced sterilization for mentally ill patients.

RESPONDING TO VISUALS

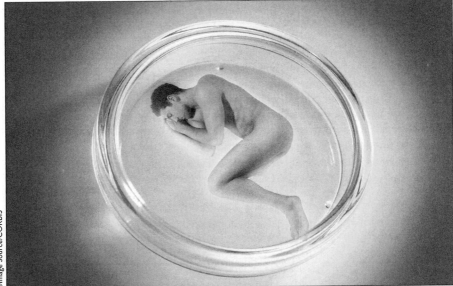

A human in a Petri dish.

1. What is the message of this image?
2. What is the symbolic significance of the naked human inside a Petri dish?
3. Why do you suppose an adult was used inside the Petri dish instead of a baby?

RESPONDING TO VISUALS

Stan Schmunk protests as a truck passes by carrying anti-stem cell research messages outside the Stem Cells and Regenerative Medicine: Commercial Implications for the Pharmaceutical and Biotech Industries meeting October 8, 2002 in San Diego, California. The protesters are demonstrating on behalf of the anti-abortion California Life Coalition that opposes all embryonic stem cell research.

1. What comment does the photograph make on opposition to stem-cell research?
2. To what extent does this photograph summarize the reasons some people are opposed to stem cell research?
3. To what extent do you agree with the messages photographed here?

CHAPTER 21

PUBLIC HEALTH

Epidemics, pandemics, and plagues have been much dreaded realities from the very beginning of human existence. Consider such major outbreaks of disease as the bubonic plague in thirteenth- and fourteenth-century Europe; cholera epidemics in various parts of the world from time to time, up to the present; the smallpox epidemic that swept Sweden in 1764; the typhus epidemic that killed more than three million Russians during World War I; or the influenza plague of 1918 to 1919 that killed more than twenty million people around the world. More recently, untreatable, deadly viruses have infected populations in certain areas of the world, worrying health officials that they may spread elsewhere. The Ebola virus in Africa, for instance, produces acute suffering in its victims, most of whom die within days of being infected. Viruses are particularly difficult to contain, because they live inside body cells, where antibiotics cannot reach them. Worse, once a person is infected with a virus, it can continue to live in the body's cells, waiting to strike again many years later.

Even such previously treatable diseases as herpes, hepatitis, and chicken pox are becoming resistant to treatment and causing deaths in increasingly higher numbers. Cases of deaths caused by herpes simplex 1 (HSV1) and related members of the herpes family, such as cytomegalovirus (CVM), chicken pox, and genital herpes (HSV2), have been reported. Although certain groups such as pregnant women are particularly vulnerable to these diseases, these and other viruses pose a considerable threat to the general population. More than three million Americans are believed to harbor the mysterious and deadly hepatitis C virus, for instance, with even more people harboring the less-mysterious but potentially life-threatening hepatitis A and hepatitis B viruses.

This chapter features articles on issues related to several aspects of public health, both national and global, beginning with Charles Krauthammer's "Smallpox Shots: Make Them Mandatory." Smallpox was supposedly eradicated for good almost three decades ago, but the possibility that hostile nations might be developing strains to attack the U.S. leads Krauthammer to argue that preventive vaccinations should be reintroduced and made mandatory, not voluntary.

Another serious public-health issue is the rising cost of U.S. health care. Arnold S. Relman gives an overview of the current health-care system in "Restructuring the U.S. Health Care System." Relman outlines the problems inherent in rising health-care costs and discusses the perspectives of insurance companies, physicians, and patients. He concludes by recommending a restructuring of the system that he believes would benefit all parties.

The focus then shifts to global health concerns with Richard D. Smith's "Global Public Goods and Health." Smith explains what "global public goods" are and suggests applying that model to global health issues. Finally, Jessica Reaves in "What the Rest of Africa Could Learn About AIDS" reports on the success that the African nation Senegal has had in reducing the spread of AIDS. She explains how the Senegalese model works in three separate areas: government involvement, religious attitudes, and the country's legalization and regulation of prostitution. From Senegal, she suggests, the rest of the continent can learn much about aggressively fighting this devastating disease.

SMALLPOX SHOTS: MAKE THEM MANDATORY

Charles Krauthammer

Charles Krauthammer is a contributing editor to the New Republic *and writes a weekly syndicated column for the* Washington Post. *A political scientist, psychiatrist, journalist, and speech writer, Krauthammer won a Pulitzer Prize in 1981 for his commentary on politics and society and was the winner of the first $250,000 Bradley Prize in 2003. He has published a book,* Cutting Edges: Making Sense of the Eighties *(1985). While serving as chief resident in psychiatry at Massachusetts General Hospital, he published scientific papers, including his co-discovery of a form of bipolar disease that continues to be cited in psychiatric literature. In 2001, he was appointed to the President's Council on Bioethics. Krauthammer also contributes to* Time *magazine, where the following essay appeared in December 2002.*

The eradication of smallpox was one of humanity's great success stories. After thousands of years of suffering at the hands of the virus, the human race gathered all its wit and cunning and conquered the scourge, eradicating it forever. Well, forever lasted less than 25 years. It does not bode well for the future of our species that it took but a blink of the eye for one of history's worst killers to make a comeback—not on its own, mind you, but brought back by humans to kill again.

During the age of innocence—the '90s, during which it seemed history had ended—the big debate was whether the two remaining known stocks of smallpox in the world, one in Russia and the other in the U.S., should be destroyed. It seemed like a wonderful idea, except that no one could be absolutely sure that some smallpox stores had not fallen into other hands. In fact, we now think Iraq is working on weaponizing smallpox, and perhaps North Korea and others too.

The danger is greater now than ever—first, and ironically, because of our very success in eradicating it in the past. People today have almost no experience with, and therefore no immunity to, the virus. We are nearly as virgin a population as the Native Americans who were wiped out by the various deadly pathogens brought over by Europeans. Not content with that potential for mass murder, however, today's bad guys are reportedly trying to genetically manipulate the virus to make it even deadlier and more resistant to treatment. Who knows what monstrosities the monsters are brewing in their secret laboratories.

4   What to do? We have enough vaccine on hand, some diluted but still effective, to vaccinate everyone in the U.S., with more full-strength versions to come. President Bush has just announced that his Administration will take the concentric-circle approach: mandatory inoculations for certain soldiers, voluntary inoculations for medical and emergency workers, and then inoculations available to, but discouraged for, everybody else.

It sounds good, but it is not quite right. If smallpox were a threat just to individuals, then it could be left up to individuals to decide whether or not they want to protect themselves. When it comes to epidemic diseases, however, we don't leave it up to individuals to decide. The state decides.

Forget about smallpox. This happens every day with childhood diseases. No child can go to school unless he's been immunized. Parents have no choice. Think of it: we force parents to inject healthy children with organisms—some living, some dead—that in a small number of cases will cripple or kill the child. It is an extraordinary violation of the privacy and bodily integrity of the little citizen. Yet it is routine. Why? Because what is at stake is the vulnerability of the entire society to catastrophic epidemic. In that case, individuals must submit.

Which is why smallpox vaccines were mandatory when we were kids. It wasn't left up to you to decide if you wanted it. You might be ready to risk your life by forgoing the vaccine, but society would not let you—not because it was saving you from yourself but because it had to save others from you. The problem wasn't you getting smallpox; the problem was you giving smallpox to others if you got it. Society cannot tolerate that. We forced vaccination even though we knew it would maim and kill a small but certain number of those subjected to it.

8   Today the case for mandatory vaccination is even stronger. This is war. We need to respond as in war. The threat is not just against individuals, but against the nation. Smallpox kills a third of its victims. If this epidemic were to take hold, it could devastate America as a functioning society. And the government's highest calling is to protect society—a calling even higher than protecting individuals.

That is why conscription in wartime is justified. We violate the freedom of individuals by drafting them into combat, risking their lives—suspending, in effect, their right to life and liberty, to say nothing of the pursuit of happiness—in the name of the nation.

Vaccination is the conscription of civilians in the war against bioterrorism. I personally would choose not to receive the smallpox vaccine. I would not have my family injected. I prefer the odds of getting the disease vs. the odds of inflicting injury or death by vaccination on my perfectly healthy child.

Nonetheless, it should not be my decision. When what is at stake is the survival of the country, personal and family calculation must yield to national interest. And a population fully protected from smallpox is a supreme national interest.

12   If it is determined that the enemy really has smallpox and might use it, we should vaccinate everyone. We haven't been called upon to do very much for the country since Sept. 11. We can and should do this.

PERSONAL RESPONSE

Would you choose to have a smallpox vaccination if it were available and voluntary? Explain your answer.

QUESTIONS FOR CLASS OR SMALL-GROUP DISCUSSION

1. Comment on the effectiveness of Krauthammer's opening paragraph.

2. Analyze Krauthammer's argumentative strategy. Where does he state his position? What supporting proofs does he provide? What is his chief evidence in support of his position? How convincing is it?

3. How effective is Krauthammer's comparison of mandatory smallpox vaccination to conscription in wartime (paragraph 9)?

4. Are you persuaded by Krauthammer's argument?

RESTRUCTURING THE U.S. HEALTH CARE SYSTEM

Arnold S. Relman

Arnold S. Relman, Professor Emeritus of Medicine and Social Medicine at Harvard Medical School, is the former editor of the New England Journal of Medicine. *He was the co-editor, with F. J. Ingelfinger and M. Finland, of two volumes of* Controversy in Internal Medicine *(1974). In recent years he has written widely on the economic, ethical, legal, and social aspects of healthcare and is an advocate for reform in the healthcare system. This article appeared in the Summer 2003 issue of* Issues in Science and Technology.

The past two decades have seen major economic changes in the health care system in the United States, but no solution has been found for the basic problem of cost control. Per-capita medical expenditures increased at an inflation-corrected rate of about 5 to 7 percent per year during most of this period, with health care costs consuming an ever-growing fraction of the gross national product. The rate of increase slowed a little for several years during the 1990s, with the spread of managed care programs. But the rate is now increasing more rapidly than ever, and control of medical costs has reemerged as a major national imperative. Failure to solve this problem has resulted in most of the other critical defects in the health care system. Half of all medical expenditures occur in the private sector, where employment-based health insurance provides at least partial coverage for most (but by no means all) people under age 65. Until the mid-1980s, most private insurance was of the indemnity type, in which the insurer simply paid the customary bills of hospitals and physicians. This coverage was offered by employers as a tax-free fringe benefit to employees (who might be required to contribute 10 to 20 percent of the cost as a copayment), and was tax-deductible for employers as a business cost. But the economic burden and unpredictability of ever-increasing premiums caused employers ultimately to abandon indemnity insurance for most of their workers. Companies increasingly turned to managed care plans, which contracted with employers to provide a given package of health care benefits at a negotiated and prearranged premium in a price-competitive market.

When the Clinton administration took office in 1993, one of its first initiatives was an ambitious proposal to introduce federally regulated competition among managed care plans. The objective was to control premium prices while ensuring that the public had universal care, received quality care, and could choose freely among care providers. It was hoped that all kinds of managed care plans, including the older not-for-profit plans as well as the more recent plans offered by investor-owned companies, would be attracted to the market and would want to compete for patients on a playing field kept level by government regulations.

But this initiative was sidetracked before even coming to a congressional vote. There was strong opposition from the private insurance industry, which saw huge profit-making opportunities in an unregulated managed care market but not under the Clinton plan. Moreover, the proposed plan's complexity and heavy dependence on government regulation frightened many people—including the leaders of the American Medical Association—into believing it was "socialized medicine."

4   The failure of this initiative delivered private health insurance into the hands of a new and aggressive industry that made enormous profits by keeping the lid on premiums while greatly reducing its expenditures on medical services—and keeping the difference as net income. This industry referred to its expenditures on care as "medical losses," a term that speaks volumes about the basic conflict between the health interests of patients and the financial interests of the investor-owned companies. But, in fact, there was an enormous amount of fat in the services that had been provided through traditional insurance, so these new managed care insurance businesses could easily spin gold for their investors, executives, and owners by eliminating many costs. They did this in many different ways, including denial of payment for hospitalizations and physicians' services deemed not medically essential by the insurer. The plans also forced price discounts from hospitals and physicians and made contracts that discouraged primary care physicians from spending much time with patients, ordering expensive tests, or referring patients to specialists. These tactics were temporarily successful in controlling expenditures in the private sector. Fueled by the great profits they made, managed care companies expanded rapidly. It then consolidated into a relatively few giant corporations that enjoyed great favor on Wall Street, and quickly came to exercise substantial influence over the political economy of U.S. health care.

The other half of medical expenditures is publicly funded, and this sector was not even temporarily successful in restraining costs. The government's initial step was to adopt a method of reimbursing hospitals based on diagnostic related groupings (DRGs). Rather than paying fees for each hospital day and for individual procedures, the government would pay a set amount for treating a patient with a given diagnosis. Hospitals were thus given powerful incentives to shorten stays and to cut corners in the use of resources for inpatient care. At the same time, they encouraged physicians to conduct many diagnostic and therapeutic procedures in ambulatory facilities that were exempt from DRG-based restrictions on reimbursement.

Meanwhile, the temporary success of private managed care insurance in holding down premiums—along with its much-touted (but never proven) claims of higher quality of care—suggested to many politicians that government could solve its health care cost problems by turning over much of the public system to private enterprise. Therefore, states began to contract out to private managed care plans a major part of the services provided under Medicaid to low-income people. The federal government, for political reasons, could not so cavalierly outsource care provided to the elderly under Medicare, but did begin to encourage those over 65 to join government-subsidized private plans in lieu of receiving Medicare benefits. For a time, up to 15 percent of Medicare beneficiaries chose to do so, mainly because the plans promised coverage for outpatient prescription drugs, which Medicare did not provide.

What about attempts to contain the rapidly rising physicians' bills for the great majority of Medicare beneficiaries who chose to remain in the traditional fee-for-service system? The government first considered paying doctors through a DRG-style system similar to that used for hospitals, but this idea was never implemented; and in 1990, a standardized fee schedule replaced the old "usual and customary" fees. Physicians found a way to maintain their incomes, however, by disaggregating (and thereby multiplying) billable services and by increasing the number of visits; and Medicare's payments for medical services continued to rise.

8   Cost-control efforts by for-profit managed care plans and by government have diminished the professional role of physicians as defenders of their patients' interests. Physicians have become more entrepreneurial and have entered into many different kinds of business arrangements with hospitals and outpatient facilities, in an effort not only to sustain their income but also to preserve their autonomy as professionals. Doctor-owned imaging centers, kidney dialysis units, and ambulatory surgery centers have proliferated. Physicians have acquired financial interests in the medical goods and services they use and prescribe. They have installed expensive new equipment in their offices that generates more billing and more income. And, in a recent trend, groups of physicians have been investing in hospitals that specialize in cardiac, orthopedic, or other kinds of specialty care, thus serving as competition for community-based general hospitals for the most profitable patients. Of course, all of these self-serving reactions to the cost-controlling efforts of insurers are justified by physicians as a way to protect the quality of medical care. Nevertheless, they increase the costs of health care, and they raise serious questions about financial influences on professional decisions.

In the private sector, managed care has failed in its promise to prevent sustained escalation in costs. Once all the excess was squeezed out, further cuts could only be achieved by cutting essentials. Meanwhile, new and more expensive technology continues to come online, inexorably pushing up medical expenditures. Employers are once again facing a disastrous inflation in costs that they clearly cannot and will not accept, and they are cutting back on covered benefits and shifting more costs to employees. Moreover, there has been a major public backlash against the restrictions imposed by managed care, forcing many state governments to pass laws that prevent private insurers from limiting the health care choices of patients and the medical decisions of physicians. The courts also have begun to side with complaints that managed care plans are usurping the prerogatives of physicians and harming patients.

In the public sector, a large fraction of those Medicare beneficiaries who chose to shift to managed care are now back with their standard coverage, either because they were dissatisfied and chose to leave their plans or because plans have terminated their government contracts for lack of profit. The unchecked rise in expenditures on the Medicaid and Medicare programs is causing government to cut back on benefits to patients and on payments to physicians and hospitals. Increased unemployment has reduced the numbers of those covered by job-related insurance and thus has expanded the ranks of the uninsured, which now total more than 41 million people. Reduced payments have caused many physicians to refuse to accept Medicaid patients. Some doctors are even considering whether they want to continue taking new elderly patients into their practices who do not have private Medigap insurance to supplement their Medicare coverage.

Major Changes Needed

What will the future bring? The present state of affairs cannot continue much longer. The health care system is imploding, and proposals for its rescue will be an important part of the national political debate in the upcoming election year. Most voters want a system that is affordable and yet provides good-quality care for everyone. Some people believe that modest, piecemeal improvements in the existing health care structure can do the job, but that seems unlikely. Major widespread changes will be needed.

12   Those people who think of health care as primarily an economic commodity, and of the health care system as simply another industry, are inclined to believe in market-based solutions. They suggest that more business competition in the insuring and delivering of medical care, and more consumer involvement in sharing costs and making health care choices, will rein in expenditures and improve the quality of care. However, they also believe that additional government expenditures will be required to cover the poor.

Those people who do not think that market forces can or should control the health care system usually advocate a different kind of reform. They favor a consolidated and universal not-for-profit insurance system. Some believe in funding this system entirely through taxes and others through a combination of taxes and employer and individual contributions. But the essential feature of this idea is that almost all payments should go directly to health care providers rather than to the middlemen and satellite businesses that now live off the health care dollar.

A consolidated insurance system of this kind—sometimes called a single-payer system—could eliminate many of the problems in today's hodgepodge of a system. However, sustained cost control and the realignment of incentives for physicians with the best interests of their patients will require still further reform in the organization of medical care. Fee-for-service private practice, as well as regulation of physician practices by managed care businesses, will need to be largely replaced by a system in which multispecialty not-for-profit groups of salaried physicians accept risk-free prepayment from the central insurer for the delivery of a defined benefit package of comprehensive care.

Such reform, seemingly utopian now, may eventually gain wide support as the failure of market-based health care services to meet the public's need becomes increasingly evident, and as the ethical values of the medical profession continue to erode in the rising tide of commercialism.

PERSONAL RESPONSE

What health plan, if any, do you have? Are you satisfied with your health plan?

QUESTIONS FOR CLASS OR SMALL-GROUP DISCUSSION

1. How effectively does Relman explain the problem of rising health-care costs for all parties concerned? State in your own words what you understand to be the views of physicians, insurers, employers, and the elderly on the current state of health care in the U.S.

2. How well does Relman explain the differences between those who view health care as an economic commodity and those who believe health care should not be market-driven?

3. What is Relman's argumentative strategy? Does he make a persuasive case for health care reform in the U.S.?

4. In his concluding paragraphs, Relman suggests a reform plan that he describes as "seemingly utopian." In what ways is it utopian? What is the likelihood of his plan's succeeding?

GLOBAL PUBLIC GOODS AND HEALTH

Richard D. Smith

Richard D. Smith is Senior Lecturer in Health Economics at the School of Health Policy and Practice, University of East Anglia, England. He has written and spoken extensively on health issues, particularly those affecting the elderly and disadvantaged. "Global Public Goods and Health" is an editorial that appeared in the July, 2003, issue of Bulletin of the World Health Organization.

Health improvement requires collective as well as individual action, and the health of poor populations in particular requires collective action between countries as well as within them. Initiatives such as the Global Fund to Fight AIDS, Tuberculosis and Malaria reflect a growing awareness of this fact. However, initiating, organizing and financing collective actions for health at the global level presents a challenge to existing international organizations (1).

The concept of "global public goods" (GPGs) suggests one possible framework for considering these issues (2). In this expression, "goods" encompass a range of physical commodities (such as bread, books and shoes) but include services (such as security, information and travel), distinguishing between private and public goods. Most goods are "private" in the sense that their consumption can be withheld until a payment is made in exchange for them, and once consumed they cannot be consumed again. In contrast, once "public" goods are provided no one can be excluded from consuming them (they are non-excludable), and one person's consumption of them does not prevent anyone else's (they are non-rival in consumption) (3). For example, no one in a population can be excluded from benefiting from a reduction in risk of infectious disease when its incidence is reduced, and one person benefiting from this reduction in risk does not prevent anyone else from benefiting from it as well.

Global public goods are goods of this kind whose benefits cross borders and are global in scope. For example, reductions in carbon dioxide emissions will slow global warming. It will be impossible to exclude any country from benefiting from this, and each country will benefit without preventing another from doing so. Similarly, the eradication of infectious diseases of global scope, such as smallpox or polio, provides a benefit from which no country is excluded, and from which all countries will benefit without detriment to others.

4   However, these attributes of public goods give rise to a paradox: although there is significant benefit to be gained from them by many people, there is no commercial incentive for producing them, since enjoyment cannot be made conditional on payment. With national public goods, the government therefore intervenes either financially, through such mechanisms as taxation or licensing, or with direct provision. But for global public goods this is harder to do, because no global government exists to ensure that they are produced and paid for. The central issue for health-related GPGs is how best to ensure that the collective action necessary, for health is taken at the international level.

Globalization of travel, changes in technology, and the liberalization of trade all affect health. Communicable diseases spread more rapidly, often in drug-resistant form (4), environmental degradation reduces access to clean air and water, and knowledge of traditional and modern health technologies is increasingly patented and thus made artificially excludable (5). However, discussion of GPGs to date has typically been broad-based and multisectoral (for instance on the environment, international security and trade agreements), and most of the discussion within the health sector has been focused on medical technologies (3, 6, 7).

This has left many questions unanswered (8). For example, is health itself a GPG? To what extent does my (national) health depend on your (national) health? How many of the actions necessary to global health—communicable disease control, generation and dissemination of medical knowledge, public health infrastructure—constitute GPGs? What contribution can the GPG concept make to fulfilling these needs? Is international financing for these GPGs best coordinated through voluntary contributions, global taxation systems, or market-based mechanisms? Does the concept of GPGs undermine or support concepts of equity and human rights?

The first large-scale study of the application of the GPG concept to the health sector examines questions such as these, and has just been published (8). The study finds that, while the concept has important limitations, for some areas of health work it can offer guidance in the financing and provision of global health programmes. In these areas it provides a framework for collective action at the global level, demonstrates the advantages for the rich in helping the poor, and provides a rationale for industrialized countries to use national health budgets to complement traditional aid (as seen in the Polio Eradication Initiative (9)). Overall, the GPG concept will be increasingly important as a rationale and a guide for public health work in an era of globalization.

Endnotes[1]

1. Drager N. & Beaglehole, R. Globalization: Changing the public health landscape. *Bulletin of the World Health Organization* 2001; 79: 803.
2. Kaul I & Faust, M. Global public goods and health: Taking the agenda forward. *Bulletin of the World Health Organization* 2001; 79: 869–74.
3. Kaul I, Grunberg I, Stern MA, editors. *Global public goods: International cooperation in the 21st century.* New York: Oxford University Press; 1999.
4. Smith RD, Coast J. Antimicrobial resistance: a global response. *Bulletin of the World Health Organization* 2002; 80:126–33.
5. Thorsteinsdottir H, Daar A, Smith RD, Singer P. Genomics—a global public good? *Lancet* 2003; 361:891–2.
6. Kaul I, Conceicao P, Le Goulven K, Mendoza RU, editors. *Providing global public goods: managing globalization.* New York: Oxford University Press; 2003.
7. *Macroeconomics and health: investing in health for economic development. Report of the Commission on Macroeconomics and Health.* Geneva: World Health Organization; 2001.
8. Smith RD, Beaglehole R, Woodward D, Drager N, editors. *Global public goods for health: a health economic and public health perspective.* Oxford: Oxford University Press; 2003.
9. Aylward B, Acharya A, England S, et al. Achieving global health goals: the politics and economics of polio eradication, *Lancet* (forthcoming).

PERSONAL RESPONSE

Do you agree that the issue of health care requires collective rather than individual action (paragraph 1)? How would you answer Smith's question in paragraph 6: "Is health itself a GPG"?

[1]Endnotes are reproduced as originally published and do not conform to either MLA or APA style. [Ed.]

QUESTIONS FOR CLASS OR SMALL-GROUP DISCUSSION

1. Does Smith clearly define the concept of "global public goods?" How well do his examples in paragraphs 2 and 3 serve to illustrate that concept?

2. How well does Smith explain the paradox that he mentions in paragraph 4?

3. Do you agree with Smith that the GPG model would work in the health sector?

4. What is the rhetorical effect of the series of questions in paragraph 6?

WHAT THE REST OF AFRICA COULD LEARN ABOUT AIDS

JESSICA REAVES

Jessica Reaves is a staff writer and reporter for the Chicago Tribune, *where she has worked since 2004. Before joining the* Tribune, *she wrote for Time.com in New York and as a reporter for* Ms. Magazine. *This article was published in the April 27, 2007, issue of the* Chicago Tribune.

KOLDA, Senegal—The open-air classroom, buffeted by a stiff, dusty wind, rang with the sound of children's laughter and excited chatter as their teacher paced in front of the blackboard, brandishing colored chalk. He raised his hand, and the room fell silent.

He pointed to a poster with an illustration of a man in a bar, leaning suggestively toward a woman holding a condom in her hand. "What do we think is happening here?" he asked.

The 12- and 13-year-olds raised their hands eagerly, some bouncing up and down in their seats. The teacher called on a girl sitting in the back of the room.

4   "He wants to have sex with her," she said.

"And what will she say to him?" asked the teacher.

There was some mumbling, and then a boy raised his hand.

"Not without a condom."

8   This is a scene I witnessed recently in the West African country of Senegal, one of the continent's success stories in the fight against HIV/AIDS. The infection rate in Senegal is 0.9 percent—similar to the rate in the U.S. (0.6 percent), and far lower than the soaring tolls in African countries such as Namibia (19.6 percent), South Africa (18.8 percent) and Botswana (24.1 percent).

What is Senegal doing right, I wondered, and could those practices be replicated in other countries?

I arrived in Senegal with plenty of questions and, like most Americans, a few misconceptions about Islamic West Africa. As far as AIDS in Senegal was concerned, I knew there were a few factors to consider: government involvement, religious attitudes and the country's long-standing legalization and regulation of prostitution.

The Senegalese government has taken a remarkably active role in the sex education of its citizens. In 1986, immediately after the first case of AIDS was confirmed in Senegal, the government launched a massive prevention program, pouring resources into AIDS education.

12   The Senegalese brand of Islam dictates a certain social conservatism, and there is little opportunity for teenagers to be alone together. The lack of alcohol certainly plays a role in disease prevention; drunken sex is statistically far less likely to involve condom use than sober sex. And Senegal's sex worker registration system, in place since 1969, provides prostitutes with weekly health care and free condoms. In a recent academic report, 100 percent of Senegalese sex workers surveyed (all of whom had taken part in government-sponsored classes on AIDS and sexually transmitted disease prevention) said they use condoms with every customer.

But there are plenty of other reasons for the country's low AIDS rate, including the early and intensive efforts by the country's powerful imams, some of whom use Friday services to educate their congregations about AIDS. This growing trend is a powerful indicator of the partnership between the medical community and religious leaders: While imams limit their sermons to discussions of abstinence and fidelity, doctors are often on hand to handle practical instruction and clinical questions.

One particularly warm day during my trip, I went to speak with the imam who presides over the Grand Mosque in Kolda, a city in Senegal's Casamance region, where the AIDS rate is six times higher (3 percent) than it is in the capital of Dakar (0.5 percent). I took note of the imam's kind eyes, grizzled hair and easy smile and asked him, through a translator, whether he had any hesitation incorporating AIDS into his sermons, which reach about 3,000 people each week. "We treat this like any other disease," he replied. "If someone is sick, we want to help them."

And when it comes to talking about condoms? "Teaching people to use condoms is a contradiction of Islamic law," he said. "We teach fidelity in marriage and abstinence before marriage." Outside the mosque, he said, he can discuss HIV and AIDS more directly and, like many Senegalese imams, he refers congregants to a local clinic or doctor where practical advice about contraception is readily available.

16   Imams enjoy enormous political and cultural power in Senegal. In involving its religious leaders—a process that has taken patience, time and government funding—Senegal's anti-AIDS strategy provides a useful blueprint for other countries struggling to contain the spread of the disease.

Another of Senegal's successful HIV/AIDS prevention techniques should also be duplicated and exported: Frank, open and comprehensive sex education beginning at age 12, and AIDS awareness training starting as early as 1st grade.

The emphasis on education is deeply ingrained. In 1994, Senegal's Ministry of Education requested—and received—funding from UNFPA (the United Nations Population Fund) to begin the Group for the Study and Teaching of Population

Issues, or GEEP. GEEP's mandate: to bring information about sex, contraception, health and family planning to children in Senegal's schools.

Over 13 years, GEEP has expanded; it now provides peer counselors to students and sponsors family life education clubs in schools. Since GEEP's inception, Senegalese girls have delayed sex three years longer than their mothers' generation, and a recent survey shows that condom use has risen threefold from 10 years ago, to nearly 70 percent.

20 The message is clear: Comprehensive sex education—including information about condoms and how to use them—is one of the most important weapons in the fight against AIDS.

Teaching kids about condoms doesn't promote sex. (Anyone who's been a high school student knows this makes some sense: If there's anything less romantic than unrolling condoms in front of your classmates, it's seeing graphic photographs of STD-infected genitals—available at any Senegalese health kiosk.) But the Bush administration exports a restrictive, abstinence-only agenda used in many American schools.

PEPFAR, the United States President's Emergency Plan for AIDS Relief, has made funding of sex education projects contingent on the use of extremely limited language when talking about contraception and sex. To receive PEPFAR funding, countries must severely constrain teaching about condoms in favor of abstinence-based lessons.

In Senegal and in Uganda, where the HIV infection rate has fallen from 15 percent to about 6 percent, the governments were quick to implement the "ABC" approach, which advocates "Abstinence, Be Faithful and Use Condoms." This trifecta is consistent with the teaching I saw in Senegal, where middle school pupils were told that abstinence and monogamy were the best choices—though if they were unable to maintain either, they should always use a condom.

24 That doesn't jibe with PEPFAR's logic, which hinges on "targeted" messaging. By their calculations, only sex workers and other "high risk" populations should receive information about condoms. And even then, PEPFAR policy dictates that the message has to include an abstinence component.

Many African nations, including AIDS-ravaged Botswana and South Africa, continue to receive PEPFAR money, a dependency that stifles the free exchange of information and could cost more lives than it saves. Senegal's policy of legalized prostitution means the country is ineligible for PEPFAR funding, so it relies instead on donations from the UNFPA and the Global Fund, an independent grant-making consortium of governmental, non-governmental and private-sector groups. That means Senegal's teachers and community leaders are free to discuss condom use as part of a larger prevention message—a message, it must be noted, that has been far more successful than what is offered in any of the PEPFAR recipient countries.

The hot March day when I visited a classroom in Kolda, I was struck, as the kids answered their teacher's questions without embarrassment, by their sophisticated understanding of AIDS and of the ways, including abstinence until marriage and condom use, they could prevent the disease from spreading.

As the class period ended and the kids filed out of the room, the girls whispering and giggling and the boys whooping on their way to the dirt field for a game of soccer, their teacher suddenly let out an exclamation.

28 "I forgot the condom demonstration," he said, shaking his head ruefully. "I got so wrapped up in the lesson I forgot to bring out the condoms."

"Oh, well," he said, sitting down at his desk to rewrite the next day's lesson plans. "We'll tackle that tomorrow."

PERSONAL RESPONSE

Reaves mentions that she arrived in Senegal with "a few misconceptions about Islamic West Africa," although she does not say what those misconceptions were. What do you suppose they were? What impressions or even "misconceptions," if any, did you have about Senegal before reading this article?

QUESTIONS FOR CLASS OR SMALL-GROUP DISCUSSION

1. Assess the effectiveness of Reaves's opening description of the classroom scene and her returning to it at the end of her article. What function do those references serve in relation to the rest of her article?

2. What does Reaves think that rest of Africa could learn about AIDS from Senegal?

3. Are you persuaded by Reaves's evidence that Senegal's policy toward HIV/AIDS education is a model for other countries? How likely do you think it is that other countries will adopt Senegal's policies in AIDS prevention? Explain your answer.

4. Discuss Reaves's suggestion that the U.S. policy for giving aid to African countries (PEPFAR) creates "a dependency that stifles the free exchange of information and could cost more lives than it saves" (paragraph 25). Do you agree with her?

○ PERSPECTIVES ON PUBLIC HEALTH ○

Suggested Writing Topics

1. Argue for or against making smallpox vaccinations mandatory.

2. Argue for or against the right of pharmaceutical companies to hold patents and continue to make large profits on drugs that could help fight AIDS in sub-Saharan countries.

3. Explore the role of drug companies in fighting the global AIDS epidemic.

4. Discuss your views on providing universal access to health care in light of the high cost of health care.

5. Explain your views on how best to educate the public about preventing sexually transmitted diseases.

6. Explain the role you believe that schools and other public institutions should play in disseminating information about sexually transmitted diseases.

7. Argue either for or against programs to distribute free condoms to high school students.

8. If you know someone with AIDS or another grave illness, describe that person's condition, the problems it poses for the person's family, and your concerns about the person and the illness.

9. Many writers suggest that social inequalities, such as poverty, the class system, or women's lower social status, help spread AIDS in Third World countries. Select one of those subjects and explain how working to overcome the problems associated with it is an important component in the fight against AIDS. For instance, how would helping lift people out of poverty work against the spread AID? How might improving women's rights help control the spread of AIDS.

Research Topics

1. Research the viewpoints of drug companies, economists, and health workers, among others, on this question: Should drug companies bear the financial burden of sending lifesaving drugs to developing countries?

2. In combination with library and Internet research, interview public health officials or representatives from the health center at your campus about a public health issue. Narrow your focus to one aspect of public health and explain your own view on the topic.

3. Research the controversy over government funding for AIDS research.

4. Research and assess the importance or success of the work of either a national health agency, such as the U.S. Centers for Disease Control (CDC), or an international health agency, such as the World Health Organization (WHO).

5. Research some aspect of the AIDS epidemic in the United States (or another country) and responses by public health officials to the disease. You will discover many controversies on this subject, so identify one major controversy, explore the issues involved, and arrive at your own position on the subject. You may want to take a historical approach, for instance, by exploring various theories on the origin of AIDS, or you may want to focus on controversial treatments for the disease.

6. Research one of the many contributing factors in the spread of AIDS in Africa that are mentioned by either Wayne Ellwood in "We All Have AIDS": poverty, gender, class inequality, ignorance, urbanization, colonialism, or the collapse of rural economies.

7. Research a major plague of the past, such as the bubonic plague in thirteenth- and fourteenth-century Europe, cholera epidemics, the smallpox

epidemic that swept Sweden in 1764, the typhus epidemic that killed more than three million Russians during World War I, or the influenza plague of 1918 to 1919 that killed more than 20 million people around the world. Determine the consequences for the country (or countries) affected by the plague as well as its possible origins and how it was finally conquered.

RESPONDING TO VISUALS

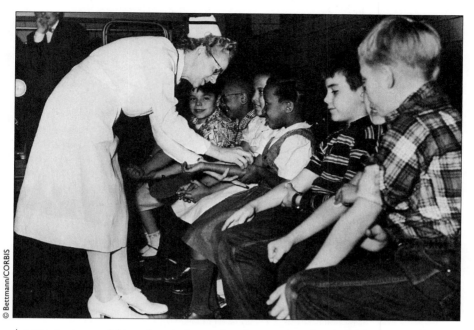

© Bettmann/CORBIS

A nurse prepares children for a polio vaccine shot as part of a city-wide testing of vaccine on elementary school students, February 23, 1954, Pittsburg, Pennsylvania.

1. What is going on in this photograph? State the details that explain what is happening.
2. What aspects of the scene does the photographer emphasize?
3. What do the facial expressions and body language indicate about how both the nurse and the children view this experience?
4. What details give clues that this picture is not current? Could you tell that the photograph was taken in the 1950s if you were not told that in the caption?

RESPONDING TO VISUALS

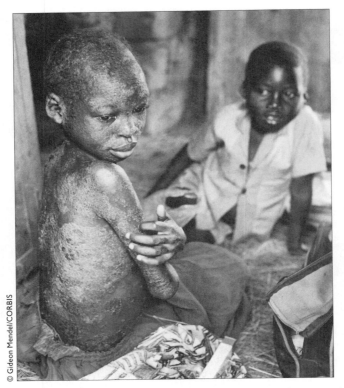

© Gideon Mendel/CORBIS

A 13-year-old Tanzanian girl suffering from an AIDS-related skin infection, at her home near Bukoba, Tanzania. She was transmitted AIDS from a blood transfusion from her father to treat malarial anaemia. Her father died from AIDS-related syndrome, and her mother is severely ill from the disease.

1. What is your emotional response to the picture?
2. What is the effect of the perspective from which the photograph was taken? What details about the children are revealed from that perspective?
3. Why does the photographer include the child who apparently is not ill? What is the effect of the juxtaposition of the two children?

CHAPTER
22

Environmental Studies

Environmental issues such as depletion of the ozone layer, global warming, deforestation, and air and water pollution are just a few of the many causes for concern over the health of animal and vegetable life on Earth. Closely connected to these environmental problems is the rapid rate of increase in the world population. As the number of people grows, pressure increases on natural resources. Will Earth provide enough food for everyone? How can water supplies be kept safe for drinking? How does pollution produced by so many humans affect the quality of the air they breathe? How can people stop the ever-widening hole in the ozone layer that protects us from the harmful rays of the sun? How will future generations sustain the rapidly increasing worldwide population? These are just some of the questions confronting scientists, civic leaders, and ordinary people everywhere.

Although most people recognize that humans must keep their environments safe, not everyone agrees on either the nature of the problems or the severity of their consequences.

For instance, resource depletion and global warming are the subjects of many debates. Researchers and scientists differ in their beliefs on questions such as Earth's ability to sustain life indefinitely and whether Earth is experiencing global warming and, if so, whether the phenomenon is cause for alarm.

In the first piece in this chapter, Aaron Sachs profiles the nineteenth-century scientist Baron Alexander von Humboldt, who, he says, is "the man most responsible for bringing the practice of science into mainstream Western culture." In "Humboldt's Legacy and the Restoration of Science," Sachs maintains that modern science would do well to adopt Humboldt's integrated vision of nature. He laments the relatively low federal allocation for furthering the understanding of the environment, and he believes that ecologists and environmentalists should adopt a broader, interdisciplinary approach to environmental problems. Although the essay was first published a decade and a half ago, you will no doubt see that what Sachs says about Humboldt resonates yet today for anyone concerned about environmentalism.

Next is an essay offering practical guides to conservation in a number of areas. Paul Hawken, in "A Declaration of Sustainability," suggests actions for both individuals and groups to help the environment. According to his "strategies for sustainability," Hawken offers "twelve steps society can take to save the whole enchilada." Like Sachs's essay on Humboldt, this piece, first published in the 1990s, remains relevant today. As you read both Sachs's and Hawken's essays, think about what you already do to conserve resources and help curb environmental problems and whether these writers persuade you to do even more.

The *American Spectator* editorial, "The Galileo of Global Warming," presents a critical view of environmentalists, at least those who maintain that humans are responsible for global warming. The article reviews some of the issues concerning global warming and reports on the findings of scientist Lloyd Keigwin, whose research about Earth's climate discredits the theory that it is humans who cause global warming.

In the last article in this chapter, Bill McKibben makes an impassioned plea for activism in "Global Warming: Get Up! Stand Up!" Pointing out that previously identified environmental problems were fixable with both changes in behavior as well as legislatively mandated changes, he maintains that Congress has "failed to take on the single greatest challenge human civilization has ever faced." His subtitle, "How to Build a Mass Movement to Halt Climate Change," is a clear indication of the subject of his essay. As you read McKibben's piece, notice his argumentative strategies and ask yourself if you are persuaded to take action as he so urgently presses his readers to do.

HUMBOLDT'S LEGACY AND THE RESTORATION OF SCIENCE

Aaron Sachs

Aaron Sachs is a research associate at Worldwatch Institute studying issues in international development, human rights, and the social and environmental impacts of technology. He has authored numerous articles and is author of Eco-Justice: Linking Human Rights and the Environment *(1994) and co-author of* The Next Efficiency Revolution: Creating a Sustainable Materials Economy *(1990) and* State of the World 1995. *This essay is from the March/April 1995, issue of* World Watch *magazine.*

On September 15, 1869, the *New York Times* ran a one-word headline: "HUMBOLDT." Every literate American knew the name. "The One Hundredth Birthday of the Philosopher," explained the subtitle. "Celebration Generally Throughout the Country." The story took up the entire front page.

It is unthinkable today that Americans would celebrate the birthday of any dead philosopher, let alone a foreign one. Yet from San Francisco to Peoria to New York, on that Tuesday afternoon, people read speeches, unrolled banners, and unveiled statues in honor of the late Baron Alexander von Humboldt. Of course, Humboldt was much more than a philosopher: He was also an explorer, a geographer, a writer, a naturalist—and the man most responsible for bringing the practice of science into mainstream Western culture.

The word *scientist* first entered the English language in the 1830s, specifically in reference to Humboldt and his disciples—Charles Darwin among them. Originally, then, the term meant "natural scientist." The new profession Humboldt had carved out and popularized took as its goal the transformation of natural history studies, to cover not just the detailed cataloging of the phenomena of the physical world, but also the formulation of a grand, unifying theory that would link all those phenomena together. Humboldt wanted to know what tied the rivers to the trees, how climate influenced vegetation, why particular animals thrived only in particular habitats; he also wanted to reveal humanity's place within these interdependent relationships. And in an early nineteenth-century culture of amateur naturalists obsessed with the romance of the wilderness, his quest struck many chords.

4   Initially, Humboldt earned his fame by exploring the New World between 1799 and 1804, when he surveyed the headwaters of the Orinoco in the jungles of Venezuela and scaled the Andes to heights never before attained in any of the world's mountain ranges. On that trip, between the ages of thirty and thirty-five, the "Rediscoverer of America" witnessed the immense diversity of humanity and nature. He saw just how different life was among the natives of the Venezuelan rainforest and the politicians of the newly formed U.S. Congress—among the insects swarming in marshlands along the Colombian coast and the birds floating above Ecuadorean volcanoes and the wildflowers lining fertile Cuban valleys. Yet he never wavered in his belief that there existed a "chain of connection," that all elements of earthly life, including humans, were "mutually dependent"—and that a knowledge of that interdependence was the "noblest and most important result" of all scientific inquiry. For the last fifty-five years of his life—he lived to age ninety—he struggled to "recognize unity in the vast diversity of physical phenomena." While acknowledging the world's chaos, he saw within it what the ancient Greeks called a *kosmos*, a beautifully ordered and harmonious system, and he coined the modern word *cosmos* to use as the title of his final, multivolume work—a book Walt Whitman kept on his desk as he was writing *Leaves of Grass*.

Today, most environmentalists would be shocked to learn that nature's interrelationships were once in the mainstream of scientific thought. The dominant theme in science over the past century has been *fission*, the breaking down of life and matter and ideas into their smaller components: Life science and its organic theories have given way to specialization, to microbiology and nuclear physics. In our rush to gain in-depth knowledge about particular elements of a complicated, seemingly chaotic world, we have tacitly decided that it would be futile to try to tie those elements together. Science has lost its delicate balance between chaos and cosmos, between diversity and unity.

It now seems clear that this century-old imbalance is inextricably linked to our global ecological crisis. If we assume that the world on which we depend is utterly chaotic, there is no reason to do anything but try to control and conquer it—which has become science's new goal. And though specialization has proved itself invaluable in the pursuit of knowledge, its narrow, short-range focus, in the absence of a complementary organic approach, is extremely dangerous. We have directed society's accumulated scientific knowledge toward constantly improving our exploitation of each individual natural resource, without recognizing the threat we are posing to the basic ecosystems that create those resources. As Rachel Carson observed in her classic *Silent Spring*, we failed to predict the environmental impacts of extensive pesticide use because chemical companies paid researchers simply to kill pests—and not to worry about the pesticides' effects on other plants and animals, or groundwater supplies, or farm workers' lungs. Perhaps the highest goal of the environmental movement, then, is to reclaim science, to ensure that we use it not for the domination of nature but for the appreciation of our connectedness to it—to restore, in other words, the legacy that Humboldt tried to leave us.

In the nineteenth century, Humboldt's appeal was wide-ranging. Many people saw him as the world's historian, the man who would explain where we came from and how we fit into the universe. He provided an enthralled public with glimpses of exotic natural worlds they would never see for themselves. Scholars flocked to his study in Germany to soak up his wisdom, to examine his field notes and sprawling maps and native artifacts. And laypeople gathered at the newly opened natural history museums to which Humboldt had donated his famous collections of intricate jungle plants and multicolored birds. By organizing lectures and workshops all over the world, he made huge numbers of people feel involved in the progress of science. Moreover, his theories themselves were attractive for their inclusiveness, their ambitious attempts at painting a unified picture of all the world's complexities.

8   Just as every lowly plant and minute insect had a crucial role in Humboldt's vision of the world, so too did every type of human being, no matter how powerless or marginalized. Humboldt was a hero to Simon Bolivar, who used the scientist's writings in his campaigns for Latin American independence, to help prove that colonialism was wreaking havoc on both the people and the environment of the New World. And Humboldt was especially popular among Americans, by the time of the 1869 centennial, because he had been one of the world's most outspoken opponents of slavery. "In maintaining the unity of the human race," he had written, "we also reject the disagreeable assumption of superior and inferior peoples." Four years after the end of the Civil War, Americans found in Humboldt's scientific work a parallel to the political heroism of President Lincoln. Both men had staked everything on the concept of Union.

In 1869, Humboldt was as well-known and respected, globally, as Lincoln and Bolivar; he had been as influential in nineteenth-century science as Beethoven had been in music, as Napoleon had been in politics. Darwin once wrote that "my whole career is due to having read and reread" Humboldt's *Personal Narrative to the Equinoctial Regions of America,* and he often sent his manuscripts to the older scientist for comment. When the great theoretician of evolution set off on his voyage aboard *The Beagle,* he brought with him only three books: the Bible, a copy of Milton, and Humboldt's *Narrative.* Humboldt's magnum opus, *Cosmos,* bore the daunting subtitle, "A Sketch of a Physical Description of the Universe," and it had an index that ran to more than one thousand pages. But it was translated into all the major languages and sold hundreds of thousands of copies. "The demand is epoch-making," Humboldt's publisher claimed. "Book parcels destined for London and St. Petersburg were torn out of our hands by agents who wanted their orders filled for the bookstores in Vienna and Hamburg." Science, it seems, could easily have gone in the direction Humboldt was taking it.

Today, Humboldt's name is woven tightly into our geographical fabric: The index of a good atlas might list it some twenty-five times, referring not only to towns like Humboldt, Iowa, and Humboldt, South Dakota, but also to the Humboldt Mountains in China, Venezuela, and Nevada; the Humboldt Current off the coast of Peru; and even a Humboldt Glacier in Greenland. But almost no one today has any idea who Humboldt was.

Science, and Western society in general, underwent a huge transformation toward the end of the nineteenth century. In 1859, Humboldt died, Darwin published *On the Origin of Species,* and the modern age was born—though the full implications of evolution did not become clear until 1871, when Darwin delivered the ultimate comeuppance of his own species in *The Descent of Man*. The theory of evolution was revolutionary both because it directly undermined the centuries-old assumption that there was a divine plan separating human beings from the lowly animals, and because it posed a significant threat to the dearly held Humboldtian notion that nature was fundamentally a harmonious, unified entity. To most educated Westerners, the Darwinian concept of "the struggle for existence" meant that humanity's origins were steeped in animal violence and conflict—that the different facets of nature were not working together to form an organic whole but were competing with each other, fighting over ecological niches, fighting just to survive.

12   The one redeeming element of Darwinism, for many shocked Victorians, was that their civilization had at least seemed to come out of the competition victorious. In the hands of so-called Social Darwinists, "the struggle for existence" became "the survival of the fittest," and theorizers were quick to assert that Darwin's explanation of biological fitness proved the superiority of white, Christian Europeans. After all, they argued, a careful reading of *On the Origin of Species* revealed that the successful animals were those that had bodies perfectly designed to perform a particular function or adapt to a particular environment. The key to a species' success, in other words, was *specialization*—a word Darwin probably coined in the 1840s. And Europeans were without question becoming the world's experts in specialization.

By the second half of the nineteenth century, specialization was beginning to seep into almost every aspect of Western culture and thought. Graduate schools were offering highly specialized training in narrow professions. Huge new businesses were dividing their production processes into the smallest possible components, with the aim of improving efficiency and becoming more fit competitors in the capitalist economy. Laborers no longer saw products through from start to finish, but rather performed their one limited function, over and over again. By the turn of the century, someone had to coin the term *Renaissance man* to refer to that rare person who hearkened back to the era before intense specialization was the norm, back when most people cultivated a variety of linked interests and skills.

Gradually, Humboldt's bigger picture came to seem neither appealing nor important, since specialization was paying off so well by making labor and the exploitation of nature so much more efficient. Now, Darwinists reasoned, man might be on his way to breaking his connections with animal savagery and freeing himself from all the other harsh forces of nature. Evolutionary progress came to mean the conquest of the natural world by science and technology, and distancing oneself from nature became a cultural imperative. Survival depended on winning an all-out competition with other living things—including other members of our own species. And knowledge depended on the ability to observe nature purely as object, as something unrelated to us and best understood when broken down mechanistically into its smallest components.

The embrace of Darwinism and the transformation of science, then, went hand in hand with rapid industrialization, the rise of free-market capitalism, and the expansion of colonialism. Social Darwinists defended empire-building on the grounds that vigorous self-aggrandizement was only natural. And they used similar arguments to validate their racism: The affluence and technological prowess of the Western world, they argued, proved that the races and nations of the "Third World" really were "less developed." As C. S. Lewis, the British writer and critic, once pointed out, the ironies of this new world order ran deep: "At the moment, then, of man's victory over nature, we find the whole human race subjected to some individual men, and individuals subjected to that in themselves which is purely 'natural'—to their irrational impulses." The leaders of a culture that worshipped civilization and science were calmly calling for the massacre or repression of several indigenous nations in the Americas, the methodical deforestation of the United States, and the military invasion of most of Africa.

16   Of course, given Humboldt's direct influence on Darwin, there had to be elements of the theory of evolution that hearkened back to the elder scientist's approach.

Indeed, the most significant implication of the *Origin* may have been its assertion that man, on the most fundamental level, was but a part of nature—as Humboldt had argued for decades. Some nineteenth-century thinkers, accordingly, managed to find in evolutionary theory a spirit of cooperation and union. To the author and naturalist W. H. Hudson, for instance, Darwin's work meant that "we are no longer isolated, standing like starry visitors on a mountain-top, surveying life from the outside; but are on a level with and part and parcel of it."

Darwin was fascinated with the idea of nature as a "web"—"we may all be netted together," he mused in the late 1830s—and strong ecological currents run through many of his early writings. The word *oecologie* was in fact coined in 1866 by Germany's foremost Darwinian scientist, Ernst Haeckel. And when Haeckel defined his new scientific discipline, he invoked his mentor by name: ecology, he explained, was "the body of knowledge concerning the economy of nature . . . , the study of all those complex interrelations referred to by Darwin."

In the end, however, Darwin chose to focus on the violent, competitive aspects of his theory. He was explicitly lending his support to the colonialist ethic when he asserted the evolutionary doctrine that an "endless number of lower races" had to be "beaten and supplanted" by "the higher civilized races." Such competitive replacement was inevitable, Darwin argued, because niches in the economy of nature were only so big—as he had learned from the work of the Reverend Thomas Malthus. To Darwin, Malthus's 1798 *Essay on Population* proved that no species could rely on the myth of nature's abundance. Since our population seems to grow at a much faster rate than our food supply, Malthus argued, human society is destined to face starvation on a massive scale. Darwin made this doomsday theme the engine of his theory of evolution: Crises caused by environmental constraints brutally forced out the species that could not compete. He considered it part of his mission to convince naive Romantics that, in the words of the evolutionary biologist Stephen Jay Gould, "we should never have sought solace or moral instruction in Nature."

20   Humboldt, conversely, held up the natural world as a model, as something worthy of our ultimate respect. In his writings, he sought "to depict the contemplation of natural objects as a means of exciting a pure love of nature." Yet he was no naive Romantic. Just as Darwin recognized the organicist ecological perspective,

so too did Humboldt recognize the elements of violence, competition, and disunity in nature. After all, he had cut his way through the swarming, dripping jungles of South America, had witnessed such bizarre events as the mass electrocution of several horses by a colony of eels—and he had seen men enslaving other men. While Darwin focused on the disunity, though, and the specialized adaptations of species to local environments, Humboldt focused on the unity, and the global forces that link different environments and their inhabitants together. Both perspectives reveal important truths.

Humboldt's ideas were marginalized simply because Darwin's were more fit in the late nineteenth century—because Darwinism in effect captured the essence of the modernizing Western world.

In general, Humboldt's work is still marginalized, but where it is known, experts accept it as good, hard science. One representative contribution he made to the development of ecology was his theory relating the geographical distribution of plants to the effects of climate—a radical idea that remains a cornerstone of our understanding of plant ecosystems. At the base of peaks like Mount Chimborazo in the Ecuadorean Andes, he found the vines and bright orchids and tall hardwoods of the rainforest, while on the snow-clad summit he found only the hardiest mosses and lichens. On mountain after mountain, vegetation got sparser at higher altitudes, as if during his ascent he were walking from the equator to one of the poles: vertical geography mirrored horizontal geography. Humboldt was the first to classify forests as tropical, temperate, or boreal. Climate, he realized, seemed to govern the development of life everywhere; all plants and animals were "subject to the same laws" of temperature.

Humboldt had traveled to a continent less touched by human influence in order to look into the past and discover the forces that had shaped nature into its present form. "In the New World," he wrote, "man and his productions almost disappear amidst the stupendous display of wild, and gigantic nature. . . . On no other part of the globe is [the naturalist] called upon more powerfully to raise himself to general ideas on the cause of phenomena and their mutual connection." This historical technique and his "habit of viewing the Globe as a great whole" allowed Humboldt to identify climate as a unifying global force, proving, in a sense, that we all live under the same roof. Changes in one locale, he pointed out, might cause, or at least signal, changes somewhere else. And by drawing lines on the map connecting points with the same mean temperature—he coined the word *isotherm*—he established permanent scientific structures that would enable future generations to think globally. Humboldt's innovations in the field of comparative climatology underlie current attempts to understand the threat of global warming.

24   Long before any suspicion of change in the atmosphere, Humboldt was worrying about the effect of humanity's actions on terra firma; his knowledge of ecology translated into a nascent environmentalism. Again, the New World taught him an important lesson. European systems of commerce insulated the wealthy from the ecological consequences of their consumption, but the less developed economies of the Americas could not hide their dependence on surrounding natural systems. A year in Mexico, for instance, showed Humboldt that "the produce of the earth is

in fact the sole basis of permanent opulence"—and that we could not afford to use that produce wastefully.

Studying a lake in Venezuela, Humboldt used his ecological perspective to relate the lake's decline to the deforestation of the surrounding watershed. Once deprived of the trees' root systems, he explained, the surrounding soils had a greatly diminished capacity for water retention, so they could no longer recharge the springs that fed the lake. And, meanwhile, because the area was deforested, "the waters falling in rain are no longer impeded in their course; and instead of slowly augmenting the level of the rivers by progressive filtrations, they furrow [the hillsides with] sudden inundations," causing widespread soil erosion. "Hence it results that the destruction of the forests, the want of permanent springs, and the existence of torrents are three phenomena closely connected together." Humboldt saw the social consequences as well: "by felling trees . . . , men in every climate prepare at once two calamities for future generations: the want of fuel and a scarcity of water."

Humboldt's fear of resource scarcity reflects his own reading of Malthus's essay, which he called "one of the most profound works of political economy ever written." Yet Humboldt's analysis of environmental limits was far more sophisticated than Malthus's: To Humboldt, increases in resource consumption reflected not inevitable demographic pressures but simple, conscious decisions. If our population increased to several billion, then perhaps our basic needs might become too much for the earth to handle, but Humboldt realized that the resource scarcities of his own day were caused by overconsumption and mismanagement. Those trees in Venezuela didn't have to be chopped down.

Even more radical was Humboldt's interest in linking such problems to the injustices of colonialism. In his analysis of the resource base of Mexico, which he published as *A Political Essay on the Kingdom of New Spain*—and which ventured into the fields of demography, medicine, anthropology, sociology, political science, economics, agriculture, biology, geology, and geography—Humboldt took great pains to show that it was not necessary for so many Mexicans to go without land and food. His multifaceted approach helped him to see that such outrages were being driven not by population pressures but by basic socioeconomic structures. Many peasants were landless, he explained, because "the property in New Spain . . . is in a great measure in the hands of a few powerful families who have gradually absorbed the smaller estates." And impoverished Mexicans were starving because wealthy landlords grew cash crops for export instead of food crops for domestic consumption. "Whenever the soil can produce both indigo and maize," Humboldt noted indignantly, "the former prevails over the latter, although the general interest requires that a preference be given to those vegetables which supply nourishment to man over those which are merely objects of exchange with strangers."

28   Humboldt was still a man of his time: In general, he approved of the development of the New World, and he never openly demanded that the Spanish American colonies receive full independence. But his interdisciplinary research did lead him to a scathing critique of colonialism. With the conviction of one who knows his subject thoroughly, Humboldt asserted that "the restless and suspicious colonial policies of the nations of Europe . . . have thrown insurmountable obstacles in the

way of the . . . prosperity of their distant possessions. . . . A colony has for ages been considered useful to the parent state only in so far as it supplied a great number of raw materials." Because Humboldt was so aware of the interdependent relationships that governed the world, his science could never have been used to validate dominance over other people or the environment; he knew the Europeans' abuse of other lands would come back to haunt them. Later in the nineteenth century, politicians would repeatedly refer to Darwinism in claiming that certain human and natural resources were expendable for the sake of the evolutionary progress of "the higher civilized races." But according to Humboldt, nothing was expendable.

Today, the destruction of the developing world's environment—the burning of the rainforest, the strip-mining of mountain ranges, the appropriation of valuable croplands for the raising of tradable commodities—is still largely driven by the demands of the world's wealthiest countries. The structure of the global economy dictates that developing nations put all their efforts into raising cash—usually by exporting whatever virgin resources the industrial world might desire. They need the cash to pay off their "debt."

Even Humboldt accepted Darwinian conflict and chaos as basic facts of life. The whole time he was working on *Cosmos*—during the last thirty years of his life—he knew that the grand, unifying theory he sought was unattainable, because the world was too complicated and chaotic and contingent. "Experimental sciences," he wrote, "based on the observation of the external world, cannot aspire to completeness; the nature of things, and the imperfection of our organs, are alike opposed to it. . . . The attempt perfectly to represent unity in diversity must therefore necessarily prove unsuccessful."

The existence of chaos, however, does not invalidate the search for a cosmos. "Even a partial solution," Humboldt wrote, "—the tendency toward a comprehension of the phenomena of the universe—will not the less remain the eternal and sublime aim of every investigation of nature." And modern chaos theory has in fact demonstrated that beneath almost every manifestation of disorder lurks some sort of pattern or equilibrium. As Daniel Botkin, author of *Discordant Harmonies: A New Ecology for the Twenty-First Century*, has noted, it is important for us to realize, with Darwin, that nature is not calm and balanced but rather constantly changing; but we must also understand that "certain rates of change are natural, desirable, and acceptable, while others are not." It is possible to differentiate between natural and unnatural rates of change and to seek to uphold nature's dynamic equilibrium.

32   Up to now, unfortunately, scientists and policy makers have put far too much emphasis on bracing for disorder—on exploiting and stockpiling natural resources in ever greater quantities, and on stockpiling weapons to defend those resources. The United States, for instance, spends $50 billion annually on the development of defense and space technologies, but less than $2 billion in furthering our understanding of the environment. There is a perfectly straightforward reason why we have more sophisticated techniques for planting land mines in the desert than for planting corn on an erodible hillside.

Restoring the balance of modern science, then, would entail devoting more time and money to the search for order in nature, to the mapping of the world's interconnections. more prominent, better-funded environmental science could help stop over-exploitation by forcing people to realize that each part of the living world is equally valuable. And a major redistribution of research dollars could produce creative, long-term solutions to the problems inherent in resource extraction. New studies could help us, for instance, to pinpoint sustainable yields from fisheries and water supplies; to harvest crops, including trees, without losing so much soil to erosion; and to harness renewable, efficient forms of energy instead of going to war to ensure a steady supply of oil.

In lobbying for the research dollars they deserve, ecologists and environmentalists should begin by spreading an ethic of interdisciplinary cooperation. Their unique perspective, which emphasizes holistic, synthetic thinking, is crucial to scientists and developers alike, who need to understand the full impacts of their work over the long term. Even more important, though, ecologists and environmentalists should extend their interdisciplinary approach to include the public at large. People everywhere need to realize that they have a stake in the direction science is taking. All over the world, people concerned about their environments are already clamoring for more information, so that they can hold developers, corporations, and governments accountable for their actions. But they need more help from the scientists themselves, who too often come across as aloof experts with little interest in the public sphere. Only by bridging the gap between "laypeople" and "specialists," only by building connections among ourselves, will we be able to alter the scientific research agenda and rebuild our connections with the natural world.

So far, what limited success environmentalists have had in broadening their coalitions and garnering more research grants has been due to their eloquent public warnings about the dangers of ignoring the ecological perspective. Over the last few years, for instance, by pointing out that most rainforests are probably nurturing valuable medicines, food crops, fibers, soil-restoring vegetation, or petroleum substitutes, environmentalists have convinced major drug companies and agribusiness firms to join with indigenous peoples in conserving tropical ecosystems. As the wilderness philosopher Aldo Leopold once noted, "To keep every cog and wheel is the first precaution of intelligent tinkering."

36   Unfortunately, though, ecological warnings sometimes deteriorate into scare tactics, and a public that already has too much to worry about is quickly becoming disdainful of doomsday scenarios. Well-meaning environmentalists too often claim that if we don't do the right thing immediately, we'll end up fighting each other for whatever resources remain—in other words, we'll be stuck in a world of Malthusian scarcity and Darwinian conflict. Yet the goal of ecological thinking should be to offer an alternative to conflict. If environmentalists truly want to restore science's balance, they will have to go beyond warnings and give us a positive reason to take an interest in scientific research priorities. They will have to popularize science the way Humboldt did—by conveying to people the exhilaration of understanding one's place in the world, the "intellectual delight and sense of freedom" that comes of "insight into universal nature."

Humboldt considered himself above all an educator, and his ultimate goal was to teach people a basic love of nature, something today's environmental movement rarely seems to do. All his life, he encouraged people simply to leave their houses and escape their specialized lifestyles, to experience the wide-open land. Once we were surrounded by nature, Humboldt felt sure, an awareness of our dependence on it would arise in us "intuitively . . . , from the contrast we draw between the narrow limits of our own existence and the image of infinity revealed on every side—whether we look upward to the starry vault of heaven, scan the far-stretching plain before us, or seek to trace the dim horizon across the vast expanse of ocean." That intuition of our indebtedness to the natural world, that recognition of our own smallness, should be the force driving scientific research.

PERSONAL RESPONSE

What did you know about Humboldt before you read this essay? What is your impression of him now that you have read about his work and his importance?

QUESTIONS FOR CLASS OR SMALL-GROUP DISCUSSION

1. What is the impact of Sachs's opening paragraph? What details does Sachs provide throughout the essay to explain why Humboldt was so highly regarded? Locate a passage that you consider especially significant in describing Humboldt and his influence.

2. Sachs writes in paragraph 19 that the perspectives of both Darwin and Humboldt "reveal important truths." Summarize the different perspectives of those two, and then discuss what truths their differing perspectives reveal.

3. Sachs reports that the United States "spends $50 billion annually on the development of defense and space technologies, but less than $2 billion on furthering our understanding of the environment" (paragraph 30). Are you comfortable with that ordering of priorities? Explain whether you would make any changes in allocations if you had the authority to do so.

4. Sachs maintains that ecologists and environmentalists should spread "an ethic of interdisciplinary cooperation" (paragraph 32). How do you think that might be done?

A DECLARATION OF SUSTAINABILITY

Paul Hawken

Paul Hawken, who writes frequently of the need for businesses to take social and environmental responsibility, dedicated his life at the age of 20 to sustainability and changing the relationship between business and the environment. The ideas in this essay, which first appeared in the September/October, 1993, issue of Utne Reader, are from his book The Ecology of Commerce: A Declaration of Sustainability *(1993) and from* Our Future and the Making of Things *(1994), which he wrote with William McDonough. He has written dozens of articles, op-ed columns, and papers as well as six books, including* Natural Capitalism: Creating the Next Industrial Revolution *(1999), and* Blessed Unrest: How the Largest Movement in the World Came Into Being, and Why No One Saw it Coming *(2007). You can read more about his work at www.paulhawken.com.*

I recently performed a social audit for Ben & Jerry's Homemade Inc., America's premier socially responsible company. After poking and prodding around, asking tough questions, trying to provoke debate, and generally making a nuisance of myself, I can attest that their status as the leading social pioneer in commerce is safe for at least another year. They are an outstanding company. Are there flaws? Of course. Welcome to planet Earth. But the people at Ben & Jerry's are relaxed and unflinching in their willingness to look at, discuss, and deal with problems.

In the meantime, the company continues to put ice cream shops in Harlem, pay outstanding benefits, keep a compensation ratio of seven to one from the top of the organization to the bottom, seek out vendors from disadvantaged groups, and donate generous scoops of their profit to others. And they are about to overtake their historic rival Häagen-Dazs, the ersatz Scandinavian originator of super-premium ice cream, as the market leader in their category. At present rates of growth, Ben & Jerry's will be a $1 billion company by the end of the century. They are publicly held, nationally recognized, and rapidly growing, in part because Ben wanted to show that a socially responsible company could make it in the normal world of business.

Ben & Jerry's is just one of a growing vanguard of companies attempting to redefine their social and ethical responsibilities. These companies no longer accept the maxim that the business of business is business. Their premise is simple: Corporations, because they are the dominant institution on the planet, must squarely face the social and environmental problems that afflict humankind. Organizations such as Business for Social Responsibility and the Social Venture Network, corporate "ethics" consultants, magazines such as *In Business* and *Business Ethics,* nonprofits including the Council on Economic Priorities, investment funds such as Calvert and Covenant, newsletters like *Greenmoney,* and thousands of unaffiliated companies are drawing up new codes of conduct for corporate life that integrate social, ethical, and environmental principles.

4   Ben & Jerry's and the roughly two thousand other committed companies in the social responsibility movement here and abroad have combined annual sales of approximately $2 billion, or one-hundredth of 1 percent of the $20 trillion sales garnered by the estimated eighty million to one-hundred million enterprises worldwide. The problems they are trying to address are vast and unremittingly complex: 5.5 billion people are breeding exponentially, and fulfilling their wants and needs is stripping the earth of its biotic capacity to produce life; a climactic burst of consumption by a single species is overwhelming the skies, earth, waters, and fauna.

As the Worldwatch Institute's Lester Brown patiently explains in his annual survey, *State of the World*, every living system on earth is in decline. Making matters worse, we are having a once-in-a-billion-year blowout sale of hydrocarbons, which are being combusted into the atmosphere, effectively double glazing the planet within the next fifty years with unknown climatic results. The cornucopia of resources that are being extracted, mined, and harvested is so poorly distributed that 20 percent of the earth's people are chronically hungry or starving, while the top 20 percent of the population, largely in the north, control and consume 80 percent of the world's wealth. Since business in its myriad forms is primarily responsible for this "taking," it is appropriate that a growing number of companies ask the question, How does one honorably conduct business in the latter days of industrialism and the beginning of an ecological age? The ethical dilemma that confronts business begins with the acknowledgment that a commercial system that functions well by its own definitions unavoidably defies the greater and more profound ethic of biology. Specifically, how does business face the prospect that creating a profitable, growing company requires an intolerable abuse of the natural world?

Despite their dedicated good work, if we examine all or any of the businesses that deservedly earn high marks for social and environmental responsibility, we are faced with a sobering irony: If every company on the planet were to adopt the environmental and social practices of the best companies—of, say, the Body Shop, Patagonia, and Ben & Jerry's—the world would still be moving toward environmental degradation and collapse. In other words, if we analyze environmental effects and create an input–output model of resources and energy, the results do not even approximate a tolerable or sustainable future. If a tiny fraction of the world's most intelligent companies cannot model a sustainable world, then that tells us that being socially responsible is only one part of an overall solution, and that what we have is not a management problem but a design problem.

At present, there is a contradiction inherent in the premise of a socially responsible corporation: to wit, that a company can make the world better, can grow, and can increase profits by meeting social and environmental needs. It is a have-your-cake-and-eat-it fantasy that cannot come true if the primary cause of environmental degradation is overconsumption. Although proponents of socially responsible business are making an outstanding effort at reforming the tired old ethics of commerce, they are unintentionally creating a new rationale for companies to produce, advertise, expand, grow, capitalize, and use up resources: the rationale that they are doing good. A jet flying across the country, a car rented at an airport, an air-conditioned hotel room, a truck full of goods, a worker commuting to his or her job—all cause the same amount of environmental degradation whether they're associated with the Body Shop, the Environmental Defense Fund, or R. J. Reynolds.

8   In order to approximate a sustainable society, we need to describe a system of commerce and production in which each and every act is inherently sustainable and restorative. Because of the way our system of commerce is designed, businesses will not be able to fulfill their social contract with the environment or society until the system in which they operate undergoes a fundamental change, a change that brings commerce and government into alignment with the natural world from

which we receive our life. There must be an integration of economic, biologic, and human systems in order to create a sustainable and interdependent method of commerce that supports and furthers our existence. As hard as we may strive to create sustainability on a company level, we cannot fully succeed until the institutions surrounding commerce are redesigned. Just as every act of production and consumption in an industrial society leads to further environmental degradation, regardless of intention or ethos, we need to imagine—and then design—a system of commerce where the opposite is true, where doing good is like falling off a log, where the natural, everyday acts of work and life accumulate into a better world as a matter of course, not a matter of altruism. A system of sustainable commerce would involve these objectives:

1. It would reduce absolute consumption of energy and natural resources among developed nations by 80 percent within forty to sixty years.

2. It would provide secure, stable, and meaningful employment for people everywhere.

3. It would be self-actuating as opposed to regulated, controlled, mandated, or moralistic.

4. It would honor human nature and market principles.

5. It would be perceived as more desirable than our present way of life.

6. It would exceed sustainability by restoring degraded habitats and ecosystems to their fullest biological capacity.

7. It would rely on current solar income.

8. It should be fun and engaging, and strive for an aesthetic outcome.

Strategies for Sustainability

At present, the environmental and social responsibility movements consist of many different initiatives, connected primarily by values and beliefs rather than by design. What is needed is a conscious plan to create a sustainable future, including a set of design strategies for people to follow. For the record, I will suggest twelve.

1. Take Back the Charter.   Although corporate charters may seem to have little to do with sustainability, they are critical to any long-term movement toward restoration of the planet. Read *Taking Care of Business: Citizenship and the Charter of Incorporation,* a 1992 pamphlet by Richard Grossman and Frank T. Adams (Charter Ink, Box 806, Cambridge, MA 02140). In it you find a lost history of corporate power and citizen involvement that addresses a basic and crucial point: Corporations are chartered by, and exist at the behest of, citizens. Incorporation is not a right but a privilege granted by the state that includes certain considerations such as limited liability. Corporations are supposed to be under our ultimate authority, not the other way around. The charter of incorporation is a revocable dispensation that was supposed to ensure accountability of the corporation to society as a whole. When Rockwell criminally despoils a weapons facility at Rocky Flats, Colorado, with plutonium waste, or when any corporation continually harms, abuses, or violates the public trust, citizens should have the right to revoke its charter, causing the company to disband, sell off its enterprises to other companies, and effectively go out of business. The workers would have jobs with the new owners, but the executives, directors, and management would be out of jobs, with a permanent notice on their résumés that they mismanaged a corporation into a charter revocation. This is not merely a deterrent to corporate abuse but a critical element of an ecological society because it creates feedback loops that prompt accountability, citizen involvement, and learning. We should remember that the citizens of this country originally envisioned corporations to be part of a public–private partnership, which is why the relationship between the chartering authority of state legislatures and the corporation was kept alive and active. They had it right.

2. Adjust Price to Reflect Cost.   The economy is environmentally and commercially dysfunctional because the market does not provide consumers with proper information. The "free market" economies that we love so much are excellent at setting prices but lousy when it comes to recognizing costs. In order for a sustainable society to exist, every purchase must reflect or at least approximate its actual costs, not only the direct cost of production but also the costs to the air, water, and soil; the cost to future generations; the cost to worker health; the cost of waste, pollution, and toxicity. Simply stated, the marketplace gives us the wrong information. It tells us that flying across the country on a discount airline ticket is cheap when it is not. It tells us that our food is inexpensive when its method of production destroys aquifers and soil, the viability of ecosystems, and workers' lives. Whenever an organism gets wrong information, it is a form of toxicity. In fact, that is how pesticides work. A[n] herbicide kills because it is a hormone that tells the plant to grow faster than its capacity to absorb nutrients allows. It literally grows itself to death. Sound familiar? Our daily doses of toxicity are the prices in the marketplace. They are telling us to do the wrong thing for our own survival. They are lulling us into cutting down old-growth forests on the Olympic Peninsula for apple crates, into patterns of production and consumption that are not just unsustainable but profoundly shortsighted and destructive. It is surprising that "conservative" economists do not support or understand this idea, because it is they who insist that we pay as we go, have no debts, and take care of business. Let's do it.

12   *3. Throw Out and Replace the Entire Tax System.*   The present tax system sends the wrong messages to virtually everyone, encourages waste, discourages conservation, and rewards consumption. It taxes what we want to encourage—jobs, creativity, payrolls, and real income—and ignores the things we want to discourage—degradation, pollution, and depletion. The present U.S. tax system costs citizens $500 billion a year in record-keeping, filing, administrative, legal, and governmental costs—more than the actual amount we pay in personal income taxes.

The only incentive in the present system is to cheat or hire a lawyer to cheat for us. The entire tax system must be incrementally replaced over a twenty-year period by "Green fees," taxes that are added onto existing products, energy, services, and materials so that prices in the marketplace more closely approximate true costs. These taxes are not a means to raise revenue or bring down deficits, but must be absolutely revenue neutral so that people in the lower and middle classes experience no real change of income, only a shift in expenditures. Eventually, the cost of nonrenewable resources, extractive energy, and industrial modes of production will be more expensive than renewable resources, such as solar energy, sustainable forestry, and biological methods of agriculture. Why should the upper middle class be able to afford to conserve while the lower income classes cannot? So far the environmental movement has only made the world better for upper middle class white people. The only kind of environmental movement that can succeed has to start from the bottom up. Under a Green fee system the incentives to save on taxes will create positive, constructive acts that are affordable for everyone. As energy prices go up to three to four times their existing levels (with commensurate tax reductions to offset the increase), the natural inclination to save money will result in carpooling, bicycling, telecommuting, public transport, and more efficient houses. As taxes on artificial fertilizers, pesticides, and fuel go up, again with offsetting reductions in income and payroll taxes, organic farmers will find that their produce and methods are the cheapest means of production (because they truly are), and customers will find that organically grown food is less expensive than its commercial cousin. Eventually, with the probable exception of taxes on the rich, we will find ourselves in a position where we pay no taxes, but spend our money with a practiced and constructive discernment. Under an enlightened and redesigned tax system, the cheapest product in the marketplace would be best for the customer, the worker, the environment, and the company. That is rarely the case today.

4. Allow Resource Companies to Be Utilities.   An energy utility is an interesting hybrid of public–private interests. A utility gains a market monopoly in exchange for public control of rates, open books, and a guaranteed rate of return. Because of this relationship and the pioneering work of Amory Lovins, we now have markets for "negawatts." It is the first time in the history of industrialism that a corporation has figured out how to make money by selling the absence of something. Negawatts are the opposite of energy: They represent the collaborative ability of a utility to harness efficiency instead of hydrocarbons. This conservation-based alternative saves ratepayers, shareholders, and the company money—savings that are passed along to everyone. All resources systems, including oil, gas, forests, and water, should be run by some form of utility. There should be markets in negabarrels, negatrees, and negacoal. Oil companies, for example, have no alternative at present other than to lobby for the absurd, like drilling in the Arctic National Wildlife Refuge. That project, a $40 billion to $60 billion investment for a hoped-for supply of oil that would meet U.S. consumption needs for only six months, is the only way an oil company can make money under our current system of commerce. But what if the oil companies formed an oil utility and cut a deal with citizens and taxpayers that allowed them to "invest" in insulation, super-glazed windows, conservation rebates on new automobiles, and the scrapping of old cars? Through Green fees, we would pay them back a return on their conservation investment equal to what

utilities receive, a rate of return that would be in accord with how many barrels of oil they save, rather than how many barrels they produce. Why should they care? Why should we? A $60 billion investment in conservation will yield, conservatively, four to ten times as much energy as drilling for oil. Given Lovins' principle of efficiency extraction, try to imagine a forest utility, a salmon utility, a copper utility, a Mississippi River utility, a grasslands utility. Imagine a system where the resource utility benefits from conservation, makes money from efficiency, thrives through restoration, and profits from sustainability. It is possible today.

5. *Change Linear Systems to Cyclical Ones.*

Our economy has many design flaws, but the most glaring one is that nature is cyclical and industrialism is linear. In nature, no linear systems exist, or they don't exist for long because they exhaust themselves into extinction. Linear industrial systems take resources, transform them into products or services, discard waste, and sell to consumers, who discard more waste when they have consumed the product. But of course we don't consume TVs, cars, or most of the other stuff we buy. Instead, Americans produce six times their body weight every week in hazardous and toxic waste water, incinerator fly ash, agricultural wastes, heavy metals, and waste chemicals, paper, wood, etc. This does not include CO_2 which if it were included would double the amount of waste. Cyclical means of production are designed to imitate natural systems in which waste equals food for other forms of life, nothing is thrown away, and symbiosis replaces competition. Bill McDonough, a New York architect who has pioneered environmental design principles, has designed a system to retrofit every window in a major American city. Although it still awaits final approval, the project is planned to go like this: The city and a major window manufacturer form a joint venture to produce energy-saving superglazed windows in the town. This partnership company will come to your house or business, measure all windows and glass doors, and then replace them with windows with an R-8 to R-12 energy-efficiency rating within seventy-two hours. The windows will have the same casements, molding, and general appearance as the old ones. You will receive a $500 check on installation, and you will pay for the new windows over a ten- to fifteen-year period in your utility or tax bill. The total bill is less than the cost of the energy the windows will save. In other words, the windows will cost the home or business owner nothing. The city will pay for them initially with industrial development bonds. The factory will train and employ three hundred disadvantaged people. The old windows will be completely recycled and reused, the glass melted into glass, the wooden frames ground up and mixed with recycled resins that are extruded to make the casements. When the city is reglazed, the residents and businesses will pocket an extra $20 million to $30 million every year in money saved on utility bills. After the windows are paid for, the figure will go even higher. The factory, designed to be transportable, will move to another city; the first city will retain an equity interest in the venture. McDonough has designed a win-win-win-win-win system that optimizes a number of agendas. The ratepayers, the homeowners, the renters, the city, the environment, and the employed all thrive because they are "making" money from efficiency rather than exploitation. It's a little like running the industrial economy backwards.

16   **6. *Transform the Making of Things.*** We have to institute the Intelligent Product System created by Michael Braungart of the EPEA (Environmental Protection Encouragement Agency) in Hamburg, Germany. The system recognizes three types of products. The first are consumables, products that are either eaten, or, when they're placed on the ground, turn into dirt without any bio-accumulative effects. In other words, they are products whose waste equals food for other living systems. At present, many of the products that should be "consumable," like clothing and shoes, are not. Cotton cloth contains hundreds of different chemicals, plasticizers, defoliants, pesticides, and dyes; shoes are tanned with chromium and their soles contain lead; neckties and silk blouses contain zinc, tin, and toxic dye. Much of what we recycle today turns into toxic by-products, consuming more energy in the recycling process than is saved by recycling. We should be designing more things so that they can be thrown away—into the compost heap. Toothpaste tubes and other nondegradable packaging can be made out of natural polymers so that they break down and become fertilizer for plants. A package that turns into dirt is infinitely more useful, biologically speaking, than a package that turns into a plastic park bench. Heretical as it sounds, designing for decomposition, not recycling, is the way of the world around us.

The second category is *durables,* but in this case, they would not be sold, only licensed. Cars, TVs, VCRs, and refrigerators would always belong to the original manufacturer, so they would be made, used, and returned within a closed-loop system. This is already being instituted in Germany and to a lesser extent in Japan, where companies are beginning to design for disassembly. If a company knows that its products will come back someday, and that it cannot throw anything away when they do, it creates a very different approach to design and materials.

Last, there are *unsalables*—toxins, radiation, heavy metals, and chemicals. There is no living system for which these are food and thus they can never be thrown away. In Braungart's Intelligent Product System, unsalables must always belong to the original maker, safeguarded by public utilities called *parking lots* that store the toxins in glass-lined barrels indefinitely, charging the original manufacturers rent for the service. The rent ceases when an independent scientific panel can confirm that there is a safe method to detoxify the substances in question. All toxic chemicals would have molecular markers identifying them as belonging to their originator, so that if they are found in wells, rivers, soil, or fish, it is the responsibility of the company to retrieve them and clean up. This places the problem of toxicity with the makers, where it belongs, making them responsible for full-life-cycle effects.

7. *Vote, Don't Buy.* Democracy has been effectively eliminated in America by the influence of money, lawyers, and a political system that is the outgrowth of the first two. While we can dream of restoring our democratic system, the fact remains that we live in a plutocracy—government by the wealthy. One way out is to vote with your dollars, to withhold purchases from companies that act or respond inappropriately. Don't just avoid buying a Mitsubishi automobile because of the company's participation in the destruction of primary forests in Malaysia, Indonesia, Ecuador, Brazil, Bolivia, Chile, Siberia, and Papua New Guinea. Write and tell them why you won't. Engage in dialogue, send one postcard a week, talk, organize, meet, publish newsletters, boycott, patronize, and communicate with companies like General Electric. Educate nonprofits, organizations, municipalities, and pension funds to act affirmatively, to support the ecological CERES (formerly *Valdez*) Principles for business, to invest intelligently, and to *think* with their money, not merely spend it. Demand the best from the companies you work for and buy from. You deserve it and your actions will help them change.

20   **8. Restore the "Guardian."**   There can be no healthy business sector unless there is a healthy governing sector. In her book *Systems of Survival,* author Jane Jacobs describes two overarching moral syndromes that permeate our society: the commercial syndrome, which arose from trading cultures, and the governing, or guardian, syndrome that arose from territorial cultures. The guardian system is hierarchical, adheres to tradition, values loyalty, and shuns trading and inventiveness. The commercial system, on the other hand, is based on trading, so it values trust of outsiders, innovation, and future thinking. Each has qualities the other lacks. Whenever the guardian tries to be in business, as in Eastern Europe, business doesn't work. What is also true, but not so obvious to us, is that when business plays government, governance fails as well. Our guardian system has almost completely broken down because of the money, power, influence, and control exercised by business and, to a lesser degree, other institutions. Business and unions have to get out of government. We need more than campaign reform. We need a vision that allows us all to see that when Speaker of the House Tom Foley exempts the aluminum industry in his district from the proposed Btu tax, or when Philip Morris donates $200,000 to the Jesse Helms Citizenship Center, citizenship is mocked and democracy is left gagging and twitching on the Capitol steps. The irony is that business thinks that its involvement in governance is good corporate citizenship or at least is advancing its own interests. The reality is that business is preventing the economy from evolving. Business loses, workers lose, the environment loses.

9. Shift from Electronic Literacy to Biologic Literacy.   That an average adult can recognize one thousand brand names and logos but fewer than ten local plants is not a good sign. We are moving not to an information age but to a biologic age, and unfortunately our technological education is equipping us for corporate markets, not the future. Sitting at home with virtual reality gloves, 3D video games, and interactive cable TV shopping is a barren and impoverished vision of the future. The computer revolution is not the totem of our future, only a tool. Don't get me wrong. Computers are great. But they are not an uplifting or compelling vision for culture or society. They do not move us toward a sustainable future any more than our obsession with cars and televisions provided us with newer definitions or richer meaning. We are moving into the age of living machines, not, as Corbusier noted, "machines for living in." The Thomas Edison of the future is not Bill Gates of Microsoft, but John and Nancy Todd, founders of the New Alchemy Institute, a Massachusetts design lab and think tank for sustainability. If the Todds' work seems less commercial, less successful, and less glamorous, it is because they are working on the real problem—how to live—and it is infinitely more complex than a microprocessor. Understanding biological processes is how we are going to create a new symbiosis with living systems (or perish).What we can learn online is how to model complex systems. It is computers that have allowed us to realize how the synapses in the common sea slug are more powerful than all of our parallel processors put together.

10. Take Inventory.   We do not know how many species live on the planet within a factor of ten. We do not know how many are being extirpated. We do not know what is contained in the biological library inherited from the Cenozoic age. (Sociobiologist E. O. Wilson estimates that it would take 25,000 person-years to catalog most of the species, putting aside the fact that there are only 1,500 people with the taxonomic ability to undertake the task.) We do not know how complex systems interact—how the transpiration of the giant lily, *Victoria amazonica,* of Brazil's rainforests affects European rainfall and agriculture, for example. We do not know what happens to 20 percent of the C02 that is off-gassed every year (it disappears without a trace).We do not know how to calculate sustainable yields in fisheries and forest systems. We do not know why certain species, such as frogs, are dying out even in pristine habitats. We do not know the long-term effects of chlorinated hydrocarbons on human health, behavior, sexuality, and fertility. We do not know what a sustainable life is for existing inhabitants of the planet, and certainly not for future populations. (A Dutch study calculated that your fair share of air travel is one trip across the Atlantic in a lifetime.) We do not know how many people we can feed on a sustainable basis, or what our diet would look like. In short, we need to find out what's here, who has it, and what we can or can't do with it.

11. Take Care of Human Health.   The environmental and socially responsible movements would gain additional credibility if they recognized that the greatest amount of human suffering and mortality is caused by environmental problems that are not being addressed by environmental organizations or companies. Contaminated water is killing a hundred times more people than all other forms of pollution combined. Millions of children are dying from preventable diseases and malnutrition. The movement toward sustainability must address the clear and present dangers that people face worldwide, dangers that ironically increase population levels because of their perceived threat. People produce more children when they're afraid they'll lose them. Not until the majority of people in the world, all of whom suffer in myriad preventable yet intolerable ways, understand that environmentalism means improving their lives directly will the ecology movement walk its talk. Americans will spend more money in the next twelve months on the movie and tchotchkes of *Jurassic Park* than on foreign aid to prevent malnutrition or provide safe water.

24   **12. Respect the Human Spirit.**   If hope is to pass the sobriety test, then it has to walk a pretty straight line to reality. Nothing written, suggested, or proposed here is possible unless business is willing to integrate itself into the natural world. It is time for business to take the initiative in a genuinely, open process of dialogue, collaboration, reflection, and redesign. "It is not enough," writes Jeremy Seabrook

of the British Green party, "to declare, as many do, that we are living in an unsustainable way, using up resources, squandering the substance of the next generation however true this may be. People must feel subjectively the injustice and unsustainability before they will make a more sober assessment as to whether it is worth maintaining what is, or whether there might not be more equitable and satisfying ways that will not be won at the expense either of the necessities of the poor or of the wasting fabric of the planet."

Poet and naturalist W. S. Merwin (citing Robert Graves) reminds us that we have one story, and one story only, to tell in our lives. We are made to believe by our parents and businesses, by our culture and televisions, by our politicians and movie stars that it is the story of money, of finance, of wealth, of the stock portfolio, the partnership, the country house. These are small, impoverished tales and whispers that have made us restless and craven; they are not stories at all. As author and garlic grower Stanley Crawford puts it, "The financial statement must finally give way to the narrative, with all its exceptions, special cases, imponderables. It must finally give way to the story, which is perhaps the way we arm ourselves against the next and always unpredictable turn of the cycle in the quixotic dare that is life; across the rock and cold of lifelines, it is our seed, our clove, our filament cast toward the future." It is something deeper than anything commercial culture can plumb, and it is waiting for each of us.

Business must yield to the longings of the human spirit. The most important contribution of the socially responsible business movement has little to do with recycling nuts from the rainforest, or employing the homeless. Their gift to us is that they are leading by trying to do something, to risk, take a chance, make a change— change. They are not waiting for "the solution," but are acting without guarantees of success or proof of purchase. That is what all of us must do. Being visionary has always been given a bad rap by commerce. But without a positive vision for humankind we can have no meaning, no work, and no purpose.

PERSONAL RESPONSE

In what way or ways has this essay changed or influenced your views about your personal consumption habits and about the steps society must take to require socially responsible actions by businesses? If you are not persuaded by the essay that changes must be made, explain why.

QUESTIONS FOR CLASS OR SMALL-GROUP DISCUSSION

1. How effectively does Hawken define "socially responsible" (paragraph 2)? Can you give examples, other than those Hawken names, of businesses that do not meet this "socially responsible" criterion?

2. In paragraph 8, Hawken lists the objectives involved in his proposed "system of sustainable commerce." Discuss those objectives and the likelihood that the majority of commercial enterprises worldwide would adopt them and work toward such a system.

3. Discuss the twelve steps Hawken lists. Include in your discussion an assessment of how effective you believe the steps to be as reasonable conservation measures, what their adoption would entail, and how likely you think it is that Hawken's recommendations will be adopted.

4. How well does Hawken support the following statements: "Democracy has been effectively eliminated in America by the influence of money, lawyers, and a political system that is the outgrowth of the first two" (paragraph 18) and "Computers are great. But they are not an uplifting or compelling vision for culture or society" (paragraph 20)?

THE GALILEO OF GLOBAL WARMING

AMERICAN SPECTATOR EDITORIAL

American Spectator *is a national opinion magazine whose target audience is leaders in business, government, and media. It covers matters of business, politics, economics, foreign policy, and culture. This editorial appeared in the May 2001, issue of* American Spectator.

Now the global warming debate reveals that what Bob Tyrrell calls the plutomores (from the Greek plutos, "riches," and moros, "fools") have reached high positions in the Bush administration. Fooled entirely by the copious press and television coverage of the Democratic victory in Florida, for example, Treasury Secretary Paul O'Neill seems to believe he was summoned to Washington to serve as a token Republican in the administration of Al Gore. The Alcoa corpocrat devoted his first presentation to the Cabinet to an earnest plutomoronic tract on global warming, urging his baffled companions to save the planet from Republican religionists (apparently awaiting the Second Coming in rubber boots on Long Island beaches and golf courses). He all but said the Earth is in the Balance.

O'Neill and his Cabinet colleague Christie Whitman had provided the high point of this comic opera until this month's assault on Exxon Mobil by a group of angry shareholders, including a medley of nuns and Capuchin friars from New Jersey, inspired by Lloyd Keigwin, a good scientist panicked by pressures of political correctness. Collaborating in the panic is a writer from the *Wall Street Journal* named Thaddeus Herrick, who reports lugubriously that Exxon Mobil is "increasingly isolated on the issue, not only from the international scientific community, but also from European competitors . . . which largely accept the premise that the Earth is warming because of heat-trapping greenhouse gases."

Hardly heroic is Exxon Mobil, backpedaling from its denial of global warming risks. Its own plutomores seem increasingly ready to capitulate to the idea that their energy products imperil the planet.

4   Keigwin, though, is the more intriguing case. A 54-year-old oceanographer at Woods Hole Observatory near the Massachusetts Cape, he found a way to concoct a 3,000-year record of the temperatures of the Sargasso Sea near Bermuda through

analyzing thermally dependent oxygen isotopes in fossils on the ocean floor. He discovered that temperatures a thousand years ago, during the so-called medieval climate optimum, were two degrees Celsius warmer than today's and that the average temperature over the last three millennia was slightly warmer than today's. Roughly confirming this result are historical records—the verdancy of Greenland at the time of the Vikings, the little ice age of the mid-1700s, a long series of temperature readings collected in Britain over the last 300 years documenting a slow recovery from the ice age, reports of medieval temperatures from a variety of sources, and records of tree rings and ice cores.

These previous findings, echoed by Keigwin's, are devastating to the theory of human-caused global warming. If the Earth was significantly warmer a thousand years ago, if we have been on a rewarming trend for three centuries, if, as other even more voluminous evidence suggests, the Earth has repeatedly seen mini-cycles of warming and cooling of about 1,500 years duration, then any upward drift in temperatures we may be seeing now—included scattered anecdotes of thinning arctic ice—is likely to be the result of such cycles.

Thus the case for human-caused global warming can no longer rest on the mere fact of contemporary warming. To justify drastic action like the Kyoto treaty requiring a reduction in U.S. energy consumption of some 30 percent, unfeasible without destroying the U.S. economy, the human-caused global warming advocates would have to demonstrate a persuasive mechanism of human causation. This they show no sign of being able to do. Grasping the point, scientists at Exxon Mobil recently used the Keigwin data in a *Wall Street Journal* ad and the PC bees hit the fan.

By all reasonable standards, Keigwin is a hero. Not only did he invent an ingenious way to compile an early temperature record, but he made a giant contribution to discrediting a movement that would impose a deadly energy clamp on the world economy. But soon enough his government-financed colleagues began to exert pressure. Was he a tool of the oil companies? Lordy no, he wrote, in an indignant letter to Exxon Mobil, denying that his findings had anything much to do with the global warming issue.

8   As the *Wall Street Journal* reported, "Dr. Keigwin warns that the results are not representative of the Earth as a whole. He says that the importance of his research isn't in the data per se, but rather that marine geologists can undertake such a study at all. . . . He wants to put the issue behind him." Hey, he's got a new government grant to find out "what's causing a substantial warming in the Atlantic Ocean off Nova Scotia." He has not reached any conclusion—but according to the *Journal*, "he gives a nod to global warming concerns, saying 'I'd take a guess.'" Scores of scientists have been pressured to embrace the cult pressures that befall any critic of the cult of human-caused global warming. In a scientific establishment 50 percent financed by government, few can resist. An eminent scientist who was once the leading critic of global warming had to stop writing on the subject in order to continue his research. The source of the pressure that ended his publications was then-Senator Al Gore. Later this scientist coauthored a key paper with Arthur Robinson—organizer of a petition against Kyoto signed by 17,000 scientists—but had to remove his name under pressure from Washington.

Keigwin's denials of his own significance are all pathetically misleading. The temperature pattern he found in the Sargasso Sea is indeed a global phenomenon. Sallie Baliunas and Willi Soon of Harvard have uncovered a new oxygen isotope study that extends this temperature record another 3,000 years based on six millennia of evidence from peat bogs in northeastern China. The peat bog records both confirm Keigwin and demonstrate an even warmer period that lasted for 2,000 years. During this era, beginning some 4,000 years ago and running until the birth of Christ, temperatures averaged between 1.5 and 3 degrees Celsius higher than they do today.

Summing up the case is an article published earlier this year by Wallace Broecker in the prestigious pages of *Science* entitled "Was the Medieval Warm Period Global?" His answer is a resounding yes. As Craig and Keith Idso report in a March 7 editorial on their Webpage www.c02science.org, Broecker recounts substantial evidence for a series of climatic warmings spaced at roughly 1,500-year intervals. Broecker explains the science of reconstructing the histories of surface air temperatures by examining temperature data from "boreholes." From some 6,000 boreholes on all continents, this evidence confirms that the Earth was significantly warmer a thousand years ago and two degrees Celsius warmer in Greenland. This data, Robinson warns, is less detailed and authoritative than the evidence from the Sargasso Sea and from the Chinese peat bogs. But together with the independent historical record, the collective evidence is irrefutable. Thousands of years of data demonstrate that in the face of a few hundred parts per million increase in CO_2, temperatures today, if anything, are colder than usual. Temperatures in Antarctica, for example, have been falling for the last 20 years. The global satellite record of atmospheric temperature, confirmed by weather balloons, shows little change one way or another for the last three decades. Terrestrial temperature stations, on average, show more warming over the past century, but many are located in areas that were rural when the stations were established and are densely urban today, a change which causes local warming. The dominance of natural cycles globally is not surprising since, as Baliunas and Soon report, the impact of changes in sun energy output are some 70,000 times more significant than all human activity put together.

In the end, the global warming panic will take its place in the history books next to other environmental chimeras, such as the threat of DDT (but not of pandemic malaria), the peril of nuclear power (but not of coal mining), the brain-curdling effect of cellphones (but not of far more potent sun rays), the menace of powerlines (but not of poverty), the poison of alar (though not of rotten apple juice), the danger of asbestos in walls (but not of fire), the carcinogenic impact of PCBs (but not of carrots, peanut butter, coffee and other items that test more toxic in the same way) and the horror of radon and other sources of low-level radiation (despite its beneficial effect on health through a process called hormesis).

12   Overall, the situation is simple. Politicized scientists with government grants and dubious computer temperature models persuaded the world's politicians to make pompous fools of themselves in Kyoto. Socialist politicians were happy to join an absurd movement to impose government regulations over the world energy

supply and thus over the world economy. The scientific claims and computer models have now blown up in their faces. But rather than admit error they persist in their fearmongering. When this happened with DDT, hundreds of millions of people died of malaria. They continue to die. How many people would die as a result of an energy clamp on global capitalism?

PERSONAL RESPONSE

Explore your reactions to the position this article takes on the subject of global warming.

QUESTIONS FOR CLASS OR SMALL-GROUP DISCUSSION

1. What evidence does this article present to support its major argument? Are you persuaded by that evidence?

2. Discuss your understanding of the Kyoto Treaty referred to in this article. Did you know that 17,000 scientists had signed a petition against the treaty (paragraph 8)? Does that information in any way change your thinking about the treaty?

3. Comment on the editorial's use of the term *cult* to describe the views of those who believe that there is global warming occurring and that humans are responsible for it (paragraph 8).

4. Look carefully at paragraph 11 and discuss your understanding of the implications of all of the parenthetical asides. For instance, the editorial expands on the second one—"the threat of DDT (but not of pandemic malaria)"—in paragraph 12 when it suggests that when DDT was banned, it resulted in a resurgence of malaria, which has killed hundreds of millions of people. What is your response to that claim and to the implications in paragraph 11?

GLOBAL WARNING: GET UP! STAND UP!

Bill McKibben

Bill McKibben, author, educator, and environmentalist, is contributing editor of OnEarth. *His books include* The End of Nature, *the first book for a general audience on global warming (1989);* The Age of Missing Information *(1992);* Hope, Human and Wild: True Stories of Living Lightly on Earth *(1995);* Maybe One: The Case for Smaller Families *(1998);* Long Distance: Testing the Limits of Body and Spirit in a Year of Living Strenuously *(2000);* Enough: Staying Human in an Engineering Age *(2003); and* Deep Economy: The Wealth of Communities and the Durable

Future *(2007)*. OnEarth, *the quarterly journal of the Natural Re-*
sources Defense Council, explores politics, nature, wildlife, culture, sci-
ence, health, the challenges that confront our planet, and the solutions
that promise to heal and protect it. This article appeared in the Spring
2007 issue of OnEarth.

Here's a short list of the important legislation our federal government has enacted
to combat global warming in the years since 1988, when a NASA climatologist,
James Hansen, first told Congress that climate change was real:
1.
2.
4   3.
And what do you know? That bipartisan effort at doing nothing has been
highly successful: Our emissions of carbon dioxide have steadily increased over that
two-decade span.

Meanwhile, how have the lone superpower's efforts at leading international
action to deal with climate change gone? Not too well. We refused to ratify the
Kyoto treaty, while the rest of the developed world finally did so. And while we've
pressured China over world-shaking issues like DVD piracy, we've happily sold
them the parts to help grow their coal-fired electric utility network to a size that
matches ours.

In other words, Washington has utterly and completely failed to take on the
single greatest challenge human civilization has ever faced.

8   What's more, Washington, at least so far, couldn't care less about the failure. A
flurry of legislation has been introduced in the last couple of months, but scarcely a
member of Congress felt compelled to answer in the last election for failing to deal
with climate change. A simple "I'm concerned" was more than enough.

Not only that, but scientists revealed last December that a piece of ice the size
of 11,000 football fields had broken off an Arctic ice shelf.

So, and here I use a technical term that comes from long study of the intricate
science, we're screwed. Unless.

If we're going to change any of those nasty facts, we need a movement. A real,
broad-based public movement demanding transformation of the way we power our
world. A movement as strong, passionate, and willing to sacrifice as the civil rights
movement that ended segregation more than a generation ago. This essay is about
the possible rise of such a movement—about the role that you might play in making
it happen.

12   It's not the fault of our environmental organizations that such a movement
doesn't yet exist. It's the fault of the molecular structure of carbon dioxide.

Modern environmentalism arose in the early 1960s in the wake of *Silent*
Spring. That's the moment advocates of "conservation"—the idea that we should
protect some areas as refuges amid a benign modernity—began to realize that modernity itself might be a problem, that the bright miracles of our economic life
came with shadows. First DDT, but before long phosphates in detergent and sulfur in the smoke stream of coal plants and chlorofluoro-carbons (CFCs) in our air

conditioners. And carbon monoxide, carbon with one oxygen atom, the stuff that was helping turn the air above our cities brown.

All were alike in one crucial way: You could take care of the problems they caused with fairly easy technical fixes. Different pesticides that didn't thin eggshells; scrubbers on smokestacks. DuPont ended up making more money on the stuff that replaced CFCs, which had been tearing a hole in the ozone layer. None of these battles was easy: The Natural Resources Defense Council (NRDC) and Greenpeace and Environmental Defense and the Sierra Club and the Union of Concerned Scientists and a thousand Friends of the You-Name-It had to fight like hell to make sure that the fixes got made. But that was the war we armed for: We had the lawyers and the scientists and the regulatory experts and the lobbyists and the fund-raisers. We didn't always win, but the batting average was pretty high: You can swim in more rivers, breathe in more cities. It was a carbon monoxide movement, and the catalytic converter, which washed that chemical from your exhaust, was its emblem. You could drive your car; you just needed the right gear on your tailpipe.

But carbon dioxide—carbon with two oxygen atoms—screwed everything up. Carbon dioxide in itself isn't exactly a pollutant. It doesn't hurt you when you breathe it; in fact, for a very long time engineers described a motor as "clean-burning" if it gave off only CO_2 and water vapor. The problem that emerged into public view in the late 1980s was that its molecular structure trapped heat near the planet that would otherwise radiate back out to space. And, worse, there wasn't a technofix this time—CO_2 was an inevitable by-product of burning fossil fuels. That is to say, the only way to deal with global warming is to move quickly away from fossil fuels.

16   When you understand that, you understand why Congress has yet to act, and why even big and talented environmental organizations have been largely stymied. Fossil fuel is not like DDT or phosphates or CFCs. It's the absolute center of modern life. An alien scientist arriving on our planet might well conclude that Western human beings are devices for burning coal and gas and oil, since that is what we do from dawn to dusk, and then on into the brightly lit night. When societies get richer, they start reducing other pollutants—even in China some cities have begun to see reductions in sulfur and nitrogen as people demand better pollution controls. But as the Harvard economist Benjamin Friedman conceded in a landmark book in 2005, The Moral Consequences of Economic Growth, carbon dioxide is the only pollutant that economic growth doesn't reduce. It is economic growth. It's no accident that the last three centuries, a time of great prosperity, have also been the centuries of coal and oil and gas.

Which means that this is a war that environmentalism as currently constituted simply can't win. Our lobbyists can sit down with congressional staffers and convince them of the need for, say, lower arsenic levels in water supplies; they have enough support to win those kinds of votes. We've managed, brilliantly, to save the Arctic National Wildlife Refuge from drilling. But we lack (by a long shot) the firepower to force, say, a carbon tax that might actually cut fossil fuel use. We've been outgunned by the car companies and the auto unions when it comes to gasoline mileage. We can save the Arctic refuge from oil drilling, but we can't save it from thawing into a northern swamp no caribou would ever wander through. In essence, we have a problem opposite to that of the American military: Well armed for small battles with insurgent polluters, we suddenly find ourselves needing to fight World War II.

What we have now is the superstructure of a movement. We have brilliant scientists, we have superb economists, we have some of the most battle-hardened lawyers and lobbyists you could hope for. The only thing the climate movement lacks is the movement part.

Consider this: Last Labor Day weekend, a few of us led a five-day, 50-mile march across our home state of Vermont to demand that our candidates for federal office take stronger stands on climate legislation. We started at Robert Frost's summer writing cabin high in the Green Mountains, happy with the symbolism of choosing a road less taken. As we wandered byways and main roads, we were happy too with the reception we got—crowds waiting to greet us at churches and senior centers and farms, motorists waving and honking even from the largest SUVs. By the time we reached Burlington, the state capital, we had a thousand marchers. (It was more than enough to convince all our candidates, even the conservative Republicans, to endorse strong carbon reductions; they all signed a pledge backing 80 percent cuts in carbon emissions by 2050.) But here's the not-so-happy thing: The newspapers said that a rally of 1,000 people was the largest that had yet taken place in this nation against global warming. That's pathetic.

20   But not hopeless. Because that movement is starting to gather, less inside the main environmental organizations than on their fringes.

The student movement, for instance, has come out of nowhere in the last three years. All of a sudden there are hundreds of high schools and college campuses where kids are working for real change in how their dorms and classrooms are heated and lit. And emboldened by their success on campus, they're increasingly involved in state and national and international efforts. Whenever I'm feeling disheartened about how slowly change is coming, I stop by a meeting of the Sunday Night Group at Middlebury College, the campus where I work. A hundred or more students show up for the weekly meetings, and they get right down to business— some on making sure that every light bulb in town is a compact fluorescent, some on making sure that every legislator in the state is a climate convert. On the national level, the group Energy Action has joined 16 student organizations into an effective force. The group's Campus Climate Challenge will soon involve a thousand schools, and its leaders are planning a summer of marches and a platoon of youth to bird-dog presidential candidates.

Or look at the churches and synagogues. Ten years ago there was no religious environmental movement to speak of. Now, "creation care" is an emerging watchword across the spectrum, from Unitarians to evangelicals among the Christian traditions and in Jewish, Buddhist, and Muslim communities as well. And the rhetoric is increasingly matched by action: Groups such as Interfaith Power and Light are organizing congregations to cut energy use, and groups such as Religious Witness for the Earth are organizing people of faith for marches of their own.

There's even one very sweet by-product of the roadblock in Washington: In cities and states across the union, big environmental groups and local citizen activists have focused their energy on mayors and governors and learned a good deal in the process. Including this: It's possible to win. If California's Republican governor can decide it's in his interest to embrace strong climate legislation, you know people have done good groundwork. They've worked in public as well as behind the scenes. Activists from the Maryland-based Chesapeake Climate Action Network were arrested last fall for blocking the doors to federal offices to demand more accurate federal science.

24   The moment is ripe. Hurricane Katrina blew open the door of public opinion, and Al Gore walked valiantly through it with his movie. There are, finally, lots and lots of people who want to know how they can make a difference. Not 51 percent of the people, but we don't need 51 percent. We can do just fine with 15 percent. As long as they're active. As long as they're a movement.

Which brings me, finally, to the point. It's time to unleash as much passion and energy as we can. It's movement time.

What we need is nothing less than a societal transformation. Not a new gizmo, not a few new laws, but a commitment to wean America from fossil fuels in our lifetime and to lead the rest of the world, especially India and China, in the same direction. The shorthand we're using in our April stepitup07.org campaign is the same as it was in our Vermont march: 80 percent cuts by 2050. What we need is big change, starting right now.

And that's a message Congress needs to hear. Though the November elections opened new possibilities, they also raised new perils. Instead of James Inhofe, who thought global warming was a hoax, the relevant Senate committee now answers to Barbara Boxer, who understands that it's very real. But the very chance of a deal raises the specter of a bad deal—some small-potatoes around-the-edges kind of action that substitutes the faux realism of Washington politics for the actual physics-and-chemistry realism of our predicament. For instance, when John McCain introduced legislation five years ago that asked for small and more or less voluntary cuts, it was a step forward, and I saluted him on the cover of this magazine. But the current draft of his bill is fairly weak. Even the strongest bills, introduced by Henry Waxman and Bernie Sanders, barely meet the test for what the science demands. And chances are, unless we really do our job on the ground, the measures they're proposing will barely be discussed.

28   NASA's James Hansen—our premier climatologist—has made it clear we have 10 years to reverse the flow of carbon into the atmosphere. Actually, he made it clear in the fall of 2005, so we have eight and a half years before we cross certain thresholds (Arctic melt, for instance) that commit us to an endless cycle of self-reinforcing feedback loops and, in Hansen's words, a "totally different planet."

That requires transformation, not tinkering. It's not like carbon monoxide or DDT—it's like the women's movement or the civil rights movement, which changed the basic taken-for-granted architecture of our nation. Except it's harder, because this time we don't need the system to accommodate more people; we need the system to change in profound ways.

The only chance is for those of us who see the risk and the opportunity to act—as quickly and as powerfully as ever we can.

PERSONAL RESPONSE

How committed are you to the kind of activism that McKibben calls for?

QUESTIONS FOR CLASS OR SMALL-GROUP DISCUSSION

1. Describe the tone in the opening paragraphs. What is the effect of that tone? Where does the tone change?
2. In paragraph 4, McKibben writes that Washington has failed "to take on the single greatest challenge human civilization has ever faced." What is that challenge? Do you agree that it is the greatest challenge humans have faced? If not, what other challenge(s) are greater?
3. The subtitle of this essay is "How to Build a Mass Movement to Halt Climate Change." Summarize in your own words what actions McKibben recommends for building a mass movement to halt climate change. Do you agree with him that such a movement will work?
4. How persuasive do you find this article? Are you moved to act?

○ PERSPECTIVES ON ENVIRONMENTAL STUDIES ○

Suggested Writing Topics

1. Explain your own position on global warming or any of the environmental issues mentioned in the readings in this chapter.
2. Write an essay that offers possible solutions to one of the major environmental issues confronting people today.
3. Write an essay in response to the *American Spectator* editorial "The Galileo of Global Warming," or Paul Hawken's "A Declaration of Sustainability."
4. Taking into account the opinion of Paul Hawken in "A Declaration of Sustainability," argue the extent to which you think pressure from lobbyists should influence the thinking of legislators considering measures that would tighten regulations on environmental issues.
5. Write a letter to the editor of your campus or community newspaper in which you urge students on your campus and citizens in the community to take actions to reverse the current abuse of natural resources. Or, propose practical conservation steps that students on your campus can take.
6. Write a letter to the president of a corporation that you know abuses the environment urging him or her to make changes in the way the company produces its product. If you refuse to buy the product because of its production methods, say so.

7. Although the writers in this chapter address a wide range of environmental issues, these selections do not provide exhaustive coverage. Select an environmental issue that is not addressed in these essays, then explain the problem in detail, and if possible, offer solutions.

Research Topics

1. Research the work of Baron Alexander von Humboldt, Charles Darwin, or Thomas Malthus and write a paper arguing the relevance of their ideas to today's environmental issues.

2. Conduct library research on the impact of socioeconomic inequities on environmental issues and argue your position on the subject. Consider including interviews of environmentalists, sociologists, and/or economists from your campus in your research.

3. Research the Kyoto Treaty referred to in the *American Spectator* editorial "The Galileo of Global Warming," explain the controversy that surrounds the treaty, and explain your own viewpoint on it.

4. Select any of the environmental issues mentioned in this chapter as a research subject. Make sure that you fairly present both sides of the issue as you explain your own position.

RESPONDING TO VISUALS

Mexican Greenpeace activists on deforested land in Ocuyoapan, Lagunas de Zempoala, Mexico, February 3, 2004.

1. Describe the details in the picture.
2. What is the photographer's subject? Is it the SOS sign, or is it something else?
3. How effectively does the activists' banner convey their protest?
4. What does the photograph say about deforestation?

RESPONDING TO VISUALS

©Ed Oudenaarden/AFP/Getty Images

Members of an environmental group Milieudefensie [Dutch for "environmental defense"] dressed as burnt tree stumps demonstrate in front of the Dutch Parliament in The Hague to protest against the use of palm oil as a bio-fuel, 29 October 2007. Green campaigners warn that proposals for certifying palm oil as sustainable are flawed. Banner reads: "No tropical forest in my tank."

1. What do you understand the message on the banner—"No tropical forest in my tank"—to mean?
2. How effective do you find dressing as burnt tree stumps to be as a protest strategy?
3. What message does the photograph convey about environmentalism?

PART • FIVE

Business and Economics

CHAPTER
23

Marketing and the American Consumer

In their characteristic consumption and materialism, Americans are both the envy of people in other nations and the objects of their criticism. America has long been regarded as the "land of plenty," with a plethora of products to buy and a standard of living that allows most citizens to buy them. Yet such plenitude can lead to overconsumption, creating a need to buy for the sake of buying that can become a kind of obsession. Some people seek psychological counseling for this compulsion, whereas others seek financial counseling to manage the debts they have built up as a result of their need to buy things.

Indeed, shopping is so central to the lives of Americans that malls have become more than places to find virtually any product people want and need; they have become social centers, where people gather to meet friends, eat, hang out, exercise, and be entertained. Some regard this penchant for spending money and acquiring goods as a symptom of some inner emptiness, with malls, shopping strips, and discount stores replacing the spiritual centers that once held primary importance in people's lives. Others, especially manufacturers of products and the people who sell them, regard consumerism as a hearty indicator of the nation's economic health.

The selections in this chapter begin with "In Praise of Consumerism," an essay by James B. Twitchell, who writes often on American consumerism and materialism. Twitchell discusses the social aspect of the consumerism concept in America, suggesting that it is the consumer who directs the marketplace, not the manufacturers and marketers of products. "We like having stuff," he asserts. As you read his essay, think about your own spending habits. Do you buy just to have things, or do you buy just those things necessary for living?

In an essay that also acknowledges the influence of advertising but that sees its influence in a different light, Richard Wolkomir and Joyce Wolkomir, in "You Are What You Buy," profile James B. Twitchell, author of "In Praise of Consumerism," based on his book *Lead Us Into Temptation: The Triumph of American Materialism*. Their article provides a historical overview of mass marketing, using many examples of successful advertising campaigns as they follow Twitchell through a Wal-Mart.

In the next article, Gary Ruskin and Juliet Schor discuss the negative effects of the pervasive spread of commercialism throughout far too many aspects of American life. "Every Nook and Cranny: The Dangerous Spread of Commercialized Culture" cites numerous examples of the commercialization of government and culture and argues that the effects are almost all negative. Noting that advertising has only recently "been recognized as having political and social merit," Ruskin and Schor complain that it now invades "nearly every nook and cranny of life." You may find yourself nodding in agreement as they mention many ways in which advertising has invaded everyday life. Whether you agree with them that such pervasiveness is dangerous is something you will have to decide for yourself.

Finally, Phyllis Rose takes an amused look at consumerism in America in "Shopping and Other Spiritual Adventures in America Today." Although her essay was written in 1991, her astute observations on why people shop remains relevant today. Using her own experiences, Rose elaborates on what she means when she writes: "It is a misunderstanding of the American retail store to think we go there necessarily to buy. Some of us shop. There's a difference." As you read what Rose has to say about shoppers, think about your own shopping behavior. Do you see yourself in her description of the behavior of shoppers?

As you read each of the selections in this chapter, think of your own consumer habits. Are you "addicted" to shopping? Do you like to buy for the sake of buying, whether you need a product or not? Do you buy products that are endorsed by celebrities for that reason alone? Did you (or do you) go to malls in order to socialize, or do you visit them frequently now?

IN PRAISE OF CONSUMERISM

James B. Twitchell

James B. Twitchell teaches English and Advertising at the University of Florida. He is author of Carnival Culture: The Trashing of Taste in America *(1992);* Adcult USA: The Triumph of Advertising in American Culture *(1995);* Twenty Ads that Shook the World: The Century's Most Groundbreaking Advertising and How It Changed Us All *(2000);* Living it Up: America's Love Affair with Luxury *(2003);* Branded Nation: The Marketing of Megachurch, College Inc., and Museumworld *(2004);* Where Men Hide *(2006); and* Shopping for God: How Christianity Went from In Your Heart to In Your Face *(2007). This article, which is based on his book* Lead Us Into Temptation: The Triumph of American Materialism *(1999), appeared in the August/September 2000, issue of* Reason.

Sell them their dreams, sell them what they longed for and hoped for and almost despaired of having, sell them hats by splashing sunlight across them. Sell them dreams—dreams of country clubs and proms and visions of what might happen if only. After all, people don't buy things to have things. They buy things to work for them. They buy hope—hope of what your merchandise will do for them. Sell them this hope and you won't have to worry about selling them goods.

—Helen Landon Cass

Those words were spoken some years ago by a female radio announcer to a convention of salesmen in Philadelphia. *The Philadelphia Retail Ledger* for June 6, 1923, recorded Ms. Cass' invocations with no surrounding explanation. They were simply noted as a matter of record, not as a startling insight.

There are two ways to read her spiel. You can read it like a melancholy Marxist and see the barely veiled indictment of the selling process. What does she think consumers are—dopes to be duped? What is she selling? Snake oil?

Or you can read it like an unrepentant capitalist and see the connection between consuming goods and gathering meaning. The reason producers splash magical promise over their goods is because consumers demand it. Consumers are not sold a bill of goods; they insist on it. Snake oil to the cynic is often holy water to the eager. What looks like exploiting desire may be fulfilling desire.

4   How you come down in this matter depends on your estimation of the audience. Does the audience manipulate things to make meaning, or do other people use things to manipulate the audience? Clearly, this is a variation of "I persuade, you educate, they manipulate," for both points of view are supportable. Let's split the difference and be done with it.

More interesting to me, however, is to wonder why such a statement, so challenging, so revolutionary, so provocative in many respects was, in the early 1920s, so understandable, so acceptable, even so passé that it appears with no gloss. Why is it that when you read the early descriptions of capitalism, all the current bugaboos—advertising, packaging, branding, fashion, and retailing techniques—seem so much better understood?

And why has the consumer—playing an active, albeit usually secondary, part in the consumptive dyad of earlier interpretations—become almost totally listless in our current descriptions? From Thomas Hobbes in the mid-17th century ("As in other things, so in men, not the seller but the buyer determines the price") to Edwin S. Gingham in the mid-20th century ("Consumers with dollars in their pockets are not, by any stretch of the imagination, weak. To the contrary, they are the most merciless, meanest, toughest market disciplinarians I know"), the consumer was seen as participating in the meaning-making of the material world. How and why did the consumer get dumbed down and phased out so quickly? Why has the hypodermic metaphor (false needs injected into a docile populace) become the unchallenged explanation of consumerism?

I think that much of our current refusal to consider the liberating role of consumption is the result of who has been doing the describing. Since the 1960s, the primary "readers" of the commercial "text" have been the well-tended and -tenured of members of the academy. For any number of reasons—the most obvious being their low levels of disposable income, average age, and gender, and the fact that these critics are selling a competing product, high-cult (which is also coated with its own dream values)—the academy has casually passed off as "hegemonic brainwashing" what seems to me, at least, a self-evident truth about human nature: We like having stuff.

8   In place of the obvious, they have substituted an interpretation that they themselves often call vulgar Marxisms. It is supposedly vulgar in the sense that it is not as sophisticated as the real stuff, but it has enough spin on it to be more appropriately called Marxism lite. Go into almost any cultural studies course in this country and you will hear the condemnation of consumerism expounded: What we see in the marketplace is the result of the manipulation of the many for the profit of the few. Consumers are led around by the nose. We live in a squirrel cage. Left alone we would read Wordsworth, eat lots of salad, and have meetings to discuss Really Important Subjects.

In cultural studies today, everything is oppression and we are all victims. In macrocosmic form, the oppression is economic—the "free" market. In microcosmic form, oppression is media—your "free" TV. Here, in the jargon of this downmarket Marxism, is how the system works: The manipulators, a.k.a. "the culture industry," attempt to enlarge their hegemony by establishing their ideological base in the hearts and pocketbooks of a weak and demoralized populace. Left alone, we would never desire things (ugh!). They have made us materialistic. But for them, we would be spiritual.

To these critics, the masters of industry and their henchmen, the media lords, are predators, and what they do in no way reflects or resolves genuine audience concerns. Just the opposite. The masters of the media collude, striving to infantilize us so that we are docile, anxious, and filled with "reified desire." While we may think advertising is just "talking about the product," that packaging just "wraps the object," that retailing is just "trading the product," or that fashion is just "the style of the product," this is not so. That you may think so only proves their power over you. The marginalized among us—the African American, the child, the immigrant, and especially the female are trapped into this commodifying system, this false consciousness, and this fetishism that only the enlightened can correct. Legendary ad man David Ogilvy's observation that, "The consumer is no fool, she is your wife" is just an example of the repressive tolerance of such a sexist, materialist culture.

Needless to say, in such a system the only safe place to be is tenured, underpaid, self-defined as marginalized, teaching two days a week for nine months a year, and writing really perceptive social criticism that your colleagues can pretend to read. Or rather, you would be writing such articles if only you could find the time.

The Triumph of Stuff

12   The idea that consumerism creates artificial desires rests on a wistful ignorance of history and human nature, on the hazy, romantic feeling that there existed some halcyon era of noble savages with purely natural needs. Once fed and sheltered, our needs have always been cultural, not natural. Until there is some other system to codify and satisfy those needs and yearnings, capitalism—and the culture it carries with it—will continue not just to thrive but to triumph.

In the way we live now, it is simply impossible to consume objects without consuming meaning. Meaning is pumped and drawn everywhere throughout the modern commercial world, into the farthest reaches of space and into the smallest divisions of time. Commercialism is the water we all swim in, the air we breathe, our sunlight and shade. Currents of desire flow around objects like smoke in a wind tunnel.

This isn't to say that I'm simply sanguine about such a material culture. It has many problems that I have glossed over. Consumerism is wasteful, it is devoid of otherworldly concerns, it lives for today and celebrates the body. It overindulges and spoils the young with impossible promises. It encourages recklessness, living beyond one's means, gambling. Consumer culture is always new, always without a past. Like religion, which it has displaced, it afflicts the comfortable and comforts the afflicted. It is heedless of the truly poor who cannot gain access to the loop of meaningful information that is carried through its ceaseless exchanges. It is a one-dimensional world, a wafer-thin world, a world low on significance and high on glitz, a world without yesterdays.

On a personal level, I struggle daily to keep it at bay. For instance, I am offended by billboards (how do they externalize costs?); I fight to keep Chris Whittle's Channel One TV and all placed-based advertising from entering the classroom; political advertising makes me sick, especially the last-minute negative ads; I contribute to PBS in hopes they will stop slipping down the slope of commercialism (although I know better); I am annoyed that Coke has bought all the "pouring rights" at my school and is now trying to do the same to the world; I think it's bad enough that the state now sponsors gambling, do they also have to support deceptive advertising about it?; I despise the way that amateur athletics has become a venue for shoe companies (why not just replace the football with the Nike swoosh and be done with it?); and I just go nuts at Christmas.

16   But I also realize that while you don't have to like it, it doesn't hurt to understand it and our part in it. We have not been led astray. Henry Luce was not far off when he claimed in a February 1941 editorial in *Life* magazine that the next era was to be the American Century: "The Greeks, the Romans, the English and the French had their eras, and now it was ours." Not only that, but we are likely to commandeer much of the 21st century as well.

Almost a decade ago, Francis Fukuyama, a State Department official, contended in his controversial essay (and later book) "The End of History?" that "the ineluctable spread of consumerist Western culture" presages "not just the end of the Cold War, or the passing of a particular period of postwar history, but the end of history as such: that is, the end point of mankind's ideological evolution." OK, such predictions are not new. "The End of History" (as we know it) and "the end point of mankind's ideological evolution" have been predicted before by philosophers. Hegel claimed it had already happened in 1806 when Napoleon embodied the ideas of the French Revolution, and Marx said the end was coming soon with world communism. What legitimizes this modern claim is that it is demonstrably true. For better or for worse, American commercial culture is well on its way to becoming world culture. The Soviets have fallen. Only quixotic French intellectuals and anxious Islamic fundamentalists are trying to stand up to it.

To some degree, the triumph of consumerism is the triumph of the popular will. You may not like what is manufactured, advertised, packaged, branded, and broadcast, but it is far closer to what most people want most of the time than at any other period of modern history.

Trollope and *The Jerk*

Two fictional characters personify to me the great divide: Augustus Melmotte, the protagonist of Anthony Trollope's 19th-century novel, *The Way We Live Now,* and Navin R. Johnson, the eponymous hero of Steve Martin's 1979 movie, *The Jerk.*

20   Melmotte, a Jew, comes from Paris to London with his daughter and his Bohemian wife. When the action of the novel is over and Augustus has committed suicide because he cannot fit in to proper Victorian society, wife and daughter head off to America—to San Francisco, to be exact. Trollope is always exact in letting you know that geography determines character. So too we know that Ruby Ruggles and her bumpkin brother belong at Sheep's Acres Farm and that Roger Carbury should preside over Carbury Hall. Sir Felix Carbury, fallen from grace, must go to Germany—there is no room for his kind, no club that will accept him. Mrs. Hurtle comes from San Francisco and in the end must return there.

Any Trollope lover worth his salt can tell you much about the protagonists simply by such comings and goings. These paths are the code by which our grandparents recognized, in Dominick Dunne's felicitous title, those who are "people like us": our kind/not our kind. The Victorian reading public needed such shorthand because things had no brand personalities—manners, places, sinecures—and bloodlines did. Salaries meant little, accomplishments even less. The central acts of *The Way We Live Now* are the attempts by Augustus Melmotte to buy a titled husband for his daughter and get a named estate for himself. He can't do it, of course—how silly to try, even if he is the "City's most powerful financier." In his world, meaning was generated through such social conventions as the abstract concept of bloodline, the value of patina, your club, owning land, acceptable in-laws, your accent, the seating chart for dinner, the proper church pew—all things Melmotte could never master. It was a stultifying system—a real old-boy network, but one that to Trollope still worked. It was a system presided over by chummy squires, comfortable gentlemen, and twinkling clerics.

Compare that to the world of *The Jerk*. Here, the story is held together by the running joke that when Navin R. Johnson is being the most idiotic, he is really being the most savant. After a series of misadventures, Navin amasses a fortune by inventing a way to keep eyeglasses from slipping down the nose (the "Opti-grab"). He wins the hand of his sweetheart, buys incredibly gauche gold chains, swag lamps, outrageous golf carts, and ersatz Grecian mansions. Surrounded by things, he is finally happy. But then—curses!—he loses his possessions as a google-eyed litigant wins a class action lawsuit because the Opti-grab has made many wearers cross-eyed. Navin's wife is distraught. She bursts into tears. "I don't care about losing the money, it's losing all this stuff."

Navin, as innocent as he is honest, says he doesn't really care about these things, he knows who he is without possessions. His sense of self is certainly not tied to the material world. "I don't want stuff . . . I don't need anything," he says to her as he starts to leave the room in his pajamas. He sees an old ashtray. "Except this ashtray, and that's the only thing I need is this," he says, as he leans over to pick it up. Navin walks to the door. "Well, and this paddle game and the ashtray is all I need. And this, this remote control; that's all I need, just the ashtray, paddle game, and this remote control."

24   Navin is growing progressively more frantic in vintage Steve Martin fashion. He is in the hall now, pajamas down around his knees and his arms full of stuff.

"And these matches. Just the ashtray, paddle ball, remote control, and these matches . . . and this lamp, and that's all I need. I don't need one other thing . . . except this magazine." We hear him gathering more things as he disappears down the hall. Navin, jerk enough to think he needs nothing, is sage enough not to leave home without a few of his favorite things.

Augustus Melmotte, certified world-class financier, is forever kept at bay. He never achieves his goal and finally commits suicide. Navin R. Johnson, certified consumer jerk, achieves (if only for a while) the objects of his heart's desire. He finally becomes a bum on Skid Row, true, but a bum who at least can try it all over again. In a consumerist culture, the value-making ligatures that hold our world together come from such conventions as advertising, packaging, branding, fashion, and even shopping itself. It is a system presided over by marketers who deliver the goods and all that is carried in their wake. It is a more democratic world, a more egalitarian world, and, I think, a more interesting world.

That said, commercialism can be a stultifying system too, and wasteful. It would be nice to think that this eternally encouraging market will result in the cosmopolitanism envisioned by the Enlightenment philosophers, that a "universalism of goods" will end in a crescendo of hosannas. It would be nice to think that more and more of the poor and disenfranchised will find their ways into the cycle of increased affluence without contracting "affluenza," the "disease" of buying too much. It would be nice to think that materialism could be heroic, self-abnegating, and redemptive. It would be nice to think that greater material comforts will release us from racism, sexism, and ethnocentrism, and that the apocalypse will come as it did at the end of Shelley's *Prometheus Unbound*, leaving us "Sceptreless, free, uncircumscribed . . . Equal, unclassed, tribeless; and nationless . . . Pinnacled dim in the intense inane."

But it is more likely that the globalization of capitalism will result in the banalities of an ever-increasing, worldwide consumerist culture. Recall that Athens ceased to be a world power around 400 B.C., yet for the next three hundred years Greek culture was the culture of the world. The Age of European Exposition ended in the mid-20th century; the Age of American Markets—Yankee imperialism—is just starting to gather force. The French don't stand a chance. The Middle East is collapsing under the weight of dish antennas and Golden Arches. The untranscendent, repetitive, sensational, democratic, immediate, tribalizing, and unifying force of what Irving Kristol calls the American Imperium need not result in a Bronze Age of culture, however. In fact, who knows what this Pax Americana will result in? But it certainly will not produce what Shelley had in mind.

28   We have been in the global marketplace a short time, and it is an often scary and melancholy place. A butterfly flapping its wings in China may not cause storm clouds over Miami, but a few lines of computer code written by some kid in Palo Alto may indeed change the lives of all the inhabitants of Shanghai.

More important, perhaps, we have not been led into this world of material closeness against our better judgment. For many of us, especially when young, consumerism is not against our better judgment. It is our better judgment. And this is true regardless of class or culture. We have not just asked to go this way, we have demanded. Now most of the world is lining up, pushing and shoving, eager to elbow into the mall. Woe to the government or religion that says no.

Getting and spending have been the most passionate, and often the most imaginative, endeavors of modern life. We have done more than acknowledge that the good life starts with the material life, as the ancients did. We have made stuff the dominant prerequisite of organized society. Things "R" Us. Consumption has become production. While this is dreary and depressing to some, as doubtless it should be, it is liberating and democratic to many more.

PERSONAL RESPONSE

Do you think that consumerism creates artificial values? Do you consider yourself "an unrepentant capitalist" (paragraph 4)? Explain your answer.

QUESTIONS FOR CLASS OR SMALL-GROUP DISCUSSION

1. How does the Helen Landon Cass quotation that precedes the text work to introduce Twitchell's subject? How effective do you find Twitchell's references to Trollope and *The Jerk* (paragraph 20)? What is their function?

2. Look at what Twitchell says in paragraph 4 about consumers demanding that "producers splash magical promise over their goods." What do you think he means when he says that consumers "insist on" a bill of goods and that "what looks like exploiting desire may be fulfilling desire"? To what extent do you agree with him?

3. Comment on Twitchell's use of the phrase "liberating role of consumption" in paragraph 8. Do you agree with him that "we like having stuff?" Do you think it is a fair representation of Americans? What do you think of Twitchell's critique of academics who view consumerism as oppression (paragraphs 8–12)?

4. Twitchell seems to see consumerism as both good and bad. State in your own words what he sees as good about it and what he sees as bad. To what extent do you share his viewpoint?

YOU ARE WHAT YOU BUY

RICHARD WOLKOMIR AND JOYCE WOLKOMIR

Richard Wolkomir and Joyce Wolkomir are writers whose work appears often in Smithsonian *magazine. He is a former editor at the McGraw-Hill Publishing Company, and she is a former Scholastic Magazines editor. They are authors of* Junkyard Bandicoots and Other Tales of the World's Endangered Species *(1992). Their writing has received a number of awards, including the Clarion*

*Award and the American Association for the Advancement of Science
Award for Distinguished Science Writing in Magazines. This article
was published in the October 2000, issue of* Smithsonian.

Along with two friends who need a new plastic dish drainer, James Twitchell, a
professor of 19th-century poetry at the University of Florida in Gainesville, is visiting a Wal-Mart. Twitchell gazes raptly upon the aisles stacked with TV sets in
boxes, and picnic baskets and T-shirts and beach balls. So much mass-produced
stuff! Twitchell is energized—as any dedicated scholar would be upon entering an
archive packed with new material.

    "Look at this wire shopping cart—it's the equivalent of the Las Vegas poker
chip," he says. "In a casino, instead of gambling with your real money, you use little
colored plastic disks, so it seems OK. This huge cart is something like that: it's so
roomy you don't feel you're buying too much. Marketers fooled around with the
size of these carts, getting them just right."

    Twitchell loves this stuff. He loves it so much that he has switched from teach-
ing and writing solely about Romantic-era poetry to buzzier issues, such as adolescents wearing dungarees slung low to reveal their Joe Boxers, and whether the
Jolly Green Giant is an avatar of Zeus. And now, reveling in all these bedspreads
and CD players and croquet sets and yellow raincoats, Twitchell tells his friends
that one reason he began studying such fine points of mass marketing is that his
parents, long ago, denied him Wonder Bread.

4   Twitchell's father, a Vermont physician, dismissed Wonder Bread as "air and
water." His mother warned that Coca-Cola was sugar water that would "rot your
teeth." Now he keeps a cellophane-wrapped loaf of Wonder Bread and an aluminum can of Coke—icons among American consumables—atop his computer monitor. In one of Twitchell's recent books, *Lead Us Into Temptation: The Triumph of
American Materialism,* he wrote that everything he loved as a youth was from the
forbidden mass culture: "It was mass produced, mass marketed and consumed en
masse." And if he wanted to savor Pepsi and Whoppers and Dairy Queen sundaes,
he had to do it on the sly, "for we would not countenance them inside the family
circle."

    Twitchell—who is now in his 50s, trim and urbane—says his study of mass
culture, especially advertising, began 15 years ago, when he was teaching a class on
the Romantic poets. "I suddenly realized my students had no interest in what I had
to say." He asked them to complete a line from Wordsworth: "My heart leaps up
when I behold a ———— in the sky." Nobody could supply the missing "rainbow,"
but his students could flawlessly recite the contents of a Big Mac: two all-beef patties, special sauce, lettuce, cheese, pickles and onions on a sesame-seed bun.

    "It was an epiphany," he says.

    At the time, the much-discussed book by E. D. Hirsch, et al., *Cultural Lit-
eracy: What Every American Needs To Know,* argued that cultures need the glue of
shared knowledge, like who Napoleon was or where Beirut is. "I realized he was
right, we do need a body of information," explains Twitchell. "But he was wrong
about what body of information we share, because it isn't from high culture—it's

from pop culture, the world my students knew so well." His students knew little about Dickens or Keats. "But they could recite the 'Mmm, mmm good' Campbell's Soup jingle," he says. "They didn't know Rembrandt, but they could tell you Ben's and Jerry's last names." Twitchell was stunned. "I wanted to know why the stuff they knew was so powerful it pushed my stuff out of the way."

8   Since then, he has been observing himself, his law professor wife, his two daughters, now grown, his colleagues, students, neighbors. He has invited himself into advertising agencies as an academic gadfly on the wall. He has explored advertising's history. And he has learned the average adult now encounters some 3,000 advertisements every day, from bus flanks to messages over the telephone as the caller waits on hold. He has probed the impact of all that mass marketing in such works as *ADCULT USA* and his latest book, *Twenty Ads That Shook the World*.

Academics usually excoriate modern materialism as spiritually deadening and socially corrupting, he observes. "My own take is that humans love things, and we've always been materialistic, but until the Industrial Revolution only the wealthy had things—now the rest of us are having a go at arranging our lives around things." Especially in the past 20 years, young people have had lots more money to spend. "Now they're driving the market for mass-produced objects." And especially for youths, Twitchell maintains, advertising has become our social studies text. "Ask 18-year-olds what freedom means, and they'll tell you, 'It means being able to buy whatever I want!'"

But advertising's job is not just urging, "Buy this!" Twitchell cites 1950s ad ace Rosser Reeves, who created a television commercial in which a hammer clangs an anvil to remind viewers how a headache feels (or maybe to induce one) while reporting good news: Anacin is "for fast, Fast, FAST relief. . . ." Reeves would hold up two quarters. It was advertising's task, he said, to make you believe those two quarters were different. Even more important, the ad had to persuade you that one of those quarters was worth more.

To illustrate the process, Twitchell points to 1930s ads claiming Schlitz steam-cleaned its beer bottles. What the ads omitted was that all brewers steamcleaned their bottles. Thus, through advertising, the company achieved "ownership" of product purity—it created for itself what the ad industry calls a USP (Unique Selling Proposition).

12   According to Twitchell, it was in the Victorian era that mass culture reared up, driven by the steam-powered printing press, which spewed out text and images and notions for the "mob." Victorians invented the word "mob," he says, by shortening the Latin *mobile vulgus*, "rabble on the move." Victorian education strove to differentiate literature from pulp novels, to show classical music's superiority to dance-hall tunes, to instill "art appreciation." But with the machine age churning out cheap goods, consumerism was erupting all over, and so was advertising.

Thomas J. Barratt, the 19th-century manufacturer of Pears' Soap, noted: "Any fool can make soap. It takes a clever man to sell it." And Barratt was just that man. "The manufacture of soap is a turning point in civilization," says Twitchell. Originally, farmers boiled animal fats with wood ashes and molded the result into soap balls, which soon stank. With the machine age came soap concocted from caustic soda and vegetable fats, pressed into bars that lasted forever. But one soap was much like another.

In 1881, at James Gamble's soap factory in Cincinnati, a worker forgot to turn off the mixing machinery, inadvertently producing a batch of soap so air-filled it floated. Gamble claimed his new soap, Ivory, floated because it was pure—in fact, 99 44/100 percent pure.

Earlier, England's Andrew Pears—the father-in-law of Thomas J. Barratt—had developed a translucent soap. It seemed a natural to appeal to the class-conscious Briton's desire for whiter skin, versus a laborer's weathered tan. Barratt got the message across in such ways as plastering his company's new slogan, an early version of Nike's "Just Do It," on walls all over the British Empire: "Good Morning! Have You Used Your Pears' Soap?"

16   But Barratt's greatest coup was co-opting Bubbles, a John Everett Millais painting of the artist's angelic grandson watching a just-blown soap bubble waft upward. Barratt sold Millais on the notion that, distributed as a free poster, his painting would reach thousands upon thousands of potential new art lovers, for their edification. For their further edification, Barratt had a cake of the soap lying in the painting's foreground, inscribed "Pears.'"

Branding made advertising possible. In the early 1800s, soap was just soap. Like biscuits or nails, it came in barrels, and to get some, you told the store clerk, "Two bars of soap, please." By the late 1800s—nudged by Barratt's advertising—you might specify Pears' Soap. Twitchell says Barratt's hijacking of art to sell soap "blurred, for the first time and forevermore, the bright line between art and advertising, between high culture and the vulgar, between pristine and corrupt." Today, art co-opted by advertising is so commonplace we do not blink at Michelangelo's David wearing Levi's cutoffs.

Back in the Wal-Mart, Twitchell veers toward a barrel displaying kitchen floor mats. "Two for five dollars!" he says, reading a sign. It is clearly tempting. Two floor mats, one price. But he pulls himself away from the alluring floor mats to ruminate about literature. "I'm supposed to teach English Romantic poetry," he says. "That period, the beginning of the 19th century, is where many of our views on materialism came from, because that was when the Industrial Revolution began producing the surfeit of things that will cause the trouble."

Surpluses produced by the new technologies, like steam power, were particularly apt to pile up after wars, and that was especially true in the aftermath of the Civil War. "What it takes to win a war is the ability to produce more war materials than your opponent, but when the war ends you have too many blankets, boots, rifles, and too much patent medicine—which was the subject of the first real advertising," he explains. "In the 1870s we had the rise of advertising, along with the rise of newspapers, and now we start talking about two nostrums or two pairs of boots as if they were different, when we know they are the same."

20   Modern advertising, Twitchell insists, learned its stuff from religion. "I grew up a Vermont Congregationalist. My father was a doctor in our town, and his father had been a doctor in our town, and my mother's family had lived around there since the Revolution." His was, except for Wonder Bread denial, a stable life.

"In the world where I grew up, you knew who you were by a series of time-tested anchors—ancestry, land, religion, where you went to school, your accent, your job—but we've been rapidly losing those anchors," he argues. "One marriage out of two ends in divorce, the average person changes jobs seven or eight times during a lifetime." With the old determinants of social position shifting or gone, he says, "we're starting to build our identity around driving a Lexus or displaying Ralph Lauren's polo player on our shirt."

He notes that many of modern advertising's founders had religious backgrounds. A Baptist minister's son, Bruce Barton, cofounded the large ad agency Batten, Barton, Durstine & Osborne (which comedian Fred Allen suggested sounded like "a trunk falling downstairs"). Artemus Ward, who wrote psalms to Sapolio Soap, was the son of an Episcopal minister. John Wanamaker, whose marketing genius helped create the modern department store, once considered becoming a Presbyterian minister. Rosser Reeves, creator of the Anacin anvils, was the son of a Methodist minister.

Twitchell contends that these founders of modern advertising, and others like them, modeled their messages on parables they heard in church. He sketches a typical TV commercial in which someone is distressed. Perhaps it is a young woman, if the product is a dish detergent. Perhaps it is a middle-aged man, if the product is a cold remedy. The heroine or hero consults another person who gives witness: a certain product "works miracles." The product is tried. Relief! Ads create and then promise to absolve you of secular sins, such as halitosis or dandruff, or "ring around the collar" or "dishpan hands."

But Twitchell says that advertising also reaches back to paganism. Instead of Zeus in the clouds and dryads in trees, we have televisions that are inhabited by the Jolly Green Giant, the Michelin Man, the Man from Glad, Mother Nature, Aunt Jemima, the White Knight, the Energizer Bunny and Speedy Alka-Seltzer with his magical chant: "Plop, plop, fizz, fizz. . . ."

24   Commercial culture is so potent, Twitchell believes, that it has "colonized" society. For instance, Christmas was low-key until the 1800s, when stores reinvented the holiday to sell off their surpluses. On December 24, 1867, R. H. Macy kept his Manhattan store open until midnight, setting a one-day sales record of more than $6,000.

Santa started as "a weird conflation of St. Nicholas (a down-on-his-luck nobleman who helped young women turn away from prostitution) and Kriss Kringle (perhaps a corruption of the German Christkindl, a gift giver)." Today's familiar Santa, Twitchell continues, originated in the 1930s, because Coca-Cola's sales slumped in winter. Ads began showing Santa—in his modern persona—relaxing in a living room after toy delivery, quaffing a Coke apparently left for him by the home's children. "Coke's Santa was elbowing aside other Santas—Coke's Santa was starting to own Christmas." Rudolph the Red-Nosed Reindeer was a 1930s creation of a Montgomery Ward copywriter. And Twitchell says Kodak ads universalized the tradition of blowing out birthday-cake candles and other "Kodak Moments" to "show what you can do with fast Kodak film and the Kodak Flashmatic attachment on your Kodak camera."

Ads have even changed our attitude toward debt, which once could lead to prison. "Think only of how consumer debt was merchandised until it became an accepted habit, not an abhorred practice," observes Twitchell. "Think only of how the concept of shine and 'new and improved' replaced the previous value of patina and heirloom." Twitchell says politics hit its modern ad-driven stride starting with the 1952 "Eisenhower Answers America" Presidential campaign, designed by Rosser Reeves. Regarding his own ads, Ike said ruefully: "To think an old soldier should come to this."

Athletes have become logo-bedecked living billboards. But Twitchell argues that commercial culture has affected us all. Cereal, for example, is now synonymous with breakfast. "Before Messrs. Post and Kellogg, this meal consisted of breaking fast by finishing last night's dinner," he says, adding that leftovers went to the family dog. Dog food was a creation of Ralston Purina's ad agency. Twitchell says that some marketing ploys fizzled, of course, citing an old ad headlined: "Sunday is Puffed Grain Day."

28   Mother's Day began in the early 1900s when Philadelphia merchandiser John Wanamaker elevated to stardom a local woman mourning for her mother. He ran fullpage ads in the *Philadelphia Inquirer*. Soon only a blackguard would fail to buy Mom a present on her newly special day. Wanamaker reportedly gloated that he would rather be the founder of Mother's Day than the king of England.

Twitchell is no longer amazed that his students, inundated with commercial messages, display their status with manufacturers' logos on their shirt pockets or on their sunglasses. "At a Palm Beach store a woman explained to me that the more expensive the sunglasses, the smaller the logo, so that with Cartier you can barely see the Cy." His students derogatorily refer to certain classmates as "Gaps," after the retail chain where they buy their clothes. In the 19th century, people learned manners from novels and magazines; in the 20th from sitcoms and ads. When his daughter was a teenager, he heard her telling friends, after watching a teen TV show, *90210*, "Can you believe how cool Kelly looked in Dylan's Porsche!" Twitchell shrugs: "That's all they have for Trollope."

Economist Thorstein Veblen coined the term "conspicuous consumption": displaying possessions to impress others. "Between ages 15 and 25, we males consume the most as a percentage of our disposable income because we're displaying our feathers to potential mates," says Twitchell. "Now it's more complicated because females are working and they can display too." But the urge wanes. "After about age 45, many people start moving away from acquisition. Thus, ads, TV shows, and movies, which are studded with paid-for product placements, concentrate ferociously on youths, who seem to get the message.

But not all analysts agree with Madison Avenue's youth fixation. In fact, according to Beth Barnes, an associate professor at Syracuse University and chair of the advertising department at the S. I. Newhouse School of Public Communications, advertisers are increasingly recognizing that the over-45 age-group is growing fast. And older Americans often have the magic ingredient: disposable income. "I think the change is slow, but inevitable," Barnes says. For one thing, she notes, advertising is increasingly segmented, exploiting today's highly segmented media to aim finetuned messages at specific subcultures, including age-groups. "Advertising for soft drinks may stay aimed at youth," she says. "But the trick is to go after older people with products in which they are not set in their ways—computers, for instance, or travel and tourism, or financial services, or new products, like Chrysler's PT Cruiser."

32   About a year ago, marketing circles buzzed over the surprising number of over-45 online shoppers. "It makes sense. They're amazingly machine savvy—my mother just got a new computer because her old one was too slow." It is true, Barnes continues, that younger people may be less loyal to brands, and easier to woo away. But she adds: "There's a flip side to that—young people are lot more skeptical too!"

Perhaps. "Why," asks James Twitchell, "are my daughters willing to buy a bottle of water worth two cents and pay $1.50?" They aren't buying the product itself; they're buying the values that advertising has attached to the product, such as being hip. He cites a Madison Avenue adage: "You don't drink the beer; you drink the advertising."

Many of today's ads leave the average reader or viewer totally confused about what is being sold. For instance, in one current TV commercial, a cool young couple is driving down a city street, their car's windshield wipers clacking. They are so tuned in, they notice that the passing scene is rife with tempos, such as a boy bouncing a basketball, all in perfect sync with the rhythmic clack of their windshield wipers. What is going on?

"Often advertising is not about keeping up with the Joneses, but about separating you from them," Twitchell points out. "That's especially true of advertising directed at a particular group, such as adolescents or young-adult males—it's called 'dog-whistle' advertising because it goes out at frequencies only dogs can hear." In this case, the "dogs" are the commercial's target group of young adults. The young couple is hip enough to be driving their model of Volkswagen. "The idea is, your parents can't understand this, but you can." He cites a recent advertisement for a new sport utility vehicle that actually has the headline: "Ditch the Joneses!"

36   The most egregious example of this oblique marketing ploy was, of course, Benetton's spate of ads that employed the force of shock in order to create product recognition. The image of a nun and a priest, locked in a passionate kiss, was offensive to many people. But the pieces de resistance were Benetton's portraits of 25 death row inmates in America's prisons. This ad campaign cost Benetton its lucrative contract with Sears, Roebuck & Company and ended Oliviero Toscani's 18-year career as Benetton's creative director.

Such an ad may look senseless to a 50-year-old, Twitchell says, "but it's being properly decoded by a 23-year-old." It works. Today's average American consumes twice as many goods and services as in 1950, and the average home is twice as large as a post-World War II average home. A decade ago, most grocery stores stocked about 9,000 items; today's stores carry some 24,000.

Twitchell says he does not believe for a minute that our commercial society is a better world. "But it might be a safer world, oddly enough, if we value machine-made objects about which lies are told, rather than feuding over how to save souls," he says. "And we may be moving into a quieter world as people who were never able to consume before begin getting and spending."

He points upward, to the Wal-Mart's ceiling, with its exposed girders, pipes, wires and ducts, painted industrial gray. "That's to give you the illusion that you're buying stuff as close to the factory as possible," he says. His eyes fix upon Kraft Macaroni & Cheese boxes, each inscribed "The Cheesiest." He says, "It looks like a cornucopia, and the message is, 'Take one!' And see, the stack still sits on its freight pallet, to give you the idea there aren't many middlemen between you and the factory price."

40   Everything in the store is a brand-name product. "See, a stack of Fedders' air conditioners in their boxes. It was Wal-Mart founder Sam Walton's great insight that if he sold only branded items and negotiated lower prices, the manufacturers would do all the advertising for him."

Twitchell wanders back to the alluring display of floor mats that had first attracted his eye. He stares, transfixed. "Two for five dollars! I came in here meaning to buy one. That idea of two seemingly for the price of one took hold in the 1940s, especially with Alka-Seltzer, which you originally took as only one tablet until they halved the dosage so you'd take two: 'Plop, plop. . . . '" A few steps farther, he eyes a display of bottled mineral water. "This one is made by Pepsi. When they studied its marketing in Wichita, they were astonished to find out that buyers of these lower priced mineral waters didn't care if it came from underground springs or run-off from Alpine glaciers—they bought the water because they liked the name and the feel of the bottle in their hand."

He pauses at a rack of greeting cards. "It's how we exchange emotions now, the commercializing of expression. The most touching are the cards to send to kids, offering your sympathy because their parents just got divorced." Such cards perform a useful service. "They're facilitators of difficulty, and they help us handle emotionally fraught events quickly and efficiently."

As his friends prepare to leave the Wal-Mart, without the dish drainer they had sought, Twitchell stops. "I'm going to go buy those two floor mats, but after you leave, because I'm ashamed to be seen succumbing to that two-for-the-price-of-one deal," he says.

44   Even so, Twitchell—deprived as a boy of Wonder Bread and Coke—believes the stuff cramming our stores, which advertisements strain to get us to buy, is not necessarily invidious to our cultural health. "After all," he says, "we don't call them 'bads'—we call them 'goods!'"

PERSONAL RESPONSE

Wolkomir and Wolkomir mention James B. Twitchell's comments on students wearing manufacturers' logos (paragraph 30). Do you wear such logos with pride, or do you avoid wearing them? Explore your viewpoint on this very popular practice.

QUESTIONS FOR CLASS OR SMALL-GROUP DISCUSSION

1. Wolkomir and Wolkomir conducted their interview of James B. Twitchell in a Wal-Mart store. Discuss the appropriateness of that location as a site

for the interview. What is your impression of Twitchell as a result of this interview?

2. What do you understand Twitchell to mean by this comment: "[E]specially for youths [. . .] advertising has become our social studies text" (paragraph 9). To what extent do you think he is correct?

3. In response to Thomas J. Barratt's observation, "Any fool can make soap. It takes a clever man to sell it" (paragraph 13), discuss current advertising campaigns that you think are particularly clever, like the Pears' Soap campaign that Wolkomir and Wolkomir describe.

4. State in your own words what advertisers do to sell their products, commenting on some of the techniques to which Wolkomir and Wolkomir refer. How does the placing of manufacturers' logos on their products help sell the products? Why do you think that young people especially like those products?

EVERY NOOK AND CRANNY: THE DANGEROUS SPREAD OF COMMERCIALIZED CULTURE

Gary Ruskin and Juliet Schor

Gary Ruskin is Executive Director of Commercial Alert. Juliet Schor is a professor of sociology at Boston College, and author of Born to Buy: The Commercialized Child and the New Consumer Culture. *She serves on the Board of Directors of Commercial Alert. This article was first published in the January/February 2005 issue of* Multinational Monitor, *a mo lication that tracks activity in the corporate world, especially in third world countries.*

In December, many people in Washington, D.C. paused to absorb the meaning in the lighting of the National Christmas Tree, at the White House Ellipse. At that event, President George W. Bush reflected that the "love and gifts" of Christmas were "signs and symbols of even a greater love and gift that came on a holy night."

But these signs weren't the only ones on display. Perhaps it was not surprising that the illumination was sponsored by MCI, which, as MCI WorldCom, committed one of the largest corporate frauds in history. Such public displays of commercialism have become commonplace in the United States.

The rise of commercialism is an artifact of the growth of corporate power. It began as part of a political and ideological response by corporations to wage pressures, rising social expenditures, and the successes of the environmental and consumer movements in the late 1960s and early 1970s. Corporations fostered the anti-tax movement and support for corporate welfare, which helped create funding crises in state and local governments and schools, and made them more willing to carry commercial advertising. They promoted "free market" ideology, privatization and consumerism, while denigrating the public sphere. In the late 1970s, Mobil Oil began its decades-long advertising on the New York Times op-ed page, one example of a larger corporate effort to reverse a precipitous decline in public approval of corporations. They also became adept at manipulating the campaign finance system, and weaknesses in the federal bribery statute, to procure influence in governments at all levels.

4   Perhaps most importantly, the commercialization of government and culture and the growing importance of material acquisition and consumer lifestyles was hastened by the co-optation of potentially countervailing institutions, such as churches (papal visits have been sponsored by Pepsi, Federal Express and Mercedes-Benz), governments, schools, universities and nongovernmental organizations.

While advertising has long been an element in the circus of U.S. life, not until recently has it been recognized as having political or social merit. For nearly two centuries, advertising (lawyers call it commercial speech) was not protected by the U.S. Constitution. The U.S. Supreme Court ruled in 1942 that states could regulate commercial speech at will. But in 1976, the Court granted constitutional protection to commercial speech. Corporations have used this new right of speech to proliferate advertising into nearly every nook and cranny of life.

Entering the Schoolhouse

During most of the twentieth century, there was little advertising in schools. That changed in 1989, when Chris Whittle's Channel One enticed schools to accept advertising, by offering to loan TV sets to classrooms. Each school day, Channel One features at least two minutes of ads, and 10 minutes of news, fluff, banter and quizzes. The program is shown to about 8 million children in 12,000 schools.

Soda, candy and fast food companies soon learned Channel One's lesson of using financial incentives to gain access to schoolchildren. By 2000, 94 percent of high schools allowed the sale of soda, and 72 percent allowed sale of chocolate candy. Energy, candy, personal care products, even automobile manufacturers have entered the classroom with "sponsored educational materials"—that is, ads in the guise of free "curricula."

8   Until recently, corporate incursion in schools has mainly gone under the radar. However, the rise of childhood obesity has engendered stiff political opposition to junk food marketing, and in the last three years, coalitions of progressives, conservatives and public health groups have made headway. The State of California has banned the sale of soda in elementary, middle and junior high schools. In Maine, soda and candy suppliers have removed their products from vending machines in all schools. Arkansas banned candy and soda vending machines in elementary schools. Los Angeles, Chicago and New York have city-wide bans on the sale of soda in schools. Channel One was expelled from the Nashville public schools in the 2002–3 school year, and will be removed from Seattle in early 2005. Thanks to activist pressure, a company called ZapMe!, which placed computers in thousands

of schools to advertise and extract data from students, was removed from all schools across the country.

Ad Creep and Spam Culture

Advertisers have long relied on 30-second TV spots to deliver messages to mass audiences. During the 1990s, the impact of these ads began to drop off, in part because viewers simply clicked to different programs during ads. In response, many advertisers began to place ads elsewhere, leading to "ad creep"—the spread of ads throughout social space and cultural institutions. Whole new marketing sub-specialties developed, such as "place-based" advertising, which coerces captive viewers to watch video ads. Examples include ads before movies, ads on buses and trains in cities (Chicago, Milwaukee and Orlando), and CNN's Airport channel. Video ads are also now common on ATMs, gas pumps, in convenience stores and doctors' offices.

Another form of ad creep is "product placement," in which advertisers pay to have their product included in movies, TV shows, museum exhibits, or other forms of media and culture. Product placement is thought to be more effective than the traditional 30-second ad because it sneaks by the viewer's critical faculties. Product placement has recently occurred in novels, and children's books. Some U.S. TV programs (*American Idol, The Restaurant, The Apprentice*) and movies (*Minority Report, Cellular*) are so full of product placement that they resemble infomercials. By contrast, many European nations, such as Austria, Germany, Norway and the United Kingdom, ban or sharply restrict product placement on television.

Commercial use of the Internet was forbidden as recently as the early 1990s, and the first spam wasn't sent until 1994. But the marketing industry quickly penetrated this sphere as well, and now 70 percent of all e-mail is spam, according to the spam filter firm Postini Inc. Pop-ups, pop-unders and ad-ware have become major annoyances for Internet users. Telemarketing became so unpopular that the corporate-friendly Federal Trade Commission established a National Do Not Call Registry, which has brought relief from telemarketing calls to 64 million households.

12   Even major cultural institutions have been harnessed by the advertising industry. During 2001–2002, the Smithsonian Institution, perhaps the most important U.S. cultural institution, established the General Motors Hall of Transportation and the Lockheed Martin Imax Theater. Following public opposition and Congressional action, the commercialization of the Smithsonian has largely been halted. In 2000, the Library of Congress hosted a giant celebration for Coca-Cola, essentially converting the nation's most important library into a prop to sell soda pop.

Targeting Kids

For a time, institutions of childhood were relatively uncommercialized, as adults subscribed to the notion of childhood innocence, and the need to keep children from the "profane" commercial world. But what was once a trickle of advertising to children has become a flood. Corporations spend about $15 billion marketing to children in the United States each year, and by the mid-1990s, the average child was exposed to 40,000 TV ads annually.

Children have few legal protections from corporate marketers in the United States. This contrasts strongly to the European Union, which has enacted restrictions. Norway and Sweden have banned television advertising to children under 12 years of age; in Italy, advertising during TV cartoons is illegal, and toy advertising is illegal in Greece between 7 AM and 11 PM. Advertising before and after children's programs is banned in Austria.

Government Brought to You by . . .

As fiscal crises have descended upon local governments, they have turned to advertisers as a revenue source. This trend began inauspiciously in Buffalo, New York in 1995 when Pratt & Lambert, a local paint company, purchased the right to call itself the city's official paint. The next year the company was bought by Sherwin-Williams, which closed the local factory and eliminated its 200 jobs.

16   In 1997, Ocean City, Maryland signed an exclusive marketing deal to make Coca-Cola the city's official drink, and other cities have followed with similar deals with Coke or Pepsi. Even mighty New York City has succumbed, signing a $166 million exclusive marketing deal with Snapple, after which some critics dubbed it the "Big Snapple."

At the United Nations, UNICEF made a stir in 2002 when it announced that it would "team up" with McDonald's, the world's largest fast food company, to promote "McDonald's World Children's Day" in celebration of the anniversary of the United Nations adoption of the Convention on the Rights of the Child. Public health and children's advocates across the globe protested, prompting UNICEF to decline participation in later years.

Another victory for the anti-commercialism forces, perhaps the most significant, came in 2004, when the World Health Organization's Framework Convention on Tobacco Control became legally binding. The treaty commits nations to prohibit tobacco advertising to the extent their constitutions allow it.

Impacts

Because the phenomenon of commercialism has become so ubiquitous, it is not surprising that its effects are as well. Perhaps most alarming has been the epidemic of marketing-related diseases afflicting people in the United States, and especially children, such as obesity, type 2 diabetes and smoking-related illnesses. Each day, about 2,000 U.S. children begin to smoke, and about one-third of them will die from tobacco-related illnesses. Children are inundated with advertising for high calorie junk food and fast food, and, predictably, 15 percent of U.S. children aged 6 to 19 are now overweight.

20   Excessive commercialism is also creating a more materialistic populace. In 2003, the annual UCLA survey of incoming college freshmen found that the number of students who said it was a very important or essential life goal to "develop a

meaningful philosophy of life" fell to an all-time low of 39 percent, while succeed-ing financially has increased to a 13-year high, at 74 percent. High involvement in consumer culture has been show (by Schor) to be a significant cause of depression, anxiety, low self-esteem and psychosomatic complaints in children, findings which parallel similar studies of materialism among teens and adults. Other impacts are more intangible. A 2004 poll by Yankelovich Partners, found that 61 percent of the U.S. public "feel that the amount of marketing and advertising is out of control," and 65 percent "feel constantly bombarded with too much advertising and market-ing." Is advertising diminishing our sense of general well-being? Perhaps.

The purpose of most commercial advertising is to increase demand for a prod-uct. As John Kenneth Galbraith noted 40 years ago, the macro effect of advertising is to artificially boost the demand for private goods, thereby reducing the "demand" or support for unadvertised, public goods. The predictable result has been the back-lash to taxes, and reduced provision of public goods and services.

This imbalance also affects the natural environment. The additional consump-tion created by the estimated $265 billion that the advertising industry will spend in 2004 will also yield more pollution, natural resource destruction, carbon dioxide emissions and global warming.

Finally, advertising has also contributed to a narrowing of the public discourse, as advertising-driven media grow ever more timid. Sometimes it seems as if we live in an echo chamber, a place where corporations speak and everyone else listens.

24   Governments at all levels have failed to address these impacts. That may be because the most insidious effect of commercialism is to undermine government integrity. As governments adopt commercial values, and are integrated into corpo-rate marketing, they develop conflicts of interest that make them less likely to take stands against commercialism.

Disgust among Yourselves

As corporations consolidate their control over governments and culture, we don't expect an outright reversal of commercialization in the near future.

That's true despite considerable public sentiment for more limits and regula-tions on advertising and marketing. However, as commercialism grows more intru-sive, public distaste for it will likely increase, as will political support for restricting it. In the long run, we believe this hopeful trend will gather strength.

In the not-too-distant future, the significance of the lighting of the National Christmas Tree may no longer be overshadowed by public relations efforts to create goodwill for corporate wrongdoers.

PERSONAL RESPONSE

Ruskin and Schor ask in paragraph 20: "Is advertising diminishing our sense of general well-being?" Look at the examples they give in that and the previous para-graph and then answer the question by examining whether your own general well-being has been affected by advertising.

QUESTIONS FOR CLASS OR SMALL-GROUP DISCUSSION

1. Ruskin and Schor mention ways in which commercialism has entered the schoolroom (paragraphs 6–8). Were any of the examples they cite part of your own school experience? Can you give other examples of the invasion of commercialism into schools?

2. What other examples of "ad creep" (paragraph 9) can you give besides the ones that Ruskin and Schor mention? Discuss whether you believe that such advertising should be banned or restricted in the United States, as it is in other countries.

3. Summarize the effects cited by Ruskin and Schor of the "ubiquitous" nature of commercialization (paragraph 19). Do you think that they provide enough evidence to support their contention?

4. Are you convinced by Ruskin and Schor's argument that the spread of commercialism is "dangerous"? Explain your answer.

SHOPPING AND OTHER SPIRITUAL ADVENTURES IN AMERICA TODAY

PHYLLIS ROSE

Phyllis Rose is the author of the following books: Woman of Letters: A Life of Virginia Woolf *(1978);* Parallel Lives: Five Victorian Marriages *(1983);* Jazz Cleopatra: Josephine Baker in Her Time *(1989);* The Norton Book of Women's Lives *(1993);* The Year of Reading Proust: A Memoir in Real Time *(1999); and* Never Say Good-Bye: Essays *(1991), from which this essay is taken.*

Last year a new Waldbaum's Food Mart opened in the shopping mall on Route 66. It belongs to the new generation of super-duper markets open twenty-four hours that have computerized checkout. I went to see the place as soon as it opened and I was impressed. There was trail mix in Lucite bins. There was freshly made pasta. There were coffee beans, four kinds of tahini, ten kinds of herb teas, raw shrimp in shells and cooked shelled shrimp, fresh-squeezed orange juice. Every sophistication known to the big city, even goat's cheese covered with ash, was now available in Middletown, Conn. People raced from the warehouse aisle to the bagel bin to the coffee beans to the fresh fish market, exclaiming at all the new things. Many of us felt elevated, graced, complimented by the presence of this food palace in our town.

This is the wonderful egalitarianism of American business. Was it Andy Warhol who said that the nice thing about Coke is, no can is any better or worse than any other? Some people may find it dull to cross the country and find the same chain stores with the same merchandise from coast to coast, but it means that my

town is as good as yours, my shopping mall as important as yours, equally filled
with wonders.

Imagine what people ate during the winter as little as seventy-five years ago.
They ate food that was local, long-lasting, and dull, like acorn squash, turnips, and
cabbage. Walk into an American supermarket in February and the world lies before
you: grapes, melons, artichokes, fennel, lettuce, peppers, pistachios, dates, even
strawberries, to say nothing of ice cream. Have you ever considered what a triumph
of civilization it is to be able to buy a pound of chicken livers? If you lived on a farm
and had to kill a chicken when you wanted to eat one, you wouldn't ever accumulate a pound of chicken livers.

4   Another wonder of Middletown is Caldor, the discount department store. Here
is man's plenty: tennis racquets, panty hose, luggage, glassware, records, toothpaste.
Timex watches, Cadbury's chocolate, corn poppers, hair dryers, warm-up suits,
car wax, light bulbs, television sets. All good quality at low prices with exchanges
cheerfully made on defective goods. There are worse rules to live by. I feel good
about America whenever I walk into this store, which is almost every midwinter
Sunday afternoon, when life elsewhere has closed down. I go to Caldor the way
English people go to pubs: out of sociability. To get away from my house. To widen
my horizons. For culture's sake. Caldor provides me too with a welcome sense of
seasonal change. When the first outdoor grills and lawn furniture appear there, it's
as exciting a sign of spring as the first crocus or robin.

Someone told me about a Soviet émigré who practices English by declaiming,
at random, sentences that catch his fancy. One of his favorites is, "Fifty percent
off all items today only." Refugees from Communist countries appreciate our supermarkets and discount department stores for the wonders they are. An Eastern
European scientist visiting Middletown wept when she first saw the meat counter
at Waldbaum's. On the other hand, before her year in America was up, her pleasure turned sour. She wanted everything she saw. Her approach to consumer goods
was insufficiently abstract, too materialistic. We Americans are beyond a simple,
possessive materialism. We're used to abundance and the possibility of possessing
things. The things, and the possibility of possessing them, will still be there next
week, next year. So today we can walk the aisles calmly.

It is a misunderstanding of the American retail store to think we go there necessarily to buy. Some of us shop. There's a difference. Shopping has many purposes,
the least interesting of which is to acquire new articles. We shop to cheer ourselves
up. We shop to practice decision making. We shop to be useful and productive
members of our class and society. We shop to remind ourselves how much is available to us. We shop to remind ourselves how much is to be striven for. We shop to
assert our superiority to the material objects that spread themselves before us.

Shopping's function as a form of therapy is widely appreciated. You don't really need, let's say, another sweater. You need the feeling of power that comes with
buying or not buying it. You need the feeling that someone wants something you
have—even if it's just your money. To get the benefit of shopping, you needn't actually purchase the sweater, any more than you have to marry every man you flirt
with. In fact, window-shopping, like flirting, can be more rewarding, the same

high without the distressing commitment, the material encumbrance. The purest form of shopping is provided by garage sales. A connoisseur goes out with no goal in mind, open to whatever may come his or her way, secure that it will cost very little. Minimum expense, maximum experience. Perfect shopping.

8   I try to think of the opposite, a kind of shopping in which the object is all important, the pleasure of shopping at a minimum. For example, the purchase of blue jeans. I buy new blue jeans as seldom as possible because the experience is so humiliating. For every pair that looks good on me, fifteen look grotesque. But even shopping for blue jeans at Bob's Surplus on Main Street—no frills, bare-bones shopping—is an event in the life of the spirit. Once again I have to come to terms with the fact that I will never look good in Levi's. Much as I want to be mainstream, I never will be.

In fact, I'm doubly an oddball, neither Misses nor Junior, but Misses Petite. I look in the mirror, I acknowledge the disparity between myself and the ideal, I resign myself to making the best of it: I will buy the Lee's Misses Petite. Shopping is a time of reflection, assessment, spiritual self-discipline.

It is appropriate, I think, that Bob's Surplus has a communal dressing room. I used to shop only in places where I could count on a private dressing room with a mirror inside. My impulse then was to hide my weaknesses. Now I believe in sharing them. There are other women in the dressing room at Bob's Surplus trying on blue jeans who look as bad as I do. We take comfort from one another. Sometimes a woman will ask me which of two items looks better. I always give a definite answer. It's the least I can do. I figure we are all in this together, and I emerge from the dressing room not only with a new pair of jeans but with a renewed sense of belonging to a human community.

When a Solzhenitsyn rants about American materialism, I have to look at my digital Timex and check what year this is. Materialism? Like conformism, a hot moral issue of the fifties, but not now. How to spread the goods, maybe. Whether the goods are the Good, no. Solzhenitsyn, like the visiting scientist who wept at the beauty of Waldbaum's meat counter but came to covet everything she saw, takes American materialism too materialistically. He doesn't see its spiritual side. Caldor, Waldbaum's, Bob's Surplus—these, perhaps, are our cathedrals.

PERSONAL RESPONSE

Explain your attitude toward shopping. Do you go to discount stores or malls to shop or to buy? Does shopping give you the pleasure that Rose says it gives most Americans?

QUESTIONS FOR CLASS OR SMALL-GROUP DISCUSSION

1.   How does the list of foods that Rose mentions in paragraph one relate to her central point? What function do the references to the Soviet émigré and the Eastern European scientist in paragraph 5 serve?

2. Discuss whether you get the pleasure from shopping in American discount stores and supermarkets that Rose describes in her essay. Consider, for instance, Rose's comment in paragraph 9 that "shopping is a time of reflection, assessment, spiritual self-discipline."

3. What criticisms of American consumerism does Rose imply in her ironic descriptions of shopping as a spiritual adventure and department stores as America's cathedrals?

4. In paragraph 10, Rose describes trying on jeans in a communal dressing room and of taking comfort from other women there. Do men experience the same kind of camaraderie when shopping that women often do? To what extent do you think there are differences between the way men and women view shopping in general?

○ PERSPECTIVES ON MARKETING AND THE AMERICAN CONSUMER ○

Suggested Writing Topics

1. Argue against or in support of the contention of Gary Ruskin and Juliet Schor in "Every Nook and Cranny" that commercialism is "dangerous" to the public.

2. Drawing on readings in the chapter, write an essay on the importance of young consumers for the American economy.

3. Drawing on readings in this chapter, explain the pressures you think America's high-consumption society puts on young people and the effects of those pressures.

4. Drawing on the comments of at least two writers in this chapter, write an essay on the image you think that American consumerism presents to the rest of the world and whether you think that image is a good or a bad one.

5. Argue for or against the proposition that the United States should "ban or sharply restrict product placement on television" (Gary Ruskin and Juliet Schor, "Every Nook and Cranny," paragraph 10).

6. Phyllis Rose suggests in "Shopping and Other Spiritual Adventures in America Today" that malls, discount stores, and supermarkets are America's cathedrals, while James B. Twitchell, in "In Praise of Consumerism," asserts that consumerism has displaced religion. Write an essay explaining the extent to which you agree with these writers. Can you name other structures that would be more appropriate symbols of America's spiritual center? Is consumerism America's main religion?

7. In "Shopping and Other Spiritual Adventures in America Today," Phyllis Rose refers to the "wonderful egalitarianism of American business" (paragraph 2), and in James Twitchell's "In Praise of Consumerism," he notes that consumerism makes for a "more egalitarian world" (paragraph 25).

Using those comments as a starting point, write an essay on American consumerism as a social equalizer.

8. Explain why you agree or disagree with the following remark by James B. Twitchell in Richard Wolkomir and Joyce Wolkomir's "You Are What You Buy." Referring to his daughters' willingness to spend $1.50 on a bottle of water worth two cents, Twitchell says, "'They aren't buying the product itself; they're buying the values that advertising has attached to the product'" (paragraph 35).

9. Imagine that you are marketing a product that has traditionally been sold to one particular segment of the market, such as white, middle-class males. Now you want to increase your sales by targeting other groups. Select a particular group and create a sales campaign aimed at that group.

10. Using examples of people you know, either support or refute James B. Twitchell's contention in "In Praise of Consumerism" that Americans are committed to consumerism because "We like having stuff " (paragraph 8).

11. Explain the effects on you or someone you know of a change in income, suddenly coming into money, or acquiring some coveted material possession.

12. Analyze the positive and negative effects of America's emphasis on consumerism on one particular group of people, such as young people, the elderly, working-class people, the wealthy, or those living in poverty.

13. Explain what you think shopping malls, discount stores, and overstocked supermarkets suggest about Americans' values. For instance, what impression do you think that foreign visitors get of America when they see the sizes of and selections in those marketplaces?

Research Topics

1. Research one of the many subjects raised by Gary Ruskin and Juliet Schor in "Every Nook and Cranny," such as their assertion in paragraph four that "the commercialization of government and culture and the growing importance of material acquisition and consumer lifestyles was hastened by the co-optation of potentially countervailing institutions, such as churches, . . . governments, schools, universities, and nongovernmental organizations."

2. Research the marketing strategies of a major business, perhaps one mentioned in this chapter. Assess what you see as its successes and/or failures in promoting its products.

3. Select a particular product (such as automobiles, cosmetics, clothing, or beer) or a particular target population (such as children, overweight women, or the elderly) and research the market strategies used by major companies for that particular product or group.

4. Research the recent advertising campaign of a major corporation whose product poses a threat to the environment or to human health and well-being.

5. Research the subject of American consumerism and arrive at your own conclusion about its effects on Americans and American values. This is a broad subject, so look for ways to narrow your focus as quickly as you can.

6. Research the impact of suburban malls on city-center or small "Mom and Pop," neighborhood businesses.

RESPONDING TO VISUALS

A pedestrian looks at an advertisement featuring Eva Longoria at the New York & Co. store on Lexington Ave in New York, Thursday, Dec. 1, 2005. New York & Co.'s November same-store sales rose 13% as the company's merchandise assortments and advertising campaign helped boost traffic.

1. How does the ad make use of the fame of actress Eva Longoria? How effective do you find celebrity endorsement as a selling tool?
2. In what ways does the advertisement use sex to sell its product?
3. What details of the advertisement do you find persuasive? Does it matter that even though the window advertises a sale on sweaters, Eva Longoria is apparently wearing nothing as she enjoys her bubble bath?

RESPONDING TO VISUALS

©AP Photo/Scott Sady

Shoppers pass through the checkout counters of the Wal-Mart Supercenter in Reno, Nevada, July 7, 2003.

1. What is your first impression of this picture? Which details contribute to that impression?
2. What impressions of Wal-Mart are conveyed by viewing the store from this perspective?
3. Find details in the photograph that indicate this is a "supercenter."

CHAPTER

24

The Workplace

The workplace can have enormous influence on people's lives. Most Americans work outside the home, either full-time or part-time, spending significant portions of their lives on the job. The physical atmosphere of the workplace, the friendliness of coworkers, wages and benefits, and the attitudes of supervisors or bosses play pivotal roles not only in the way workers perform but also in the way they feel about themselves. Tension, anxiety, and stress in the workplace can lower production for the company and produce actual illnesses in workers, whereas a pleasant atmosphere, good benefits, and relatively low stress can boost production and make employees look forward to going to work. The quality of life in the workplace has a direct effect on the quality of work employees do and on their general well being.

If, like most college students, you have had a job or are currently working, think about your own experiences as a worker. Do you feel a sense of community in your workplace? Is your work fun? Tedious? Challenging? How would you characterize the relationship between management and employees where you work (or have worked)? Is what you earn adequate enough to meet your financial needs? Do you have benefits with your job? These questions all relate to the quality of your work experience, and how you answer them reveals a great deal about your workplace.

The first essay in this chapter focuses on an issue of particular importance for mothers who work outside the home. In "You've Been Mommified," Ellen Goodman looks at "family responsibility discrimination," specifically discrimination against women workers who are also mothers. Suggesting that such women are looked at almost as a "third gender," she reports on the findings of a research center on worklife law and on the results of a study to determine if there is a "motherhood penalty in the job market." Given that a large portion of women in the workforce also have children, this subject is a compelling one. As you read Goodman's piece, think about the women you know who are mothers and work outside the home. Does what Goodman says ring true to your own observations or even your own experience?

Then Judith Warner takes up the subject of working mothers who wish that they could afford to work part time, but in the course of her piece expands her focus to include all workers. In "The Full-Time Blues," she notes that most part-time work does not have the pay and benefits to make it a viable choice for those women who prefer not to work full time because of the demands of family. In proposing solutions to the problem, Warner calls for the adoption of the kind of family-friendly practices and even legislation currently operative in many European countries. Consider whether you agree with her that flexible scheduling, better benefits and pay for part-time workers, or even paid family leave would benefit all workers, male or female, with or without children.

Next, Terry Golway's "Rewriting the Old Rules" suggests that, despite women's advancement in the corporate world, too often women have had to adopt male values. Using the example of women lawyers, he argues that a "macho" work ethic has been imposed on women. Golway notes: "In fact, in nearly every profession, in every factory, workers are expected to think of their lives and their jobs as one, to the detriment of family, friends, outside interests and other small pleasures." Such an ethic, he believes, should be replaced by one that values a balance of work and life. As you read his discussion about the demands that some professions place on their employees, think about your own employment future. Are you willing to follow what he calls the traditional business model, one that affects both male and female workers? Is your college education preparing you for the kind of work life that Golway says men and women must accept in order to succeed?

The chapter ends with an excerpt from Barbara Ehrenreich's *Nickel and Dimed: On (Not) Getting By in America.* Ehrenreich worked for a month each in three different areas of the United States to discover how full-time, year-round workers earning poverty-level wages manage to get by. The selection included here, "Serving in Florida," describes her experiences looking for a place to live, finding a job, and surviving on her earnings as a waitress at a restaurant in Key West. Although wages have increased in the decade since Ehrenreich's research, so have living expenses. Her findings are surely as relevant today as they were in 1998 because millions of workers still toil at low-wage, dead-end jobs.

YOU'VE BEEN MOMMIFIED

Ellen Goodman

Ellen Goodman began her career as a reporter for Newsweek, *worked for a time at the* Detroit Free Press, *and became a columnist for the* Boston Globe *in 1967. Her column, "At Large," has been syndicated by the* Washington Post *Writers Group since 1976. In 1980, she won a Pulitzer Prize for distinguished commentary. She has published a study of human change,* Turning Points *(1979), and many of her columns have been collected in* Close to Home *(1979),* At Large *(1981),* Keeping in Touch *(1985),* Making Sense *(1989),* Value Judgments *(1993), and* Paper Trail *(2004). She is author, with Patricia O'Brien, of* I Know Just What You Mean: The Power of Friendship in Women's Lives *(2000). This article was published in the May 10, 2007, issue of the* Boston Globe.

It's become a Mother's Day tradition on a par with candy, flowers and guilt. While advertisers wax poetically about the priceless work of motherhood, economists tally up the paycheck for the services she performs.

This year, salary.com estimates the value of a full-time mom at $138,095, up 3 percent from last year. The monetary value of a second-shift mom is $85,939, on top of her day job.

But, alas, the check is not in the mail. Nor will mom find it next to the maple syrup on her bed tray. Motherhood is what the economists call a monopsony, a job for which there is only one employer. And it's a rare child who's saved up to fill mom's piggybank, let alone a 401(k).

4   The real story of the Mother's Day economy is less rosy. This is what to expect when you are expecting—expecting to be a mom and a paid worker at the same time. You can expect to be mommified.

Mothers are still treated as if they were a third gender in the workplace. Among people ages 27 to 33 who have never had children, women's earnings approach 98 percent of men's. Many women will hit the glass ceiling, but many more will crash into the maternal wall.

Here's a Mother's Day card from a study just published by Shelley Correll in the American Journal of Sociology. Correll performed an experiment to see if there was a motherhood penalty in the job market. She and her colleagues at Cornell University created an ideal job applicant with a successful track record, an uninterrupted work history, a boffo resume, the whole deal.

Then they tucked a little telltale factoid into some of the resumes with a tip-off about mom-ness. It described her as an officer in a parent-teacher association. And—zap—she was mommified.

8   Moms were seen as less competent and committed. Moms were half as likely to be hired as childless women or men with or without kids. Moms were offered $11,000 less in starting pay than non-moms. And, just for good measure, they were also judged more harshly for tardiness.

"Just the mention of the PTA had that effect," says Correll. "Imagine the effect of a two-year absence from the work force or part-time work."

If this is true in the lab, it's true in real life. Joan C. Williams, who runs the Center for WorkLife Law at Hastings Law School, says discrimination against women may have gone underground but "the discrimination against mothers is breathtakingly open. Mothers are told, 'You belong at home with the kids, you're fired.'"

In the stories from the center's hot line and in the growing case law they've accumulated on family responsibility discrimination, you hear about women overtly denied promotions for having a child, told to have an abortion to keep a job, or rejected for a new job because "it was incompatible with being a mother." Family emergencies are treated differently than other timeouts. And things are at least as bad for dads when they take on mommy's work of caregiving.

12   I'm not suggesting that mothers quit the PTA, hide the kids or even sue, although the 400 percent increase in FRD suits has, um, raised some corporate consciousness. But at the very least, we have to turn the story line around.

No, mothers are not actually a third gender. More than 80 percent of American women have children and 80 percent of those are employed by the time their kids are 12. The reality of the workplace affects us all.

The much-touted mommy wars are as useful in solving our problems as a circular firing squad. And tales of women "opting out" of professional careers squeeze out the tales of women being pushed out.

As for the idea that women's lives are an endless array of choices? Williams says ruefully, "An awful lot of what gets interpreted as a mother's choice to drop out is really a 'take this job and shove it' reaction by mothers who encounter discrimination."

16   How many mothers would choose to spend more time at home if the fear of re-entry weren't so daunting? How many would choose to stay in the work force except for one sick child, one snow day, one emergency room visit? And how many dads would choose to live up to their own family ideals?

On Mother's Day 2007 there is still a deep-seated bias that puts the image of a "good mother" at odds with that of an "ideal worker." Until we wrestle down the beliefs and the rules of the workplace, our annual homage to the family values keeper will be as sentimental as this year's $138,095 paycheck.

PERSONAL RESPONSE

How would you define a "'good mother'" and an "'ideal worker'" (paragraph 17). Do you believe that the two are incompatible?

QUESTIONS FOR CLASS OR SMALL-GROUP DISCUSSION

1. What do you understand Goodman to mean by the term "mommified" (title and paragraph 7)?

2. How effective do you find Goodman's opening paragraphs about the monetary value of a full-time mother? How do they relate to her central idea?

3. Define in your own words what you believe the terms "glass ceiling" and "maternal wall" mean (paragraph 5).

4. Discuss whether you agree with Goodman when she says that "the reality of the workplace affects us all" (paragraph 13).

THE FULL-TIME BLUES

Judith Warner

Judith Warner writes the "Domestic Disturbances" column for the New York Times *and is the host of "The Judith Warner Show" on XM Satellite Radio. She is also the author of the best-selling biography* Hillary Clinton: The Inside Story *(1993);* You Have the Power: How to Take Back Our Country and Restore Democracy to America *(with Howard Dean) (2004); and* Perfect Madness: Motherhood in the Age of Anxiety *(2005). A former special correspondent for* Newsweek *in Paris, she reviews books for the* New York Times *and has written about politics and women's issues for magazines including the* New Republic *and* Elle. *This piece was published in the July 24, 2007, issue of the* New York Times.

The news from the Pew Research Center this month—that 60 percent of working mothers say they'd prefer to work part time—was barely out before it was sucked up into the fetid air of the mommy wars, with all the usual talk on "opting out" and guilting out, and the usual suspects lining up to slug it out on morning talk TV.

But the conversation we should be having these days really isn't one about What Mothers Want. (This has been known for years; surveys dating back to the early 1990s have shown that up to 80 percent of mothers—working and at-home alike—consistently say they wish they could work part time.) The interesting question is, rather, why they're not getting it.

Only 24 percent of working mothers now work part time. The reason so few do isn't complicated: most women can't afford to. Part-time work doesn't pay.

4   Women on a reduced schedule earn almost 18 percent less than their full-time female peers with equivalent jobs and education levels, according to research by Janet Gornick, a professor of sociology and political science at City University of New York, and the labor economist Elena Bardasi. Part-time jobs rarely come with benefits. They tend to be clustered in low-paying fields like the retail and service industries. And in better-paid professions, a reduced work schedule very often can mean cutting down from 50-plus hours a week to 40-odd—hardly a "privilege" worth paying for with a big pay cut.

It doesn't have to be this way. In Europe, significant steps have been made to make part-time work a livable reality for those who seek it. Denying fair pay and benefits to part-time workers is now illegal. Parents in Sweden have the right to work a six-hour day at prorated pay until their children turn 8 years old. Similar legislation helps working parents in France, Austria, and Belgium and any employee in Germany and the Netherlands who wants to cut back.

Even Britain has a (comparatively tame) pro-family law that guarantees parents and other caregivers the right to request a flexible schedule from their employers. European employers have the right to refuse workers' requests, but research shows that very few actually do. And workers have the right to appeal the denials.

None of this creates a perfect world. Feminists have long been leery of part-time work policies, which tend to be disproportionately used by women, mommy-tracking them and placing them at an economic disadvantage within their marriages and in society. The American model of work-it-out-for-yourself employment is Darwinian, but women's long working hours have gone a long way toward helping them advance up the career ladder.

8   "We know that family-friendly policies encourage work force participation," says Professor Gornick, who has extensively studied family policy on both sides of the Atlantic. "But do they lower the glass ceiling or make it thicker? That's the million-euro question."

I think that when it comes to setting priorities for (currently nonexistent) American work-family policy, we ought to go for the greatest good for the greatest number.

The place to start, ideally, would be universal health care, which is really the necessary condition for making freedom of choice a reality for working parents. European-style regulations outlawing wage and benefit discrimination against part-time workers would be nice, too, though it's not a terribly realistic goal for the U.S., where even unpaid family leave is still a hot-button issue for employers.

A British-style "soft touch" law could, however, be within the realm of the possible. Senator Edward Kennedy and Representative Carolyn Maloney are circulating draft legislation modeled on the British workplace flexibility law that would give employees—all workers, not just moms or parents—the right to request a flexible schedule. The legislation—which would require employers to discuss flexibility with workers who request it, but wouldn't require them to honor the requests—has a little bit of something for everyone: protection from retaliation for workers who fear letting on that they're eager to cut back, protection from "unfunded mandates" for businesses.

12   Critics might say the proposed legislation's touch is so soft as to be almost imperceptible, but it's a start. At the very least, it's a chance to stop emoting about maternal love and war and guilt and have a productive conversation.

PERSONAL RESPONSE

Discuss whether you think the United States should make it illegal to deny fair pay and benefits to part-time workers, as some European countries have done.

QUESTIONS FOR CLASS OR SMALL-GROUP DISCUSSION

1. Comment on the effectiveness as an argumentative strategy of Warner's use of statistics in the first four paragraphs.

2. What do you think the term "mommy-tracking" means in the context of paragraph 7? What does Warner mean by the term "Darwinian" (paragraph 7)?

3. How likely do you think it is that the United States will enact universal health care, as some European countries have done (paragraph 10)?

4. To what extent are you convinced by Warner's proposal that the United States enact a law "modeled on the British workplace flexibility law" (paragraph 11)? Do you agree that flexibility in scheduling would be a good option for all employees to have available to them?

REWRITING THE OLD RULES

TERRY GOLWAY

Terry Golway, columnist and city editor of the New York Observer *and a frequent columnist for* America *magazine, is author of* Irish Rebel: John Devoy and America's Fight for Ireland's Freedom *(1998);* For the Cause of Liberty: The Story of Ireland's Heroes *(2000);* Full of Grace: An Oral Biography of John Cardinal O'Connor *(2001);* So Others Might Live: A History of New York's Bravest: The FDNY from 1700 to the Present *(2002);*

Washington's General: Nathanael Greene and the Triumph of the American Revolution *(2005); and, with Robert Dallek,* Let Every Nation Know *(2006). This essay was originally published in the April 23, 2001, issue of* America.

Women are about to outnumber men in the nation's law schools, a development heralding yet another milestone for women and a foreshadowing of great cultural change in the way law is practiced in this country.

There can be no doubt about the former. The latter may not be so easy.

Women have been breaking through glass ceilings in the workplace for more than 30 years, and with each new achievement (the first woman to run for national office, to pilot the space shuttle, to serve as attorney general), society has changed for the better. Young girls now have role models in fields ranging from politics to the sciences to professional sports. Can there be any doubt that historians will one day agree that the civil rights movement and the women's movement were among the transforming events of the 20th century?

4   What these historians will say about the impact of women in the workforce, however, remains to be seen. At the moment, it would be fair to argue that women have not changed the American workplace as much as the workplace has changed women.

Take law, for example. Even with women pouring into law firms across the country, the macho culture of the partner track remains undisturbed. Young men and women still are obliged to perform high-end penal servitude if they wish to become partners at a white-shoe, big-city law firm. Yes, they get paid startling amounts of money—first-year associates in New York during the recently departed boom were commanding salaries approaching six figures—but they are expected to work absurd hours. It is the law culture's equivalent of boot camp, except that the military puts its new recruits through only a few months of terror, while the fresh-faced associate can expect to spend his or her 20's living and breathing for the firm and the firm alone. At the end, of course, there are no guarantees. Those long hours and work-filled weekends may be for naught, at which time an associate had best look for work elsewhere.

Not to make any sweeping generalizations, but only a man could have come up with so ruthless a scheme.

We can be grateful that some law firms have begun to concede that their associates are entitled to a life outside the office and, under pressure from women, have adopted measures like flex-time and part-time work. For the most part, however, the remorseless, endless paper chase remains a signature part of big-time law's partner track culture.

8   It isn't only law, however, that remains in the thrall of the otherwise discredited macho ethic. In fact, in nearly every profession, in every factory, workers are expected to think of their lives and their jobs as one, to the detriment of family, friends, outside interests and other small pleasures.

Despite the historic entry of millions of women into the workforce, the workplace rules and traditions that men enforce and celebrate have not been repealed. The hoary custom of measuring one's dedication, value and, yes, toughness by the number of hours logged per week hasn't changed. And managers still shake their heads disapprovingly when, in the phrase of one former colleague, a "clockwatcher" begins packing up at 5 P.M. The clockwatcher might have children who need help with homework, or an aged parent to care for, or an anniversary to celebrate. Under the rules of the macho workplace, however, those who let such considerations get in the way of all work, all the time, are considered slackers.

The global marketplace and the technological revolution have made matters worse for those trying to balance their work lives with real life. For millions of workers, there is no escape from professional obligations. I know men and women who feel obliged to bring along their laptop computers when they are on "vacation"—a concept, incidentally, that is beginning to be thought of as yet another outdated ritual from the industrial age. I've been out to dinner with men and women who keep their cell phones ready on the table, just in case the boss (and the boss is not always a male) wants to reach them.

Recent data indicate that the culture of overwork is pervasive in American society. A survey conducted by the National Sleep Association found that 40 percent of the 1,004 adults polled said they worked longer hours than they did five years ago. The average work-week, according to the poll, was 46 hours, but 38 percent said they worked 50 hours or more a week. And then there are those, like the well-dressed fellow who sat next to me on the commuter train the other day, who keep working even when they're home. My seatmate put aside his work-related reading material to call his wife (from his cell phone) to make sure everybody at home knew he needed to use the family computer after dinner. Something to do with developments in the Asian markets.

12   Is it sexist to suggest that women—at least most women I know—have a far saner perspective on the balance between work and life? I hope not. I certainly believe it's true.

For the time being, women probably have little choice but to adhere to the old rules written by corporate America's macho men. But as more women gain power in corporate America, they will have a chance to rewrite the old rules and abolish the macho-overwork ethic for good.

Or so this macho-challenged male hopes.

PERSONAL RESPONSE

Does it surprise you that a man wrote this essay? Do you think that your response to the essay would be any different were the author a woman?

QUESTIONS FOR CLASS OR SMALL-GROUP DISCUSSION

1. Explain your understanding of what Golway means when he refers to "the workplace rules and traditions that men enforce and celebrate" (paragraph 9), that is, what he calls "the macho culture" (paragraph 5).
2. Golway writes that women "have a far saner perspective on the balance between work and life" (paragraph 12). What do you think he means? In what ways might women have "a saner perspective" than men?

3. Golway refers to women's "breaking through glass ceilings" (paragraph 3). Does he explain that phrase clearly? What examples, other than the ones he mentions, can you give to illustrate it?

4. How effective do you think Golway's final paragraphs and especially his final sentence are? Do they bring the piece to a satisfying conclusion?

SERVING IN FLORIDA

Barbara Ehrenreich

Barbara Ehrenreich's articles appear in a variety of popular magazines and newspapers, including Time, *the* Progressive, Ms., *and the* New York Times, *among many others. Her books include* Witches, Midwives, and Nurses: A History of Women Healers *(with Deirdre English) (1973)*; Hearts of Men: American Dreams and the Flight from Commitment *(1984);* For Her Own Good: 150 Years of the Experts' Advice to Women *(with Deirdre English) (1989);* Blood Rites: Origins and History of the Passions of War *(1997);* Fear of Falling: The Inner Life of the Middle Class *(2000);* Nickel and Dimed: On (Not) Getting By in America *(2001);* Global Woman, *a collection of essays co-edited with Arlie Russell Hochschild (2002);* Bait and Switch: The (Futile) Pursuit of the American Dream *(2006); and* Dancing in the Streets: A History of Collective Joy *(2007). Reprinted here is an excerpt from* Nickel and Dimed.

Mostly out of laziness, I decide to start my low-wage life in the town nearest to where I actually live, Key West, Florida, which with a population of about 25,000 is elbowing its way up to the status of a genuine city. The downside of familiarity, I soon realize, is that it's not easy to go from being a consumer, thoughtlessly throwing money around in exchange for groceries and movies and gas, to being a worker in the very same place. I am terrified, especially at the beginning, of being recognized by some friendly business owner or erstwhile neighbor and having to stammer out some explanation of my project. Happily, though, my fears turn out to be entirely unwarranted: during a month of poverty and toil, no one recognizes my face or my name, which goes unnoticed and for the most part unuttered. In this parallel universe where my father never got out of the mines and I never got through college, I am "baby," "honey," "blondie," and, most commonly, "girl."

My first task is to find a place to live. I figure that if I can earn $7 an hour—which, from the want ads, seems doable—I can afford to spend $500 on rent or maybe, with severe economies, $600 and still have $400 or $500 left over for food and gas. In the Key West area, this pretty much confines me to flophouses and trailer homes—like the one, a pleasing fifteen-minute drive from town, that has no air-conditioning, no screens, no fans, no television, and, by way of diversion, only the challenge of evading the landlord's Doberman pinscher. The big problem with this place, though, is the rent, which at $675 a month is well beyond my reach. All right, Key West is expensive. But so is New York City, or the Bay Area, or Jackson, Wyoming, or Telluride, or Boston, or any other place where tourists and the wealthy compete for living space with the people who clean their toilets and fry their hash browns. Still, it is a shock to realize that "trailer trash" has become, for me, a demographic category to aspire to.

So I decide to make the common trade-off between affordability and convenience and go for a $500-a-month "efficiency" thirty miles up a two-lane highway from the employment opportunities of Key West, meaning forty-five minutes if there's no road construction and I don't get caught behind some sun-dazed Canadian tourists. I hate the drive, along a roadside studded with white crosses commemorating the more effective head-on collisions, but it's a sweet little place—a cabin, more or less, set in the swampy backyard of the converted mobile home where my landlord, an affable TV repairman, lives with his bartender girlfriend. Anthropologically speaking, the trailer park would be preferable, but here I have a gleaming white floor and a firm mattress, and the few resident bugs are easily vanquished.

4   The next piece of business is to comb through the want ads and find a job. I rule out various occupations for one reason or another: hotel front-desk clerk, for example, which to my surprise is regarded as unskilled and pays only $6 or $7 an hour gets eliminated because it involves standing in one spot for eight hours a day. Waitressing is also something I'd like to avoid, because I remember it leaving me bone-tired when I was eighteen, and I'm decades of varicosities and back pain beyond that now. Telemarketing, one of the first refuges of the suddenly indigent, can be dismissed on grounds of personality. This leaves certain supermarket jobs, such as deli clerk, or housekeeping in the hotels and guest houses, which pays about $7 and, I imagine, is not too different from what I've been doing part-time, in my own home, all my life.

So I put on what I take to be a respectable-looking outfit of ironed Bermuda shorts and scooped-neck T-shirt and set out for a tour of the local hotels and supermarkets. Best Western, Econo Lodge, and HoJo's all let me fill out application forms, and these are, to my relief, mostly interested in whether I am a legal resident of the United States and have committed any felonies. My next stop is Winn-Dixie, the supermarket, which turns out to have a particularly onerous application process, featuring a twenty-minute "interview" by computer since, apparently, no human on the premises is deemed capable of representing the corporate point of view. I am conducted to a large room decorated with posters illustrating how to look "professional" (it helps to be white and, if female, permed) and warning of the slick promises that union organizers might try to tempt me with. The interview is multiple-choice: Do I have anything, such as child care problems, that might make it hard for me to get to work on time? Do I think safety on the job is the responsibility of management? Then, popping up cunningly out of the blue: How many dollars' worth of stolen goods have I purchased in the last year? Would I turn in a fellow employee if I caught him stealing? Finally, "Are you an honest person?"

Apparently I ace the interview, because I am told that all I have to do is show up in some doctor's office tomorrow for a urine test. This seems to be a fairly general rule: if you want to stack Cheerios boxes or vacuum hotel rooms in chemically fascist America, you have to be willing to squat down and pee in front of a health worker (who has no doubt had to do the same thing herself.)[1] The wages Winn-Dixie is offering—$6 and a couple of dimes to start with—are not enough, I decide, to compensate for this indignity.

I lunch at Wendy's, where $4.99 gets you unlimited refills at the Mexican part of the Super-bar, a comforting surfeit of refried beans and cheese sauce. A teenage employee, seeing me studying the want ads, kindly offers me an application form, which I fill out, though here, too, the pay is just $6 and change an hour. Then it's off for a round of the locally owned inns and guest houses in Key West's Old Town, which is where all the serious sightseeing and guzzling goes on, a couple of miles removed from the functional end of the island, where the discount hotels make their homes. At The Palms, let's call it, a bouncy manager actually takes me around to see the rooms and meet the current housekeepers, who, I note with satisfaction, look pretty much like me—faded ex-hippie types in shorts with long hair pulled back in braids. Mostly, though, no one speaks to me or even looks at me except to proffer an application form. At my last stop, a palatial B & B, I wait twenty minutes to meet "Max," only to be told that there are no jobs now but there should be one soon, since "nobody lasts more than a couple weeks."

8   Three days go by like this and, to my chagrin, no one from the approximately twenty places at which I've applied calls me for an interview. I had been vain enough to worry about coming across as too educated for the jobs I sought, but no one even seems interested in finding out how overqualified I am. Only later will I realize that the want ads are not a reliable measure of the actual jobs available at any particular time. They are, as I should have guessed from Max's comment, the employers' insurance policy against the relentless turnover of the low-wage workforce. Most of the big hotels run ads almost continually, if only to build a supply of applicants to replace the current workers as they drift away or are fired, so finding a job is just a matter of being in the right place at the right time and flexible enough to take whatever is being offered that day. This finally happens to me at one of the big discount chain hotels where I go, as usual, for housekeeping and am sent instead to try out as a waitress at the attached "family restaurant," a dismal spot looking out on a parking garage, which is featuring "Polish sausage and BBQ sauce" on this 95-degree day. Phillip, the dapper young West Indian who introduces himself as the manager, interviews me with about as much enthusiasm as if he were a clerk processing me for Medicare, the principal questions being what shifts I can work and when I can start. I mutter about being woefully out of practice as a waitress, but he's already

---

[1]Eighty-one percent of large employers now require preemployment drug testing, up from 21 percent in 1987. Among all employers, the rate of testing is highest in the South. The drug most likely to be detected—marijuana, which can be detected weeks after use—is also the most innocuous, while heroin and cocaine are generally undetectable three days after use. Alcohol, which clears the body within hours after ingestion, is not tested for.

on to the uniform: I'm to show up tomorrow wearing black slacks and black shoes; he'll provide the rust-colored polo shirt with "Hearthside," as we'll call the place, embroidered on it, though I might want to wear my own shirt to get to work, ha ha. At the word *tomorrow*, something between fear and indignation rises in my chest. I want to say, "Thank you for your time, sir, but this is just an experiment, you know, not my actual life."

So begins my career at the Hearthside, where for two weeks I work from 2:00 till 10:00 P.M. for $2.43 an hour plus tips.[2] Employees are barred from using the front door, so I enter the first day through the kitchen, where a red-faced man with shoulder-length blond hair is throwing frozen steaks against the wall and yelling, "Fuck this shit!" "That's just Billy," explains Gail, the wiry middle-aged waitress who is assigned to train me. "He's on the rag again"—a condition occasioned, in this instance, by the fact that the cook on the morning shift had forgotten to thaw out the steaks. For the next eight hours, I run after the agile Gail, absorbing bits of instruction along with fragments of personal tragedy. All food must be trayed, and the reason she's so tired today is that she woke up in a cold sweat thinking of her boyfriend, who was killed a few months ago in a scuffle in an upstate prison. No refills on lemonade. And the reason he was in prison is that a few DUIs caught up with him, that's all, could have happened to anyone. Carry the creamers to the table in a "monkey bowl," never in your hand. And after he was gone she spent several months living in her truck, peeing in a plastic pee bottle and reading by candlelight at night, but you can't live in a truck in the summer, since you need to have the windows down, which means anything can get in, from mosquitoes on up.

At least Gail puts to rest any fears I had of appearing overqualified. From the first day on, I find that of all the things that I have left behind, such as home and identity, what I miss the most is competence. Not that I have ever felt 100 percent competent in the writing business, where one day's success augurs nothing at all for the next. But in my writing life, I at least have some notion of *procedure:* do the research, make the outline, rough out a draft, etc. As a server, though, I am beset by requests as if by bees: more iced tea here, catsup over there, a to-go box for table 14, and where are the high chairs, anyway? Of the twenty-seven tables, up to six are usually mine at any time, though on slow afternoons or if Gail is off, I sometimes have the whole place to myself. There is the touch-screen computer-ordering system to master, which I suppose is meant to minimize server-cook contacts but in practice requires constant verbal fine-tuning: "That's gravy on the mashed, OK? None on the meatloaf," and so forth. Plus, something I had forgotten in the years since I was eighteen: about a third of a server's job is "side work" invisible to customers—sweeping, scrubbing, slicing, refilling, and restocking. If it isn't all done, every little

---

[2]According to the Fair Labor Standards Act, employers are not required to pay "tipped employees," such as restaurant servers, more than $2.13 an hour in direct wages. However, if the sum of tips plus $2.13 an hour falls below the minimum wage, or $5.15 an hour, the employer is required to make up the difference. This fact was not mentioned by managers or otherwise publicized at either of the restaurants where I worked.

bit of it, you're going to face the 6:00 P.M. dinner rush defenseless and probably go down in flames. I screw up dozens of times at the beginning, sustained in my shame entirely by Gail's support—"It's OK, baby, everyone does that sometime"—because, to my total surprise and despite the scientific detachment I am doing my best to maintain, I *care.*

The whole thing would be a lot easier if I could just skate through it like Lily Tomlin in one of her waitress skits, but I was raised by the absurd Booker T. Washingtonian precept that says: If you're going to do something, do it well. In fact, "well" isn't good enough by half. Do it better than anyone has ever done it before. Or so said my father, who must have known what he was talking about because he managed to pull himself, and us with him, up from the mile-deep copper mines of Butte to the leafy suburbs of the Northeast, ascending from boilermakers to martinis before booze beat out ambition. As in most endeavors I have encountered in my life, "doing it better than anyone" is not a reasonable goal. Still, when I wake up at 4 A.M. in my own cold sweat, I am not thinking about the writing deadlines I'm neglecting; I'm thinking of the table where I screwed up the order and one of the kids didn't get his kiddie meal until the rest of the family had moved on to their Key lime pies. That's the other powerful motivation—the customers, or "patients," as I can't help thinking of them on account of the mysterious vulnerability that seems to have left them temporarily unable to feed themselves. After a few days at Hearthside, I feel the service ethic kick in like a shot of oxytocin, the nurturance hormone. The plurality of my customers are hardworking locals—truck drivers, construction workers, even housekeepers from the attached hotel—and I want them to have the closest to a "fine dining" experience that the grubby circumstances will allow. No "you guys" for me; everyone over twelve is "sir" or "ma'am." I ply them with iced tea and coffee refills; I return, midmeal, to inquire how everything is; I doll up their salads with chopped raw mushrooms, summer squash slices, or whatever bits of produce I can find that have survived their sojourn in the cold storage room mold-free.

12   There is Benny, for example, a short, tight-muscled sewer repairman who cannot even think of eating until he has absorbed a half hour of air-conditioning and ice water. We chat about hyperthermia and electrolytes until he is ready to order some finicky combination like soup of the day, garden salad, and a side of grits. There are the German tourists who are so touched by my pidgin *"Wilkommen"* and *"Ist alles gut?"* that they actually tip. (Europeans, no doubt spoiled by their trade union-ridden, high-wage welfare states, generally do not know that they are supposed to tip. Some restaurants, the Hearthside included, allow servers to "grat" their foreign customers, or add a tip to the bill. Since this amount is added before the customers have a chance to tip or not tip, the practice amounts to an automatic penalty for imperfect English.) There are the two dirt-smudged lesbians, just off from their shift, who are impressed enough by my suave handling of the fly in the piña colada that they take the time to praise me to Stu, the assistant manager. There's Sam, the kindly retired cop who has to plug up his tracheotomy hole with one finger in order to force the cigarette smoke into his lungs.

Sometimes I play with the fantasy that I am a princess who, in penance for some tiny transgression, has undertaken to feed each of her subjects by hand. But the nonprincesses working with me are just as indulgent, even when this means flouting management rules—as to, for example, the number of croutons that can go on a salad (six). "Put on all you want," Gail whispers "as long as Stu isn't looking." She dips into her own tip money to buy biscuits and gravy for an out-of-work mechanic who's used up all his money on dental surgery, inspiring me to pick up the tab for his pie and milk. Maybe the same high levels of agape can be found throughout the "hospitality industry." I remember the poster decorating one of the apartments I looked at, which said, "If you seek happiness for yourself you will never find it. Only when you seek happiness for others will it come to you," or words to that effect—an odd sentiment, it seemed to me at the time, to find in the dank one-room basement apartment of a bellhop at the Best Western. At Hearthside, we utilize whatever bits of autonomy we have to ply our customers with the illicit calories that signal our love. It is our job as servers to assemble the salads and desserts, pour the dressings, and squirt the whipped cream. We also control the number of butter pats our customers get and the amount of sour cream on their baked potatoes. So if *you* wonder why Americans are so obese, consider the fact that waitresses both express their humanity and earn their tips through the covert distribution of fats.

Ten days into it, this is beginning to look like a livable lifestyle. I like Gail, who is "looking at fifty," agewise, but moves so fast she can alight in one place and then another without apparently being anywhere between. I clown around with Lionel, the teenage Haitian busboy, though we don't have much vocabulary in common, and loiter near the main sink to listen to the older Haitian dishwashers' musical Creole, which sounds, in their rich bass voices, like French on testosterone. I bond with Timmy, the fourteen-year-old white kid who buses at night, by telling him I don't like people putting their baby seats right on the tables: it makes the baby look too much like a side dish. He snickers delightedly and in return, on a slow night, starts telling me the plots of all the *Jaws* movies (which are perennial favorites in the shark-ridden Keys): "She looks around, and the water-skier isn't there anymore, then SNAP! The whole boat goes . . ."

I especially like Joan, the svelte fortyish hostess, who turns out to be a militant feminist, pulling me aside one day to explain that "men run everything—we don't have a chance unless we stick together." Accordingly, she backs me up when I get overpowered on the floor, and in return I give her a chunk of my tips or stand guard while she sneaks off for an unauthorized cigarette break. We all admire her for standing up to Billy and telling him, after some of his usual nastiness about the female server class, to "shut the fuck up." I even warm up to Billy when, on a slow night and to make up for a particularly unwarranted attack on my abilities, or so I imagine, he tells me about his glory days as a young man at "coronary school" in Brooklyn, where he dated a knockout Puerto Rican chick—or do you say "culinary"?

16   I finish up every night at 10:00 or 10:30, depending on how much side work I've been able to get done during the shift, and cruise home to the tapes I snatched at random when I left my real home—Marianne Faithfull, Tracy Chapman, Enigma, King Sunny Adé, Violent Femmes—just drained enough for the music to

set my cranium resonating, but hardly dead. Midnight snack is Wheat Thins and Monterey Jack, accompanied by cheap white wine on ice and whatever AMC has to offer. To bed by 1:30 or 2:00, up at 9:00 or 10:00, read for an hour while my uniform whirls around in the landlord's washing machine, and then it's another eight hours spent following Mao's central instruction as laid out in the Little Red Book, which was: Serve the people.

I could drift along like this, in some dreamy proletarian idyll, except for two things. One is management. If I have kept *this* subject to the margins so far it is because I still flinch to think that I spent all those weeks under the surveillance of men (and later women) whose job it was to monitor my behavior for signs of sloth, theft, drug abuse, or worse. Not that managers and especially "assistant managers" in low-wage settings like this are exactly the class enemy. Mostly, in the restaurant business, they are former cooks still capable of pinch-hitting in the kitchen, just as in hotels they are likely to be former clerks, and paid a salary of only about $400 a week. But everyone knows they have crossed over to the other side, which is, crudely put, corporate as opposed to human. Cooks want to prepare tasty meals, servers want to serve them graciously, but managers are there for only one reason—to make sure that money is made for some theoretical entity, the corporation, which exists far away in Chicago or New York, if a corporation can be said to have a physical existence at all. Reflecting on her career, Gail tells me ruefully that she swore, years ago, never to work for a corporation again. "They don't cut you no slack. You give and you give and they take."

Managers can sit—for hours at a time if they want—but it's their job to see that no one else ever does, even when there's nothing to do, and this is why, for servers, slow times can be as exhausting as rushes. You start dragging out each little chore because if the manager on duty catches you in an idle moment he will give you something far nastier to do. So I wipe, I clean, I consolidate catsup bottles and recheck the cheesecake supply, even tour the tables to make sure the customer evaluation forms are all standing perkily in their places—wondering all the time how many calories I burn in these strictly theatrical exercises. In desperation, I even take the desserts out of their glass display case and freshen them up with whipped cream and bright new maraschino cherries; anything to look busy. When, on a particularly dead afternoon, Stu finds me glancing at a *USA Today* a customer has left behind, he assigns me to vacuum the entire floor with the broken vacuum cleaner, which has a handle only two feet long, and the only way to do that without incurring orthopedic damage is to proceed from spot to spot on your knees.

On my first Friday at Hearthside there is a "mandatory meeting for all restaurant employees," which I attend, eager for insight into our overall marketing strategy and the niche (your basic Ohio cuisine with a tropical twist?) we aim to inhabit. But there is no "we" at this meeting. Phillip, our top manager except for an occasional "consultant" sent out by corporate headquarters, opens it with a sneer: "The break room—it's disgusting. Butts in the ashtrays, newspapers lying around, crumbs." This windowless little room, which also houses the time clock for the entire hotel, is where we stash our bags and civilian clothes and take our half-hour meal breaks.

But a break room is not a right, he tells us, it can be taken away. We should also know that the lockers in the break room and whatever is in them can be searched at any time. Then comes gossip; there has been gossip; gossip (which seems to mean employees talking among themselves) must stop. Off-duty employees are henceforth barred from eating at the restaurant, because "other servers gather around them and gossip." When Philip has exhausted his agenda of rebukes, Joan complains about the condition of the ladies' room and I throw in my two bits about the vacuum cleaner. But I don't see any backup coming from my fellow servers, each of whom has slipped into her own personal funk; Gail, my role model, stares sorrowfully at a point six inches from her nose. The meeting ends when Andy, one of the cooks, gets up, muttering about breaking up his day off for this almighty bullshit.

20   Just four days later we are suddenly summoned into the kitchen at 3:30 P.M., even though there are live tables on the floor. We all—about ten of us—stand around Philip, who announces grimly that there has been a report of some "drug activity" on the night shift and that, as a result, we are now to be a "drug-free" workplace, meaning that all new hires will be tested and possibly also current employees on a random basis. I am glad that this part of the kitchen is so dark because I find myself blushing as hard as if I had been caught toking up in the ladies' room myself: I haven't been treated this way—lined up in the corridor, threatened with locker searches, peppered with carelessly aimed accusations—since at least junior high school. Back on the floor, Joan cracks, "Next they'll be telling us we can't have *sex* on the job." When I ask Stu what happened to inspire the crackdown, he just mutters about "management decisions" and takes the opportunity to upbraid Gail and me for being too generous with the rolls. From now on there's to be only one per customer and it goes out with the dinner, not with the salad. He's also been riding the cooks, prompting Andy to come out of the kitchen and observe—with the serenity of a man whose customary implement is a butcher knife—that "Stu has a death wish today."

Later in the evening, the gossip crystallizes around the theory that Stu is himself the drug culprit, that he uses the restaurant phone to order up marijuana and sends one of the late servers out to fetch it for him. The server was caught and she may have ratted out Stu, at least enough to cast some suspicion on him, thus accounting for his pissy behavior. Who knows? personally, I'm ready to believe anything bad about Stu, who serves no evident function and presumes too much on our common ethnicity, sidling up to me one night to engage in a little nativism directed at the Haitian inimigrants: "I feel like I'm the foreigner here. They're taking over the country." Still later that evening, the drug in question escalates to crack. Lionel, the busboy, entertains us for the rest of the shift by standing just behind Stu's back and sucking deliriously on an imaginary joint or maybe a pipe.

The other problem, in addition to the less-than-nurturing management style, is that this job shows no sign of being financially viable. You might imagine, from a comfortable distance, that people who live, year in and year out, on $6 to $10 an hour have discovered some survival stratagems unknown to the middle class. But no. It's not hard to get my coworkers talking about their living situations, because housing, in almost every case, is the principal source of disruption in their lives, the first thing they fill you in on when they arrive for their shifts. After a week, I have compiled the following survey:

> Gail is sharing a room in a well-known downtown flophouse for $250 a week. Her roommate, a male friend, has begun hitting on her, driving her nuts, but the rent would be impossible alone.

> Claude, the Haitian cook, is desperate to get out of the two-room apartment he shares with his girlfriend and two other unrelated people. As far as I can determine, the other Haitian men live in similarly crowded situations.

> Annette, a twenty-year-old server who is six months pregnant and abandoned by her boyfriend, lives with her mother, a postal clerk.

> Marianne, who is a breakfast server, and her boyfriend are paying $170 a week for a one-person trailer.

> Billy, who at $10 an hour is the wealthiest of us, lives in the trailer he owns, paying only the $400-a-month lot fee.

> The other white cook, Andy, lives on his dry-docked boat, which, as far as I can tell from his loving descriptions, can't be more than twenty feet long. He offers to take me out on it once it's repaired, but the offer comes with inquiries as to my marital status, so I do not follow up on it.

> Tina, another server, and her husband are paying $60 a night for a room in the Days Inn. This is because they have no car and the Days Inn is in walking distance of the Hearthside. When Marianne is tossed out of her trailer for subletting (which is against trailer park rules), she leaves her boyfriend and moves in with Tina and her husband.

> Joan, who had fooled me with her numerous and tasteful outfits (hostesses wear their own clothes), lives in a van parked behind a shopping center at night and showers in Tina's motel room. The clothes are from thrift shops.[3]

It strikes me, in my middle-class solipsism, that there is gross improvidence in some of these arrangements. When Gail and I are wrapping silverware in napkins—the only task for which we are permitted to sit—she tells me she is thinking of escaping from her roommate by moving into the Days Inn herself. I am astounded: how she can even think of paying $40 to $60 a day? But if I was afraid of sounding like a social worker, I have come out just sounding like a fool. She squints at me in disbelief: "And where am I supposed to get a month's rent and a

---

[3] I could find no statistics on the number of employed people living in cars or vans, but according to a 1997 report of the National Coalition for the Homeless, "Myths and Facts about Homelessness," nearly one-fifth of all homeless people (in twenty-nine cities across the nation) are employed in full- or part-time jobs.

month's deposit for an apartment?" I'd been feeling pretty smug about my $500 efficiency, but of course it was made possible only by the $1,300 I had allotted myself for start-up costs when I began my low-wage life: $1,000 for the first month's rent and deposit, $100 for initial groceries and cash in my pocket, $200 stuffed away for emergencies. In poverty, as in certain propositions in physics, starting conditions are everything.

24   There are no secret economies that nourish the poor; on the contrary, there are a host of special costs. If you can't put up the two months' rent you need to secure an apartment, you end up paying through the nose for a room by the week. If you have only a room, with a hot plate at best, you can't save by cooking up huge lentil stews that can be frozen for the week ahead. You eat fast food or the hot dogs and Styrofoam cups of soup that can be microwaved in a convenience store. If you have no money for health insurance—and the Hearthside's niggardly plan kicks in only after three months—you go without routine care or prescription drugs and end up paying the price. Gail, for example, was doing fine, healthwise anyway, until she ran out of money for estrogen pills. She is supposed to be on the company health plan by now, but they claim to have lost her application form and to be beginning the paperwork all over again. So she spends $9 a pop for pills to control the migraines she wouldn't have, she insists, if her estrogen supplements were covered. Similarly, Marianne's boyfriend lost his job as a roofer because he missed so much time after getting a cut on his foot for which he couldn't afford the prescribed antibiotic.

My own situation, when I sit down to assess it after two weeks of work, would not be much better if this were my actual life. The seductive thing about waitressing is that you don't have to wait for payday to feel a few bills in your pocket, and my tips usually cover meals and gas, plus something left over to stuff into the kitchen drawer I use as a bank. But as the tourist business slows in the summer heat, I sometimes leave work with only $20 in tips (the gross is higher, but servers share about 15 percent of their tips with the busboys and bartenders). With wages included, this amounts to about the minimum wage of $5.15 an hour. The sum in the drawer is piling up but at the present rate of accumulation will be more than $100 short of my rent when the end of the month comes around. Nor can I see any expenses to cut. True, I haven't gone the lentil stew route yet, but that's because I don't have a large cooking pot, potholders, or a ladle to stir with (which would cost a total of about $30 at Kmart, somewhat less at a thrift store), not to mention onions, carrots, and the indispensable bay leaf. I do make my lunch almost every day—usually some slow-burning, high-protein combo like frozen chicken patties with melted cheese on top and canned pinto beans on the side. Dinner is at the Hearthside, which offers its employees a choice of BLT, fish sandwich, or hamburger for only $2. The burger lasts longest, especially if it's heaped with gut-puckering jalapeños, but by midnight my stomach is growling again.

So unless I want to start using my car as a residence, I have to find a second or an alternative job. I call all the hotels I'd filled out housekeeping applications at weeks ago—the Hyatt, Holiday Inn, Econo Lodge, HoJo's, Best Western, plus a half dozen locally run guest houses. Nothing. Then I start making the rounds again, wasting whole mornings waiting for some assistant manager to show up, even dipping into places so creepy that the front-desk clerk greets you from behind bulletproof glass and sells pints of liquor over the counter. But either someone has exposed my real-life housekeeping habits—which are, shall we say, mellow—or I am at the wrong end of some infallible ethnic equation: most, but by no means all, of the working housekeepers I see on my job searches are African Americans, Spanish-speaking, or refugees from the Central European post-Communist world, while servers are almost invariably white and monolingually English-speaking. When I finally get a positive response, I have been identified once again as server material. Jerry's—again, not the real name—which is part of a well-known national chain and physically attached here to another budget hotel, is ready to use me at once. The prospect is both exciting and terrifying because, with about the same number of tables and counter seats, Jerry's attracts three or four times the volume of customers as the gloomy old Hearthside.

PERSONAL RESPONSE

Write about any aspect of Ehrenreich's experiences that reminds you of your own experience looking for work, finding affordable housing, or earning enough to meet your living expenses.

QUESTIONS FOR CLASS OR SMALL-GROUP DISCUSSION

1. What strategies does Ehrenreich use to convey a genuine sense of "poverty and toil" during her period of working in Key West (paragraph 1)?

2. What details does Ehrenreich give that might help explain "the relentless turnover of the low-wage workforce" (paragraph 8)? What overall impression do you have of life as a low-wage worker after reading this excerpt from her book?

3. What do you understand Ehrenreich to mean by the phrase "service ethic" (paragraph 11)? What is the purpose of her reference to Mao at the end of this excerpt?

4. Comment on Ehrenreich's use of specific individuals when describing her coworkers and customers. What do they add to her general description of her job and the people she works with?

○ PERSPECTIVES ON THE WORKPLACE ○

Suggested Writing Topics

1. Ellen Goodman in "You've Been Mommified" writes that "there is still a deep-seated bias that puts the image of a 'good mother' at odds with that of an 'ideal worker'" (paragraph 17). Define each of those terms and explain whether you agree that there is a still a bias.

2. Select one of these phrases from Ehrenreich's "Serving in Florida" and define it: "chemically fascist America" (paragraph 6), or "service ethic" (paragraph 11).

3. Explain what you value most in a job and why. Is it having fun, making lots of money, meeting challenges, or some other aspect of it? Or conduct your own informal interview on the subject of expectations for a job and report your results.

4. Drawing on at least one of the essays in this chapter, describe what you see as the ideal job or ideal working conditions.

5. Describe your work experiences and the extent to which self-satisfaction or self-motivation contributes to your performance.

6. Argue in support of or against the contention made by many workers and implied by a couple of the authors in this chapter that employers unfairly violate the basic rights of workers. Read Barbara Ehrenreich's *Nickel and Dimed: On (Not) Getting By in America* and write a critique of it.

7. Argue in support of or against drug testing in the workplace.

8. Write an essay explaining whether you believe this statement by Terry Golway in "Rewriting the Old Rules" to be true: "Women have been breaking through glass ceilings in the workplace [. . .] and with each new achievement [. . .] society has changed for the better" (paragraph 3).

Research Topics

1. Both Ellen Goodman and Judith Warner use the term "mommy wars" ("You've Been Mommified," paragraph 14; "The Full-Time Blues," paragraph 1). Research the subject of the "mommy wars," report your conclusions, and, if possible, take a position on the subject.

2. Research the topic of "family responsibility discrimination" (Ellen Goodman's "You've Been Mommified," paragraph 11).

3. Research the "European-style regulations outlawing wage and benefit discrimination against part-time workers" referred to by Judith Warner in "The Full-Time Blues" (paragraph 10) and argue whether you think the United States ought to have such a goal and, if so, whether it could realistically attain it.

4. Combine library research and personal interviews with area employers on the subject of employer attitudes toward female employees with children. Then report your conclusions.

5. Terry Golway in "Rewriting the Old Rules" suggests that women's ways of doing things are "saner" than men's ways. Research this topic, including interviews, if possible.

6. Research the topic of the effect of workplace environment on employee productivity and morale.

7. Research the subject of the right to free speech or the right to privacy in the work place.

8. Research workers' perceptions of their work places. If possible, interview people who work full-time about their work place experiences and combine the results of your interview(s) with your other sources.

RESPONDING TO VISUALS

A waitress carries plates of food from the kitchen at Jimmy's Grille in Bridgeville, Delaware.

1. How does the photographer give the impression of movement?
2. How does the photographer convey the stress of the woman's job?
3. What emotions does the server's face reveal?

RESPONDING TO VISUALS

©FogStock LLC/Index Open

Working mother with baby in arms, home office.

1. What image of working at home does the photograph convey?
2. What do the looks on the faces of both mother and child suggest about how each felt at the moment the photograph was taken?
3. What details of the photograph convey the tensions between being simultaneously a mother and a worker?
4. Do you think that companies should accommodate working parents?

CHAPTER

25

The Economic Impact of Outsourcing

Throughout the twentieth century, American wholesalers and retailers imported goods that were made abroad. American consumers were used to seeing the words "made in China" or "made in Taiwan," for instance, on the products that they purchased. Then, it became popular in the last decades of the century for American manufacturers to either outsource the labor to make their products in a foreign country or physically to move abroad. Workers in other countries could be hired to make parts and/or assemble products at wages considerably less than what manufacturers would have to pay workers in the United States, and many American manufacturers found it just as cost-effective to relocate their factories. Central and South America were particularly appealing for such moves because transportation of the products into the United States was fairly easy.

Now, with the development of high-tech telecommunications and the globalization of the economy, many businesses are outsourcing their work to countries all over the world, or they are offshoring completely. Now not only Central and South America, but also India, Eastern Europe, North and South Africa, Asia Pacific, and New Zealand have all become outsourcing centers for American businesses.

The practice of outsourcing—that is, hiring people outside one's own company to do work previously done on-site, or offshoring, physically relocating to another country—has always been subject to criticism from American workers and consumers. These critics charge that it is unethical, unfair, and damaging to the U.S. economy. Its defenders point out that such a practice is highly beneficial to the company's economic health. The articles in this chapter look at both sides of the issue and explore some of the economic benefits and drawbacks of offshore outsourcing.

First, Michael Mandel, in a *BusinessWeek* cover story, examines the data on U.S. economy and concludes that there is "a gaping flaw in the way statistics treat offshoring." This flaw, he maintains, has "serious economic and political implications." Offshoring to low-cost countries, he maintains, creates what *BusinessWeek* calls "phantom GDP." The article raises some intriguing questions, though Mandel admits that it is not clear whether the figure *BusinessWeek* arrives at for the amount that phantom GDP accounts for overstates or understates the seriousness of its impact.

In contrast to Mandel, Daniel W. Drezner argues in "The Outsourcing Bogeyman" that the uproar over the outsourcing of American jobs is both alarmist and damaging to the U.S. economy and American workers. He maintains that outsourcing actually brings far more benefits than costs, not just in the present but in the long run as well. Although his article was published in the 2004 election year in response to the allegations of politicians about the perceived threat of sending jobs overseas, the details of his argument are still relevant to any discussion of the pros and cons of outsourcing.

The other two pieces in this chapter look at specific aspects of the outsourcing controversy. "The Wal-Mart You Don't Know" by Charles Fishman examines the world's largest retailer in terms of what being able to offer products at low cost actually costs Wal-Mart's suppliers and the people who work for them. Wal-Mart exerts enormous pressure on its suppliers to outsource in order to sell at low wholesale prices to Wal-Mart. Fishman wonders, Are we shopping our way straight to the unemployment line? Then, Thomas L. Friedman in "30 Little Turtles" reports on his visit to a training center in India where young Indians are being taught to speak with a Canadian accent for their telephone service jobs. Friedman describes it as "an uplifting experience" and explains why he believes there is more to outsourcing than econom-ics: "There's also geopolitics."

THE REAL COST OF OFFSHORING

MICHAEL MANDEL

Michael Mandel is an economist and economic journalist. Currently chief economist for BusinessWeek *magazine, he is author of a number of books, including the following:* The High Risk Society*(1996);* The Coming Internet Depression *(2000); and* Rational Exuberance: Silencing the Enemies of Growth and Why the Future Is Better Than You Think *(2004). This article appeared in the June 18, 2007, issue of* BusinessWeek.

Whenever critics of globalization complain about the loss of American jobs to low-cost countries such as China and India, supporters point to the powerful perfor-mance of the U.S. economy. And with good reason. Despite the latest slow quarter, official statistics show that America's economic output has grown at a solid 3.3% annual rate since 2003, a period when imports from low-cost countries have soared. Similarly, domestic manufacturing output has expanded at a decent pace. On the face of it, offshoring doesn't seem to be having much of an effect at all.

But new evidence suggests that shifting production overseas has inflicted worse damage on the U.S. economy than the numbers show. *BusinessWeek* has learned of a gaping flaw in the way statistics treat offshoring, with serious economic and politi-cal implications. Top government statisticians now acknowledge that the problem exists, and say it could prove to be significant.

The short explanation is that the growth of domestic manufacturing has been substantially overstated in recent years. That means productivity gains and overall economic growth have been overstated as well. And that raises questions about U.S. competitiveness and "helps explain why wage growth for most American workers has been weak," says Susan N. Houseman, an economist at the W.E. Upjohn Insti-tute for Employment Research who identifies the distorting effects of offshoring in a soon-to-be-published paper.

Fly in the Ointment

4 The underlying problem is located in an obscure statistic: the import price data published monthly by the Bureau of Labor Statistics (BLS). Because of it, many of the cost cuts and product innovations being made overseas by global compa-nies and foreign suppliers aren't being counted properly. And that spells trouble because, surprisingly, the government uses the erroneous import price data directly and indirectly as part of its calculation for many other major economic statistics,

including productivity, the output of the manufacturing sector, and real gross domestic product (GDP), which is supposed to be the inflation-adjusted value of all the goods and services produced inside the U.S.

The result? *BusinessWeek*'s analysis of the import price data reveals offshoring to low-cost countries is in fact creating "phantom GDP"—reported gains in GDP that don't correspond to any actual domestic production. The only question is the magnitude of the disconnect. "There's something real here, but we don't know how much," says J. Steven Landefeld, director of the Bureau of Economic Analysis (BEA), which puts together the GDP figures. Adds Matthew J. Slaughter, an economist at the Amos Tuck School of Business at Dartmouth College who until last February was on President George W. Bush's Council of Economic Advisers: "There are potentially big implications. I worry about how pervasive this is."

By *BusinessWeek*'s admittedly rough estimate, offshoring may have created about $66 billion in phantom GDP gains since 2003. That would lower real GDP today by about half of 1%, which is substantial but not huge. But put another way, $66 billion would wipe out as much as 40% of the gains in manufacturing output over the same period.

It's important to emphasize the tenuousness of this calculation. In particular, it required *BusinessWeek* to make assumptions about the size of the cost savings from offshoring, information the government doesn't even collect.

Getting Worse

8   As a result, the actual size of phantom GDP could be a lot larger, or perhaps smaller. This estimate mainly focuses on the shift of manufacturing overseas. But phantom GDP can be created by the introduction of innovative new imported products or by the offshoring of research and development, design, and services as well—and there aren't enough data in those areas to take a stab at a calculation. "As these [low-cost] countries move up the value chain, the problem becomes worse and worse," says Jerry A. Hausman, a top economist at Massachusetts Institute of Technology. "You've put your finger on a real problem."

Alternatively, as Landefeld notes, the size of the overstatement could be smaller. One possible offset: Machinery and high-tech equipment shipped directly to businesses from foreign suppliers may generate less phantom GDP, just because of the way the numbers are constructed.

Depending on your attitude toward offshoring, the existence of phantom GDP is either testimony to the power of globalization or confirmation of long-held fears. The U.S. economy no longer stops at the water's edge. Global corporations often provide their foreign suppliers and overseas subsidiaries with business knowledge, management practices, training, and all sorts of other intangible exports not picked up in the government data. In return, they get back cheap products.

But the new numbers also require a reassessment of productivity and wages that could add fire to the national debate over the true performance of the economy in President Bush's second term. The official statistics show that productivity, or output per hour, grew at a 1.8% rate over the past three years. But taking the phantom GDP effect into account, the actual rate of productivity growth might be closer to 1.6%—about what it was in the 1980s.

12 More broadly, it becomes clear that "gains from trade are being measured instead of productivity," according to Robert C. Feenstra, an economist at the University of California at Davis and the director of the international trade and investment program at the National Bureau of Economic Research. "This has been missed."

  Pat Byrne, the global managing partner of Accenture Ltd.'s (**ACN**) supply-chain management practice, goes even further, suggesting that "at least half of U.S. productivity [growth] has been because of globalization." But quantifying this is tough, he notes, because most companies don't look at how much of their productivity growth is onshore and how much is offshore. "I don't know of any companies or industries that have tried to measure this. Maybe they don't even want to know."

  Phantom GDP helps explain why U.S. workers aren't benefiting more as their companies grow ever more efficient. The cost savings that companies are reaping "don't represent increased productivity of American workers producing goods and services in the U.S.," says Houseman. In contrast, compensation of senior executives is typically tied to profits, which have soared alongside offshoring.

Importing Earnings

But where are those vigorous corporate profits coming from? The strong earnings growth of U.S.-based corporations is still real, but it may be that fewer of the gains are coming from improvements in domestic productivity. In fact, holding down costs by moving key tasks overseas could be having a greater impact on corporate earnings than anyone guessed—or measured.

16 There are investing implications, too, although those are harder to quantify. Companies with their primary focus in the U.S. might suddenly seem less attractive, since underlying economic growth is slower here than the numbers show. But if the statistical systems of other developed countries suffer from the same problem—and they might—then growth in Europe and Japan might be overstated, too.

  When Houseman first uncovered the problem with the numbers that is created by offshoring, she was primarily focused on manufacturing productivity, where the official stats show a 32% increase since 2000. But while some of the gains may be real, they also include unlikely productivity jumps in heavily outsourced industries such as furniture and audio and video equipment such as televisions. "In some sectors, productivity growth may be an indicator not of how competitive American workers are in international markets," says Houseman, "but rather of how cost-uncompetitive they are." For example, furniture manufacturing has been transformed by offshoring in recent years. Imports have surged from $17.2 billion in 2000 to $30.3 billion in 2006, with virtually all of that increase coming from low-cost China. And the industry has lost 21% of its jobs during the same period.

  Yet Washington's official statistics show that productivity per hour in the furniture industry went up by 23% and output by 3% between 2000 and 2005. Those numbers baffle longtime industry consultant Arthur Raymond of Raleigh, N.C., who has watched factory after factory close. "And we haven't pumped any money into the remaining plants," says Raymond. "How anybody can say that domestic production has stayed level is beyond me."

Wrenching Process

Paul B. Toms Jr., CEO of publicly traded Hooker Furniture Corp., (HOFT) recently closed his company's last remaining domestic wood-furniture manufacturing plant, in Martinsville, Va. It was the culmination of a wrenching process that started in 2000, when Hooker still made the vast majority of its products in the U.S. Toms didn't want to go overseas, he says, but he couldn't pass up the 20% to 25% savings to be gleaned from manufacturing there.

20   The lure of offshoring works the same way for large companies. Byrne of Accenture is working with a "major transportation equipment company" that's planning to offshore more than half of its parts procurement over the next few years. Most of it will go to China. "We're talking about 30% to 40% cost reductions," says Byrne.

Yet no matter how hard you look, you can't find any trace of the cost savings from offshoring in the import price statistics. The furniture industry's experience is particularly telling. Despite the surge of low-priced chairs, tables, and similar products from China, the BLS is reporting that the import price of furniture has actually risen 6.7% since 2003.

The numbers for Chinese imports as a whole are equally out of step with reality. Over the past three years, total imports have climbed by 89%, as U.S.-based companies have rushed to take advantage of the enormous cost advantages. Yet over the same period, the import price index for goods coming out of China has declined a mere 2.3%.

Facade of Growth

The import price index also misses the cost cut when production of an item, such as blue jeans, is switched from a country such as Mexico to a cheaper country like China. That's especially likely to happen if the item goes through a different importer when it comes from a new country, because government statisticians have no way of linking the blue jeans made in China with the same pair that had been made in Mexico.

24   Phantom GDP can also be created in import-dependent industries with fast product cycles, because the import price statistics can't keep up with the rapid pace of change. And it can happen when foreign suppliers take on tasks such as product design without raising the price. That's an effective cost cut for the American purchaser, but the folks at the BLS have no way of picking it up.

The effects of phantom GDP seem to be mostly concentrated in the past three years, when offshoring has accelerated. Indeed, the first time the term appeared in *BusinessWeek* was in 2003. Before then, China and India in particular were much smaller exporters to the U.S.

The one area where phantom GDP may have made an earlier appearance is information technology. Outsourcing of production to Asia really took hold in the late 1990s, after the Information Technology Agreement of 1997 sharply cut the duties on IT equipment. "At least a portion of the productivity improvement in the late 1990s ought to be attributed to falling import prices," says Feenstra of UC Davis, who along with Slaughter and two other co-authors has been examining this question.

What does phantom GDP mean for policymakers? For one thing, it calls into question the economic statistics that the Federal Reserve uses to guide monetary policy. If domestic productivity growth has been overstated for the past few years, that suggests the nation's long-term sustainable growth rate may be lower than thought, and the Fed may have less leeway to cut rates.

28   In terms of trade policy, the new perspective suggests the U.S. may have a worse competitiveness problem than most people realized. It was easy to downplay the huge trade deficit as long as it seemed as though domestic growth was strong. But if the import boom is actually creating only a facade of growth, that's a different story. This lends more credence to corporate leaders such as CEO John Chambers of Cisco Systems Inc. (**CSCO**) who have publicly worried about U.S. competitiveness—and who perhaps coincidentally have been the ones leading the charge offshore.

In a broader sense, though, the problem with the statistics reveals that the conventional nation-centric view of the U.S. economy is completely obsolete. Nowadays we live in a world where tightly integrated supply chains are a reality.

For that reason, Landefeld of the BEA suggests perhaps part of the cost cuts from offshoring are being appropriately picked up in GDP. In some cases, intangible activities such as R&D and design of a new product or service take place in the U.S. even though the production work is done overseas. Then it may make sense for the gains in productivity in the supply chain to be booked to this country. Says Landefeld: "The companies do own those profits." Still, counters Houseman, "it doesn't represent a more efficient production of things made in this country."

What Landefeld and Houseman can agree on is that the rush of globalization has brought about a fundamental change in the U.S. economy. This is why the methods for measuring the economy need to change, too.

PERSONAL RESPONSE

What is your opinion of businesses moving jobs overseas? Do you think it has hurt the economy? Do you know anyone who has lost a job because of offshoring?

QUESTIONS FOR CLASS AND SMALL-GROUP DISCUSSION

1. State in your own words what Mandel says are the effects of erroneous input price data (paragraph 4).
2. What do you understand the term "phantom GPD" to be? What does Mandel say are the possible effects or over- or understating that figure? To

what extent are you convinced by Mandel's argument that the effects of phantom GDP are significant?

3. Summarize what Mandel argues are the possible effects of inaccurate import price statistics.

4. Although Mandel does not overtly discuss the broader implications of increased reliance on cheap imports, what do you think the effects are likely to be?

THE OUTSOURCING BOGEYMAN

Daniel W. Drezner

Daniel W. Drezner is associate professor of international politics at the Fletcher School of Law and Diplomacy at Tufts University. He has previously taught at the University of Chicago and the University of Colorado at Boulder. He is the author of All Politics is Global: Explaining International Regulatory Regimes *(2008);* U.S. Trade Policy: Free Versus Fair *(2006); and* The Sanctions Paradox *(1999). He is the editor of* Locating the Proper Authorities *(2003). Professor Drezner has published articles in numerous scholarly journals as well as the* New York Times, Washington Post, Wall Street Journal, Foreign Affairs, Foreign Policy, Reason, *and* Slate. *He has provided expert commentary on U.S. foreign policy and the global political economy for C-SPAN, CNNfn, CNN International, and ABC's* World News Tonight. *He keeps a daily weblog at www .danieldrezner.com. This article was published in the May/June 2004 issue of* Foreign Affairs. *Full references and data sources for it can be found at http://www.danieldrezner.com/archives/001155.html.*

The Truth Is Offshore

When a presidential election year coincides with an uncertain economy, campaigning politicians invariably invoke an international economic issue as a dire threat to the well-being of Americans. Speechwriters denounce the chosen scapegoat, the media provides blanket coverage of the alleged threat, and legislators scurry to introduce supposed remedies.

The cause of this year's commotion is offshore outsourcing—the alleged migration of American jobs overseas. The depth of alarm was strikingly illustrated by the firestorm of reaction to recent testimony by N. Gregory Mankiw, the head of President George W. Bush's Council of Economic Advisers. No economist really disputed Mankiw's observation that "outsourcing is just a new way of doing international trade," which makes it "a good thing." But in the political arena, Mankiw's comments sparked a furor on both sides of the aisle. Democratic presidential candidate John Kerry accused the Bush administration of wanting "to export more of our jobs overseas," and Senate Minority Leader Tom Daschle quipped, "If this is the administration's position, I think they owe an apology to every worker in America." Speaker of the House Dennis Hastert, meanwhile, warned that "outsourcing can be a problem for American workers and the American economy."

Critics charge that the information revolution (especially the Internet) has accelerated the decimation of U.S. manufacturing and facilitated the outsourcing of service-sector jobs once considered safe, from backroom call centers to high-level software programming. (This concern feeds into the suspicion that U.S. corporations are exploiting globalization to fatten profits at the expense of workers.) They are right that offshore outsourcing deserves attention and that some measures to assist affected workers are called for. But if their exaggerated alarmism succeeds in provoking protectionist responses from lawmakers, it will do far more harm than good, to the U.S. economy and to American workers.

4   Should Americans be concerned about the economic effects of outsourcing? Not particularly. Most of the numbers thrown around are vague, overhyped estimates. What hard data exist suggest that gross job losses due to offshore outsourcing have been minimal when compared to the size of the entire U.S. economy. The outsourcing phenomenon has shown that globalization can affect white-collar professions, heretofore immune to foreign competition, in the same way that it has affected manufacturing jobs for years. But Mankiw's statements on outsourcing are absolutely correct; the law of comparative advantage does not stop working just because 401(k) plans are involved. The creation of new jobs overseas will eventually lead to more jobs and higher incomes in the United States. Because the economy—and especially job growth—is sluggish at the moment, commentators are attempting to draw a connection between offshore outsourcing and high unemployment. But believing that offshore outsourcing causes unemployment is the economic equivalent of believing that the sun revolves around the earth: intuitively compelling but clearly wrong.

Should Americans be concerned about the political backlash to outsourcing? Absolutely. Anecdotes of workers affected by outsourcing are politically powerful, and demands for government protection always increase during economic slowdowns. The short-term political appeal of protectionism is undeniable. Scapegoating foreigners for domestic business cycles is smart politics, and protecting domestic markets gives leaders the appearance of taking direct, decisive action on the economy.

Protectionism would not solve the U.S. economy's employment problems, although it would succeed in providing massive subsidies to well-organized interest groups. In open markets, greater competition spurs the reallocation of labor and capital to more profitable sectors of the economy. The benefits of such free trade—to both consumers and producers—are significant. Cushioning this process for displaced workers makes sense. Resorting to protectionism to halt the process, however, is a recipe for decline. An open economy leads to concentrated costs (and diffuse benefits) in the short term and significant benefits in the long term. Protectionism generates pain in both the short term and the long term.

The Sky Is Falling

Outsourcing occurs when a firm subcontracts a business function to an outside supplier. This practice has been common within the U.S. economy for some time. (Witness the rise of large call centers in the rural Midwest.) The reduction of communication costs and the standardization of software packages have now made it possible to outsource business functions such as customer service, telemarketing, and document management. Other affected professions include medical transcription, tax preparation, and financial services.

8   The numbers that are bandied about on offshore outsourcing sound ominous. The McKinsey Global Institute estimates that the volume of offshore outsourcing will increase by 30 to 40 percent a year for the next five years. Forrester Research estimates that 3.3 million white-collar jobs will move overseas by 2015. According to projections, the hardest hit sectors will be financial services and information technology (IT). In one May 2003 survey of chief information officers, 68 percent of IT executives said that their offshore contracts would grow in the subsequent year. The Gartner research firm has estimated that by the end of this year, 1 out of every 10 IT jobs will be outsourced overseas. Deloitte Research predicts the outsourcing of 2 million financial-sector jobs by 2009.

At first glance, current macroeconomic indicators seem to support the suspicion that outsourcing is destroying jobs in the United States. The past two years have witnessed moderate growth and astonishing productivity gains, but overall job growth has been anemic. The total number of manufacturing jobs has declined for 43 consecutive months. Surely, many observers insist, this must be because the jobs created by the U.S. recovery are going to other countries. Morgan Stanley analyst Stephen Roach, for example, has pointed out that "this is the first business cycle since the advent of the Internet—the enabler of a new real-time connectivity to low-cost offshore labor pools." He adds, "I don't think it's a coincidence that this jobless recovery has occurred in such an environment." Those who agree draw on anecdotal evidence to support this assertion. CNN's Lou Dobbs routinely harangues U.S. companies engaged in offshore outsourcing in his "Exporting America" series.

Many IT executives have themselves contributed to this perception. When IBM announced plans to outsource 3,000 jobs overseas this year, one of its executives said, "[Globalization] means shifting a lot of jobs, opening a lot of locations in places we had never dreamt of before, going where there's low-cost labor, low-cost competition, shifting jobs offshore." Nandan Nilekani, the chief executive of the India-based Infosys Technologies, said at this year's World Economic Forum, "Everything you can send down a wire is up for grabs." In January testimony before Congress, Hewlett-Packard chief Carly Fiorina warned that "there is no job that is America's God-given right anymore."

That last statement chills the blood of most Americans. Few support the cause of free trade for its own sake, out of pure principle. The logic underlying an open economy is that if the economy sheds jobs in uncompetitive sectors, employment in competitive sectors will grow. If hi-tech industries are no longer competitive, where will new jobs be created?

Inside the Numbers

12   Before answering that question, Americans need to separate fact from fiction. The predictions of job losses in the millions are driving the current outsourcing hysteria. But it is crucial to note that these predictions are of gross, not net, losses. During the 1990s, offshore outsourcing was not uncommon. (American Express, for one, set up back-office operations in India more than a decade ago.) But no one much cared because the number of jobs leaving U.S. shores was far lower than the number of jobs created in the U.S. economy.

Similarly, most current predictions are not as ominous as they first sound once the numbers are unpacked. Most jobs will remain unaffected altogether: close to 90 percent of jobs in the United States require geographic proximity. Such jobs include everything from retail and restaurants to marketing and personal care—services that have to be produced and consumed locally, so outsourcing them overseas is not an option. There is also no evidence that jobs in the high-value-added sector are migrating overseas. One thing that has made offshore outsourcing possible is the standardization of such business tasks as data entry, accounting, and IT support. The parts of production that are more complex, interactive, or innovative—including, but not limited to, marketing, research, and development—are much more difficult to shift abroad. As an International Data Corporation analysis on trends in IT services concluded, "the activities that will migrate offshore are predominantly those that can be viewed as requiring low skill since process and repeatability are key underpinnings of the work. Innovation and deep business expertise will continue to be delivered predominantly onshore." Not coincidentally, these are also the tasks that generate high wages and large profits and drive the U.S. economy.

As for the jobs that can be sent offshore, even if the most dire-sounding forecasts come true, the impact on the economy will be negligible. The Forrester prediction of 3.3 million lost jobs, for example, is spread across 15 years. That would mean 220,000 jobs displaced per year by offshore outsourcing—a number that sounds impressive until one considers that total employment in the United States is roughly 130 million, and that about 22 million new jobs are expected to be added between now and 2010. Annually, outsourcing would affect less than .2 percent of employed Americans.

There is also reason to believe that the unemployment caused by outsourcing will be lower than expected. Gartner assumed that more than 60 percent of financial-sector employees directly affected by outsourcing would be let go by their employers. But Boston University Professor Nitin Joglekar has examined the effect of outsourcing on large financial firms and found that less than 20 percent of workers affected by outsourcing lose their jobs; the rest are repositioned within the firm. Even if the most negative projections prove to be correct, then, gross job loss would be relatively small.

16   Moreover, it is debatable whether actual levels of outsourcing will ever match current predictions. Despite claims that the pace of onshore and offshore outsourcing would quicken over time, there was no increase in 2003. In fact, TPI Inc., an outsourcing advisory firm, even reports that the total value of business process outsourcing deals in the United States fell by 32 percent in 2003.

There is no denying that the number of manufacturing jobs has fallen dramatically in recent years, but this has very little do with outsourcing and almost everything to do with technological innovation. As with agriculture a century ago, productivity gains have outstripped demand, so fewer and fewer workers are needed for manufacturing. If outsourcing were in fact the chief cause of manufacturing losses, one would expect corresponding increases in manufacturing employment in developing countries. An Alliance Capital Management study of global manufacturing trends from 1995 to 2002, however, shows that this was not the case: the United States saw an 11 percent decrease in manufacturing employment over the course of those seven years; meanwhile, China saw a 15 percent decrease and Brazil a 20 percent decrease. Globally, the figure for manufacturing jobs lost was identical to the U.S. figure—11 percent. The fact that global manufacturing output increased by 30 percent in that same period confirms that technology, not trade, is the primary cause for the decrease in factory jobs. A recent analysis of employment data from U.S. multinational corporations by the U.S. Department of Commerce reached the same conclusion.

What about the service sector? Again, the data contradict the popular belief that U.S. jobs are being lost to foreign countries without anything to replace them. In the case of many low-level technology jobs, the phenomenon has been somewhat exaggerated. For example, a Datamonitor study found that global call-center operations are being outsourced at a slower rate than previously thought—only five percent are expected to be located offshore by 2007. Dell and Lehman Brothers recently moved some of their call centers back to the United States from India because of customer complaints. And done properly, the offshore outsourcing of call centers creates new jobs at home. Delta Airlines outsourced 1,000 call-center jobs to India in 2003, but the $25 million in savings allowed the firm to add 1,200 reservation and sales positions in the United States.

Offshore outsourcing is similarly counterbalanced by job creation in the high-end service sector. An Institute for International Economics analysis of Bureau of Labor Statistics employment data revealed that the number of jobs in service sectors where outsourcing is likely actually increased, even though total employment decreased by 1.7 percent. According to the Bureau of Labor Statistics "Occupation Outlook Handbook," the number of IT-related jobs is expected to grow 43 percent by 2010. The case of IBM reinforces this lesson: although critics highlight the offshore outsourcing of 3,000 IT jobs, they fail to mention the company's plans to add 4,500 positions to its U.S. payroll. Large software companies such as Microsoft and Oracle have simultaneously increased outsourcing and domestic payrolls.

20   How can these figures fit with the widespread perception that IT jobs have left the United States? Too often, comparisons are made to 2000, an unusual year for the technology sector because Y2K fears and the height of the dot-com bubble had pushed employment figures to an artificially high level. When 1999 is used as the starting point, it becomes clear that offshore outsourcing has not caused a collapse in IT hiring. Between 1999 and 2003, the number of jobs in business and financial operations increased by 14 percent. Employment in computer and mathematical positions increased by 6 percent.

It is also worth remembering that many predictions come from management consultants who are eager to push the latest business fad. Many of these consulting firms are themselves reaping commissions from outsourcing contracts. Much of the perceived boom in outsourcing stems from companies' eagerness to latch onto the latest management trends; like Dell and Lehman, many will partially reverse course once the hidden costs of offshore outsourcing become apparent.

If offshore outsourcing is not the cause of sluggish job growth, what is? A study by the Federal Reserve Bank of New York suggests that the economy is undergoing a structural transformation: jobs are disappearing from old sectors (such as manufacturing) and being created in new ones (such as mortgage brokering). In all such transformations, the creation of new jobs lags behind the destruction of old ones. In other words, the recent recession and current recovery are a more extreme version of the downturn and "jobless recovery" of the early 1990s—which eventually produced the longest economic expansion of the post-World War II era. Once the structural adjustments of the current period are complete, job growth is expected to be robust. (And indeed, current indicators are encouraging: there has been a net increase in payroll jobs and in small business employment since 2003 and a spike in IT entrepreneurial activity.)

Offshore outsourcing is undoubtedly taking place, and it will likely increase over the next decade. However, it is not the tsunami that many claim. Its effect on the U.S. economy has been exaggerated, and its effect on the U.S. employment situation has been grossly exaggerated.

The Upside of Outsourcing

24   To date, the media's coverage of outsourcing has focused on its perceived costs. This leaves out more than half of the story. The benefits of offshore outsourcing should not be dismissed.

The standard case for free trade holds that countries are best off when they focus on sectors in which they have a comparative advantage—that is, sectors that have the lowest opportunity costs of production. Allowing countries to specialize accordingly increases productivity across all countries. This specialization translates into cheaper goods, and a greater variety of them, for all consumers.

The current trend of outsourcing business processes overseas is comparative advantage at work. The main driver of productivity gains over the past decade has been the spread of information technology across the economy. The commodification of simple business services allows those benefits to spread further, making growth even greater.

The data affirm this benefit. Catherine Mann of the Institute for International Economics conservatively estimates that the globalization of IT production has boosted U.S. GDP by $230 billion over the past seven years; the globalization of IT services should lead to a similar increase. As the price of IT services declines, sectors that have yet to exploit them to their fullest—such as construction and health care—will begin to do so, thus lowering their cost of production and improving the quality of their output. (For example, cheaper IT could one day save lives by reducing the number of "adverse drug events." Mann estimates that adding bar codes to prescription drugs and instituting an electronic medical record system could reduce the annual number of such events by more than 80,000 in the United States alone.)

28   McKinsey Global Institute has estimated that for every dollar spent on outsourcing to India, the United States reaps between $1.12 and $1.14 in benefits. Thanks to outsourcing, U.S. firms save money and become more profitable, benefiting shareholders and increasing returns on investment. Foreign facilities boost demand for U.S. products, such as computers and telecommunications equipment, necessary for their outsourced function. And U.S. labor can be reallocated to more competitive, better-paying jobs; for example, although 70,000 computer programmers lost their jobs between 1999 and 2003, more than 115,000 computer software engineers found higher-paying jobs during that same period. Outsourcing thus enhances the competitiveness of the U.S. service sector (which accounts for 30 percent of the total value of U.S. exports). Contrary to the belief that the United States is importing massive amounts of services from low-wage countries, in 2002 it ran a $64.8 billion surplus in services.

Outsourcing also has considerable noneconomic benefits. It is clearly in the interest of the United States to reward other countries for reducing their barriers to trade and investment. Some of the countries where U.S. firms have set up outsourcing operations—including India, Poland, and the Philippines—are vital allies in the war on terrorism. Just as the North American Free Trade Agreement (NAFTA) helped Mexico deepen its democratic transition and strengthen its rule of law, the United States gains considerably from the political reorientation spurred by economic growth and interdependence.

Finally, the benefits of "insourcing" should not be overlooked. Just as U.S. firms outsource positions to developing countries, firms in other countries outsource positions to the United States. According to the Bureau of Labor Statistics, the number of outsourced jobs increased from 6.5 million in 1983 to 10 million in 2000. The number of insourced jobs increased even more in the same period, from 2.5 million to 6.5 million.

Political Economy

When it comes to trade policy, there are two iron laws of politics. The first is that the benefits of trade diffuse across the economy, but the costs of trade are concentrated. Thus, those made worse off by open borders will form the more motivated interest group. The second is that public hostility toward trade increases during economic downturns. When forced to choose between statistical evidence showing that trade is good for the economy and anecdotal evidence of job losses due to import competition, Americans go with the anecdotes.

32   Offshore outsourcing adds two additional political pressures. The first stems from the fact that technological innovation has converted what were thought to be nontradeable sectors into tradeable ones. Manufacturing workers have long been subject to the rigors of global competition. White-collar service-sector workers

are being introduced to these pressures for the first time—and they are not happy about it. As Raghuram Rajan and Luigi Zingales point out in "Saving Capitalism From the Capitalists," globalization and technological innovation affect professions such as law and medicine that have not changed all that much for centuries. Their political reaction to the threat of foreign competition will be fierce.

The second pressure is that the Internet has greatly facilitated political organization, making it much easier for those who blame outsourcing for their troubles to rally together. In recent years, countless organizations—with names such as Rescue American Jobs, Save U.S. Jobs, and the Coalition for National Sovereignty and Economic Patriotism—have sprouted up. Such groups have disproportionately focused on white-collar tech workers, even though the manufacturing sector has been much harder hit by the recent economic slowdown.

It should come as no surprise, then, that politicians are scrambling to get ahead of the curve. During the Democratic primary in South Carolina—a state hit hard by the loss of textile jobs—billboards asked voters, "Lost your job to free trade or offshore outsourcing yet?" Last Labor Day, President Bush pledged to appoint a manufacturing czar to get to the bottom of the outflow of manufacturing positions. In his stump speech, John Kerry bashes "Benedict Arnold CEOs [who] send American jobs overseas."

Where presidential candidates lead, legislators are sure to follow. Senator Charles Schumer (D-N.Y.) claimed in a January "New York Times" op-ed authored with Paul Craig Roberts that because of increased capital mobility, the law of comparative advantage is now null and void. Senator Tom Daschle (D-S.D.) has observed, "George Bush says the economy is creating jobs. But let me tell you, China is one long commute. And let me tell you, I'm tired of watching jobs shift overseas." Senator Christopher Dodd (D-Conn.) and Representative Nancy Johnson (R-Conn.) are sponsoring the USA Jobs Protection Act to prevent U.S. companies from hiring foreign workers for positions when American workers are available. In February, Senate Democrats announced their intentions to introduce the Jobs for America Act, requiring companies to give public notice three months in advance of any plan to outsource 15 or more jobs. In March, the Senate overwhelmingly approved a measure banning firms from federal contracts if they outsource any of the work overseas. In the past two years, more than 20 state legislatures have introduced bills designed to make various forms of offshore outsourcing illegal.

Splendid Isolation?

36   There are clear examples of jobs being sent across U.S. borders because of U.S. trade policy—but not for the reasons that critics of outsourcing believe. Consider the example of candy-cane manufacturers: despite the fact that 90 percent of the world's candy canes are consumed in the United States, manufacturers have sent much of their production south of the border in the past five years. The attraction of moving abroad, however, has little to do with low wages and much to do with protectionism. U.S. quotas on sugar imports have, in recent years, caused the domestic price of sugar to become 350 percent higher than world market prices. As candy makers

have relocated production to countries where sugar is cheaper, between 7,500 and 10,000 workers in the Midwest have lost their jobs—victims not of outsourcing but of the kind of protectionism called for by outsourcing's critics.

A similar story can be told of the steel tariffs that the Bush administration foolishly imposed from March 2002 until December 2003 (when a ruling by the World Trade Organization prompted their cancellation). The tariffs were allegedly meant to protect steelworkers. But in the United States, steel users employ roughly 40 times more people than do steel producers. Thus, according to estimates by the Institute for International Economics, between 45,000 and 75,000 jobs were lost because higher steel prices made U.S. steel-using industries less competitive.

These examples illustrate the problem with relying on anecdotes when debating the effects of offshore outsourcing. Anecdotes are incomplete narratives that fail to capture opportunity costs. In the cases of steel and sugar, the opportunity cost of using protectionism to save jobs was the much larger number of jobs lost in sectors rendered less productive by higher input prices. Trade protectionism amounts to an inefficient subsidy for uncompetitive sectors of the economy, which leads to higher prices for consumers and a lower rate of return for investors. It preserves jobs in less competitive sectors while destroying current and future jobs in sectors that have a comparative advantage. Thus, if barriers are erected to prevent offshore outsourcing, the overall effect will not be to create jobs but to destroy them.

So if protectionism is not the answer, what is the correct response? The best piece of advice is also the most difficult for elected officials to follow: do no harm. Politicians never get credit for inaction, even when inaction is the best policy. President George H.W. Bush, for example, was pilloried for refusing to follow Japan's lead by protecting domestic markets—even though his refusal helped pave the way for the 1990s boom by letting market forces allocate resources to industries at the technological frontier. Restraint is anathema to the political class, but it is still the most important response to the furor over offshore outsourcing. As Robert McTeer, president of the Federal Reserve Bank of Dallas, said when asked about policy responses to outsourcing, "If we are lucky, we can get through the year without doing something really, really stupid."

40   The problem of offshore outsourcing is less one of economics than of psychology—people feel that their jobs are threatened. The best way to help those actually affected, and to calm the nerves of those who fear that they will be, is to expand the criteria under which the Trade Adjustment Assistance (TAA) program applies to displaced workers. Currently, workers cannot apply for TAA unless overall sales or production in their sector declines. In the case of offshore outsourcing, however, productivity increases allow for increased production and sales—making TAA out of reach for those affected by it. It makes sense to rework TAA rules to take into account workers displaced by offshore outsourcing even when their former industries or firms maintain robust levels of production.

Another option would be to help firms purchase targeted insurance policies to offset the transition costs to workers directly affected by offshore outsourcing. Because the perception of possible unemployment is considerably greater than the actual likelihood of losing a job, insurance programs would impose a very small cost on firms while relieving a great deal of employee anxiety. McKinsey Global Institute estimates that such a scheme could be created for as little as four or five cents per dollar saved from offshore outsourcing. IBM recently announced the creation of a two-year, $25 million retraining fund for its employees who fear job losses from outsourcing. Having the private sector handle the problem without extensive government intervention would be an added bonus.

The Best Defense

Until robust job growth returns, the debate over outsourcing will not go away—the political temptation to scapegoat foreigners is simply too great.

The refrain of "this time, it's different" is not new in the debate over free trade. In the 1980s, the Japanese variety of capitalism—with its omniscient industrial policy and high nontariff barriers—was supposed to supplant the U.S. system. Fifteen years later, that prediction sounds absurd. During the 1990s, the passage of NAFTA and the Uruguay Round of trade talks were supposed to create a "giant sucking sound" as jobs left the United States. Contrary to such fears, tens of millions of new jobs were created. Once the economy improves, the political hysteria over outsourcing will also disappear.

44   It is easy to praise economic globalization during boom times; the challenge, however, is to defend it during the lean years of a business cycle. Offshore outsourcing is not the bogeyman that critics say it is. Their arguments, however, must be persistently refuted. Otherwise, the results will be disastrous: less growth, lower incomes—and fewer jobs for American workers.

PERSONAL RESPONSE

Are you convinced that it is alarmist to view outsourcing of American jobs as a problem?

QUESTIONS FOR CLASS OR SMALL-GROUP DISCUSSION

1. In paragraph 4, Drezner answers his question "Should Americans be concerned about the economic effects of outsourcing?" by saying "Not particularly." State in your own words the points he raises to support his position.

2. What benefits does Drezner say that outsourcing brings to the American economy and American workers? To what extent are you convinced by his argument that outsourcing actually brings far more benefits than costs?

3. Summarize Drezner's argument against protectionism. Do you agree with him that the consequences of a new wave of American protectionism would be disastrous for the American economy and workers?

4. What options does Drezner suggest in answer to his question, "So if protectionism is not the answer, what is the correct response?" Can you suggest other options?

THE WAL-MART YOU DON'T KNOW

CHARLES FISHMAN

Charles Fishman began his writing career at the Washington Post *and held positions on the* Orlando Sentinel *and* Raleigh News & Observer *before joining the staff of* Fast Company, *where he is a senior writer. Andrew Moesel provided research assistance for this story, which appeared in the December 2003 issue of* Fast Company.

A gallon-sized jar of whole pickles is something to behold. The jar is the size of a small aquarium. The fat green pickles, floating in swampy juice, look reptilian, their shapes exaggerated by the glass. It weighs 12 pounds, too big to carry with one hand. The gallon jar of pickles is a display of abundance and excess; it is entrancing, and also vaguely unsettling. This is the product that Wal-Mart fell in love with: Vlasic's gallon jar of pickles.

Wal-Mart priced it at $2.97—a year's supply of pickles for less than $3! "They were using it as a 'statement' item," says Pat Hunn, who calls himself the "mad scientist" of Vlasic's gallon jar. "Wal-Mart was putting it before consumers, saying, This represents what Wal-Mart's about. You can buy a stinkin' gallon of pickles for $2.97. And it's the nation's number-one brand."

Therein lies the basic conundrum of doing business with the world's largest retailer. By selling a gallon of kosher dills for less than most grocers sell a quart, Wal-Mart may have provided a service for its customers. But what did it do for Vlasic? The pickle maker had spent decades convincing customers that they should pay a premium for its brand. Now Wal-Mart was practically giving them away. And the fevered buying spree that resulted distorted every aspect of Vlasic's operations, from farm field to factory to financial statement.

4   Indeed, as Vlasic discovered, the real story of Wal-Mart, the story that never gets told, is the story of the pressure the biggest retailer relentlessly applies to its suppliers in the name of bringing us "every day low prices." It's the story of what that pressure does to the companies Wal-Mart does business with, to U.S. manufacturing, and to the economy as a whole. That story can be found floating in a gallon jar of pickles at Wal-Mart.

Wal-Mart is not just the world's largest retailer. It's the world's largest company—bigger than ExxonMobil, General Motors, and General Electric. The scale can be hard to absorb. Wal-Mart sold $244.5 billion worth of goods last year. It sells in three months what number-two retailer Home Depot sells in a year. And in its own category of general merchandise and groceries, Wal-Mart no longer has any real rivals. It does more business than Target, Sears, Kmart, J.C. Penney, Safeway, and Kroger combined. "Clearly," says Edward Fox, head of Southern Methodist University's J.C. Penney Center for Retailing Excellence, "Wal-Mart is more powerful than any retailer has ever been." It is, in fact, so big and so furtively powerful as to have become an entirely different order of corporate being.

Wal-Mart wields its power for just one purpose: to bring the lowest possible prices to its customers. At Wal-Mart, that goal is never reached. The retailer has a clear policy for suppliers: On basic products that don't change, the price Wal-Mart will pay, and will charge shoppers, must drop year after year. But what almost no one outside the world of Wal-Mart and its 21,000 suppliers knows is the high cost of those low prices. Wal-Mart has the power to squeeze profit-killing concessions from vendors. To survive in the face of its pricing demands, makers of everything from bras to bicycles to blue jeans have had to lay off employees and close U.S. plants in favor of outsourcing products from overseas.

Of course, U.S. companies have been moving jobs offshore for decades, long before Wal-Mart was a retailing power. But there is no question that the chain is helping accelerate the loss of American jobs to low-wage countries such as China. Wal-Mart, which in the late 1980s and early 1990s trumpeted its claim to "Buy American," has doubled its imports from China in the past five years alone, buying some $12 billion in merchandise in 2002. That's nearly 10% of all Chinese exports to the United States.

8   One way to think of Wal-Mart is as a vast pipeline that gives non-U.S. companies direct access to the American market. "One of the things that limits or slows the growth of imports is the cost of establishing connections and networks," says Paul Krugman, the Princeton University economist. "Wal-Mart is so big and so centralized that it can all at once hook Chinese and other suppliers into its digital system. So—wham!—you have a large switch to overseas sourcing in a period quicker than under the old rules of retailing."

Steve Dobbins has been bearing the brunt of that switch. He's president and CEO of Carolina Mills, a 75-year-old North Carolina company that supplies thread, yarn, and textile finishing to apparel makers—half of which supply Wal-Mart. Carolina Mills grew steadily until 2000. But in the past three years, as its customers have gone either overseas or out of business, it has shrunk from 17 factories to 7, and from 2,600 employees to 1,200. Dobbins's customers have begun to face imported clothing sold so cheaply to Wal-Mart that they could not compete even if they paid their workers nothing.

"People ask, 'How can it be bad for things to come into the U.S. cheaply? How can it be bad to have a bargain at Wal-Mart?' Sure, it's held inflation down, and it's great to have bargains," says Dobbins. "But you can't buy anything if you're not employed. We are shopping ourselves out of jobs."

The gallon jar of pickles at Wal-Mart became a devastating success, giving Vlasic strong sales and growth numbers—but slashing its profits by millions of dollars.

12   There is no question that Wal-Mart's relentless drive to squeeze out costs has benefited consumers. The giant retailer is at least partly responsible for the low rate of U.S. inflation, and a McKinsey & Co. study concluded that about 12% of the economy's productivity gains in the second half of the 1990s could be traced to Wal-Mart alone.

There is also no question that doing business with Wal-Mart can give a supplier a fast, heady jolt of sales and market share. But that fix can come with long-term consequences for the health of a brand and a business. Vlasic, for example, wasn't looking to build its brand on a gallon of whole pickles. Pickle companies make money on "the cut," slicing cucumbers into spears and hamburger chips. "Cucumbers in the jar, you don't make a whole lot of money there," says Steve Young, a former vice president of grocery marketing for pickles at Vlasic, who has since left the company.

At some point in the late 1990s, a Wal-Mart buyer saw Vlasic's gallon jar and started talking to Pat Hunn about it. Hunn, who has also since left Vlasic, was then head of Vlasic's Wal-Mart sales team, based in Dallas. The gallon intrigued the buyer. In sales tests, priced somewhere over $3, "the gallon sold like crazy," says Hunn, "surprising us all." The Wal-Mart buyer had a brainstorm: What would happen to the gallon if they offered it nationwide and got it below $3? Hunn was skeptical, but his job was to look for ways to sell pickles at Wal-Mart. Why not?

And so Vlasic's gallon jar of pickles went into every Wal-Mart, some 3,000 stores, at $2.97, a price so low that Vlasic and Wal-Mart were making only a penny or two on a jar, if that. It was showcased on big pallets near the front of stores. It was an abundance of abundance. "It was selling 80 jars a week, on average, in every store," says Young. Doesn't sound like much, until you do the math: That's 240,000 gallons of pickles, just in gallon jars, just at Wal-Mart, every week. Whole fields of cucumbers were heading out the door.

16   For Vlasic, the gallon jar of pickles became what might be called a devastating success. "Quickly, it started cannibalizing our non–Wal-Mart business," says Young. "We saw consumers who used to buy the spears and the chips in supermarkets buying the Wal-Mart gallons. They'd eat a quarter of a jar and throw the thing away when they got moldy. A family can't eat them fast enough."

The gallon jar reshaped Vlasic's pickle business: It chewed up the profit margin of the business with Wal-Mart, and of pickles generally. Procurement had to scramble to find enough pickles to fill the gallons, but the volume gave Vlasic strong sales numbers, strong growth numbers, and a powerful place in the world of pickles at Wal-Mart. Which accounted for 30% of Vlasic's business. But the company's profits from pickles had shriveled 25% or more, Young says—millions of dollars.

The gallon was hoisting Vlasic and hurting it at the same time.

Young remembers begging Wal-Mart for relief. "They said, 'No way,'" says Young. "We said we'll increase the price"—even $3.49 would have helped tremendously—"and they said, 'If you do that, all the other products of yours we buy, we'll stop buying.' It was a clear threat." Hunn recalls things a little differently, if just as ominously: "They said, 'We want the $2.97 gallon of pickles. If you don't do it, we'll see if someone else might.' I knew our competitors were saying to Wal-Mart, 'We'll do the $2.97 gallons if you give us your other business.'" Wal-Mart's business was so indispensable to Vlasic, and the gallon so central to the Wal-Mart relationship, that decisions about the future of the gallon were made at the CEO level.

20   Finally, Wal-Mart let Vlasic up for air. "The Wal-Mart guy's response was classic," Young recalls. "He said, 'Well, we've done to pickles what we did to orange juice. We've killed it. We can back off.'" Vlasic got to take it down to just over half a gallon of pickles, for $2.79. Not long after that, in January 2001, Vlasic filed for

bankruptcy—although the gallon jar of pickles, everyone agrees, wasn't a critical factor.

By now, it is accepted wisdom that Wal-Mart makes the companies it does business with more efficient and focused, leaner and faster. Wal-Mart itself is known for continuous improvement in its ability to handle, move, and track merchandise. It expects the same of its suppliers. But the ability to operate at peak efficiency only gets you in the door at Wal-Mart. Then the real demands start. The public image Wal-Mart projects may be as cheery as its yellow smiley-face mascot, but there is nothing genial about the process by which Wal-Mart gets its suppliers to provide tires and contact lenses, guns and underarm deodorant at every day low prices. Wal-Mart is legendary for forcing its suppliers to redesign everything from their packaging to their computer systems. It is also legendary for quite straightforwardly telling them what it will pay for their goods.

John Fitzgerald, a former vice president of Nabisco, remembers Wal-Mart's reaction to his company's plan to offer a 25-cent newspaper coupon for a large bag of Lifesavers in advance of Halloween. Wal-Mart told Nabisco to add up what it would spend on the promotion—for the newspaper ads, the coupons, and handling—and then just take that amount off the price instead. "That isn't necessarily good for the manufacturer," Fitzgerald says. "They need things that draw attention."

It also is not unheard of for Wal-Mart to demand to examine the private financial records of a supplier, and to insist that its margins are too high and must be cut. And the smaller the supplier, one academic study shows, the greater the likelihood that it will be forced into damaging concessions. Melissa Berryhill, a Wal-Mart spokeswoman, disagrees: "The fact is Wal-Mart, perhaps like no other retailer, seeks to establish collaborative and mutually beneficial relationships with our suppliers."

24 For many suppliers, though, the only thing worse than doing business with Wal-Mart may be not doing business with Wal-Mart. Last year, 7.5 cents of every dollar spent in any store in the United States (other than auto-parts stores) went to the retailer. That means a contract with Wal-Mart can be critical even for the largest consumer-goods companies. Dial Corp., for example, does 28% of its business with Wal-Mart. If Dial lost that one account, it would have to double its sales to its next nine customers just to stay even. "Wal-Mart is the essential retailer, in a way no other retailer is," says Gib Carey, a partner at Bain & Co., who is leading a year-long study of how to do business with Wal-Mart. "Our clients cannot grow without finding a way to be successful with Wal-Mart."

Many companies and their executives frankly admit that supplying Wal-Mart is like getting into the company version of basic training with an implacable Army drill sergeant. The process may be unpleasant. But there can be some positive results.

"Everyone from the forklift driver on up to me, the CEO, knew we had to deliver [to Wal-Mart] on time. Not 10 minutes late. And not 45 minutes early, either," says Robin Prever, who was CEO of Saratoga Beverage Group from 1992 to 2000, and made private-label water sold at Wal-Mart. "The message came through clearly: You have this 30-second delivery window. Either you're there, or you're out.

With a customer like that, it changes your organization. For the better. It wakes everybody up. And all our customers benefited. We changed our whole approach to doing business."

But you won't hear evenhanded stories like that from Wal-Mart, or from its current suppliers. Despite being a publicly traded company, Wal-Mart is intensely private. It declined to talk in detail about its relationships with its suppliers for this story. More strikingly, dozens of companies contacted declined to talk about even the basics of their business with Wal-Mart.

28   Here, for example, is an executive at Dial: "We are one of Wal-Mart's biggest suppliers, and they are our biggest customer by far. We have a great relationship. That's all I can say. Are we done now?" Goaded a bit, the executive responds with an almost hysterical edge: "Are you meshuga? Why in the world would we talk about Wal-Mart? Ask me about anything else, we'll talk. But not Wal-Mart."

No one wants to end up in what is known among Wal-Mart vendors as the "penalty box"—punished, or even excluded from the store shelves, for saying something that makes Wal-Mart unhappy. (The penalty box is normally reserved for vendors who don't meet performance benchmarks, not for those who talk to the press.)

"You won't hear anything negative from most people," says Paul Kelly, founder of Silvermine Consulting Group, a company that helps businesses work more effectively with retailers. "It would be committing suicide. If Wal-Mart takes something the wrong way, it's like Saddam Hussein. You just don't want to piss them off."

As a result, this story was reported in an unusual way: by speaking with dozens of people who have spent years selling to Wal-Mart, or consulting to companies that sell to Wal-Mart, but who no longer work for companies that do business with Wal-Mart. Unless otherwise noted, the companies involved in the events they described refused even to confirm or deny the basics of the events.

32   To a person, all those interviewed credit Wal-Mart with a fundamental integrity in its dealings that's unusual in the world of consumer goods, retailing, and groceries. Wal-Mart does not cheat suppliers, it keeps its word, it pays its bills briskly. "They are tough people but very honest; they treat you honestly," says Peter Campanella, who ran the business that sold Corning kitchenware products, both at Corning and then at World Kitchen. "It was a joke to do business with most of their competitors. A fiasco."

But Wal-Mart also clearly does not hesitate to use its power, magnifying the Darwinian forces already at work in modern global capitalism. What does the squeeze look like at Wal-Mart? It is usually thoroughly rational, sometimes devastatingly so.

John Mariotti is a veteran of the consumer-products world—he spent nine years as president of Huffy Bicycle Co., a division of Huffy Corp., and is now chairman of World Kitchen, the company that sells Oxo, Revere, Corning, and Ekco brand housewares.

He could not be clearer on his opinion about Wal-Mart: It's a great company, and a great company to do business with. "Wal-Mart has done more good for America by several thousand orders of magnitude than they've done bad," Mariotti says. "They have raised the bar, and raised the bar for everybody."

36   Mariotti describes one episode from Huffy's relationship with Wal-Mart. It's a tale he tells to illustrate an admiring point he makes about the retailer. "They demand you do what you say you are going to do." But it's also a classic example of the damned-if-you-do, damned-if-you-don't Wal-Mart squeeze. When Mariotti was at Huffy throughout the 1980s, the company sold a range of bikes to Wal-Mart, 20 or so models, in a spread of prices and profitability. It was a leading manufacturer of bikes in the United States, in places like Ponca City, Oklahoma; Celina, Ohio; and Farmington, Missouri.

One year, Huffy had committed to supply Wal-Mart with an entry-level, thin margin bike—as many as Wal-Mart needed. Sales of the low-end bike took off. "I woke up May 1"—the heart of the bike production cycle for the summer—"and I needed 900,000 bikes," he says. "My factories could only run 450,000." As it happened, that same year, Huffy's fancier, more-profitable bikes were doing well, too, at Wal-Mart and other places. Huffy found itself in a bind.

With other retailers, perhaps, Mariotti might have sat down, renegotiated, tried to talk his way out of the corner. Not with Wal-Mart. "I made the deal up front with them," he says. "I knew how high was up. I was duty-bound to supply my customer." So he did something extraordinary. To free up production in order to make Wal-Mart's cheap bikes, he gave the designs for four of his higher-end, higher-margin products to rival manufacturers. "I conceded business to my competitors, because I just ran out of capacity," he says. Huffy didn't just relinquish profits to keep Wal-Mart happy—it handed those profits to its competition. "Wal-Mart didn't tell me what to do," Mariotti says. "They didn't have to." The retailer, he adds, "is tough as nails. But they give you a chance to compete. If you can't compete, that's your problem."

In the years since Mariotti left Huffy, the bike maker's relationship with Wal-Mart has been vital (though Huffy Corp. has lost money in three out of the last five years). It is the number-three seller of bikes in the United States. And Wal-Mart is the number-one retailer of bikes. But here's one last statistic about bicycles: Roughly 98% are now imported from places such as China, Mexico, and Taiwan. Huffy made its last bike in the United States in 1999.

40   As Mariotti says, Wal-Mart is tough as nails. But not every supplier agrees that the toughness is always accompanied by fairness. The Lovable Company was founded in 1926 by the grandfather of Frank Garson II, who was Lovable's last president. It did business with Wal-Mart, Garson says, from the earliest days of founder Sam Walton's first store in Bentonville, Arkansas. Lovable made bras and lingerie, supplying retailers that also included Sears and Victoria's Secret. At one point, it was the sixth largest maker of intimate apparel in the United States, with 700 employees in this country and another 2,000 at eight factories in Central America.

Eventually Wal-Mart became Lovable's biggest customer. "Wal-Mart has a big pencil," says Garson. "They have such awesome purchasing power that they write their own ticket. If they don't like your prices, they'll go vertical and do it themselves—or they'll find someone that will meet their terms."

In the summer of 1995, Garson asserts, Wal-Mart did just that. "They had awarded us a contract, and in their wisdom, they changed the terms so dramatically that they really reneged." Garson, still worried about litigation, won't provide details. "But when you lose a customer that size, they are irreplaceable."

Lovable was already feeling intense cost pressure. Less than three years after Wal-Mart pulled its business, in its 72nd year, Lovable closed. "They leave a lot to be desired in the way they treat people," says Garson. "Their actions to pulverize people are unnecessary. Wal-Mart chewed us up and spit us out."

44   Believe it or not, American business has been through this before. The Great Atlantic & Pacific Tea Co., the grocery-store chain, stood astride the U.S. market in the 1920s and 1930s with a dominance that has likely never been duplicated. At its peak, A&P had five times the number of stores Wal-Mart has now (although much smaller ones), and at one point, it owned 80% of the supermarket business. Some of the antipredatory-pricing laws in use today were inspired by A&P's attempts to muscle its suppliers.

There is very little academic and statistical study of Wal-Mart's impact on the health of its suppliers and virtually nothing in the last decade, when Wal-Mart's size has increased by a factor of five. This while the retail industry has become much more concentrated. In large part, that's because it's nearly impossible to get meaningful data that would allow researchers to track the influence of Wal-Mart's business on companies over time. You'd need cooperation from the vendor companies or Wal-Mart or both—and neither Wal-Mart nor its suppliers are interested in sharing such intimate detail.

Bain & Co., the global management consulting firm, is in the midst of a project that asks, How does a company have a healthy relationship with Wal-Mart? How do you avoid being sucked into the vortex? How do you maintain some standing, some leverage of your own?

Bain's first insights are obvious, if not easy. "Year after year," Carey, a partner at Bain & Co., says, "for any product that is the same as what you sold them last year, Wal-Mart will say, 'Here's the price you gave me last year. Here's what I can get a competitor's product for. Here's what I can get a private-label version for. I want to see a better value that I can bring to my shopper this year. Or else I'm going to use that shelf space differently.'"

48   Carey has a friend in the umbrella business who learned that. One year, because of costs, he went to Wal-Mart and asked for a 5% price increase. "Wal-Mart said, 'We were expecting a 5% decrease. We're off by 10%. Go back and sharpen your pencil.'" The umbrella man scrimped and came back with a 2% increase. "They said, 'We'll go with a Chinese manufacturer'—and he was out entirely."

The Wal-Mart squeeze means vendors have to be as relentless and as microscopic as Wal-Mart is at managing their own costs. They need, in fact, to turn themselves into shadow versions of Wal-Mart itself. "Wal-Mart won't necessarily say you have to reconfigure your distribution system," says Carey. "But companies recognize they are not going to maintain margins with growth in their Wal-Mart business without doing it."

The way to avoid being trapped in a spiral of growing business and shrinking profits, says Carey, is to innovate. "You need to bring Wal-Mart new products— products consumers need. Because with those, Wal-Mart doesn't have benchmarks to drive you down in price. They don't have historical data, you don't have competitors, they haven't bid the products out to private-label makers. That's how you can have higher prices and higher margins."

Reasonable advice, but not universally useful. There has been an explosion of "innovation" in toothbrushes and toothpastes in the past five years, for instance; but a pickle is a pickle is a pickle.

52   Bain's other critical discovery is that consumers are often more loyal to product companies than to Wal-Mart. With strongly branded items people develop a preference for—things like toothpaste or laundry detergent—Wal-Mart rarely forces shoppers to switch to a second choice. It would simply punish itself by seeing sales fall, and it won't put up with that for long.

But as Wal-Mart has grown in market reach and clout, even manufacturers known for nurturing premium brands may find themselves overpowered. This July, in a mating that had the relieved air of lovers who had too long resisted embracing, Levi Strauss rolled blue jeans into every Wal-Mart doorway in the United States: 2,864 stores. Wal-Mart, seeking to expand its clothing business with more fashionable brands, promoted the clothes on its in-store TV network and with banners slipped over the security-tag detectors at exit doors.

Levi's launch into Wal-Mart came the same summer the clothes maker celebrated its 150th birthday. For a century and a half, one of the most recognizable names in American commerce had survived without Wal-Mart. But in October 2002, when Levi Strauss and Wal-Mart announced their engagement, Levi was shrinking rapidly. The pressure on Levi goes back 25 years—well before Wal-Mart was an influence. Between 1981 and 1990, Levi closed 58 U.S. manufacturing plants, sending 25% of its sewing overseas.

Sales for Levi peaked in 1996 at $7.1 billion. By last year, they had spiraled down six years in a row, to $4.1 billion; through the first six months of 2003, sales dropped another 3%. This one account—selling jeans to Wal-Mart—could almost instantly revive Levi.

56   Last year, Wal-Mart sold more clothing than any other retailer in the country. It also sold more pairs of jeans than any other store. Wal-Mart's own inexpensive house brand of jeans, Faded Glory, is estimated to do $3 billion in sales a year, a house brand nearly the size of Levi Strauss. Perhaps most revealing in terms of Levi's strategic blunders: In 2002, half the jeans sold in the United States cost less than $20 a pair. That same year, Levi didn't offer jeans for less than $30.

For much of the last decade, Levi couldn't have qualified to sell to Wal-Mart. Its computer systems were antiquated, and it was notorious for delivering clothes late to retailers. Levi admitted its on-time delivery rate was 65%. When it announced the deal with Wal-Mart last year, one fashion-industry analyst bluntly predicted Levi would simply fail to deliver the jeans.

But Levi Strauss has taken to the Wal-Mart Way with the intensity of a neardeath religious conversion—and Levi's executives were happy to talk about their experience getting ready to sell at Wal-Mart. One hundred people at Levi's headquarters are devoted to the new business; another 12 have set up in an office in Bentonville, near Wal-Mart's headquarters, where the company has hired a re-spected veteran Wal-Mart sales account manager.

Getting ready for Wal-Mart has been like putting Levi on the Atkins diet. It has helped everything—customer focus, inventory management, speed to market. It has even helped other retailers that buy Levis, because Wal-Mart has forced the company to replenish stores within two days instead of Levi's previous five-day cycle.

60   And so, Wal-Mart might rescue Levi Strauss. Except for one thing.

Levi didn't actually have any clothes it could sell at Wal-Mart. Everything was too expensive. It had to develop a fresh line for mass retailers: the Levi Strauss Sig-nature brand, featuring Levi Strauss's name on the back of the jeans.

Two months after the launch, Levi basked in the honeymoon glow. Overall sales, after falling for the first six months of 2003, rose 6% in the third quarter; profits in the summer quarter nearly doubled. All, Levi's CEO said, because of Signature.

But the low-end business isn't a business Levi is known for, or one it had been particularly interested in. It's also a business in which Levi will find itself compet-ing with lean, experienced players such as VF and Faded Glory. Levi's makeover might so improve its performance with its non-Wal-Mart suppliers that its estab-lished business will thrive, too. It is just as likely that any gains will be offset by the competitive pressures already dissolving Levi's premium brands, and by the can-nibalization of its own sales. "It's hard to see how this relationship will boost Levi's higher-end business," says Paul Farris, a professor at the University of Virginia's Darden Graduate School of Business Administration. "It's easy to see how this will hurt the higher-end business."

64   If Levi clothing is a runaway hit at Wal-Mart, that may indeed rescue Levi as a business. But what will have been rescued? The Signature line—it includes cloth-ing for girls, boys, men, and women—is an odd departure for a company whose brand has long been an American icon. Some of the jeans have the look, the fin-gertip feel, of pricier Levis. But much of the clothing has the look and feel it must have, given its price (around $23 for adult pants): cheap. Cheap and disappointing to find labeled with Levi Strauss's name. And just five days before the cheery profit news, Levi had another announcement: It is closing its last two U.S. factories, both in San Antonio, and laying off more than 2,500 workers, or 21% of its workforce. A company that 22 years ago had 60 clothing plants in the United States—and that was known as one of the most socially responsible corporations on the planet—will, by 2004, not make any clothes at all. It will just import them.

In the end, of course, it is we as shoppers who have the power, and who have given that power to Wal-Mart. Part of Wal-Mart's dominance, part of its insight, and part of its arrogance, is that it presumes to speak for American shoppers.

If Wal-Mart doesn't like the pricing on something, says Andrew Whitman, who helped service Wal-Mart for years when he worked at General Foods and Kraft, they simply say, "At that price we no longer think it's a good value to our shopper. Therefore, we don't think we should carry it."

Wal-Mart has also lulled shoppers into ignoring the difference between the price of something and the cost. Its unending focus on price underscores something that Americans are only starting to realize about globalization: Ever-cheaper prices have consequences. Says Steve Dobbins, president of thread maker Carolina Mills: "We want clean air, clear water, good living conditions, the best health care in the world—yet we aren't willing to pay for anything manufactured under those restrictions."

68   Randall Larrimore, a former CEO of MasterBrand Industries, the parent company of Master Lock, understands that contradiction too well. For years, he says, as manufacturing costs in the United States rose, Master Lock was able to pass them along. But at some point in the 1990s, Asian manufacturers started producing locks for much less. "When the difference is $1, retailers like Wal-Mart would prefer to have the brand-name padlock or faucet or hammer," Larrimore says. "But as the spread becomes greater, when our padlock was $9, and the import was $6, then they can offer the consumer a real discount by carrying two lines. Ultimately, they may only carry one line."

In January 1997, Master Lock announced that, after 75 years making locks in Milwaukee, it would begin importing more products from Asia. Not too long after, Master Lock opened a factory of its own in Nogales, Mexico. Today, it makes just 10% to 15% of its locks in Milwaukee—its 300 employees there mostly make parts that are sent to Nogales, where there are now 800 factory workers.

Larrimore did the first manufacturing layoffs at Master Lock. He negotiated with Master Lock's unions himself. He went to Bentonville. "I loved dealing with Wal-Mart, with Home Depot," he says. "They are all very rational people. There wasn't a whole lot of room for negotiation. And they had a good point. Everyone was willing to pay more for a Master Lock. But how much more can they justify? If they can buy a lock that has arguably similar quality, at a cheaper price, well, they can get their consumers a deal."

It's Wal-Mart in the role of Adam Smith's invisible hand. And the Milwaukee employees of Master Lock who shopped at Wal-Mart to save money helped that hand shove their own jobs right to Nogales. Not consciously, not directly, but inevitably. "Do we as consumers appreciate what we're doing?" Larrimore asks. "I don't think so. But even if we do, I think we say, Here's a Master Lock for $9, here's another lock for $6—let the other guy pay $9."

PERSONAL RESPONSE

Do you shop at Wal-Mart? Has this article changed in any way your view of Wal-Mart?

QUESTIONS FOR CLASS OR SMALL-GROUP DISCUSSION

1. Comment on the effectiveness as a rhetorical strategy of Fishman's references to the gallon-sized jar of whole pickles throughout the essay.
2. What is "the real story of Wal-Mart, the story that never gets told" (paragraph 4)?

3. Comment on Fishman's use of examples. How do they work to illustrate his major points? Which do you think are the most effective or most dramatic examples?

4. Fishman reveals that he had trouble finding sources to corroborate his findings (paragraph 31). Does that weaken his article? Does he provide enough evidence to outweigh the drawbacks of uncooperative sources?

30 LITTLE TURTLES

Thomas L. Friedman

Thomas L. Friedman has written for the New York Times *since 1981. In 1995, he became the paper's foreign affairs columnist. Friedman was awarded the 1983 Pulitzer Prize for international reporting (from Lebanon) and the 1988 Pulitzer Prize for international reporting (from Israel). In 2002, he won the Pulitzer Prize for commentary. His book* From Beirut to Jerusalem *(1989) won the National Book Award for nonfiction in 1989.* The Lexus and the Olive Tree: Understanding Globalization *(2000) won the 2000 Overseas Press Club award for best nonfiction book on foreign policy and has been published in twenty languages. He is also author of* Longitudes and Attitudes: Exploring the World after September 11 *(2002) and* The World is Flat: A Brief History of the Twenty-first Century *(2005). This op-ed column was published in the February 29, 2004, issue of the* New York Times.

Indians are so hospitable. I got an ovation the other day from a roomful of Indian 20-year-olds just for reading perfectly the following paragraph: "A bottle of bottled water held 30 little turtles. It didn't matter that each turtle had to rattle a metal ladle in order to get a little bit of noodles, a total turtle delicacy. The problem was that there were many turtle battles for less than oodles of noodles."

I was sitting in on an "accent neutralization" class at the Indian call center 24/7 Customer. The instructor was teaching the would-be Indian call center operators to suppress their native Indian accents and speak with a Canadian one—she teaches British and U.S. accents as well, but these youths will be serving the Canadian market. Since I'm originally from Minnesota, near Canada, and still speak like someone out of the movie "Fargo," I gave these young Indians an authentic rendition of "30 Little Turtles," which is designed to teach them the proper Canadian pronunciations. Hence the rousing applause.

Watching these incredibly enthusiastic young Indians preparing for their call center jobs—earnestly trying to soften their t's and roll their r's—is an uplifting experience, especially when you hear from their friends already working these jobs how they have transformed their lives. Most of them still live at home and turn over part of their salaries to their parents, so the whole family benefits. Many have credit cards and have become real consumers, including of U.S. goods, for the first time. All of them seem to have gained self-confidence and self-worth.

4   A lot of these Indian young men and women have college degrees, but would never get a local job that starts at $200 to $300 a month were it not for the call centers. Some do "outbound" calls, selling things from credit cards to phone services to Americans and Europeans. Others deal with "inbound" calls—everything from tracing lost luggage for U.S. airline passengers to solving computer problems for U.S. customers. The calls are transferred here by satellite or fiber optic cable.

I was most taken by a young Indian engineer doing tech support for a U.S. software giant, who spoke with pride about how cool it is to tell his friends that he just spent the day helping Americans navigate their software. A majority of these call center workers are young women, who not only have been liberated by earning a decent local wage (and therefore have more choice in whom they marry), but are using the job to get M.B.A.'s and other degrees on the side.

I gathered a group together, and here's what they sound like: M. Dinesh, who does tech support, says his day is made when some American calls in with a problem and is actually happy to hear an Indian voice: "They say you people are really good at what you do. I am glad I reached an Indian." Kiran Menon, when asked who his role model was, shot back: "Bill Gates—I dream of starting my own company and making it that big." I asked C. M. Meghna what she got most out of the work: "Self-confidence," she said, "a lot of self-confidence, when people come to you with a problem and you can solve it—and having a lot of independence." Because the call center teams work through India's night—which corresponds to America's day—"your biological clock goes haywire," she added. "Besides that, it's great."

There is nothing more positive than the self-confidence, dignity and optimism that comes from a society knowing it is producing wealth by tapping its own brains—men's and women's—as opposed to one just tapping its own oil, let alone one that is so lost it can find dignity only through suicide and "martyrdom."

8   Indeed, listening to these Indian young people, I had a déjà vu. Five months ago, I was in Ramallah, on the West Bank, talking to three young Palestinian men, also in their 20's, one of whom was studying engineering. Their hero was Yasir Arafat. They talked about having no hope, no jobs and no dignity, and they each nodded when one of them said they were all "suicide bombers in waiting."

What am I saying here? That it's more important for young Indians to have jobs than Americans? Never. But I am saying that there is more to outsourcing than just economics. There's also geopolitics. It is inevitable in a networked world that our economy is going to shed certain low-wage, low-prestige jobs. To the extent that they go to places like India or Pakistan—where they are viewed as high-wage, high-prestige jobs—we make not only a more prosperous world, but a safer world for our own 20-year-olds.

PERSONAL RESPONSE

Are you sympathetic with Friedman's view of the young Indians that he describes in his essay?

QUESTIONS FOR CLASS OR SMALL-GROUP DISCUSSION

1. Do you think that Friedman anticipated an audience who would be supportive or critical of him? How can you tell?

2. Do you find the title effective? How does it relate to the essay?

3. How well do Friedman's examples of individual Indians help convey his view that being with them was an "uplifting experience" (paragraph 2)?

4. How adequately does Friedman make his case that "there is more to outsourcing than just economics" (paragraph 8)? Are you convinced?

○ PERSPECTIVES ON THE ECONOMIC IMPACT OF OUTSOURCING ○

Suggested Writing Topics

1. Write a response to Michael Mandel's "The Real Cost of Offshoring" by explaining whether you are convinced by his arguments of the importance of statistics in the overall assessment of the effects of offshoring.

2. Select one of the arguments in Daniel W. Drezner's "The Outsourcing Bogeyman" and explain whether you are convinced by what he says.

3. In response to Charles Fishman's "The Wal-Mart You Don't Know," defend Wal-Mart's business practices.

4. Write a critique of Thomas L. Friedman's "30 Little Turtles."

5. Describe your own buying habits in terms of whether you are socially conscious or not. Do you consciously buy only "fair trade" products, for instance? Do you boycott products of companies that employ sweatshop labor?

6. Select a statement from any of the essays in this chapter that you would like to respond to, elaborate on, or argue for or against.

7. Drawing on the readings in this chapter, compare and contrast the benefits of offshore outsourcing.

8. If you know someone who has lost a job because the company moved offshore, narrate that person's experience.

Research Topics

1. Daniel W. Drezner cites many studies and reports in his 2004 essay "The Outsourcing Bogeyman." Research the data he uses, update it, and draw your own conclusions about the extent to which outsourcing should be cause for concern.

2. Research Wal-Mart's business practices that make it a model of success.

3. Research one of the companies that supplies products to Wal-Mart, as mentioned in Charles Fishman's "The Wal-Mart You Don't Know," and chart its progress or decline.

4. Research the economic impact of outsourcing by focusing on one particular type of business.

5. Research the subject of "phantom GDP," as discussed by Michael Mandel in "The Real Cost of Offshoring."

6. Research the subject of non-economic benefits or drawbacks to outsourcing. For instance, Daniel W. Drezner says that outsourcing has resulted in creating allies in the war on terrorism. Can you confirm or refute that claim?

7. Research the effects of the North American Free Trade Agreement (NAFTA) on the American economy and workers.

8. Research the subject of trade protectionism and state your conclusions on its positive or negative effects.

RESPONDING TO VISUALS

©Jagadeesh/Reuters/CORBIS

Indian employees work at a call center in Bangalore, India, June 23, 2003.

1. What details contribute to your first impression of this picture?
2. How does the photographer use symmetry in the composition of the photograph?
3. Why does the photographer shoot the picture from this angle, when about half of the workers have their back to the camera?
4. What do the facial expressions and body language of those facing the camera suggest about their work experience?

RESPONDING TO VISUALS

©AP Photo/Mario Lopez

A Taiwanese manager, left, walks past seamstresses in the Chentex factory in Tipitapa, Nicaragua, near Managua, Dec. 13, 2000. Four hundred of the plant's 2,000 workers were fired in August after a four-day strike last summer to demand better pay and working conditions at a factory that sews blue jeans for the U.S. military.

1. What impression of the workplace does the photograph convey?
2. What does the fact that 20% of the plants workers were fired after striking for better pay and working conditions add to the image of workers in this plant?
3. What does the information that the factory sews blue jeans for the U.S. military add to the impact of the photograph?

CHAPTER
26

The Global Marketplace

If we live in a "global village," we also buy and sell in a "global marketplace." Manufacturers that once exported goods to other nations now build plants and sell goods directly in those countries. American businesses that once limited themselves to the domestic market are now expanding operations beyond the United States as they compete in foreign markets. Indeed, most trade analysts predict that the twenty-first century will see enormous growth in global prosperity as businesses compete for foreign trade and increase their expansion in the global marketplace. Certainly, the ease of international travel makes the process of conducting business with other countries not much more difficult than travel from state to state was in former days, and the fax machine and Internet capabilities have had enormous impacts on business communication. Combine those factors with the rise in market economies in previously communist countries, and you have some compelling reasons to account for optimistic forecasts for the global economy in the twenty-first century.

The essays in this chapter focus on the issue of globalization, the place of the United States in the global market, and the effects of globalization. First, Former UN Secretary-General Kofi Annan, in "Development without Borders," comments on the issue of globalization, including its benefits, how to get the most out of it, and how to expand opportunities for all nations, including underdeveloped ones. Then, in "Mixing '60s Activism and Anti-Globalization," Robert Borosage reports on the increased activism of today's college students in their efforts to oppose what they see as the exploitative aspects of globalization. Taking on the global corporation might have seemed an impossible goal, but students influenced major American corporations to make changes in the way they conduct their manufacturing abroad. Borosage writes: "Already, even pundits who disparage the demonstrators have begun to accept that worker rights and the environment, food and workplace safety can no longer be ignored in the global market."

In defense of globalization, Murray Weidenbaum's speech, "Dispelling the Myths about the Global Economy," addresses ten myths or misunderstandings that he says people have about the global economy and its impact on the American business system. Taking each one in turn, he explains why the belief is a myth and what the reality is. As you read his responses to the attacks of student groups, environmentalists, unionists, and human-rights groups, among others, against globalization, consider the extent to which you agree with him. Can you offer counterarguments to his assertions?

The final essay also defends globalization, this time in terms of its effects on China and India. Robyn Meredith and Suzanne Hoppough, in "Why Globalization is Good," argue that, far from making the rich richer and further impoverishing the poor, globalization has lifted millions of people out of poverty. Citing statistics and giving examples of the effects of globalization on both China and India, they counter the criticisms of such groups as Public Citizen and Global Trade Watch who are critical of globalization's effect on Third World countries. As you read this and the rest of the readings in this chapter, consider what implications America's place in the global market has for your own future.

DEVELOPMENT WITHOUT BORDERS

KOFI ANNAN

Kofi Annan of Ghana was the seventh Secretary-General of the United Nations, serving from 1997 to 2006, and the first to be elected from the ranks of the United Nations staff. He joined the United Nations in the early 1970s and has held many positions, including Assistant Secretary-General for Program Planning, Budget and Finance; head of human resources; director of the budget; chief of personnel for the High Commissioner for Refugees; administrative officer for the Economic Commission for Africa; and Under-Secretary-General for Peacekeeping Operations. Kofi Annan and the United Nations were awarded the 2001 Nobel Peace Prize. This paper was published in the Summer 2001, issue of the Harvard International Review.

What is globalization? More than ever before, groups and individuals are interacting directly across borders without involving the state. This happens partly due to new technology and partly because states have found that prosperity is better secured by releasing the creative energies of their people than by restricting them.

The benefits of globalization are obvious: faster growth, higher standards of living, and new opportunities. However, globalization's benefits are very unequally distributed; the global market is not yet underpinned by shared social objectives, and if all of today's poor follow the same path that brought the rich to prosperity, the earth's resources will soon be exhausted. The challenge we face is to ensure that globalization becomes a positive force for all people instead of leaving billions in squalor.

If we are to get the most out of globalization, we must learn how to provide better governance at the local, national, and international levels. We must think afresh about how we manage our joint activities and our shared interests, since so many challenges that we confront today are beyond the reach of any state acting on its own.

This should not be seen as a future of world government or the eclipse of nation states. On the contrary, states will draw strength from each other by acting together within the framework of common institutions based on shared rules and values. Governments must work together to make these changes possible, but governments alone cannot make them happen. Much of the heavy lifting will be done by private investment and charitable foundations.

The best ideas, however, will come from nongovernmental sources: from academic researchers, nonprofit organizations, business, the media, and the arts. These elements compose civil society, and they have a vital role to play.

At the UN Millennium Summit in September 2000, world leaders resolved to halve three figures: the number of people whose income is less than one US dollar a day, the proportion of people who suffer from hunger, and the proportion of people who are unable to reach or afford safe drinking water. They resolved to accomplish these goals by 2015. History will judge this generation by what it did to fulfill that pledge.

Success in achieving sustained growth depends on expanding access to the opportunities of globalization. That in turn depends in large measure on the quality of governance a country enjoys. Countries can only compete in the global market if their people benefit from the rule of law, effective state institutions, transparency and accountability in the management of public affairs, and respect for human rights. Their people must have a say in the decisions that affect their lives.

8   If developing countries succeed in creating the right economic and social environment, new technology can put many opportunities within their reach. That is especially true of information technology, which does not require vast amounts of hardware, financial capital, or even energy, and which is relatively environment-friendly. What information technology does require is brain power—the one commodity that is equally distributed among the peoples of the world. So for a relatively small investment—for example, an investment in basic education—we can bring all kinds of knowledge within reach of the world's poor and enable poor countries to leapfrog some of the long and painful stages of development that other nations had to go through.

In short, there is much that poor countries can do to help themselves. But rich countries have an indispensable role to play. For wealthy nations to preach the virtues of open markets to developing countries is mere hypocrisy if they do not open their own markets to those countries' products or stem the flooding of the world market with subsidized food exports that make it impossible for farmers in developing countries to compete. Nor can they expect developing countries to protect the global environment, unless they are ready to alter their own irresponsible patterns of production and consumption.

Developing countries must be helped to export their way to prosperity. Everyone now agrees that the burden of debt must be lifted from the poorest countries, but developed countries have not yet come forward with sufficient resources to alleviate this burden. Nations, whether in debt or not, need help to reach the stage where they can produce goods and services that the rest of the world wants to buy. Many also need help in resolving destructive conflicts and rebuilding a peaceful, productive society.

Long ago, all members of the Organization for Economic Cooperation and Development committed 0.7 percent of their gross domestic product to development aid. Very few made good on that commitment. Private companies, as well as governments, have an obligation to consider the interests of the poor when making investment choices and when pricing their products. Companies are the largest beneficiaries of globalization; it is in their interest to make this trend sustainable, by helping it work for all.

12   Only when the lives of ordinary men, women, and children in cities and villages around the world are made better will we know that globalization is becoming inclusive, allowing everyone to share in its opportunities. This is the key to eliminating world poverty.

PERSONAL RESPONSE

Do you agree with Annan that rich countries have an obligation to help developing countries?

QUESTIONS FOR CLASS OR SMALL-GROUP DISCUSSION

1. How well does Annan support his statement that "the benefits of globalization are obvious" but that they "are very unequally distributed" (paragraph 2)?

2. Do you think it possible for world leaders to achieve the goals resolved upon at the UN Millennium summit (paragraph 6)? What do you think they will have to do to accomplish these goals?

3. Discuss ways in which rich or strong nations could help poor or developing countries enhance their brain power (paragraph 8).

4. Explain the extent to which you agree with this statement: "Private companies, as well as governments, have an obligation to consider the interests of the poor when making investment choices and when pricing their products" (paragraph 11).

MIXING '60S ACTIVISM AND ANTI-GLOBALIZATION
ROBERT BOROSAGE

Robert Borosage is a cofounder and codirector, with Roger Hickey, of the Campaign for America's Future. He is also president of its sister organization, the Institute for America's Future. He has written on political, economic, and national security issues for publications including the New York Times, *the* Washington Post, *and the* Nation. *He is a frequent commentator on television and radio, including* Fox Morning News, *RadioNation, National Public Radio, C-SPAN and Pacifica Radio. He teaches on presidential power and national security as an adjunct professor at American University's Washington School of Law. Borosage is co-editor of* The Next Agenda: Blueprint for a New Progressive Movement *(2000). This article appeared in the April 23, 2000, issue of the* Los Angeles Times.

Kids today can't get any respect. First, their generation was described as apathetic, stirred only by dreams of dot-com fortunes. Then, when students stunned the world by joining turtle lovers and Teamsters to shut down the World Trade Organization meeting in Seattle last December, they were disparaged as "flat-Earth advocates." Last week, when they rallied against the World Bank and International Monetary Fund in Washington and 1,300 were arrested in nonviolent protest, they were labeled "imitation activists," filling the time between "spring break and summer vacation, and between the last body-piercing and the first IPO." At least Washington and Seattle captured headlines. For the most vibrant student movement in years is roiling America's university campuses in relative obscurity.

Here's the reality so many can't see. Activist, idealistic students are in motion once again, seized of a morally compelling cause. Their target, amazingly, is nothing less than the global corporation. They are challenging the conservative free-trade agenda that dominates both major political parties. Already, they are forcing global companies such as Nike to scramble for cover. They've only just begun.

The most vital part of this growing movement is, perhaps, the least noticed. On more than 175 campuses, students are calling global corporations to account for their exploitation of workers abroad. They are mounting demonstrations, going on hunger strikes, seizing administration buildings, confronting university trustees and administrators, and getting arrested by the dozens in nonviolent protests. The two-person staff of the coordinating group, United Students Against Sweatshops, can't keep up with the e-mail from students seeking to get involved both here and abroad.

4   This movement is less than four years old. Its roots trace back to 1996, when human-rights advocate Charles Kernaghan focused national attention on Honduran sweatshops in which young women worked at poverty wages, surrounded by barbed wire and armed guards, to sew clothes for a Kathie Lee Gifford fashion line. That summer, hundreds of university students joined worker struggles in this country as part of the AFL-CIO's Union Summer. Since then, groups of students have visited Central America to witness how women their own age work and live.

The students had a compelling moral argument: Let's not support companies that profit from exploiting workers abroad—and they acted on it. They targeted university apparel shops that buy logo clothing from global corporations with factories in Honduras, Indonesia and China, where worker rights are trampled. The $2.5-billion collegiate retail-apparel industry represents just 1% of the U.S. apparel market but is key to the youth market. So students started calling for their universities to enforce a code of conduct on suppliers.

University administrators didn't need the hassle but had no ready response for the students. The companies realized they were in trouble. Nike's swoosh symbol started being associated less with Michael Jordan than with impoverished young women abroad. Nike and others circled the wagons, enlisting a few human-rights groups to form the Fair Labor Assn., establishing their own code of conduct with the companies in control. Company-paid consultants did inspections, with factories notified ahead of time. Reports were kept private while the company "remedied" any problem. The Clinton administration pumped money into the operation. Relieved university administrators signed up.

But the students weren't buying. As Marikah Mancini, a graduate student at Purdue, said, "The basic question was whether you were empowering the companies or the workers." The result of the FLA, Sarah Jacobson of the University of Oregon argued, "would be to hide, not expose sweatshop conditions." The students insisted that any code of conduct include protections for the rights of women and workers, require a living wage and ban production from countries where workers had no right to organize. Most important, the students demanded that companies disclose the location of all factories. This would allow local church and human-rights groups to do independent monitoring. Nike and others refused.

8   So the students organized a Worker Rights Consortium to monitor company practices, financed by 1% of the revenues produced by university garment sales. It would sponsor independent monitoring by local human-rights groups and make findings public.

When university administrators resisted, the students upped the ante. At the University of Pennsylvania, the University of Wisconsin and elsewhere, students took over administration buildings. At Purdue, students camped out on the square, with several risking an 11-day hunger strike. At the University of Wisconsin, Eric Brakken was told he didn't have the student body's support. So he ran for student-government chairman on a no-sweatshops platform and won. Even at the University of Oregon, next door to Nike's corporate headquarters, students took over the president's office until he agreed to join the WRC.

Last year, facing suspension of contracts with Duke and other universities, Nike blinked and disclosed its factory locations. The other companies soon followed suit.

Forty-four universities have now joined the WRC, including six Big 10 universities, Brown, Columbia and Georgetown. Two weeks ago, the entire University of California system signed up, issuing a code of conduct that demands a living wage of all contractors.

12   The students have identified an issue—the spread of sweatshop labor—that cuts through the cant about free trade. They have found the leverage to move not just their campuses, but global corporations—and maybe even the entire debate about globalization. They are directly challenging the laissez-faire assumptions of the last quarter-century, demanding corporations be held to some basic moral standards of conduct. Their focus on global corporations enlists the energies of many student passions, from the environmentalists to pro-Tibetan activists. And unlike the antiwar movement in the 1960s that was confronted by "hard hats," the SAS is forging links between students and workers, and between the environment and worker rights.

As President Bill Clinton and anyone active in the 1960s understands, when students are aroused about a moral issue, they can change the direction of the country. Already, even pundits who disparage the demonstrators have begun to accept that worker rights and the environment, food and workplace safety can no longer be ignored in the global market.

But the students are making the larger connections. Last week, SAS activists gathered in Washington for the march against the World Bank and IMF, arguing that their "structural adjustment programs," in the words of Erica Hiegelke, Smith College freshman, "press governments to attract Western investment by denying workers fundamental, internationally recognized rights."

These are not Neanderthal protectionists, nor bored kids looking for something to do. This student movement is internationalist, passionate and on the rise.

And it is raising questions that might well mark the end of the conservative era of the last quarter-century.

PERSONAL RESPONSE

Write for a few minutes about your opinion of the kind of student activism Borosage describes. Are you personally involved in the anti-globalization movement? If not, would you like to become involved or would you rather not? Explain your reasons for being involved, wanting to become involved, or avoiding such involvement.

QUESTIONS FOR CLASS OR SMALL-GROUP DISCUSSION

1. How effective do you find Borosage's opening and closing paragraphs?

2. To what extent do you agree with students who argue that we should "not support companies that profit from exploiting workers abroad" (paragraph 5)? In what ways, according to this article, do companies exploit workers abroad? Can you give other examples of such exploitation?

3. Borosage writes: "[Students] are directly challenging the laissez-faire assumptions of the last quarter-century, demanding corporations be held to some basic moral standards of conduct" (paragraph 11). What do you understand by the term *laissez-faire assumptions?* What examples of those assumptions does Borosage provide? How do "basic moral standards of conduct" apply to those examples?

4. Discuss your opinion of the student movement Borosage describes. Do you admire the students who are involved in the organizations he mentions, or not?

DISPELLING THE MYTHS
ABOUT THE GLOBAL ECONOMY

Murray Weidenbaum

Murray Weidenbaum is Mallinckrodt Distinguished University Professor and honorary chairman of the Weidenbaum Center on the Economy, Government, and Public Policy at Washington University in St. Louis. He has written and edited a number of books on business and the economy, including An Agnostic Examination of the Case for Action Against Global Warming *(1998) and the textbook* Business and Government in the Global Marketplace, *now in its seventh edition (2003). Weidenbaum's international activities include serving as Chairman of the Economic Policy Committee of the Organization for Economic Cooperation and Development and lecturing at universities and research institutes throughout Western Europe and Asia. He*

*received the National Order of Merit from France in recognition of his
contributions to foreign policy. In 1989 he was a member of a Presidential Mission to Poland. In 1999–2000, he was chairman of the new
Congressional Commission to Review the Trade Deficit. This speech
was presented to the Economic Club of Detroit on January 22, 2001.*

Today I want to deal with a perplexing conundrum facing the United States: this is
a time when the American business system is producing unparalleled levels of prosperity, yet private enterprise is under increasing attack. The critics are an unusual
alliance of unions, environmentalists, and human rights groups and they are focusing on the overseas activities of business. In many circles, globalization has become
a dirty word.

How can we respond in a constructive way? In my interaction with these interest groups, I find that very often their views arise from basic misunderstandings
of the real world of competitive enterprise. I have identified ten myths about the
global economy—dangerous myths—which need to be dispelled. Here they are:

1. Globalization costs jobs.
2. The United States is an island of free trade in a world of protectionism.
3. Americans are hurt by imports.
4. U.S. companies are running away, especially to low-cost areas overseas.
5. American companies doing business overseas take advantage of local peo-
    ple, especially in poor countries. They also pollute their environments.
6. The trade deficit is hurting our economy and we should eliminate it.
7. It's not fair to run such large trade deficits with China or Japan.
8. Sanctions work. So do export controls.
9. Trade agreements should be used to raise environmental and labor stan-
    dards around the world.
10. America's manufacturing base is eroding in the face of unfair global
    competition.

That's an impressive array of frequently heard charges and they are polluting
our political environment. Worse yet, these widely held myths fly in the face of the
facts. I'd like to take up each of them and knock them down.

1. Globalization Costs Jobs

4   This is a time when the American job miracle is the envy of the rest of the world,
so it is hard to take that charge seriously. Yet some people do fall for it. The facts
are clear: U.S. employment is at a record high and unemployment is at a 30-year
low. Moreover, the United States created more than 20 million new jobs between
1993 and 2000, far more than Western Europe and Japan combined. Contrary to a
widely held view, most of those new jobs pay well, often better than the average for
existing jobs.

Of course, in the best of times, some people lose their jobs or their businesses fail, and that happens today. However, most researchers who have studied this question conclude that, in the typical case, technological progress—not international trade—is the main reason for making old jobs obsolete. Of course, at the same time, far more new jobs are created to take their place.

2. The United States Is an Island of Free Trade in a World of Protectionism

Do other nations erect trade barriers? Of course they do—although the trend has been to cut back these obstacles to commerce. But our hands are not as clean as we like to think. There is no shortage of restrictions on importers trying to ship their products into this country. These exceptions to free trade come in all shapes, sizes, and varieties. They are imposed by federal, state, and local government. U.S. import barriers include the following and more:

- Buy-American laws give preference in government procurement to domestic producers. Many states and localities show similar favoritism. Here in Michigan, preference is given to in-state printing firms;
- The Jones Act prohibits foreign ships from engaging in waterborne commerce between U.S. ports; many statutes limit the import of specific agricultural and manufactured products, ranging from sugar to pillowcases;
- We impose selective high tariffs on specific items, notably textiles; and many state and local regulatory barriers such as building codes, are aimed at protecting domestic producers.

It's strange that consumer groups and consumer activists are mute on this subject. After all, it is the American customer who has to pay higher prices as a result of all of this special interest legislation. But these barriers to trade ultimately are disappointing. Nations open to trade grow faster than those that are closed.

3. Americans Are Hurt by Imports

8   The myth that imports are bad will be quickly recognized by students of economics as the mercantilist approach discredited by Adam Smith over two centuries ago. The fact is that we benefit from imports in many ways. Consumers get access to a wider array of goods and services. Domestic companies obtain lower cost components and thus are more competitive. We get access to vital metals and minerals that are just not found in the United States. Also, imports prod our own producers to improve productivity and invest in developing new technology.

I'll present a painful example. By the way, I have never bought a foreign car. But we all know how the quality of our domestic autos has improved because of foreign competition. More recently, we had a striking example of the broader benefits of imports. In 1997–98, the expanded flow of lower-cost products from Asia kept inflation low here at a time when otherwise the Fed would have been raising interest rates to fight inflation. The result would have been a weaker economy. Moreover, in a full employment economy, imports enable the American people to enjoy a higher living standard than would be possible if sales were limited to domestic production.

In our interconnected economy, the fact is that the jobs "lost" from imports are quickly replaced by jobs elsewhere in the economy—either in export industries or in companies selling domestically. The facts are fascinating: the sharp run-up in U.S. imports in recent years paralleled the rapid growth in total U.S. employment. Both trends, of course, reflected the underlying health of our business economy.

The special importance of imports was recently highlighted by the director of the Washington State Council on International Trade. "The people who benefit most critically are families at the lower end of the wage scale who have school-age children and those elderly who must live frugally." She goes on to conclude: "It is a cruel deception that an open system of free trade is not good for working people."

4. U.S. Companies Are Running Away, Especially to Low-Cost Areas Overseas

12   Right off the bat, the critics have the direction wrong. The flow of money to buy and operate factories and other businesses is overwhelmingly into the United States. We haven't had a net outflow of investment since the 1960s. That's the flip side of our trade deficit. Financing large trade deficits means that far more investment capital comes into this country than is leaving.

But let us examine the overseas investments by American companies. The largest proportion goes not to poor countries, but to the most developed nations, those with high labor costs and also high environmental standards. The primary motive is to gain access to markets. That's not too surprising when we consider that the people in the most industrially advanced nations are the best customers for sophisticated American products. By the way, only one-third of the exports by the foreign branches of U.S. companies goes to the United States. About 70 percent goes to other markets, primarily to the industrialized nations.

Turning to American investments in Mexico, China, and other developing countries, the result often is to enhance U.S. domestic competitiveness and job opportunities.

This is so because many of these overseas factories provide low-cost components and material to U.S.-based producers who are thus able to improve their international competitiveness.

16   In some cases, notably the pharmaceutical industry, the overseas investments are made in countries with more enlightened regulatory regimes, such as the Netherlands. "More enlightened" is not a euphemism for lower standards. The Dutch maintain a strong but more modern regulatory system than we do.

5. American Companies Doing Business Overseas Take Advantage of Local People and Pollute Their Environments

There are always exceptions. But by and large, American-owned and managed factories in foreign countries are top-of-the-line—in terms of both better working conditions and higher environmental standards than locally-owned firms. This is why so many developing countries compete enthusiastically for the overseas ocation of U.S. business activities—and why so many local workers seek jobs at the American factories. After all, American companies manufacturing overseas frequently follow the same high operating standards that they do here at home. I serve on a panel of Americans who investigate the conditions in some factories in China. I wish the critics could see for themselves the differences between the factories that produce for an American company under its worldwide standards and those that are not subject to our truly enlightened sense of social responsibility.

I'll give you a very personal example of the second category of facilities. While making an inspection tour, I tore my pants on an unguarded piece of equipment in one of those poorly-lit factories. An inch closer and that protruding part would have dug into my thigh. I also had to leave the factory floor every hour or so to breathe some fresh air. When I said that, in contrast, the American-owned factories were top-of-the-line, that wasn't poetry.

Yes, foreign investment is essential to the economic development of poor countries.

20   By definition, they lack the capability to finance growth. The critics do those poor countries no favor when they try to discourage American firms from investing there. The critics forget that, during much of the nineteenth century, European investors financed many of our canals, railroads, steel mills, and other essentials for becoming an industrialized nation. It is sad to think where the United States would be today if Europe in the nineteenth century had had an array of powerful interest groups that were so suspicious of economic progress.

6. The Trade Deficit Is Hurting Our Economy and We Should Eliminate It

Yes, the U.S. trade deficit is at a record high. But it is part of a "virtuous circle" in our economy. The trade deficit mainly reflects the widespread prosperity in the United States, which is substantially greater than in most of the countries we trade with. After all, a strong economy such as ours—operating so close to full employment and full capacity—depends on a substantial amount of imports to satisfy our demands for goods and services. Our exports are lower primarily because the demand for imports by other nations is much weaker.

The acid test is that our trade deficit quickly declines in the years when our economy slows down and that deficit rises again when the economy picks up. Serious studies show that, if the United States had deliberately tried to curb the trade deficit in the 1990s, the result would have been a weak economy with high inflation and fewer jobs. The trade deficit is a byproduct of economic performance. It should not become a goal of economic policy.

There is a constructive way of reducing the trade deficit. To most economists, the persistence of our trade imbalance (and especially of the related and more comprehensive current account deficit) is due to the fact that we do not generate enough domestic saving to finance domestic investment. The gap between such saving and investment is equal to the current account deficit.

24 Nobel laureate Milton Friedman summed up this point very clearly: "The remarkable performance of the United States economy in the past few years would have been impossible without the inflow of foreign capital, which is a mirror image of large balance of payments deficits."

The positive solution is clear: increase the amount that Americans save. Easier said than done, of course. The shift from budget deficits (dissaving) to budget surpluses (government saving) helps. A further shift to a tax system that does not hit saving as hard as ours does would also help. The United States taxes saving more heavily than any other advanced industrialized nation. Replacing the income tax with a consumption tax, even a progressive one, would surely be in order—but that deserves to be the subject of another talk.

7. It's Not Fair to Run Such Large Trade Deficits with China or Japan

Putting the scary rhetoric aside, there really is no good reason for any two countries to have balanced trade between them. We don't have to search for sinister causes for our trade deficits with China or Japan. Bilateral trade imbalances exist for many benign reasons, such as differences in per capita incomes and in the relative size of the two economies. One of the best kept secrets of international trade is that the average Japanese buys more U.S. goods than the average American buys Japanese goods, Yes, Japan's per capita imports from the United States are larger than our per capita imports from Japan ($539 versus $432 in 1996). We have a large trade deficit with them because we have more "capita" (population).

8. Sanctions Work, So Do Export Controls

It is ironic that so many people who worry about the trade deficit simultaneously support sanctions and export controls. There is practically no evidence that unilateral sanctions are effective in getting other nations to change their policies or actions. Those restrictions on trade do, however, have an impact: they backfire. U.S. business, labor, and agriculture are harmed. We lose an overseas market for what is merely a symbolic gesture. Sanctions often are evaded. Shipping goods through third countries can disguise the ultimate recipient in the nation on which the sanctions are imposed. On balance, these sanctions reduced American exports in 1995 by an estimated $15–20 billion.

28   As for export controls, where American producers do not have a monopoly on a particular technology—which is frequent—producers in other nations can deliver the same technology or product without the handicap imposed on U.S. companies. A recent report at the Center for the Study of American Business showed that many business executives believe that sanctions and export controls are major obstacles to the expansion of U.S. foreign trade.

9. Trade Agreements Should Be Used to Raise Environmental and Labor Standards around the World

At first blush, this sounds like such a nice and high-minded way of doing good. But, as a practical matter, it is counterproductive to try to impose such costly social regulations on developing countries as a requirement for doing business with them. The acid test is that most developing nations oppose these trade restrictions. They see them for what they really are—a disguised form of protectionism designed to keep their relatively low-priced goods out of the markets of the more advanced, developed nations. All that feeds the developing nations' sense of cynicism toward us.

In the case of labor standards, there is an existing organization, the International Labor Organization, which has been set up to deal specifically with these matters. Of all the international organizations, the ILO is unique in having equal representation from business, labor, and government. The United States and most other nations are members. The ILO is where issues of labor standards should be handled. To be taken more seriously, the United States should support the ILO more vigorously than it has.

As for environmental matters, we saw at the unsuccessful meetings on climate change at the Hague late last year how difficult it is to get broad international agreement on environmental issues even in sympathetic meetings of an international environmental agency. To attempt to tie such controversial environmental matters to trade agreements arouses my suspicions about the intent of the sponsors. It is hard to avoid jumping to the conclusion that the basic motivation is to prevent progress on the trade front.

32   I still recall the signs carried by one of the protesters in Seattle, "Food is for people, not for export." Frankly, it's hard to deal with such an irrational position. After all, if the United States did not export a major part of its abundant farm output, millions of people overseas would be starving or malnourished. Also, thousands of our farmers would go broke.

The most effective way to help developing countries improve their working conditions and environmental protection is to trade with and invest in them. As for the charge that companies invest in poor, developing nations in order to minimize their environmental costs, studies of the issue show that environmental factors are not important influences in business location decisions. As I pointed out earlier, most U.S. overseas direct investment goes to developed nations with high labor costs and also high environmental standards.

10. America's Manufacturing Base Is Eroding in the Face of Unfair Global Competition

Unfortunately, some of our fellow citizens seem to feel that the only fair form of foreign competition is the kind that does not succeed in landing any of their goods on our shores. But to get to the heart of the issue, there is no factual basis for the charge that our manufacturing base is eroding—or even stagnant. The official statistics are reporting record highs in output year after year. Total industrial production in the United States today is 45 percent higher than in 1992—that's not in dollars, but in terms of real output.

Of course, not all industries or companies go up—or down—in unison. Some specific industries, especially low-tech, have had to cut back. But, simultaneously, other industries, mainly high-tech, have been expanding rapidly. Such changes are natural and to be expected in an open, dynamic economy. By the way, the United States regularly runs a trade surplus in high-tech products.

36   It's important to understand the process at work here. Technological progress generates improved industrial productivity. In the United States, that means to some degree fewer blue-collar jobs and more white-collar jobs. That is hardly a recent development.

The shift from physical labor to knowledge workers has been the trend since the beginning of the 20th century. On balance, as I noted earlier, total U.S. employment is at an all-time high.

If you have any doubt about the importance of rising productivity to our society, just consider where we would be if over the past century agriculture had not enjoyed rising productivity (that is, more output per worker/hour). Most of us would still be farmers.

It is vital that we correct the erroneous views of the anti-globalists. Contrary to their claims, our open economy has raised living standards and helped to contain inflation.

40   International commerce is more important to our economy today than at any time in the past. By dollar value and volume, the United States is the world's largest trading nation. We are the largest importer, exporter, foreign investor, and host to foreign investment. Trying to stop the global economy is futile and contrary to America's self-interest.

Nevertheless, we must recognize that globalization, like any other major change, generates costs as well as benefits. It is essential to address these consequences. Otherwise, we will not be able to maintain a national consensus that responds to the challenges of the world marketplace by focusing on opening markets instead of closing them. The challenge to all of us is to urge courses of action that help those who are hurt without doing far more harm to the much larger number who benefit from the international marketplace.

We need to focus more attention on those who don't share the benefits of the rapid pace of economic change. Both private and public efforts should be increased to provide more effective adjustment assistance to those who lose their jobs. The focus of adjustment policy should not be on providing relief from economic change, but on positive approaches that help more of our people participate in economic prosperity.

As you may know, I recently chaired a bipartisan commission established by Congress to deal with the trade deficit. Our commission included leaders of business and labor, former senior government officials, and academics. We could not agree on all the issues that we dealt with. But we were unanimous in concluding that the most fundamental part of an effective long-run trade adjustment policy is to do a much better job of educating and training. More Americans should be given the opportunity to become productive and high-wage members of the nation's workforce.

44   No, I'm not building up to a plea to donate to the college of your choice, although that's a pretty good idea.

Even though I teach at major research universities—and strongly believe in their vital mission—let me make a plea for greater attention to our junior colleges. They are an overlooked part of the educational system. Junior colleges have a key role to play. Many of these community-oriented institutions of learning are now organized to specially meet the needs of displaced workers, including those who need to brush up on their basic language and math skills. In some cases, these community colleges help people launch new businesses, especially in areas where traditional manufacturing is declining. A better trained and more productive workforce is the key to our long-term international competitiveness. That is the most effective way of resisting the calls for economic isolationism.

Let me leave you with a final thought. The most powerful benefit of the global economy is not economic at all, even though it involves important economic and business activities. By enabling more people to use modern technology to communicate across traditional national boundaries, the international marketplace makes possible more than an accelerated flow of data. The worldwide marketplace encourages a far greater exchange of the most powerful of all factors of production—new ideas. That process enriches and empowers the individual in ways never before possible.

As an educator, I take this as a challenge to educate the anti-globalists to the great harm that could result from a turn to economic isolationism. For the twenty-first century, the global flow of information is the endless frontier.

PERSONAL RESPONSE

To what extent are you convinced that the "myths" Weidenbaum discusses are truly "myths"?

QUESTIONS FOR CLASS OR SMALL-GROUP DISCUSSION

1. Weidenbaum says that there are "ten myths about the global economy—dangerous myths—which need to be dispelled" (paragraph 2). Discuss each of the "myths" in turn, examining his rationale for why they are not myths and explaining the extent to which you are convinced by his argument.

2. What do you think Weidenbaum means when he says, "Trying to stop the global economy is futile and contrary to America's self-interest" (paragraph 34)? What is your response to that statement?

3. Weidenbaum suggests: "More Americans should be given the opportunity to become productive and high-wage members of the nation's workforce" (paragraph 37). Does he adequately explain how those goals can be accomplished? Do you agree that both of those goals are achievable?

WHY GLOBALIZATION IS GOOD

ROBYN MEREDITH AND SUZANNE HOPPOUGH

Robyn Meredith was a Detroit correspondent for the New York Times, *wrote for* USA Today *as a business reporter, and spent two years as a reporter in the Washington bureau of the* American Banker *newspaper before joining* Forbes *magazine. She is now Senior Editor, Asia division, of* Forbes. *Suzanne Hoppough is a reporter for* Forbes. *This piece was adapted from Meredith's* The Elephant and the Dragon: The Rise of India and China, and What It Means for All of Us *(2007) and first appeared in the April 16, 2007, issue of* Forbes.

A ragtag army of save-the-world crusaders has spent years decrying multinational corporations as villains in the wave of globalization overwhelming the Third World. This ominous trend would fatten the rich, further impoverish and oppress the poor and crush local economies.

The business-bashing group Public Citizen argued as much in a proclamation signed by almost 1,500 organizations in 89 countries in 1999. Whereupon hundreds of protesters rioted outside a conference of the World Trade Organization in Seattle, shattering windows, blocking traffic and confronting cops armed with tear gas and pepper spray. Six hundred people were arrested.

Cut to 2007, and the numbers are in: The protesters and do-gooders are just plain wrong. It turns out globalization is good—and not just for the rich, but *especially* for the poor. The booming economies of India and China—the Elephant and the Dragon—have lifted 200 million people out of abject poverty in the 1990s as globalization took off, the International Monetary Fund says. Tens of millions more have catapulted themselves far ahead into the middle class.

4   It's remarkable what a few container ships can do to make poor people better off. Certainly more than $2 trillion of foreign aid, which is roughly the amount (with an inflation adjustment) that the U.S. and Europe have poured into Africa and Asia over the past half-century.

In the next eight years almost 1 billion people across Asia will take a Great Leap Forward into a new middle class. In China middle-class incomes are set to rise threefold, to $5,000, predicts Dominic Barton, a Shanghai managing partner for McKinsey & Co.

As the Chindia revolution spreads, the ranks of the poor get smaller, not larger. In the 1990s, as Vietnam's economy grew 6% a year, the number of people living in poverty (42 million) fell 7% annually; in Uganda, when GDP growth passed 3%, the number fell 6% per year, says the World Bank.

China unleashed its economy in 1978, seeding capitalism first among farmers newly freed to sell the fruits of their fields instead of handing the produce over to Communist Party collectives. Other reforms let the Chinese create 22 million new businesses that now employ 135 million people who otherwise would have remained peasants like the generations before them.

8   Foreign direct investment, the very force so virulently opposed by the do-gooders, has helped drive China's gross domestic product to a more than tenfold increase since 1978. Since the reforms started, $600 billion has flooded into the country, $70 billion of it in the past year. Foreigners built hundreds of thousands of new factories as the Chinese government built the coal mines, power grid, airports and highways to supply them.

As China built infrastructure, it created Special Economic Zones where foreign companies willing to build modern factories could hire cheap labor, go years without paying any taxes and leave it to government to build the roads and other infrastructure they needed. All of that, in turn, drove China's exports from $970 million to $974 billion in three decades. Those container loads make Americans better off, too. You can get a Chinese DVD at Wal-Mart for $28, and after you do you will buy some $15 movies made in the U.S.A.

Per-person income in China has climbed from $16 a year in 1978 to $2,000 now. Wages in factory boomtowns in southern China can run $4 a day—scandalously low in the eyes of the protesters, yet up from pennies a day a generation ago and far ahead of increases in living costs.

Middle-class Chinese families now own TVs, live in new apartments and send their children to private schools. Millions of Chinese have traded in their bicycles for motorcycles or cars. McDonald's has signed a deal with Sinopec, the huge Chinese gasoline retailer, to build drive-through restaurants attached to gas stations on China's new roads.

12   Today 254 Starbucks stores serve coffee in the land of tea, including one at the Great Wall and another at the Forbidden Palace. (The latter is the target of protesters.) In Beijing 54 Starbucks shops thrive, peddling luxury lattes that cost up to $2.85 a cup and paying servers $6 for an 8-hour day. That looks exploitative until you peek inside a nearby Chinese-owned teahouse where the staff works a 12-hour day for $3.75.

Says one woman, 23, who works for an international cargo shipper in Beijing: "My parents were both teachers when they were my age, and they earned 30 yuan [$3.70] a month. I earn 4,000 yuan ($500) a month, live comfortably and feel I have better opportunities than my parents did."

Tony Ma, age 51, was an unwilling foot soldier in Mao's Cultural Revolution. During that dark period from 1966 to 1976 universities were closed, and he was sent at age 16 to work in a steel mill for $2 a month. He cut metal all day long for seven years and feared he might never escape.

When colleges reopened, he landed a spot to study chemistry, transferred to the U.S., got a Ph.D. in biochemistry and signed on with Johnson & Johnson at $45,000 a year. Later he returned to the land he fled and now works for B.F. Goodrich in Hong Kong.

16   The young college grads in China today wouldn't bother immigrating to the U.S. for a job that pays $45,000, he says—because now they have better opportunities at home.

Capitalism alone, however, isn't enough to remake Third World economies—globalism is the key. A big reason India trails behind its bigger neighbor to the northeast in lifting the lower classes is that, even after embracing capitalism, it kept barriers to the flow of capital from abroad.

Thus 77% of Indians live on $2 a day or less, the Asian Development Bank says, down only nine percentage points from 1990. A third of the population is illiterate. In 1980 India had more of its population in urban centers than China did (23% versus 20% for China). But by 2005 China had 41% in cities, where wages are higher; India's urbanites had grown to only 29%.

Freed of British colonial rule in 1947 and scarred by its paternalistic effects, India initially combined capitalism with economic isolationism. It thwarted foreign companies intent on investing there and hampered Indian firms trying to sell abroad. This hurt Indian consumers and local biz: A $100 Microsoft operating system got slapped with duties that brought the price to $250 in India, putting imported software and computers further from reach for most people and businesses. Meanwhile, the government granted workers lavish job protections and imposed heavy taxes and regulations on employers. Government jobs usually were by rote and paid poorly, but they guaranteed lifetime employment. They also ensured economic stagnation.

20   Financial crisis struck in 1991. Desperate for cash, India flew a planeload of gold reserves to London and began, grudgingly, to open its economy. Import duties were lowered or eliminated, so India's consumers and companies could buy modern, foreign-made goods and gear. Overseas firms in many industries were allowed to own their subsidiaries in India for the first time since 1977. India all but banned foreign investment until 1991. Since then foreign companies have come back, but not yet on the scale seen in China. Foreign companies have invested $48 billion in India since 1991—$7.5 billion of that just in the last fiscal year—the same amount dumped into China every six weeks. By the mid-1990s the economy boomed and created millions of jobs.

By the late 1990s U.S. tech companies began turning to India for software design, particularly in the Y2K crunch. The Indians proved capable and cheap, and the much-maligned offshoring boom began. Suddenly Indian software engineers were programming corporate America's computers. New college graduates were answering America's customer service phone calls. Builders hired construction workers to erect new high-rise buildings suddenly in demand as American and European firms rushed to hire Indian workers.

The new college hires, whose older siblings had graduated without finding a job, tell of surpassing their parents' salaries within five years and of buying cell phones, then motorcycles, then cars and even houses by the time they were 30. All of that would have been impossible had India failed to add globalization to capitalism.

Today, despite its still dilapidated airports and pothole-riddled highways, the lumbering Elephant now is in a trot, growing more than 7% annually for the last decade. In 2005, borrowing from the Chinese, India began a five-year, $150 billion plan to update its roads, airports, ports and electric plants. India is creating free trade zones, like those in China, to encourage exports of software, apparel, auto parts and more.

24   S.B. Kutwal manages the assembly line where Tata Motors builds Safari SUVs. He remembers how, in the 1980s, people waited five years to buy a scooter and cars were only for the rich. "Since we've liberated the economy, lots of companies have started coming into India," says Kutwal. "People couldn't afford cars then. Now the buying power is coming."

In Mumbai (formerly Bombay), Delhi, Bangalore and other big cities, shopping malls have sprung up, selling everything from Levi's jeans to Versace. India still has raggedy street touts, but when they tap on car windows at stoplights, instead of peddling cheap plastic toys, they sell to the new India: copies of *Vogue* and *House & Garden* magazines. Western restaurants are moving in, too: Domino's Pizza and Ruby Tuesday's have come to India, and 107 McDonald's have sprung up, serving veggie burgers in the land where cattle are sacred.

None of this gives pause to an entity called International Forum on Globalization. The group declares that globalism's aim is to "benefit transnational corporations over workers; foreign investors over local businesses; and wealthy countries over developing nations. While promoters . . . proclaim that this model is the rising tide that will lift all boats, citizen movements find that it is instead lifting only yachts."

"The majority of people in rich and poor countries aren't better off" since the World Trade Organization formed in 1995 to promote global trade, asserts Christopher Slevin, deputy director of Global Trade Watch, an arm of Ralph Nader's Public Citizen. "The breadth of the opposition has grown. It's not just industrial and steel workers and people who care about animal rights. It includes high-tech workers and the offshoring of jobs, also the faith-based community."

28   While well-off American techies may be worried, it seems doubtful that an engineer in Bangalore who now earns $40,000 a year, and who has just bought his parents' house, wants to ban foreign investment.

Slevin's further complaint is that globalism is a creature of WTO, the World Bank and other unelected bodies.

But no, the people do have a voice in the process, and it is one that is equivocal on the matter of free market capitalism. The Western World's huge agriculture subsidies—$85 billion or more annually, between the U.S., Japan and the European Union—are decreed by democratically elected legislatures. The EU pays ranchers $2 per cow in daily subsidies, more than most Indians earn. If these farmers weren't getting handouts, and if trade in farm products were free, then poor farmers in the

Third World could sell more of their output, and could begin to lift themselves out of poverty.

PERSONAL RESPONSE

Whom do you find yourself agreeing with, those who believe that globalization is exploitative of poor nations or those who believe that it is good for poor nations?

QUESTIONS FOR CLASS OR SMALL-GROUP DISCUSSION

1. Comment on the use of loaded language in the opening paragraphs. Do you find it effective?

2. What do Meredith and Hoppough say are the effects of capitalism on China? What might protesters against globalization in China say about those examples? Do you agree with the authors that the effects are all good?

3. What do you understand the authors to mean when they say that capitalism alone is not enough? How do the details about India support that statement?

4. To what extent are you convinced that "globalization is good" (title)?

○ PERSPECTIVES ON THE GLOBAL MARKETPLACE ○
Suggested Writing Topics

1. Compare and/or contrast the positions of any two of the writers in this chapter on the subject of globalization of the economy.

2. Drawing on at least two of the essays in this chapter, discuss possible solutions to the problem of how to moderate the desire of corporations to make money in the global marketplace with the altruistic goal of providing adequate attention to the needs of poor or developing countries.

3. Kofi Annan writes in "Development without Borders": "In short, there is much that poor countries can do to help themselves. But rich countries have an indispensable role to play." Drawing on Annan's article, write an essay explaining what poor countries can do and how rich countries can help them.

4. Read and write a critique of Robyn Meredith's *The Elephant and the Dragon: The Rise of India and China, and What It Means for Us*, from which the article "Why Globalization is Good" has been adapted.

5. Discuss the implications for both American consumers and American businesses of the rapid expansion of the global marketplace.

6. Write an essay explaining how you see changes in the global economy affecting you personally, both as a consumer and as a (perhaps future) member of the workforce.

7. Assess the impact of foreign products on a typical day in your life. Which imported items are important to your daily life?

8. Interview a specialist in international marketing or economics about the global market and its importance for the American economy in the twenty-first century. Then write an essay on America's future in the global economy in which you include both the specialist's remarks and those of any of the authors in this chapter.

9. Write an essay from the point of view of a market researcher for a new corporation looking for rapid growth through global marketing. Make up a product and a corporation name; then prepare a report for the board of directors of your company in which you recommend expanding efforts in one of the world's newest market areas.

10. Select a statement from any of the readings in this chapter and write a response in support of or against it.

Research Topics

1. Research the economic changes in the past decade in any of these geographic areas: Asia, Asia Pacific, Latin America, Eastern Europe, or sub-Saharan Africa. Read about developments in the area and projections for the future, and then report your findings and conclusions.

2. Research the global investment strategies of any major American corporation. Draw some conclusions about the effectiveness of such strategies in your paper.

3. Analyze the connections between the information revolution and the global spread of market economies. How do they affect or influence one another?

4. Select an area such as politics, technology, or economics. Then conduct library research to determine both the positive and negative implications of the enormous global changes in that area, including a prediction of the effects of these changes on the American economy in the next decade.

5. Research and assess the effectiveness of any of the following: the UN Millennium Summit of September, 2000, or the Organization for Economic Cooperation and Development (Kofi Annan's "Development without Borders"); the United Students Against Sweatshops, the Fair Labor Association, or the Worker Rights Consortium (Robert Borosage's "Mixing '60s Activism and Anti-Globalization").

RESPONDING TO VISUALS

©AP Photo/Bela Szandelszky

Hungarian Fair Trade activists protest with sewing machines in Budapest, Hungary, against claimed exploitation of third-world workers, Thursday, June 7, 2007. The demonstration took place during the G8 summit in Heiligendamm, Germany.

1. Why do you think the protesters are wearing masks? How do the masks comment on their claim that third world workers are exploited?
2. What do the sewing machines and the shirts being sewn add to the protest? What do the passersby in the background contribute to the photograph?
3. How effective do you find this kind of "performance" protest, as opposed to people carrying posters and banners and shouting?

RESPONDING TO VISUALS

Depiction of globalization; world with shopping carts.

1. What comment on the global economy does this image make?
2. What do the shopping carts represent? Why do you think the perspective highlights the shopping carts and puts the globe in the background?
3. Why do you think that North and South America are represented rather than other continents? The artist could have had the shopping carts on the other side of the globe, for instance. Why do you think he made this choice?

APPENDIX

1

Glossary of Terms

Abstract. A summary of the essential points of a text. It is usually quite short, no more than a paragraph.

Ad hominem arguments. Attacking the character of the arguer rather than the argument itself.

Analysis. Dividing a subject into its separate parts for individual study.

Appeal. A rhetorical strategy used in argumentation to be persuasive; a persuasive technique that goes beyond fact or logic to engage audience's sympathy, sense of higher power or authority, or reasoning. Classic persuasion relies on a combination of ethical, logical, and emotional appeals to sway an audience.

Argument/persuasion. An argument is an attempt to prove the validity of a position by offering supporting proof. Persuasion takes argument one step further by convincing an audience to adopt a viewpoint or take action.

Attributive tag. This is a short identifying phrase or clause that identifies ("attributes") the source of a quotation or paraphrase: *Mugabane explains . . . ; According to Sissela Bok, . . . ; Singer, a Princeton University professor who publishes widely on bioethics issues, recommends . . .*

Backing. According to the Toulmin model of reasoning, the support or evidence for a warrant.

Begging the question (Circular reasoning). Making a claim that simply rephrases another claim in other words.

Blog. A personal website which the owner uses for whatever purpose he or she likes, such as a daily record of thoughts or experiences or links to other sites. The term derives from the phrase "web log."

Book review. A report that summarizes only the main ideas of a book and provides critical commentary on it. Usually in a book review, you will also be asked to give your personal response to the book, including both your opinion of the ideas it presents and an evaluation of its worth or credibility.

Case study. A situation or profile of a person or persons, for which you provide a context and background information.

Citation. A reference that provides supporting illustrations or examples for your own ideas; the authority or source of that information is identified.

Comparison. A likeness or strong similarity between two things.

Concession. Agreement with an opponent on certain points or acknowledging that an opposing argument cannot be refuted.

Contrast. A difference or strong dissimilarity between two things.

Critique. An evaluation of a work's logic, rhetorical soundness, and overall effectiveness.

Debate. A discussion involving opposing points in an argument. In formal debate, opposing teams defend and attack a specific proposition.

Deductive reasoning. In argumentation, the movement from a general principle or shared premise to a conclusion about a specific instance.

Description. A conveyance through words of the essential nature of a thing.

Diction. A writer's word choice and level of usage, which varies in informal and formal language; slang, regional, nonstandard, and colloquial language; and jargon.

Dropped quotation. A quotation that appears without an introduction, as if it had just been dropped into a paper.

Either–or reasoning. Admitting only two sides to an issue and asserting that the writer's is the only possible correct one.

Ellipsis points. Used in quoting source material, three spaced periods indicate that words have been omitted.

Evaluation. A judgment about worth, quality, or credibility.

Exemplification. Showing by example; using specific details or instances to illustrate, support, or make specific.

Fallacy. A component of argument that is false or misleading, thus making the reasoning illogical and the argument essentially invalid.

False analogy. Falsely claiming that, because something resembles something else in one way, it resembles it in all ways.

Figurative language. Non-literal or imaginative language used to make abstract words or ideas more concrete. *Simile* and *metaphor* are two common figures of speech.

Forum. An open discussion or exchange of ideas among many people.

Freewriting. The act of writing down every idea that occurs to you about your topic without stopping to examine what you are writing.

Hasty or faulty generalization. The drawing of a broad conclusion on the basis of very little evidence.

Hypothesis. A tentative explanation to account for some phenomenon or set of facts. It is in essence a theory or an assumption that can be tested by further investigation and is assumed to be true for the purpose of argument or investigation.

Illustration. An explanation or clarification, usually using example or comparison.

Inductive reasoning. In argumentation, the movement from a number of specific instances to a general principle.

Introduction. The opening words, sentences, or paragraphs that begin a piece of writing.

Invention. Generating ideas for writing.

Journal. A personal record of experiences, thoughts, or responses to something, usually kept separate from other writings, as in a diary or notebook.

Listserv. An e-mail based discussion group of a specific topic.

Literature search. A process of locating titles of articles, books, and other material on a specific subject.

Loaded words (Emotionally charged language). Language guaranteed to appeal to audiences on an emotional rather than an intellectual level. A loaded word has highly charged emotional overtones or connotations that evoke a strong response, either positive or negative, that goes beyond the denotation or specific definition given in a dictionary. Often the meaning or emotional association of the words varies from person to person or group to group.

Metaphor. An implied comparison; comparing one thing to another without using the words "like" or "as." For instance, the metaphor "my love is a rose" makes the comparison between love and rose without explicitly saying so.

Narration. Telling a story.

Non sequitur. Drawing inferences or conclusions that do not follow logically from available evidence.

Oversimplification. Offering a solution or an explanation that is too simple for the problem or issue being argued.

Panel discussion. A small group of people (usually between three and six) gathered to discuss a topic. Often each member of a panel is prepared to represent a certain position or point of view on the subject of discussion, with time left after the presentations for questions from audience members.

Paraphrase. A restatement of a passage in your own words. A paraphrase is somewhat shorter than the original but retains its essential meaning.

Point of view. The perspective from which a piece is written: first person (I, we), second person (you), or third person (he/she/it/one, they).

Position paper. A detailed report that explains, justifies, or recommends a particular course of action.

Post hoc, *ergo propter hoc* reasoning. Assuming that something happened simply because it followed something else without evidence of a causal relationship.

Premise. An assumption or a proposition on which an argument is based or from which a conclusion is drawn.

Proposition. A statement of a position on a subject, a course of action, or a topic for discussion or debate.

Rebuttal. Response addressed to opposing arguments, such as demonstrating a flaw in logic or reasoning or exposing faulty or weak supporting evidence.

Red herring. Diverting the audience's attention from the main issue at hand to an irrelevant issue.

Reflective writing. A process of drawing on personal experience to offer your own response to something. For this kind of writing, use the first person.

Report. A detailed account of something.

Rhetoric. That art or study of using language effectively.

Rhetorical method. The strategy used to organize and develop ideas in a writing assignment.

Simile. An express comparison; using the words "like" or "as" to make a comparison. For instance: "My love is like a red, red rose" is a simile.

Slanted word. A word whose connotations (suggestive meaning as opposed to actual meaning) is used to advance an argument for its emotional association.

Stereotyping. A form of generalization or oversimplification in which an entire group is narrowly labeled or perceived on the basis of a few in the group.

Strategy. A plan of action to achieve a specific goal; the way that an assignment is organized and developed.

Subject. A general or broad area of interest.

Summary. A shortened version of a passage, stated in your own words. A summary resembles a paraphrase, in that you are conveying the essence of the original, but it is shorter than a paraphrase.

Syllogism. Traditional form of deductive reasoning that has two premises and a conclusion.

Synthesis. Combining the ideas of two or more authors and integrating those ideas into your own discussion.

Thesis statement. A statement of the specific purpose of a paper. A thesis is essentially a one-sentence summary of what you will argue, explain, illustrate, define, describe, or otherwise develop in the rest of the paper. It usually comes very early in a paper.

Tone. A writer's attitude toward the subject and the audience, conveyed through word choice and diction.

Topic. A specific, focused, and clearly defined area of interest. A topic is a narrow aspect of a subject.

Topic sentence. Sentence stating the focus or central idea of a paragraph.

Warrant. According to the Toulmin model of reasoning, the underlying assumptions or inferences that are taken for granted and that connect the claim to the data.

Workshop. Similar in intent to a forum, a workshop is characterized by exchanges of information, ideas, and opinions, usually among a small group of people. Both workshops and forums involve interaction and exchange of ideas more than panel discussions, which typically allot more time to panel members than to audience participants.

APPENDIX 2

Formatting Guidelines for Course Papers

Your instructor may give you formatting guidelines for your papers, but if not, the following guidelines should serve you well in most cases. They follow MLA recommended guidelines for student papers, as do the student papers that appear in this textbook.

MARGINS, SPACING, AND PAGE NUMBERS

Leave a one-inch margin on both sides and at the top and bottom of each page, except for the page number. Double space everything throughout the paper. Number pages consecutively throughout the paper. MLA guidelines show the page number on the first page, but if your instructor asks you not to put it there, follow the instructor's directions. Place page numbers on the right-hand side, one-half inch from the top of the paper, flush with the right margin. MLA guidelines require your last name with each page number, including the first.

HEADING AND TITLE ON FIRST PAGE

If your instructor tells you to put the endorsement on the first page of your paper rather than on a separate title page, drop down one inch from the top of the first page and write all the information your instructor requires flush with the left margin. This information includes your name, your instructor's name, the course number and section, and the date (using day/month/year format). Then write your title, centered on the page. Double space between all lines, including between the date and the title and between the title and the first line of the paper. Do not underline your own title or put it in quotation marks.

Konrad 1

Elizabeth Konrad

Professor Lee

English 102-12

28 November 2008

The Place of Spirituality in the College Curriculum

Education today is more complicated than ever before. The rapid rate at which knowledge increases and the almost constantly changing nature of our society and the jobs required to sustain it put great pressure on institutions of higher education and students alike.

TITLE PAGE

If your instructor requires a title page, center your title about a third of the way down the page. Do not underline your title or use quotation marks around it. Underneath the title, about halfway down, write your name. Then drop down the page and put your instructor's name, the course number and section, and the date.

The Place of Spirituality in the College Curriculum

Elizabeth Konrad

Professor Lee

English 102-12

28 November 2008

CREDITS

Adams, Mike, and Dan Berger. "HPV Vaccine Texas Tyranny" (cartoon and commentary). © 2007 Truth Publishing. <www.NewsTarget.com>.

Allen, Arthur. "The HPV Debate Needs an Injection of Reality." From *The Washington Post*, April 8, 2007. Reprinted by permission.

American Spectator commentary. "The Galileo of Global Warming," May 2001. Reprinted by permission of *American Spectator*.

Annan, Kofi. "Development Without Borders." *Harvard International Review*, 23.2 (Summer 2001): 84. Reprinted by permission.

Arnold, Andrew D. "Comix Poetics." *World Literature Today*, March-April 2007. Reprinted by permission.

Ash, Timothy Garton. "Fortress America." Reprinted by permission of the author.

Baldwin, James. "Fifth Avenue, Uptown: A Letter from Harlem" Originally published in *Esquire*, Copyright © 1960 by James Baldwin. Copyright renewed. Collected in *Nobody Knows My Name*, published by Vintage Books. Used by arrangement with the James Baldwin Estate.

Bayles, Martha. "Now Showing: The Good, the Bad, and the Ugly Americans." First appeared in *The Washington Post*, August 28, 2005. Reprinted by permission of the author.

Begley, Josanne. "The Gettysburg Address and the War Against Terrorism." Copyright © 2007 Josanne Begley. Reprinted by permission of author.

Bernikow, Louise. "Cinderella at the Movies," pp. 17–37 of *Among Women* by Louise Bernikow. Reprinted by permission of the author.

Blume, Judy. "Censorship: A Personal View." Reprinted with the permission of Simon & Schuster Books for Young Readers, an imprint of Simon &Schuster Children's Book Division, from *Places I Never Meant to Be* by Judy Blume. Copyright © 1999 by Judy Blume. All rights reserved.

Bok, Sissela. "Aggression: The Impact of Media Violence." From *Mayhem: Violence as Public Entertainment by Sissela Bok*. Copyright © 1998 by Sissela Bok. Reprinted by permission of Da Capo Press, a member of Perseus Books Group.

Booth, William. "One Nation Indivisible: Is It History?" Copyright 1998 by Washington Post Writers Group. Reprinted with permission of Washington Post Writers Group in the format textbook via Copyright Clearance Center.

Borosage, Robert. "Mixing '60s Activisim and Anti-Globalization." *Los Angeles Times*, April 23, 2000. Reproduced with permission of Los Angeles Times Syndicate in the format textbook via Copyright Clearance Center.

Jenkins, Henry. "Art Form for the Digital Age" *Technology Review,* Sept. 2000. Reproduced by permission of the publisher via Copyright Clearance Center, Inc.

Johnson, Paul. "American Idealism and Realpolitik," *Forbes,* March 12, 2007. Reprinted by permission of Forbes Magazine © 2007 Forbes LLC.

Kilbourne, Jean. "Advertising's Influence on Media Content." Reprinted with the permission of The Free Press, a Division of Simon & Schuster, Inc., from *Can't Buy My Love: How Advertising Changes the Way We Think and Feel* (originally published as *Deadly Persuasion*) by Jean Kilbourne. Copyright © 1999 by Jean Kilbourne. All rights reserved.

Kingsbury, Alex. "The Measure of Learning." Copyright 2007 *U.S. News & World Report,* L. P. Reprinted with permission.

Kingsolver, Barbara. "A Pure, High Note of Anguish." Copyright © 2001 by Barbara Kingsolver. Reprinted by permission of the Frances Goldin Literary Agency.

Koppel, Ted. "The Long, Cost-Free War." From *The New York Times,* November 6, 2006. The New York Times, Inc. All Rights Reserved. Used by permission and protected by the Copyright Laws of the United States. The printing, copying, redistribution, or retransmission of the Material without express written permission is prohibited.

Kotlowitz, Alex. "Colorblind." Copyright © 1998 by The New York Times Co. Reprinted by permission.

Krauthammer, Charles. "Smallpox Shots: Make them Mandatory." Copyright © 2002 by Time, Inc. Reprinted by permission.

——. "The War and the Words." Copyright © 2007. The Washington Post Writers Group. Reprinted with permission.

Lewan, Todd. "CHIPS: High-Tech Aids or Tracking Tools?" AP Wire Service, July 22, 2007.

Long, Cindy. "I Need My Space!" *NEA Today, April 2007.* Reprinted by permission.

Love, MaryAnn Cusimano. "Race in America: We Would Like to Believe We are Over the Problem." *America,* Feb. 12, 2007. Copyright © 2007 by America Press, Inc. Reproduced with permission of America Press, Inc., in the format Textbook via Copyright Clearance Center.

Males, Mike. "Stop Blaming Kids and TV." Reprinted by permission from the October, 1997 issue of *The Progressive,* 409 East Main Street, Madison, WI 53703.

Magubane, Zine. "Why 'Nappy' is Offensive." *The Boston Globe,* April 12, 2007. Reprinted by permission of the author.

Mandel, "The Real Cost of Offshoring." *BusinessWeek,* June 18, 2007. Reprinted by permission.

McClure, Jennifer. "Hip-Hop's Betrayal of Black Women." *ZMagazine Online* July/August 2006. Reprinted by permission.

McCullough, David. "No Time to Read?" Reprinted with the permission of *Family Circle* magazine.

McKibben, Bill. "Global Warning: Get Up! Stand Up!" *OnEarth,* Spring 2007. Reprinted by permission of Bill McKibben.

Meredith, Robyn and Suzanne Hoppough. "Why Globalization is Good." Reprinted by permission of Forbes Magazine. Copyright © 2007 Forbes LLC.

Mitchell, Whitney. "Deconstructing Gender, Sex, and Sexuality as Applied to Identity." Reprinted with permission of *The Humanist.*

Moody Howard. "Sacred Rite or Civil Right?" Reprinted with permission from the June 5, 2004 issue of *The Nation.* For subscription information, call 1-800-333-8536. Portions of each week's Nation magazine can be accessed at http://www.thenation.com.

Wallis, David. "The Wrong Lesson: Teaching College Students to be Meek." From the August/September 2004 issue of *Reason*. Reprinted by permission of *Reason* and *Reason.com*.

Warner, Judith. "The Full-Time Blues." *The New York Times*, July 24, 2007. Copyright © 2007 New York Times. Reprinted by permission.

Watson, James D. "All for the Good." Copyright © 1999 by Time, Inc. Reprinted by permission.

Weidenbaum, Murray. "Dispelling the Myths about the Global Economy." Reprinted by permission of the author.

Wilmut, Ian. "Dolly's False Legacy," *Time* magazine, January 11, 1999. Reprinted by permission of the author.

Wolkomir, Joyce, and Richard Wolkomir. "You are What You Buy." Reprinted with permission from the October 2000 *Smithsonian*. Copyright © 2000 by Richard and Joyce Wokomir.

Young, Cathy. "Terror Then and Now." From the November 2006 issue of *Reason*. Reprinted by permission of *Reason* and *Reason.com*.

Zimbardo, Philip G. "Revisiting the Stanford Prison Experiment: A Lesson in the Power of Situation." *The Chronicle of Higher Education*, March 30, 2007. Reprinted by permission of Philip G. Zimbardo.

Zine, Magubane. "Why 'Nappy' is Offensive." From *The Boston Globe*, April 12, 2007. Reprinted by permission of the author.

PHOTO/REALIA CREDITS

INDEX